Photoshop CS4
THE MISSING MANUAL

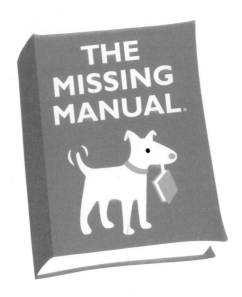

Lesa Snider King

POGUE PRESS™
O'REILLY®

Beijing • Cambridge • Farnham • Köln • Sebastopol • Taipei • Tokyo

Photoshop CS4: The Missing Manual

by Lesa Snider King

Published by O'Reilly Media, Inc., 1005 Gravenstein Highway North, Sebastopol, CA 95472.

O'Reilly books may be purchased for educational, business, or sales promotional use. Online editions are also available for most titles (*safari.oreilly.com*). For more information, contact our corporate/institutional sales department: (800) 998-9938 or *corporate@oreilly.com*.

Printing History:

December 2008:   First Edition.

ISBN: 978-0-596-52296-4
[V]

Table of Contents

Chapter 3: Layers: The Key to Nondestructive Editing 69

Chapter 4: Selections: Choosing What to Edit 124

Part Three: The Artistic Side of Photoshop

Part Four: Printing and the Web

Part Five: Photoshop Power

Part Six: Appendixes

> **NOTE**   In addition to the two appendixes printed in this book, we've posted three more online. To download them visit *www.missingmanuals.com* and click the Missing CD link.

Foreword

In the short but crowded history of consumer technology, only two products ever became so common, influential, and powerful that their names become verbs.

Google is one.

Photoshop is the other.

("Did you Google that guy who asked you out?" "Yeah—he's crazy. He Photoshopped his last girlfriend out of all his pictures!")

It's safe to say that these days, not a single photograph gets published, in print or online, without having been processed in Photoshop first. It's usually perfectly innocent stuff: a little color adjustment, contrast boosting, or cropping.

But not always. Sometimes, the editing actually changes the photo so that it no longer represents the original, and all kinds of ethical questions arise. Remember when TV Guide Photoshopped Oprah's head onto Ann-Margaret's body? Or when Time magazine darkened O.J. Simpson's skin to make him look more menacing on the cover? Or when National Geographic moved one of the pyramids closer together to improve the composition?

Well, you get the point: Photoshop is magic. Thanks to Photoshop, photography is no longer a reliable record of reality.

And now, all that magic is in your hands. Use it wisely.

There's only one problem: Photoshop is a monster. It's huge. Just opening it is like watching a slumbering beast heave into consciousness. Dudes: Photoshop CS4 has over 500 menu commands.

In short, installing Photoshop is like being told that you've just won a 747 jumbo jet. You sit down in the cockpit and survey the endless panels of controls and switches. Now what?

You don't even get a printed manual anymore.

If there were ever a piece of software that needed the Missing Manual treatment, it's Photoshop. And yet, despite having published over 100 books since I started this series in 1999, we've never tackled Photoshop. It's been the elephant in the room for all those years, and it's been bugging me.

Frankly, we were terrified.

But no longer; the beast has at last been tamed. I'm delighted to introduce its new master, Lesa Snider King: a first-time author with Missing Manual credentials as long as your arm.

She worked on Missing Manuals, side-by-side with me in my office, for four years, in all kinds of editorial and production capacities. And when she wasn't at my place, she was out in the real world, teaching Photoshop seminars, writing Photoshop how-to articles for the Web, retouching hundreds of photos in Photoshop, and eventually becoming a Photoshop master (which I would define as, "anyone who knows what more than 50 percent of those 500 menu commands actually do").

Even more important, the Missing Manual mantra runs through her blood: make it clear, make it entertaining, make it complete (hence the thickness of the book in your hands). And above all, don't just identify a feature: tell us what it's for. Tell us when to use it. (And if the answer is "you'll never use it," tell us that, too.)

Now, Photoshop CS4: The Missing Manual is not for everybody; I'll be the first to admit it. In fact, the book is aimed primarily at two kinds of people: Photoshop beginners and Photoshop veterans.

But seriously, folks. If you're new to Photoshop, you'll find patient, friendly introductions to all those nutty Photoshoppy concepts like layers, color spaces, image resolution, and so on. And, mercifully, you'll find a lot of loving attention to a time-honored Missing Manual specialty—tips and shortcuts. As Photoshop pros can tell you, you pretty much have to learn some of Photoshop's shortcuts, or it will crush you like a bug.

On the other hand, if you already have some Photoshop experience, you'll appreciate this book's coverage of CS4's new features. Some of them are pretty sweet indeed. (Continuous zoom, content-aware scaling, and flick-panning—mmm.) There's a redesign to contend with, too; CS4 can be like coming home from college to find that your parents have moved around everything in your old room.

In any case, get psyched. You now have both the most famous, powerful, magical piece of software on earth—and an 800-page treasure map to help you find your way.

The only missing ingredients are time, some photos to work on, and a little good taste. You'll have to supply those yourself.

Good luck!

David Pogue

David Pogue is the weekly tech columnist for the New York Times, an Emmy-winning TV correspondent (CBS News and CNBC), and the creator of the Missing Manual series.

The Missing Credits

About the Author

 Lesa Snider King is on a mission to teach the world to create—and use—better graphics. She's a stock photographer and chief evangelist for iStockphoto.com and founder of the creative tutorial site GraphicReporter.com. Lesa is the author of many video training titles including *Graphic Secrets for Business Professionals* (Lynda.com, 2007), *From Photo to Graphic Art*, and *Practical Photoshop Elements* (KelbyTraining.com, 2008). She writes regularly for *Macworld* magazine, the National Association of Photoshop Professionals (*www.photoshopuser.com*), Elements Techniques (*www.photoshopelementsuser.com*), and *Layers* magazine. Lesa is also a corporate trainer and teaches at many industry conferences including Photoshop World, Macworld Expo, Mac Mania Cruises, and the esteemed Santa Fe Workshops.

You can catch her Graphics Tip of the Week live each Wednesday night on the Your Mac Life Internet radio show (*www.yourmaclifeshow.com*), which she also co-hosts with husband Shawn King. During her free time, you'll find her carving the twisties on her sportbike or hanging with fellow Mac geeks. Lesa is a proud member of the BMWMOA, F800 Riders Club, DACS, NCMUG, Washington Apple Pi, and LiMac.

About the Creative Team

Dawn Frausto (editor) is assistant editor for the Missing Manual series. When not working, she likes rock climbing, playing soccer, and causing trouble. Email: *dawn@oreilly.com*.

Peter Meyers (editor) is the managing editor of O'Reilly Media's Missing Manual series. He lives with his wife, daughter, and cats in New York City. Email: *meyers@oreilly.com*.

Nellie McKesson (production editor) lives in Jamaica Plain, Mass., where she makes t-shirts (*http://mattsaundersbynellie.etsy.com*) and plays music with her band Dr. & Mrs. Van Der Trampp (*http://myspace.com/drmrsvandertrampp*). Email: *nellie@oreilly.com*.

Carol Thoma (copy editor) has a PhD in English with a specialty in British Romantic poetry. After completing a 630-page dissertation on a biographer of Percy Bysshe Shelley named Thomas Jefferson Hogg, she contributed three articles on friends of Shelley to the *New Oxford Dictionary of National Biography*. She's a huge fan of the Harry Potter series and a loyal supporter of King Richard III who enjoys spending her free time with her grandchildren.

Melissa Findley (technical reviewer) is a freelance digital artist and illustrator specializing in fantasy art. Her work has been featured in Ballistic Publishing's *Exotique 4*, *Art Scene International* magazine, and Imagine FX. She also does book covers for Cobblestone Press. Melissa lives with her husband, tech writer John Welch, and stepson, Alex, in Tallahassee, FL. For more of her work visit her Web site: *www.WickedFae.com*.

Shangara Singh (technical reviewer) is a photographer and a heavy Photoshop and Lightroom user. He owns *www.examaids.com* and is the author of the popular Photoshop and Lightroom ACE Exam Aids—study guides for people who want to become Adobe Certified Experts. He also shoots stock and has his own stock photo Web site: *www.mpxstockimages.com*.

John C. Welch (technical reviewer) is an IT Manager for The Zimmerman Agency, freelance writer, and whatever else comes up. He's contributed to multiple technical books on Mac OS X and co-written two. He's a regular speaker at Macworld Conference & Expo on Mac IT issues, and lives in Tallahassee, FL with his wife, teenaged son, and two cats. He can be reached via his Web site: *http://www.bynkii.com/*.

Acknowledgements

This book is dedicated to the Greek god of wine, Bacchus, and all the brave little grapes who so valiantly sacrificed their lives so this book could be written. In vino veritas!

I'd like to express galactic thanks to iStockphoto.com for providing the beautiful imagery you see throughout this book. I truly believe an image is worth a thousand words, and thus made the screenshots as visually pleasing as possible. If you ever need high-quality, affordable images, iStockphoto.com is the way to go! A big hug and thanks go to David Pogue who got me involved in this project to begin with, and so graciously wrote the foreward of this book (while we were in disturbingly rough seas teaching on MacMania 8, no less). To Scott and Jeff Kelby for believing in me and nurturing my career in *immeasurable* ways throughout the last several years. To John "Bynkii" Welch for convincing me during our annual Macworld pub crawl that I should say yes to taking on this monstrous project should I be asked, and to Derrick Story for his wisdom and guidance before this book technically became my project, and my project alone. Also, a big fancy dinner and jugs of Umbrian vino rosso go to Pete Meyers and Dawn Frausto for editing this book and keeping me on track. Their input has made me a better writer and I will forever be grateful to them both.

You would not, however, be holding this book if it weren't for Jeff Gamet, managing editor of MacObserver.com, Design-Tools.com, and author of *Designers Guide to Mac OS X* (Peachpit), who cleared his schedule to help meet the world's ugliest deadline, and for staying up with me on iChat more nights than I can count (it's all one big blur). Here's to the Sugar-Free Red Bull and the Mozart station we made on Pandora.com that got us through the last of it! And when I ended up working straight through my Italian vacation, I'm *really* glad you kept me from jumping overboard while in the middle of the Mediterranean. In hindsight, I shudder to think of all the shopping in Firenze I would have missed.

Special thanks to Richard Harrington (*www.photoshopforvideo.com*) for his help on video layers and the Actions chapter, to Taz Tally (http://*taztallyphotography.com*) for helping with the Photoshop and Print chapter, to Marcus Conge (*www. digitalmanipulation.com*) and Bert Monroy (*www.bertmonroy.com*) for their help with all things 3D and vector-related, and to the wonderfully brilliant Veronica Hanley who sacrificed two days at sea in order to make the vector chapter make sense! To Melissa Findley (*www.wickedeye.com*) for her superb guidance on the Painting in Photoshop chapter, and to photographer extraordinaire, Tony Corbell (*www.corbellproductions.com*), for his guidance on the plug-ins chapter (meet you at the Inn of the Anasazi in Santa Fe next year!).

To my esteemed colleagues—and good friends—Taz (again!), Ben Willmore, Trevor Perry, Terry White, Dave Cross, Jack Davis, Kevin Ames, and Jay Nelson who all expressed how *very* proud of me they are and who each, in their own special way, convinced me I could survive writing a book of this magnitude.

To all my friends who continually gave their support when I needed it the most: Pat Fauquet, Jean MacDonald, Sly Marton, Kirk Aplin, George Canellis, Loren Finkelstein, Lorene Romero, Leslie Hollis, Maurice Shevalier, Leslie Raguso, Kathryn Kroll, and Tiffani Barnes. And to the best mama a girl could have, Fran Snider, who sat on the phone with me while I cried tears of stress more nights than I care to admit.

And finally, many thanks go to my husband, Shawn King, who kept the house stocked with food and who forced me away from my Mac to climb onto my beloved bike, Saphira, for a much needed break now and then. I can't believe you didn't strangle me when I bit your head off so many times, and I'm amazed at how you rigged wireless Internet access in our Umbrian farmhouse so I could send off the last few files. Thanks for putting up with me! I'm really glad I didn't shoot you.

—*Lesa Snider King*

Introduction

Congratulations on buying one of the most complicated pieces of software ever created. Fortunately, it's also one of the most rewarding. No other program on the market lets you massage, beautify, and transform your images like Photoshop. It's so popular that people use its name as a verb: "Dude, you Photoshopped the *heck* out of her!" You'd be hard pressed to find a published image that *hasn't* spent some quality time in this program, and those that didn't probably should have.

The bad news is that it's a tough program to learn; you won't become a Photoshop guru overnight. Luckily, you hold in your hot little hands a book that covers Photoshop from a *practical* standpoint, so you'll learn the kinds of techniques you can use every day. It's written in plain English for normal people, so you don't have to be any kind of expert to understand it. You'll also learn just enough theory (where appropriate) to help you understand *why* you're doing what you're doing.

> **NOTE** This book focuses primarily on the standard edition of Photoshop CS4, which runs about $650. Adobe also offers Photoshop CS4 Extended, which costs about $1,000 and offers more features primarily designed for folks who work in fields like architecture and medical science. Page 4 lists some of the new Extended-only goodies.

What's New in Photoshop CS4

Adobe has made some pretty serious changes in Photoshop CS4, especially to the program's overall look. It's a change that's long overdue, as each version of the software piles new tools on top of old ones, and some get lost in the shuffle.

Heck, you're liable to notice several "new" tools in Photoshop CS4 that aren't new at all—they've just clawed their way to the surface. Here's an overview:

- **Workspace overhaul.** Your whole Photoshop world now exists within a compact frame that you can move around and resize (this is new for Mac users, anyway). Using the new Arrange Documents menu (page 63), you can see and work with several documents at once, whether they're side-by-side or stacked on top of each other. And you can create even more room for your images by collapsing panels with a single click (page 17). The new Application bar (page 12) gives you quick access to zoom controls, the Hand tool, screen modes, and the brand-new Rotate View tool (page 61) that lets you spin your canvas around so you can work with it at an angle.

- **Adjustments panel.** Adjustment layers (page 71) have long been Photoshop pros' tool of choice for nondestructive editing (that is, editing that preserves your original image). Problem is, lots of folks didn't know where to find these layers. Now these adjustments take center stage in their very own panel, which not only makes them easier to find and work with—who knew there were so many presets?—but also keeps your image from getting covered up by dialog boxes. Also new are "on-image" adjustments for Curves and Hue/Saturation Adjustment layers. So instead of selecting part of your image and adjusting it, you can adjust a specific range of color by clicking and dragging on the image. You'll also find a new type of Adjustment layer: Vibrance. Snatched straight from Camera Raw (page 53), you can use it make your colors pop without completely messing up skin tones.

- **Masks panel.** The new Masks panel is even more exciting because, for the first time, you can feather masks on the fly—nondestructively!—with a handy slider. You can also control their opacity with the new Density slider, and access the Refine Edges and Color Range controls all in the same panel. These last two controls are great for fine-tuning your selections, as you can read in Chapter 4.

- **Smoother panning and zooming.** Photoshop CS4 displays smooth-looking (non-jagged) images at odd zoom percentages (like 33%) and lets you quickly "toss" your image across the screen with your space bar (this feature is called *flick-panning*—see page 59). If you're zoomed way in on your image, Bird's eye view (page 60) lets you zoom back out instantly by pressing one key for a bird's-eye look at where you are in your image. If you zoom in to 501 percent or more, you see a pixel-grid view that lets you retouch images with amazing precision; page 56 has the scoop.

- **Content-Aware Scaling.** If you've ever needed to make an image just a bit larger or smaller, or move your subjects closer together, Photoshop's new Content-Aware Scale tool (page 242) can help you do just that. Using the same simple controls as the Free Transform tool (page 245) and some revolutionary new technology, Photoshop analyzes your image and alters only less important areas of your image like the ground or sky, leaving your subject completely intact.

- **Enhanced Smart Objects.** You can now use the full range of Transform tools (page 245) on Smart Objects (page 115), including the Perspective, Distort, and Warp options. Smart Objects also now work with linked Layer masks (page 105), so you can move an object and its mask as one unit.

- **Adobe Kuler.** The new Kuler panel is an amazingly useful, people-powered color theme generator. If you get stuck trying to choose a color scheme for your design, you can pick one from the growing number of shared themes posted by other designers—and you can join the fun and upload your own (page 454).

- **Drag-resize cursors.** Whether you're retouching or painting, you'll spend a lot of time using brush-based tools, and Adobe has made it easier than ever to resize them: Ctrl-Option-drag (Alt+right-click+drag on a PC) to the left to make them smaller or to the right to make them bigger. To change brush hardness, ⌘-Ctrl-Option-drag (Alt+Shift+right-click+drag on a PC) to the left to make it softer or to the right to make it harder.

- **"Spring-loaded" tools.** Need to temporarily switch from one tool to another? No problem: Just press and hold the tool's keyboard shortcut and then release the key when you're ready to switch back to the tool you were originally using.

- **Enhanced Auto-Blend and Auto-Align.** If you want to combine several images into one to create extended depth-of-field effects (where you take several photos of an object that have different parts in focus and put them together to make it look like the whole thing is in focus), complex collages, or 360-degree panoramas, these two tools make Photoshop do the heavy lifting for you. They're covered on page 288 and page 283, respectively.

- **Improved Dodge and Burn tools.** Long considered too destructive for serious use, Adobe has reengineered these two tools so they now preserve color and details. That said, page 414 shows you how to use a better alternative: the Brush tool. You can make it behave *like* the Dodge and Burn tools *and* it's nondestructive.

- **Cloning and Healing previews.** Now you can see what you're about to paint *before* you actually use the Cloning and Healing tools. Once you tell Photoshop which part of the image you want to clone or heal with, it shows you a preview of that area inside your brush cursor. You can learn about these tools in Chapter 7 (page 288) and Chapter 10 (page 394).

- **Enhanced printing.** The Mac version of Photoshop lets you create 16-bit images (page 43) so your printouts can include even richer details. And you can now preview out-of-gamut colors (ones outside the range of what the printer can reproduce) right in the Print dialog box—see page 652.

- **64-bit support in Windows Vista.** The new buzzword in graphics circles is "64-bit". All it really means is that some programs (ones that can read 64-bit files) let you open and edit honkin' big files—ones that are over 4 gigabytes. Unfortunately, the Mac version of Photoshop doesn't yet support 64-bit files (that'll likely happen in the *next* version). If you're on a Mac, you can still share

Photoshop files with PC folks just like you always have, and aside from the Mac's 4-GB file size limit, you shouldn't see any big performance difference. And unless you plan on working with files that are bigger than 4 GB, the difference between the 64-bit and 32-bit versions of Photoshop CS4 doesn't mean a hill of beans to you.

- **Upgraded Camera Raw.** The newest version of the Camera Raw plug-in (page 53) sports major improvements like selective editing with the new Adjustments brush, the ability to add nondestructive gradient masks with Graduated Filters, and so on. You'll learn about all these features in Chapter 9 (beginning on page 354).

- **Beefed-up Bridge.** Adobe Bridge (a separate program that ships with Photoshop) lets you preview, organize, and process image files. Bridge now boasts better speed, a much-improved workspace, one-click previews, a search bar, and more. Photographers will love the new Review mode, where you see a big, floating carousel of all the photos you've selected. And the new Adobe Output Module lets you export your images as PDFs and Web galleries. See Appendix C for full coverage of Bridge.

There are also a few features that you'll only find in Photoshop CS4 Extended:

- **3D editing.** Adobe has added a couple of new items to the Tools panel—3D Rotate and 3D Orbit—as well as a new 3D menu stuffed full of commands for working with 3D objects. With CS4, Photoshop has stepped into the realm of 3D modeling, letting you convert 2D objects into 3D ones and adjust textures and lighting. You can even paint on 3D models in real time and open models you've downloaded. This book doesn't cover all the new 3D features in detail, but the box on page 72 has the highlights.

- **Enhanced video features.** If you're a videographer, you'll appreciate Photoshop Extended's single-letter keyboard shortcuts, the way it smoothly displays pixels that aren't perfectly square (see the box on page 74), and the ability to preview and export audio. You can also turn any 3D object into a video display area.

There are also tons of little changes in Photoshop CS4, too. For example, you can finally delete layers by pressing the Delete key (Mac) or Backspace (PC)—yay! And you can now use Photoshop with multi-touch trackpads on Mac laptops, generate color profiles for color-blind folks, view a 6-color histogram in the Histogram panel (page 363), and access a new online help system.

With the good comes a little bad: To make room for new features, Adobe left some plug-ins on the cutting room floor, like the Extract filter, Picture Package, Contact Sheets, and PDF Presentations. Thankfully, the older versions of those plug-ins still work in CS4 (save for PDF Presentations—that one's a goner); you just have to download them from Adobe's Web site or snatch them from Photoshop CS3, if you have it (this book shows you how). The drag-and-drop Photomerge dialog box has also passed quietly into the night, as has the ability to create a PDF of a layer comp in Photoshop (though you can still do that in Bridge).

About This Book

Adobe has pulled together an amazing amount of information in its new online help system (page 729), but despite all these efforts, it's geared toward seasoned Photoshop jockeys and assumes a level of skill that you may not have. The explanations are very clipped and to the point, which makes it difficult to get a real feel for the tool or technique you're learning about.

That's where this book comes in. It's intended to make learning Photoshop CS4 tolerable and even enjoyable by avoiding technical jargon as much as possible and explaining *why* and *when* you'll want to use (or avoid) certain features in the program. It's a conversational and friendly approach intended to speak to beginners and seasoned pixel pushers alike.

Some of the tutorials in this book refer to files you can download from the Missing Manuals Web site (*www.missingmanuals.com*) so you can practice the techniques you're reading about. And throughout the book, you'll find several kinds of sidebar articles. The ones labeled "Up to Speed" help newcomers to Photoshop CS4 do things or explain concepts that veterans are probably already familiar with. Those labeled "Power Users' Clinic" cover more advanced topics for the brave of heart.

> **NOTE** Photoshop CS4 now functions almost identically on Macs and Windows computers, but the screenshots in this book were all taken on a Mac for the sake of consistency. However, the keyboard shortcuts for the two operating systems are different, so you'll find both included throughout this book—Mac shortcuts first, followed by Windows shortcuts in parentheses. In a few instances, the locations of certain folders differ and in those cases, you get the directions for both operating systems.

About the Outline

This hefty book is divided into six parts, each devoted to the type of things you'll do in Photoshop CS4:

- **Part One: The Basics.** Here's where you'll learn the essential skills you need to know before moving forward. Chapter 1 gives you the lay of the land and teaches you how to work with panels and make the Photoshop workspace your own. You'll also find out the many ways of undoing what you've done, which is crucial when you're still learning. Chapter 2 covers how to open and view your documents efficiently, and how to set up new documents so you have a solid foundation on which to build your masterpieces.

  Chapter 3 dives into the most powerful feature in all of Photoshop: layers. You'll learn about the different kinds of layers and how to manage them, the power of layer masks, and how to use Layer styles for special effects. Chapter 4 explains how to select part of an image so you can edit just that area. In Chapter 5, you'll dive head first into the science of color as you explore channels (Photoshop's way of isolating the colors that make up your image) and learn how to use channels to create selections; you'll also pick up some channel-specific editing tips along the way.

- **Part Two: Editing Images.** Chapter 6 starts off by explaining a variety of ways you can crop images, both in Photoshop and in Camera Raw. The chapter then demystifies resolution once and for all so you'll understand how to resize images without reducing their quality. In Chapter 7, you'll learn how to combine your images in a variety of ways, from simple techniques to more complex ones. Chapter 8 covers draining, changing, and adding color, arming you with several techniques for creating gorgeous black-and-white images, delicious duotones, partial-color effects, and more. You'll also learn how to change the color of almost anything.

  Chapter 9 focuses on color-correcting images, beginning with auto fixer-uppers, moving on to the wonderfully simple world of Camera Raw, and then into the more complicated realm of Levels and Curves Adjustment layers. Chapter 10 is all about retouching people and is packed with practical techniques for slimming, trimming, and beautifying the faces and bodies that grace your pictures. It also explains how to use the Dodge and Burn tools in ways that won't harm your images. Chapter 11 covers all kinds of ways to sharpen images to make them look especially crisp.

- **Part Three: The Artistic Side of Photoshop.** This part of the book is all about creativity. Chapter 12 explains the many ways of choosing colors for your documents, and teaches you how to create a painting from scratch. Chapter 13 focuses on using the mighty Pen tool to create complex illustrations and selections, and you'll learn how to use Photoshop's Shape tools. Chapter 14 teaches you the basics of typography and then moves on to how to create and format text in Photoshop. You'll find out how to outline, texturize, and place text, among other fun stuff. Chapter 15 covers the wide world of filters; you'll come away with at least one practical use for one or more of the filters in each filter category.

- **Part Four: Printing and the Web.** In Chapter 16, you'll learn about printing your images, beginning with why it's so darn hard to make what comes out of your printer match what you see onscreen. You'll learn about the different color modes and how to prepare your images for printing, whether you're using an inkjet printer or sending your files to a commercial printing press. Chapter 17 focuses on preparing images for the Web, and walks you through the various file formats you can use, how to protect your images online, and using Adobe Bridge to create Web galleries. Rounding out the chapter is info on using the Slice tool on a Web page design, and step-by-step instructions for creating an animated GIF.

- **Part Five: Photoshop Power.** This part is all about working smarter and faster. It starts with an entire chapter devoted to using actions (Chapter 18), which help you automate tasks you perform regularly. Chapter 19 covers installing and using plug-ins (small programs you can add on to Photoshop) and recommends some of the best ones.

- **Part Six: Appendixes.** Appendix A covers installing and uninstalling Photoshop. Appendix B gives you some troubleshooting tips, explains Photoshop's help system, and points you to resources other than this book. Appendix C gets you up to speed on using Adobe Bridge to import, organize, and export your images. Appendix D walks you through Photoshop CS4's 244 menu items. And Appendix E gives you a tour of the mighty Tools panel.

NOTE Appendixes A, D, and E are available online at *www.missingmanuals.com*.

For Photographers

If you're relatively new to digital-image editing or you've always shot film and are taking your first brave steps into the world of digital cameras, you'll be amazed at what you can do in Photoshop, but there's a lot to learn. By breaking Photoshop down into digestible chunks that are most important to *you*, the learning process will feel less overwhelming. (There's no sense in tackling the whole program when you'll only use a quarter of it—if that much). The most important thing to remember is to be patient and try not to get frustrated.

With patience and practice, you *can* master the bits of Photoshop that you need to help do your job better. And with the help of this book you'll conquer everything much faster than you might think. As you gain confidence, you can start branching out into other parts of the program to broaden your skills. Here's a suggested roadmap for quickly learning the most useful aspects of the program as you're starting out:

1. **Read all of Chapters 1 and 2 (or at the very least skim them).**

   These two chapters show you where to find all of Photoshop's tools and features and explain how the program is organized. You'll learn how to open, view, and save your images, which is vital stuff to know.

2. **If your photos aren't on your computer already, read Appendix A about Adobe Bridge.**

   Bridge is an amazingly powerful image organizer and browser that can help get your images onto your computer. Bridge takes care of importing, renaming, and backing up your precious photos.

3. **If you're shooting in Raw format (page 53) and need to color-correct your images in a hurry, skip ahead to the section on editing in Camera Raw in Chapter 9 (page 354).**

   This chapter includes an entire section on practical editing techniques you can use in Camera Raw, and a quick reference that points you to where you'll find other Camera Raw techniques throughout this book.

4. **If you're not shooting in Raw and you need to resize your images before you edit them, start with Chapter 6.**

   Chapter 6 explains resolution and how to resize images without reducing their quality.

5. Proceed with Chapters 8, 9, and 10 to learn about color effects, color-correcting, and retouching people, respectively.

6. When you're ready to sharpen your images, read Chapter 11.

7. Finally, when you want to print your photos, read the section on printing with an inkjet printer in Chapter 16 (page 625).

    This chapter walks you through the maze of dialog boxes you have to go through to print your photos. It even has advice on how to print borderless images.

That's all you need to get started. When you're ready to dive more fully into Photoshop, pick back up at Chapter 3, which covers layers, and move on through the book as time permits.

The Very Basics

This book assumes that you know how to use a computer and that, to some extent, you're an expert double-clicker, drag and dropper, and menu opener. If not, here's a quick refresher:

To *click* means to move the point of your mouse or trackpad cursor over an object on your screen and press the left mouse or trackpad button once. To *right-click* means to press the right mouse button once, which produces a menu of special features called a *shortcut menu*. To *double-click* means to press the left button twice, quickly, without moving the mouse between clicks. To *drag* means to click an object and use the mouse to move it while holding down the left mouse button. Most selection buttons onscreen are pretty obvious, but you may not be familiar with *radio buttons*: To choose an option, you click one of these little empty circles that are arranged like a list. If you're comfortable with basic concepts like these, you're ready to get started with this book.

You'll find tons of keyboard shortcuts along the way, and they're huge timesavers. If you see "Press ⌘-S (Ctrl+S on a PC) to save your file," that means to hold down the ⌘ (or Ctrl) key while pressing the S key. Press one and keep holding it as you press the other. (This book lists Mac keyboard shortcuts first, followed by Windows shortcuts in parentheses.) Other keyboard shortcuts are so complex that you'll need to use multiple fingers, both hands, and a well-placed elbow. Use them at your own risk!

About → These → Arrows

Throughout *Photoshop CS4: The Missing Manual* (and in all Missing Manuals, for that matter), you'll see arrows sprinkled throughout each chapter in sentences like this: "Choose Filter → Blur → Gaussian Blur." This is a shorthand way of helping you find files, folders, and menu choices without having to read through painfully long and boring instructions. For example, the sentence in the previous paragraph is a short way of saying: "At the top of the Photoshop window, locate the Filter menu. Click it and, in the list that appears, look for the Blur category. Point to the word Blur without clicking and, in the resulting submenu, click Gaussian Blur."

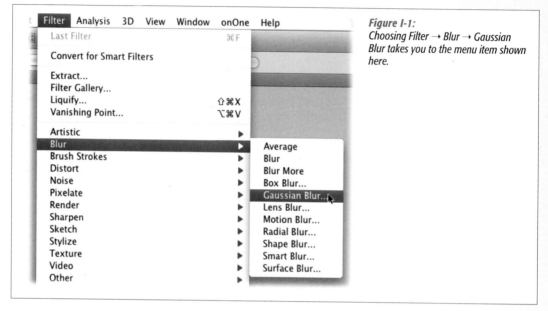

Figure I-1:
Choosing Filter → Blur → Gaussian Blur takes you to the menu item shown here.

About MissingManuals.com

On the Missing Manuals Web site (*www.missingmanuals.com*), you can find links to downloadable images mentioned in the tutorials in this book, in case you want to practice techniques without using your own photos.

A word about the image files for the tutorials: To make life easier for people with dial-up Internet connections, the file sizes have been kept pretty small. This means you probably won't want to print the results of what you create (you'll end up with a print about the size of a matchbook). But that doesn't really matter because the files are only meant for onscreen use. You'll see notes throughout the book about which practice images are available for any given chapter.

At the Web site, you can also find articles, tips, and updates to this book. If you click the Errata link, you'll see any corrections we've made to the book, too. If you find something in this book that you think is wrong, feel free to report it by clicking that link. Each time the book is printed, we'll update it with any confirmed corrections. If you want to be certain that your own copy is up to the minute, this is where to check for any changes. And thanks for reporting any errors or suggesting corrections.

We'd love to hear your suggestions for new books in the Missing Manual line. There's a place for that on *missingmanuals.com*, too. And while you're online, you can also register this book at *www.oreilly.com* (you can jump directly to the registration page by going here: *http://tinyurl.com/yo82k3*). Registering means we can send you updates about this book, and you'll be eligible for special offers like discounts on future editions.

Safari® Books Online

 When you see a Safari® Books Online icon on the cover of your favorite technology book, that means the book is available online through the O'Reilly Network Safari Bookshelf.

Safari offers a solution that's better than e-books. It's a virtual library that lets you easily search thousands of top tech books, cut and paste code samples, download chapters, and find quick answers when you need the most accurate, current information. Try it for free at *http://safari.oreilly.com*.

Photoshop CS4 Guided Tour

Photoshop CS4 is bursting with amazing features that'll help you edit and create digital masterpieces. If this is your first foray into the world of Photoshop, all these features will be new to you. If you're an experienced pixel pusher, there are surprises a-plenty waiting for you, too. With Photoshop CS4, Adobe introduced major changes to the work environment, and while these changes make Photoshop easier to use, they take some getting used to.

Throughout the rest of this book, you'll dive much deeper into specific tools and techniques, but this chapter gives you a good, solid foundation on which to build your Photoshop skills. You'll learn how to work with the new Application Frame and Application bar and how to wrangle all the windows and panels filling your screen. Once you've gotten them placed just right, you'll learn how to save your setup as a custom workspace. If you're a beginner, the section on using Undo commands and history states will show you how to fix mistakes and back out of almost anything you've done. Finally, you'll learn how to fine-tune Photoshop's behavior through preferences and built-in tools (called presets) that let you personalize your work environment even more.

Meet the Application Frame

When you launch Photoshop CS4 for the first time, you'll be greeted by the new *Application Frame* shown in Figure 1-1. It's part of Adobe's effort to consolidate your work environment and lessen clutter; the frame confines all things Photoshop to a single resizable and movable window. You can grab the whole mess—documents, panels, and all—and move it to one side of your screen (or better yet, to another monitor) so it's out of your way. If you open more than one document, they're displayed in handy tabs that you can rearrange by dragging to the left or right.

Close frame
Minimize frame
Maximize frame
Application Bar
Options Bar
Document tab
Panels
Workspace menu

Tools panel
Document Window
Drag to resize frame

Figure 1-1:
Click an image's document tab to summon it front and center. Photoshop stores the vast majority of its tools in the panels on the left and right sides; a full introduction to panels starts on page 17.

The upside of using the Application Frame is that all of Photoshop's bits and pieces stay together as you move things around. Resizing the frame also automatically changes the size of your panels and windows to fit within it. The downside is that this kind of all-encompassing worldview is pretty radical for Mac fans though it should feel familiar to folks who use PCs. Chances are, you'll either love it or hate it!

If you find the Application Frame isn't your style, you can turn it off by choosing Window → Application Frame to make Photoshop switch to the floating-window view used in previous versions of the program.

TIP If you need to do some work on your desktop or in another program, you can temporarily *hide* Photoshop. On a Mac, press ⌘-Ctrl-H or click the red dot at the top left of the Application Frame. Your workspace disappears, but Photoshop keeps running in the background, standing by. To bring the program back to the forefront, just click its shrunken icon in the Dock. If you're on a PC, click the upper-right – sign button and Windows tucks the program down into your taskbar. To get it back, click its taskbar icon.

The Application Bar

At the very top of the Application Frame is a row of tools called the *Application bar* (Figure 1-2). Here, you've got one-click access to handy stuff like Adobe Bridge (covered in Appendix C), extras (guides, grids, and rulers), zoom controls, and more. The real gems, though, are the new Rotate View tool and the Arrange Documents menu. Rotate View will make graphics tablet users squeal with delight because it creates a more natural way to paint or draw (see page 61 for details). The Arrange Documents menu lets you view several open documents so you can see them all at one time, which is handy for evaluating before and after versions of images or just managing a bunch of open windows. Flip over to Chapter 2 for more on using these features (beginning on page 62).

TIP If you're on a Mac and you turned off the Application Frame by choosing Window → Application Frame and don't see the Application bar anymore, you can create a floating Application bar by choosing Window → Application Bar.

Launch Bridge
View Extras   Hand tool
Zoom Level   Zoom tool   Arrange Documents

Rotate View   . Screen Mode

Figure 1-2:
The new Application bar includes features like Rotate View (page 61), Arrange Documents (page 63), and Screen Mode (page 14). It also makes some old tools easier to reach. For example, the extras (guides, grids, and rulers) used to be buried deep within menus, the zoom controls were stuck at the bottom of the document window, and the Hand and Zoom tools hung out at the far end of the Tools panel.

NOTE In the PC version of Photoshop CS4, the Application bar is also home to all the program's main menus (File, Edit, Image, Layer, and so on); in the Mac version, those menus appear at the top of your screen instead.

The Almighty Options Bar

Lording over your document window is the Options bar, which lets you customize the settings for every tool in the program (see Figure 1-3). The bar automatically changes to show settings related to the tool you're currently using. Unfortunately, its labels are fairly cryptic, so it can be hard to figure out what the heck all that stuff does. Luckily, you can hover your cursor over any item to see a little pop-up description called a *tooltip* (you don't need to click—just wait a couple seconds). When you move your cursor away from the item, the tooltip disappears.

When you first install Photoshop, the Options bar is perched near the top of the screen underneath the Application bar. If you'd rather put it somewhere else, grab its left end and drag it wherever you want, as shown in Figure 1-3, bottom. If you decide to put it back later, drag it to the top of the screen and, when you see a thin blue line appear at the bottom of the Application bar, release your mouse button.

Figure 1-3:
Top: The Options bar is customization central for whatever tool you're currently using. Incidentally, if a tool seems to be misbehaving, it's usually because you changed one of the Options bar's settings and forgot to change it back! The settings are "sticky": once you change them, they stay that way until you change them back.

Bottom: To move the Options bar, grab the tiny dotted lines at its far left end and drag the bar somewhere else.

Swapping Screen Modes

Photoshop also includes three different *screen modes* for your document viewing pleasure. Depending on what you're doing, one will suit you better than another. For example, you can make your image take up your whole screen (with or without the Application and Options bars), you can hide your panels, and so on (see Figure 1-4).

> **NOTE** Flip ahead to page 47 to learn how to open an image. The short version: Choose File → Open, navigate to where the image lives, and click Open.

It's a snap to jump between modes—just press the F key repeatedly (as long as you're not using the Type tool—if you are, you'll type a bunch of *f*s) or use the new Screen Mode pop-up menu in the Application bar (see Figure 1-2). Your choices are:

- **Standard Screen Mode** is the view you see when you launch Photoshop for the first time. This mode shows menus, the Application Frame and Application bar, panels, and document windows. Use this mode when the Application Frame is active and you need to move the whole Photoshop application—windows and all—around on your monitor.

- **Full Screen Mode With Menu Bar** completely takes over your screen, puts your currently open document in the center, places it on a gray background, and attaches any open panels to the left and right edges of your monitor. This mode is great for day-to-day editing because you can see all your tools and menus without being distracted by all the files and folders on your desktop. The gray background is also easy on your eyes.

Figure 1-4:
The many faces of Photoshop: Standard with Application Frame (top left); Full Screen With Menu Bar (bottom top right); Full Screen with menu bar and panels hidden (bottom left); and Full Screen (bottom right). You can edit images in any of the modes. Pressing the Tab key displays menus and panels if they're hidden.

- **Full Screen Mode** hides all of Photoshop's menus and panels, centers your document on your screen, and puts it on a black background. This mode is great for displaying and evaluating your work or for editing distraction-free. The black background really makes images pop off your screen, too.

TIP You can free up precious screen real estate by pressing the Tab key to hide your panels. This trick is a great way to get rid of distracting elements when you're editing images, especially if you've got a small monitor. Pressing Shift-Tab hides everything except the Tools panel, Options bar, and Application bar. To turn the panels back on, press Tab or mouse over to the edge of your monitor where the panels should be. When you move your mouse away from the panels, they'll disappear again.

Customizing Your Workspace

The folks at Adobe understand that once you arrange your panels just so, you want to keep them that way. That's why Photoshop lets you save your setup as a *workspace* by using the Workspace Switcher menu at the top right of the Application bar. This menu, which is set to Essentials when you first open the program, always shows the name of the currently selected workspace. To change workspaces, click the menu and pick one of the presets (built-in settings) to make Photoshop rearrange your panels accordingly. The list of presets includes customized panel groups for things like painting, working with video, and so on (see Figure 1-5).

Figure 1-5:
Most of the preset workspaces are designed to help you perform specialized tasks. For example, the Painting workspace puts the Brushes and Navigation panels at the top right and groups together the color-related panels you'll undoubtedly use while you're painting your masterpiece. Take the built-in workspaces for a test drive—they may give you customizing ideas you hadn't thought of.

> **TIP** If you're familiar with Photoshop but new to CS4, try out the "What's New in CS4" workspace. Because it literally highlights all the menu item that are new in Photoshop CS4, it's a great way to see the additions at a glance.

To save your own custom workspace, first get things looking the way you want. (The next section has details on working with panels.) Next, click the Workspace Switcher menu and choose Save Workspace (it's at the bottom of the menu). In the resulting dialog box, give your workspace a name and turn on the options for the features you want to include. You can pick from panel locations, keyboard shortcuts, and menu settings; just be sure to turn on the options for *all* the features you changed or they won't be included in your custom workspace. After you click Save, your custom workspace shows up in the Workspace Switcher menu along with all the built-in workspaces.

> **TIP** Some workspaces hide menu items so you see only the ones you're most likely to use for a specific editing task. If you need to get at hidden menu items temporarily, look for the Show All Menu Items option at the bottom of any menu list. If you don't see that option, it means all of that menu's items are visible.

If you've created some custom workspaces that you'll never use again, you can get rid of them (sorry, you can't get rid of the presets!). First, make sure the workspace you want to delete isn't selected. Next, choose Delete Workspace from the Workspace Switcher menu. In the resulting Delete Workspace dialog box, pick the offending workspace and click Delete.

Working with Panels

The far right side of the Application frame is home to a slew of small windows called *panels* (they were called palettes in previous versions of Photoshop). They let you work with commonly used features like colors, adjustments, layers, and so on. Panels don't have to live alone; you can link them together in groups, which you can then move around. Feel free to organize the panels you use most however you like, and you can position them anywhere you want. Panels can be free floating or *docked* (attached) to the left, top, or right side of your screen (or the Application Frame).

Photoshop starts you off with three docked panel groups filled with the panels it thinks you'll most likely need first. The first group includes the Colors, Swatches, and Styles panels; the second group includes Adjustments and Masks; and the third includes Layers, Channels, and Paths panels (there's more on docked panels coming up shortly).

To work with a panel, select it by clicking its tab. Panels are like Silly Putty—they're incredibly flexible. You can collapse, expand, move, and resize them or swap 'em for other panels (the Windows menu lists all the panels in Photoshop). Here's how:

- **Collapse or expand panels.** If the panels are encroaching on your editing space, you can shrink them both horizontally and vertically so they look and behave like buttons (see Figure 1-6). To collapse a panel horizontally into a button nestled against the side of another panel (or the edge of your screen), click the tiny double arrow in its top-right corner (click this same button again to expand the panel). To collapse a panel vertically against the bottom of the panel above it, click a blank spot in the dark gray area near the panel's tab to make the panel roll up like a window shade (click it again to roll it back down). To adjust a panel's width, hover your cursor over its left edge; when your cursor turns into a double-headed arrow, drag left or right to make the panel bigger or smaller. Collapsing and expanding panels works exactly the same for individual panels and panel groups.

- **Modify panel groups.** As mentioned earlier, Photoshop clumps frequently used panels into *panel groups*. If you don't use certain a panel in a group, replace it with a panel you *do* use. To remove a panel, click its tab and drag it out of the panel group to a different area on your screen (see Figure 1-7, top). Then click the tiny circle in the panel's top-left corner to close it. (On a PC, click the X button in the panel's top-right corner instead.) Don't worry—the panel isn't gone forever; if you want to reopen it, simply choose it from the Windows menu.

Click here to collapse
panels vertically

Click here to collapse
panels horitzontally

Figure 1-6:
Here you can see the difference between expanded (left) and collapsed (right) panels. Click the medium gray bar at the top of a panel to collapse it vertically (circled on the left), rolling it up like a window shade. Click the bar again to expand it. You can also collapse them horizontally by clicking the double arrows at the top right of the panel (circled on the right).

To add a panel to a group, first make sure the panel is open (if not, select it from the Windows menu). Then grab the top of the panel near its tab and drag it into the group you want to add it to; when you see a blue outline appear inside the panel group, release your mouse button (see Figure 1-7, middle).

TIP To rearrange panels within a group, drag their tabs left or right.

- **Dock and undock panels.** The first time you open Photoshop, it docks three sets of panel groups to the right side of your screen (or Application Frame). But you're not stuck with your panels glued to this spot; you can set them free by turning them into *floating* panels. To liberate a panel, grab its tab, pull it out of the group it's in, and then move it anywhere you want. When you let go of your mouse button, the panel appears where you put it—all by itself.

Figure 1-7:

Top: You can remove panels you don't use to free up space. For example, if you never use the Styles panel (and you probably won't use it much), drag it out of the panel group and close it.

Middle: When you're dragging a panel into a panel group, wait until you see a blue line around the inside of the group before you release your mouse button. Here the Kuler panel is being added to a panel group.

Bottom: When you release your mouse button, the new panel becomes part of the group.

To undock a whole panel group, click an empty spot in the group's tab area and drag it out of the Dock (Figure 1-8, top). Once you release your mouse button, you can drag the panel group around by clicking the same empty spot in the tab area. Or, if the group is collapsed, click the tiny dotted lines at the top of the group, just below the dark gray bar (Figure 1-8, bottom). To dock the panel (or panel group) again, drag it back to the right side of your screen. Getting the hang of undocking, redocking, and arranging panels takes a little practice because it's tough to control where the little buggers *land*. When the panel you're dragging is about to join the Dock area at the right side of your screen (or a different panel group), a thin blue line appears showing you where the panel or group will go. Unfortunately, the line can be tough to spot because it's so thin and light colored.

TIP   If the thin blue highlight lines are hard to see when you're trying to group or dock panels, try dragging the panels more slowly. When you drag the panel into a group or dockable area, the blue highlight hangs around longer.

Drag this way to undock the panel

Click and drag to move vertical panels

Drag this way to dock the panel

Figure 1-8:
Left: To undock a panel or panel group, grab a free area to the right of the tabs at the top of the panel and drag it somewhere else on your screen. To dock it again, drag it to the right side of your screen—on top of the other panels. When you see a thin blue line appear where you want the panel or group to land, release your mouse button.

Right: You can move vertically collapsed panels in the same way, but you grab them by the row of tiny dots that appears at the top (shown here).

Using the Tools Panel

The most important panel in Photoshop is the one named Tools (Figure 1-9, left); it serves as home base for all of Photoshop's editing tools. When you first launch the program, you'll see the Tools panel on the left side of your screen, but you can drag it anywhere you want by clicking the double row of dots near its top (Figure 1-9, right).

Unfortunately, there's not enough room in the Tools panel for every tool to have its own button (or the panel would be a mile long), so related tools are grouped together into *toolsets*. The microscopic black triangle at the bottom right of each tool's button lets you know it represents more than one tool (the Move and Zoom tools are the only ones that live alone). To see the other tools, hold down the tool's button and Photoshop displays a list of the other tools it harbors in a fly-out menu, as shown in Figure 1-9, left.

Once you expand each toolset, you'll see each tool's keyboard shortcut listed to the right of its name. These shortcuts are great timesavers because they let you switch between tools without moving your hands off the keyboard. To access a tool that's hidden deep within a toolset, add the Shift key to the tool's shortcut and you'll cycle through all the tools in that toolset. For example, to select the Elliptical Marquee tool, press Shift-M repeatedly until that tool appears in the Tools panel.

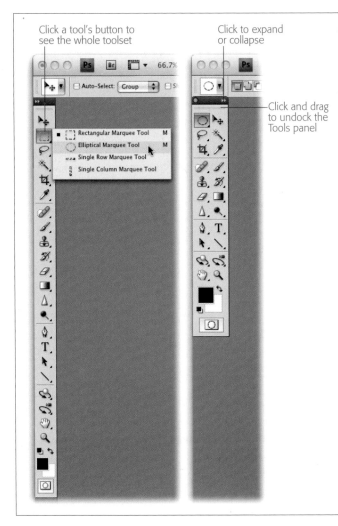

Click a tool's button to
see the whole toolset

Click to expand
or collapse

Click and drag
to undock the
Tools panel

Figure 1-9:
*Click and hold any tool to expand its toolset.
Photoshop starts you off with a one-column
Tools panel, but you can collapse it into two
columns by clicking the dark gray bar shown
here (click it again to expand it back to one
column). If you want to undock the Tools panel
from the Application Frame (page 11), grab
the dotted bar labeled here and drag the panel
wherever you want it.*

TIP   If you need to switch tools only *temporarily*—for a quick edit—you can use Photoshop CS4's new spring-loaded tools feature. Just press and hold a tool's keyboard shortcut to switch to that tool and then perform your edit. As soon as you release the key, you'll jump back to the tool you were using before. For example, if you're painting with the Brush and suddenly make an error, press and hold E to switch to the Eraser and fix your mistake. Once you release the E key, you're back to using the Brush tool. Sweet!

For an overview of all the tools in this panel, check out online Appendix E. For a quick reminder of what each tool does, hover your mouse pointer over its icon for a couple of seconds; Photoshop displays a handy tooltip that includes the tool's name and its keyboard shortcut (you have to keep your mouse perfectly still or release your mouse button for the tooltip to appear).

Foreground and background color chips

Photoshop can handle millions of colors, but it lets you work with only two at a time: a foreground color and a background color. Each of these is visible as a square *color chip* near the bottom of the Tools panel (in Figure 1-9, they're black and white, respectively). Photoshop uses your foreground color when you paint or fill something with color. It uses your background color to do things like setting the second color of a *gradient* (page 265) and erasing parts of a locked Background layer (page 80). It's also helpful when you're running special effects like the Clouds filter (page 486). In other words, the foreground color is where most of the action is. If you want to change either color, click its color chip once to make Photoshop open the Color Picker (page 457), which lets you pick another color for that particular color chip. To swap your foreground and background colors, click the double-headed arrow just above the two chips or press X. (Remember this shortcut; it's extremely handy when you work with layer masks, which are discussed in Chapter 3.)

Colors

In the upper-right part of your screen, you'll see the Color panel, which also displays your current foreground and background color chips. This panel lets you pick a new color for either chip *without* having to open the just-mentioned Color Picker (which also means Photoshop won't pop open a big dialog box that hides part of your image). The Color panel is discussed in Chapter 12 on page 461.

Swatches

The Swatches panel holds miniature samples of colors, giving you easy access to them for use in painting or colorizing your images. This panel also stores a variety of color libraries like the Pantone Matching System (special inks used in professional printing processes). You'll learn all about the Swatches panel in Chapter 12 on page 460.

Styles

Styles are saved special effects created with a variety of layer styles (page 119). For example, if you've created a glass-button look by using several layer styles, you can save the whole lot of 'em as a *single* style—which means you can apply it with a swift double-click (instead of adding each layer style individually). You can choose from tons of built-in styles; they're all discussed starting on page 122.

Adjustments

The Adjustments panel, new in Photoshop CS4, gives you one-stop access to all the Adjustment layers in Photoshop. Instead of making color and lighting changes to your original image, these Adjustment layers make the change on a separate layer, giving you all kinds of editing flexibility and keeping your original image out of harm's way. They're defined in detail in Chapter 3 (page 71).

Masks

Also new in CS4, the Masks panel lets you create and fine-tune layer masks. You'll dive headfirst into masks in Chapter 3 (page 105), but, for now, you can think of them as digital masking tape that lets you hide the contents of a layer, whether that's an adjustment of some sort (color or lighting change) or parts of an image.

Layers

The Layers panel is the single most important panel in Photoshop. Layers let you work with your images as if they were a stack of transparencies, so you can create one image from many. With layers, you can resize, adjust, and add special effects to each element independently. Understanding layers is the key to Photoshop success, and you'll learn all about them in Chapter 3.

Channels

Channels are containers in which Photoshop stores the color information your images are made from, whether that's RGB (red, green, blue), CMYK (cyan, magenta, yellow, black), grayscale, and so on. Channels are extremely powerful, and you can use them to edit the individual colors in your image, which is helpful in sharpening images, creating selections (telling Photoshop which part of an image you want to work with), and so on. Chapter 5 has the scoop on channels.

Paths

Paths are the lines you make with the Pen and Shape tools. They're not your average, run-of-the-mill lines; because they're comprised of points and paths instead of pixels, they'll always print perfectly crisp, and you can make them bigger or smaller without losing any quality. You'll learn all about paths in Chapter 13.

Navigator

Think of the Navigator panel as a map. It displays a mini version of your image with a frame around the area you're currently zoomed into. You can use the Navigator panel to move around in your document, and change magnification levels. The Navigator panel is especially useful when you're working with really big images and you're zoomed in to work on fine details. To see the Navigator panel in action, flip to Chapter 2, page 60.

Histogram

A histogram is a graph that shows a visual representation of the color info contained in your image. The left side of the graph shows how much of the image falls into the darkest colors (shadows), the far right shows the brightest colors (highlights), and the area in the middle represents colors in between (midtones). Histograms are crucial when you're color-correcting images, and they're discussed at length in Chapter 9, beginning on page 363.

Info

The Info panel is your command center for general info about the image you're working on. It shows you the color values of certain pixels, your mouse pointer location, image size, and other useful bits of, well, image info. It also changes on the fly to show info that relates to the currently selected tool and gives you a handy tip about using the currently active tool. You can find out more on pages 68 and 373.

The Power of Undo

Thankfully, Photoshop is extremely forgiving: It'll let you back out of almost anything you do, which is *muy importante* when you're first learning.

You've got several ways to retrace your steps, including the lifesaving Undo command—just choose Edit → Undo or press ⌘-Z (Ctrl+Z on a PC). Unfortunately, the Undo command lets you undo only the last edit you made.

If you need to go back *more* than one step, use the Step Backward command—choose Edit → Step Backward or press ⌘-Option-Z (Ctrl+Alt+Z on a PC). Out of the box, this command lets you undo the last 20 things you did, one at a time. If you want to go back even further, you can change that number by digging into Photoshop preferences, as the next section explains. You can step forward through your edit history, too, by choosing Edit → Step Forward or ⌘-Shift-Z (Shift+Ctrl+Z on a PC).

> **TIP** Photoshop lets you undo up to 20 changes, back to the point when you first opened the document, which means you can't close a document and then undo the changes you made *before* you closed it.

Changing How Far Back You Can Go

If you think you might someday need to go back *further* than your last 20 steps, you can make Photoshop remember up to 1,000 steps by changing the program's preferences. Here's how:

1. **Choose Photoshop → Preferences.**

   On a Mac, doing this opens the Preferences dialog box. Click Performance in the left-hand column to see the history preferences. On a PC, choosing Photoshop → Preferences opens another submenu. Choose Performance from the submenu to see the history preferences.

2. **Look for the History States field in the upper right corner of the Preferences dialog box and then pick the number of Undo steps you want Photoshop to remember.**

   Choose any number between 1 and 1,000. While increasing the number of history states might help you sleep better, doing so means Photoshop has to keep track of that many versions of your document, which requires memory and processing power. If you increase this setting and notice that the program is running like molasses, try lowering it.

3. **Click OK when you're finished.**

Turning Back Time with the History Panel

The History panel is like your very own time machine. Whereas the Undo and Step Backward commands let you move back through changes one step at a time, the History panel (see Figure 1-10) kicks it up a notch and lets you jump back *several* steps at once. (You can step back through as many history states as you set in Photoshop's preferences, as mentioned earlier.) The History panel is much quicker than undoing a long list of changes one by one, and it gives you a nice list of *exactly* what you've done to your image—in chronological order from top to bottom—letting you pinpoint the exact state you want to jump back to. You can also take snapshots of your image at various points in the editing process to make it easier to jump back to the state you want (covered later in this section).

After you make a few changes to your image, pop open the History panel by choosing Window → History to see a list of everything you've done to the image, including opening it. To jump back in time, click the step you want to go back to, making Photoshop return your image to the way it looked at that point. The tiny pointer in the panel's left column (circled in Figure 1-10, top) shows which step you selected (and the step itself is highlighted). If you stepped back further than you meant to, just pick a more recent step in the list.

Each time you save your image, a thumbnail preview of what it looked like appears at the top of the History panel. Clicking the thumbnail is a fast and easy way to jump back to the last saved version of your document without having to close and reopen it.

> **TIP** You can also get back to the last saved version of your document by choosing File → Revert, as discussed later in this chapter.

Taking *snapshots* of your image along the way lets you mark key points in the editing process. A snapshot is more than a preview of your image because it also includes all the edits you've made up to that point. Think of snapshots as milestones in your editing work: When you reach a critical point that you might want to return to, take a snapshot so you can easily get back to that particular version of your document. To take a snapshot, click the little camera icon at the bottom of the History panel (shown in Figure 1-10). Photoshop adds the snapshot to the top of the panel, just below the saved-state thumbnail. The snapshots you take appears in the list in the order you took them.

> **NOTE** History states don't hang around forever: As soon as you close your document, they're gone. If you think you'll ever want to return to an earlier version of your document, use the "Create new document from current state" button at the bottom of the History panel. That way you've got a brand new document to return to, instead of having to recreate it.

Figure 1-10:
Top: The History panel keeps track of everything you do to your images, beginning with opening them. The tiny pointer (circled) lets you know which editing step you're on. And you can also take snapshots of your image at crucial points during the editing process like when you convert it to black and white and add a color tint.

Bottom: If you take a snapshot, you can revert to that state later on with a single mouse click. For example, if you've given your image a sepia (brown) tint and later changed it to blue, you can easily go back to the sepia version by clicking the snapshot you took, as shown here, without working your way back through all the other changes you made.

The History Brush

The History Brush takes the power of the History panel and lets you focus it on specific parts of your image. Instead of sending your *entire* image back in time, you can use the History brush to paint your edits away *selectively*, revealing the previous state of your choosing. For example, you could blur the heck out of a portrait with the Gaussian Blur filter (page 591) and then use the History Brush to revert to the original, sharp version of your subject's face, as shown in Figure 1-11. Of course, you paint away other edits, too, like color changes, filter effects, or any other changes you made in between.

Figure 1-11:
By using the History Brush set to your image's Open state—see step 4 on page 28—you can undo all kinds of effects, including a severe Gaussian Blur.

NOTE The Art History Brush works similarly, but it adds bizarre, stylized effects as it returns your image to a previous state (see the box on page 493).

Here's how to use the History Brush to undo a serious Gaussian Blur you've applied:

1. **Open an image—in this example, a photo of a person—and run the Gaussian Blur filter.**

    You'll learn all about opening images on page 47, but, for now, choose File → Open and then navigate to where the image lives on your computer. Then choose Filter → Blur → Gaussian Blur. (You'll learn all about using filters in Chapter 15.)

2. **In the resulting dialog box, enter a radius of 10 and then click OK.**

    This setting blurs your image pretty severely, giving you a *lot* to undo with the History Brush.

3. **Grab the History Brush by pressing Y and choose a brush from the Options bar.**

    Once you've grabbed the History Brush, hop up to the Options bar's Brush menu and pick a large, soft-edged brush (one that's pretty big and blurry around the edges). You'll learn about brushes in Chapter 12.

4. **Open your History panel (Window → History) and click a saved state or snapshot.**

   This is where you pick which version of the image you want to revert to. Since all you've done is open the image and run the Gaussian Blur filter, choose the Open state. Just click within the panel's left-hand column next to that state to choose it (you'll see the History Brush's icon appear in the column).

5. **Mouse over to your image and paint over the person's eyes to reveal the unblurred eyes of the original image.**

   If you keep painting in the same place, you'll expose more and more of the original image. For example, a quick swipe over the eyes reveals traces of the original while a good scrubbing back and forth in one area reveals the original in its full glory.

   As you can see, you can use the History Brush to easily undo any kind of change. Just pick the state you want to revert to in the History panel and paint away!

POWER USERS' CLINIC

Erasing to History

At some point you'll realize that the perfect fix for your image is something you zapped about 10 steps ago. For example, you may change the color of an object only to decide later that it looked better the way it was. Argh.

Thanks to Photoshop's "Erase to History" feature, you can jump back in time and paint away the edits you no longer want. Choose the Eraser tool by pressing E and then turn on the "Erase to History" checkbox in the Options bar. Choose the layer you want to edit from your Layers panel and then start erasing the areas you want to restore to their former glory.

Erasing to history is a really handy way to leave *some* changes in place while recovering your original image in other areas.

Revert Command

If you've taken your image down a path of craziness from which you *can't* rescue it by using Undo or the History panel, you can revert back to its most recent saved state by choosing File → Revert. This command opens the previously saved version of your image, giving you a quick escape route back to square one.

> **NOTE** If you haven't made any changes to your image since it was last saved, the Revert option is disabled.

Tweaking Photoshop's Preferences

As you learned earlier in this chapter, Photoshop is pretty darn customizable. In addition to personalizing the way your tools behave and how your workspace looks, you can make lots of changes using the program's preferences, which control different aspects of Photoshop and let you turn features on or off, change how tools act, and fine-tune how the program performs on your computer.

To open the Preferences dialog box, choose Photoshop → Preferences (Edit → Preferences → General on a PC), or press ⌘-K (Ctrl+K). When you choose a category from the left side of the dialog box, you see tons of settings related to that category appear on the right side. In the following pages, you'll get an idea of the types of goodies each category contains.

General

The General section in the Preferences dialog box (Figure 1-12) is a kind of catch-all for preferences that don't fit anywhere else. Most of these options are either self-explanatory (Beep When Done, for example) or covered elsewhere in this book. A few, however, are worth taking a closer look at here.

Unless you tell it otherwise, Photoshop displays the Adobe Color Picker (see page 457) anytime you choose a color. If you're more comfortable using your operating system's color picker instead, choose it from the Color Picker pop-up menu. If you download and install third-party color pickers like Painter's Picker (page 457), they show up in this menu, too. However, since the Adobe Color Picker is designed to work with Photoshop and all its built-in options, using another color picker may mean losing quick access to critical features like Color Libraries (page 459).

Figure 1-12:
The General section of Photoshop's Preferences dialog box is home to the History Log settings. If you turn on the History Log checkbox, Photoshop keeps track of everything that happens to your images. The History Log is an invaluable tool for folks who need to prove what they've done to an image for billing clients or to produce legal documentation of all the edits they've made to an image (think law enforcement professionals and criminal investigators).

Another notable option in this dialog box involves a couple of cool new features called animated zoom and flick-panning (both covered in Chapter 2). If your computer is running at a snail's pace, try turning off one or both features by turning off their checkboxes. Both features can *really* tax slower computers, and while they're sure fun to use, you can edit without 'em.

Interface

The Interface preferences control how Photoshop looks on your screen. You can squeeze a little more performance out of slower computers by setting the Border pop-up menus at the top of the dialog box to None. That way, Photoshop won't waste any processing power generating those pretty drop shadows around your images or around the Photoshop window itself.

Also, if you're familiar with all of Photoshop's tools and don't care to see the little yellow tooltips that appear when you hover over them (page 13), turn off the Show Tool Tips checkbox (you can find the setting in the middle of the dialog box below the screen mode pop-up menus). If you'd like new documents to open in separate windows instead of in new tabs, turn off the "Open Documents as Tabs" checkbox.

File Handling

The File Handling settings control how Photoshop opens and saves files. If you're a Mac user and you plan on working with images that'll be opened on both Macs and PCs, you need to make sure Append File Extension is set to Always and that Use Lower Case is turned on. These settings improve the chances that your files will open on *either* type of computer without hassle. PC users can leave their File Handling settings alone because Mac users can open their Photoshop files just fine.

Straight from the factory, Photoshop is set to display a dialog box each time you save a file that asks if you want to save your images for maximum compatibility with *PSD* and *PSB* files (the native Photoshop format and the format for really big files, respectively; see page 46). Saving your documents with maximum compatibility improves the chances that your document can be understood by other programs like Adobe InDesign. If the pesky dialog box annoys you, change the "Maximize PSD and PSB File Compatibility" pop-up menu to Always and you'll never see the dialog box again (plus you'll have the peace of mind that comes with knowing your images will play nice with other programs).

Another handy option lies at the very bottom of the dialog box. Here you can change the number of documents Photoshop remembers in its Recent files menu (found by choosing File → Open Recent). This field is automatically set to 10, but you can change it if you like.

Performance

The Performance preferences (shown in Figure 1-13) control how efficiently Photoshop runs on your computer. For example, the amount of memory the program has to work with affects how well it performs. In the Memory Usage section's Let Photoshop Use field, Photoshop's factory setting tells the program to use up to 70 percent of your machine's available memory. If you're tempted to increase it to 100 percent for better performance, don't. Remember that other programs need to use your computer's memory, too, and leaving it set to 70 percent ensures that all of them get their fair share (after Photoshop takes the biggest chunk, of course).

Customizing Keyboard Shortcuts and Menus

Keyboard shortcuts can make the difference between working fast and working at warp speed. They can drastically reduce the amount of time you spend taking your hands off the keyboard to do things like use your mouse to choose menu items or grab tools. Photoshop has a ton of built-in keyboard shortcuts and menu groups, but that doesn't mean you're stuck with 'em. You can reassign shortcuts, add new ones, and show or hide menu options. Here's how to add or change keyboard shortcuts:

1. Choose Edit → Keyboard Shortcuts to open the "Keyboard Shortcuts and Menus" dialog box.

2. Choose which type of shortcuts you want to add or change from the Shortcuts For pop-up menu. You options are Application Menus (like the File and Edit menus), Panel Menus (the menus on the program's various panels), and Tools.

3. In the list below the Shortcuts For menu, select the shortcut you want to change.

4. Enter a new shortcut in the Shortcut field and then click Accept.

5. To save your new shortcut set, click the floppy-disk icon near the top of the dialog box to the right of the Set pop-up menu. In the resulting dialog box, give your custom set of keyboard shortcuts a name and then click Save.

To help you remember the new keyboard shortcuts, Photoshop lets you print a handy chart to tack up on the wall. In the Keyboard Shortcuts and Menus dialog box, select your custom set from the Set pop-up menu and then click Summarize. In the resulting Save dialog box, give the keyboard shortcut list a name, choose where to save it, and click Save. Photoshop creates an HTML file that you can open in any Web browser and then print.

When you're finished, you can impress your colleagues by telling them that you *reprogrammed* Photoshop to do your bidding. Unless they've been in this dialog box themselves, they'll have no idea how easy this stuff is to change.

In the Keyboard Shortcuts and Menus dialog box, you can modify the program's menus by clicking the Menus tab near the top of the box. In the Menu For pop-up menu, choose Application Menus or Panel Menus, depending on which ones you want to tweak. Click the little flippy triangle next to each menu to see the items it includes. To hide a menu item, select it and then click its visibility eye; to show a hidden item, click within its Visibility column. If you want, you can colorize menu items so they're easier to spot. To do that, select the item you want to highlight, click within the Color column, and choose a color from the resulting pop-up menu. Click OK and enjoy your new customizations.

However, if you just have to tweak this setting, type a new number in the field or drag the slider below it.

The Performance category is also where you can also change the number of history states that Photoshop remembers, as explained on page 25. If your computer's hard drive is running low on space, consider adding another drive that Photoshop can use as a *scratch disk*—the place where it stashes the bazillions of temporary files it makes when you're editing images like those various history states. (If you don't have a separate scratch disk, Photoshop stores those temporary files on your computer's hard drive, taking up space you could be using for other documents.) When you add a new internal hard drive or plug in an external drive, that drive appears in the Scratch Disks list shown in Figure 1-13. You can give Photoshop the green light to use it by putting a checkmark in the disk's "Active?" column.

Figure 1-13:
To add one or more scratch disks (page 31), click the "Active?" column next to each hard drive you want to use. Avoid using USB-based hard drives as they tend to be sluggish and can actually make Photoshop run slower.

If you need to squeeze a little more performance out of your machine, turn off the Enable OpenGL Drawing checkbox (see the box on page 60). The drawback to disabling this setting is that you won't be able to use features that rely on it like flick-panning (page 59) and Rotate View (page 61).

> **TIP** When it comes to Photoshop's scratch disk, speed matters, and faster means better. Since the speed at which the disk spins plays a big role in scratch disk performance, always try to use disks rated 7200 RPM (revolutions per minute) or faster. Slower 5400 RPM disks can take a toll on Photoshop's performance, and 4200 RPM drives slow…Photoshop…to…a…crawl.

Cursors

These preferences control how your cursors look when you're working with images. There are no right or wrong choices for you to make here, so try out the different cursor styles and see what works for you. Photoshop includes two types of cursors: painting cursors and everything else. When you choose different options, Photoshop shows you a preview of what each cursor looks like. At the bottom of the dialog box is a Brush Preview color swatch that controls the color of the brush preview when you resize your brush by Ctrl-Option-dragging (Alt+right-click+dragging on a PC) to the left or right. To change the swatch's color, click the color chip, choose a new color from the Color Picker dialog box, and then click OK. (See page 464 to learn how these options affect the Brush tool.)

Transparency & Gamut

The Transparency settings let you fine-tune what the background layer looks like when part of your image is transparent. Like the cursor settings, these options are purely cosmetic, so feel free to experiment. You can learn more about transparency and the Background layer in Chapter 3. The Gamut Warning option lets you set a highlight color showing where colors in your image fall outside the safe range for the color mode you're working in or the printer you're using. (You'll learn more about all these advanced color issues in Chapter 16.)

Units & Rulers

The Units & Rulers category (see Figure 1-14) lets you determine the unit of measurement Photoshop uses. The Rulers pop-up menu, not surprisingly, controls the unit of measurement displayed in your document rulers (see page 64); your choices are pixels, inches, centimeters, millimeters, points, picas, and percent. If you work on a lot of documents destined for print, inches or picas are probably your best bet. If you create images primarily for the Web, choose pixels. Leave the Type pop-up menu set to points unless, for whatever reason, you need to work with type measured in pixels or millimeters, which can be handy if you need to align type for a Web page layout.

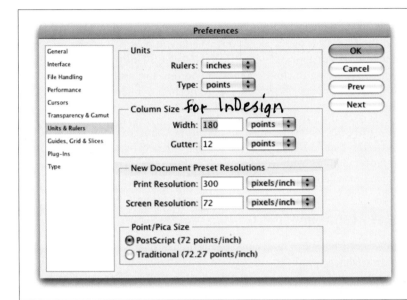

Figure 1-14:
To really save some time, take a moment to adjust the settings in the New Document Preset Resolutions section. From that point on, Photoshop automatically fills in the New Document dialog box with the settings you entered here (you'll learn about creating new documents on page 37).

The Column Size settings are handy when you're designing graphics that need to fit into specific-sized columns in a page layout program like Adobe InDesign. Just ask the person who's designing the layout in InDesign which measurements you should use.

Guides, Grid & Slices

These preferences let you choose the colors for your guides (page 64), gridlines (page 66), and slice lines (page 679). You can also set your gridlines' spacing and the number of subdivisions that appear between each major gridline with the "Gridline every" and Subdivisions fields, respectively.

Plug-ins

You can make Photoshop do even more cool stuff by installing third-party programs called *plug-ins*. There are so many useful plug-ins that this book has an entire chapter devoted to them (Chapter 19). The preferences in this category let you store plug-ins somewhere other than the Photoshop folder, which can help you avoid losing your plug-ins if you have to reinstall Photoshop at some point. Leave both checkboxes in the Extension Panels section turned on so Photoshop can connect to the Internet if a plug-in or panel needs to grab information from a Web site. For example, the Kuler panel (covered on page 454) lets you use color themes posted on the Web by folks in the Kuler community. If you turn off these checkboxes, Photoshop can't connect to the Internet and you can't use the Kuler panel.

Type

Photoshop has an amazing type engine under its hood, and you'll learn all about it in Chapter 14. The preferences here let you toggle Smart Quotes (the curly kind) on or off, as well as control the Font Preview Size used in the Options bar's font menu and in the Character panel (page 556). When you pick a size from this pop-up menu, the font names appears *in their actual typefaces*. This preview is *extremely* helpful when you're trying to choose a font. If you don't want to see typeface previews, turn off Font Preview Size to make Photoshop display only the typeface names (yawn).

If you work with Asian characters, turn on the Show Asian Text Options checkbox and make sure the Enable Missing Glyph Protection checkbox is also turned on. That way you don't end up with weird symbols or boxes if you try to use a letter or symbol that isn't installed on your machine.

The Preset Manager

Once you get comfortable in Photoshop, you can customize all kinds of stuff like brushes, color swatches, gradients, and so on. The Preset Manager handles loading, saving, and storing your personalized goodies, as well as all the presets (built-ins like brushes, color swatches, patterns, and so on) that came with the program. You can open it by choosing Edit → Preset Manager or by clicking the right-facing triangle at the top right of any tool's preset picker menu in the Options bar and then choosing Preset Manager.

Each group of settings, like a category of brushes, is called a *preset library*. To see a certain preset library, choose it from the Preset Type pop-up menu at the top of the Preset Manager dialog box (Figure 1-15).

Clicking the button that's circled in Figure 1-15 lets you set the category of presets you're viewing to the factory-fresh settings (choose "Reset [name of category]") and then click OK. You can make these same adjustments when you're using the tools themselves, but the Preset Manager gives you a bigger preview space than the individual tool's preset pickers, which makes these organizational chores a little more tolerable.

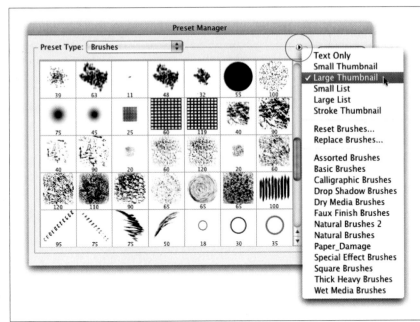

Figure 1-15:
You can open the Preset Manager's panel menu by clicking the right-facing triangle (circled). This menu lets you change the size of the previews you see in Photoshop's preset picker menus. Large thumbnails make it easier to see what your options are.

Sharing Presets

Once you've made your own brushes, styles, or what have you, feel free to share them with the masses. You can share them with other computers (which is handy when the whole team needs to use the same color swatches or brushes), and upload them to the Web (for the whole world to download).

To create a preset library of your own, open the Preset Manager and click the Save Set button. In the resulting Save dialog box, give your custom library a name. Photoshop automatically saves it in the folders where it stores *all* custom settings unless you pick a different location on your hard drive (which is handy if you plan on sharing the library with other folks). When everything looks good, click Save.

> **TIP** If you're saving a custom preset to share with others, save it in a spot that's easy for you to find. For example, if you plan on emailing your preset library, your desktop might be a good option. If you're sharing your presets with coworkers who work in the same office, your local file server works well.

Once you've saved your custom preset library, you can email it to folks or upload it to a Web site for others to download. If you're uploading to the Web, make sure the file doesn't have any spaces in its name. For example, instead of naming your file "Dragon Scale Brushes", name it "DragonScaleBrushes".

If you're on the receiving end of a new preset library, open the Preset Manager by choosing Edit → Preset Manager and then click the Load button. Navigate to where the library lives and click Load. The next time you use a tool that has custom presets, you'll see the new library's options in the tool's preset picker menu.

To add to the fun, you can also rename preset libraries. In the Preset Manager dialog box, select the relevant library from the Preset Type pop-up menu and click Rename. Type a new name in the Name field and click OK. To delete a preset library you never use, select it from the Preset Manager's Preset Type pop-up menu and click Delete.

> **TIP**   If you've managed to mess up one of Photoshop's built-in preset libraries by adding settings that don't work the way you want, you can easily restore the original libraries. Open the Preset Manager and choose the library you want to reset. From the panel menu (click the button that's circled in Figure 1-15), choose "Reset [type of preset]". Photoshop asks if you want to replace the current brushes or append (add to) them instead. Click OK to replace the brushes and you'll be back to the factory-fresh settings.

Opening, Viewing, and Saving Files

Chances are good that if you're holding this book, you'll be spending a lot of time in Photoshop. So the ability to shave off a minute here and there from routine stuff can really add up. Heck, if you're lucky, you'll save enough time to read a book, ride your bike, or catch an episode of *Battlestar Galactica*.

One way to steal back some of that time is to work more efficiently, and that means learning a slew of tricks for the less glamorous stuff like opening, viewing, and saving files. And since you'll be doing these things so often, it's important to form good habits up front so your documents are set up properly from the get-go. It's truly heartbreaking to find that the artwork you've spent weeks creating is too small to print, or you saved the file in such a way that you can't change it later on. Finally, since a key part of working with images is navigating around these vast pixel landscapes, tis chapter teaches you some handy ways to move around within your onscreen images.

Creating a New Document

Photoshop gives you plenty of ways to accomplish most tasks, including creating a new document. You can choose File → New, but it's faster to press ⌘-N (Crtl+N on a PC). Either way, you'll be greeted with the New dialog box shown in Figure 2-1.

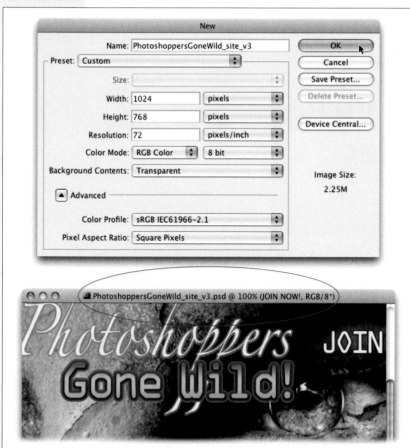

Figure 2-1:
The New dialog box (top) is where life begins for any Photoshop file you create. The settings here let you pick, among other things, your document's size, resolution, and color mode, all of which affect the quality and size of your image. You'll learn more about all these options in the following pages. Whatever you type in the Name box appears in the document's title bar (bottom).

You'd think that naming your document would be simple: Just type something in the Name box and you're done, right? Not quite. Here are a few things to keep in mind:

- If you're working on a Mac, don't start your file names with a period. Files whose names start with periods are invisible in Mac OS X (meaning neither you nor Photoshop can see them), which makes 'em darn hard to work with.

- If folks need to open your files on both Mac and Windows machines, don't put slashes (/), colons (:), angle brackets (< >), pipes, (|), asterisks (*), or question marks (?) in the file names, either.

- Mac users need to leave *file extensions* (the period and three letters at the end of the file name, like .psd, .jpg, and so on) on the file name. The file extension tells Photoshop, Microsoft's Windows operating system, and other programs what kind of file it is.

Photoshop's Ready-Made Documents

After you've named your document, you need to pick a size for it. You've got two choices here: Enter the dimensions you'd like in the Width and Height boxes or pick one of Photoshop's canned choices (4"×6" landscape photo, 640×480 pixel Web page, and so on) from the Preset and Size menus (see Figure 2-2).

The advantage of picking a canned option is that, in addition to filling out the dimensions for you, Photoshop plugs in resolution and color mode settings. You'll learn more about these two options in a minute, but if you're new to the program, these *presets* (ready-to-use document settings) are a great way to make sure you're starting off with a well-configured document. Besides, the presets can be helpful even if they're not *exactly* what you need. For example, if you find one that lists the right size but the wrong resolution, just select it, adjust the resolution, and you're on your way.

> **NOTE** Two Preset choices worth remembering: If you copy all or part of an image, Clipboard grabs that image's settings for you. This preset makes it easy to match a document's settings without having to copy them first. And if you choose 5"×7" from the Preset menu, you get a document perfectly set up for onscreen viewing.

Figure 2-2:
Once you make a selection from the Preset menu (which includes different types of paper, electronic formats, and recently used document sizes), Photoshop fills the Size menu and its related fields with the appropriate settings—including Width, Height, Resolution, and Color Mode (page 40). Presets are great timesavers, and they help you avoid mistakes when you're making new documents.

Setting Size and Resolution

In Photoshop, size refers to two different things: file size (640 kilobytes or 2.4 megabytes, for example) and dimensions (like 4"×6" or 640×480 pixels). You'll find plenty of advice throughout this book on how to control file size, but here you're concerned with the size of your document's canvas.

Photoshop can measure size in pixels, inches, centimeters, millimeters, points, picas, and columns. Just pick the one that's appropriate for your project—or the easiest for you to work with—from the pop-up menus to the right of the Width and Height fields. If you're designing a piece for the Web or a slideshow presentation, pixels are your best bet. If you're going to print the image, inches are a common choice. Columns come in handy when you're making an image destined for a page-layout program like Adobe InDesign that has to fit within a specific number of columns.

NOTE Photoshop assumes you want to use the same unit (say, inches) to measure width and height, so it automatically changes both fields when you adjust one. If you really *do* need to work with different units, just hold the Shift key while you pick the second unit to make Photoshop leave the other field alone.

The Resolution fields control the number of pixels per inch or per centimeter in your document. High-resolution documents typically contain more details in the same amount of space than low-resolution documents of the same size. (You'll learn all about resolution in Chapter 6, starting on page 221.)

For now, here's some ready-to-use guidance if you haven't yet mastered the fine art of resolution: If you're designing an image that will be viewed only onscreen (in a Web browser or a slideshow presentation, for example) enter *72* in the Resolution field—it's really only the pixel dimensions that matter in this situation, but you'll learn more about that later. If you're going to print the image, set the resolution to at least 150 pixels per inch.

Once you enter values in the Width, Height, and Resolution fields, Photoshop calculates the document's *file size*—the amount of space it takes up on your hard drive—and displays it in the New dialog box's bottom-right corner (in Figure 2-1, for example, the file size is 2.25 megabytes).

TIP If you don't know the exact size your document needs to be, it's better to make it really big; you can always make it smaller later. See page 220 for more info.

Just because you make your document a certain size doesn't mean you can't have artwork that's bigger than the document's dimensions in that file. Photoshop is perfectly fine with objects that extend beyond your document's edges (also called *document boundaries*), though you can't see or print those parts. It may sound odd, but if you paste a photo or a piece of vector art (page 48) that's larger than your document, those extra bits will dangle off the edges. To resize your document so that you can see everything—even the stuff that doesn't quite fit—choose Image → Reveal All to make Photoshop modify your document's dimensions so everything fits.

Choosing a Color Mode

The New dialog box's Color Mode field (see Figure 2-1) determines which colors you can use in your document. You'll spend most of your time working in RGB mode (which stands for red, green, and blue), but you can switch modes whenever you like (see Chapter 16 for more info). The pop-up menu to the right of the Color Mode field controls your document's *bit depth*, which is explained in the box on page 43.

Unless you choose a different color mode, Photoshop automatically uses RGB mode (which is the one you'll be using most often). The Color Mode menu gives you the following choices:

Stealing Document Settings

Need to create a document that's the same size and resolution as an existing document? No problem—just snag one file's settings and use them to make another. You can steal document settings in several ways:

- Open the existing document and press ⌘-N (Ctrl+N on a PC) to open the New dialog box. Click the Preset pop-up menu, which lists the names of all open documents. When you pick the one you want, Photoshop adjusts all the dialog box's settings to match.

- With the existing document open, press ⌘-A (Ctrl+A) to select everything in it and press ⌘-C (Ctrl+C) to copy the document's contents to your

computer's memory. If you choose File → New or press ⌘-N (Ctrl+N on a PC), Photoshop automatically fills in the document's settings for you.

- If you want to base your new document on the *last* document you created, hold Option (Alt on a PC) while you choose File → New or press ⌘-Option-N (Ctrl+Alt+N).

- If you need to create a new document that's the same size and resolution as your current selection, choosing File → New or pressing ⌘-N (Ctrl+N on a PC) makes Photoshop create a document that matches your selection's dimensions. (See Chapter 4 for the full story on selections.)

- **Bitmap** restricts you to two colors: black and white. (Shades of gray aren't welcome at the Bitmap party.) This mode is useful when you're scanning high-contrast items like black-and-white text documents or when you're creating graphics for handheld devices that don't have color screens.

- **Grayscale** expands on Bitmap mode by adding shades between pure black and pure white. The higher the document's bit depth, the more shades of gray—and so the more details—your document can contain. Eight-bit documents include 256 shades of gray, 16-bit documents extend that range to over 65,000, and 32-bit documents crank it up to 16.7 million (see the box on page 43 for more on bit depth).

- **RGB Color** is the color mode you'll use most often when you're working in Photoshop, and it's also the mode your monitor and digital camera use to represent colors. This mode shows colors as a mix of red, green, and blue light (page 172), with each having a numeric value between 0 and 255 that describes the brightness of each color present (for example, fire-engine red has an RGB value of 250 for red, 5 for green, and 5 for blue). As with Grayscale mode, the higher your document's bit depth, the more details it can contain. In this mode, you can choose among 8-, 16-, and 32-bit documents. (See Chapters 5, 9, and 16 for more info on RGB.)

- **CMYK Color** simulates the colors used in printing and its name stands for cyan, magenta, yellow, and black ink. It doesn't have as many colors as RGB because it's limited to the colors a printer—whether it's an inkjet, commercial offset, or digital press—can reproduce with ink and dyes on paper (you'll learn more about CMYK in Chapters 5 and 16). Cahpter 16fs has the scoop on if and when you should switch to CMYK mode.

- **Lab Color** mode, which is based on the way humans see color, lets you use all the colors human eyes can detect. It represents how colors *should look* no matter which device they're displayed on, whereas other modes (RGB and CMYK) limit a file's colors to what's visible onscreen or in a printed document, respectively. Lab's upside is that it can handle color management—a concept you'll learn more about in Chapter 16—better than other modes. The downside is that many folks have a hard time learning to create the colors they want in Lab mode. You'll find various techniques involving Lab mode sprinkled throughout Part 2 of this book.

Choosing Your Background

The New dialog box's Background Contents pop-up menu lets you choose what's on the Background layer—the only layer you start out with in a new document. Your choices are White, Background Color (which uses the color that the background color chip is set to [page 22]), and Transparent (which leaves the background completely empty).

What you choose here isn't that crucial—if you don't like your choice, you can simply turn off the Background layer's visibility (see page 78). Choosing a color is handy if you plan to use images that share a background color, so you can preview your artwork. In that case, you need to make sure your background color chip is set to the right color before you create your new document and then choose Background Color from this menu. The Transparent option is handy if your document is part of a bigger project where it'll be placed in front of other documents or images. When you choose this option, you see a gray-and-white checkerboard pattern in the Background layer, as explained in the box on page 44.

NOTE For more on the mysterious Background layer, see the box on page 80.

Advanced Options

A quick click of the Advanced button at the bottom of the New dialog box reveals a couple of pop-up menus:

- **Color Profile.** A *color profile* is a set of instructions that determine how computer monitors and printers display or print your document's colors. Unless you change it, this menu is set to "sRGB IEC61966-2.1". Unless you know ahead of time that you need to use a specific color profile for your project, leave this setting alone; otherwise, your colors may not look the way you expect them to on other computers or when they're printed. You'll learn about color profiles in Chapter 16.

Understanding Bit Depth

You may have heard the terms "8-bit" and "16-bit" tossed around in graphics circles. When people use these terms, they're talking about how many colors an image file contains. Photoshop's color modes (page 40) determine whether your document is an 8- or a 16-bit image (other, less common options are 1-bit and 32-bit). Since you'll run into these labels fairly often, it helps to understand more about what these numbers mean.

A *bit* is the smallest unit of measurement that computers use to store information. Each pixel in an image has a *bit depth,* which controls how much color information that pixel can hold. So an image's bit depth determines how much color info the image contains. The higher the bit depth, the more colors the image can display. And the more colors in your image, the more info (details) you've got to play with in Photoshop.

Understanding bit depth also means you need to know a little about *channels,* where Photoshop stores your image's color info (see Chapter 5) on separate layers (see Chapter 3). For example, in an RGB image you have three channels: one each for red, green, and blue. If you combine the info contained in each channel, you can figure how many colors are in your image.

With all that in mind, here's a quick tour of your various bit choices in Photoshop:

- In Bitmap color mode, your pixels can be only black or white. Images in this mode are called **1-bit** images because each pixel can be only one color—black or white (they're also known simply as *bitmap* images).

- An **8-bit** image can hold two values in each bit, which equals 256 possible color values. Why 256? Since each of the eight bits can hold two possible values, you get 256 combinations. (For math fans: it's two to the eighth power, which equals 256). Images in Grayscale mode contain one channel, so that's 8 bits per channel, equaling 256 colors. Since images in RGB mode contain three channels

(one each for red, blue, and green), folks refer to them as 24-bit images (8 bits per channel $\times 3$ = 24), but they're still really just 8-bit images. With 256 combinations for each channel (that's $2^8 \times 2^8 \times 2^8$), you can have over 16 million colors in your RGB image. Since CMYK images have four channels, folks refer to them as 32-bit images (8 bits per channel $\times 4$ = 32), but again, these are *still* 8-bit images. Over 200 combinations per channel and four channels add up to a massive number of possible color values, but since you're dealing with printed ink, your color range in CMYK is dictated by what can actually be reproduced on paper, which reduces it to about 55,000 colors.

- **16-bit** images contain 65,536 colors in a single channel and are produced by high-end digital cameras (digital single-lens reflex, or dSLR, cameras) shooting in Raw format (page 53) or by really good scanners. These files don't look any different from other images on your screen, but they take up twice as much hard drive space. Photographers really like them because the extra colors give them more flexibility when they're making Curves and Levels adjustments (see Chapter 9) though the larger file sizes can *really* slow Photoshop down. Also, not all of Photoshop's tools and filters work with 16-bit images, but that list of tools grows with each new version of the program.

- **32-bit** images, referred to as high dynamic range (HDR), contain more colors than you can shake a stick at. See the box on page 387 for more info.

For the most part, you'll be dealing with 8-bit images, but if you've got a camera that shoots at higher bit depths, by all means, take a weekend and experiment to see if the difference in quality is worth the sacrifice of hard drive space (and editing speed). And if you're restoring a really old photo, it may be helpful to scan it at a high bit depth so you have a wider range of colors to work with. (See the box on page 52 for more scanning tips.)

FREQUENTLY ASKED QUESTION

Seeing Transparency

Dude, what's up with the gray-and-white checkerboard pattern in my new document? I thought it was supposed to be blank!

When you tell Photoshop to make your background layer transparent (page 42), it fills your new document with a checkerboard pattern. Don't worry: That checkerboard is just what the program uses to represent transparency on the Background layer. In other words, the checkered pattern is just a reminder that there aren't any pixels on that layer to hide what's behind your image if you add it to another document later on.

You can change how the checkerboard pattern looks by choosing Photoshop → Preferences → Transparency & Gamut. In the Transparency Settings section, you can tweak the settings to make the squares bigger or smaller or to change their colors. If you can't stand seeing the checkered pattern no matter what it looks like, you can turn it off by setting the Grid Size field to None.

- **Pixel Aspect Ratio.** This setting determines the shape of your pixels by changing their size, or aspect ratio. This setting gets its name from the term *aspect ratio*—the relationship between an image's width and height. (For example, a widescreen television has an aspect ratio of 16:9.) Out of the box, Photoshop's pixels are set to Square. Although square pixels are fine for photos, printed images, and onscreen use, they look funky and distorted in video, which has a tendency to make everything look short and fat (including people). So if you're using Photoshop to work on a movie, try to find out which video format the filmmakers are using and then select it here.

Saving your custom settings

If you've gone to the trouble of getting your document's settings just right and you expect to create lots of similar documents, save those settings as a preset. Click the Save Preset button to open the dialog box show in Figure 2-3. If you save your settings *before* you click the New dialog box's OK button to create your new document, you can choose a descriptive name for your new preset.

Figure 2-3:
Use these checkboxes to tell Photoshop which settings you want it to remember. When you create a new document, Photoshop grabs the settings you don't include here from the last new document you made. For example, if you don't include the color profile (by turning on the Profile checkbox shown here), Photoshop assigns the currently active color profile to your new image. See page 617 for more about color profiles.

Going Mobile with Device Central

To see what your graphics look like on a wide range of cell phones and other portable electronic devices, you can use Device Central, a program that comes with Photoshop. (You need an active Internet connection to use it since it downloads handheld device profiles stored online.) It lets you preview all kinds of files on a bunch of different simulated gadget screens, and it even lets you test interactive elements and record videos showing how your images look on specific devices.

You can use Device Central from the get-go to make sure your file is set up properly and take the guesswork out of which size to make your images. Here's how:

1. Create a new document by choosing File → New, or by pressing ⌘-N (Ctrl+N on a PC).

2. Click the Device Central button on the right side of the New dialog box (shown in Figure 2-1).

3. Select a gadget from the Local Library list on the left side of the Device Central window (or Shift-click to choose more than one). If the device you're designing for isn't in that list, select it in the Online Library list, drag it into the Local Library list, and then select it there.

4. Click Create to open a new file in Photoshop tailored to the device(s) you picked. If you picked more than one device, the dimensions are set to best work on all of them.

5. When you're finished editing your mobile masterpiece, choose File → Save For Web & Devices (page 665). Be sure to pick a file format from the Preset pop-up menu and then click the Device Central button at the bottom of the dialog box to preview your document on the device (see the figure on page 671).

Saving Files

After you've put a ton of work into whipping up a lovely Photoshop creation, don't forget to save it or you'll never see it again. As in any program, be sure to save early and often so your efforts don't go to waste if your computer crashes or the power goes out.

The simplest method is to choose File → Save or press ⌘-S (Ctrl+S on a PC). If you haven't previously saved the file, Photoshop pops open the Save As dialog box where you can pick where to save the file, give it a name, and select the file format you want to save it as. If you *have* already saved the file, Photoshop replaces the previously saved version with the *current* version without asking if that's what you want to do. In some situations, that's fine, but it can be disastrous if you were planning to keep more than one version of your image around.

You can play it safe by using the Save As dialog box instead; it *always* prompts you for a new file name (see Figure 2-4), which is handy when you want to save another version of your document or save it in a different format. Choose File → Save As or press ⌘-Shift-S (Ctrl+Shift+S on a PC) to summon the dialog box. When you first use Photoshop, the Format pop-up menu is set to Photoshop, which makes sense because you're working in Photoshop. But, as the next section explains, you can save files in lots of other formats.

Figure 2-4:
The Save As dialog box lets you save a copy of your file with a different name in a different location and even in a different format.

File Formats

You'll learn much more about file formats in Chapters 16 and 17, but here's a quick overview. If you remember nothing else, remember to save your images as PSD files (Photoshop documents) because that's the most flexible format (see the box on page 47). That said, sometimes you need to save your document in other formats because of where the file is *headed*. For example, Adobe InDesign (a popular page-layout program) is adept at handling PSD files, but QuarkXPress is a little different. While QuarkXPress can indeed open Photoshop documents, not everyone is comfortable working *with* PSD files in Quark. In that case, try saving your document as a TIFF file because nearly every image-handling program ever invented can open TIFF files just fine.

> **NOTE** If you need to save a Photoshop document that's bigger than two gigabytes, save it as a PSB file instead. That format lets you get past the PSD file's two GB limit on file sizes.

Graphics destined for the Web are a different animal because they're especially designed for onscreen viewing and faster downloads. Here's a quick cheat sheet to tide you over until you've got time and energy to make your way to Chapter 17:

- **JPEG** is commonly used for graphics that include a wide range of colors like photos. It compresses images so they take up less space, but the smaller file size comes at a price: loss of quality.

- **GIF** is a popular choice for graphics that include a limited number of colors (think cartoon art) or when you need to save a see-through (transparent) background.

- **PNG** is the up-and-comer because it offers true transparency and a wide range of colors. It produces a higher-quality image than a JPEG, but it generates larger files.

For more on creating and preparing images for the Web, head over to Chapter 17. If your image is headed for a professional printer, visit Chapter 18 instead.

UP TO SPEED

Save Your Master

Experimenting with your image is fine—until you accidentally ruin the original and don't have a backup. To avoid losing a critical file and having to explain to your boss, coworkers, or client why the project is behind schedule, save your master file as a PSD file so that your layers, Smart Filters (page 588), and Smart Objects (page 115) remain intact. (It's also a good idea to save a copy somewhere other than your hard drive in case something happens to your computer. Burn it onto a CD or DVD, save it on a Flash drive, or use an online storage service.) That way, if something goes wrong while you're working on the project, you've always got the original to fall back on. And if something *does* go wrong, duplicate the master file again and then work on the copy. There's no point in tempting fate!

Opening an Existing Document

In most programs, opening files is simple and that holds true in Photoshop, too. But Photoshop gives you a few more options than you'll find in some other programs because Photoshop can open files saved in its own format (PSD files), as well as a slew of other formats both common and obscure (a feature that makes Photoshop amazingly versatile at working with a wide range of images). Even better, if the program doesn't recognize a particular format, there's a good chance someone has developed a plug-in (companion program) that can (see Chapter 19 for more on plug-ins).

Photoshop knows how to open Adobe Illustrator, Camera Raw (page 53), JPEG, GIF, PNG, TIFF, EPS, and PDF files (page 620), along with Collada DAE, Google Earth 4 KMZ, Scitex CT, Targa, and several other kinds of files most folks have never even heard of.

You can open files in Photoshop in several ways, including:

- Double-clicking the document icon, no matter where it's stored on your computer.

- Dragging the document's icon onto the Photoshop program icon (the blue square with "Ps" on it).

- Ctrl-clicking (right-clicking on a PC) the document icon and choosing Open With → Photoshop from the resulting shortcut menu.

• Launching Photoshop and then choosing File → Open or pressing ⌘-O (Ctrl+O) to call up the Open dialog box, discussed in the next section.

• You can also use Adobe Bridge to preview and open your documents. Head over to Appendix C to learn all about using Bridge.

UP TO SPEED

Raster Images vs. Vector Images

The images you'll work with and create in Photoshop fall into two categories: those made from pixels and those made from paths. It's important to understand that they have different characteristics and you have to open them in different ways.

• **Raster** images are made from tiny blocks of color called *pixels*, the smallest element of a digital image. The number of pixels in an image depends on the device that captured it (a digital camera or scanner) or the settings you entered when you created the document in Photoshop (page 37). The size of the pixels depends on the image's *resolution* (see page 221), which specifies the number of pixels in an inch. Usually pixels are so small that you can't see individual ones. But if you enlarge a raster image, the pixels appear bigger, and the image starts to look like a bunch of blocks instead of a smooth image.

• **Vector** images are made up of points and paths that form shapes; these shapes are filled and stroked (outlined) with color. You can create vector images in drawing programs like Adobe Illustrator and CorelDraw. The paths are based on mathematical equations that tell monitors and printers how to draw the image. Because there aren't any pixels involved, you can make vector images as big or small you want, and they'll still look as smooth and crisp as the original. Photoshop can open vector images, but unless you open them as Smart Objects (discussed later in this chapter—see page 50), Photoshop will turn them into pixel-based raster images. (This process is called *rasterizing*.)

In the figure below, the upper image is a vector image (the right-hand version shows the paths it's made from) and the bottom image is a raster image. Vectors are handy when you're designing logos and other illustrations that you might need to make bigger at some point. But you'll end up working with rasters more often because all photos are raster images and because Photoshop is a pixel-based program (as are all image-editing and painting programs). That said, you can use some of its tools to draw vectors (see Chapter 13), and it lets you open vector files (discussed in the next section). You can also create some amazing artwork by combining raster and vector images as described on page 293.

The Open Dialog Box

When you choose File → Open (Ctrl+O on a PC) or press ⌘-O (Ctrl+O), Photoshop brings up the dialog box shown in Figure 2-5. All you need to do is navigate to the file on your hard drive and then click the Open button. In addition to helping hunt through the murky depths of your hard drive, the dialog box sports the ability to limit the files you can open via the Enable pop-up menu. If you use this menu to select just the format you want to see, Photoshop will dutifully dim everything else (dimmed items aren't selectable), which is handy when you've saved a file in several different formats—like PSD, JPEG, and TIFF files of the same image.

> **NOTE** PC users don't get as many options in the Open dialog box as Mac users do. Instead of the Enable pop-up menu, PC folks get a "Files of type" menu, and the Format pop-up menu doesn't appear at all. Also, the PC version of the Open dialog box hides files that you can't select.

Figure 2-5:
The Open dialog box lets you navigate to the image you want to open. The Format pop-up menu at the bottom left automatically changes to match the format of the document you select.

> **TIP** To open more than one file, ⌘-click (Ctrl-click) to select files that aren't next to each other or Shift-click to select files that are. When you click Open, Photoshop opens each file in a separate tab if you're using the new CS4 Application Frame (page 47).

If you leave the Enable pop-up menu set to All Readable Documents (set the "Files of type" menu to All Formats on a PC), you tell Photoshop that it's okay to open *any* file format it recognizes. If you try to open a format Photoshop should know how to open but for some mysterious reason thinks it doesn't (see page 47 for a list of formats Photoshop recognizes), someone may have saved the document with the wrong file extension. (Since all programs, including Photoshop, rely on the file extension to figure out which type of document they're looking at, be careful not to change these multi-letter codes that appear after a document's name.) If you run into this problem, Mac users can use the Format pop-up menu (PC users can choose File → Open As instead) to tell Photoshop which format the document *should* be, and the program will ignore the file's extension and try to open it based on the format you picked.

> **TIP**   If you're looking for a specific image but can't remember its name, try using Bridge (Appendix C) to find it. Bridge shows you a preview of each image along with a ton of other info like keywords, ratings, and more. It also gives you filtering and search options to help hunt down the image you want.

Opening Files as Smart Objects

Smart Objects are one of those glorious features that make Photoshop truly amazing. You'll learn a lot more about Smart Objects in Chapter 3, but here's a quick overview: Smart Objects are basically containers that can store raster, vector, or Camera Raw files (page 53) in their original formats. Smart Objects keep track of the original file so you can undo any changes you make to them (this process, called *nondestructive* editing, is discussed at length in Chapter 3). In addition to the image types just mentioned, you can also import TIFF, PDF, and JPEG files as Smart Objects.

To open an image as a Smart Object, choose File → "Open as Smart Object". In the resulting dialog box, choose the file you want to open. When you click Open, Photoshop opens it as a Smart Object layer in a new document. See Chapter 3 for more about layers and page 238 for the skinny on resizing Smart Objects.

Opening Recent Files

This one's a real timesaver. Like many programs, Photoshop keeps track of the documents you've recently opened. Choose File → Open Recent to see a list of the last ten documents you worked on, with the latest one at the top of the list (see Figure 2-6). If you've moved or renamed the file since you last opened it in Photoshop (put it in a different folder on your hard drive, say), the program will try to find it for you when you select it from this list. If the document isn't on your hard drive anymore, Photoshop displays a message box with a considerate message telling you it can't find the file.

> **TIP**   If you want Photoshop to remember more or fewer than 10 files, choose File → Preferences → File Handling (Edit → Preferences → File Handling on PCs) and change the number in the "Recent file list contains" field at the bottom of the Preferences dialog box. You can set it as low as 2 or as high as 30. Just remember that a higher number means a longer list of recent documents to search through.

Figure 2-6:
The Open Recent menu option is a
handy shortcut for getting at files
without traipsing through the Open
dialog box. If you want to erase the
list, click Clear Recent.

Working with PDFs

Saving a document as a PDF file is kind of like taking a picture of it so others can open the file without needing the program you used to create it. They just need the free Adobe Reader (or any other PDF-viewing program like Preview on the Mac). PDFs can store text, images, and even video at a variety of quality settings. PDFs are also *cross-platform*, which means they play nice with both Macs and PCs. It's an amazingly useful file format that will only become more common (see Chapter 16 for a peek into the future).

You can open PDFs the same way you open any file: by choosing File → Open, selecting the PDF you want, and then clicking the Open button. If someone created the PDF in Photoshop, it opens right up. If someone created it in another program, Photoshop displays the Import PDF dialog box (Figure 2-7) where you can choose which parts of the document you want to import (full pages or just the images) and set resolution, dimensions, and so on.

Working with Scanned Images

The Open dialog box isn't the only way to get images into Photoshop. If you have a scanner that knows how to talk to Photoshop, you can use it to import images straight into the program. But, first, you need to install your scanner's software *and* the Photoshop plug-in for your scanner. (Check the owner's manual to learn how to install the software, and then flip to Chapter 19, which covers plug-ins in detail. To find the plug-in for your scanner, check the manufacturer's Web site for the most recent version.) Once everything is all set, you can start importing scanned documents.

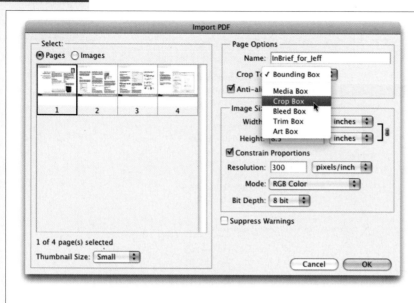

Figure 2-7:
If you decide to import multiple pages (as shown here), Photoshop creates a new document for each one.

If you're lucky and the person who created the document was a PDF pro, she may have included size-specification goodies like crop size, bleed area, trim, and art size (you'll learn about most of these terms in Chapter 16). If so, you can eliminate some resizing work on imported files by choosing one of the size elements from the Crop To pop-up menu (shown here, right).

To import an image from your scanner into Photoshop, choose File → Import and then select your scanner from the resulting list. Each scanner has its own software, so there's no standard set of steps to work through—they're all different. Unfortunately, that means you have to read the documentation that came with your scanner to figure out how to import files from it. The box below has some advice on scanning images.

UP TO SPEED

Scanning 101

Just because all scanning software is different doesn't mean there aren't a few guidelines you can follow to produce good scans. Keep these things in mind when you scan:

- Scan at a higher bit depth than you need for the edited image. This means your files will be larger, but they'll contain lots of color info you can work with when you're editing them. (See the box on page 43 for more on bit depth.)

- Scan at a higher resolution than you need for the finished image to make your files larger and include more details. You can always lower the resolution later, but you can't increase it...or, rather, you *shouldn't* increase it without knowing the trick (see page 221 to learn about resolution).

- If you can use your scanner software to adjust your image's color *before* you import the file into Photoshop, take the time to use it. Making adjustments before you import the image lets you take advantage of all of the info your scanner picked up. The amount of information that your scanner passes along to Photoshop when you import the file is almost *always* less than the amount of info in the original image.

Working with Raw Files

Of all the file formats Photoshop can understand, *Raw* is the most useful and flexible. Professional-grade digital cameras (and many high-end consumer cameras, too) use this format. The info in a Raw file is the exact same information your camera recorded when you took the picture; it's uncompressed and unchanged. (Other file formats, like JPEG, compress images and in the process slightly reduce the image's quality.) Raw files contain the most detailed information you can get from a digital camera, including what's known as *metadata* (info on all the settings your camera used to capture the image like shutter speed, aperture, and so on). You can edit Raw files using a Photoshop plug-in called *Adobe Camera Raw* (shown in Figure 2-8), which you'll learn more about in Chapter 9.

Figure 2-8:
Raw files get their own separate editing program called Camera Raw, which launches automatically when you open a Raw file in Photoshop.

NOTE Camera Raw is one of the most frequently updated plug-ins known to man—which is good because manufacturers release new camera models faster than photographers can buy them. If you've got a sparkling new camera, you may have to update the Camera Raw plug-in before you can open your file, which means it's time for a trip to the Adobe Updater program. To run it, choose Help → Updates (Appendix A—online at *www.missingmanuals.com*—has more about checking for updates). If there's a newer version of Camera Raw, Photoshop lets you know so you can install it.

Opening Raw files

Opening a Raw file in Photoshop is no different from opening any other kind of image except that it opens in the Camera Raw window instead of the main Photoshop window. You can open Raw files by:

- Double-clicking the Raw file's icon. Your computer launches Photoshop (if it wasn't running already) and then opens the Camera Raw window.

- Ctrl-clicking (right-clicking on a PC) the Raw file's icon and choosing Open With → Photoshop. (Since Camera Raw is a plug-in that runs inside Photoshop and Bridge, it doesn't get listed separately, but your computer knows to open the file in Camera Raw.)

- Using Bridge (see Appendix C) to select the file you want to open and then choosing File → "Open in Camera Raw" or pressing ⌘-R (Ctrl+R on a PC). You can also Ctrl-click (right-click) the file in Bridge and then choose "Open in Camera Raw" from the resulting shortcut menu.

TIP If you've got a bunch of Raw images that need similar edits (cropping, color-correcting, and so on), you can open them all at once by Shift or ⌘-clicking (Ctrl-clicking on a PC) them in Bridge or by selecting multiple files on your desktop and then double-clicking or dragging them onto the Photoshop icon. When you click the Select All button in the top-left corner of the Camera Raw window, any edits you make afterwards affect all your open images. See the box on page 390 for more on editing multiple files.

POWER USERS' CLINIC

Opening Images as a Stack

If you sprang for Photoshop CS4 Extended (page 1), you've got a bonus feature called *Stacks* that lets you open multiple images on separate layers in the same document. It's a *huge* timesaver when you need to combine several images—like when you want to make several group shots into one perfect shot where everyone's eyes are open and they're all smiling—or when you're editing individual frames of a video.

To open a group of images as a Stack, choose File → Scripts → Load Files into Stack. In the resulting Load Layers

dialog box, tell Photoshop where the images are stored on your hard drive and click OK.

The Load Layers dialog box's Use pop-up menu lets you choose what you want to open: individual images or whole folders of images. If you're combining several shots into one, turn on the "Attempt to Automatically Align Source Images" checkbox. To convert all the layers into a single Smart Object (page 117) so you can resize the image later, turn on the "Create Smart Object after Loading Layers" checkbox.

Duplicating Files

If your client or boss asks you to alter an image and you suspect they'll change their mind later, it's wise to edit a *copy* of the image instead of the original file. That way, when they ask you to change everything back, you don't have to sweat bullets hunting for a backup of the original or try to recreate the earlier version.

Duplicating files is also handy when you want to experiment with a variety of different effects.

You can duplicate a file by choosing File → Save As and renaming the image, but there's a faster way: Make sure the file you want to copy is in the currently active window (just click the window to activate it), and then choose Image → Duplicate. In the Duplicate Image dialog box (Figure 2-9), give your file a new name and click OK. You've just set yourself up to be the office hero.

Figure 2-9:
A duplicate file has everything in the original, including layers, Layer styles, and so on. If you need to create a single-layer (flattened) version of your file, turn on the Duplicate Merged Layers Only checkbox. Page 104 has more about flattening files.

Changing Your Image View

Photoshop gives you a variety of ways to look at your images; different views are better for doing different things. For example, you can get rid of the Application Frame (page 11), view images full screen, zoom in and out, or rotate your canvas to view images at an angle (that last one is new in Photoshop CS4). This section teaches you how to do all that and more.

Zooming In and Out

Being able to zoom in on your image is crucial; it makes fixing imperfections, doing detailed clean-up work, and drawing accurate selections a hundred times easier. One way to zoom is to click with the Zoom tool, which looks like a magnifying glass. You can find it at the bottom of the Tools panel or the top of your screen in the Application bar, or you can grab it by pressing Z (see Figure 2-10). Simply click repeatedly to get as close to your pixels as you want. When you're ready to zoom back out, just Option-click (Alt-click on a PC) instead. You can also zoom using your keyboard: press ⌘ and the + or – key (Ctrl + or –). To zoom in on a specific area, drag with the Zoom tool to draw a box around the pixels you want to look at. As soon as you let go of your mouse button, Photoshop zooms in until the area you selected fills your document window.

> **NOTE** In older versions of Photoshop, zooming in to certain percentages made your image look jagged and blocky. In Photoshop CS4, you see a smooth image no matter which magnification level you choose (though you do need OpenGL [see the box on page 60]).

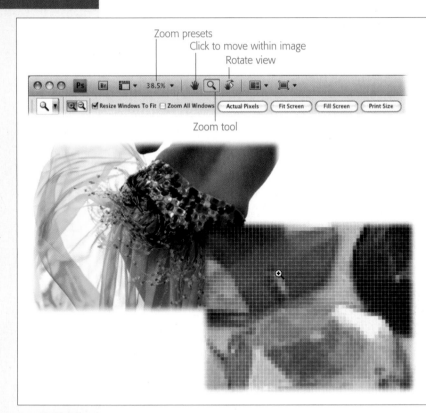

Zoom presets
Click to move within image
Rotate view

Zoom tool

Figure 2-10:
Top: You can grab the Zoom tool from the Tools panel or the Application bar at the top of your screen. You can also zoom by selecting an item from the Zoom preset menu or typing a percentage into the lower-left corner of your document window (not shown).

Bottom: If you zoom in to 501 percent or closer in CS4, you'll get this handy pixel-grid view that lets you edit precisely, pixel by pixel (it also makes it easy to see whether pixels are perfectly aligned horizontally and vertically).

If your computer can handle *OpenGL* (see the box on page 60), Photoshop CS4 lets you hold down your mouse button—while the Zoom tool is active—or hold ⌘-+ (Ctrl-+) to *fly* into your image, zooming to up to 3,200 percent. Then simply Option-click (Alt-click) and hold down your mouse button or hold ⌘-- (that's ⌘ plus the minus sign) or Ctrl-- on a PC to zoom back out. This animated zooming makes you feel like you're flying into and out of your image—and it saves you several mouse clicks along the way.

When you have the Zoom tool active, the Options bar gives you the following choices:

• **Resize Windows To Fit.** If you want Photoshop to resize your document window to accomodate the current magnification level, turn on this checkbox. You can also access it by choosing Photoshop → Preferences → General (Edit → Preferences → General on a PC) and turning on the Zoom Resizes Window checkbox though as of this writing the two settings cancel each other out.

The Status Bar: Document Info Central

At the bottom of each document window is the *status bar,* shown in the figure below, which gives you a quick peek at important info about your document. When you first start using Photoshop, the status bar shows the size of your document (K stands for kilobytes and M for megabytes). If you don't see any status information, your document window may be too small. Just drag outward from the lower-right edge of the window so it's big enough for you to see it.

Click the little triangle to the status bar's right (circled) and you get a menu that lets you control which information the bar displays. Here's what you can choose from:

- If you're using Adobe Version Cue (see the box on page 58), choose **Show Versions** to see a list of older or newer versions of the file if any are available on the Version Cue server.

- Choose **Reveal in Bridge** to make Photoshop display the file and its metadata in Bridge (see Appendix C).

- If you select **Show**, Photoshop presents you with a bunch of other options. The submenu that appears lets you pick from all kinds of info about the file you're working on:

–Version Cue shows whether the Version Cue workgroup thinks your document is open, unsaved, or unmanaged.

–Document Size displays the approximate size of your image for printing (on the left) and the approximate saved size of your image (on the right).

–Document Profile shows the color profile (page 617) for your image.

–Document Dimensions displays the dimensions (width and height) of your image.

–In Photoshop CS4 Extended, Measurement Scale shows the scale of pixels compared with other units of measurement. For example, an image from a microscope can measure objects in microns, and each micron can equal a certain number of pixels.

–Scratch Sizes tells you how much memory and hard disk space is being used to display your open images.

–Efficiency lets you know if Photoshop is performing tasks as fast as it possibly can. A number below 100 percent means Photoshop is running slowly because it's relying on scratch disk (page 30) space.

–Timing shows how long it took Photoshop to perform the most recent activity.

–Current Tool displays the name of the selected tool.

–32-bit Exposure lets you adjust the preview image for HDR images (see the box on page 387).

Zoom percentage

Status bar

Version Cue and You

Photoshop is packed with other little programs that can help you get things done quicker, faster, and better. One of those programs is *Version Cue CS4*. If you work with other folks who use Photoshop or Adobe's Creative Suite and exchange files with them, Version Cue can keep track of the changes each person makes to each file (technically called *asset management*). Version Cue acts like a librarian, letting you check out files when you need to work on them. It also organizes documents and records other important bits of information about the files you use.

To let Version Cue manage files, you need to save them on a shared computer, which Version Cue calls the *Adobe*

Drive (for best performance, this computer should be dedicated to Version Cue, not a coworker's design computer). It looks and acts like a regular hard drive, which means you can easily open files stored on it and save files to it. When you open a shared document with Photoshop or Bridge CS4, Version Cue automatically locks that file so your coworkers can't open it and overwrite your edits with theirs.

A great resource for learning more about Version Cue is Lynda.com's *Bridge and Version Cue Essential Training*, a video-based training course available online and on DVD.

- **Zoom All Windows.** Turn on this checkbox to use the Zoom tool to zoom in on all open windows by the same amount simultaneously. This checkbox is helpful if you've opened a duplicate of your image as described on page 54. You can also use the Window → Arrange menu to do pretty much the same thing. Your options there include:

    — **Match Zoom.** Zooms all open windows to the same magnification level.

    — **Match Location.** Zooms to the same spot in each window.

    — **Match Rotation.** Rotates the canvas of each window to the same angle.

    — **Match All.** Does all of the above.

- **Actual Pixels.** Click this button to see your image at 100 percent magnification. You can do the same thing by pressing ⌘-1 (Ctrl+1 on a PC), by double-clicking the Zoom tool, by entering *100* into the zoom percentage field at the bottom-left corner of the document window, or by choosing View → Actual Pixels.

- **Fit Screen.** Clicking this button makes Photoshop resize the active image window to fit the available space on your screen and fit the image inside the document window. You can also press ⌘-0 (Ctrl+0) or choose View → "Fit on Screen".

- **Fill Screen.** This button enlarges your image to the largest possible dimensions within the window. Clicking Fill Screen makes your image a little bigger than it gets when you use Fit Screen because it uses all the available vertical space.

- **Print Size.** If you click this button, Photoshop makes your image the size it will be when you print it; you can do the same thing by choosing View → Print Size. Keep in mind that the resolution settings for your monitor can make the print size sample look bigger or smaller than it really will be, so use this feature only as an approximation.

TIP   If your image is smaller than the document window (meaning you see a gray border around the edges of the image) or if the document window itself is smaller than the available space in the Application Frame (page 11), you can double-click the Hand tool in the Tools panel (*not* in the Application bar) to make Photoshop enlarge your image to fill the document window.

POWER USERS' CLINIC

Zooming with Mac Gestures

If you use a MacBook, MacBook Air, or MacBook Pro with a multi-touch trackpad, you've got yet another way to zoom in or out of your images: use the finger pinch gesture even if the Zoom tool isn't active. You can also flick left or right with two fingers to move across your image or twist with your finger and thumb to rotate the canvas.

If your Mac includes a multi-touch trackpad, you can see examples of each of these gestures in the Keyboard & Mouse Preference Pane. From the menu, choose System Preferences → Keyboard & Mouse and then select the Trackpad tab. Click an item in the action list on the left side of the dialog box to see that gesture in action. Sweet!

TIP   If you've got a scroll wheel on your mouse, you can use that to zoom, too. Just choose Photoshop → Preferences → General (Edit → Preferences → General on a PC), turn on "Zoom with Scroll Wheel" in the Options section, and then click OK.

Moving Around in Your Image

Once you've zoomed into your image, you can use the Hand tool to move to another area without zooming back out. Grab this tool from the Tools panel or the Application bar, or just press and hold the space bar on your keyboard (unless you're typing with the Type tool—then you'll just type a bunch of spaces). When your cursor turns into a hand, hold your mouse button down and then drag to move your image. When you get to the right spot, just let go of your mouse button.

TIP   If you press and hold the Shift key while you're using the Hand tool, Photoshop moves all your open windows at the same time. You can do the same thing by turning on the Scroll All Windows checkbox in the Options bar.

In Photoshop CS4, Adobe has given you a couple of other ways to move around your document: *flick-panning* and the *birds-eye view* feature. If you've got a computer that can run OpenGL (see the box on page 60), you can use these fast and efficient ways to move around your image. Here's how they work:

- **Flick-panning** lets you "toss" an image from one side of the document window to the other. Just grab the Hand tool, click your image, and hold down the mouse button. Then, quickly move your mouse in the direction you want to go and release your mouse button. The image slides along and slowly comes to a stop. You can do the same thing by holding your space bar and moving your mouse quickly while you hold the mouse button down.

NOTE If you're not a fan of flick-panning, you can turn it off by choosing Photoshop → Preferences → General (Edit → Preferences → General on a PC) and, in the resulting dialog box, turn off the Enable Flick Panning checkbox.

- **Birds-eye view** lets you zoom out of your document quickly to see the whole thing. To use it, just press and hold the H key and click within your image. You'll get an instant aerial view of your image with a box marking the area you're zoomed in on. Let go of the H key (and your mouse button) to zoom back to where you were.

UP TO SPEED

Understanding OpenGL

OpenGL is a technology that helps newer computers draw graphics faster and more efficiently. (To learn more about it, go to *www.opengl.org*.) You can tell whether your computer uses OpenGL by going to Photoshop → Preferences → Performance (Edit → Preferences → Performance on a PC). If the Enable OpenGL Drawing checkbox is turned on, you're all set. If it's not checked but you *can* turn it on, do it. If the checkbox is grayed out (meaning you can't turn it on), then your computer's video card isn't fast enough to run OpenGL. Bummer!

If your computer can't run OpenGL, some Photoshop features will take a long time to run, and others, like flick-panning, canvas rotating, and pixel-grid overlay (Figure 2-10), won't work at all. Other nifty CS4 features that require OpenGL include Photoshop CS4 Extended's 3D Axis, Toggle Ground Plate, and Toggle Lights.

Zooming with the Navigator Panel

You can think of the Navigator panel as your one-stop zooming shop. If you want to know *exactly* which part of an image you're zoomed in on, it can show you. To open it, go to Window → Navigator. The panel displays a smaller version of your image called a *thumbnail* and marks the area you're zoomed in on with a red box called the *proxy preview*. At the bottom of the panel, the zoom text field shows your current magnification level. You can zoom into or out of your image by clicking the zoom buttons (which look like little mountains) at the bottom of the panel or by using the slider in between them (see Figure 2-11). To zoom to a specific level, enter a number in the zoom text field.

TIP To make the Navigator panel bigger, drag its bottom-right corner. You can change the color of the proxy preview box by choosing Panel Options from the top-right corner of the Navigator panel's menu. Click the red color swatch, pick another color from the resulting Color Picker, and then click OK.

Figure 2-11:
As you zoom into your image, the proxy preview box shrinks. You can drag it around to cruise to another area in your image.

- Proxy preview
- Increase panel size
- Zoom out
- Zoom slider
- Zoom in

Rotating Your Canvas

If you're an artist, you're going to love this new feature! The Rotate View tool rotates your canvas—without harming any pixels—so you can edit, draw, or paint at a more natural angle (see Figure 2-12). It's like shifting a piece of paper or angling a painting canvas, but it doesn't rotate the actual image; it just rotates your *view* of the image. If you're using a graphics tablet (see the box on page 477), this feature alone may be worth the price of upgrading from previous versions of Photoshop. Bear in mind, though, that your computer needs to be able to run OpenGL (page 60) for this feature to work. To use this tool, click its button in the Application bar or select it from the Tools panel (where it hides in the Hand tool's toolset).

TIP MacBook, MacBook Air, and MacBook Pro users with multi-touch trackpads (page 59) can rotate the canvas by using the two-finger rotate gesture.

UP TO SPEED

Document Size vs. Canvas Space

One thing that's super confusing to Photoshop beginners is the difference between document size (also known as image size) and canvas size because you can change one without changing the other. In Photoshop, the *canvas* is the amount of editable area inside your document, or its dimensions, and nothing else—it has nothing to do with resolution. Document size, on the other hand, is the image size, which can be smaller than the canvas size.

Let's say you're designing a poster for a chili cook-off and you're experimenting with the design. Instead of limiting your work area to the final size of the poster, you can make your canvas bigger than that (page 240) so you have room to spread out and try different things. Once you've got the final design, you can crop (page 202) or trim (page 215) either the document or the canvas area back down to size.

Figure 2-12:
Grab the Rotate View tool and then drag your image up or down to rotate it. When you start to drag, you see a compass that shows how far from "north" you're rotating the canvas. Instead of dragging, you can type a number into the Options bar's Rotation Angle field or spin the little round dial to the field's right. To straighten your image, click the Reset View button in the Options bar. To rotate all open images, turn on the Rotate All Windows checkbox.

Arranging Open Images

In Photoshop CS4, the new Application Frame (page 11) and tabbed document workspace can help you keep track of several open documents. If you've decided to turn off the Application Frame, your documents can get scattered across your screen. But you can herd those open windows together by using the list of commands that appears when you choose Window → Arrange (see Figure 2-13).

Here are your choices:

- **Cascade** stacks your windows on top of each other, putting the largest one on the bottom and the smallest on the top.

- **Tile** resizes your windows to identical sizes and arranges them in rows and columns.

Figure 2-13:
You can use the Arrange command to create order out of chaos by tiling (top) or cascading (bottom) your windows. You can also use the new Arrange Documents menu (shown opened here) in the Application bar to view your windows in a variety of ways.

- **Float in Window** puts the current document in its own window if it's part of a document group sharing the same window (a tabbed window group).

- **Float All Windows** splits all tabbed documents out into their own windows and cascades the new windows.

- **Consolidate All Tabs** groups your open images in a single tabbed window (as shown in Figure 2-14, top left).

TIP   You can cycle through all your open documents by using the ⌘-~ keyboard shortcut (Ctrl+Tab on a PC). To cycle through documents in the reverse order, press Shift-⌘-~ (Shift+Ctrl+Tab).

Guides, Grids, and Rulers

Placing all the components of your design in just the right spot can be challenging, and if you're a real stickler for details, close enough isn't good enough. This section teaches you how to use Photoshop's guides, grids, and rulers to get everything positioned *perfectly*. In Photoshop CS4, these little helpers are called *Extras*. You can access them using the new Application bar's Extras pop-up menu, shown in Figure 2-15.

Figure 2-14:
Photoshop CS4's new tabbed document feature is a handy way of organizing open windows. For example, you can slide the tabs left or right to rearrange them (top left) or drag a tab out of the window group to create a floating window (bottom left). To redock a floating window, just drag its tab back into the main tab area (right). You can close all tabbed documents by Option-clicking (Shift-clicking on a PC) the little X to the right of each document tab.

Figure 2-15:
The Extras pop-up menu gives you easy access to guides, grids, and rulers.

Rulers and Guiding Lines

Positioning objects on your canvas properly can make the difference between a basic design and a masterpiece. The quickest way to position and align objects is by drawing a straight line to nestle them against. You can do just that using Photoshop's nonprinting *guides*—vertical and horizontal lines you can place anywhere you want (see Figure 2-16).

Before you can create guides, you need to turn on Photoshop's rulers. The fastest way to do that is by pressing ⌘-R (Ctrl+R on a PC) though you can also turn them on by choosing View → Rulers or selecting Rulers from the Extras pop-up menu (see Figure 2-15). Whichever method you use, the rulers appear on the top and left edges of your image window. The units you see on the rulers are controlled by the settings in the Units & Rulers preferences (page 33).

Once you've turned your rulers on, you can add a guide by clicking in either the horizontal or vertical ruler, and then drag into your document as shown in Figure 2-16. After you've drawn a guide, you can:

Figure 2-16:
*Guides help you position items exactly where you want
'em. Here the green guides help you make sure all the
text is the same width and the edges of the poster are
kept free of clutter. The guides won't show up when you
print your image, so you don't have to worry about
deleting them.*

- **Move a guide** by grabbing the Move tool (see Appendix E, online at *www.
missingmanuals.com*) from the Tools panel (or by pressing V), and then dragging the guide to a new position (your cursor turns into a double-sided arrow
like the one circled in Figure 2-16).

TIP   If you're having trouble grabbing a guide, try making your document window bigger than
your canvas (drag any edge of the document window, or its lower-right corner, diagonally). That
way your guides extend beyond the canvas so they don't overlap other elements that you might
accidentally select and move.

- **Snap objects to your guides** by turning on Photoshop's *snap* feature. This feature makes it super easy to align objects because, when they get close to one of
your guides, they jump to it as if they were magnetized. To turn on this behavior, choose View → Snap To → Guides. You can tell that an object has snapped
to the nearest guide because it pops into place. After the object aligns to a guide,
you can move it along that line to snap it into place with other guides, too. If
you don't want an object aligned with a certain guide, just keep moving it—it'll
let go of the guide as soon as you move it far enough.

TIP   You can make objects snap to grids (page 66), layers (Chapter 3), slices (Chapter 17), and the edges of your document. Just go to View → Snap To and choose the elements you want objects to align with. For example, choosing both Guides and Layers makes the object you're moving snap to guides *and* the edges of objects on other layers.

- **Hide your guides** temporarily by pressing ⌘ (Ctrl on a PC) and the semicolon key (;).
- **Delete a guide** by dragging it back where it came from (into the ruler area).
- **Delete all guides** by choosing View → Clear Guides.

Smart Guides

Smart Guides are a little different from regular guides in that they automatically appear onscreen to show the spatial relationship between objects. For example, they pop up when objects are aligned or evenly spaced in your document. As you drag an object, Smart Guides appear whenever the current object is horizontally, vertically, or centrally aligned with other objects on other layers. To enable Smart Guides, choose View → Show → Smart Guides. You can see them in action in Chapter 3 (page 91).

Using the Document Grid

If you want *lots* of guides without all the work of placing them, you can add a grid to your image by choosing View → Show → Grid (see Figure 2-17). Straight from the factory, Photoshop's gridlines appear an inch apart with four subdivisions though you can change that spacing by choosing Photoshop → Preferences → "Guides, Grid & Slices" (Edit → Preferences → "Guides, Grid & Slices" on a PC). In the Preferences dialog box, adjust the gridline marks by changing the "Gridline every" field and use the pop-up menu next to it to choose the unit of measurement the grid uses: pixels, inches, centimeters, millimeters, points, picas, or percent. Just below the "Gridline every" field is the Subdivisions field, which you can use to set how many lines appear between each gridline—if any.

The Ruler Tool

In addition to the rulers you learned about earlier, Photoshop also gives you a virtual tape measure: the Ruler tool. It lets you measure the distance between two points in your document. Grab the tool (it's hiding in the Eyedropper toolset; it looks like a little ruler) by pressing Shift-I repeatedly and click and hold your mouse button where you want to start measuring. Drag across the area or object with your mouse and you'll see a line appear in your document. To draw a perfectly straight horizontal or vertical line, press and hold the Shift key as you drag. When you release your mouse button to let go of the ruler, Photoshop displays the measurement between the start and end points of the line in the Options bar (see Figure 2-18).

Figure 2-17:
Photoshop's grid is helpful when you need to align lots of different items like the text shown here.

Within the image:
iStock_000000832473Medium.jpg @ 33.3% (...

Bra/skirt with tassels: $325
Red cape: $75
Being seen belly-dancing
by your ex: Priceless

33.33%   1130 pixels x 1699 pixels (300 ppi)

The Options bar's measurements can be a little confusing. Here's what they mean:

- **X and Y.** These *axes* mark the horizontal and vertical coordinates (respectively) at the start of your ruler line. For example, if you start your line at the four-inch mark on the horizontal ruler and the seven-inch mark on the vertical ruler, your coordinates are X: 4 and Y: 7.

- **W and H.** Calculates the distance your line has traveled from the X and Y axes.

- **A.** Displays the angle of your line relative to the X axis.

- **L1.** Shows the length of the line you drew.

- **L2.** You see a number here only if you use a virtual *protractor.* (Thought you left protractors behind in high school, didn't you? Quick refresher: Protractors help you measure angles.) To create a protractor, Option-drag (Alt-drag on a PC) at an angle from the end of your ruler line (or just double-click the line and drag). This number represents the angle between the two lengths when you use a protractor.

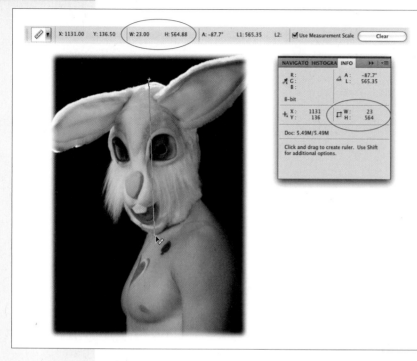

Figure 2-18:
The Info panel (page 24) and Ruler tool make a great tag team when it comes to taking measurements or finding angles in your image. When you're using the Ruler tool, the Info panel's CMYK section gets replaced with angle (A) and length (L) info. As you can see here, Bunny Boy's head is 564 pixels high.

- **Use Measurement Scale.** Turn on this checkbox to copy the unit of measurement set in your preferences (choose Photoshop → Preferences → Units & Rulers or Edit → Preferences → Units & Rulers on a PC). You can change the unit of measurement you see in the Info panel by choosing Panel Options from the Info panel's menu.

- **Clear.** Any ruler line you draw hangs around until you tell it to go away by clicking the Clear button in the Options bar or draw another ruler line. But the line won't print even if you forget to clear it, so don't lose any sleep over it.

TIP To reposition a ruler line, just grab one of its end points and drag it to another position.

Layers: The Key to Nondestructive Editing

Photoshop gives you two ways to edit your files: the destructive way and the non-destructive way. *Destructive editing* means you're changing your original image—once you exceed the limit of your History panel (page 25), those changes are (gulp) permanent. *Nondestructive editing* means you're not changing the original file and you can go back to it at any time. Folks new to image editing tend to use the first method and experienced pixel-jockeys the second—and you'll likely see a tiny cloud of smugness floating above the pixel-jockeys.

When you're working in Photoshop, you need to keep your documents as flexible as possible. People (even you!) change their minds hourly about what looks good, what they want, and where they want it—all of which is no big deal if you're pre-pared for that. If not, you'll spend a ton of time *redoing* what you've done from scratch. To avoid this kind of suffering, you can use *layers*, a set of stackable trans-parencies that together form your whole image (see Figure 3-1). Layers are your key to nondestructive editing.

With layers, you can make all kinds of changes to your image without altering the original. For example, you can use one layer to color-correct your family reunion photo (page 345), another to whiten Aunt Bessie's teeth (page 402), and yet another to add a photo of the Great Pyramid, making your reunion look like it was in Egypt instead of the local park (page 260). Using layers also lets you:

• Resize an object independently of everything else in your document, without changing the size of your document (page 89).

• Move an object around without moving anything else (page 90).

• Combine several images into one document to make a collage (page 93).

Figure 3-1:
Think of layers as a stack of slides. If a layer is partially transparent, you can see through the transparent parts to the layers below. If you look down through the top of the stack, you see a single image even though it's made from many different slides (this kind of image is called a composite).

- Hide parts of your image so you can see through to layers below (page 105).

- Change the opacity of a layer to make it more or less see-through (page 87).

- Change the way colors on various layers interact (page 267).

- Fix the color and lighting of your whole photo (or just parts of it) without harming your original (page 109).

The best part about using layers is that once you save your document as a PSD file (page 46), you can close it, forget about it, and open it next week to find your layers—and all of your changes—intact. Learning to love layers is your key to a successful Photoshop career: They let you edit with maximum flexibility.

Throughout this chapter, you'll learn about the different kinds of layers, when to use them, and how to create them. You'll also learn about the fun and useful features that tag along with layers like Layer styles and layer masks. By the time you're done, you'll be shouting the praises of nondestructive editing from the highest rooftop! (Whether you do it smugly is up to you.)

Layer Basics

Layers come in many flavors, all of which have their own special purpose. They include:

- **Image layers.** These layers are pixel-based (page 48), and you'll work with them *all* the time. If you open a photo or make a new layer (page 76), you've got yourself an Image layer.

- **Type layers.** Photoshop text isn't made from pixels, so it gets its own kind of layer. Anytime you grab the Type tool and start pecking away, Photoshop creates a Type layer for you automatically. See Chapter 14 for the full story on creating type in Photoshop.

- **Shape layers.** These layers are vector-based (page 48), meaning they're not made from pixels. You get a lot of flexibility with these babies because you can resize them without losing quality, *and* you can change their fill color by double-clicking their layer thumbnails (page 73). Photoshop creates a Shape layer automatically anytime you use a shape tool (see Chapter 13).

- **Fill and Adjustment layers.** When it comes to adjusting the color of your image (by changing, draining, or adding color), these layers are your best friends. Fill layers let you fill a layer with a solid color, gradient, or pattern (shown later in this chapter), which comes in handy when you want to create new backgrounds. Adjustment layers let you apply color and lighting changes to the layer directly underneath them, but the actual changes happen on the Adjustment layer. For example, if you want to change a color image to black and white, you can use a Black & White Adjustment layer (page 301) and the color removal will happen on its own layer, leaving your original unharmed. These layers don't contain any pixels, just the instructions that tell Photoshop which changes you want to make. The Adjustments panel (new in CS4) lives on the right side of your screen (if you don't see it, choose Window → Adjustments). You'll also find an Adjustment layer menu at the bottom of the Layers panel (it looks like a half-black/half-white circle), as well as in the Layers menu (choose Layers → New Adjustment layer). There are 18 kinds of Adjustment layers, and you'll learn how to use them in Part 2 of this book.

- **Smart Objects.** Adobe refers to this kind of layer as a *container*, though "miracle layer" is a better description. Smart Objects let you work with files that weren't created with Photoshop, like Raw (page 53) and vector files (page 48). The best thing about a Smart Object is that you can resize its content without trashing its quality. Flip over to page 238 to for more info.

- **3D and Video layers.** In the extended version of Photoshop (page 1), you can import 3D and video files into their own special layers, which is helpful if you want to do some custom painting and transformations of individual video frames or 3D objects. See the box on page 72 for the scoop on 3D, and the box on page 74 for more on video.

POWER USERS' CLINIC

The 3D Experience

If you ponied up for Photoshop CS4 Extended (page 1), you'll notice a couple of new tools gracing your Tools panel: 3D Rotate and 3D Orbit, as well as a new menu stuffed full of commands like New Mesh from Grayscale, Invert Visible Surfaces, and Create UV Overlays. What's up with all that?

With each new version of Photoshop, Adobe dives a little deeper into the 3D waters, and not without good reason. 3D technologies are developing at warp speed, and soon you'll be able to snap a camera's shutter twice (hopefully once at some point!) and your camera will create a 3D model for you on the fly.

But if you don't know anything about 3D, does all this new functionality mean anything to you? It could. If you've ever dreamt of dabbling in 3D modeling, Photoshop is a great place to start. Just as you can buy stock images, video clips, and audio clips, you can also buy 3D objects. Do a quick Google search and you'll find oceans of 3D models for sale. If those objects are already painted and lit (some aren't), you can bring all that info into Photoshop. You've also got a fair amount of control over the object's textures and lighting. If the object came with a separate texture file, you can edit it in Photoshop and see your updated model when you save it. You can also add and adjust lighting to make the model blend into your scene better.

If you're feeling particularly brave, you can paint directly on the surface of a 3D model in real time (meaning you see your brushstrokes as you make them). It's *really* nice to be able to do this kind of painting in Photoshop, especially if you don't have a dedicated 3D painting program. Adobe also added a *reparameterize* command (try saying that 10 times fast!) that can quickly rebuild the surface geometry of your 3D object—called a *mesh*—for smoother painting. So if you come upon a seam while you're painting or your brush isn't behaving like you'd expect, give this command a spin.

Learning to do a little 3D work can be both fun and beneficial. For example, you can build your own props. Let's say you forgot to include a stick of butter in the croissant shop shoot last week in France. Do you fly back and redo the lighting, hire talent, and so on? Heck, no. You can churn a stick of butter right here in Photoshop and then toss it into your shot. Adobe has also made it fairly easy for you, too, since Photoshop treats 3D objects like souped-up layers—you can run filters on them, add Layer styles, and so on (they're similar to Smart Objects [page 115]).

Photoshop CS4 Extended can't do everything a traditional 3D modeling program can, but it's a good place to start.

The Layers Panel

No matter which kinds of layers your document contains, the one that's most important to you at any given time is the currently active layer. You can tell which layer is active by peeking at the Layers panel where Photoshop highlights the active layer, as shown in Figure 3-2. No matter which tool you're wielding, your changes will affect *only* that layer. To open the Layers panel, click its tab in the panel dock on the right side of your screen, or choose Window → Layers.

> **TIP**   If you're trying to use a tool and Photoshop doesn't seem to be responding, take a peek in your Layers panel and make sure you've got the right layer selected. Nine times out of ten, you'll find that you don't!

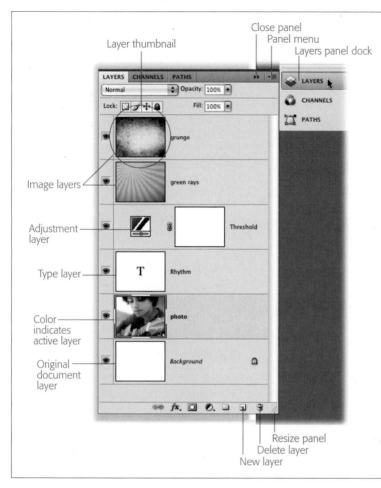

Figure 3-2:
In your Layers panel, Photoshop highlights the currently active layer as shown here. Each kind of layer has its own little preview called a layer thumbnail (circled).

Selecting Layers

About the easiest thing you'll ever do in Photoshop is select a layer—just mouse over to your Layers panel and click it. However, just because it's easy doesn't mean it isn't important. As you learned in the last section, whatever you're doing in Photoshop will affect only the *currently active layer*—the one that's selected.

As your document gets more complex and your Layers panel starts to grow (and it will), it can be hard to figure out which layer each part of your image lives on. If you want, you can make Photoshop *guess* which layer an object is on: Press V to activate the Move tool, head up to the Options bar at the top of your screen, turn on the Auto-Select checkbox, and then choose Layer from the pop-up menu to its right (the other option, Groups, is discussed on page 98).

POWER USERS' CLINIC

Working with Video

You may be thinking, "I can work with video in Photoshop?" Actually, unless you've sprung for Photoshop CS4 Extended (page 1), you can't (but you can still import video as still frames as discussed later in this box). Remember: Photoshop isn't just for graphic designers and photographers; it's used in many professions. For example, law enforcement officers use it to enhance surveillance footage, and TV show editors use video clips as reference images when they're designing type and logos in Photoshop.

If you want to work with a video clip in Photoshop or Photoshop CS4 Extended, you need to make sure you have the latest and greatest version of QuickTime. If you're using a Mac, you've probably already got it; if you're on a PC, you can download it free from *www.apple.com*. You also need to save the video file in a format that QuickTime can play, like .mov, .avi, .flv, or .mp4.

You've got two ways to load video into Photoshop, and the method depends on your particular needs and which version of Photoshop you have.

If you've got Photoshop CS4 Extended, you can import video as a *video layer:*

1. To open the video file, choose File → Open. To import the video into an existing document, choose Layer → Video Layers → "New Video Layer from File".

2. In the Open dialog box, make sure the Enable pop-up menu is set to "All Readable Documents" or "QuickTime Movies" (on a PC, the menu is called "Files of type" and the option you want is "All Formats"). Otherwise, your computer won't let you select your video.

3. Select a video file, click Open, and Photoshop opens the file as a video layer. Since video files are linked to your Photoshop document (meaning it references the video file instead of embedding it in your document), you need to keep the original file hanging around. It's a good idea to put it in the same folder as your Photoshop document.

4. If you want to adjust the clip's playback options, choose Window → Animation and tweak the settings to your liking.

That's it. If you want to *export* a video from Photoshop, choose File → Export → Render Video. You can export it as a QuickTime movie, animated GIF, or a sequence of images.

If you're using Photoshop CS3 or CS4 standard version, you can convert a video clip to still frames on individual layers. (Most video formats use between 24 and 30 frames per second.) This technique is a handy way to snatch an image from a video clip to use in another document, as a video link on a Web site, or to create a frame-by-frame animation (like an animated GIF—see page 671). To load video as images on individual layers:

1. Choose File → Import → "Video Frames to Layers". Head to where the video clip lives on your hard drive and click Load.

2. In the resulting Import Video To Layers dialog box, specify the range you want to import. You can load the whole clip or just a portion of it. If you like, turn on the Limit To Every __ Frames checkbox to load just a few frames of your video instead of the whole thing.

3. If you want to create an animation, leave the Make Frame Animation setting turned on; if you're going to use the frames in a still project, turn it off.

4. Click OK to load the video.

Once Photoshop puts the frames on separate layers, you can edit them just like any other layer. If you're creating an animation, you can see a preview by choosing Window → Animation and then clicking the play button.

Working with video in Photoshop can be a little tricky, but it gives you a ton of options for multimedia and video projects. To find out more, visit *www.PhotoshopforVideo.com*.

Now when you click an object in your document, Photoshop selects the layer it *thinks* the object is on (it'll do this next time you use the Move tool, too, unless you turn off the Auto-Select option). The program may or may not guess right, and it really works only if your layers don't completely cover each other up. If you've got a document full of isolated objects—ones without backgrounds—on different layers, give it a shot. If you're working on a multi-layered collage, forget it. For those reasons, you usually want to leave Auto-Select turned *off*.

> **TIP** You can have Photoshop narrow down your layer hunting options by prodding it to give you a list of layers it *thinks* your object is on. Press V to select the Move tool, Ctrl-click (right-click) an object in your document, and choose one of the layers from the resulting shortcut menu. This trick works only if you click an area that's more than 50 percent opaque.

Selecting multiple layers

You'd be surprised how often you need to do the same thing to more than one layer. If you want to rearrange a few of them in your layers stack (page 79), move them around in your document together (page 90), or resize them simultaneously (page 89), you need to select them first. Photoshop lets you select as few or as many as you want though how you go about it depends on where they live in your Layers panel and which kind of layers they are. Here's how:

- **Consecutive layers.** To select layers that are next to each other in the Layers panel, click the first one and then Shift-click the last one. Photoshop automatically selects everything in between (see Figure 3-3, left).

- **Nonconsecutive layers.** To select layers that *aren't* next to each other, click the first one's name and then ⌘-click (Ctrl-click on a PC) the rest of them (see Figure 3-3, right).

- **Similar layers.** To select layers similar to the active layer, choose Select → Similar Layers. This command is handy, for example, if you want to select all the Type layers so you can change the font (page 554) or all the Shape or Fill layers to change their color (page 85).

- **All layers.** To select the whole kit and caboodle, choose Select → All Layers. Choosing Deselect → All Layers (you guessed it) deselects everything.

- **Linked layers.** If you've linked any layers together (page 96), you can select them all by choosing Layer → Select Linked Layers (you can also find this command in the Layers panel menu).

> **NOTE** Selecting a layer is *completely* different from loading a layer's contents as a selection. When you load a layer as a selection, you see marching ants running around your image. Selecting a layer simply makes that layer active so you can perform other edits. See Chapter 4 for more on selections.

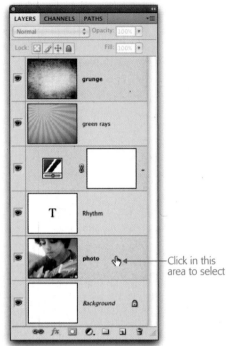

Figure 3-3:
You can select consecutive layers (left) or random layers (right). To avoid loading the layer as a selection (page 125) when you're selecting nonconsecutive layers, make sure you ⌘-click (Ctrl-click) the area to the right of the layer thumbnail, as shown here.

Click in this area to select

Adding New Layers

Most of the time, Photoshop creates new layers *for* you, like when you copy and paste an image (page 85), create text (page 537), and so on. But if you want to do something like paint with the Brush tool—to colorize a grayscale image (page 333) or to make a colorful new background (page 85), say—you need to create a new layer. Otherwise, you'll paint on or over your original image.

Photoshop gives you four ways to create a new layer:

- Click the "Create a new layer" button at the very bottom of the Layers panel (it looks like a piece of paper with a folded corner)

- Choose Layer → New → Layer

- Choose New Layer from the Layers panel menu

- Press Shift-⌘-N (Shift+Ctrl+N on a PC)

> **TIP:** If your fingers are flexible enough, you can create a new layer *and* bypass the New Layer dialog box by pressing Shift-Option-⌘-N (Shift+Alt+Ctrl+N on a PC). This shortcut is handy if you want to make new layers and don't care what they're called.

Shortcuts for Selecting and Moving Layers

It's a little known fact that you can use keyboard shortcuts to select and move layers. This trick can be a real time saver since you don't have to lift your hands from your keyboard, and it's helpful when you're creating actions and don't want Photoshop to capture a layer's name (see Chapter 18).

Here's the rather complicated list of shortcuts:

- To select the layer below the current layer, press Option-[(Alt+[on a PC). To select the layer above the current layer, press Option-] (Alt+]).

- To grab a bunch of layers in a row, select the first layer and then press Option-Shift-[(Alt+Shift+[) to select layers below the first one, or Option-Shift-] (Alt+Shift+]) to select layers above it. This shortcut lets you grab one layer at a time. Just type the shortcut again to grab another layer.

- To select the top layer in your Layers panel, press Option-. (Alt+.)—that's Option or Alt plus the period key. To select the bottom layer, press Option-, (Alt+,)—Option or Alt plus the comma key.

- To select all the layers between the currently active layer and the top layer, press Option-Shift-. (Alt+Shift+.)—Option or Alt plus Shift and the period key.

- To select all the layers between the currently active layer and the bottom layer, press Option-Shift-, (Alt+Shift+,)—Option or Alt plus Shift and the comma key.

- To select every layer *except* the locked Background layer, press ⌘-Option-A (Ctrl+Alt+A). If you've unlocked the Background layer (page 80), it gets selected, too.

- To move the current layer up one slot in your layer stack, press ⌘-] (Ctrl+]). To move it down one slot in your layer stack, press ⌘-[(Ctrl+[).

- To move the current layer to the top of the layers stack, press Shift-⌘-] (Shift+Ctrl+]). To move it to the bottom of your layers stack, press Shift-⌘-[(Shift+Ctrl+[).

Turns layer visibility off/on

Color code

Figure 3-4:
In the New Layer dialog box (top), you can give your layer a name and a colored label. Color-coding your layers makes them easier to spot in the Layers panel (bottom). You can double-click a layer's name to rename it or turn its visibility on or off by clicking the little eyeball to the left of its thumbnail. The new layer's thumbnail shown here is the checkerboard pattern (page 44) because the layer is empty and transparent.

When you click the "Create a new layer" button, Photoshop creates an empty layer called "Layer 1". If you already have a layer called "Layer 1", Photoshop names the new one "Layer 2", and so on. If you use the menu options or keyboard shortcut, the program displays the New Layer dialog box (Figure 3-4) where you can name the layer, color code it (page 95), choose its blend mode (page 267), set its opacity, and use it in a clipping mask (page 114).

> **TIP** If you want to create a new layer *below* the one you're currently on, ⌘-click (Ctrl-click) the "Create a new layer" button at the bottom of the Layers panel. This shortcut saves you the extra step of dragging the new layer to a lower position later. This tip, when it's used over the course of a year, has been known to produce an *entire* vacation day! (But if the only layer in your document is the locked Background layer, you've got to double-click it to make it editable before you can add a new layer below it.)

Hiding and Showing Layers

The little visibility eye to the left of each layer lets you turn layers off and on (Figure 3-4, bottom). Photoshop calls this incredibly useful feature *hiding*. For example, hiding layers lets you:

- **See an instant before-and-after preview.** If you've spent some time color-correcting (Chapter 9) or retouching people (Chapter 10) on duplicate layers, hiding those layers is an easy way to see the effect of your handiwork.

- **Experiment with different looks.** If you're trying out different backgrounds, you can add them all to your document and turn them on one at a time to see which one looks best.

- **See what you're doing.** When you're working on a document that has a bunch of layers, some of them may hide an area you need to see or work on. The solution is to hide in-the-way layers while you're working on those parts of the image and then turn them back on when you're done.

- **Print certain layers.** Only layers that are visible in your document will print, so if you want to print only parts of your image, you can hide the other layers first.

To turn a layer off, simply click the little eye to the left of its layer thumbnail; to turn it back on, click the empty square where the visibility eye used to be. To turn off *all* layers except one, Option-click (Alt-click on a PC) the visibility eye of the one layer you want to see. You can turn the other layers back on again by Option-clicking (Alt-clicking) that same layer's visibility eye again. Alternatively, you can Ctrl-click (right-click) a layer's visibility eye (or the spot where it used to be if the layer is turned off) and choose "Show/Hide this layer" or "Show/Hide all other layers" from the shortcut menu. You can also find the Show/Hide layer command in the Layers menu.

> **TIP** To turn several layers on or off, drag up or down over the visibility eyes in your Layers panel while you hold down your mouse button.

Restacking Layers

Once you start adding layers, you can rearrange their *stacking order*—the order in which they appear in your Layers panel—to control what's visible and what's not. When you think about stacking order, pretend you're peering down at your Layers panel from above: The layer at the very top can hide any layers below. For example, if you fill a layer with color (page 85) and then place it above another layer containing a photo, the color will completely cover the photo. If you've merely painted a swish or two with the Brush tool, though, your brushstrokes will cover just that part of your photo.

You can rearrange your layers manually, or you can make Photoshop do it for you:

- **By dragging.** Click a layer's thumbnail and drag it up or down to change its position as shown in Figure 3-5. When you get it in the right place, let go of your mouse button.

Figure 3-5:
To rearrange your layers, drag the layer's thumbnail up or down. When you drag, your cursor turns into a tiny closed fist as shown here (left). When you see the dividing line between the layers darken (left), let go of your mouse button to make the layer hop into place (right).

- **Using the Arrange command.** If you've got one or more layers selected, you can choose Layer → Arrange to move them somewhere else in the layers stack. Depending on that layer's location in your Layers panel, you can choose from:

  — **Bring to Front** moves your layer all the way to the top of the layers stack. Keyboard shortcut: Shift-⌘-] (Shift+Ctrl+] on a PC).

  — **Bring Forward** moves your layer up one level. Keyboard shortcut: ⌘-] (Ctrl-]).

  — **Send Backward** sends your layer down one level. Keyboard shortcut: ⌘-[(Ctrl-[).

  — **Send to Back** sends your layer all the way to the bottom of the layers stack. Keyboard shortcut: Shift-⌘-[(Shift+Ctrl-[).

  — **Reverse.** If you've got two or more layers selected (page 75), this command inverts the stacking order of the selected layers. You probably won't use this command very often, but give it a try just for fun; it can produce some mildly interesting results (Photoshop doesn't have a keyboard shortcut for this one).

NOTE   If you've got a long Layers panel, these keyboard shortcuts can save you lots of time.

The only layer you *can't* move around (at least not without giving it some special treatment) is the *Background layer.* The Background layer isn't really a layer, though it looks like one. It behaves a little differently from other layers, as the box explains, so if you want to rearrange it in your Layers panel, you have to double-click its thumbnail (circled back in Figure 3-2) and rename it in the resulting New Layer dialog box. When you click OK, it becomes a normal, everyday layer that you can put wherever you want.

UP TO SPEED

The Background Layer and You

Only a handful of image file formats understand Photoshop's layer system: PSD (Photoshop) files and TIFF files are the two most popular. Most other image file formats can handle only *flat* images (unlayered files). If you save a multi-layered PSD file as a JPEG, EPS, or PNG file, for example, Photoshop will flatten it for you, smashing all your layers into one. (See page 104 for more on flattening files.)

When you open an image created by a device or program that *doesn't* understand layers, like your digital camera or desktop scanner, Photoshop opens it as a flat image named Background. Though it looks like a regular layer, it's not nearly as flexible as the layers you create in Photoshop. For example, you can paint on it with the Brush tool (page 461), make a selection and fill the selection with color (page 168), or use any of the retouching tools (Chapter 10) on it, but you can't use the Move tool to make it hang off the edges of your document or make any part of it transparent—if you try to use the Eraser tool, nothing happens other than painting with the background color (and you can almost *hear* Photoshop snickering at your efforts). Also, if you make a selection and press Delete (Backspace on a PC), Photoshop fills that area with the color of your background chip (page 22).

When you create a *new* document in Photoshop, the program opens a more universally compatible flat file containing a single Background layer. You can convert the Background layer into a fully editable and movable layer in a couple of different ways:

- The easiest method is to double-click the Background layer in your Layers panel, give it a new name in the resulting New Layer dialog box, and then click OK.

- You can select the Background layer in the Layers panel and then choose Layer → New → "Layer from Background".

- You can also ⌘-click (Right-click) the Background layer and choose "New layer from Background".

If you want, you can convert a normal layer into a Background layer by choosing Layer → New → "Background from Layer", though it'd be tough to think of a reason why you would want to.

The only way to create a new document *without* a Background layer is to choose Transparent from the Background Contents pop-up menu (see page 42). Otherwise, you're doomed to double-clicking and renaming the Background layer every time you create a new document.

To *really* understand how layer stacking works, it helps to put theory into practice. Let's say you want to make a photo look like one side fades to white and then add some text on top of the white part. To do that, you need to place the photo at the bottom of the layers stack, the white paint layer in the middle, and the text layer at the top (see Figure 3-6).

Figure 3-6:
The stacking order of your layers determines what you can see and what you can't.

Top: With the Type layer at the top of the stack, you can see the text because it's sitting on top of everything else. And because the white fade layer is partially transparent (you can tell by the checkerboard pattern in its thumbnail), you can see through it to the photo on the very bottom of the stack.

Bottom: If you drag the Type layer below the white fade layer, you can't see the text anymore because it's hidden by the white paint.

Here's a quick bonus lesson in how to softly fade your photo to white and then add some text to it:

1. **Open a soon-to-be-faded photo and add a new layer to your document.**

   To safeguard your photo, you need to put the white paint on another layer. Press ⌘-Shift-N (Ctrl+Shift+N on a PC) to create a new layer, give it a clever name like *white fade*, and click OK.

2. **Set your foreground color chip to white.**

   Peek at the color chips at the bottom of your Tools panel (page 22). If they're black and white, just press X to flip-flop them until white hops on top. If your chips are other colors, press D to set them back to the factory setting of black and white.

3. **Grab the Gradient tool and set it to create a "Foreground to Transparent" linear gradient.**

Press G to select the Gradient tool and then head up to the Options bar at the top of your screen. Open the Gradient picker (near the left end of the bar) by clicking the down arrow next to the gradient preview and click once on the "Foreground to Transparent" swatch (second from the left in the top row). Move your mouse just a hair to the right in the Options bar to the gradient style buttons and click the first one, named Linear Gradient. (For more on gradients, see pages 87, 265, 338.)

4. **Back in your document, create a white-to-transparent fade by positioning your mouse just to the right of the photo's center and then dragging from right to left for about a quarter of inch (a little line appears as you drag).**

To paint a good-sized chunk of white, place your mouse near the right side of the photo (just past center) and then drag to the left for about a quarter of an inch and release your mouse button. The farther you drag, the wider the faded area. Don't worry if you don't get it right the first time; just keep clicking and dragging until you get the look you want.

> **TIP** If you want to start over, select all by pressing ⌘-A (Ctrl+A on a PC) and then press Delete (Backspace). That keystroke zaps everything on the layer so you can start your white gradient from scratch.

5. **Press T to grab the Type tool and add some text.**

You haven't learned about the Type tool yet, but be brave and press T to activate it and then hop up to the Options bar and pick a font and type size from the pop-up menus (see Chapter 14 for a proper introduction to the Type tool). Click once on your document where you want the text to begin and start typing. When you're finished typing, click the little checkmark at the top right of the Options bar to let Photoshop know you're done (pressing Enter—not Return—or selecting another tool works, too).

6. **You're finished! If you want to move your text around, you can temporarily select the Move tool by holding down the V key (this spring-loaded tool behavior is new in Photoshop CS4). When your cursor turns into a little arrow, click and move your mouse to move the text.**

If you followed these steps in order, you won't need to rearrange your layers in the Layers panel, but if you do, just grab the layer's thumbnail and drag it either up or down to change its position By the way, this technique is great for making your own personalized postcards and invitations.

Duplicating and Deleting Layers

Duplicating a layer comes in handy when you want to do something destructive like sharpen it (page 428) or soften Great Grandma's skin (page 410). By duplicating the layer first, you can work on a *copy* of the image instead of the original. But duplicating isn't limited to whole layers; you can duplicate just *part* of a layer. That technique comes in handy when you want to whiten teeth or make multiple copies of an object and move it around (like the hippy chicks in Figure 3-7).

Figure 3-7:
By selecting each of the silhouettes (top) and then pressing ⌘-J (Ctrl+J on a PC), you can jump copies of them onto their own layers (bottom). To move them around in your document, select one of the new layers, press V to grab the Move tool, and then drag to reposition the selected figure. Chapter 4 has more on how to make selections.

You can duplicate a layer in a gazillion ways:

- **Press ⌘-J (Ctrl+J on a PC)** or choose Layer → New → "Layer via Copy" to copy your entire layer onto another layer just like it.

- **Drag the original layer atop the** "Create a new layer" button at the bottom of the Layers panel. When Photoshop highlights the button, let go of your mouse button (the button looks like a piece of paper with a folded corner).

- **Option-drag (Alt-drag on a PC) the layer somewhere else in your Layers panel.** Your cursor will turn into a double black-and-white arrowhead as soon as you start to drag. When you let go of your mouse button, Photoshop duplicates the layer.

- **Choose Duplicate Layer from the Layers panel's option menu** (Figure 3-2) or choose Layer → Duplicate Layer. This method gives you a chance to name your layer, as well as send it to a new document. If you choose to send it to a new document, pick an open document from the Destination section's Document pop-up menu or choose New to create a new document (enter a name for the new document in the Name field).

- **Ctrl-click (right-click on a PC) the layer itself.** From the resulting shortcut menu, choose Duplicate Layer.

- **To duplicate part of layer,** create a selection using any of the tools discussed in Chapter 4 and then press ⌘-J (Ctrl+J) to move your selection onto its own layer. If you want to *delete* the selected area from the original layer, press Shift-⌘-J (Shift+Ctrl+J). You can think of this trick as a *cut* to another layer instead of a *copy* since you'll have a hole in the original layer where the selection used to be.

Adding layers can *really* increase your document's file size, so if you have a slow computer or very little memory (RAM), you'll want to delete the layers you don't need. To delete a layer, select it in the Layers panel and then:

- **Press Delete (Backspace on a PC).** This option is new in Photoshop CS4, and it's the fastest deletion method in the West.

- **Drag it onto the trash can at the bottom of your Layers panel.** The layer vanishes before your eyes.

- **Click the trash can.** When Photoshop asks if you're *sure* you want to delete the layer, click Yes and turn on the "Don't show again" checkbox if you don't want to see this confirmation box in the future.

> **TIP** If you delete a layer and then wish you had it back, just use Photoshop's Undo command. You can find it by choosing Edit → Undo or just pressing ⌘-Z (Ctrl+Z on a PC).

- **Ctrl-click (right-click on a PC) the layer's name and choose Delete Layer from the shortcut menu.** Be sure to click the layer's *name*—if you click the thumbnail itself you won't see the Delete Layer item in the shortcut menu. When Photoshop asks if you really want to delete the layer, click Yes to send it packin'.

- **Open the Layers panel menu and choose Delete Layer or choose Layer → Delete.** You'll get the confirmation dialog box here, too, so just smile sweetly, click Yes, and be on your way.

TIP   If you've hidden multiple layers (page 78), you can delete them all at once by opening the Layers panel menu and choosing Delete → Hidden Layers (hey, if you're not using 'em, you might as well toss 'em!). Getting rid of extra layers shortens your Layers panel *and* reduces your document's file size.

Copying and Pasting Layers

You can use the regular ol' copy and paste commands to move whole or partial layers between Photoshop documents:

- **To copy part of a layer into another document,** create your selection first and then press ⌘-C (Ctrl+C on a PC) to copy it. Then open the other document and press ⌘-V (Ctrl+V); Photoshop pastes those pixels onto a new layer.

- **To copy and paste a whole layer into another document,** choose Select → All (or press ⌘-A [Ctrl+A]) to select the layer and then press ⌘-C (Ctrl+C). Next, click the other document's window and press ⌘-V (Ctrl+V) to add the layer to that document's Layers panel.

TIP   When you copy an image from another program and paste it right into a Photoshop document, it lands on its very own layer. If the pasted image is *bigger* than your document, you may need to resize the image using Free Transform (page 245).

Filling a Layer with Color

One of the most common things you'll do with a new layer is fill it with color. If you've hidden the original background of your image (page 105) or added an interesting edge effect (see Figure 12-18 on page 475), for example, you can spice up the image by adding a solid-colored background. Photoshop gives you a couple of different ways to tackle this task:

- **Fill an existing layer with color.** After you've created a new layer using one of the methods listed on page 76, choose Edit → Fill. In the resulting Fill dialog box (Figure 3-8), pick a color from the Use pop-up menu and then click OK. You can also fill a layer with your foreground color chip by pressing Option-Delete (Alt+Backspace on a PC).

NOTE   If you increase your canvas size (page 240) after you've filled a layer with color, you'll need to refill the layer or it'll be smaller than your document and you'll see the contents of layers below it peeking through. If you want to avoid this extra step, use a Fill layer, as discussed in the following bullet point.

- **Create a Fill layer.** If you're not sure which color you want to use, choose Layer → New Fill Layer and pick Solid Color. In the New Layer dialog box that appears, name your new layer and then click OK. Next, Photoshop displays the Color Picker so you can choose the fill color you want. If you decide to change the fill color, double-click the Fill layer's thumbnail and Photoshop opens the Color Picker, letting you pick a new color or steal one from the image itself (as shown in Figure 3-9).

The Fill setting is different from the Opacity setting in that it doesn't affect the whole layer. For example, if you create a Shape layer or Type layer (both described on page 71), lowering its Fill will lower only the opacity of the color *inside* the shape or letters. Changing a layer's Fill setting won't affect the opacity of any layer styles you've added (page 119); it affects only the opacity of the color on the *inside* of the object.

The Opacity and Fill settings live at the top of your Layers panel (see Figure 3-11). To change Opacity or Fill, mouse over to your Layers panel, select the layer you want to tweak, and then:

- **Enter a new value in the Opacity or Fill field.** Double-click the current value in either field to highlight it, enter a new value, and then press Return (Enter on a PC).

Figure 3-11:
If you lower the opacity of the white fade layer to 50 percent, as shown here, the white paint becomes partially transparent, letting you see through to the photo layer below. If you want to look like a real Photoshop pro, hover your cursor near the word Opacity. You'll get a little scrubby cursor that you can drag to the left or right to lower or raise the layer's opacity (you can even drag the scrubby cursor off the Layers panel if you want to). This trick works for many settings with similar controls, too, including the Fill setting.

- **Use the field's slider.** Click the down arrow to the right of the Opacity or Fill field (on a PC, the arrow points to the right) and drag the resulting slider to the left or right to decrease or increase that setting, respectively.

- **Use your keyboard.** Press V to activate the Move tool (think "moVe") and change the Opacity by typing *1* for 10 percent, *2* for 20 percent, *35* for 35 percent, and so on (type *0* for 100 percent). If you've got any other tool selected besides the Move tool, you'll change the opacity setting for that particular *tool* instead.

TIP You can use the same keyboard trick to adjust the Opacity settings for the Fill tool, too. Just hold down the Shift key while you type the numbers.

Resizing and Rotating Layers

If you want to resize the contents of a layer—or many layers—*without* changing the size of your document, you can use the Free Transform tool (shown in Figure 3-12). You'll learn a lot more about this tool in Chapter 6 (page 245), so consider this a sneak peek.

To resize or rotate a layer, follow these steps:

1. **In your Layers panel, select the layers you want to adjust (see page 75 for the scoop on selecting multiple layers).**

2. **Press ⌘-T (Ctrl+T on a PC) to summon the Free Transform tool.**

   Photoshop puts a box (called a *bounding box*) lined with small square white handles around the content of your layer or layers (see Figure 3-12).

   NOTE If you're resizing a Smart Object (page 238), the little handles will be black instead of white. The difference is cosmetic—the handles work exactly the same.

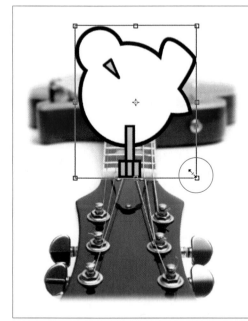

Figure 3-12:
You can drag any of the square handles on the bounding box to resize your object. To adjust all four sides of the box simultaneously, hold down Option (Alt on a PC) as you drag a corner handle. Don't forget to press Return (Enter) when you're finished because Photoshop won't let you do anything else while you've got an active bounding box.

3. **Drag one of the corner handles inward to make the layers smaller.**

   Grab any of the white corner handles and drag inward to make the layers smaller. If you want to resize the object proportionately so it doesn't get squished or stretched, hold down the Shift key as you drag one of the handles.

4. To rotate your layers, position your cursor outside the bounding box and when it turns into a curved, double-head arrow, drag up or down in the direction you want to turn the layers.

5. Press Return (Enter on a PC) or double-click inside the bounding box to let Photoshop know you're done.

> **TIP** To see the Free Transform tool's resizing handles all the time, you can turn on the Show Transform Controls in the Options bar. Seeing the handles is handy if you're jumping between layers to resize or rotate objects and don't want to stop and summon Free Transform each time.

Do you risk reducing your image's quality by resizing layers this way? Sure. Anytime you alter pixel size (page 222), you alter the quality a little bit, too, whether it's a single layer or your whole document. But as long as you *decrease* the layer's size, you won't lose much quality (though you don't want to decrease its size *repeatedly*—try to do it once or twice and be done with it). You definitely risk losing quality if you *increase* the size of a pixel-based Image layer because when pixels get bigger, they also get blockier.

That said, if you're working with a Smart Object (page 115), Shape layer (page 509), or Type layer (page 537), you've got no worries; you can resize those babies all day long—larger or smaller, as many times as you want—and you won't affect the quality, which is why you want to use those kinds of layers whenever you can.

> **TIP** The rest of the transform tools, including Skew, Distort, and so on, work on layers, too. See page 248 for details.

Moving and Aligning Layers

One of the many advantages of using layers is that you can scoot 'em around independent of everything else in your document. To move a layer, you have to select it in your Layers panel first. Press V to grab the Move tool and drag the layer wherever you want. For example, if you want to move the text in Figure 3-11 a bit to the left, press V and drag it to a new spot. To move the layer in a perfectly vertical or horizontal line, hold down the Shift key while you drag. You can also nudge the layer by using the arrows on your keyboard (holding down the Shift key while you press the arrow keys scoots the layer by 10 pixels per keystroke).

If you want to move only *part* of a layer, you need to select that portion first using one of the methods explained in Chapter 4. Then you can grab the Move tool and move just the selected bits.

Aligning layers

When you need to position your layers, Photoshop has several tools that can help you get them lined up just right. If you're trying to align one layer perfectly with the layer below, it's a good idea to lower the top layer's opacity temporarily (page 87) so you can actually *see* the layer below.

Photoshop tries to help you align layers by *snapping* the one you're moving to the *boundaries* (content edges) of other layers. As you drag a layer with the Move tool, Photoshop tries to pop the layer into place when you get near another layer's edge (if you want to make the program stop popping them into place, choose View → Snap). If you'd like to *see* the boundaries of your layer, press V to activate the Move tool, hop up to the Options bar, and turn on Show Transform Controls (Figure 3-13).

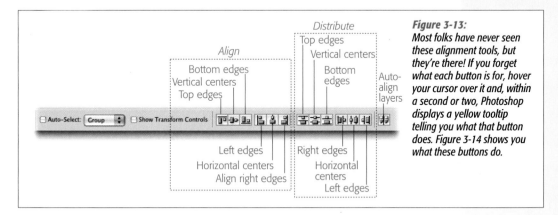

Figure 3-13:
Most folks have never seen these alignment tools, but they're there! If you forget what each button is for, hover your cursor over it and, within a second or two, Photoshop displays a yellow tooltip telling you what that button does. Figure 3-14 shows you what these buttons do.

In addition to snapping and showing you boundaries, Photoshop offers you the following alignment helpers:

- **Alignment tools.** If you need to align the edges of more than one layer, these tools come in handy. You'll see them in the Options bar at the top of your screen when the Move tool is active *and* you have more than one layer selected (see Figure 3-13 for details). You can also find them by choosing Layer → Align (you still need to have more than one layer selected, but you don't have to activate the Move tool). Figure 3-14 shows you what each alignment button does.

- **Distribute tools.** Nestled snugly to the right of the alignment tools are the distribute tools (Figure 3-13) Their mission is to evenly space the contents of the selected layers (you need to have at least *three* layers selected to use them) based on each layer's horizontal or vertical center. But, honestly, they just don't work like you'd think they would. Most folks find them funky, and you probably will, too, so you're better off just moving layers around manually.

- **Smart Guides.** Unlike the regular guides your learned about in Chapter 2 (page 64), Smart Guides show up automatically anytime you drag a layer near another layer's boundaries (see Figure 3-15). They're extremely helpful when you're manually aligning layers with the Move tool since they make it easier to position layers precisely in relation to each other. To turn them on, choose View → Show → Smart Guides.

Align top edges

Align vertical centers

Align bottom edges

Figure 3-14:
Each of these guitars is on its own layer, so you can see the effect of each alignment tool.

Align left edges

Align horizontal centers

Align right edges

Figure 3-15:
When you turn on Smart Guides, Photoshop alerts you with a thin red line anytime you approach the boundaries of another layer so you know if you're about to move past the edge of other layers.

- **Auto-alignment.** If you choose Edit → Align → Auto-Align Layers, Photoshop does the aligning for you by looking at the corners and edges of objects on selected layers. This command is really handy when you're combining images into a panorama (see page 283), but it doesn't work on Adjustment layers, Smart Objects, or Vector layers.

WORKAROUND WORKSHOP

When Layers Won't Align

If you try to align the bottoms of two Type layers using the Align Bottom Edges command, you may run into trouble. If there's a *descender* (a letter that goes below the baseline, like the letters *y* and *p* in *type*) in one layer but not the other, the two layers won't align properly because they're not even on the bottom. The fix is to replace the troublesome letter(s) temporarily with one that doesn't have a descender and *then* click the Align Bottom Edges button. Once the layers are aligned, you can change the letter back. It's not elegant, but it works.

Photoshop can also do strange things when you're using the alignment tools on layers that have layer masks (page 105). Instead of aligning the layers according to what you've hidden with the mask (which is probably what you're trying to do), Photoshop tries to align your layers using the actual pixel information. In that case, you may need to turn on your Rulers (page 64), create a few guides (page 65), and manually align your layers with the Move tool (page 90).

Moving layers between documents

In addition to copying and pasting layers from one document to another (as described back on page 85), you can also drag and drop them straight from your Layers panel to another document as shown in Figure 3-16. Photoshop leaves the layer in your original document and places a copy in the target document, so you don't have to worry about losing anything from either file. This technique is really helpful if you want to create a collage (page 390), swap backgrounds, or share color corrections across documents.

Here's how to move a layer from one document to another:

1. **Open the documents you want combine.**

2. **Click the Arrange Documents button at the top of your screen (page 63) and choose one of the 2-Up display options or "Float All in Windows" from the pop-up menu.**

   To drag from one document to the other, you need to *see* both documents. Choosing either the 2-Up display option or "Float All in Windows" makes Photoshop rearrange your document windows so you can see them both at the same time. (Page 62 has more on display options.)

Figure 3-16:
Top: To combine two images into one document, first arrange your workspace so that you can see both windows at the same time. Then drag one layer's thumbnail from your Layers panel into the other document.

Bottom: When you release your mouse button, the new layer appears in the other document's Layers panel, as shown here.

3. **Click the document that contains the layer you want to move and then drag the layer's thumbnail onto the other document.**

   As you drag, your cursor turns into a tiny closed fist, as you can see in Figure 3-16. When Photoshop highlights the inside border of the destination window with a faint black outline, let go of the mouse button to make Photoshop add the layer to the new document.

   TIP   To center the moved layer perfectly in its new home, hold the Shift key as you drag the layer between documents.

Exporting layers to separate files

If you've got a bunch of layers that you want to separate into individual files (with each layer in its own file), Photoshop is happy to do it for you. Choose File → Scripts → "Export Layers to Files". In the resulting dialog box (Figure 3-17), use the Destination field to tell Photoshop where you want it to save the files. In the File Name Prefix box, create a naming scheme (Photoshop uses whatever you enter in the prefix field as the first part of your file names), and, in the File Type pop-up menu, choose a file format. When you're finished, click Run and sit back while Photoshop does all the work.

Figure 3-17:
The Export Layers To Files dialog box lets you choose where to put the new files and what to name them. If you want to exclude any hidden layers (page 78), turn on the Visible Layers Only checkbox. In the File Type pop-up menu, you can choose any of the following file formats: BMP, JPEG, PDF, PSD, TARGA, TIFF, PNG-8, or PNG-24 (all of which are discussed on page 46). Each format gives you different options (for example, JPEG lets you pick a quality setting). Photoshop includes your document's ICC profile (page 630) in each file unless you turn off the lower checkbox shown here.

Managing Layers

If there's one thing for certain in Photoshop, it's that your Layers panel will get long and unwieldy in a hurry. Now that you've seen a smidgeon of the increased editing flexibility layers give you (moving, resizing, and so on) you'll want to put *everything* on its own layer—and you *should*. However, learning a wee bit of layer organization can keep you from spending ages digging through your Layers panel to find the layer you want. This section gives you the lowdown.

Naming and Color-Coding Layers

The simplest way to organize layers is to name the darn things something other than Layer 1, Layer 2, and so on. If you didn't name them when you made them, you can always double-click a layer's name in your Layers panel and rename it right there (Photoshop highlights the name when you double-click it, so you can just start typing). When you're done, press Return (Enter on a PC).

> **TIP** If you double-click in the Layers panel *near* the layer's name but not directly on it, Photoshop opens the Layer Style dialog box (discussed on page 119) instead of highlighting the layer's name. No problem: Just close the dialog box and try again.

Another renaming option is to open the Layer Properties dialog box where you can give the layer a new name *and* assign it a color. When you assign a color to a layer, its visibility control (page 77) changes to the highlight color. Color coding is useful when you've got a ton of layers because it lets you distinguish them at a glance. For example, you could color code sections of a document like the header, footer, body, and so on. You can open the Layer Properties dialog box in a few different ways:

- Open the Layers panel menu and choose Layer Properties.

- Ctrl-click (right-click on a PC) the layer in the Layers panel and choose Layer Properties from the shortcut menu.

- Press Option (Alt) as you double-click near the layer's name (but not directly on it) in the Layers panel.

Next, choose a highlight color from the Color pop-up menu in the Layer Properties dialog box. Click OK to close the dialog box and apply the color label, too.

Linking and Locking Layers

Editing layers can be a lot of work, and once you get them just right, you want to make darn sure they stay that way. You can arm yourself with a little protection by linking layers together or locking down certain aspects of them. Read on to learn how.

Linking layers

If you need to move something in your image that's made from several layers, it'd be a real pain to move each layer individually and then reconstruct the image. Fortunately, you can *link* layers before you grab the Move tool. Linked layers move together as if they were one unit. Linking related layers can help you avoid accidentally misaligning layers with a careless flick of the Move tool. For example, if you're working with a headshot that has some Adjustment layers associated with it, linking the photo layer with those Adjustments layers will ensure that they stay perfectly aligned. Figure 3-18 shows you how to link layers.

Locking 'em down

You can add a more serious level of protection to layers by using *layer locks*, which prevent layers from being edited or moved. Take a peek at the top of the Layers panel and you'll spot a row of four buttons (Figure 3-19) that you can use to lock various aspects of your layers. First select the layer you want to lock and then click the lock button to prevent any changes.

> **TIP** If you want to lock more than one layer, select them in the Layers panel and then choose Layers → Lock Layers or choose Lock Layers from the Layers panel menu.

Figure 3-18:
Once you've got more than one layer selected (page 75), you can link them by clicking the tiny chain at the bottom of the Layers panel. The same chain appears to the right of each layer's name (circled) to show that the layers are linked. To unlink them, select a layer and then click the chain at the bottom of the Layers panel again.

Link layers

Lock transparent pixels
Lock image pixels
Lock position
Lock all

Figure 3-19:
Use the lock buttons at the top of the Layers panel to protect your layers from accidental editing or repositioning. Your keyboard's forward slash key (/) acts like a switch; tap it once to unlock a locked layer. Tapping the slash key while you have an unlocked layer selected causes Photoshop to apply the transparent lock. You'll see the padlock to the right of a locked layer's name no matter which lock you apply.

Layer lock

You can choose from several kinds of layer locks:

- **Lock transparent pixels.** This lock protects the layer's transparent pixels so they don't change *even* if you paint across them or use the Edit → Fill command. For example, if you created the faded-color effect described on page 81, you could apply this lock to change the color of the fade without affecting the layer's see-through bits. Its button looks like the transparency checkerboard pattern.

- **Lock image pixels.** This lock won't let you do *anything* to a layer but nudge it around with the Move tool. The button for this lock looks like the Brush tool.

- **Lock position.** If you've carefully positioned a layer and want to make sure it stays put, turn on this option. You can still *edit* the layer; you just can't move it. This lock's button looks like a four-headed arrow.

- **Lock all.** This is your deadbolt. Click this button to prevent the layer from being edited *or* moved. You know this lock means business because its layer icon is a solid black padlock (the other layer locks are gray).

   TIP   If you've taken the time to create a layer group (page 98), you can lock all the layers in the group at once by selecting the group and then choosing Layers → "Lock All Layers in Group". Photoshop pops open a dialog box where you can turn on any of the locks listed above. Click OK to apply them. You can also find this same menu item in the Layers panel menu.

Grouping Layers into Folders

You can put a rein on your fast-growing Layers panel by tucking your layers into folders called *layer groups*. You can expand and collapse layer groups just like the folders on your hard drive, and they'll save you a heck of a lot of scrolling when you're layer hunting, as you can see in Figure 3-20.

Figure 3-20:
Layer groups not only help you shorten your Layers panel, they also let you apply masks, Layer styles, and so on to all the layers in the group simultaneously. The down-pointing flippy triangle next to the Background group's folder shows that it's expanded. The Text and Photos groups are collapsed. Just click a layer group's flippy triangle to expand or collapse that group.

Expanded group—

Collapsed groups—

New group

Here's an example of how useful layer groups are: Say you're building a concert poster, and you've got several layers that comprise the background, some photos of the band, some text, and so on. With layer groups, you can put all the layers associated with the background in a group cleverly named *Background*, the photos in a group called *Photos*, and the Type layers in a group called *Text*. By adding some color-coding (blue for background, red for photos, and so on), you can quickly spot the layer group you want to work with instead of wasting time scrolling through your Layers panel.

Here are the different ways you can group layers:

- **Create the group first** by clicking the "Create a new group" button at the bottom of your Layers panel (it looks like a tiny folder) or by choosing New Group from the Layers panel menu. If you make a new group by using the menu option, you'll get a dialog box where you can name the group (and pick a color code if you want). Photoshop adds the group to your layers panel; just drag the layers you want to group together into it. You can add layers to the group any time you want, so you don't have to add everything at once.

- **Select your layers first** and then press ⌘-G (Ctrl+G on a PC) or choose "New Group from Layers" in the Layers panel menu. Photoshop adds a group named "Group 1" to your Layers panel; double-click its name to rename it.

- **Option-drag (Alt-drag on a PC) layers** onto the "Create a new group" button at the bottom of your Layers panel.

You can do the same things to layer groups that you can to regular layers: duplicate them, hide them, lock them, and so on. You can also create nested groups by dragging and dropping one group into another.

If you want to split apart grouped layers, select the group and then choose Layer → Ungroup Layers or press Shift-⌘-G (Shift+Ctrl+G on a PC). You can also run this command by going to the Layers panel menu or Ctrl-clicking (right-clicking) the group and choosing Ungroup from the shortcut menu. Photoshop deletes the group but leaves your layers intact.

Layer Comps: Presenting Different Versions

Speaking of that hypothetical concert poster, you'll probably want to show your client different versions and let the client pick the one she likes best. Photoshop can help by saving multiple versions of your document as *layer comps*—snapshots of your Layers panel in various states (see Figure 3-21). It's much better than having to juggle multiple files you could lose track of. Layer comps can record the position and visibility of your layers, as well as the blend modes (page 267) and layer styles (page 119) you've applied.

> **TIP**   Layer comps may be great for showing alternate designs in a single file, but they work only if your document has more than one layer. Like layer groups, layer comps aren't available if your document has just one layer.

You capture layer comp "snapshots" as you're working. For instance, you could start off with a baseline version and record what it looks like. Then make some changes and record that new version. And so on. When you're ready to save your first layer comp, follow these steps:

1. **Choose Window → Layer Comps to summon the Layer Comps panel. Then click the Create New Layer Comp button at the bottom of the panel.**

   This button looks just like the New Layer button—a piece of paper with a folded corner.

Figure 3-21:
Top: Give each of your layer comps a name that describes that version of your design. To cycle through each comp using the arrow buttons at the bottom of the panel, first summon the arrows by choosing Window → Layer Comps.

Bottom: Showing, hiding, and rearranging layers lets you quickly produce several versions of the same design.

2. **In the New Layer Comp dialog box, give your snapshot a meaningful name and then tell Photoshop which attributes you want to save.**

The dialog box has three settings you can turn on or off:

- **Visibility** captures the visibility of your layers.

- **Position** captures your layer stacking order.

- **Appearance** captures blend modes (page 119) and layer styles.

Turn on all three capture options in the New Layer Comp dialog box *just in case* you decide to tweak that stuff later. Add a comment if you'd like and then click OK.

3. **Back in the Layers panel, rearrange, show, or hide layers, add layer styles, or change blend modes to produce another version of your image.**

   Unfortunately, if you change a layer's color, opacity, or fill, Photoshop can't capture that in a layer comp. But there is a workaround: Duplicate those layers, make the changes, and then show or hide them when you save the next layer comp.

4. **Click the Create New Layer Comp button at the bottom of the Layer Comps panel to create another layer comp and give it a name.**

   Repeat these steps as many times as you want to save lots of different layout versions in your document.

When you're ready stroll through the different versions of your document, click the little forward and back arrows at the bottom of the Layer Comps panel as shown in Figure 3-21. To get back to the way your document looked when you last tweaked it (or when you saved your last layer comp), at the top of the Layer Comps panel, click the visibility eye to the left of the words Last Document State.

You can duplicate and delete layer comps just like layers and layer groups. If you want to *change* a layer comp, select it in the Layer Comps panel and then change whatever you want in your Layers panel. When you're finished, click the Update button at the bottom of the Layer Comps panel, shown in Figure 3-21.

Some edits, like cropping, deleting a layer, or changing a layer's color, opacity, or fill—and basically any edit that falls beyond the limits of the layer comp's tracking capabilities—cause Photoshop to cross its arms and lock you out of your layer comps. They all fall beyond the limits of the Layer Comp's tracking capabilities

You can tell which Layer Comps are affected because they'll have a little warning triangle to the right of their name (see Figure 3-22). This triangle means Photoshop needs you to update that layer comp because it can't keep track of every change you made. (Don't worry, it's not a sign that you lost your changes.) Fixing the problem is easy: Just select the affected layer comps and click the update button shown in Figure 3-21.

Exporting layer comps

When you're ready for your client to see the layer comps, you can export them by choosing File → Scripts → "Layer Comps to Files" to create a separate file for each layer comp in whatever format you choose (you get the same options as when you export layers to files; see Figure 3-17).

Previous versions of Photoshop let you export your layer comps as both PDF files *and* Web Photo Gallery (WPG) files right from the Scripts menu, but in CS4 that kind of stuff has been handed off to the *Adobe Output Module* over in Bridge (see Appendix C), which adds a few extra steps to the export process. Figure 3-23 explains how to export your layer comps into a single PDF file; creating a Web gallery is covered on page 689.

Figure 3-22:
If you click the little warning triangle next to your layer comp (circled), you see this dialog box, which gently chastises you for messing up your layer comp. Click Clear to get rid of the warning. If you turn on the "Don't show again" checkbox, Photoshop won't display the message any more, but you'll still have to update your layer comps when you see that warning triangle.

Figure 3-23:
Once you've exported your layer comps as separate files (File → Scripts → "Layer Comps to Files"), you can use Bridge to turn them into a single PDF file. Launch Bridge (Appendix C), click the Output button at the top of the window (circled, top) and then choose "Output to Web or PDF". Navigate to the files you've exported by using the Folder or Favorites panel on the left of the Bridge window. Then, in the Content panel toward the bottom of the window (circled, bottom), ⌘-click (Ctrl-click on a PC) to select your files (also circled).

In the Output panel, click the PDF button (where the cursor is here) to make Photoshop display a host of options on the right side of the window that let you set paper size, quality, background color, and so on. If you choose a black background and add a watermark in the center, you can create a professional-looking PDF ready to fire off to your client (foreground). When you've got all the settings just right, scroll to the bottom of the Output panel, click the Save button, and give your file a name.

Rasterizing Layers

If you try to paint (Chapter 12) or run a filter (Chapter 15) on a vector layer, Photo-shop puts up a fuss: It displays a dialog box letting you know—in no uncertain terms—that you've got to *rasterize* that layer first. Why? Because as you learned back in Chapter 2 (page 48), vectors aren't made of pixels, and to use pixel-based tools—like the Brush, Eraser, and Clone Stamp—on a vector-based layer, you have to convert it to pixels first. This process is called *rasterizing*.

Beware: There's no going back once you've rasterized a layer. You can't resize Smart Objects or Shape layers without losing quality, you can't double-click a Fill layer and change its color, and you can't edit a Type layer. That's why it's a good idea to do your rasterizing on a duplicate layer—that way, you can always go back to the original. Just duplicate the layer (page 82) before you rasterize and then turn off the original layer's visibility so you don't accidentally rasterize the wrong layer.

Rasterizing is easy. Just select a vector-based layer and choose Layer → Rasterize. From the resulting menu, pick the kind of layer you want to rasterize (Type, Shape, Fill Content, and so on) or choose Layer to rasterize the layer you're on or All Layers to rasterize everything (shudder).

Merging Layers

Layers are supremely awesome, but sometimes you need to squash layers together. Yes, this goes against what you've learned in this chapter so far—that you should keep everything on its own layer—but in some situations you have no choice but to *merge* or *stamp* layers, or worse, completely *flatten* your file. Here's what those scary-sounding words mean, along with how and why you might need these features:

- **Merge.** If you've whipped pixels into perfection and know in the deepest cockles of your heart that you'll *never* want to change them, you can merge two or more layers into one. Not only will you reduce the length of your Layers panel by merging your layers, you'll knock a few pounds off your file's size, too.

  NOTE You can merge any kind of layers, but you need to have a *pixel-based* layer selected in your Layers panel to use the merge commands (or else they'll be grayed out). Photoshop merges everything onto the selected layer.

  Photoshop gives you several ways to merge layers:

  — **Merge down.** If you want to merge two layers that live next to each other in your Layers panel—and the bottom one is a pixel-based layer—select the top layer and go to Layers → Merge Down, choose Merge Down from the Layers panel menu or press ⌘-E (Ctrl+E on a PC).

  — **Merge visible.** To merge some layers but not all, you can hide the ones you *don't* want to squash, select a pixel-based layer as your target, and then go to Layers → Merge Visible, choose Merge Visible from the Layers panel menu or press Shift-⌘-E (Shift+Ctrl+E).

— **Merge selected.** Select the layers you want to merge (either pixel or vector-based) as explained on page 75 and then go to Layers → Merge Layers, choose Merge Layers from the Layers panel menu or press ⌘-E (Ctrl+E).

— **Merge linked.** If you've linked layers together (page 96), you can merge them in one fell swoop (though you've got to select them first) by going to Layers → Select Linked Layers or choosing Select Linked Layers from the Layers panel menu and then following the instructions to merge selected layers (above).

• **Stamp.** You can think of stamping as a safer version of merging because it combines the selected layers on a *new* layer, leaving the original layers intact. This command is great when you need to edit *more* than one layer with tools that affect only *one* layer at a time (like filters and Layer styles). The only downside is that stamping adds a layer, which adds fat to your file (see Figure 3-24). Here are your stamping options:

— **Stamp selected.** Choose the layers you want to stamp and then press ⌘-Option-E (Ctrl+Alt+E).

— **Stamp visible.** Turn off the layers you *don't* want to stamp by clicking their visibility eyes and then press ⌘-Shift-Option-E (Ctrl+Shift+Alt+E). You can also hold Option (Alt) as you choose Merge Layers from the Layers panel menu to make Photoshop merge everything onto a new layer.

• **Flatten.** This command makes your file flatter than a pancake, giving you a locked background that, as you know from the box on page 80, doesn't allow for transparency (any areas that were transparent become white instead). Alas, you have no choice but to flatten your file if you're exporting it to a format that doesn't *support* layers (like JPEG, PNG, and so on); just be sure to save your document as a PSD file *first* so you can go back and edit it later. You've got three flattening options:

— **Flatten image.** To flatten your whole file, go to Layers → Flatten Image or choose Flatten Image from the Layers panel menu.

WARNING   Danger, Will Robinson! After flattening your file, be sure to choose File → Save As, instead of File → Save to avoid saving over your original.

— **Flatten All Layer Effects.** Instead of flattening your whole file, you can flatten just the layer styles (page 119) so they become one with the layer they're attached to. But be aware that, if you've applied any Layer styles to vector-based layers (like Type or Shape layers), those layers will get rasterized in the process. To flatten your Layer styles, choose File → Scripts → Flatten All Layer Effects.

— **Flatten All Masks.** You can also flatten layers that you've applied layer masks to (page 105), so the mask is permanently applied by choosing File → Scripts → Flatten All Masks.

TIP   If you flatten your document by accident, you can get your layers back using your History panel (page 63) or by pressing ⌘-Z (Ctrl+Z on a PC). Whew!

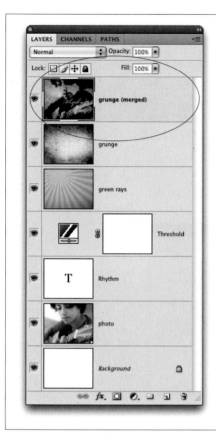

Figure 3-24:
If you need to edit a multi-layer file using tools that affect one layer at a time, you can stamp your layers into a merged-layer copy (circled here) to avoid having to flatten your file.

Layer Blending

In Photoshop, *blending* refers to the way colors on one layer interact with colors on other layers. You get some pretty powerful blending options with layers in the form of general blend modes, advanced blending, and "blend if" sliders. You can do some amazing stuff with these tools, and since they're used in combining images, you'll learn all about them in Chapter 7, beginning on page 267.

Layer Masks: Digital Masking Tape

Remember the last time you gave your walls a fresh coat of paint? You probably broke out a roll of masking tape and taped up your baseboards and molding so you wouldn't get paint all over them. Sure, you could've have taken the baseboards *off* and put them back on once the paint dried, but, *dadgum,* that's a lot of work. Besides, masking tape covers everything just fine. Hiding and protecting is masking tape's special purpose in life and—what luck!—you've got its *digital* equivalent right in Photoshop: *layer masks.*

A layer mask lets you hide the content on a layer, whether it's a pixel-based image layer, Smart Object, Shape layer, Fill layer or—in the case of Adjustment layers—a color or lighting change (page 71 covers all the layer types). Learning to use masks will keep you from having to *erase* parts of your image to produce the effect you want. Once you erase, there's no going back, and if your hand isn't steady enough to erase around detailed areas, you can start hunting for a paddle on eBay now. So, for example, instead of *deleting* your background to swap it with another one, you can use a layer mask to *hide* it, as shown in Figure 3-25. (You'll find all kinds of other uses for layer masks sprinkled throughout this book.) As long as you save your document as a PSD file, you can go back and edit your mask any time.

Add
layer
mask

Layer
masks

Figure 3-25:
Left: Wanna be a rock star? No problem: A layer mask can make it happen. Here you can see the original, boring blue background, as well as the new, exciting, clamoring crowd.

Right: If you peek at the Layers panel, you can see that the original background wasn't deleted–it was hidden with a mask instead. (To make the color of the guitarist and the crowd match a bit more, you can add an Adjustment layer– page 71–that uses the same mask.)

Adding Layer Masks

You can add a mask to any layer, though some layers come with them automatically, like Fill and Adjustment layers (page 71) and Shape layers (page 509). As you can see in Figure 3-25, the mask shows up in your Layers panel as a thumbnail to the right of the layer thumbnail.

> **NOTE**   You can't add a layer mask to a locked Background layer; you first have to double-click the background to make it editable *and then* add a mask.

Layer masks are grayscale creatures, so when you're dealing with them you work only in black, white, and shades of gray, depending on what you want to do. A black mask hides your layer completely and a white mask reveals it completely. A gray mask falls somewhere in between—it's partially transparent. All this is easy to remember if you memorize the rhyme, "Black conceals and white reveals."

To add a layer mask, choose Layer → Layer Masks and then pick one of the following:

- **Reveal All.** Creates a solid white mask that shows everything on your layer, so it doesn't change anything in your image. You can also add a white (or empty) mask by clicking the Add Layer Mask button at the bottom of your Layers panel (it looks like a circle within a square, as you can see in Figure 3-25). If you want to hide just a *little* bit of your layer, Reveal All is the way to go; after you add the mask, you can paint the areas you want to hide with a black brush.

- **Hide All.** Creates a solid black mask that conceals everything on your layer. (Option-clicking, or Alt-clicking on a PC, the Add Layer Mask button does the same thing.) If you want to hide the majority of your layer, the fastest way is to hide everything and then go back with a white brush to reveal specific areas.

- **Reveal Selection.** Choose this option if you've created a selection and want to hide everything else. Photoshop makes your selected area white and the background black. (You'll learn all about selections in Chapter 4.)

- **Hide Selection.** This command makes your selected area black and the background white.

NOTE   To learn about vector masks, flip over to page 527.

Using Layer Masks

You can use any tool you want to add black, white, or gray paint to your mask though the Brush tool is especially handy (Chapter 12 covers all your brush options), and the Gradient tool is great if you want to create a smooth transition from black to white (see the color fade effect on page 310). Selection tools (Chapter 4) also work in masks, and once you have a selection you can fill it with black, white, or shades of gray by choosing Edit → Fill.

One of the simplest uses for layer masks is to hide bits of text, as shown in Figure 3-26, so the text looks like it's behind a person or object in a photo.

Here's how to create the text-behind effect:

1. **Open a photo and press T to select the Type tool.**

   Don't worry about double-clicking the Background layer to make it editable; you don't need to touch your original image in this technique.

2. **From the Options bar at the top of your screen, pick a font, a size, and a color.**

   For this technique, you need to pick a nice thick font like Impact and set it to a fairly large size, like 84 points. (You'll learn all about text formatting in Chapter 14, so don't worry about it too much here.)

3. **Mouse over to your document and type some text.**

   Click where you want the text to begin and start typing. If you want to move the text around, mouse away from the text and your cursor turns into a little arrow. At that point you can drag the text anywhere you'd like in your document.

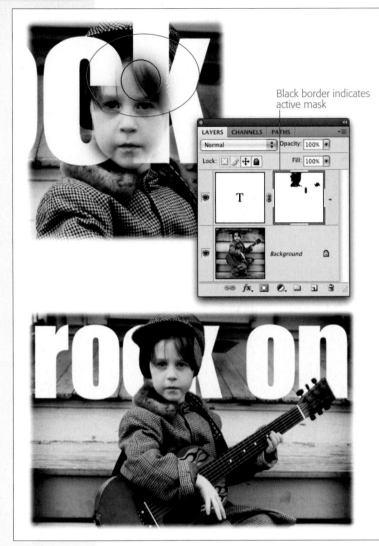

Black border indicates
active mask

Figure 3-26:
*Top: Here you can see a boy and
some text that live on different
layers. If you add a layer mask to
the text layer and then paint within
the mask with a black brush
(circled), you can hide parts of the
text, revealing the boy's face. Over
in the Layers panel, the little black
border lets you know which part of
the document is active: the layer
or, in this case, the mask.*

*Bottom: Magazines use this trick
all the time on their covers to
make text look like it's behind a
person.*

4. **Add a layer mask to your Type layer by clicking the circle-within-a-square button
at the bottom of the Layers panel.**

   Take a look at your Layers panel and you'll see the mask thumbnail next to the
   Type layer's thumbnail. See the thin black border around the mask thumbnail?
   That means it's active and you're about to paint on the mask (good) instead of
   the photo (bad).

   TIP   One of the biggest mistakes folks make is not paying attention to which thumbnail they've
   selected in the Layers panel (it takes a single click to activate either thumbnail). The little black border always lets you know which part of the document is active.

5. **Press B to select the Brush tool and pick a soft-edge brush set to black.**

As soon as you activate the Brush tool, head up to the left side of the Options bar and open the Brush menu (page 461) by clicking the down-pointing triangle next to the little brush preview. Pick a soft-edge brush that's about 60 pixels. Since you want to *hide* bits of text (remember, black conceals and white reveals), you need to choose black as your foreground color. To do that, take a peek at your color chips at the bottom of the Tools panel (page 22) and press X until black hops on top. Now you're ready to start painting.

6. **Mouse over to your document and paint the parts of the text you want to hide.**

In the example in Figure 3-26, position your mouse over the little boy's face and click to start painting (and hiding) parts of the *c* and *k*. When you release your mouse button—you don't have to do all your painting with one brushstroke—you'll see black paint on your layer mask in the Layers panel.

7. **If you accidentally hide too much of the text, press X to swap color chips so you're painting with white and then paint that area back in.**

When you're working with a layer mask, you'll do tons of color-chip swapping (from black to white and vice versa). You'll also use a variety of brush sizes to paint the fine details as well as large areas. To keep from going blind when you're doing detailed work like this, zoom in or out of your document by pressing ⌘ and then the + or – key (Ctrl and then the + or – key on a PC).

TIP   In Photoshop CS4, you can change the size of your brush and its hardness by dragging with your mouse, which is super handy when it comes to painting on layer masks. To resize your brush, Ctrl-Option-drag (Alt+right-click+drag on a PC) to the left to decrease brush size or to the right to increase it. To change the brush's hardness, ⌘-Ctrl-Option-drag (Shift+Alt+right-click+drag) to the left to soften it or to the right to harden it. Inside your brush cursor, you'll see a red preview of what your new brush will look like—if your computer supports OpenGL (page 60). See page 464 if you want to change that color to something other than red. If you're using an earlier version of Photoshop, you can decrease your brush size by pressing the left bracket key ([) and increase it pressing the right bracket key (]).

That wasn't too bad, was it? You just learned *core* Photoshop skills that you'll use over and over. The more you use masks, the more natural this stuff will feel.

Fixing exposure with masks

Masks are especially handy for quickly fixing an over- or underexposed image (one that's too light or too dark). This trick is important to have up your sleeve if you're short on time, or if other lighting fixes (see Chapter 9) aren't working. Here's what you do:

1. **Open your image and duplicate the background by pressing ⌘-J (Ctrl+J on a PC).**

2. **Change the duplicate layer's blend mode from Normal to Multiply using the pop-up menu at the top of your Layers panel.**

Blend modes control how color on one layer interacts with colors on other layers, which is terrific when it comes to combining images (you'll learn all about blend modes in Chapter 7). For now, you'll focus on two blend modes that you'll use often because they let you quickly darken or lighten an image, respectively: Multiply and Screen (see Figure 3-27). For this example, pick Multiply from the menu at the top of the Layer's panel to darken your image dramatically. You'll hide the too dark bits with a layer mask in the next step.

Figure 3-27:
You can darken or lighten your image by using a brush to fine-tune the mask. Photo-editing veterans call this technique "painting with light."

Top: You can see that this guy's shirt and arms are too light in the original image (left). If you change the duplicate layer's blend mode to Multiply, his face and guitar are too dark (middle). But if you hide his face and guitar with a layer mask, he looks much better (right).

Bottom: You can do the same thing to a photo that's too dark. On the left is the super dark original. The middle image shows what happens when you change the duplicate layer's blend mode to Screen. You can use a layer mask to hide the overlightened areas (mainly the background) as shown on the right. Now you can see the rocker dude's face which, on second thought, maybe isn't such a good idea, after all!

3. **Add a layer mask to the duplicate layer.**

   With the duplicate layer selected (it should be highlighted in the Layers panel), click the circle-within-a-square button at the bottom of the Layers panel to add a layer mask, which allows you to hide the parts of your image that don't need darkening.

4. **Press B to grab the Brush tool and set your foreground color chip to black.**

   To hide the overdarkened areas, paint them with black because—all together now!—black conceals and white reveals. Peek at your color chips, and if black isn't on top, press X. Now you're ready to paint.

5. **With a big soft brush, paint the areas of your image that are too dark.**

   At this point, those keyboard shortcuts for resizing and changing the hardness of your brush come in handy (see the Tip on page 109). Remember, if you mess up and hide too much of the darkened part of your image, simply flip-flop your color chips by pressing X and then reveal the dark part by painting it with white.

6. **If your image is still a little too dark, you can lower the opacity (page 87) of the duplicate layer.**

UP TO SPEED

Unlinking a Layer from Its Mask

Photoshop assumes that if you reposition the contents of your layer, you want your mask to come along for the ride, too. However, that's not always the case.

For example, if you use a mask to frame your photo (see the oval vignette instructions on page 137), you may want to move what's *inside* the mask (your photo) independent of the mask itself, or vice versa. No problemo—you just need to unlink them first.

Over in the Layers panel, you'll see a tiny chain between the layer's thumbnail and the mask's thumbnail (you can see this chain in Figure 3-27). Click the chain once or choose Layer → Layer Mask → Unlink to unlink the layer from the mask (you'll know you got it right when the chain disappears). Then press V to grab the Move tool, click the thumbnail of the piece you want to move (the layer or the mask), and then drag. Once you've got everything where you want it, click the chain's previous position (between the layer and mask thumbnails) or choose Layer → Layer Mask → Relink to relink them. Easy, huh?

Editing a Mask

Once you add a mask, you'll undoubtedly need to fine-tune it, turn it off or on, and so on. In earlier versions of Photoshop, you had to mouse *all* over the Photoshop workspace to do that stuff. But in CS4, all of your mask tasks are consolidated in the new Masks panel (Figure 3-28).

Pixel Mask
Close panel
Add a vector Mask
Panel menu

Figure 3-28:
The Masks panel is your one-stop shop for working with layer masks. Heck, you can even add a layer mask right from this panel!

Mask preview

Masks panel dock

Load Selection from Mask

Apply Mask

Disable/Enable Mask

Delete Mask

You'll find the following controls roosting comfortably in the Masks panel:

- **Density.** Photoshop sets the opacity for new layer masks to 100 percent, which means you can't see through them. If you want to make your mask semitransparent so the contents of the layer (like the original background) start to show through, drag this slider to the left. Dragging it *all* the way to the left makes your mask completely transparent.

- **Feather.** If you want to soften the edges of your mask so that it blends into the background a little better, this slider will get it done. Drag it to the right to soften the mask's edges and to the left to sharpen them (new layer masks don't have any automatic feathering, so their edges are always sharp).

- **Mask Edge.** When you click this button, Photoshop opens the Refine Mask dialog box where you can smooth mask edges, contract or expand your mask (make it smaller or bigger), and so on. Page 155 has the details on this dialog box.

- **Color Range.** This button opens the Color Range dialog box where you can add to or subtract from your mask based on the colors in your image. You can use this button to help create a selection that you can make a mask *from*. Page 143 has more info.

- **Invert.** This button lets you flip-flop your mask so what *was* masked isn't and what *wasn't* masked is.

- **Load Selection from Mask.** Once you've created a layer mask, you can load it as a selection that you can use somewhere else like in an Adjustment layer (see Figure 3-25, right).

- **Apply Mask.** Once you get the mask just right, you can permanently (eek!) apply it to your layer by clicking this button. Applying a mask permanently alters the layer and limits the changes you can make later, so don't use this option unless you're certain you won't need to change the mask down the road. If you click this button by accident, use your History panel or undo command to get your mask back (⌘-Z or Ctrl+Z on a PC) or you won't be able to edit it ever again.

- **Disable/Enable Mask.** This visibility eye works just like the one in the Layers panel (page 78). Click it to turn your mask off or on.

- **Delete.** If you decide you don't want the mask, you can kick it to the curb by clicking the little trash can at the bottom of the Masks panel.

> **TIP** If you want to copy a mask to another layer, click the mask in your Layers panel and Option-drag (Alt-drag on a PC) it to another layer. Your cursor turns into a double black-and-white arrowhead when you start to drag.

Opening the Masks panel menu by clicking the panel's upper-right corner reveals these goodies (see Figure 3-28):

- **Mask Options.** When you're editing masks, you've got a few different viewing options. Which one you choose will depend on the colors in your image and the area you're trying to select. Pick a color that makes it easy for you to distinguish the mask from the unmasked parts of your image. In the masking examples discussed earlier, the mask was edited while the image was viewed in full color. However, as Figure 3-29 shows, you can also work on a mask while you're looking at a grayscale version of your image or turn the mask into a color overlay. If you choose the color overlay and Photoshop's standard red isn't doing it for you, use the Mask Options dialog box to pick another color.

- **Add Mask to Selection.** If you have an existing selection (see Chapter 4), you can choose this option to add the mask to your selection. "Add Mask to Selection" makes it easy to expand the currently selected area to include the mask in one quick step.

- **Subtract Mask from Selection.** This option will delete the shape of the mask from your selection.

- **Intersect Mask with Selection.** To select only areas where your selection and mask overlap (if you need to add a color or pattern only to those places, for example) choose this option.

Figure 3-29:

Left: If you want to edit a grayscale version of your mask—a good option if your image has lots of colors—Option-click (Alt-click on a PC) the mask's thumbnail in the Layers panel. Now you can copy and paste pixels—including text—right into your layer mask. (Page 579 has a cool example involving textured text.) When you're finished editing the mask, click the layer's thumbnail.

Right: To edit your mask with a red overlay, press the backslash key (\). To change the overlay's color, open the Masks panel menu and choose Mask Options. In the Layer Mask Display Options dialog box (shown here), click the little color swatch and pick a new color. Press the backslash key again to see your full-color image.

FREQUENTLY ASKED QUESTION

Clipping Masks

What the heck is a clipping mask? Is it similar to a layer mask?

Clipping masks and layer masks are similar in that they both hide parts of your image, but that's about it. Clipping masks are like Photoshop's version of stencils: they let you take the contents of one layer (like bluebonnets) and shove it through the contents of the layer directly below (for example, text that says "Texas"). The result? The image on the top layer is "clipped" so that you see the bluebonnets inside the text. Hop on over to page 583 for step-by-step instructions on this technique.

You can give clipping masks a spin by first opening a photo and double-clicking the Background layer to make it editable (page 80). Add a layer below it by using one of the methods described on page 76. Press B to grab the Brush tool and then paint a big ol' brushstroke across your

new layer. In your Layers panel, select the photo layer (which should be on top of your layers stack) and then choose Layer → Create Clipping Mask or press ⌘-Option-G (Ctrl+Alt+G on a PC). Photoshop makes your photo visible *only* through your brushstroke.

When you use a clipping mask, you don't get another thumbnail in your Layers panel like you do with a layer mask. Instead, the photo layer's thumbnail scoots to the right and you see a tiny down arrow letting you know that it's clipped to the layer below. You can clip as many layers together as you want.

To release a clipping mask, select the clipped layer (the top layer, or in this example, the Brush layer), go to Layer → Release Clipping Mask, and choose Release Clipping Mask from the Layer panel menu or press ⌘-Option-G (Ctrl+Alt+G). You should see your entire photo again.

Using Smart Objects

A *Smart Object* is a container-like layer into which you can plop all kinds of stuff like Camera Raw files (page 53), vectors (drawings) from programs like Adobe Illustrator (Chapter 13), whole PSD files, and even other layers. Smart Objects are smart because Photoshop remembers the original content and which program created it, which lets you:

- **Transform or resize without losing quality.** Instead of resizing the *instance* (a copy) of the content that you inserted into your document, Photoshop remembers info about the *original*, resizes that, and then places that information back into your image (leaving the actual original file safely unaltered). It doesn't matter whether that original lives elsewhere on your hard drive (a vector, Raw file, and so on) or right there in your Photoshop document (on another layer, say). In the blink of an eye, Photoshop updates your document with the newly resized content *without* making it look blocky. You can also use the full range of transform tools (page 245) on Smart Objects.

  NOTE   Smart Objects are especially useful when you're working with Raw files because you can double-click them in Photoshop to open them in Camera Raw (page 53). However, placing multiple Smart Objects in a single document—especially one containing Raw files—will bloat your file size in a hurry and cause Photoshop to run as fast as molasses.

- **Compress a bunch of layers into a single layer nondestructively.** Unlike merging layers (page 103), converting several layers into a single Smart Object preserve the original layers. This ability is super helpful if Photoshop is choking on the number of layers in your document or if you want to edit several layers as if they were one, which you may want to do if you're applying layer styles (page 119).

- **Run filters nondestructively.** When you run a filter on a Smart Object, the filtering happens on a new layer. That way, you can tweak, hide, or undo the effects of the filter. See Chapter 15 (page 588) to learn how to run filters on Smart Objects.

- **Update multiple instances of the same content.** If you've placed the same content in several places in your document—like a big logo in one spot and a smaller version of the same logo somewhere else—and you make changes to the original file, Photoshop automatically updates it for you wherever it appears in your document.

- **Swap content.** Once you've formatted a Smart Object just right, you can swap its contents for another image, and the new image takes on the original's attributes. This content swapping is powerful magic when it comes to making creative templates that you can use over and over but with different images (photographers love this kind of thing). Figure 3-30 has the details.

Figure 3-30:
You can create some pretty amazing templates using Smart Objects. Just open an image as a Smart Object (described later in this section) and make all the changes you want like giving it a sepia tint (page 304), adding a dark-edge vignette (page 598), and sharpening it (page 428). To swap the photo for another one, select the Smart Object layer (note the little badge that indicates it's a Smart Object, circled) and choose Layers → Smart Objects → Replace Contents. Navigate to another photo on your hard drive, click Open, and it'll take on the same characteristics automatically! Thank ya, thank ya very much.

NOTE   As you learned back on page 46, JPEG is a "lossy" format, meaning you lose a little bit of quality each time you open and resave it. If you open or place a JPEG as a Smart Object (explained next), the image quality may already be lower than you want, and the file may already show visible flaws thanks to its "lossy" compression—before you even start making your own edits. For the best image results, avoid JPEG images or any other file format that uses "lossy" file compression. For that reason, you'll want to stick with formats that *aren't* compressed with your Smart Objects like Raw, PSD, and TIFF files.

The following sections teach you how to create and manage Smart Objects.

Creating Smart Objects

How you create a Smart Object depends on two things: Where the original content lives and which document you want to put it in. Here are your options:

- **To create a new document containing a file that lives on your hard drive, choose File → "Open as Smart Object".** In the resulting Open dialog box, navigate to the file and click Open to make Photoshop create a new document containing a single Smart Object (without a Background layer). The image you've opened appears at its original size, and you'll see the Smart Object badge on its layer thumbnail (circled in Figure 3-30).

TIP   You can Shift-click multiple files in the Open dialog box to open more than one file as a Smart Object. Each file will open as its own document with a single Smart Object layer.

- **To import a file into a document that's currently open, choose File → Place.** You get the same Open dialog box so you can navigate to the file, but this time the file opens as a Smart Object *inside* the document you're in. Photoshop also puts little handles around the object so you can resize it. When you press Return (Enter on a PC) to accept the object, you'll see the Smart Object badge appear on the new layer's thumbnail.

- **Copy and paste an Adobe Illustrator file.** If you copy Illustrator art into your computer's memory, you can paste it into an open Photoshop document using ⌘-V (Ctrl+V on a PC). You'll be asked whether you want to paste it as a Smart Object, pixels, path (page 497), or Shape layer (page 509).

- **In Bridge, choose File → Place → In Photoshop.** If you're using Bridge to peruse your files, you can pop 'em open as Smart Objects in Photoshop with this command (see Appendix C for more on Bridge).

- **To turn existing layers into a Smart Object in the current document, choose Layers → Smart Objects → "Convert to Smart Object", or choose "Convert to Smart Object" from the Layers panel menu.** If you're working with an image that has a bunch of Adjustment layers associated with it (to change stuff like color and lighting), you can group the whole mess into a single Smart Object. That way, you can apply additional changes to all those layers at *once* with tools that work only on individual layers (like filters and layer styles). As a bonus, Photoshop will run a little faster because your document's file size decreases when you get rid of extra layers (Figure 3-31 has the details).

TIP   You can apply a mask to Smart Objects just like you can on any other layer. Unlike previous versions, Photoshop CS4 automatically *links* the mask to the layer so you can move them around together. If you want to unlink them, just click the little chain between their thumbnails in the Layers panel.

Managing Smart Objects

Once you've created a Smart Object, you can duplicate it, edit it, and export its contents. You'll find the following options in both the Layers → Smart Objects menu and the Layer panel options menu:

- **New Smart Object via Copy.** When you choose this command, Photoshop makes a duplicate of your Smart Object that's *not linked* to the original, so if you edit the content of the original Smart Object, the duplicate won't change. This unlinked copy is helpful if you want to create more than one instance of the same Smart Object in a single file and edit them in different ways.

Figure 3-31:
Left: To convert multiple layers to a Smart Object, select them in your Layers panel and then choose "Convert to Smart Object" from the Layers panel menu.

Right: Photoshop converts all those layers into a single Smart Object that you can run filters on nondestructively. The filter shows up on its own layer as shown here.

If you want to edit the Smart Object's contents, choose Edit Contents from the Layers panel menu and Photoshop opens a new document containing your original layers. When you're finished editing, press ⌘-S (Ctrl+S on a PC) to save your changes and then close the document. Photoshop updates your Smart Object in the original document automatically. How cool is that?

TIP To create a duplicate Smart Object that *is* linked to the original, choose Layers → Smart Objects → "New Layer via Copy" from the Layers panel menu or drag the Smart Object onto the "Create a new layer" button at the bottom of your Layers panel. This is handy if you've repeated a graphical element in your design—if you edit that element in the original Smart Object, Photoshop updates all the copies of that Smart Object in your document.

- **Edit Contents.** Choose this option or double-click the Smart Object's thumbnail in your Layers panel if you want to edit the original file in the program that created it (for example, Adobe Illustrator).

- **Export Contents.** This command pulls the contents of the selected Smart Object out of the current document and puts it into a new file that's the same format as the original. If it began life as a Raw file, for example, Photoshop will save it in Raw format. When you choose this command, Photoshop displays a dialog box where you can name the new file and choose where to save it.

- **Replace Contents.** As you learned back in Figure 3-30, you can use this command to swap the contents of a Smart Object so the new image takes on the appearance of the old one.

- **Rasterize.** You can't paint or edit directly on a Smart Object like you can on its contents. But if you're ready to give up all the goodness that comes with using a Smart Object, you can choose this option to rasterize it and make it behave like any other layer.

WORKAROUND WORKSHOP

Nested Smart Objects

If you've got a Smart Object that contains several layers and you try to apply a Layer style to it, you'll run into some difficulty. For example, if you apply a drop shadow (page 119) to a Smart Object full of layers, Photoshop tacks a drop shadow onto *every* layer. So instead of a nice, subtle shadow, you end with a shadow on top of a shadow on top of a shadow—yuck. The fix is to convert your Smart Object into *another* Smart Object inside the original before you add the Layer style.

In your Layers panel, select the Smart Object you want to convert and then choose Layers → Smart Objects → Convert to Smart Object. Photoshop creates a new Smart Object within the original (which is why it's called a *nested* Smart Object). Now you can apply the Layer style to the new Smart Object and your Layer style will look like you expect it to.

Layer Styles

After all that hard work learning about layers, you're probably ready for some fun. This section is all about *layer styles:* a set of ten fully adjustable, ready-made special effects for your layers that you can apply in all kinds of cool ways. Consider this section your reward for sticking through the chapter till the bitter end.

Layer styles are a lot of fun and, since they appear on their own layers, they're non-destructive *and* they remain editable as long as you save the document as a PSD file. Layer styles are great for adding finishing touches to your designs, and they can really make text and graphical elements pop off the page (see Figure 3-32). They also change as your layer content changes.

Here's how to add The Lord of All Styles, the drop shadow, to your layer:

1. **Select the soon-to-be-shadowed layer in your Layers panel.**

   Photoshop limits you to selecting just one layer when you're adding a style.

2. **Click the "Add a layer style" button at the bottom of the Layers panel and choose Drop Shadow.**

   The button looks like a tiny cursive *fx*.

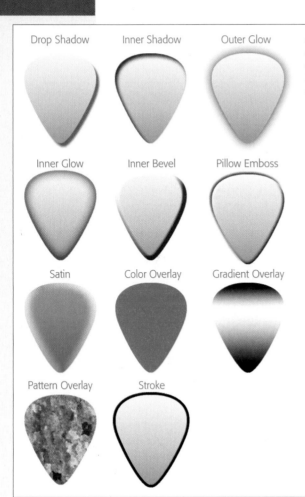

Figure 3-32:
Here's a sneak peek at all the cool styles you can tack onto your layers. Adobe refers to them individually as styles and collectively as effects though most folks just call them Layer styles.

3. **In the Layer Style dialog box that appears, adjust the settings to produce a respectable (soft)—not overly gaudy (black and 10 feet away)—drop shadow.**

   There are a bazillion options for each style in the Layer Style dialog box, and it's a good idea to experiment so you know how they work. When it comes to drop shadows, the biggies are changing its color by clicking the black rectabgular swatch (the classiest drop shadows are rarely black—instead they pick up a color from your image) and lowering its opacity so it's nice and soft. You can also use the Spread and Size sliders to make it wider. Don't bother messing with the Angle dial or the Distance slider because you can change those settings visually by heading over to your document and dragging the shadow around with your mouse.

4. **Click OK when you're satisfied with what you see in your document, then marvel at your very first drop shadow. Whee!**

If you want to edit the style, just double-click it. If you want to move it to another layer, just grab it and drag.

You can add as many styles to a layer as you want, all from the Layer Style dialog box. Just turn on the options you want (they're all in the Styles column on the left) and then click a style's *name* to see its options. And remember the Fill setting discussed back on page 87? You can use it to make the *contents* of your layer see-through while the *style* remains 100 percent solid.

> **TIP** You can also open the Layer Style dialog box by double-clicking a layer's thumbnail or double-clicking near the layer's name.

FREQUENTLY ASKED QUESTION

Hiding Styles with Masks

Help! I have a mask on my layer and Photoshop is showing the styles through the darn mask! How do I hide those pesky styles?

Ah, you seek the elusive style cloak. To summon it, you must boil the stalk of a West Texas tumbleweed, season it with eye of toad, and drink it from the shell of an armadillo three days dead…Just kidding.

To hide styles with a layer mask, you've got to change your layer's blending options (see the figure on page 280). Double-click the style in your Layers panel and, in the Layer Styles dialog box, click Blending Options at the top left.

In the Advanced Blending section in the center of the dialog box (shown here), you'll see a list of checkboxes that includes "Layer Mask Hides Effects" and "Vector Mask Hides Effects".

Turn on the appropriate option (according to which kind of layer you're working with: Vector Mask [page 527] for vector-based layers, and Layer Mask for all other layers) and then click OK. Back in your document, your mask should hide any styles you've applied to that layer.

Now, back to that magic potion….

Managing Layer Styles

Once you've tacked on a layer style or two, you'll undoubtedly want to apply them to other layers and turn them off or on. Here's how:

- **To copy a style from one layer to another,** hover your cursor above the style in your Layers panel and then Option-drag (Alt-drag on PC) the style to the new layer. Your cursor turns into a double black-and-white arrowhead when you drag.

- **To turn a style off,** click the visibility eye to the style's left in the Layers panel.

If you Ctrl-click (right-click) a style in your Layers panel, you'll get a shortcut menu with these options:

- **Disable Layer Effects** turns off all the styles on that layer. To turn them back on, open the menu again and choose Enable Layer Effects.

- **Copy Style** copies all the styles you've applied to the selected layer so you can apply them to other layers. After you select this command, Shift or ⌘-click (Ctrl-click on a PC) to select the layers you want to apply the styles to and then Ctrl-click (right-click) to open the shortcut menu again and choose **Paste Style**.

- **Clear Layer Style** deletes the style from the selected layers. You can also drag a style to the trash can at the bottom of your Layers panel to remove it from a layer.

- **Global Light** tells Photoshop to use the same lighting angle in every style you add, which is useful when you're applying drop shadows or inner shadows. If you've got more than one drop shadow in your document, turn on this option so your lighting stays consistent.

- **Create Layer** takes the style applied to the selected layer and converts it into a regular image layer, but you lose the ability to edit the style later. Though it sounds limiting, you can use this option to further customize a Layer style into your own personal vision; once it's a regular layer, you can run filters on it, use the painting tools, and so on.

- **Hide All Effects** turns off the styles applied to *every* layer. After you've hidden them, this menu item changes to Show Effects, so you can select it to turn them back on.

- **Scale Styles** lets you resize the style itself, independent of the layer contents, by entering a percentage. This option is useful if you want to fine-tune drop shadows and glows by making them slightly larger or smaller.

Using the Styles Panel

Photoshop comes with all kinds of styles made from some pretty psychedelic style combinations. You'll find a couple of them useful, but most of them are just funky. To get at them, open the Styles panel by clicking its tab in the panels dock on the right side of your screen or by choosing Window → Styles (see Figure 3-33).

Admittedly, the preloaded styles aren't anything to write home about, but if you open the Styles panel menu, you'll see ten *more* sets you can load: Abstract Styles, Buttons, and so on. To load another set, just choose it from the panel's menu; Photoshop asks if you'd like to add them to the existing styles or replace the existing ones. If you're a Web designer, you may find the Glass Buttons and Web Styles sets useful for that clear, plastic look. Otherwise, you probably won't find much use for many of these styles.

To apply one of these styles, simply select the layer you want to use it on and click once on the style's thumbnail. You can tweak the style by double-clicking the style's layer in your Layers panel or by choosing it from the Layer Style dialog box. You can also drag and drop a style thumbnail onto your layer, but that style replaces any styles already applied to that layer. To add a saved style on *top* of existing styles, hold down the Shift key as you drag and drop or as you click the style's thumbnail.

> **TIP** To make the style thumbnails larger or to view them in a list, open the Styles panel menu and choose Text Only, Small Thumbnail, Large Thumbnail, Small List, or Large List.

Close panel
Options menu
Styles panel dock

Delete style
Create new style
Clear style

Figure 3-33:
You'll find all manner of weird and wacky presets in the Styles panel (top left), some more useful than others (top right). You can add your own creations to the mix by selecting the layer where your styles are and then clicking the "Create new style" button shown here or choosing New Style from the Styles panel menu.

In the resulting dialog box (bottom), give your style a name, turn on the Include Layer Effects checkbox to make sure you don't lose any of your changes, and if you've changed any layer blending options (page 280), turn on Include Layer Blending Options checkbox, too. When you click OK, Photoshop saves your style for prosperity in the Styles panel. If you want to bypass this dialog box next time, Option-click (Alt-click on a PC) the New Style button. You'll get a new Style called "Style" that you can rename later, but you don't get to change any other settings.

Exporting and loading styles

If you're really proud of the styles you've created and want to share them with the masses (or at least load them onto another computer), here's what you do: From the Styles panel menu, choose Save Styles, give your style a name, and tell Photoshop where you want to save it. You can take the resulting file to another computer, launch Photoshop, and pick one of the following options from the Styles panel menu:

- **Load Styles** will add the new styles to the ones currently in your Styles panel.

- **Replace Styles** will zap the ones you've got in favor of the new ones.

- **Reset Styles** will return your styles to the factory settings.

Selections: Choosing What to Edit

Life is all about making choices, and the time you spend in Photoshop is no exception. Perhaps the biggest decision you'll make is which part of the image to edit. After all, your edits don't have to affect the *whole* image. Using a variety of Photoshop tools, you can tell the program exactly which portion of the image you want to tinker with—right down to the pixel, if you so desire. This process is called making a *selection*.

As you'll learn in this chapter, Photoshop has a bunch of tools that you can use to create selections based on shape, color, and other attributes. You can also draw selections by hand though that requires a bit of mouse prowess. True selection wisdom lies in learning which selection tool to start with, how to use the tools together, and how to fine-tune your selections quickly and efficiently. The following pages will help you reach selection enlightenment.

Selection Basics

What's so great about selections, anyway? Lots. After you make a selection, you can do all kinds of neat things with it, like:

- **Fill it with color.** Normally, the Edit → Fill command (page 85) floods an entire layer with color, but by creating a selection first, you can color only that area. For example, you can use the Fill command in conjunction with the Rectangular Marquee (one of the bread-and-butter selection tools you'll learn about in this chapter) to create a colorful photo border (shown later in this chapter on page 168).

- **Add an outline.** You can add a *stroke* (Photoshop's term for an outline) to any selection. For example, you can use selections to give your photo a black border (page 168) or to circle yourself in a group photo (page 169).

- **Move it around.** To move part of an image, you need to select it first. You can even move selections from one document to another, as discussed on page 164. For example, a little head swapping is great fun after family reunions and break-ups. If you want to stick your ex's head onto a ballerina's body, hop on over to page 166.

- **Resize or transform it.** Need to change the size or shape of your selection? No problem: Just make a selection and then transform it into whatever size or shape you need (page 161). Photoshop won't reshape any pixels that are in your selected area, just the selection itself.

- **Use it as a mask.** When you create a selection, Photoshop protects the area outside it—anything you do to the image affects only the selected area. For example, if you move the Eraser tool (see Appendix E, online at *www.missingmanuals.com*) across the edge of a selection, it erases only the area *inside* the selection.

  Likewise, if you create a selection before adding a layer mask (page 105), Photoshop loads the selected area into the mask automatically, letting you adjust only that part of the image. So selections are crucial when you need to correct the lighting in just one area (Chapter 9), or change the color of an object (see the figure on page 324).

This chapter discusses all these options and more. But, first, you need to understand how Photoshop marks your selections.

Meet the Marching Ants

When you create a selection, Photoshop calls up a lively army of animated "marching ants" (shown in Figure 4-1). These tiny soldiers dutifully march around the edge of the selected area, awaiting your command. You can select part of an image, everything on a single layer, or a whole document. Whenever you have an active selection (that is, whenever you see marching ants), Photoshop has eyes only for that portion of your document—any tool you use (except the Type and Shape tools) will affect only the area *inside* the selection.

> **NOTE** Selections don't hang around forever—when you click somewhere else on your screen with a selection tool, your original selection disappears, forcing you to redraw it. If you want to save a selection to use again later, flip to page 166.

Here are the commands you'll use most often when you make selections:

- **Select All.** This command selects your whole document and places marching ants around the perimeter, which is helpful when you want to copy and paste an entire image into another program or create a border around a photo (see page 168). To run this command, go to Select → All or press ⌘-A (Ctrl+A on a PC).

Figure 4-1:
To let you know an area is selected, Photoshop surrounds it with tiny, moving dashes that look like marching ants. Here you can see the ants running around the armadillo. (FYI, the nine-banded armadillo is the state animal of Texas. Aren't you glad you bought this book?)

- **Deselect.** To get rid of the marching ants after you've finished working with the selection, choose Select → Deselect or press ⌘-D (Ctrl+D). Alternatively, if you've got one of the selection tools activated in the Tools panel, you can click once on another part of the image to get rid of your selection.

- **Reselect.** To resurrect your last selection, choose Select → Reselect or press ⌘-Shift-D (Ctrl-Shift-D). This command reactivates the last selection you made, even if it was five filters and twenty brushstrokes ago (unless you've used the Crop and Type tools, which render this command powerless). Reselecting is helpful if you accidentally deselect a selection you've been working on for a long time. (The Undo command [⌘-Z or Ctrl+Z] can also help you in that situation.)

- **Inverse.** This command, which you run by going to Select → Inverse or pressing ⌘-Shift-I (Ctrl-Shift-I), lets you flip-flop your selection to select everything you *didn't* select before. You'll often find it easier to select what you *don't* want and then inverse the selection to get what you *do* want (see the box on page 143).

- **Load a layer as a selection.** When talking to people about Photoshop, you'll often hear the phrase "load as a selection," which is (unavoidable) Photoshop-speak for activating a layer that contains the object you want to work with and then summoning the marching ants so they run around that object; that way, whatever you do next affects *only* that object. To load everything that lives on a single layer as a selection, mouse over to the Layers panel and ⌘-click (Ctrl+click) the layer's thumbnail (page 73); you don't need to have the layer selected. Photoshop responds by putting marching ants around everything on that layer. Alternatively, you can Ctrl-click (right-click on a PC) the layer's thumbnail and then choose Select Pixels from the resulting shortcut menu.

TIP Although you can find most of the commands in this list in the Select menu at the top of your screen (except for loading a layer as a selection), you need to memorize their keyboard shortcuts if you want to be smokin' fast in Photoshop.

These next three items live in the Select menu, but they don't actually call up marching ants. Instead, they tell Photoshop to select entire layers (for the low-down on layers, see Chapter 3):

- **All Layers.** Use this command if you want to select every layer in your document (so you can move several layers at one time, for example). To select all layers, choose Select → All Layers or press ⌘-Option-A (Ctrl+Alt+A).

- **Deselect Layers.** This command does the exact opposite of the previous one: It deselects all the layers in your Layers panel, leaving nary a layer highlighted. To run it, choose Select → Deselect layers.

- **Similar Layers.** Choose this command if you want to select all layers of the same kind (page 71 lists the different types of layers). For example, say you want to change the font in all the Type layers in your document. Just select a Type layer and choose Select → Similar. Photoshop selects all your Type layers and highlights them in your Layers panel so you can modify them all at once. (See Chapter 14 for more on Type layers.)

> **TIP** When you move objects around with the Move tool, you can enlist Photoshop's help in selecting individual layers by turning on Auto-Select in the Options bar. As you click an object in your document, Photoshop will try to guess which layer it's on and select that layer for you.

Now it's time to discuss the tools you can use to make selections. Photoshop has a ton of 'em, so in the next several pages, you'll find them grouped according to which *kind* of selections they're best at making.

Selecting by Shape

Selections based on shape are probably the easiest ones you can make. Whether the object you need to grab is rectangular, elliptical, or rectangular with rounded corners, Photoshop has just the tool for you. You'll use the first couple of tools described in this section often, so think of them as your bread and butter when it comes to making selections.

The Rectangular and Elliptical Marquee Tools

Photoshop's most basic selection tools are the Rectangular and Elliptical Marquees. Anytime you need to make a selection that's squarish or roundish, reach for these little helpers, which live at the top of the Tools panel, as shown in Figure 4-2.

To make a selection with either marquee tool, just grab the tool by clicking its icon in the Tools panel or by pressing M and mouse over to your document. When your cursor turns into a tiny + sign, drag across the area you want to select (you'll see the marching ants appear as soon as you start to drag). Photoshop starts the selection where you clicked and continues it in the direction you drag as long as you press the mouse button. When you've got marching ants around the area you want to select, release the mouse button.

Figure 4-2:
You'll spend loads of time making selections with the Rectangular and Elliptical Marquees. To summon this pop-up menu, click the second item from the top on the Tools panel and hold down your mouse button until the menu appears.

You can use a variety of tools and techniques to modify your selection, most of which you can find in the Options bar (Figure 4-3). For example, you can:

- **Move the selection.** Clicking anywhere within the selected area and dragging to another part of your document (your cursor turns into a tiny arrow) moves the selection where you want it.

    TIP   You can move your selection as you're drawing it by moving your mouse while pressing your mouse button and the space bar. When you've got your selection where you want it, release the space bar and continue drawing it.

- **Add to the selection.** When you click the "Add to selection" button in the Options bar (see Figure 4-3) or press and hold the Shift key, Photoshop puts a tiny + sign beneath your cursor to let you know that it will add whatever you select to your current selection. This mode is handy when you've selected most of what you want but notice that you missed a spot. Instead of starting over, you can switch to Add to selection mode and draw around that area as if you were creating a new selection. You can also use this mode to select areas that don't touch each other, like the iris in your dog's eyes (see page 422).

- **Subtract from the selection.** Clicking the "Subtract from selection" button in the Options bar (also shown in Figure 4-3) or pressing and holding the Option key (Alt on a PC) has the opposite effect. You'll see a tiny – sign beneath your cursor to let you know you're in this mode. Mouse over to your document and draw a box (or oval) around the area you no longer want to select.

- **Intersect one selection with another.** If you click the "Intersect with selection" button after you draw a selection, Photoshop lets you draw another selection that overlaps the first. The marching ants then surround only the area where the two selections overlap. It's a little confusing, but don't worry because you'll rarely use this mode (if at all). The keyboard shortcut is Shift-Option (Shift+Alt on a PC). Photoshop puts a tiny multiplication sign ($\times$) beneath your cursor when you use this mode.

- **Feather.** If you want to soften the edges of your selection so that it blends into the background or another image, use *feathering*. (You can enter a value in pixels this field *before* you create the selection.) As you'll learn later in this chapter, feathering a selection lets you gently fade one image into another. (See the box on page 132 for more on feathering.)

- **Anti-alias.** Turn on the Anti-alias checkbox to make Photoshop smooth the color transition between the pixels around the edges of your selection and the pixels in your background. Like feathering, antialiasing softens your selection's edges slightly so that they blend better though you can't control the *amount* of softening Photoshop applies. It's a good idea to leave this checkbox turned on unless you want your selection to have super crisp—and possibly jagged and blocky—edges.

- **Style.** If you want to constrain your selection to a fixed size or a fixed aspect ratio (so that the relationship between its width and height stays the same), you can select Fixed Ratio or Fixed Width from the Style pop-up menu and then enter the size you want in the resulting width and height fields. Be sure to enter a unit of measurement into each field, such as *px* for pixels. If you leave the Normal option selected, you can draw any size selection you want.

Here's how to select two doors in the same photo, as shown in Figure 4-3:

1. **Click the marquee tool icon in the Tools panel and choose the Rectangular Marquee from the pop-up menu (shown in Figure 4-2).**

   The Tools panel remembers which marquee tool you last used, so you'll see that tool's icon on top of the selection tools pop-up menu. If that's the one you want to use, just press M to activate it. If not, in the Tools panel, click and hold whichever marquee tool is showing until the pop-up menu appears and then choose the tool you want.

   TIP To cycle through the different marquee tools, press M to activate the marquee toolset (the pop-up menu shown in Figure 4-2) and then press Shift-M repeatedly to activate each one in turn. If that doesn't work, make sure that a gremlin hasn't turned off the preference that makes this trick possible. Choose Photoshop → Preferences → General (Edit → Preferences → General on a PC) and make sure "Use Shift Key for Tool Switch" is turned on.

2. **Drag to draw a box around the first door.**

   To select the blue door shown in Figure 4-3, click its top-left corner and drag diagonally toward the bottom-right corner of the same door. When you get the whole door in your selection, release the mouse button. Don't worry if you don't get the selection in exactly the right spot; you can move it around in the next step.

3. **Move your selection into place if necessary.**

   If you need to move the selection, just click *inside* the selected area (your cursor turns into a tiny arrow) and drag the selection box where you want it. You can also use the arrows on your keyboard to nudge the selection in one direction or another (you don't need to click it first).

New selection
Add to selection
Subtract from selection
Intersect with selection

Feather: 0 px · Anti-alias · Style: Normal · Width: · H·

iStock_000004492075Medium.jpg @ 50% (RGB/8*) *

Figure 4-3:
Using the buttons in the Options bar, you can add to or subtract from a selection, as well as create a selection from two intersecting areas. Since all selections begin at the point where you first click, you can easily select one of these doors by dragging diagonally from the top-left corner to the bottom right as shown here. You can tell from the tiny + sign next to the crosshair-shaped cursor that you're in "Add to selection" mode, so this figure now has two selections: the blue door and the red door.

4. **Press the "Add to selection" button in the Options bar and then select the second door by drawing a selection around it.**

Photoshop lets you know that you're in "Add to selection" mode by placing a tiny + sign beneath your cursor. Once you see it, mouse over to the second door and drag diagonally from the top-left corner to the bottom right, as shown in Figure 4-3.

If you need to move this second selection around, do that *before* you release the mouse button or you'll end up moving both selections instead of just one. To move a selection while you're drawing it, hold down your mouse button, press and hold the space bar, and then move your mouse to move the selection.

When you've got the selection in the right place, release the space bar—but keep holding the mouse button—and continue dragging to draw the selection. This maneuver feels a bit awkward at first and requires coordination, but you'll get used to it.

Congratulations! You've just made your first selection and added to it. Way to go!

> **TIP** To draw a perfectly square or circular selection, press and hold the Shift key as you drag with either the Rectangular or Elliptical Marquee tool. If you want to draw the selection from the center outward (instead of from corner to corner), press and hold the Option key (Alt on a PC). If you want to draw a perfectly square or circular selection from the center outward, press and hold Shift-Option (Shift+Alt) as you drag with either marquee tool. Whew—that's a lot of keys! Be sure to use this trick only on new selections—if you've already got a selection, the Shift key pops you into "Add to selection" mode (page 130).

Creating a soft vignette

The Elliptical Marquee tool works just like the Rectangular Marquee tool except that it draws round or oval selections. It's the perfect tool for selecting eyes (page 422), circling yourself in a group photo (page 169), or creating the ever-popular, oh-so-romantic, soft oval vignette shown in Figure 4-4.

Here's how to create a vignette:

1. **Open two images and combine them into one document.**

   Simply drag one image from its Layers panel into the other document's window, as described on page 103.

2. **Reposition the layers so the soon-to-be-vignetted photo is at the top of the Layers panel.**

   Over in the Layers panel, make sure that both layers are unlocked so you can change their stacking order. If you see a tiny padlock to the right of either layer's name, double-click that layer in the Layers panel to make it editable. Then drag the layer containing the photo you want to vignette (in Figure 4-4, that's the picture of the armadillo) to the top of the Layers panel.

3. **Grab the Elliptical Marquee tool and select the part of the image you want to vignette (here, it's the armadillo's head).**

   Peek at your Layers panel to make sure the correct photo layer is selected (the armadillo) and position your mouse near the center of the image. Press and hold the Option key (Alt on a PC), mouse over to the image, and drag to draw an oval-shaped selection from the inside out. When you've got the selection big enough, release the Option (or Alt) key and your mouse button.

The Softer Side of Selections

How come my selections always have a hard edge? Can I make them soft instead?

When you first install Photoshop, any selection you make has a hard edge, but you can apply *feathering* to blur its edges. Feathered selections are perfect for blending one image—or a portion of an image—into another, as in the soft oval vignette effect, an oldie but goody shown on page 133. You can also feather a selection when you retouch an image, so the retouched area fades gently into the surrounding pixels, making it look more realistic. This technique is especially helpful when you're whitening teeth (page 402), fixing animal white-eye (page 422), or swapping heads (page 166).

You can feather a selection, either before or after you've created it, in a variety of ways:

After you choose a selection tool from the Tools panel—but *before* you draw your selection—hop up to the Options bar and enter a Feather amount in pixels (you can enter whole numbers or decimals, like *0.5*). Feathering by just a few pixels will blur and soften the selection's edges only slightly, whereas increasing the Feather setting will create a wider, more intense blur and a super-soft edge.

After you draw the selection, you can change the Feather setting either by choosing Select → Modify → Feather and entering a number of pixels or by Ctrl-clicking (right-clicking on a PC) the selection and choosing Feather from the shortcut menu.

However, by far the best method is to use the Refine Edge dialog box, which lets you *see* what the feathered edge will look like before you commit to it. To use this method, draw a selection and then head up to the Options bar and click the Refine Edge button. The dialog box that appears has five preview buttons that show a loopy metallic ring. Click one of these buttons to put a temporary background behind your selection (making its edges more visible) and then adjust the Feather slider to your liking. Once you've got the feather just right, press OK to dismiss the dialog box.

It's worth noting that the settings in the Refine Edges dialog box are "sticky", meaning that once you change them, they stay changed until you modify them again. For that reason, you should set the other sliders to 0 to keep your selection from changing in unexpected ways. (Page 155 has more about the Refine Edge dialog box.)

You won't notice a change to your marching ants (unless you enter a *huge* amount of feathering on a rectangular selection, which makes the corners look rounded), but, rest assured, Photoshop has indeed feathered your selection. Once you delete the rest of the image (or hide it with a layer mask, as shown on page 105), you'll see the newly softened edges.

4. Feather the selection's edges by clicking the Refine Edge button in the Options bar.

In the resulting dialog box, make sure all the sliders are set to 0 and then drag the Feather slider to the right. If you want to see what the feathered edge will look like, release your mouse button and take a peek at your document—you'll see the newly softened edge against a temporary white background. If you want to preview the feather against a different background, click any of the other preview buttons toward the bottom of the Refine Edge dialog box. (Page 155 covers the Refine Edge dialog box in greater detail.) When it looks good, click OK to close the dialog box.

Figure 4-4:
By feathering a selection you've made with the Elliptical Marquee tool and adding a layer mask (page 105), you can create a quick two-photo collage like this one. Wedding photographers and moms—not to mention armadillo fans—love this kind of thing!

5. **Hide the area outside the selection with a layer mask.**

You *could* simply inverse the selection (page 126) and then press the Delete key (Backspace on a PC) to zap the area outside the selection, but that'd be mighty reckless. What if you changed your mind? You'd have to undo several steps or—curses—start over completely! A less destructive and more flexible approach, which you learned about back on page 105, is to *hide* the area outside the selection with a layer mask. Over in the Layers panel, make sure you have the correct layer selected (in this case, the armadillo) and then add a layer mask by clicking the tiny circle-within-a-square icon at the bottom of the Layers panel. Photoshop hides everything outside the selection area, letting you see through to the bluebonnet layer below. Beautiful!

You'll want to memorize these steps because this method is perhaps the easiest—and most romantic!—way to combine two images into a new and unique piece of art. That armadillo looks right at home, doesn't he?

The Single Row and Column Marquee Tools

The Marquee toolset also contains the Single Row Marquee and Single Column Marquee tools, which can select exactly one row or one column's worth of pixels, spanning either the width or the height of your document. (You don't need to drag with your mouse to create a selection with these tools. Just click once in your document and the marching ants appear.)

Now, you may be asking, "Why on earth would I want to do that?" Not often, it's true, but consider these circumstances:

- **Mocking up a Web page design.** If you need to simulate a column or row of space between certain areas in a Web page, you can use either tool to create a selection that you fill with the Web site's background color, or you can just delete the existing pixels by pressing the Delete key (Backspace on a PC).

- **Stretching an image to fill a space.** If you're designing a Web page, for example, you can use these tools to extend the image by a pixel or two. Use either tool to select a row of pixels at the bottom or side of the image, grab the Move tool by pressing V, and tap the arrow keys on your keyboard while holding the Option key (Alt on a PC) to nudge the selection in the direction you need and duplicate it at the same time.

- **Making an image look like it's melting or traveling through space at warp speed.** You can use either tool to create a selection and then stretch it with the Free Transform tool (see Figure 4-5).

The Vector Shape Tools

Okay, *technically*, vector shapes aren't selection tools at all, but you can use them to create selections (turn to page 509 to learn more about vector shapes). Perhaps the most useful of this bunch is the Rounded Rectangle tool.

If you ever need to select an area that's rectangular but has rounded corners, the Rounded Rectangle tool is your best bet. If you're creating an ad for a digital camera, say, you can use this technique in a product shot to swap the image shown on the camera's display screen with a different image. Or more practically, you can use it to give your photos rounded corners, as shown in Figure 4-6.

TIP   To cycle through all the Shape tools, press Shift-U repeatedly.

Here's how to round the corners of your photos:

1. **Open a photo and double-click the Background layer to make it editable.**

   Because you'll add a mask to the photo layer in step 6, you need to make sure the Background layer is unlocked or Photoshop won't let you add the mask.

Figure 4-5:
To achieve the melting strawberry look shown here, start by using the Single Row Marquee to select a row of pixels. Then "jump" the selection onto its own layer by pressing ⌘-J (Ctrl+J on a PC). Next, summon the Free Transform tool by pressing ⌘-T (Ctrl+T), and drag one of the square, white center handles downward.

2. Select the Rounded Rectangle tool (see Appendix E, online at *www. missingmanuals.com*) from the Tools panel.

   Near the bottom of the Tools panel, you'll find the Vector Shape toolset. Unless you've previously selected a different tool, you'll see the Rectangle tool's icon. Click the icon and hold down your mouse button until the pop-up menu appears and then choose the Rounded Rectangle tool.

3. In the Options bar, make sure that you've selected the "Shape layers" button and change the Radius field to 40 pixels.

   As you'll learn on page 496, the vector Shape tools can operate in various modes, which you set in the Options bar. For this particular technique, you need to make sure that the Rounded Rectangle tool is in "Shape layer" mode (the button looks like a square with a tiny dot on each corner; it's the second button from the left in the Options bar). Next, change the number in the Options bar's Radius field, which controls how rounded the image's corners will be: the lower the number, the less rounded; the higher the number, the more rounded. This field was set to 40 pixels to create the corners shown in Figure 4-6.

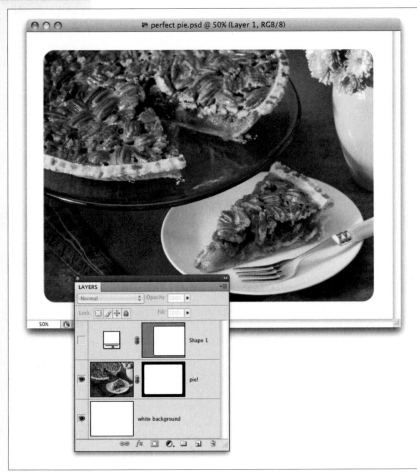

Figure 4-6:
If you're tired of boring, straight corners on your images, use the Rounded Rectangle tool to produce smooth corners like the ones shown here.

4. **Draw a box around the image.**

   Mouse over to your image and, starting in one corner, drag diagonally to draw a box around it. When you let go of the mouse button, Photoshop creates a new Shape layer containing the box, which appears over your image. Don't worry about what color the box is; you'll throw the box away as soon as you've loaded it as a selection. If you need to move the box, you can use the arrow keys on your keyboard or press V to grab the Move tool.

5. **Load the Shape layer as a selection.**

   Hop over to the Layers panel and load the new Shape layer as a selection by ⌘-clicking (Ctrl-clicking on a PC) its layer thumbnail (page 73). Photoshop selects the rectangle you just drew, which, it just so happens, has rounded corners. Once you see marching ants around the rectangle, you don't need the Shape layer anymore (and you certainly don't want it covering your photo). You can hide the Shape layer by turning off its visibility (page 78) or drag it to the tiny trash can icon at the bottom right of the Layers panel.

6. **Hide the area outside the selection by adding a layer mask.**

Over in the Layers panel, click the photo layer once to select it and then add a layer mask by clicking the tiny circle-within-a-square icon at the bottom of the Layers panel. When you do, Photoshop hides the old, boring square photo edges. Sweet!

Who knew that giving your photo rounded corners was so simple?

> **TIP** If you want rounded corners that fade into the background (like the vignette shown on page 133), use the Rectangular Marquee tool and then feather the selection you've drawn (page 132).

Selecting by Color

In addition to giving you the tools to select an area by shape, Photoshop lets you select an area by color. This option is helpful when you want to select a chunk of canvas with fairly uniform color, like someone's skin, the sky, or the paint job on a car. Photoshop has lots of tools to choose from, and in the next several pages, you'll learn how to pick the one that best suits your needs.

The Quick Selection Tool

The Quick Selection tool, which made its debut in Photoshop CS3, is the first new selection tool to grace the Tools panel in several versions of the program. This tool is shockingly easy to use and lets you create complex selections with a few strokes of an adjustable brush. As you paint with the Quick Selection tool, your selection expands outward to encompass pixels similar in color to the ones you're brushing across. It works insanely well if there's a fair amount of contrast between what you want to select and everything else. This tool lives in the same toolset as the Magic Wand (page 140), as you can see in Figure 4-7.

Figure 4-7:
When you activate the Quick Selection tool, the Options bar sports buttons that let you create a new selection and add to or subtract from the current selection.

> **TIP** You can press the W key to activate the Quick Selection tool. To switch between it and the Magic Wand, press Shift-W.

To use this wonderfully friendly tool, click anywhere in the area you want to select or *drag* the brush cursor across it, as shown in Figure 4-8. When you do that, Photoshop thinks for a second and then creates a selection based on the color of the pixels you brushed across. The size of the area Photoshop selects is proportional to the brush size you're using: a larger brush creates a larger selection, and a smaller brush creates a smaller selection. You can adjust the Quick Selection tool's brush size in the Option bar's Brush menu. (Chapter 12 covers brushes in detail.) For the best results, use a hard-edged brush to produce more defined edges (instead of the slightly transparent edges produced by a soft-edge brush; see page 463) and turn on the Auto-Enhance setting (shown in Figure 4-7 and discussed in the box on page 139).

Figure 4-8:
If the color of the objects you want to select differs greatly from the color of their background, like these chili peppers, take the Quick Selection tool for a spin. With this tool activated, you can either single-click the area you want to select or drag your cursor (circled) across the area as if you were painting. When the tool is in "Add to selection" mode, you see a tiny + sign inside it, as shown here. As you learned earlier in the chapter, this mode lets you add to an existing selection or make multiple selections.

When you activate the Quick Selection tool, the Options bar offers three modes (see Figure 4-7), just like the marquee tools (page 128):

- **New selection.** When you first grab the Quick Selection tool, it's automatically set to create a brand-new selection, which is helpful since creating a new selection is sort of the whole point.

- **Add to selection.** Once you've clicked or made an initial brushstroke, the Quick Selection tool automatically goes into "Add to selection" mode (indicated by the tiny + sign inside the cursor, as shown in Figure 4-8). Now Photoshop adds any additional brushstrokes or clicked areas to your current selection. If you don't like the selection Photoshop has created and want to start over, press ⌘-Z (Ctrl+Z on a PC) to undo it, or click the "New selection" button and then brush across the area again. (The old selection disappears as soon as you start to make a new one.) To get rid of the marching ants altogether, choose Select → Deselect.

- **Subtract from selection.** Adding to a selection can make Photoshop select more than you really want it to. If you have this problem, click the "Subtract from selection" button (a tiny – sign appears in your cursor). Simply paint across the area you *don't* want selected to make Photoshop exclude it.

> **NOTE**   To get the most out of the Quick Selection tool, you'll probably need to do a fair amount of adding to and subtracting from your selections. Keyboard shortcuts can help speed up the process: Press and hold the Shift key to enter "Add to selection" mode. Press and hold the Option key (Alt on a PC) to enter "Subtract from selection" mode. If these shortcuts sound familiar, they should—they're identical to the marquee tools' keyboard shortcuts.

- **Brush Size.** Use a larger brush to select big areas and a smaller brush to select small or hard-to-reach areas. As explained earlier, you'll get better results with this tool by using a hard-edged brush instead of a soft-edged one.

> **TIP**   In Photoshop CS4, you can change your brush size by dragging: press Ctrl-Option and drag to the left or right (right-click+Alt on a PC). In other versions of the program, you can decrease your brush size by pressing the left bracket key ([); increase it by pressing the right bracket key (]).

- **Sample All Layers.** This setting is initially turned off, which means Photoshop examines only the pixels in the active layer (the one that's selected in your Layers panel) and ignores pixels in any other. If you turn on this setting, Photoshop examines the whole enchilada—everything in your document—and grabs all similar pixels no matter which layer they're in.

- **Auto-Enhance.** Because the Quick Selection tool makes selections extremely fast, the selection's edges can end up looking blocky and imperfect. To tell Photoshop to take its time and think more carefully about the selections it makes, turn on the Options bar's Auto-Enhance checkbox. This feature gives your selections smoother edges, but if you're working with a really big file, you could do your taxes while it's processing. The box below has tips for using this feature.

WORKAROUND WORKSHOP

Smart Auto-Enhancing

The Quick Selection tool's Auto-Enhance feature is pretty spiffy, but it's a bit of a processing hog and you'll need a fast computer to use it on anything but the smallest images. If you have an older computer, you may have better luck using the Refine Edge dialog box (page 155) to create selections with smooth edges.

That being said, you don't have to avoid Auto-Enhance altogether. When you're working with a large file (anything over 5 MB), try leaving the Options bar's Auto-Enhance checkbox turned off until you're *almost* finished making the selection. When you've got just one or two brushstrokes left to complete your selection, turn on the checkbox to make Photoshop re-examine all the edges it's already created for your selection to see if it needs to extend them. That way, you get the benefit of using Auto-Enhance and keep your computer running quickly until the last possible moment.

The Magic Wand

The Magic Wand lets you select areas of color by clicking (you can't drag with it). It's in the same toolset as the Quick Selection tool, and you can grab it by pressing Shift-W (it looks like a wizard's wand, as shown back in Figure 4-7). Use the Magic Wand to select solid-colored backgrounds or large bodies of similar color, like a cloudless sky, with just a couple of clicks. The Quick Selection tool, in contrast, is better at selecting objects rather than big swaths of color.

When you click once with the Magic Wand in the area you want to select, Photoshop magically (hence the name) selects all the pixels on the currently selected layer that are both similar in color *and* touching one another (see page 141 to learn how to tweak this behavior). If the color in the area you want to select varies a bit, Photoshop may not select all of it. If that's the case, you can add to the selection by either pressing and holding the Shift key as you click nearby areas or by modifying the Magic Wand's *tolerance* in the Options bar as described later in this section and shown in Figure 4-9. To subtract from your selection, just press and hold the Option key (Alt on a PC) while you click the area you don't want included.

Figure 4-9:
With its tolerance set to 32, the Magic Wand did a good job of selecting the sky behind downtown Dallas. You've got several ways to select the spots it missed like the area circled at the bottom left: You can add to the selection by pressing the Shift key as you click in that area, increase the tolerance setting in the Options bar and then click the sky again to create a new selection, or skip to page 142 to learn how to expand your selection with the Grow and Similar commands.

When you activate the Magic Wand, the Options bar lets you adjust the following settings:

- **Tolerance.** This setting controls the Magic Wand's sensitivity—how picky the tool is about which pixels it considers similar in color. If you increase this setting, Photoshop gets less picky (in other words, more tolerant) and selects every pixel that could possibly be described as similar to the one you originally clicked. If you decrease this setting, Photoshop gets pickier and selects only pixels that closely match the original.

Out of the box, the tolerance is set to 32 though it can go all the way up to 255. (If you set it to 0, Photoshop selects only pixels that *exactly* match the one you clicked; if you set it to 255, the program selects every color in the image.) It's usually a good idea to keep the tolerance set fairly low (somewhere between 12 and 32); you can always click an area to see what kind of selection you get, increase the tolerance if you need to, and then click the area again (or add to the selection using the Shift key, as described above).

NOTE When you adjust the Magic Wand's tolerance, Photoshop won't automatically rethink your current selection. You have to click the area again to make Photoshop recalculate its selection.

- **Anti-alias.** Leave this setting turned on to make Photoshop soften the edges of your selection ever so slightly. If you want a super-crisp edge, turn it off.

- **Contiguous.** You'll probably want to leave this checkbox turned on; it makes the Magic Wand select pixels that are adjacent to one another. If you turn this setting off, Photoshop goes hog wild and selects all similar-colored pixels no matter where they are.

- **Sample all layers.** If your document has multiple layers and you leave this checkbox turned off, Photoshop examines only pixels on the active layer and ignores the pixels on other layers. If you turn this setting on, Photoshop examines the whole image and selects all pixels that are similar in color, no matter which layer they're on.

GEM IN THE ROUGH

Changing the Magic Wand's Sample Size

Did you know you can change the way the Magic Wand calculates which pixels to select? Of course, you didn't; that's because the setting that controls the Magic Wand's selections appears only when you have the *Eyedropper tool* selected. (Makes perfect sense, doesn't it?) You can read about the Eyedropper tool—see Appendix E, online at *www.missingmanuals.com*—but here's what you need to know about it to adjust how the Magic Wand works:

Over in the Tools panel, select the Eyedropper tool (its icon, not surprisingly, looks like an eyedropper; it lives beneath the Crop tool. When you do that, a Sample Size pop-up menu containing a slew of settings appears in the Options bar.

From the factory, the Sample Size menu is set to Point Sample, which makes the Magic Wand look only at the color of the pixel you clicked when determining its selection.

However, the menu's other options cause it to look at the original pixel *and* average it with the colors of surrounding pixels.

Depending on which option you choose, you can make the Magic Wand average the pixel you clicked plus the eight surrounding pixels (by choosing "3 by 3 Average") or the surrounding 10,200 pixels (by choosing "101 by 101 Average"). The "3 by 3 Average" setting works well for most images. If you need to select a really big area, you can experiment with one of the higher settings like "31 by 31 Average".

After you make your selection, simply activate the Magic Wand and then click somewhere in your image to see the effect of the new setting. It's that simple.

Who knew?

Expanding your selection

Sometimes the Magic Wand makes a *nearly* perfect selection, leaving you with precious few pixels to add to it. If this happens, it simply means that the elusive pixels are just a little bit lighter or darker in color than what the Magic Wand's tolerance setting allows for. You could Shift-click the elusive areas to add them to your selection, but the Select menu has a couple of options that can quickly expand the selection for you:

- **Grow.** Choose Select → Grow to make Photoshop expand your selection to all similar-colored pixels adjacent to the selection (see Figure 4-10, top).

- **Similar.** Choose Select → Similar to make Photoshop select similar-colored pixels throughout the *whole* image even if they're not touching the original selection (see Figure 4-10, bottom).

NOTE   Because both these commands base their calculations on the Magic Wand's tolerance setting (page 140), you can adjust their sensitivity by adjusting the Wand's tolerance setting in the Options bar. You also can run these commands more than once to get the selection you want.

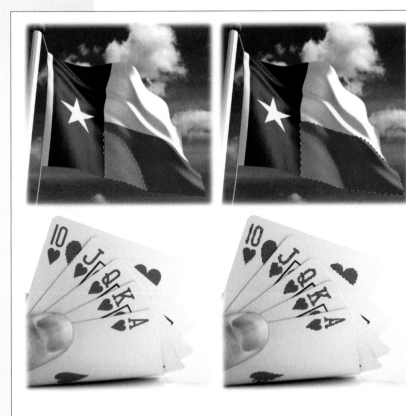

Figure 4-10:
Top: Say you're trying to select the red part of this Texas flag. After clicking once with the Magic Wand (with a tolerance of 32), you still need to select a bit more of the red (left). Since the red pixels are all touching each other, you can use the Grow command to expand your selection. After you've run this command a couple of times, Photoshop selects all the red (right).

Bottom: If you want to select the red in these playing cards (what a poker hand!), the Grow command won't help because the red pixels aren't touching each other—they're spread throughout the whole image. In this case, click once with the Magic Wand to select one of the red areas (left) and then use the Similar command to grab the rest of them (right). Read 'em and weep, boys!

Selecting the Opposite

You'll often find it easier to select what you *don't* want in order to get the selection you really *do* want. For example, look back at the photo of the Dallas skyline shown in Figure 4-9 (page 140). If you want to select the buildings, it's easier to select the sky because its color is practically uniform. (It'd take you a lot longer to select the buildings because they're irregular in shape and vary so much in color.)

After grabbing the sky, you can inverse (flip-flop) your selection to select the buildings instead. Simply choose Select → Inverse or press Shift-⌘-I (Shift+Ctrl+I on a PC).

The lesson here is that it pays to spend a few moments studying the area you want to select, as well as the area *around* it. If the color of the surrounding area is uniform, reach for one of the tools described in this section and then inverse your selection. It can save you tons of time!

The Color Range Command

The Color Range command is similar to the other tools in that it makes selections based on the colors you pick, but it's much better at selecting areas that contain a lot of details (for example, the flower bunches in Figure 4-11). The Magic Wand tends to select *whole* pixels, whereas Color Range is more fine-tuned and tends to select more partial pixels than whole ones. This fine-tuning lets Color Range produce selections with smoother edges (less blocky and jagged than the ones you get with the Magic Wand) and get in more tightly around areas with lots of details. As a bonus, you also get a handy preview in the Color Range dialog box, showing you which pixels it'll select before you commit to the selection (unlike the Grow and Similar commands discussed earlier in this section).

Open the Color Range dialog box by choosing Select → Color Range, either before or after you make a selection. If you already have a selection, Color Range looks only at the pixels within the selected area, which is helpful if you want to isolate a certain area. For example, you could throw a quick selection oval (page 127) around the red flower shown in the center of Figure 4-11 and use Color Range's subtract from selection capabilities (explained later in this section) to carve out just the red petals. By contrast, if you want to use Color Range to help expand your selection, press and hold the Shift key while you choose Select → Color Range. If you haven't yet made a selection, Color Range examines your entire image.

Use the Select pop-up menu at the top of the Color Range dialog box to tell Photoshop which colors to include in your selection. The menu is automatically set to Sampled Colors, which lets you mouse over to your image (your cursor turns into a tiny eyedropper; see Figure 4-11) and click the color you want to select. If you change the Select menu's setting to Reds, Blues, Greens, or whatever, Color Range will examine your image and grab that range of colors all by itself—once you click OK.

Figure 4-11:
The Color Range command is handy when you need to select an area with a lot of details, like the red and blue petals of these flowers. The image in the dialog box's preview area shows the part that Photoshop will select when you click the OK button.

NOTE   As mentioned in the box on page 143, it's sometimes easier to select what you *don't* want in order to select what you need. In the Color Range dialog box, you can select what you don't want by turning on the Invert checkbox.

If you're trying to select adjacent pixels, turn on Localized Color Clusters. You can tweak the area Color Range selects by adjusting its Fuzziness setting. Its factory setting is 40, but you can change this number to anything between 0 and 200. If you increase it, Photoshop includes more colors and makes larger selections. If you lower it, Photoshop creates a smaller selection because it gets pickier about matching colors. As you move the Fuzziness slider (or type a number in the text box), keep an eye on the dialog box's preview area—all the parts of the image that Photoshop will include in your selection appear white (see Figure 4-11).

Use the eyedroppers on the right side of the dialog box to add or subtract colors from your selection. Like the other selection tools discussed so far, the eyedropper with the tiny + sign adds to your selection and the one with the – sign subtracts from it. (Use the plain eyedropper to make your initial selection.) When you click one of the eyedroppers, mouse over to your document, and click the color you want to add or subtract, Photoshop updates the Color Range dialog box's preview area to show what the new selection looks like. It sometimes helps to keep the Fuzziness setting fairly low (around 50 or so) while you click repeatedly with the eyedropper.

TIP You can use the radio buttons beneath the Color Range dialog box's preview area to see either the selection area (which appears white) or the image itself. But there's a better, faster way to switch between the two views: With Selection turned on, press the ⌘ key (Ctrl on a PC) to switch temporarily to Image preview. When you let go of the key, you're back to Selection preview.

The Selection Preview pop-up menu at the bottom of the dialog box lets you display a selection preview on the image itself. In other words, instead of using the dinky preview in the dialog box, you can see your proposed selection right on your image. But you'll probably want to leave this menu set to None because the preview options that Photoshop offers (Grayscale, Black Matte, White Matte, and so on) get really distracting!

The Background and Magic Erasers

The two erasers covered here let you erase parts of your image based on the color you touch with your cursor. You're probably thinking, "Hey, I want to create a selection, not go around erasing stuff!" And you'd have a valid point except that, after you've done a little erasing, you can always *load* that area as a selection. All you have to do is think ahead and create a duplicate layer before you start erasing, as this section explains.

Say you have an image with a decent amount of contrast between the item you want to keep and its background (like a dead tree against the sky). In that case, Photoshop has a couple of eraser tools that can help you erase the sky super fast (see Figure 4-12). Sure, you could use the Magic Wand or Quick Selection tool to select the sky and then delete or mask it (page 105), but using the Background Eraser lets you erase more carefully around the edges and then add a layer mask to hide the rest of it.

Figure 4-12:
You may never see these tools because they're hidden inside the same toolset as the regular Eraser tool. Just click and hold the Eraser tool until the little pop-up menu appears. Pick an eraser based on how you want to use it: You drag to erase with the Background Eraser (as if you were painting, which is great for getting around the edges of an object), whereas you simply click with the Magic Eraser.

TIP The keyboard shortcut for activating the Eraser tool is the E key. To switch among the various eraser tools, press Shift-E repeatedly.

The Background Eraser

This tool lets you delete an image's background by painting (dragging) across the pixels you want to delete. When you activate the Background Eraser by choosing it from the Tools panel, your cursor turns into a circle with a tiny crosshair in its center. This crosshair controls which pixels Photoshop deletes, so be extra careful and let it touch only the pixels you want to erase. Up in the Options bar, you can tweak the following settings for this tool (see Figure 4-13):

- **Brush Preset Picker.** This is where you choose the shape and size of your brush. For best results, stick with a soft-edge brush. Just click the down-pointing triangle next to the Brush Preset Picker to grab one.

- **Sampling.** Made up of three buttons whose icons all include eyedroppers, this setting controls how often Photoshop looks at the color the crosshair is touching to decide what to erase. If your background has a lot of color variations, leave this set to Continuous so Photoshop keeps a constant watch on what-which color pixels the crosshair is touching. However, if the color of background you're erasing is fairly uniform, you can change this setting to Once; Photoshop then checks the color the crosshair touches just once and resolves to erase only pixels that closely match it. If you're dealing with an image with only a small area for you to paint (like a tiny portion of sky showing through a lush tree), you can change this setting to Background Swatch, which instructs Photoshop to erase only the color of your current background color chip. To choose the color, click the background color chip at the bottom of your Tools panel (page 22), mouse over to your image, and then click an area whose color is similar to the color you want to erase.

- **Limits.** When you first launch Photoshop, you'll find Limits set to Contiguous, which means you can erase only pixels adjacent to those that you touch with the crosshair. If you want to erase similar-colored pixels elsewhere in your image (for example, the background behind a really thick tree or a bunch of flowers), change the setting to Discontiguous.

- **Tolerance.** This setting works just like the Magic Wand's Tolerance setting (page 140): Choosing a lower number makes the tool pickier about the pixels it selects, whereas a higher number makes it less picky.

- **Protect Foreground Color.** If you can't seem to get the Tolerance setting high enough and you're still erasing some of the area you want to keep, turning on this setting can help. When it's on, you can tell Photoshop which area you want to keep (the foreground) by Option-clicking (Alt-clicking on a PC) in that area. If the area you want to keep is a different color in different parts of your image, you can turn this setting off or Option-click (Alt-click) to resample the foreground area.

Here's how to use the Background Eraser to erase the sky behind a dead tree without harming the original pixels, as shown in Figure 4-13:

TIP If you want to practice erasing this background, you can download DeadTree.jpg from the Missing CD page at *www.missingmanuals.com*.

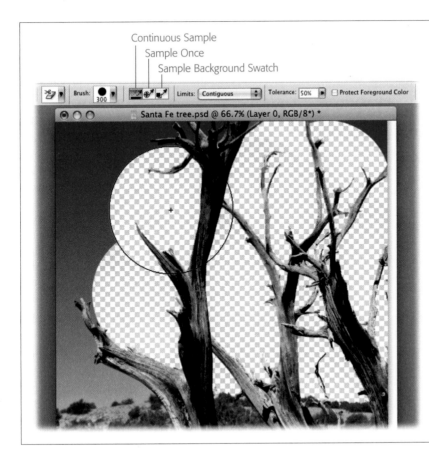

Continuous Sample
Sample Once
Sample Background Swatch

Figure 4-13:
Even though the Background Eraser is destructive because it erases pixels, you can use it in a nondestructive way by remembering to duplicate the soon-to-be-erased layer first. Then load the erased layer as a selection and use it as a layer mask on the original layer.

As you can see here, Photoshop pays attention only to the color you touch with the crosshair in the center of the brush. Even though the tree's branches are within the brush area (the circle), Photoshop deletes only the blue pixels.

1. **Open a photo and double-click its Background layer to make it editable (page 80) and then duplicate the Background by pressing ⌘-J (Ctrl+J on a PC).**

   Since you'll add a layer mask to the original layer in the last step of this list, you need to unlock the Background to make it editable. And because you'll do your erasing on the duplicate layer, you don't need to see the original layer. Over in your Layers panel, click the little visibility eye to the left of the original layer's thumbnail to turn it off.

2. **Grab the Background Eraser tool and paint away the background.**

   The Background Eraser tool is part of the same toolset as the Eraser tool (see Figure 4-12). Once you've activated it, mouse over to your document and your cursor morphs into a circle with a tiny crosshair in the center. Remember that the trick is to let the crosshair touch *only* the pixels you want to erase (it doesn't matter what the circle part of the cursor touches, as Figure 4-13 shows). If you need to, you can increase and decrease your brush size by pressing the left and right bracket keys on your keyboard, respectively.

3. **If the tool is erasing too much or too little of your image, tweak the Tolerance setting in the Options bar (also shown in Figure 4-13).**

   If an area in your image is *almost* the same color as the background, lower the tolerance to make the tool pickier about the colors it's erasing; that way, it erases only pixels that closely match the ones you touch with the crosshair. Likewise, if it's not erasing enough of the background, raise the tolerance to make it less picky about the pixels it zaps.

   TIP It's better to erase small sections at a time instead of painting around the entire object in one continuous stroke. Hold your mouse button to erase a bit of the area around the object, let go of the button, click it again to erase a little more, and so on. That way, if you need to undo your erasing using the History panel (page 25) or the Undo command (⌘-Z; Ctrl+Z on a PC), you won't have to watch all that erasing unravel before your eyes.

4. **Once you get a clean outline around the object, switch to the regular Eraser tool (see Appendix E, online at *www.missingmanuals.com*) or the Lasso tool (page 151) to get rid of the remaining background.**

   After you erase the hard part—the area around the edges—with the Background Eraser, you can use the regular Eraser tool, set to a large brush, to get rid of the remaining background quickly. You can also use the Lasso tool to select the remaining areas and then press the Delete key (Backspace on a PC) to get rid of them.

5. **Load the erased layer as a selection and turn off its visibility.**

   Over in your Layers panel, ⌘-click (Ctrl-click on a PC) the thumbnail of the layer you did the erasing work on to create a selection around the tree. When you see the marching ants, click the layer's visibility eye to turn it off.

6. **Select the original layer, turn on its visibility, and then put a layer mask over it.**

   In the Layers panel, click once to select the original layer (the unlocked Background) and then click the area to the left of its thumbnail to make it visible again. While you have marching ants running around the newly erased area, add a layer mask (page 106) to the original layer by clicking the circle-within-a-square icon at the bottom of the Layers panel.

7. **You're basically done at this point. But if you need to do any cleanup work (if the Background Eraser didn't do a perfect job getting around the edges, say), now's the time to edit the layer mask.**

   To edit the mask, click its layer thumbnail over in the Layers panel. Then press B to grab the Brush tool and set your foreground color chip to black (page 22). Now, when you brush across your image, you'll hide more of the sky. If you need to reveal more of the tree, set your foreground color chip to white, and then paint the area you want to reveal. (See page 105 for a detailed discussion of creating and editing layer masks.)

Sure, duplicating the layer you're erasing takes an extra step, but that way you're not deleting any pixels—you're just hiding them with a layer mask, so you can get them back if you want to. How cool is that?

WORKAROUND WORKSHOP

The Missing Extract Filter

Ever heard the expression, "Out with the old and in with the new"? Well, that's sort of what happened to the Extract filter, which used to be one of the easiest-to-use background zappers in the program. While it's possible that Photoshop may reincorporate the Extract filter in the future, it's gone for now. Fortunately, you've got a couple of different ways to get the old Extract filter back *into* Photoshop CS4.

Getting the filter back is a worthwhile endeavor because unless you spring for one of the third-party masking plug-ins mentioned in Chapter 19, you'll have one heck of a time deleting backgrounds behind fur or hair. Once you've got it installed (as described in a sec), choose Filter → Extract. In the resulting dialog box, use the Edge Highlighter (it's automatically selected) to mark the edges of the item you want to isolate. Just place your cursor half on and half off the object's edge and then trace all the way around the object (a nice, green outline appears). Be careful to surround the area you want to keep completely with the Edge Highlighter.

Next, switch to the Fill tool at the top left of the dialog box (it looks like a paint bucket) and click within the area you want to keep (it will turn purple). When you click the Preview button, Photoshop analyzes the edge you've marked and throws away the background. If you're satisfied with the results, click OK to exit the dialog box. If you're not, use the Cleanup tool (also on the left side of

the dialog box) to fine-tune the edges or Option-click (Alt-click on a PC) the Cancel button (it turns into a Reset button).

This filter is destructive, meaning that Photoshop gets rid of the deleted areas for good. The fix is to duplicate the original layer by pressing ⌘-J (Ctrl+J on a PC) and then run the filter on the copy. When the filter has finished processing, load the duplicate layer as a selection and then add a layer mask to the original layer (just like you did with the Background Eraser on page 145). That way, you can edit the mask if you need to clean up any of the edges.

You've got two ways to get the Extract filter into Photoshop CS4. It's available as a download that you can find by choosing Filter → Browse Filters Online and searching for Extract Filter. Or, if you own Photoshop CS3, you can drag and drop it from the older version of the program into the new one. Quit Photoshop and locate the Adobe Photoshop CS3 application folder on your hard drive and then find the Filters → *ExtractPlus.plugin* file (it's named *ExtractPlus.8BF* on a PC). Drag it to the Filters folder inside the Adobe Photoshop CS4 folder on your hard drive and then launch Photoshop CS4. You should see the Extract filter in the Filter menu from now on.

If you don't want to go this route, take a peek at Chapter 19, which mentions other masking plug-ins.

The Magic Eraser

This tool works just like the Background Eraser except that, instead of a brush cursor that you paint with, you get a cursor that looks like a cross between the Eraser tool and the Magic Wand. Just as the Magic Wand can select color with a single click, the Magic Eraser can *zap* color with a single click (it's great for erasing big areas of solid color instantly). Since this tool is an eraser, it really will delete pixels, so you'll want to duplicate your Background layer before using it.

You can alter the Magic Eraser's behavior by adjusting these settings in the Options bar:

- **Anti-alias.** The Anti-alias checkbox works the same way as in the other selection tools described in this chapter: Turning it on makes Photoshop slightly soften the edges of your selection.

- **Contiguous.** If you want to erase pixels that touch each other, leave this checkbox turned on. If you want to erase similar-colored pixels no matter where they are in your image, turn this checkbox off.

- **Sample All Layers.** If you have a multi-layer document, you can turn on this checkbox to make Photoshop look at the pixels on all the layers instead of just the active layer.

- **Opacity.** If you want to control how strong the Magic Eraser is, you can enter that value (as a percent) here. For example, entering *50* makes it wipe away 50 percent of the image's opacity, entering *100* removes the image entirely, and so on.

WORKAROUND WORKSHOP

Erasing Every Bit of Background

Now that you know how to use the Background and Magic Erasers, keep in mind that you can't always believe what you see onscreen. Most of the time, you'll use these tools to erase to a transparent (checkerboard) background like the one shown in Figure 4-13. And while it may *appear* that you've erased all the background, you may not have. The checkerboard background is notorious for making it hard to see if you've missed a pixel or two here and there. If the background you're trying to delete is white or gray (like clouds), stray pixels will be especially tough to see.

Fortunately, it's easy to overcome this checkered obstacle. The next time you're ready to use one of these eraser tools, first create a new layer filled with a bright color that contrasts with what you're trying to delete and then place it at the bottom of the layers stack. That way, you can see whether you've erased everything you wanted to.

To create a new layer filled with color, click the New Layer icon at the bottom of the Layers panel (it looks like a piece of paper with its lower-left corner upturned; see page 76). Then choose Edit → Fill, click the Use pop-up menu, and choose Color. Select a bright color from the resulting Color Picker and then press OK twice to exit the dialog boxes. Finally, drag the new layer beneath the layer you're erasing, and you're good to go. (See Chapter 3 for more on creating layers and filling them with color.)

Selecting Irregular Areas

As you might imagine, areas that aren't uniform in shape *or* color can be a real bear to select. Luckily, Photoshop has a few tools in its arsenal to help you get the job done as easily as possible. In this section, you'll learn about the three lassos and the Pen tool, as well as a few ways to use the various tools together to select hard-to-grab areas.

Using the Lasso Tools

The Lasso toolset contains three freeform tools that let you draw an outline around the area you want to select. If you've got an amazingly steady mouse hand or if you use a graphics tablet (see the box on page 477), you may fall in love with the plain ol' Lasso tool. If you're trying to select an object with a lot of straight edges, the Polygonal Lasso tool will do you proud. And the Magnetic Lasso tries to create the selection *for* you by examining the color of the pixels your cursor is hovering above. The following sections explain all three lassos, which live under the same icon at the top of the Tools panel (see Figure 4-14).

Figure 4-14:
So many lassos, so little time! The regular Lasso tool is great for drawing a selection freehand, the Polygonal Lasso is good for drawing selections around shapes that have a lot of straight lines, and the Magnetic Lasso is like an automatic version of the regular Lasso—it tries to make the selection for you.

Lasso tool

The regular Lasso tool lets you draw a selection completely freeform as if you were drawing with a pencil. To activate this tool, simply click it in the Tools panel (its icon looks like a tiny lasso—no surprise there) or press the L key. Then just click your document where you want the selection to start and drag to create a selection. Once you stop drawing and release your mouse button, Photoshop automatically completes the selection with a straight line (that is, if you don't complete it yourself by mousing over your starting point) and you see marching ants.

> **TIP**   It's nearly impossible to draw a straight line with the Lasso tool, unless you've got the steady hand of a surgeon. But if you press and hold the Option key (Alt on a PC) and then release your mouse button, you'll temporarily switch to the Polygonal Lasso tool so you can draw a straight line (see the next section). When you release the Option (Alt) key, Photoshop will complete your selection with a straight line.

The Options bar (shown in Figure 4-14) sports the same settings whether you have the Lasso tool or the Polygonal Lasso tool active. Here's what you've got:

- **Mode.** These four buttons (whose icons look like pieces of paper) let you choose among the same modes you get for most of the selection tools: New, "Add to selection", "Subtract from selection", and "Intersect with selection". They're discussed in more detail back on page 128.

- **Feather.** If you want Photoshop to blur the edges of your selection, enter a pixel value in this field. Otherwise, Photoshop won't do any feathering. (See the box on page 132 for more on feathering.)

- **Anti-alias.** If you leave this setting turned on, Photoshop slightly softens the edges of your selection, making them less jagged—page 129 has the details.

Polygonal Lasso tool

If your image has a lot of straight lines in it (like the star in Figure 4-15), the Polygonal Lasso tool is your ticket. Instead of letting you draw a selection that's any shape at all, the Polygonal Lasso draws only straight lines. To use it, click once to set the starting point and move your cursor along the shape of the item you want to select; click again where the angle changes. Simply repeat this process until you've outlined the whole shape. It's super simple to use, as Figure 4-15 illustrates. To close your selection, hover above the first point you created. When you see a tiny circle appear below your cursor (it looks like a degree symbol), click once to close the selection and summon the marching ants.

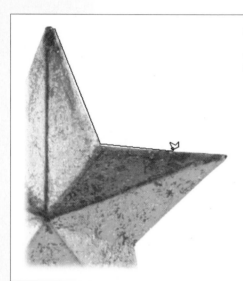

Figure 4-15:
The Polygonal Lasso tool is perfect for selecting geometric shapes and areas that have a lot of angles. However, if you want to temporarily switch to the regular Lasso tool, press and hold Option (Alt on a PC) to draw freehand.

TIP   If you want to bail out of a selection you've started to draw with the Polygonal or Magnetic Lasso tools, just press the Esc key.

Magnetic Lasso tool

This tool has all the power of the other Lasso tools, except that it's smart—or at least it tries to be! Click once to set a starting point, and from there the Magnetic Lasso tries to *guess* what you want to select by examining the colors of the pixels your cursor's hovering above (you don't even need to hold your mouse button down). As you move your cursor over the edges you want to select, it sets additional *anchor points* for you (think of anchor points as fastening points that latch onto the path you're tracing; they look like tiny, square, see-through boxes). To close the selection, hover above your starting point. When a tiny circle appears below your cursor, click once to close the selection and summon the marching ants (or you can close the selection with a straight line by triple-clicking).

As you might imagine, the Magnetic Lasso tool works best when there's a lot of contrast between the item you want to select and the area around it (see Figure 4-16). However, if you reach an area that doesn't have much contrast—or if you reach a sharp corner—you can give the tool a little nudge by clicking to set a few anchor points of your own. If it goes astray and sets an erroneous anchor point, just hover over the bad point with your mouse and press the Delete key (Backspace on a PC). Then move back to the troubled area of your selection and click to set more anchor points until you reach an area of greater contrast where the tool can be trusted to set its own points.

Starting point   Anchor   Cursor   Use tablet pressure
                  points   to change pen width

iStock_000004167025Medium.jpg @ 50% (RGB/8*)

Figure 4-16:
If you're trying to select an object on a white or other plain, high-contrast background, the Magnetic Lasso works great because it can easily find the edge of the object. For best results, glide your cursor slowly around the edge of the item you want to select (you don't need to hold your mouse button down).

If you want to draw a straight line, you can temporarily switch to the Polygonal Lasso tool. Just Option-click (Alt-click on a PC) where you want the line to start, click where you want it to end, and then switch back to the Magnetic Lasso. Then you're free to continue gliding around the rest of the object's jagged edges as you did before.

TIP   If you're not crazy about the Magnetic Lasso's cursor (which looks like a triangle and a horseshoe magnet), press the Caps Lock key and it'll change to a brush cursor with a crosshair at its center. Press Caps Lock again to switch back to the standard cursor.

You can get better results with this tool by adjusting the Options bar's settings (see Figure 4-16). Besides the usual suspects like selection modes, Feather, and anti-alias settings (all discussed on page 128), the Magnetic Lasso also lets you adjust the following:

- **Width** determines how close your cursor needs to be to an edge for the Magnetic Lasso to select it. Out of the box, this field is set to 10 px, but you can enter a value between 1 and 256. You'll want to use a lower number when you're trying to select an area whose edge has a lot of twists and turns and a higher number when you're selecting an area with fairly smooth edges. (To select the yellow rose in Figure 4-16, you'd use a higher setting around the petals and a lower setting around the leaves because they're so jagged.)

  TIP   You can change the Width setting as you're drawing with the Magnetic Lasso by pressing the open and close bracket keys. Press Shift-[to set the width to 1 and Shift-] to set it to 256.

- **Contrast** controls how much color difference between neighboring pixels the Magnetic Lasso needs before it recognizes an edge. You can try increasing this percentage when you want to select an edge that isn't well defined, but you might have better luck with a different selection tool.

- **Frequency** determines how many anchor points the tool lays down. If you're selecting an area with lots of details, you'll need more anchor points, whereas smooth areas don't require as many. Setting this field to 0 makes Photoshop add very few points, and 100 makes it have a point party. The factory setting—57—will probably suit you just fine.

- **Use tablet pressure to change pen width.** If you're using a pressure-sensitive graphics tablet, turning on this setting—whose button looks like a pen tip with circles around it—lets you override the Width setting by pressing harder or softer on your tablet with the stylus. (Flip to the box on page 477 to learn about graphics tablets.)

Selecting with the Pen Tool

Another great way to select an irregular object or area is to trace its outline with the Pen tool. Technically, you're not drawing a selection; you're drawing a *path* (page 497), which you can then *load* as a selection (page 521).

This method requires quite a bit of skill because the Pen tool isn't your average, everyday, well...*pen*, but it will produce the smoothest-edged selections this side of the Rio Grande. Head on over to Chapter 13 to read all about it.

Creating Selections with Channels

As you'll learn in Chapter 5, the images you see on your screen are made up of various colors. In Photoshop, each color is stored in its own *channel* (which is kind of like a layer) that you can view and manipulate.

If the object or area you're trying to select is one that you can isolate in a channel, you can load that channel as a selection with a click of your mouse. Chapter 5 discusses this incredibly useful technique in detail, starting on page 190.

Using the Tools Together

As wonderful as the aforementioned selection tools are *individually*, they're much more powerful if you learn to use them *together*. In fact, you'll find that making selections becomes a lot easier if you get used to a little tool collaboration.

Remember that every tool discussed so far has an "Add to selection" and "Subtract from selection" mode? This means that, no matter which tool you start with, you can add to—or take away from—the active selection with a completely different tool. Check out Figure 4-17, which gives you a couple of ideas for using the selection tools together. And thanks to the new spring-loaded tools feature (see the tip on page 23), switching between tools has never been easier.

Modifying Selections

As you've learned in the previous pages, some tools are better at making certain types of selections than others. However, no matter which tool (or tools) you use, your selection will probably need some fine-tuning. Photoshop gives you lots of ways to modify, reshape, and even save your selections, all explained in the following pages. But before you do any of those things, you'll likely want to fine-tune your selection's *edges*. The difference between a pretty-good-around-the-edges selection and a perfect one is what separates Photoshop pros from mere dabblers. Read on to learn some simple edge-polishing techniques.

Refining Edges

The newest selection modifier in town is the Refine Edge dialog box (Figure 4-18), which made its debut in Photoshop CS3. It combines several edge-adjustment tools that were scattered around on different menus in previous versions of the program into one spot and includes an extremely handy preview area. Anytime you have a selection tool active and a set of marching ants on your screen, you'll see the Refine Edge button sitting pretty up in the Options bar; simply click it to open the dialog box. You can also open it by choosing Select → Refine Edge or use its keyboard shortcut ⌘-Option-R (Ctrl+Alt+R on a PC).

> **NOTE**   In Photoshop CS4 you can access Refine Edge through the new Adjustments panel (page 302).

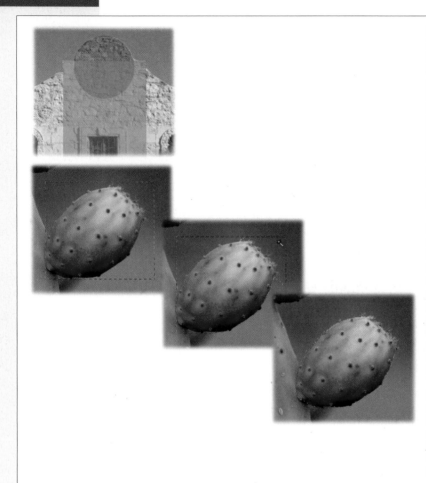

Figure 4-17:
Top: It's worth taking a moment to try to see the shapes that make up the area you want to select. For example, you can select the circular top of this famous Texas building using the Elliptical Marquee (shown in red), and then switching to the Rectangular Marquee (shown in green) set to "Add to selection" mode.

Bottom: Another way to use the selection tools together is to draw a rectangular selection around the object you want to select (like this prickly pear), and then switch to the Magic Wand to subtract the areas you don't want. While holding down the Option key (Alt on a PC) so you're in "Subtract from selection" mode, click the areas you don't want included in your selection, like this grayish background. With just a couple of clicks, you can select the prickly pear.

In the dialog box, you can tweak the following settings (and for best results, Adobe suggests you adjust them in this order):

- **Radius.** This setting controls the size of the area affected by the settings in this dialog box, or rather how far beyond the edge of your selection the edge polishing happens. You might find it helpful to think of this setting as the selection edge's degree of difficulty. For example, if your selection is really complex and has a lot of details (like hair or fur) or areas of softness (like shadows), increase this setting to polish edges that extend beyond the selection boundary (which also results in a slight softening of the selection edge). If your selection is fairly simple, lower this setting so the polishing takes place only around the selection boundary.

Figure 4-18:
The Refine Edge dialog box made quite a splash in Photoshop CS3. It lets you—for the first time ever in Photoshop—see a live, continuously updated preview of what your selection will look like after fine-tuning it in various ways.

If you forget what the dialog box's settings do, Photoshop is happy to provide a quick reminder. Just click the little triangle to the left of the word Description (circled), and as you hover above each setting, an explanation of what it does appears at the bottom of the dialog box.

- **Contrast.** This setting sharpens your selection's edge, even if you softened it by increasing the Radius as mentioned above. A higher number will create a sharper edge and can actually reduce the noisy or grainy look that sometimes comes from a high Radius setting.

- **Smooth.** Increasing this setting makes Photoshop smooth the selection's edges so they're less jagged. But if you increase it too much, you risk losing details (especially on selections of hair and the like). To bring back some details without decreasing this setting, try increasing the Radius and Contrast settings.

- **Feather.** This setting controls how much Photoshop blurs the edges of your selection, which is useful when you're combining images, as discussed in the box page 132.

- **Contract/Expand.** Moving this slider makes your selection smaller or larger. Contracting your selection (moving the slider to the left) can help reduce *edge halos*, leftover pixels around the edges of selections that you see only after you put the object on a new background (see the figure on page 159). Expanding your selection (moving the slider to the right) can help grab extra pixels you may have missed when you made the selection.

For your viewing pleasure, the dialog box also gives you five different ways to preview your altered selection. Because the preview itself happens in the main document window, you'll want to move the Refine Edge dialog box aside so it's not covering your image. Depending on the colors in your image, one of these backgrounds will let you see the selection better than the rest:

- **Standard.** This option just shows the selection on the image itself.

   TIP   You can cycle through the preview modes by pressing the F key repeatedly. To preview the changes you've made in this dialog box, be sure that the Preview option is turned on (you can press P to toggle it off and on). To see your original image temporarily, press the X key.

- **Quick Mask.** As the name indicates, this option displays your selection overlaid with the Quick Mask (see page 162). Unless you've changed its color, the overlay will be light red; to change that color, see the box on page 167.

- **On Black.** This option displays the selection on a black background, which is helpful if your image is light colored and doesn't have a lot of black in it.

- **On White.** Choose this option if your image is mostly dark. The stark white background makes it easy to see your selection.

- **Mask.** This option displays your selection as an *alpha channel* (page 185). Photoshop shows your selection in white and the mask in black; transitions between the two areas are gray.

Fixing Edge Halos

When you're making selections, you may encounter *edge halos* (also called *fringing* or *matting*). An edge halo is a tiny portion of the background that stubbornly remains even after you try to delete it (or hide it with a layer mask, page 105). They usually show up after you replace the old background with something new (see Figure 4-19). This aggravatingly tiny rim of color—a sure sign that an image has done time in Photoshop—can be your undoing when it comes to creating realistic images. Edge halos make a new sky look fake and don't help convince anyone that Elvis actually came to your cookout.

Here are a few ways to fix edge halos:

- **Contract your selection.** Use the Refine Edge dialog box (page 155) or choose Select → Modify → Contract (though the latter method won't give you a preview) to contract your selection. Use this technique while you still have marching ants—before you delete the old background (or, better yet, hide the background with a layer mask [page 105]).

- **Run the Minimum filter on a layer mask.** Once you've hidden an image's background with a layer mask, you can run the Minimum filter on the mask to tighten the mask around the object. Page 609 explains this super-useful trick.

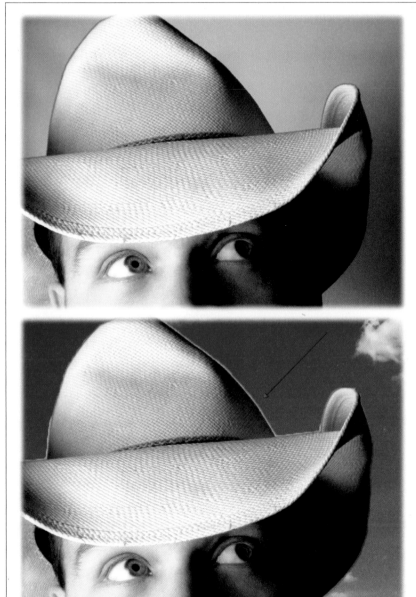

Figure 4-19:
Here you can see the intrepid cowboy on his original green background (top) and on the new background (bottom). The green pixels stubbornly clinging to his hat are an edge halo.

- **Use the Defringe command.** Run this command after you delete the background (alas, it doesn't work on layer masks or while a selection is active). Choose Layer → Matting → Defringe and then enter a value in pixels. Photoshop analyzes the active layer and deletes that many pixels from around the edge of the object. For example, if you enter *2 px*, it'll delete a 2-pixel rim all the way around the object.

- **Remove Black/White Matting.** If Photoshop has blessed you with a halo that's either black or white, you can make the program try to remove it automatically. After you've deleted the background, make sure you've selected the offending layer and then choose Layer → Matting → Remove Black Matte or Remove White Matte. (Like Defringe, this command doesn't work on layer masks or while you have an active selection.)

Creating a Border Selection

If you peek at the Select → Modify menu, you'll find the same options as in the Refine Edge dialog box (but without a preview). There is, however, one addition: the Border option, which lets you turn a solid selection into a hollow one.

Let's say you drew a circular selection with the Elliptical Marquee. You can turn that selection into a ring by choosing the Border option (which is handy if you want to make a neon sign or select the outer rim of an object). Just enter a pixel width, press OK, and poof! Your formerly solid selection is now as hollow as can be, like the one shown in Figure 4-20.

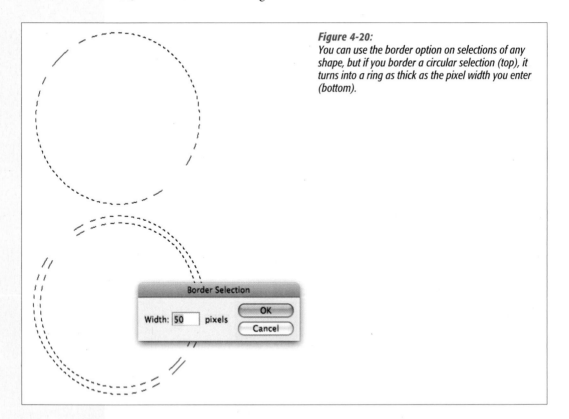

Figure 4-20:
You can use the border option on selections of any shape, but if you border a circular selection (top), it turns into a ring as thick as the pixel width you enter (bottom).

Transforming a Selection

Have you ever tried to make a slanted rectangular selection like the one shown at right in Figure 4-21? If so, you may have found the experience a little frustrating. Sure, you can try using one of the Lasso tools, but it's quicker to *transform*—meaning reshape—a rectangular selection instead. (Page 245 in Chapter 6 has more about Photoshop's Transform tools.)

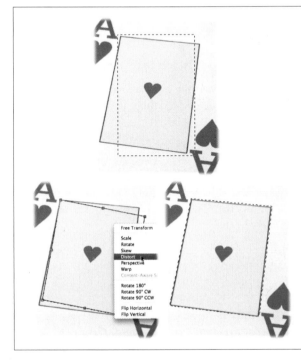

Figure 4-21:
Top: You can easily select the center part of this playing card with the Rectangular Marquee tool (page 127). Once you see marching ants, choose Select → Transform Selection and rotate the resulting bounding box to get the angle you need.

Bottom Left: Next, Ctrl-click (right-click on a PC) inside the bounding box and choose Distort from the shortcut menu, as shown here. Then drag each corner handle so it meets up with a corner of the yellow box on the card.

Bottom Right: When you're all finished, press Return (Enter on a PC) to accept the transformation.

NOTE When you transform a selection (as opposed to part of your image), Photoshop won't mess with any of your image's pixels. Instead, the program simply changes the shape of the selection—the shape of the marching ants.

Once you've made a selection, choose Select → Transform Selection, or Ctrl-click (right-click on a PC) inside the selection and, from the shortcut menu that appears, choose Transform Selection. Photoshop puts a rectangular box with little, square resizing handles on its four sides around your selection (it's called a *bounding box*). You can move your selection around by clicking inside the bounding box and dragging in any direction. The resizing handles let you:

- **Scale (resize).** You can drag any handle to change the size and shape of your selection. Drag inward to make it smaller and outward to make it bigger.

- **Rotate.** If you position your cursor outside one of the bounding box's corners, your cursor turns into a curved, double-headed arrow. That's your cue that you can drag to rotate your selection (just drag up or down in the direction you want to rotate).

If you need to change the shape of your selection, just Ctrl-click (right-click on a PC) inside the bounding box and you'll get yet another shortcut menu with the following options (see Figure 4-21, bottom left):

- **Free Transform.** This option lets you apply any of the transformations listed below freely and in one action (instead of having to choose and apply them one at a time).

- **Scale and Rotate.** These options work as described above.

- **Skew.** Choosing this option lets you slant your selection by dragging one of the bounding box's side handles.

- **Distort.** Picking this option lets you drag any handle to reshape your selection.

- **Perspective.** This option lets you drag any corner handle to give your selection a one-point perspective—that is, a vanishing point where it seems to disappear into the distance.

- **Warp.** When you choose this option, Photoshop places a grid over your selection that lets you reshape it in any way you want. Drag any *control point* (the two evenly spaced points on all four sides of the selection) or line on the grid to twist your selection however you like, or choose a ready-made preset from the Warp pop-up menu in the Options bar. This option is your ticket to a quick page-curl effect, as shown in Figure 4-22.

- **Content-Aware Scale.** New in Photoshop CS4, this option can intelligently resize the unimportant background areas of your image while the subject of your image (Aunt Edna, for example) remains unchanged. You can learn all about it on page 242.

- **Rotate 180°, Rotate 90° CW, Rotate 90° CCW.** These options turn your selection 180 degrees, 90 degrees clockwise, or 90 degrees counterclockwise, respectively.

- **Flip Horizontal, Flip Vertical.** Choose one of these options to flip your selection either horizontally (like it's reflected in a mirror) or vertically (like it's reflected in a puddle).

When you're finished transforming your selection, press Return (Enter on a PC) to accept the changes. If you want to exit the bounding box without making any changes, press the Esc key.

Using Quick Mask Mode

If you'd rather fine-tune your selections by painting with a brush (brushes are covered in detail in Chapter 12), no problem; in fact, you can create a selection from scratch using this method. Just enter Quick Mask mode and you'll find all of Photoshop's painting tools (even filters!) waiting to help you tweak your selection. Quick Mask mode gives you the freedom to work on selections with any tool you want.

Figure 4-22:
Use the Warp option to create a quick page-curl effect.

Top left: Start by creating a rectangular selection (page 127) and then choose Select → Transform Selection. Then go to Edit → Transform → Warp to get the grid shown here.

Top right: Drag to reposition the various control points and handles on the mesh so that you get the approximate shape of a page-curl. For example, start by dragging the bottom left control point in toward the middle and continue dragging the other points in the direction shown here until your mesh grid looks like the one on the right. Press Return (Enter on a PC) when you're finished.

Bottom: Create a new layer (page 76) and fill the selection with a gray-white-gray-white gradient (see Appendix E, online at www. missingmanuals.com). Add a drop shadow (page 119) to the page-curl layer, and you're done!

You can enter Quick Mask mode by clicking the button at the bottom of the Tools panel that looks like a circle within a square or by pressing the Q key. Photoshop looks to see if you have an active selection. If you do, it puts a red overlay over everything *but* your selection. (If you don't, you won't see any change though you can still use the directions in this section to *create* one.) This color-coded environment makes it easy to edit your selection visually by painting.

While you're in Quick Mask mode, you can use the Brush tool (page 461) to paint with black (to conceal portions of the selection), white (to reveal portions of the mask), or shades of gray (to, well, read on):

• **To deselect a portion of your selection**—in other words, to add an area to the mask—make black your foreground color chip (page 22) and then paint the area.

- **To extend the area covered by your selection,** paint the area you want to add white (you may need to press X to flip-flop your color chips).

- **To create a soft-edged selection or semi-transparent area,** paint with gray. For example, by painting with 50 percent gray—by lowering a black brush's opacity in the Options bar to 50 percent—you'll create a selection that's half see-through. You can create a similar effect by painting with a soft-edge brush (page 463).

All your usual tools and document tricks work while you're in Quick Mask mode: You can zoom in or out by pressing ⌘ and the + or – key (Ctrl and + or – on a PC), press and hold the space bar to move around within the document once you're zoomed in, and use any of the selection tools covered in this chapter. Even the Marquee and Lasso tools work in this mode. You can also fill the entire mask, or your selection, with black or white (see page 168). This technique is helpful when you have a large area to paint or when you want to paint the entire selection by hand. You can run filters in this mode to create interesting edges (page 595) or use the Gradient tool, set to a black-to-white gradient, to create a fade (page 310).

Once you finish fine-tuning your selection, press the Q key to exit Quick Mask mode and the marching ants come rushing back, as shown in Figure 4-23, so you can see your newly edited selection.

Moving Selections

If you create a selection that's not exactly in the right spot or you've got several objects of the same shape to alter, you may need to move the selection itself. Or maybe you need to move the pixels *underneath* the selection, or onto their own layer. No matter what you want to do, you've got plenty of options, including:

- **To move the selection (the marching ants) within the same layer,** make sure you have a selection tool active (it doesn't matter which one). Then, click inside the selection and drag to move it to another part of your document. You can also nudge the selection into place with the arrow keys on your keyboard.

  TIP   To move a selection as you're drawing it, press and hold the space bar while you still have the mouse button pressed. Drag to move the selection, release the space bar, and continue dragging to draw the selection.

- **To move the selected object (the actual pixels) within the same document,** press V to select the Move tool and then drag with your mouse to reposition the object. Be aware that a big, gaping hole will appear where the object used to be!

- **To move the selected object onto its own new layer within the same document,** press ⌘-J (Ctrl+J on a PC). This command "jumps" the selected pixels onto their very own layer, just above the current layer. That way, whatever you do to the selected area won't harm the original image. If you don't like your changes, you can throw the extra layer away. Or, if you create an effect that's a little too strong—maybe you overwhitened a set of teeth—you can reduce the layer's opacity (page 87) to lessen the effect. (Flip back to Chapter 3 for more on using layers.)

Figure 4-23:
Top left: Start by selecting the white background of this badge with the Magic Wand tool (page 140).

Top right: When you pop into Quick Mask mode, Photoshop leaves the area you've selected in full color (in this case, white) and puts a red overlay over everything else. Now you can use Quick Mask mode to clean up the problem areas like the drop shadow peeking out from beneath the badge. You can easily fine-tune the selection in these areas—by using the Brush tool set to black or white or by using the Polygonal Lasso tool and then filling the selection area with black or white—because they're so easy to spot with the red overlay.

Bottom: Once you're finished, exit Quick Mask mode by pressing Q, and you see the fine-tuned selection marked by marching ants.

- **To move the selected object to another document,** press ⌘-C (Ctrl+C on a PC) to copy the pixels and then open the other document and press ⌘-V (Ctrl+V) to paste the pixels in. The object appears on its very own layer that you can reposition with the Move tool. This technique is essential for performing the classic head swap, shown in Figure 4-24.

- **To move the selected object to a new document,** copy it as described above and then choose File → New. Photoshop opens a new document, sized to match the object on your Clipboard, into which you can paste the object.

NOTE Although the radio buttons in the Operation section of the Load Selection dialog box let you add, subtract, or intersect with your saved selection, it's easier just to load the selection, close the dialog box, and edit it using the selection tools discussed in this chapter.

Filling a Selection with Color

After you've created the selection of your dreams, you can fill it with color. Just choose Edit → Fill and, from the "Use" pop-up menu, choose Color. Pick something nice from the resulting Color Picker and then press OK twice to dismiss the dialog boxes. Photoshop fills your selection with the color you picked. Filling selections with color is a great way to create shapes and to add colorful photo borders (see Figure 4-26).

Figure 4-26:
You should fill your selections on a brand-new layer so you don't mess up the original image (see page 76 for the scoop on creating a new layer). In doing so, you can use the Rectangular Marquee tool to make a colorful photo border. For a bit of extra pizzazz, you can add an inner shadow to the photo layer using layer styles (page 119).

Stroking (Outlining) a Selection

There will be times when you want to give your selection a *stroke* (as in outline, not the medical condition). While you can stroke selections of any shape, this technique comes in really handy when you use it in conjunction with the marquee tools. For example, you can combine a stroke with the Rectangular Marquee tool to add a thin black outline to your photo or with the Elliptical Marquee to circle yourself in a group picture.

When it comes to adding a bit of class to a photo, few effects beat a thin black outline. Whether you're floating the image within text or posting it in your blog, adding an outline gives the edge a little definition, making the design look nicely finished. Here's how to add an outline around the edge of your image (it takes only a few steps):

1. **Open your image and select it.**

   If your image is the same size as the document, you can choose Select → Select All. If it's smaller than the document and lives on its own layer, ⌘-click (Ctrl-click on a PC) the layer's thumbnail instead.

2. **Choose Edit → Stroke and tell Photoshop how thick, which color, and where you want the stroke to be.**

   In the Stroke dialog box, enter a pixel dimension in the Width box and then click the little color swatch. Choose a color from the resulting Color Picker and then press OK. Back in the Stroke dialog box's Location section, choose Inside to make the outline appear just inside the image's border.

3. **Click OK to see your new outline.**

To circle someone in a photo, as shown in Figure 4-27, you follow basically the same steps:

Figure 4-27:
Once you've created a selection, you can outline it by choosing Edit → Stroke. In the resulting dialog box (shown here), pick a width, color, and location for the outline and then press OK.

If you want to play it safe, you can add the stroke on its own layer. Just add a new layer to your document (page 76) before choosing Stroke from the Edit menu and then make sure that layer is active. When you add the stroke, it'll appear on the new layer instead of the original image.

1. **Open a photo and select the Elliptical Marquee tool (page 127) from the Tools panel.**

   Drag to draw an oval around the person's head. Remember that you can press the Shift key while you drag to draw a perfect circle or press the Option key (Alt on a PC) to draw the oval from the inside out. Move the selection if you need to by clicking inside it and dragging with your mouse.

2. **Choose Edit → Stroke, enter the stroke width, and pick a color.**

   In the Stroke dialog box, tell Photoshop how thick you want the stroke to be. You'll want to use a width of at least 2 pixels so the circle will be thick enough to see. Click the color swatch, choose a color from the resulting Color Picker, and then click OK. In the Location section, turn on the Center option so Photoshop will center the stroke over the marching ants. If you've entered a width of 2 pixels, for example, the program will put one pixel of the stroke on the outside of the selection and one on the inside (in other words, the stroke will straddle your selection).

3. **Press OK to see your newly circled head.**

   At this point you can get rid of the marching ants by pressing ⌘-D (Ctrl+D on a PC) to deselect.

Controlling Color with Channels

At the heart of any Photoshop file lie *channels*—storage containers for all your image's color information, saved selections (page 166), and instructions regarding special printing inks. Channels sound intimidating at first, and folks have been known to shudder at their mention and avoid them completely. But to really understand Photoshop, you need to understand channels. Luckily, you don't need a PhD—just a little patience.

This chapter gets a little technical at times, but if you soldier through, you'll be rewarded with wisdom that'll help you perform some amazing pixel wizardry. You'll get that warm, fuzzy enlightened feeling as you learn to:

• Use channels to make complex selections (page 190).

• Perform highly targeted color adjustments (see the figure on page 384).

• Create stunning grayscale conversions (page 305).

• Map one image to the contours of another (page 296).

• Sharpen your images without introducing *noise* (page 200).

• Save a selection so you can use it later (page 185).

And that's just the tip of the iceberg. *Everything* you do in Photoshop involves channels, so it's important to get to know them. If you understand *how* Photoshop does what it does, you can make it do even *more* in less time and with less effort. That's called working smarter, not harder—which is why, dear grasshopper, you're reading this book.

To understand how channels work, you first need to learn a bit about the two color systems you'll encounter during your Photoshop career: *additive* and *subtractive*. The additive system is at play in any image that appears onscreen; it explains how lights combine to generate color. Printed images, by contrast, are created by mixing inks together according to the substractive system. Once you've got all *that* under your belt (and fear not, there's plenty more ahead explaining how both systems work), you'll dive into the color channels themselves to see what kind of information is hiding there and how it can help you improve your images. Last but not least, you'll explore an entirely different kind of channel that can help you create the toughest selections this side of the Rio Grande: *alpha channels*. Read on!

How Color Works

The images you see on your computer monitor (or TV, for that matter) are made of light. While your eyes are sensitive to hundreds of wavelengths (each associated with a different color), it takes just three—red, green, and blue—to produce all the colors you see on screen. The screen's blank canvas is darkness (in other words, an absence of light), and to create color, the monitor *adds* individual pixels of colored light. Each tiny pixel on screen can be either red, green, or blue—or, more often, some combination of all three. That's why the onscreen color system is called additive. All image-capture devices—like digital cameras, video cameras, and scanners—use the additive color system, as do all digital-image display devices.

> **NOTE** Onscreen images are called *composite* images because they're made up of a combination of red, green, and blue light (also known as *RGB*).

In the additive color system, areas where red, green, and blue light overlap appear white (see Figure 5-1). Sound crazy (or maybe it rings a bell from high school physics)? Think about it this way: If you aimed red, green, and blue spotlights onto a stage, you'd see white where all three lights overlap. Interestingly, you'd also see cyan, magenta, or yellow where just *two* of the three lights overlap (see Figure 5-1 for a visual). Areas where no light is shining appear black.

So that's how computer monitors and TVs create onscreen color. Now it's time to talk about printed color, which—brace yourself—works in a totally different way. Printing presses use what's called a *subtractive* color system. In such a system, the colors result from a combination of light that's reflected (what you see) and light that's absorbed (subtracted from what you see). In a printed photo, magazine, or the pages of this book, that system operates as kind of a joint venture between the inks used (cyan, magenta, yellow, and black, all of which absorb color) and the paper the ink is printed on (a reflective surface).

The ink serves as a filter by absorbing part of the light that hits the paper. The paper, in turn, bounces the light back to you; the whiter the paper, the truer the colors will look when they're printed. In the subtractive system, different-colored inks absorb different-colored light. For example, cyan ink absorbs red light and

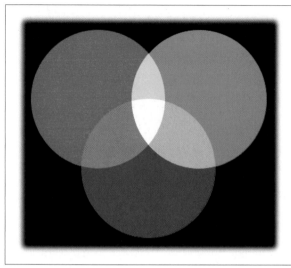

Figure 5-1:
If you overlap red, green, and blue spotlights, you see white light. This is a prime example of the additive color system, which starts with black and adds light to produce different colors. Notice how cyan, magenta, and yellow appear where just two lights overlap. You can try this spotlight experiment in Photoshop yourself by creating red, green, and blue circles on a black background. Make the circles overlap, switch the blend mode (page 267) of each layer to Lighten and voilà– the other colors appear where the circles overlap.

reflects green and blue light back to you, so you see a mix of green and blue—in other words, cyan. Similarly, magenta ink absorbs green light and reflects red and blue light; in other words, magenta. One last example: A mix of cyan, magenta, and yellow ink absorbs *most* of the primary colors—red, green, and blue—and displays what's left over: dark brown.

To produce true black, grays, and shades of color (colors mixed with black to produce darker colors), the folks who ran printing presses decided to add black as a fourth printing ink. They couldn't abbreviate it B (for "black") because they were afraid it'd be confused with blue (as in RGB), so they used K instead—as in "blacK". That's where the abbreviation CMYK comes from.

> **NOTE** To sum it all up: Subtractive color is generated by light hitting an object and bouncing back to your eye, whereas additive color is generated by different-colored light mixing together *before* you view it.

RGB Mode vs. CMYK Mode

Photoshop stores all the color information that gets relayed to your monitor, your printer, and so on, in separate *channels*. The channels' names change depending on which *color mode* you're using for a particular file. As a rule of thumb, you use RGB mode for images destined for onscreen viewing or inkjet printing and CMYK mode for images you plan on sending to a commercial printing press.

> **NOTE** To find what color mode your image is in, choose Image → Mode. The current mode will have a little checkmark to the left of its name.
>
> Spend enough time around Photoshop veterans and you'll almost certainly hear talk of "color mode" and "image mode." Don't get confused–both terms refer to the same thing.

In *RGB mode,* your file's color channels are red, blue, and green. If you look at each channel individually (which you'll learn how to do on page 174), you actually see a grayscale representation of where and at what strength that particular color appears in your image. ("Why doesn't Photoshop display them in color" you ask? The box on page 175 has the answer.) One of the best things about RGB mode is that it can display an enormous range of colors.

If you're preparing an image for a commercial printing press, on the other hand, the printed image gets composed by mixing cyan, magenta, yellow, and black inks. Enter *CMYK mode,* where your file's color channels are cyan, magenta, yellow, and black. The drawback to working in this mode is that ink can reproduce far fewer colors than light. But never fear: Even if you need to *end up* in CMYK mode, there's no harm in starting off in RGB mode. (Chapter 16 explains more than you ever wanted to know about when and how to change color modes.)

As you learned in Chapter 2 (page 40), there are other color modes, including Grayscale and Lab, that you can use for specific tasks that you'll learn about throughout this book. However, you'll spend the bulk of your time in RGB mode.

Whew! Now that the really confusing stuff is out of the way, it's time to focus on where in Photoshop you can *see* channel information and the different types of channels you can find there.

The Channels Panel and You

To peek inside a channel, you need to open Photoshop's Channels panel (see Figure 5-2). It looks and works just like the Layers panel, which you learned about in Chapter 3. You'll find the Channels panel's icon lurking in the panel dock (page 17) on the right side of your screen. (If you don't see it, choose Window → Channels.)

Just like in the Layers panel, when you click once to select a channel, Photoshop highlights that channel to let you know it's selected. Anything you do from that point on will affect only that channel. If you want to select more than one channel, Shift-click each one. You can use this trick if you want to, say, sharpen two channels at once (see page 200). You can toggle a channel's visibility on and off by clicking the visibility eye to the left of the channel's name (see Figure 5-2), or you can drag down over the eyes to turn them all on or off (you can't turn off every channel, though, since at least one has to be visible at all times).

Photoshop has several kinds of channels, all of which this chapter discusses in detail:

- **Composite.** Technically, Composite isn't really a channel; it's for your viewing pleasure only. When you're using a mode that contains more than one color channel (like RGB, CMYK, and Lab—all discussed later in this chapter), the composite channel lets you see all the channels simultaneously, revealing your image in its full-color glory. The name of the composite channel depends on which mode you're in. In RGB mode, for example, the composite channel is named RGB (creative, huh?). But no matter what Photoshop calls it, it's always at the top of your Channels panel.

Why Channels Are Gray

With all this talk about color, how come Photoshop shows color channels in black and white?

Although you *can* make Photoshop display individual color channel info in color, you really don't want to. The channel colors would be so bright and distracting that it'd be hard to see anything useful. That's why Photoshop displays color channels in grayscale as you can see in the Channels panel shown below. It's much easier to see a particular color's strength (called *luminosity*) when it's represented in shades of gray.

For example, in the figure's Red channel, the lighter-colored pixels represent high concentrations of red, whereas the darker pixels represent almost no red at all. In RGB mode, absolute white areas indicate red at full luminosity, and black areas indicate the color at its weakest. (In CMYK mode, the reverse is true—black indicates full strength and white indicates the weakest concentration.) Just glancing at grayscale channel information lets you *see* where a certain color is at full strength, where it's completely lacking, and what lies somewhere in between.

That said, if you're determined to see color channel info in full color, choose Photoshop → Preferences → Interface (Edit → Preferences → Interface on a PC). Turn on the "Show Channels in Color" option and see if you can make heads or tails out of anything!

Finally, there's one situation where you'll see the channels displayed in color whether you like it or not: If you select more than one channel, Photoshop previews your image in just those colors (see page 200). If the program displayed multiple channels in grayscale, you'd never be able to tell *which* grayscale range represented which color.

- **Color channels.** As explained earlier, if you're working in RGB mode, your color channels are Red, Green, and Blue. In CMYK mode, they're Cyan, Magenta, Yellow, and Black. In Lab mode (page 183), they're Lightness, a, and b. In all other image modes, you'll find only a single channel, named after the mode you're in.

- **Alpha channel.** If you've ever saved a selection so you can use it again later (page 166), you've created an alpha channel. They're basically grayscale representations of saved selections that come in handy when you've made a tough selection you might need to use again later (like when you're changing someone's hair color at the request of a finicky client). See page 185 for a detailed explanation of alpha channels.

Close panel — Panel menu

Currently active channel

Composite channel

Toggles channel visibility on/off

Color channels

LAYERS   CHANNELS   PATHS

RGB   ⌘2

Red   ⌘3

Green   ⌘4

Blue   ⌘5

LAYERS

CHANNELS

PATHS

Channels panel dock

Resize panel

Load channel as selection
Save selection as channel   New channel   Delete channel

Figure 5-2:
The Channels panel is your gateway to the color info that makes up your image. The composite channel at the top of the panel shows what the image looks like with all the channels turned on.

- **Spot channel.** These color channels store instructions for using special pre-mixed inks, like Pantone colors. If you're a graphic designer creating an ad for a hot new scooter that has to be Ferrari red, you can create a spot channel containing that color to make sure it prints correctly. See page 637 for details on when to use spot channels and how to create them.

At the bottom of the Channels panel, you'll find a row with the following buttons:

- **Load channel as selection.** This button, which looks like a tiny circle made of dots, selects whatever's in the active channel. This is handy when you're using channel information to create tough selections (page 190). You can also load a channel as a selection by ⌘-clicking (Ctrl-clicking on a PC) the channel's thumbnail icon.

- **Save selection as channel.** When you have an active selection, you can press this button to save it as an alpha channel so you can use it again later (page 185). You can also choose Selection → Save Selection, which lets you name your new channel.

- **Create new channel.** This button looks like a tiny piece of paper with an upturned corner. When you click it, Photoshop creates a new, empty alpha channel (page 185). Photoshop names each selection you create as Alpha 1, Alpha 2, Alpha 3, and so on. But if you want a more memorable name, you can always double-click the channel name and change it to something like "Tony's toupee" or "Lesa's Lambo." If you drag an existing channel onto this button, Photoshop duplicates it—helpful when you're modifying a channel to create a selection (page 190) or making an edge mask to sharpen your image (page 439) since you don't want to risk destroying your original image.

- **Delete current channel.** Clicking this tiny trash can deletes the current channel (you can also drag and drop a channel onto it instead). After you've tweaked a duplicate or alpha channel to create the perfect selection or edge mask, you can throw away the current channel by clicking this button. Or you can keep it hanging around and turn off its visibility eye.

> **TIP** It's okay to keep extra channels in your Photoshop files if you think you might use them again later. Channels don't increase your file size as much as layers do, so you can have lots of channels and still maintain a reasonable file size. In fact, you can have up to 56 channels in one document.

Just like every other panel in Photoshop, the Channels panel has a menu tucked into its top-right corner (it looks like a down arrow next to four little lines). This handy menu includes some of the same commands mentioned earlier and a few all its own:

- **New Channel.** This command creates a brand-new alpha channel, just like clicking the "Create a new channel" button at the bottom of the Channels panel. However, by going this route, you get a nifty dialog box that asks you to name your new channel and tell Photoshop how you'd like the channel's information displayed (see the box on page 175).

- **Duplicate Channel.** If you want to create a copy of a channel so you can edit it, choose this option. When you do, Photoshop displays a dialog box so you can name your new channel and choose its destination (the same document or a new one). The destination option is helpful when you're creating a displacement map (page 296) or using channels to make a high-contrast, black-and-white image (page 305).

- **Delete Channels.** This command deletes the current channel or, if you've Shift-clicked to select more than one channel, all the selected channels.

- **New Spot Channel.** This option lets you create a new channel for a premixed, specialty printing ink called a *spot color*. Read all about 'em on page 637.

- **Merge Spot Channel.** Only commercial printing presses can understand spot channels, so if you need to print a proof on a regular desktop printer, you'll need to use this command to merge your spot channels first. See the box on page 643 for details.

- **Channel Options.** This menu item is available only if you have an alpha channel selected. When you're creating or editing an alpha channel, you can use Channel Options to change the way Photoshop displays masked and selected areas. Page 188 has the scoop.

- **Split Channels.** If you need to split each channel in your image into its own document, choose this command. Photoshop grabs each channel and copies it into a new document (in Grayscale mode [page 306]). This technique can be useful when you're creating a grayscale image based on one of the color channels (page 305).

- **Merge Channels.** You might think this command merges more than one channel into a single channel. Negative: It merges the channels of up to four open Grayscale documents into a single RGB document (if you've got three open documents) or CMYK document (if you've got four open documents). You can also have Photoshop merge all the open documents' channels into a Multichannel document (see page 183). If you've used the Split Channels command to work on each channel separately, you can use Merge Channels to bring them back together into one document.

- **Panel Options.** In the Channels panel, Photoshop automatically displays a thumbnail preview of each channel. If you want to turn off this preview or choose a different thumbnail size, select this menu item. If you've got a decent-sized monitor (17" or larger), go for the biggest preview possible (see Figure 5-2).

- **Close and Close Tab Group.** New in Photoshop CS4, you can choose Close to make the Channels panel disappear, or Close Tab Group to get rid of a whole group of related panels (like Channels, Layers, and Paths). See Chapter 1 for more on panels.

In the next section, you'll learn about the different kinds of information you'll find in each mode's color channels.

Meet the Color Channels

Understanding what you're seeing in each channel gives you the know-how to create complicated selections and fine-tune your images. In this section, you'll look inside the different color channels, beginning with the most common image mode: RGB.

> **NOTE** This section doesn't cover alpha channels. They're so important, they get their very own section, which starts on page 185.

RGB Channels

Unless you're preparing an image that's headed for a commercial printing press (as opposed to the inkjet printer you've probably got at home), RGB mode is the place to be. After all, your monitor is RGB, as are your digital camera and scanner. But as the box on page 175 explains, Photoshop doesn't display individual channels in red, green, and blue—they're in grayscale so you can easily see where the color is most saturated. Because colors in RGB mode are made from light (page 172), white indicates areas where the color is at full strength, black indicates areas where it's weakest, and shades of gray represent everything in between (see Figure 5-3).

> **NOTE** Most likely, your image is already in RGB mode; you set an image's mode when you create a new document (page 37). For info on switching color modes, see Chapter 16.

Composite

Red

Figure 5-3:
*See how the red, green,
and blue channels differ
in this cute cowgirl
portrait? White areas
show where the color on
that channel is most
concentrated, and black
areas show where the
color is weakest.*

Green

Blue

TIP No matter which color mode you're in, you can cycle through the channels by pressing ⌘-3, 4, 5, and 6 (Ctrl+3, 4, 5, and 6 on a PC) though you'll only use that last one if you're in CMYK mode, which has four channels instead of three. To go back to the composite channel (page 174) so you can see the image in full color, press ⌘-2 (Ctrl+2). These keyboard shortcuts are new in Photoshop CS4. When you use them, be sure to hold down the ⌘ or Ctrl key; otherwise, typing numbers will change the layer's opacity instead (see page 87).

As you can see in Figure 5-3, each channel holds different information:

- **Red.** The red channel is typically the lightest of the bunch and shows the greatest difference in color range. In this example, it's very light because there's a lot of red in the woman's skin, hair, and hat. This channel can be *muy importante* when you're correcting skin tones (page 377).

- **Green.** You can think of the green channel as "contrast central" because it's usually the highest in, well, contrast. (This makes sense because digital cameras have twice as many green sensors as red or blue ones.) Remember this channel when you're creating an edge mask for sharpening (page 439) or working with displacement maps (page 296).

NOTE Back in the olden days (in previous versions of Photoshop), if you wanted to generate a grayscale version of a color photo, you had to pick the channel with the highest contrast and use that as your grayscale image. Now, Photoshop gives you much better ways to convert from color to grayscale like the Black & White Adjustment layer (page 301).

- **Blue.** Typically the darkest of the group, this channel can be useful when you want to create complex selections to isolate an object (page 190). It's where you'll find problems like *noise* and *grain* (page 200). See the box on page 427 to learn how to run the Reduce Noise filter on this channel.

CMYK Channels

Though you'll probably spend most of your time working with images in RGB mode, you may also need to work with images in CMYK mode. Its name, as you learned earlier, stands for the cyan, magenta, yellow, and black inks commercial printing presses use to print newspapers, magazines, product packaging, and so on. It, too, has a composite channel at the top of the Channels panel, and you can pop into this mode by choosing Image → Mode → CMYK Color. If you'll print your image on a regular printer—laser or inkjet—you don't need to be in CMYK mode (unless you need to create a quick, high-key effect as described on page 181). Also, you can use only a precious few filters (Chapter 15) and adjustments (Chapter 9) in this mode. (You'll learn all about converting images from one mode to another in Chapter 16.)

A professional printing press, in contrast, separates the four CMYK channels of your image into individual *color separations* (see page 633). Each separation is a perfect copy of the color channel you see in Photoshop, printed in its respective color (cyan, magenta, yellow, or black). When the printing press places these four colors atop each other, they form the full-color image. (This technique is known as *four-color process* printing.)

Because CMYK channels represent ink rather than light (as explained back on page 174), the grayscale information you see in your Channels panel represents the *opposite* of what it does in RGB mode. In CMYK mode, black indicates color at full strength and white indicates color at its weakest (see Figure 5-4). Does your brain hurt yet?

Creating a high-key portrait effect

Even if you're not sending your image to a printing press, you can still have some fun in CMYK mode. For example, you may have noticed that the Black channel in Figure 5-4 looks pretty darned neat. It resembles a popular portrait effect called *high-key* lighting, in which multiple light sources are aimed at the subject (more of a *victim* in this situation) to create a dazzling image with interesting shadows. Folks have labored long and hard to create this look in Photoshop when they could simply resort to a bit of channel theft instead. In other words, if you need to create this effect fast, just extract the black channel from a CMYK version of the image. Here's how:

1. **If your image is in RGB mode, duplicate it by choosing Image → Duplicate.**

   Because you're going to change color modes in the next step, it's a good idea to do that on a copy of your image since you lose a bit of color information when you go from one mode to another. If your image is already in CMYK mode, you can skip this step and go to step 3.

2. **In the duplicate image, choose Image → Mode → CMYK.**

3. **In your Channels panel, select the Black channel.**

   When you click to select the Black channel, Photoshop automatically turns off the other channels' visibility.

4. **Copy the Black channel.**

   With the Black channel selected, press ⌘-A (Ctrl+A on a PC) to select everything in the channel. Then copy the channel by pressing ⌘-C (Ctrl+C).

5. **Select your *original* RGB document and paste the Black channel into your Layers panel.**

   Click the document tab or inside the window of your original RGB image. Open your Layers panel by clicking its icon in the panel dock on the side of your screen or by choosing Window → Layers. Then paste the Black channel into the panel by pressing ⌘-V (Ctrl+V). You don't have to create a new layer; Photoshop does it for you.

6. **Close the duplicate document because you don't need it anymore.**

   That's it! Told ya it was fast.

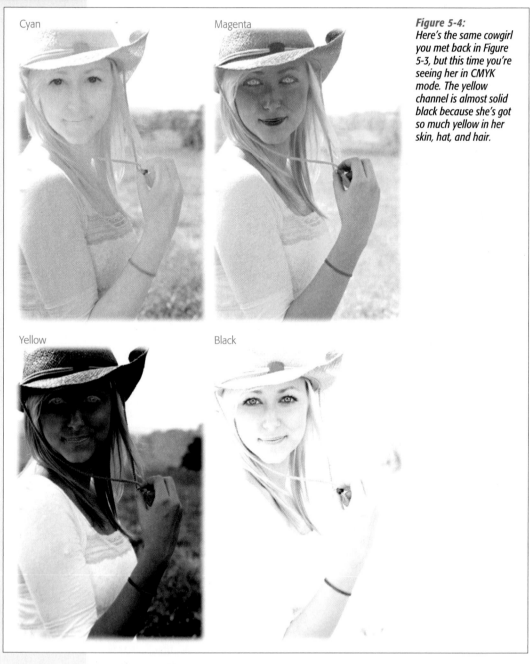

Figure 5-4:
*Here's the same cowgirl
you met back in Figure
5-3, but this time you're
seeing her in CMYK
mode. The yellow
channel is almost solid
black because she's got
so much yellow in her
skin, hat, and hair.*

Spot Channels

In the realm of CMYK printing, there's a special kind of premixed ink called a *spot color*. This ink requires a special kind of channel called a *spot channel*. If you're a graphic designer working in prepress (see the Note below), in packaging design, or at an ad agency, you need to know this stuff, and page 637 has all the details. If you're a photographer or Web designer, save your brainpower and don't bother learning about them—really.

> **NOTE** The word *prepress* refers to the preparation of images and documents–usually from a page layout program like Adobe InDesign–for printing on a commercial printing press.

Lab Channels

Lab mode (which gets its name from the channels it includes—they're listed later in this section) separates the lightness values (how bright or dark the image is) from the color information. This color mode isn't used for output like RGB and CMYK modes; instead, it's especially useful when you want to alter just the lightness values of an image (when you're sharpening or brightening, for instance) without shifting colors. Likewise, you can adjust only the color information (to get rid of a color cast) without affecting the lightness values. You can pop into Lab mode by choosing Image → Mode → Lab Color, and peek at the channel info to see the X-rayish channels shown in Figure 5-5.

When you're in Lab mode, you'll find the following channels:

- **Lightness.** Here you'll find the color-drained details of your image; it looks like a really good black-and-white version of your image. Some folks swear that by splitting this channel into its own document and then making a few adjustments, you can create a black-and-white image worthy of Ansel Adams. See page 305 for the skinny on how to do that and then judge for yourself.

- **a.** This channel contains half of your color information: a mixture of red and green.

- **b.** You'll find the other half here: a mixture of yellow and blue.

You'll see techniques that involve Lab mode sprinkled throughout Part 2 of this book.

Multichannel Mode

Unless you're preparing an image for a commercial printing press, you'll never use this mode although you may put yourself in it accidentally. If you delete one of the color channels in an RGB, CMYK, or Lab document, Photoshop plops you right into Multichannel mode without even asking. If that happens, just use your History panel to go back a step or press ⌘-Z (Ctrl+Z on a PC) to bring back the channel you accidentally deleted.

Multichannel mode doesn't have a composite channel. It's strictly for two- or three-color print jobs, so when you enter this mode—by choosing Image → Mode → Multichannel—Photoshop converts any existing color channels to spot channels (page 637).

Lightness

a (red and green)

Figure 5-5:
Here's that cowgirl again, now in Lab mode. In the a channel, lighter areas represent greens and darker areas represent reds. In the b channel, lighter areas represent blues and darker areas represent yellows.

b (yellow and blue)

When you convert your image to Multichannel mode, Photoshop promptly does one of the following (depending on which color mode you were in before):

- **Converts your RGB channels** to cyan, magenta, and yellow spot channels.

- **Converts your CMYK channels** to cyan, magenta, yellow, and black spot channels.

- **Converts your Lab channels** to alpha channels named Alpha 1, Alpha 2, and Alpha 3.

- **Converts your Grayscale channel** to a black spot channel.

With such radical channel changes, you'll get radical color shifts, but you can edit each channel individually—both its contents and its spot color—to create the image you want. When you're finished editing, save the image as a Photoshop (PSD) file (page 46) or as a DCS 2.0 file if you need to pop it into page-layout software (described on page 642).

Single-Channel Modes

The rest of Photoshop's image modes aren't very exciting when it comes to channels since they each have just one. They include Bitmap, Grayscale, Duotone, and Indexed Color mode, and they're all discussed back on page 40 in Chapter 2.

The Mighty Alpha Channel

Photoshop has one other type of channel: *alpha channels.* Their job is to store your selections so you can use or edit them again later.

These channels get their name from a process called *alpha compositing,* which combines a partially-transparent image (one that has see-through areas) with another image (which is how filmmakers create special effects and fake backdrops). But the information about the shape of the transparent area and the pixels' level of transparency has to be stored somewhere, and that somewhere is an alpha channel. This is powerful stuff because the same technology allows you to save your selections. And, as you've learned, making selections can take a *ton* of time.

Heck, you may not have the stamina to finish creating a particularly challenging selection in one sitting. And since clients change their minds occasionally—"Put the model in front of *this* bush. And change her hair color while you're at it!"—the ability to save selections so you can mess with them later is a lifesaver. As long as you save your document as a PSD file (page 46), that alpha channel will always be there for you to return to. That ought to make you sleep better at night!

> **NOTE**   You can drag alpha channels between documents as long as the documents have the same pixel dimensions.

Folks sometimes refer to alpha channels as *channel masks*. That's because once you've made an alpha channel (as the next section explains), you can use it to help you adjust certain portions of your image—kind of like when you use a layer mask (page 105). In fact, creating a layer mask by loading an alpha channel as a selection is the most common use for alpha channels. That's because, as you'll learn later in this section, you can use channels to make incredibly detailed selections that you can't get any other way.

> **NOTE** When you're in Quick Mask mode (page 162), you're actually working on a temporary alpha channel. Who knew?

Creating an Alpha Channel

It can be helpful to think of an alpha channel as a grayscale representation of your selection. Unless you change Photoshop's settings, the black parts of the channel indicate the unselected part of your image—also referred to as the *protected* or *masked* part—and the selection itself is white (see page 187 to learn how to reverse these colors). And, just like in a layer mask (page 105), shades of gray represent areas that are only partially selected, which means they're partially see-through.

You can create an alpha channel by doing any of the following:

- Click the **"Create a new channel"** button at the bottom of the Channels panel (see Figure 5-2 on page 176). Clicking this button makes Photoshop create an empty alpha channel named Alpha 1 and stick it at the bottom of the Channels panel. The channel is solid black because it's empty. To create a selection, grab your Brush tool (page 462) and paint with white (think of this process as painting a hole through the mask so you can see—and therefore select—what's below it).

> **NOTE** Though you can certainly start with an empty alpha channel, it's often easier to create your selection (or at least a rough version of it) on the full-color image before adding the alpha channel. Afterwards, you can fine-tune the alpha channel using the methods explained in the box on page 195.

- Choose **New Channel from the Channels panel menu** (see Figure 5-2). When you choose the New Channel option, Photoshop pops up a dialog box where you can name your new channel and customize how the program displays the channel's info. Out of the box, Photoshop shows selected areas (the parts of your image inside the marching ants) in white and unselected areas in black. Partially selected areas, which have soft edges, appear in shades of gray.

  If you'd rather see your selections in black and everything else in white, turn on the dialog box's "Selected Areas" option. If you want to edit your alpha channel using Quick Mask mode (as described later in this section), you can change the QuickMask color and opacity here. When you've got everything the way you want it, click OK to make Photoshop create your new alpha channel.

- Create a selection and then choose Select → Save Selection (see page 166).

- Create a selection and then click the "Save selection as channel" button at the bottom of the Channels panel. (It looks like a circle within a square and is circled in Figure 5-6.)

Alpha channel

Figure 5-6:
In most cases, you'll find it easier to create a selection first (even if it's rough) and then add your alpha channel as shown here. (That way, you see the full-color image instead of a screen full of black.) Once you've got marching ants, click the "Save selection as channel" button (circled), Photoshop adds an alpha channel—which includes your selection—to the bottom of the Channels panel.

TIP   If you Option-click (Alt-click on a PC) the "Save selection as channel" button, Photoshop displays the same dialog box you get if you choose New Channel from the Channels panel menu, so you can name your new alpha channel.

Editing Alpha Channels

Once you've got yourself an alpha channel, you can fine-tune it just like you would a layer mask (page 111). You can paint with the Brush tool or use any selection tool to modify it. If you want to use a selection tool, choose Edit → Fill and pick black or white from the Use pop-up menu, depending on what you want to do—add to or subtract from your selection (selected areas are white and everything else is black). If you want to reverse the way Photoshop displays the channel's info—if you'd rather have white mark your selection instead of black—just double-click the alpha channel's thumbnail in the Channels panel and, in the resulting Channel Options dialog box, turn on the Masked Areas option. Photoshop will instantly flip-flop your mask's colors as shown in Figure 5-7.

Figure 5-7:
Double-clicking your alpha channel's thumbnail in the Channels panel brings up this dialog box, where you can tell Photoshop to reverse what the mask color (black) represents. You can also use this dialog box to turn the alpha channel into a spot color (page 637) or change the color and opacity of the Quick Mask overlay.

NOTE   It doesn't matter whether you use black to mark the masked (protected) or selected (unprotected) areas of your image—it's a personal preference. But when you load an alpha channel as a selection, pay careful attention to what the ants are marching around; *that's* the part you'll modify when you start making changes. And, remember, as you learned in the box back on page 143, sometimes it's easier to select what you *don't* want and then use Select → Inverse to flip-flop your selection.

You can also edit your alpha channel using Quick Mask mode (page 162). In the Channels panel, select the alpha channel and then click the composite channel's visibility eye, as shown in Figure 5-8. When you do that, Photoshop puts Quick Mask mode's signature red overlay atop your image. (If you're editing an alpha channel in an image with a lot of red in it, you can't see diddly through the mask. In that case, you need to change the overlay color. Open the Channel Options dialog box by double-clicking the alpha channel's thumbnail, click the red color swatch, and then pick a new color from the resulting Color Picker. Click OK when you're finished and continue editing your alpha channel.)

You can also run filters on your alpha channel, just like you can with a layer mask. Among the most useful ones are Gaussian Blur (for softening the selection's edge, which is helpful if you're trying to select a slightly blurred area) and the Brush Stroke set (for giving your mask creative edges). Chapter 15 shows these filters in action.

Figure 5-8:
If you select your alpha channel and turn on the composite channel's visibility eye, you can edit in Quick Mask mode. In this example, the Brush tool (the black circle) is being used to touch up the area around the little cowboy's forehead. If you mess up and add too much to the mask, press X to flip-flop your color chips and paint that area with white just like you would with a layer mask (page 105).

Loading an Alpha Channel As a Selection

Once you're finished editing your mask, you can transform it into a selection so you can actually *do* something with it. You can summon the marching ants in several ways:

- ⌘-click (Ctrl-click on a PC) the alpha channel's thumbnail in your Channels panel.

- Click the "Load channel as selection" button at the bottom of the Channels panel (it looks like a tiny dotted circle) while you've got the alpha channel selected.

- Drag the alpha channel onto the "Load channel as selection" button (release your mouse as soon as Photoshop highlights the button).

Now you can perform all the amazing color and lighting adjustments explained throughout this book, and they'll affect only the area you've selected. Pretty sweet, huh?

Deleting Alpha Channels

When you're finished using an alpha channel (or if you want to start over with a new one), you can get rid of it by dragging it to the little trash can at the bottom right of the Channels panel. Or just click the trash can while the alpha channel is selected and click Yes when Photoshop asks if you're *sure* you want to throw it away.

> **NOTE** Unless you're a panel neatness freak, you don't have to throw out your alpha channels. They don't add much to your file size because they're black and white (if they contain a lot of gray, they'll add a bit to the file size but not enough that it's worth tossing them). If there's the slightest chance you'll ever use them again, save your document as a PSD file to keep the alpha channels intact.

Basic Channel Stunts

Now that you know what channels are all about, it's time to learn some of the cool things you can do with them. This section covers some of the most practical channel tricks, but you'll find techniques involving channels strewn throughout this book.

Selecting Objects with Channels

As you learned in Chapter 4, true selection wisdom lies in knowing which tool to start with so you'll have the least cleanup to do later. If you have an image with a decent amount of contrast between the object you want to select and its background, using channels is your best bet. All you need to do is create an alpha channel that contains only black-and-white objects, load it as a selection, and then use it to make a layer mask. For example, here's how to use channels to select all the balloons in Figure 5-9 in mere minutes:

> **NOTE** Want to follow along? Visit this book's Missing CD page at *www.missingmanuals.com* and download the practice file Balloons.jpg.

1. **Open an image that's in RGB mode and has a background you want to get rid of.**

   If your image came from a scanner or digital camera, it's already in RGB mode. To check, choose Image → Mode. Choose RGB Color to switch color modes if necessary.

2. **Find the channel where the objects you want to select look darkest.**

   Open your Channels panel and click each channel to find the one where the balloons appear darkest. (You can also cycle through channels by pressing ⌘-3, 4 and 5 [Ctrl+3, 4, 5 on a PC].) The objects will usually be darkest on the blue channel, as is the case here.

Figure 5-9:
Once you find the channel where the objects appear darkest (usually the blue channel), make a copy of that channel so you don't mess up your original photo. To copy a channel, simply drag it onto the "Create new channel" button, as shown in the center image. Photoshop adds the copy to the bottom of your Channels panel.

3. **Duplicate the blue channel.**

   Because you're going to tweak the blue channel to make it pure black and white, you need to duplicate it first so you don't destroy your original image. To duplicate a channel, you can either Ctrl-click (right-click on a PC) the channel in the Channels panel and select Duplicate Channel from the shortcut menu or drag the channel onto the "Create new channel" button. You can also choose Duplicate Channel from the Channels panel menu though the dragging method is quicker. Whichever method you use, Photoshop puts the duplicate channel at the bottom of your Channels panel and names it "Blue copy".

4. **Adjust the duplicate blue channel's levels to make the balloons black and the background white.**

   Chapter 9 covers levels in detail, but this exercise gives you a sneak peek at how useful they are. Choose Image → Adjustments → Levels or press ⌘-L (Ctrl+L on a PC) to summon the Levels dialog box. To make the balloons darker, in the Input Levels section of the dialog box, drag the shadows slider (it's the little black triangle that's circled in Figure 5-10) to the right until the balloons turn *almost* black. (The farther you drag the slider, the darker the background gets, too. That's okay because you'll fix the background in the next step.) Don't close the Levels dialog box just yet!

Figure 5-10:
Depending on the amount of contrast in your image, you may have to drag the shadows slider (circled) quite a ways to the right to make the objects you want to select black. But be careful: If you drag it too far to the right, you'll start to lose some of the detail around your object's edges.

Next, click the white eyedropper (also circled) and then, over in your image, click the gray background areas until the background is completely white. When your image is exclusively black and white, like the right-hand image here, you're ready to load the channel as a selection.

5. **Using the white eyedropper, click the gray background to make it white.**

You can use the little white eyedropper on the right side of the dialog box to tell Photoshop to change what it thinks should be white (image-editing pros call this technique "resetting the white point"). Click once to select the eyedropper (circled in Figure 5-10), mouse over to your document, and then click a gray part of the background. Keep clicking on different gray areas until the background is completely white (or as close to white as you can get it). When you're finished, click OK to close the Levels dialog box.

6. **If necessary, touch up the inside of the balloons with black paint and the background with white paint.**

If adjusting the shadows slider in step 4 didn't make the balloons *completely* black (see Figure 5-10), you can use the Brush tool to touch them up by hand (otherwise the balloons will be partially selected). Press B to grab the Brush tool and then set your foreground color chip to black (press D to set the color chips to black and white, and then press X until black hops on top). Mouse over to the balloons and paint them solid black. Also, if resetting the white point didn't get rid of all the gray in the background (like the bit of gray at the upper-right corner of this image), use the Brush tool to paint those areas white. When you're finished, you should have a pure black-and-white image.

7. **In the Channels panel, load the duplicate blue channel as a selection by ⌘-clicking (Ctrl-clicking on a PC) the channel's thumbnail or clicking the "Load channel as selection" button (the dotted circle) at the bottom of the panel.**

   Now that you've got a perfectly black-and-white image (it looks just like a layer mask or alpha channel, doesn't it?), you can load it as a selection. When you do, Photoshop will put marching ants around the *background* of your image, which is the opposite of what you want. No worries! You'll solve that problem in the next step.

8. **Invert the selection to select the balloons instead of the background.**

   Choose Select → Inverse or press ⌘-Shift-I (Ctrl+Shift+I on a PC) to flip-flop your selection so the marching ants run around the balloons instead of around your whole document.

9. **In the Channels panel, turn on the composite channel and hide the duplicate blue channel.**

   Scroll to the top of your Channels panel and click the visibility eye of the composite channel to turn it back on so you can see the full-color version of your image again (it's named RGB). Turn off the visibility of the duplicate blue channel or delete it by dragging it to the tiny trash can at the bottom right of your Channels panel.

10. **Open your Layers panel, select the Background layer, and then add a layer mask.**

    Use the panel dock (page 17) on the right side of your screen to open the Layers panel or choose Window → Layers. If the Background layer still has a little padlock next to it, double-click it to make the layer editable. If you like, type a name for the Background layer in the resulting dialog box and then click OK (if you're working with an image you've worked with before, you may have already named your Background layer something other than "Background"). To add a layer mask, click the circle within a square at the bottom of the Layers panel. Photoshop adds a layer mask that immediately hides the photo's original background (the sky), as shown in Figure 5-11, left. Sweet!

You're all finished! At this point you can edit the layer mask (page 111) if you need to by selecting it in the Layers panel and then painting it with either black or white. Or you can copy and paste a new background into the Layers panel and then drag it to the bottom of the layers stack to put the balloons on a new sky as shown in Figure 5-11.

Figure 5-11:
Look, Ma, no selection tools! Whenever you have an image like this one that's got a decent amount of contrast between its subject and its background, using channels is your best bet for creating an accurate selection fast.

Creating a Silhouette Effect

Attention, anyone interested in creating iPod ads: You can use the *exact* same channel selection technique described on the previous pages to create a silhouette effect. However, instead of adding a layer mask, you'll add a new layer and then fill your selection with black. That way, your silhouette will live on its own layer, making it easier for you to edit or change it later, as the Apple-esque images featured in Figure 5-12 show.

> **NOTE** Try this silhouette technique by visiting this book's Missing CD page at *www. missingmanuals.com* and downloading the practice file Indian.jpg.

To create a quick silhouette, follow steps 1–9 in the previous section (pages 190–193) so that you've got your basic selection and you're looking at the full-color image, and then start here:

1. **Create a new layer at the top of your layers stack.**

   When you see marching ants running around your subject, you're ready to create a new layer and fill your selection with black. Open the Layers panel and create a new layer by clicking the "Create a new layer" button at the bottom of the panel. Then drag the new layer to the top of the layers stack and turn off the visibility eye (page 78) of the original photo layer (which may or may not be named Background).

Touching Up Alpha Channels

When you're editing an alpha channel to make a selection, it's important that you end up with a purely black-and-white channel (the alpha channel shown in Figure 5-10 is almost there but needs a tiny bit of touch-up on the balloons). If you've got any gray areas around the edges of the object, those edges will look soft—as if you've feathered them (page 132). If you've got gray in the center of the object, those pixels will be partially selected (and if you've got white areas, they won't be selected). Adjusting the levels of your alpha channel usually gets your image *close* to pure black and white, but that method can only do so much. You're often left with stray gray pixels hiding here and there, a selection that isn't quite solid black or white, or some stuff in the background that you don't need. Your only choice at that point is to touch up your image by hand.

Sure, this kind of touch-up work is tedious, but it goes much faster if you use one of the following methods. When you're in Channels Land, it's easy to forget that you've got *most* of Photoshop's tools at your command. With that in mind, here are a few tricks for touching up alpha channels:

- **Fill the background with black or white.** If you've managed to make your object pure black, you can use a selection tool to grab everything else in the channel and make it white. For example, use the Lasso tool to draw a rough selection around your black object and then choose Select → Inverse to flip-flop the selection so Photoshop selects the background. Next, choose Edit → Fill and pick white from the Use pop-up menu and then click OK. Now, your background is solid white and your touch-up work is limited to the area right around your object. If the object you want to select is solid white, you can use the same trick to fill the background with black instead.

- **Fill in the object with black or white.** When the object you want to select isn't *quite* solid black or white, your best bet is to set the Brush tool to either black or white and paint the object by hand. However, if the area is square or oval, you're better off using the Rectangular and Elliptical Marquee

tools (page 127) to select it—yep, they work here, too!—and then choose Edit → Fill and pick black or white from the Use pop-up menu. When you click OK, Photoshop fills that area with color.

- **Get rid of stray gray pixels inside a black object.** If you've cleaned up the rest of your alpha channel but still see a few gray pixels in your black object, use Levels to turn them black. Remember how you used Levels to turn gray pixels white by resetting the white point (page 192)? You can do the same thing to make Photoshop turn gray pixels black. Just open the Levels dialog box by pressing ⌘+L (Ctrl+L on a PC), select the *black eyedropper*, mouse over to your image, and then click one of those pesky gray pixels. Photoshop turns all the gray pixels in your document black.

- **Get rid of stray gray pixels *next to* a black object.** If you end up with a few leftover gray pixels near the object you want to select, use a white Brush set to Overlay mode (see page 273) to paint them white. Press B to select the Brush tool and set your foreground color chip to white (page 22). Then hop up to the Options bar and set the Mode menu to Overlay. In this mode, the Brush tool *completely* ignores the color black and turns gray pixels white, letting you brush away gray pixels near black areas without fear of messing up the black. Even if you paint right over the black area, nothing happens to it!

- **Turn gray pixels in delicate edges black.** If you're dealing with hair or fur, some of the wispier edges may end up more gray than black. If that happens, grab the Brush tool and set your foreground color chip to black. Then trot up to the Options bar and change the Mode menu to Soft Light (page 274). Now, when you paint over the hair or fur, Photoshop turns the gray pixels back. That said, you may not want to turn those delicate parts *completely* black or they'll have a hard edge and won't blend into the background very well. You'll have to experiment on your image to see what looks best.

Figure 5-12:
Using channels to make a selection lets you create a silhouette effect in no time. You can even get a clean selection of curly hair (top) and dangling feathers (bottom).

When you're dealing with delicate edges like these, be careful not to drag the Levels dialog box's shadows slider too far to the right or the edges will disappear. You'll have a little more touch-up work to do with a black brush before you're finished, but it's worth it, and these images require less touching up than the balloons back in Figure 5-11.

2. **Fill your selection with black.**

   With the new layer selected, choose Edit → Fill and pick black from the Use pop-up menu and then click OK to close the Fill dialog box. Your silhouette is finished, but you still need to add a bright new background.

3. **Add *another* new layer and drag it below the silhouette layer.**

   This layer is for your brand new background. This time, drag it *below* the silhouette layer so the new background doesn't cover the silhouette.

4. **Fill your new layer with a bright color.**

   With the new layer selected, take a peek at the bottom of your Tools panel and click the foreground color chip. In the resulting Color Picker, pick a bright color and then click OK. Fill the new layer with color by pressing Option-Delete (Alt+Backspace on a PC), or choose Edit → Fill and then pick Foreground Color from the Use pop-up menu.

That's it! If you need to edit the silhouette—maybe you need to erase something or do a little touchup with a black brush—select that layer and have at it. Likewise, if you want to change the background color, you can select that layer and follow steps 3 and 4 again to fill it with a new color. Now you're starting to see the power of using channels to help make selections. If you used any other selection method on the photos in Figure 5-12, you'd be at it for *days!*

Selecting with the Lightest Channel

How come I always have to make the object black and the background white when I'm using channels to create a selection? Can I do it the other way around instead?

Trying to buck the system, are ya? Lucky for you, the answer is yes—you can make the object white and the background black instead if you prefer. It doesn't matter whether the area you want to select is black or white; all that matters is what the marching ants surround once you load that channel as a selection.

For example, if you're trying to select a light object that lives on a dark background, it's *much* easier to make the object white and the background black. In that case, search for the *lightest* channel (which, in RGB mode, will usually be red). Once you find it, duplicate that channel and then use levels to make it purely black and white (see page 191, step 4). You won't even need to inverse your selection; you'll see marching ants around your object as soon as you load the channel as a selection (page 193, step 7).

Lightening and Darkening Channels

There will be times when you wish a channel was lighter or darker so you'd have an easier time making your selection. Remember back in Chapter 3 when you learned how to lighten and darken a photo quickly using blend modes? While there's no blend mode pop-up menu in the Channels panel, you can make your channel lighter or darker by using the *Apply Image* command. Folks mainly use this command to blend two images together (page 281)—which is why the Apply Image dialog box has a blend mode pop-up menu—but you can also use it to apply a channel to *itself* (as if the channel were duplicated) and change its blend mode at the same time.

To lighten or darken a channel, select it in the Channels panel and create a copy of it, as explained on page 177 (otherwise you'll destroy your original image). Then choose Image → Apply Image and, at the bottom of the resulting dialog box (shown in Figure 5-13), choose either Screen (to lighten) or Multiply (to darken) from the Blending pop-up menu. When you click OK, Photoshop applies the channel to itself using the blend mode you picked. Depending on the image you're working with, your channel will lighten or darken by about 15 to 30 percent. If it needs to be even lighter or darker, you can run the Apply Image command as many times as you need to.

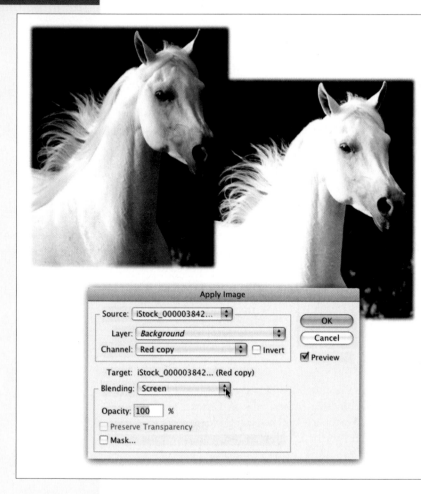

Figure 5-13:
With the Apply Image command, you can apply a channel to itself but with a different blend mode. As you can see here, applying the Screen blend mode to a duplicate of the red channel made this horse quite a bit whiter, making it easier for you to turn it solid white in an alpha channel (page 185).

TIP If the Apply Image command isn't lightening or darkening your duplicate channel enough to make a good alpha channel, you can always pump up the contrast by adding a temporary Curves or Levels adjustment layer to your Layers panel (page 379 and page 367, respectively). By using an Adjustment layer, the temporary contrast boost happens on its own layer, so you can throw it away after you've finished creating the alpha channel.

Combining Channels

Not all your images will have enough contrast to let you make a good alpha channel using just one channel—sometimes you'll have to use *two*. This process takes a bit more time, but the steps are essentially the same.

For example, if you want to select the hat and guitar in Figure 5-14, a quick glance at the Channels panel tells you that the hat is darkest in the red channel, but the guitar is darkest in the green channel. You can duplicate the red channel and adjust it using Levels, the Brush tool, and so on until you make the hat solid black. Next, duplicate the green channel and work on the guitar while you erase (or paint over) the parts of that channel you don't need (the hat). You're building your selection one channel at a time, using the best channel for each part. When you're finished, you may want to merge them, but, alas, Photoshop won't let you. But you *can* combine them into a brand-new channel using the *Calculations* command.

Figure 5-14:
Photoshop won't let you merge two channels into one, but you can combine them into a new channel by running the Calculations command.

Choose Image → Calculations and, in the dialog box shown here, set the Source 1 section's Channel pop-up menu to "Red copy" and the Source 2 section's menu to "Green copy".

Choose Multiply from the Blending pop-up menu at the bottom of the dialog box if you want to create a black object or Screen if you want to create a white one.

Choose Image → Calculations to bring up the Calculations dialog box. From the pop-up menus in the Source 1 and Source 2 areas, pick the channels you want to combine as shown in Figure 5-14, right. This dialog box also lets you set the blend mode, so if you're working with a black object and a white background as shown in the figure, set the blend mode to Multiply so Photoshop keeps the darkest parts of both channels and gets rid of everything else. If you're working with a white object and a black background, use the Screen blend mode instead so Photoshop keep the *lightest* parts of both channels instead.

> **NOTE**   You can also use the *Channel Mixer* to simulate combining channels to create grayscale images. It doesn't actually combine channels, but it makes your image look like you did. Flip to page 304 for the scoop.

Sharpening Individual Channels

As you'll learn in Chapter 11, if you sharpen an image that has a lot of noise in it, you'll sharpen the noise and grain too, making it look ten times worse than it did before (see the box on page 427). That's why it's important to get rid of—or, at the very least, reduce—those nasties *before* you sharpen your image.

> **NOTE**   What's the difference between "noise" and "grain"? They both describe tiny flecks on your image, but, technically speaking, noise occurs in digital images, whereas grain occurs on analog prints. In other words, grain becomes noise once you scan the image.

However, let's say you're in RGB mode and you dutifully followed the instructions on page 427 and ran the Reduce Noise filter on your blue channel (which is typically where most noise lives, though sometimes it can hide out in the red channel). and it didn't do squat. What do you do? You can try bringing out some of the details in your image by sharpening *only* the red and green channels, as shown in Figure 5-15.

> **TIP**   The next time you need to sharpen a portrait of someone who's sensitive about his or her appearance, try sharpening only the red channel to avoid bringing out unwanted details in the person's skin. As you learned earlier in this chapter, most of the fine details live in the high-contrast green channel.

Here's what you can do:

1. **Open your image and make a copy of the layer you're going to sharpen.**

   If you're working with a document that has just one layer, select it in your Layers panel and duplicate it by pressing ⌘-J (Ctrl+J on a PC). If you like, double-click the layer's name and rename it *Sharpen*.

   If you're working on a multi-layer document, press and hold the Option key (Alt on a PC) while choosing Merge Visible from the Layers panel menu (see the figure on page 73). Photoshop combines all the layers into a new layer. Drag this new layer to the top of your Layers panel and name it *Sharpen*.

Figure 5-15:
If you select the red and green channels before running a sharpening filter, you restrict the sharpening to those channels. That way you can avoid sharpening any noise.

2. **Open the Channels panel (page 174) and select the red and green channels.**

   Click to select one channel and then Shift-click to select the other one, so they're both highlighted in your Channels panel. Don't panic if your image turns a weird color (like the horse in Figure 5-15); Photoshop is just showing you the image using only those two color channels.

3. **Choose Filter → Sharpen → Unsharp Mask (page 428).**

   When you run a filter while you've got only certain channels selected, Photoshop applies the sharpening to just those channels. In this case, it won't apply any sharpening to the blue channel.

4. **In the Channels panel, turn on the composite channel to see your new and improved full-color image.**

   You're done! If you want to see before and after versions of your image, open the Layers panel and toggle the Sharpen layer's visibility eye (page 78) off and on.

By sharpening with this method, you won't make the noise any worse (yay!).

TIP   Another, more advanced way to sharpen your image is to use the channel with the highest contrast to create an intricate edge mask. You can read all about that process on page 439.

Cropping, Resizing, and Rotating

Cropping and resizing your images are among the most basic edits you'll ever make, but they're also among the most important. A bad crop—or no crop—can ruin an image, while a good crop can improve it tenfold by snipping away useless or distracting material. Knowing how to resize an image—by changing either its file size or its overall dimensions—can be crucial when it's time to email an image, print it, or post it on a Web site. Cropping is pretty straightforward; resizing, not so much. To resize an image correctly, you first need to understand the relationship between pixels and resolution—and how they affect image quality. (That can of worms gets opened on page 221.) Rotating images, on the other hand, is just plain fun.

In this chapter, you'll learn more than you ever wanted to know about cropping— from general guidelines to the many ways of cropping in both Photoshop and Camera Raw (a powerful photo-correcting application that's installed with Photoshop—see Chapter 9). You'll also discover how to resize images *without*—and this is crucial—losing image quality. Perhaps most important, you'll understand once and for all what resolution really is, when it matters, and how to change it without trashing your image. Finally, you'll spend some quality playtime with the Transform commands.

Cropping Images

There's a reason professional photos look so darn good. Besides being shot with fancy cameras and benefiting from a lot of post-processing voodoo, they're also composed or cropped extremely well (or both). *Cropping* means eliminating distracting elements in an image by cutting away unwanted bits around the edges. Good crops accentuate the subject, drawing the viewer's eye to it; and bad crops are, well, just bad, as you can see in Figure 6-1.

Figure 6-1:
Left: A poorly cropped image can leave the viewer distracted by extraneous elements.

Right: A well-cropped image forces the viewer to focus on the subject by eliminating distractions (in this case, the empty space in the background). This crop gives the subject a little breathing room in the direction she's facing, which is always a good idea (see the next figure).

Technically, you can crop *before* you take a photo by moving closer to the subject (also called "cropping with your feet") and repositioning the subject within the frame. However, if you don't get the shot right when you're out in the field, Photoshop can fix it after the fact. But before you go grabbing the Crop tool, you need to learn a few guidelines.

The Rule of Thirds

Once you understand the rule of thirds, a compositional guideline cherished by both photography and motion video pros, you'll spot it in almost every image you see.

The idea is to divide every picture into nine equal parts using an imaginary tic-tac-toe grid. If you position the image's horizon on either the top or the bottom line—never the center—and the focal point (the most important part of the image) on one of the spots where the lines intersect, you can create a more interesting shot. It's simpler than it sounds—just take a look at Figure 6-2.

Creative Cropping

Along with applying the rule of thirds, pros also crop in unexpected ways, as Figure 6-3 illustrates. Unconventional cropping is yet another way to add visual interest to catch the viewer's eye.

Creative cropping is especially important when you're dealing with super-small images, such as those in a thumbnail gallery or on a Web site where several images desperately vie for attention. In such small images, people can see few, if any, details; and, if the photo contains people, you can forget being able to identify them. Here are some tips for creating truly enticing, teensy-weensy images:

- **Recrop the image.** Instead of scaling down the original, focus on a single element in the image. You often don't need to include the whole subject for people to figure out what it's depicting. Figure 6-3, middle, is a good example.

Figure 6-2:
Top: Imagine a tic-tac-toe grid atop every image. Notice that the interesting bits of the photos are positioned where the lines intersect. Most digital cameras let you add such a grid to the camera's screen to help you compose your shots. To figure out how to turn it on, you may have to root through your camera's menus or (shudder) dig out your owner's manual.

Bottom: Notice the direction your subject is facing. A good crop gives the subject room to move—or, in this case, fly—through the photo. If the image were cropped tightly to the boy's face on the right side, it'd look weird because he'd (theoretically) smack into the edge of the image if he flew away.

- **Sharpen again after resizing.** Even if you sharpened (digitally enhanced the focus of) the original, go ahead and resharpen it post-resizing using the Unsharp Mask filter (page 428). Chapter 11 has the full story on sharpening.

- **Add a border.** To add a touch of class to that tiny ad or thumbnail, give it an elegant hairline border (page 168) or rounded edge (page 134).

Now that you've absorbed a few cropping guidelines, you're ready to read about the many ways you can crop in Photoshop, starting with the most common.

Figure 6-3:

Top: Think outside the box and crop in unexpected ways. You may not think cropping someone's face in two is a good idea, but here's an example where it works.

Middle: When you're close-cropping, you often don't need to reveal the whole subject. For example, this piece of zebra is more visually interesting than the whole animal, and it's still obvious what it's a photo of.

Bottom: Here's proof that you can't always trust what you see; cropping can easily alter the perceived meaning of an image. The left photo has been creatively cropped to suit the headline "Sea Muffin Wins by a Mile!" But the original photo (on the right) reveals another story.

The Crop Tool

Photoshop tools don't get much easier to use than the good ol' Crop tool, which serves all your basic cropping needs. Press C to grab it from the Tools panel and then drag to draw a box around the bits of the image you want to keep, as shown in Figure 6-4. To move the crop box *as* you're drawing it, press and hold the Space bar while dragging. When you've got the crop box where you want it, let go of the Space bar and continue drawing the box.

Figure 6-4:
Left: You can find the Crop tool (circled) in the Tools panel.

Right: After you draw a box on your image, Photoshop gives you an idea of what the end result will look like by darkening the stuff that'll get cropped out. You can easily resize, reposition, and even rotate the crop box by following the instructions lower on this page. Press Return (Enter on a PC) or double-click anywhere inside the box to accept the crop when you get it just right.

TIP   If you draw a crop box and then decide you don't want to crop your photo after all, no problem. You can bail out of a crop-in-progress by pressing the Esc key or clicking the Cancel button in the Options bar (the circle with a slash through it). Or you can just choose another tool.

As soon as you let go of the mouse, Photoshop helpfully darkens the outer portion of the image to give you an idea of what's destined for the trash bin. (This darkened portion is called a *shield*.) Grab any square handle to resize the box or click inside the box and drag to reposition it (your cursor turns into a tiny arrow). When you like what you see, press Return (Enter on a PC) or double-click inside the crop box to accept it.

Keep in mind, though, that when you accept a crop, Photoshop *deletes everything in the shielded area permanently*—unless you undo the deletion right away. So if you change your mind immediately after you wield the crop axe, just press ⌘-Z (Ctrl+Z on a PC) to undo it or step backwards in the History panel (page 25). Better yet, if you like the crop but want to make sure you keep a copy of the original, uncropped version, go to File → Save As right after you crop the photo and give it a new name.

TIP You can toggle the crop shield off and on using the forward slash key (/). You can also change the shield's color and transparency using the Options bar (see Figure 6-5) though these settings are visible only when a crop box is active. Better yet, leave the shield on and change the opacity to 100 percent for a slick, solid-black background so you can really see what the cropped image looks like. It makes a huge difference!

Cropping and hiding

Normally, when you crop an image, Photoshop deletes the portion of the photo that you cropped—it's gone forever. But if you're cropping a *layered* file (see Chapter 3 for the scoop on layers) or a single-layered file that has an unlocked Background, you can tell Photoshop not to vaporize the cropped material, making it easy to retrieve if you change your mind. To do that, head up to the Options bar and, in the Cropped Area section, turn on the Hide radio button shown in Figure 6-5; Photoshop politely *hides* the cropped area outside the document's margins instead of deleting it. In other words, though you won't see it onscreen, it's still part of your file.

If you want to resurrect the cropped portion, choose Image → Reveal All to make Photoshop resize the canvas and reveal anything that's loitering outside the edges of the document (in this case, the bits you cropped). If you want to bring back just a portion of the cropped area, press V to grab the Move tool (see Appendix E, online at *www.missingmanuals.com*) and drag the image back into view.

Figure 6-5:
If you want to hide the portion of the canvas covered by the crop shield (rather than permanently delete it), turn on the Hide radio button. After you crop, the cut bits still dangle beyond the document's new margins—so you can bring them back if you want to. For fickle folks, this is the only way to roll.

NOTE   The Hide and Delete radio buttons appear after you draw a crop box, and they're active only when you're cropping a file that doesn't have a locked Background or when you're cropping a multi-layered file (they'll be grayed out any other time).

Cropping with perspective

If you ever need to straighten an image that includes diagonal lines (like the frame shown in Figure 6-6, left), you can crop the image *and* change its perspective at the same time using the Options bar's Perspective setting. Think of it as your instant image straightener.

NOTE   Photoshop won't let you crop with perspective if you've chosen the Hide option discussed in the previous section. In that case, set the Cropped Area to Delete and *then* turn on the Perspective setting.

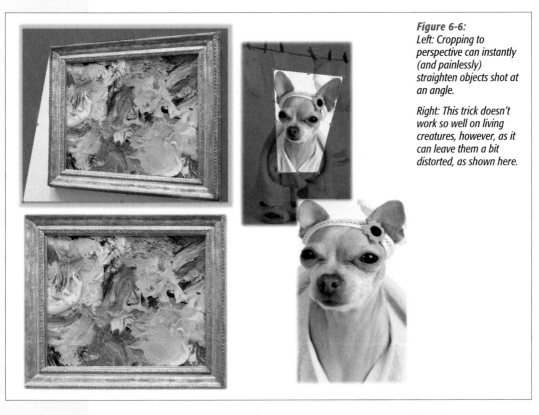

Figure 6-6:
Left: Cropping to perspective can instantly (and painlessly) straighten objects shot at an angle.

Right: This trick doesn't work so well on living creatures, however, as it can leave them a bit distorted, as shown here.

To crop with perspective, first draw your crop box around the object you want to straighten. (The box doesn't have to be exactly aligned with the object though you do want, of course, to grab the whole object.) Next, turn on the Option bar's Perspective checkbox and then drag the corner handles so that the lines of the crop box are parallel to (or on top of) the angled lines in your image. When everything's lined up, press Return (Enter on a PC) or double-click inside the box to accept the crop. If the planets are properly aligned, the cropped image looks nice and straight like the bottom-left image in Figure 6-6. Be careful, though: This tool distorts images and can leave living creatures looking like they were photographed in a funhouse mirror!

Cropping to a specific size

Sometimes you want to crop precisely, like when you're cropping a photo to fit in a 4"×6" frame. In that case, you can use the Options bar to enter the width, height, and resolution (page 221) of the final image to restrict the crop to a certain size.

> **NOTE**   As with all of Photoshop's tools, any changes you make in the Options bar *stay* changed until you change them back. So the next time you crop an image to a specific size, remember to click the Clear button (shown at the far right of Figure 6-7) to empty the dimension fields so your crop boxes won't be restricted to the last measurements you entered.

To enter custom dimensions, press C to grab the Crop tool and then head up to the Options bar and enter measurements in the width and height fields (be sure to include units—see the Note below). Alternatively, you can choose one of the generic sizes listed in the Crop tool's pull-down menu, shown in Figure 6-7. (Click the down arrow next to the Crop tool's icon to summon the menu.) If you plan to print the final result, you'll also need to enter a resolution (page 221); otherwise, you can leave this box blank.

Now, when you "draw" the crop box—actually, you just need to click your image—it's constrained to the *aspect ratio* (the relationship between width and height) of the dimensions you entered. Once you accept the crop, the area *inside* the box perfectly matches the dimensions you entered.

> **NOTE**   When you enter a custom crop size, be sure to include the unit of measurement, such as *px* for pixels or *in* for inches. Otherwise, Photoshop assumes you mean the unit of measurement that's set in Preferences, which may not be what you want (see page 33 to learn how to change this setting).

If the image gets bigger inside the document window after you've cropped to a specific size, it's a clear sign that you've enlarged the pixels by entering too high a resolution for the box you drew (flip to page 221 to learn about resolution). In that case, press ⌘-Z (Ctrl+Z on a PC) to undo the crop. Then draw a smaller crop box, or, in the Options bar, enter either smaller dimensions for the crop box or a lower resolution (or both).

Zooming in by cropping

The Crop Tool's flexibility is all well and good, but what if you want to preserve the original width-to-height relationship (the aspect ratio) of an image? Say you've been out shooting in the Texas plains and, once you're parked back at your computer, you decide to zoom in on that prairie dog you photographed by cropping

Figure 6-7:
If you know the exact dimensions you want your final cropped image to be, type them into the Width and Height fields in the Options bar (circled here). If you want to copy another image's dimensions (so that you can base a crop on those measurements), open that model image and then click the Front Image button (also circled) to snag its dimensions. When you click inside the window of the document you want to crop, the copied dimensions appear in the Options bar, ready for you to use.

out all the dirt surrounding him. Sure, you can draw a crop box around the little rodent, but you have no way of preserving the *shape* of the original photo—Photoshop doesn't have any presets for cropping to specific aspect ratios (see Figure 6-8). You can work around this problem in two ways, both of which involve selecting the whole photo first.

Here are two ways to zoom into a photo without losing its original shape:

- Open a photo and press C to grab the Crop tool. Draw a box around the entire image and, while holding the Shift key, drag one of the corner handles inward. Then click inside the box and drag it into the right position. When you've got it in just the right spot, press Return (Enter on a PC) to accept the crop.

- Open a photo, select its layer, and then press ⌘-A (Ctrl+A on a PC) to select everything on that layer. This creates a selection around the entire photo that you can resize and then use to crop. Choose Select → Transform Selection, and, while you hold down the Shift key (to preserve the selection's aspect ratio), drag one of the square corner handles inward. If you want, reposition the bounding box by dragging it just like you would a crop box. When you get the bounding box where you want it, press Return (Enter on a PC) or double-click inside the box to accept it. Now, choose Image → Crop to get rid of the portion outside the selection and then dismiss the selection itself by pressing ⌘-D (Ctrl+D).

Either way, you've just zoomed in on an item in your photo and cropped it to the same aspect ratio as the original. Give yourself a gold star.

Photoshop's Hidden Grid

Let's say you've taken a photo and didn't compose it perfectly using the rule of thirds (page 203). No biggie. Photoshop has a hidden grid that you can lay atop an image to help you crop. But like many Photoshop gems, you've got to hunt for it.

To find the grid, select the Custom Shape tool (see Appendix E, online at *www.missingmanuals.com*) from the Tools panel, head up to the Options bar and click the Custom Shape picker (circled below). Scroll through the preloaded shapes until you spot the tic-tac-toe grid and then click once to select it. Before you use this tool to draw your own grid atop a photo, you'll want to pick a grid color (so you can actually see it) and pop open the Info panel (so you can monitor its size).

To change the color of the grid, click the color swatch at the far right of the Options bar (also circled) and pick a color that will stand out well on top of your image (don't choose white if your photo has a lot of snow in it, for example). Next, open the Info panel by choosing Window → Info. This panel lets you see the width and height of the grid as you're drawing it, which is crucial for making the grid (and therefore the final cropped image) just the right size.

Now you're ready to draw the grid. Click the document once and watch the Info panel carefully as you drag diagonally to draw the grid (don't worry about *where* the grid lands because you can always move it later). You'll probably find it challenging—if not impossible—to draw the grid *exactly* the right size. So if you wind up within a few decimals of your target, that's okay (for example, a grid that's 5.01×7.01 instead of 5×7 isn't worth fussing over).

Once you draw the grid, you can reposition it with the Move tool (see Appendix E, online at *www.missingmanuals.com*) or resize it with the Free Transform command by pressing ⌘-T (Ctrl+T on a PC). (See page 245 for more on Free Transform.) You can also change the grid's color: In the Layers panel, double-click the shape layer and choose another color from the resulting Color Picker.

When everything is perfect, go to the Layers panel, select the photo layer, and then press C to activate the Crop tool. Draw a crop box around the outside edge of the grid and press Return (Enter on a PC) to accept. To get rid of the grid, drag the shape layer to the tiny trash can at the bottom of the Layers panel. Voilà—you've got yourself a perfectly composed photo.

Adding Polaroid-style photo frames

The Crop tool isn't all work and no play; you can use it for fun stuff like creating a Polaroid-style photo frame like the one in Figure 6-9. Besides being a fast way to add a touch of creativity to your image, this kind of frame lets you add a caption to commemorate those extra-special moments.

Figure 6-8:
Here you can see the original photo (top), along with the kind of crop you might perform freehand (bottom left), next to a crop that preserves the aspect ratio of the original (bottom right). Preserving the aspect ratio is handy when you're preparing photos for a slideshow and they all need to be the same shape.

Figure 6-9:
Left: To create the look of a Polaroid, use the Crop tool (page 206) to add canvas space around your photo as shown here. Be sure to add a little extra space at the bottom for a caption.

Right: When you add a solid white layer and then add even more canvas space, the Polaroid really starts to take shape. Next, add a caption, merge the layers, and then rotate your image. Finish off the effect by adding a drop shadow (page 119) large enough to show around all four edges of the photo. Engage!

Here's how to add a frame to your photo:

NOTE To practice this maneuver on your own computer, visit this book's Missing CD page at *www.missingmanuals.com* and download the practice file Trekkers.jpg.

1. **Open an image and double-click its Background layer to make it editable.**

   Remember, the Background layer is initially locked for the reasons explained in the box on page 80. Until you unlock it, Photoshop restricts what you can do with it. Just give it a quick double-click to unlock it, and—if you want—give it a name in the resulting dialog box.

2. **Enlarge the document window so you can see the gray work area all the way around the image.**

   To enlarge the window, drag its bottom-right corner until you've got a few inches of gray space on all four sides of your image. This bit of window resizing makes it easier to see what you're doing in the next step.

3. **Add canvas space with the Crop tool.**

   Draw a box around the image and, while you hold down the Option key (Alt on a PC), drag one of the crop handles outward about one-quarter inch and then release Option (or Alt).

   TIP Holding down Option (Alt) while you drag the corner handles of a crop box forces all four sides of the box to expand or shrink simultaneously by the same amount. (Otherwise, you'd have to move each handle one after another.) Press and hold the Shift key to resize the box as a perfect square.

   Next, drag the bottom-middle crop handle down another one-quarter inch (that's where the caption goes). Finally, press Return (Enter on a PC) to tell Photoshop you want to keep the new canvas space. You should see a checkerboard background around the photo (see Figure 6-9, left).

   NOTE If you don't make the Background layer editable before you increase the canvas space, the area around the photo ends up the color of your background color chip instead of transparent, so you can't see the checkerboard pattern. If you have this problem, press ⌘-Z (Ctrl+Z on a PC) and start over with step 1.

4. **Create a new layer and drag it below the original photo layer.**

   At the bottom of the Layers panel, click the new layer's icon (it looks like a piece of paper with an upturned corner). To keep from covering up the whole photo in the next step, drag the new layer's thumbnail *below* the original layer.

5. **Fill the new layer with white to form the Polaroid edges.**

   Choose Edit → Fill, pick "white" from the Use pop-up menu, and then click OK. Now you've got a Polaroid-style frame around your photo.

6. **Increase your canvas space again so you have room to rotate the image and add a drop shadow.**

   Press C to grab the Crop tool and draw a box around the image yet again. Add equal space on all four sizes by dragging any corner handle while you hold down the Option key (Alt on a PC). Press Return (Enter) to accept the crop.

7. **Add a caption with the Type tool.**

   Press T to select the Type tool (page 537) and add a caption toward the bottom of the frame. Here's your big chance to use a handwriting typeface! Bradley Hand is one good option.

8. **Merge the layers.**

   When you have everything just right, hop over to the Layers panel menu and choose Merge Visible (page 103), which lets you rotate the whole mess in the next step.

9. **If you like, rotate the image just a bit to give it more character.**

   Summon the Free Transform command by pressing ⌘-T (Ctrl+T on a PC) and then rotate your photo by positioning your cursor just below the bottom-right handle. When the cursor turns into a double-sided curved arrow, drag slightly up or down. Press Return (Enter) to accept the rotation or press Esc to reject it and try again.

10. **Finally, add a drop shadow using Layer Styles (page 119).**

    Click the tiny cursive *fx* at the bottom of the Layers panel and choose Drop Shadow (page 119), and then increase the shadow's size quite a bit so it's visible on all four sides of your new Polaroid frame. Move the shadow around by dragging in your document and soften it by lowering the opacity in the Layer Style dialog box. Finally, click OK to exit the Layer Style dialog box.

When you're all done, your image should look like Figure 6-9, right.

Cropping with Selection Tools

You can also crop an image within the boundaries of a selection. This technique is helpful if you've made a selection and then need to trim the image down to roughly that same size. The Rectangular Marquee tool (page 127) works best for this kind of cropping (though all the selection tools work) because Photoshop, bless its electronic heart, can crop only in rectangles.

After you draw a selection, choose Image → Crop. Because you're not using the Crop tool, you won't get resizing handles, a shield, or the ability to hide the crop, but the document does indeed get reduced to the edges of the selection. If you're attempting to crop with an irregular or elliptical selection, you'll *still* end up with a rectangular image that encompasses the area you selected.

Trimming Photos Down to Size

If your image has a solid-color or transparent (checkerboard) background, you may find yourself chipping away at its size to save space in the image's final destination (a Web site, a book, or whatever). The *trim* command is incredibly handy for close cropping images, especially those that include drop shadows or reflections. Such embellishments make the image's true edges hard to see—and therefore tough to crop—because they fade into the background. So it's easy to, say, accidentally chop a drop shadow in half when you're cropping. Fortunately, you can enlist Photoshop's help in finding the edges of an image and have it do the cropping for you.

To whittle down your photo, choose Image → Trim and, in the resulting dialog box (shown in Figure 6-10), use the radio buttons to tell Photoshop whether you want to zap transparent pixels or pixels that match the color at the document's top left or bottom right . (Why just those two positions? Because the solid color you want to zap is in one of those spots.) Next, choose which sides of the image you want to trim by turning their checkboxes on or off and clicking OK. Photoshop trims the document down to size with zero squinting on your part.

Figure 6-10:
If you have a hard time seeing the image's edge when you want to perform a close crop, let Photoshop do it for you by using the Trim dialog box. In this example, the goal is to get rid of the extra transparent space at the bottom so the photo is as small as possible. You can do that by choosing Transparent Pixels in the dialog box shown here.

NOTE The Trim command was used on every screenshot in this book to crop the images as closely as possible. It's a massive timesaver if you work in production!

Cropping and Straightening Photos

If you've ever painstakingly scanned a slew of photos into a single document, you can save yourself a lot of work by having Photoshop crop, straighten, and split them into separate files—all with the flick of a single menu command.

With the page of photos open, choose File → Automate → "Crop and Straighten Photos". Photoshop instantly calculates the angle of the overall image's edge (that is, the edge of the photo bits) against the white background, rotates the images, and then duplicates all the photos into their own perfectly cropped and straightened documents, as shown in Figure 6-11. It's like magic!

> **NOTE**   The "Crop and Straighten Photos" command also works on documents that contain just *one* image, provided the picture has white space on all four sides (like the white space you'd have between photos if you scanned several at once). It also works on layered files (see Chapter 3). Just select the layer of the image you want to extract, run the command, and Photoshop strips that layer out into its own document and deletes it from the original document. If that layer contains several images, they'll get stripped out into their own individual documents as well.

Figure 6-11:
It's tough to get a bunch of photos perfectly straight during the scanning process (heck, just putting the lid down moves them!). This is a prime opportunity to use Photoshop's automatic "Crop and Straighten Photos" command. In one fell swoop, the photos (top) get straightened, cropped, and copied into their own individual documents (bottom) right before your eyes.

TIP   If you want Photoshop to crop and straighten just a few photos that all reside on a single layer, draw a selection around each of them before you run the command (use any selection tool and hold the Shift key to add to the selection). Photoshop processes only those photos, provided they (and their individual selection boxes) are next to each other. If they're not, Photoshop crops and straightens everything in between, forcing you to close the new, unwanted documents.

FREQUENTLY ASKED QUESTION

Straightening a Single Image

How come there's no tool for straightening just one image?

Though Photoshop has a built-in, automatic solution for straightening multiple images in a single document (which works on a single image if it has white on all four sides), it doesn't have a tool specifically for straightening just *one* borderless image. Or at least, that tool isn't obvious.

The workaround is to use the Ruler tool (see Appendix E, online at *www.missingmanuals.com*) that hides underneath the Eyedropper in the Tools panel. Grab the Ruler tool and then drag across the horizon of your photo or some other area that should be straight. (It doesn't matter

how *far* you drag with the tool; Photoshop only cares about the *direction* you drag.)

Next, choose Image → Image Rotation → Arbitrary to bring up the angle dialog box where Photoshop has filled in the rotation measurement that it gathered from the Ruler tool. When you Click OK, the image rotates perfectly into place. With the Ruler tool still selected, click the Clear button in the Options bar to get rid of the line you drew (or it'll be there forever—at least until you grab another tool).

Press C to grab the Crop tool (page 206) and zap the newly white edges.

Cropping and Straightening in Camera Raw

Camera Raw is an amazing piece of software that photographers use to edit the color and lighting of images (you'll learn loads more about it in Chapter 9). It gets installed with Photoshop, so you don't have to download it or pay for it separately. Using Camera Raw to crop and straighten your photos has two big advantages:

- **You can undo the crop or straighten (or both) at any time**—whether the file you're working on is Raw, JPEG, or TIFF. (In Chapter 9, you'll learn how to use Camera Raw for all three file formats—not just Raw files.)

- **If you have several photos that need to be cropped in a similar manner, you can crop them all at once.** Talk about a timesaver!

To open an image in Camera Raw, select the image in Bridge (see Appendix C) and then choose File → "Open in Camera Raw", or press ⌘-R (Ctrl+R on a PC). Follow the instructions in the next section to crop one or more images.

Cropping images

It's as easy to crop images in Camera Raw as it is in Photoshop. With an image open, select the Crop tool at the top of the Camera Raw window and draw a box around the image, as Figure 6-12 illustrates. Then click the Crop tool and hold down the mouse button to reveal a handy pull-down menu that lists aspect ratios, as well as a Custom option. If you pick Custom, a dialog box appears so you can enter a specific ratio or dimensions in pixels, inches, or centimeters. Whichever method you use, Camera Raw places a crop box atop your image, which you can resize by dragging any resulting handle or dragging the box itself.

Figure 6-12:
Open one or more images in Camera Raw and use the Crop tool (circled, top) just like you would in Photoshop. (Remember, Camera Raw is actually a separate program.) Simply drag across the image to draw a box and then press Return (Enter on a PC) to accept the crop.

If you've opened multiple images (as shown here), you'll see their thumbnails in the filmstrip on the left side. To crop all the images at once, click the Select All button in the upper left (circled) and draw the crop box. You'll see the crop, along with a tiny Crop tool icon (circled, left), applied to all selected thumbnails.

The blue underlined text below the preview window (circled) changes to reflect the size of the crop box as you draw.

TIP You can exit the crop box by pressing the Esc or Delete key (Backspace on a PC) while the Crop tool is active or by choosing Clear Crop from the Crop tool's pull-down menu.

When you're finished, press Return (Enter on a PC) to see what the newly cropped image looks like. If you want to edit or undo the crop, just grab the Crop tool to make the crop box reappear for your editing pleasure.

If you have several images that need to be cropped in the same way, the steps are almost identical. Just open the images in Camera Raw by selecting them in Bridge (see Appendix C) or elsewhere on your hard drive. When the thumbnails appear in the filmstrip on the left side of the Camera Raw window, click the Select All button and then use the Crop tool as described in this section All the photos get cropped simultaneously, and each filmstrip thumbnail updates according to how you cropped the image. (A tiny Crop tool icon, circled in Figure 6-12, also appears at the bottom left of each thumbnail.)

At this point, you can:

- **Click the Save Images button to convert, rename, or relocate the file(s)—or any combination of those tasks—so you don't overwrite the original.** If you save them in Photoshop format, you can tell Camera Raw to preserve the cropped pixels in case you want to resurrect them in the future (see Figure 6-13 for details).

- **Click the Open Images button** to apply the changes and open the photo(s) inside Photoshop.

- **Click Cancel** to exit Camera Raw without applying changes.

- **Click Done** to apply the changes (which are editable the next time you open the image in Camera Raw) and exit the Camera Raw window.

Figure 6-13:
To see and work with your original, precropped image in Photoshop, click Camera Raw's Save Images button, choose Photoshop from the Format pop-up menu and then turn on the Preserve Cropped Pixels checkbox.

Next time you open that file in Photoshop, the photo appears on its own layer. If you want to see the hidden cropped bits, use the Move tool to drag them back into view or choose Image → Reveal All.

TIP   You can use all manner of keyboard shortcuts to change how the Save, Open, Cancel, and Done buttons at the bottom of the Camera Raw window behave: To open a copy of the image in Photoshop without updating the original Raw file, Option-click (Alt-click on a PC) the Open button. To open as a Smart Object (page 115), Shift-click the Open button. To skip the Save As dialog box and make Camera Raw use the same location, name, and format that you used last time you saved, Option-click (Alt-click) the Save As button. To reset the Camera Raw settings to what they were originally, Option-click (Alt-click) the Cancel button.

Straightening images

If you need to straighten a bunch of images at a similar angle, Camera Raw can handle them all at once. Open the images and grab the Straighten tool (it's just to the right of the Crop tool) and draw a line across the horizon—or anything in the image that's supposed to be straight—as shown in Figure 6-14, top.

The image won't straighten immediately—instead you see what looks like a crop box so you can check the angle (Figure 6-14, bottom). If it's okay, press Return (Enter on a PC) and Camera Raw straightens the photo. If you didn't get it perfectly straight, you can have another go by opening the image in Camera Raw (if you closed it) and choosing the Straighten tool again.

Resizing Images

No matter what you've whipped up in Photoshop, there will come a time when you need to change the size of your masterpiece. For example, if you want to print, email, or post it on a Web site, you need different-sized images for each of those tasks. Changing an image's size isn't hard; Photoshop gives you oodles of options. The challenge lies in doing it without sending the quality of your image down the tubes.

Sure, you can let the "Save for Web & Devices" dialog box (page 232) or the Print dialog box (page 628) do the resizing for you, but if you're aiming to be a serious pixel pusher, you'll want far more control. That, my friend, brings you up against the granddaddy of Photoshop principles: Image Resolution—the measurement that determines the size of the pixels in your image, which in turn controls the quality of your prints.

Arguably, resolution is one of the toughest digital-image editing concepts to wrap your brain around. Many people grapple with questions like "What the heck is resolution?" "How do I change an image's resolution?" and "What's the minimum resolution I need to print good-looking photos?"

In the following pages, you'll learn all the nitty-gritty you need to answer these—and other—questions.

NOTE   Resolution doesn't mean a hill of beans unless you're sending your image to a printer. If you're not going to print it, don't worry about resolution—think about pixel dimensions instead.

Figure 6-14:
Top: Camera Raw can't take a document full of images and then crop, straighten, and split them out into individual documents automatically like Photoshop (page 216). But you can use it to straighten one or more images simultaneously. Just activate the Straighten tool (circled) and draw a line across a part of the image that's supposed to be straight (also circled).

Bottom: You'll see what looks like a rotated crop box (shown here). Just press Return (Enter on a PC) to accept and Camera Raw straightens the image.

Pixels and Resolution

As you learned in Chapter 2 (see the box on page 48), the smallest element of a raster image is a pixel. When they're small enough and viewed together, these tiny blocks of color form an image (see Figure 6-15).

NOTE Some digital images aren't comprised of pixels—they're made up of *vectors,* a series of points and paths. One of the best things about working with vectors is that none of the size-versus-quality challenges you run into with pixel-based images apply. You can make vectors as big or as small as you like, and they'll always look great. To learn more about using vectors, trot on over to Chapter 13.

Figure 6-15:
Raster images are comprised of individual blocks of color called pixels. To see them, zoom into the image by pressing ⌘-+ (Ctrl-+ on a PC) repeatedly or use the Magnify tool in the Tools panel. (Press ⌘ or Ctrl and the – key to zoom out.) At 3,200 percent magnification, you can see the individual pixels that make up a tiny section of this sunflower.

Pixels have no predetermined size, which is where *resolution* enters the, uh, picture. Resolution is a measurement that determines how many pixels get packed into a given space, which in turn controls how big or small the pixels are. It's helpful to think of resolution as pixel density—how closely the pixels are packed together. In fact, it's measured in terms of pixels per inch—or *ppi,* as folks tend to call it.

NOTE You'll also hear resolution referred to as *dpi,* which stands for "dots per inch." This usage isn't strictly accurate because dpi is technically a measurement used by printers (since they actually print dots). Nevertheless, many folks mistakenly say "dpi" when they mean "ppi."

One helpful way to understand resolution is to relate it to something in the real world. Imagine you're baking cookies (hang in there; it'll make sense in a minute). When you pour brown sugar into a measuring cup, the sugar reaches the one-cup line. But after you pack the granules firmly into the cup, the sugar reaches only the half-cup line. You still have the same number of granules (which are like pixels), they're just packed more tightly together (they have a higher resolution) in the confines of the measuring cup (the document). The loosely packed granules you started with are like low resolution, and the firmly packed granules are like high resolution. (Anyone hungry?)

Since increasing image resolution—from, say, 72 ppi to 300 ppi—packs the pixels more tightly, it results in a smaller but smoother and better-looking printed image. Lowering image resolution, on the other hand, means loosening the pixels, which results in a larger image that, as you might suspect, is totally unsuitable for print since the pixels get so big you see each one (so the image looks like it's made from Legos).

A printer is one of the few devices capable of modifying its output (that is, the print) based on an image's resolution. In other words, send your inkjet printer a low-res version and a high-res version of the same picture and it'll spit out images that differ vastly in size and quality. The resolution on a computer monitor, on the other hand, is handled by the video driver (the software that controls what you see on the monitor), not the resolution specified in the image itself. That's why an 85 ppi image looks identical to an 850 ppi image onscreen. The bottom line: Printers can take advantage of higher resolutions (scanners can, too, but that's a story for page 52).

The Mighty Image Size Dialog Box

If you can't trust your monitor to show your image's true resolution, who can you trust? Why, the Image Size dialog box, shown in Figure 6-16. It not only displays the current resolution of any open document, it also lets you *change* the resolution.

To summon this dialog box and check your picture's resolution, choose Image → Image Size. The dialog box reveals all kinds of info about your image: its file size (that is, how much space it takes up on your hard drive), its pixel (onscreen) dimensions, how big it would be if you printed it, and its resolution. If you're pre-paring an image to send by email or post to the Web, you need concern yourself only with the pixel dimensions at the top of the dialog box. If you're going to print the image, focus your attention on the Document Size portion in the middle.

> **TIP** You can summon the Image Size dialog box by pressing ⌘-Option-I on a Mac or Ctrl+Alt+I on a PC.

The checkboxes at the bottom of the dialog box control how Photoshop resizes your image if you make changes in this dialog box. Here's what each one does:

Document file size

Image Size

Pixel Dimensions: 1.37M

Width: 655 | pixels
Height: 733 | pixels

OK
Cancel
Auto...

—Use to automatically calculate ppi from lpi

Document Size:

Width: 6.55 | inches
Physical size — Height: 7.33 | inches
when printed
Resolution: 100 | pixels/inch

☑ Scale Styles
☑ Constrain Proportions
Turn off to — ☑ Resample Image:
lock pixel
dimensions   Bicubic (best for smooth gradients)

Interpolation method

Figure 6-16:
This particular image is 655 pixels wide by 733 high and has a file size of 1.37 MB. If you were to fire it off to your trusty inkjet printer, the resulting print would be 6.55"×7.33" with a resolution (pixel density) of 100 ppi. As you'll learn from the chart on page 228, anything printed at that resolution looks super blocky–like a bad Xerox that someone keeps enlarging.

- The **Scale Styles** checkbox determines whether Photoshop scales any layer styles you've applied to the image along with the image itself. It's a good idea to leave this setting turned on; otherwise, that drop shadow you added may end up larger or smaller than the image itself. (See page 119 for more on layer styles.)

- The **Constrain Proportions** checkbox locks the aspect ratio (page 209) of the image so it doesn't get squished or stretched when you resize it. You'll want to leave this important setting turned on, too.

- The **Resample Image** checkbox is your key to changing resolution *without* changing image quality. Resampling is a process in which Photoshop responds to your size-change request either by adding or subtracting pixels. The problem, as you'll learn in a moment, is that resampling involves guesswork on Photoshop's part, which can futz with your picture's quality.

When you first launch Photoshop, the Resample Image setting is turned on, which instructs Photoshop to increase or decrease the number of pixels in your image, and both processes reduce the image's quality because Photoshop either makes up pixels or chooses which ones to eliminate, respectively. By turning Resample Image *off* you protect the quality of your image by *locking* the pixel dimensions. If you plan to print the image, turning this setting off lets you fiddle with the resolution for hours without altering the quality of your image because you're just changing how tightly the existing pixels are packed together. (Visit "Resizing Images for Print" on page 228 to see this concept in action.)

In contrast, when you turn the Resample Image checkbox on, you get to choose a resample method from the pop-up menu below it. So why would you want to go this route? Well, sometimes you need Photoshop's resampling help.

For instance, if you've got a 200-ppi image that's going to print at 4"×6" and you *really* need a 5"×7" print *and* want to maintain that 200-ppi resolution, turn on this checkbox.

The options below the Resample Image checkbox determine which kind of mathematical voodoo Photoshop uses to either add or delete pixels. Since better image quality means more work for Photoshop, the better the image, the more time Photoshop takes to perform the aforementioned voodoo. Here are your choices, listed in order of quality (worst to best) and speed (fastest to slowest):

- **Nearest Neighbor.** Though this method gives you the lowest image quality, it can be useful because it produces the smallest files, which is great if you're transferring files over the Internet and either you or the person on the other end has a slow connection. Nearest Neighbor works by looking at the colors of surrounding pixels and then copying them. It's known for creating jagged edges, so you'll want to restrict its use to images with hard edges like illustrations that aren't anti-aliased (see Chapter 13).

- **Bilinear.** If you choose this method, Photoshop guesses at the color of new pixels by averaging the colors of the pixels directly above, below, and to the left and right of the one it's adding. It produces slightly better results than Nearest Neighbor and is still pretty fast, but you're better off using one of the next three methods instead.

- **Bicubic.** Picking this method tells Photoshop to figure out the colors of new pixels by averaging the colors of the pixels directly above and below the new one and the *two* pixels to its left and its right. This method takes longer than the previous two but produces smoother color transitions in areas where one color fades into another.

- **Bicubic Smoother.** Similar to Bicubic in the way it creates new pixels, this method blurs the pixels slightly to blend the new ones into the old ones, making the image smoother and more natural looking. Adobe recommends this method for enlarging images.

- **Bicubic Sharper.** This method is also similar to Bicubic in the way it creates new pixels, but instead of blurring whole pixels to improve blending between the new and old like Bicubic Smoother, it softens only the pixel *edges*. Adobe recommends this method for downsizing images. (Some Photoshop gurus report that Bicubic Sharper also produces better *enlargements* than Bicubic Smoother.)

If you know the *lpi* (lines per inch—see the box on page 226) of your printer, you can click the Image Size dialog box's Auto button to bring up the Auto Resolution dialog box (see Figure 6-17). Just enter the lpi, pick a quality setting, and let Photoshop calculate the proper resolution for a good print.

Figure 6-17:
If you know the lpi of the printer you're using, enter it in the Screen field. Photoshop then calculates the resolution (ppi) for you. You've got a choice of three different quality settings: Draft gives you a resolution of 72 ppi, Good multiplies the lpi by 1.5, and Best multiplies it by 2.

NOTE   There are two kinds of resampling: If you delete pixels, you're *downsampling* (see page 231 for more); if you add them, you're *upsampling* (the box on page 227 has tips for upsampling). When you upsample, Photoshop adds pixels that weren't originally there through a mathematical process called *interpolation*, in which Photoshop uses the pixels that really *are* there to guess what the new ones should look like.

FREQUENTLY ASKED QUESTIONS

Understanding LPI

What the heck is lpi? I thought all I had to worry about was ppi!

Laser printers and professional printing presses print a little differently than inkjet and dye-sublimation printers. Inkjets spray dots of color onto paper and simulate shades of gray by using a wide or narrow dot dispersal pattern. Dye-subs use a process that involves fusing color dye—including shades of gray—onto paper through a heating process (they tend to produce higher-quality, water- and smudge-proof prints than inkjets but are more expensive).

Professional printing presses use yet another inting method. If you were to hold a magnifying glass to a professionally printed newspaper or magazine, you'd find that the image is comprised of a gazillion tiny shapes. Typically, those little shapes are circles though they can

be diamonds or squares, depending on the printer. If the shapes are small enough, you'll never see them with your naked eye (although some folks have been quite successful enlarging them to galactic proportions and calling it pop art—think Lichtenstein and Warhol).

The setting that determines how many little shapes get printed in an inch of space is called *lines per inch*, or lpi. (It's also referred to as screen frequency, line screen, or halftone screen.) It's important to understand lpi because there may come a day when you're forced to figure the appropriate ppi (page 222) from lpi (also helpful in scanning, see page 52). When this happens, breathe deeply, smile smugly, and proceed to Table 6-1 on page 228. Or just click the Auto button in the Image Size dialog box and let Photoshop figure out the ppi from lpi for you, as Figure 6-17 explains.

Resolution guidelines for print

Now that you understand what resolution is and how it works, the question becomes how much resolution you need when you print. Because printers print in different ways, the resolution you need for a beautiful print depends on the printing device itself: inkjets spray, dye-subs fuse, laser printers or professional presses print shapes, and so on.

It's tempting to practice resolution overkill just to be on the safe side, but doing so makes your files larger, resulting in wasted hard drive space and increased time to process, save, and print. Instead, consider the resolution guidelines listed in Table 6-1.

Upsampling Without Losing Quality

If you leave the Image Size dialog box's Resample Image checkbox (page 224) turned on and increase an image's resolution, Photoshop adds information (in the form of pixels) that wasn't originally there. Increasing the resolution this way is usually a bad idea because fake pixels never look as good as real ones. However, there may come a time when you've got no choice.

For example, maybe you've snatched an image from the Web that you need to print (see page 235) or your image needs to be printed in an extremely large format (like a billboard). If you find yourself in such a pickle, you've got a few options (happily, the first two are free):

Method 1. For some reason, adding pixels 5 to 10 percent at a time doesn't damage quality much (it causes some loss of quality, sure, but not as much as, say, increasing the size by 900 percent all at once). Here's what you do: Open the Image Size dialog box, make sure both the Resample Image checkbox and the Constrained Proportions checkbox at the bottom of the dialog box are turned on, and then choose Bicubic Smoother from the method pop-up menu. Then, in the Document Size section of the dialog box, change either the Width or Height pop-up menu to Percent (changing one menu to percent causes the other to change automatically). Enter a number between 105 and 110 into the Width field and then click OK (the Height field changes to the same number automatically). Repeat this process as many times as necessary to enlarge the image to the dimensions you need.

Method 2. Some Photoshop pros (Scott Kelby and Vincent Versace, for example) swear by this method for large-format printing. Open the Image Size dialog box and make sure that the Resample Image and Constrain Proportions checkboxes are turned on. In the Document Size section of the dialog box, enter *either* the width or the height of the desired print. Enter your desired resolution, choose Bicubic Sharper from the pop-up menu at the bottom of the dialog box, and then click OK. The pros swear this method gives them terrific results though it defies the resizing guidelines discussed so far. Give it a shot and see what happens.

Method 3. Buy a third-party plug-in specifically designed to help you upsample, like Genuine Fractals by onOne Software (*www.ononesoftware.com/detail.php?prodLine _id=2*) or PhotoZoom Pro 2 by BenVista (*www.benvista. com/main/content/content.php?page=ourproducts& section=photozoompro_1*). Both plug-ins manage to pull off some serious pixel-adding witchery with truly amazing results. See Chapter 19 for more on third-party plug-ins.

NOTE When you send files off to a professional printshop, it's always a good idea to ask how much resolution the printshop wants. If they don't know, find another printer…fast!

Table 6-1. Resolution guidelines for print

Device	Paper	Resolution	Use For
Desktop laser printer	Any kind	Resolution should match the dpi of the printer (which should be listed in the owner's manual). Some people call this resolution 1:1, which is just another way of saying the ppi matches the dpi exactly.	Documents or line art (pure black-and-white images containing no shades of gray)
Inkjet printer	Regular or textured	150–240 ppi	Color or grayscale images, black-and-white documents
Inkjet printer	Glossy or matte photo	240–480 ppi. Use the upper end of this range only for large images (13" × 19" on up).	Color or grayscale images
Dye-sublimation printer	Any kind	Resolution should match the dpi of the printer.	Color or grayscale images
Web offset press	Newsprint or uncoated stock	1.5–2 times the lpi, depending on how detailed (1.5) or smooth (2) you want the print to be (see the box on page 226)	Newspaper ads or community papers (like *Auto Trader* and *The Village Voice*)
Commercial printing press	Coated stock	2–2.5 times the lpi	Magazines, coffee table books, fancy brochures, business cards, and line art

Resizing Images for Print

Throughout your Photoshop career, you'll need to resize and change the resolution of images so they'll print well. Perhaps the most common situation where you'll need to do this is when you download stock photography or import a snapshot from a digital camera. Unless the stock photographer has changed the resolution, the images you download from stock image companies will be 72 ppi. Similarly, most digital-camera files arrive on your computer with their resolution set to 72 ppi (roughly the standard for onscreen display).

Keep in mind that today's digital cameras can capture *tons* of info: Consumer-level, 10-megapixel cameras currently produce images packed with around 3648 (width) × 2048 (height) pixels, and pro-level, 21-megapixel models capture images in excess of 4080 × 2720 pixels. That's a veritable smorgasbord of pixels, letting you crop the image (see page 206) and alter resolution however you like.

Resizing your images is a snap though the risk of reducing image quality in the process is high. As you learned in the previous section, the key to preserving quality lies in the Resample Image checkbox (shown in Figure 6-18).

NOTE   If you're printing a generic-size image (like 8" × 10" or 5" × 7") straight from Photoshop, you can use the Print dialog box's "Scale to Media" option to recalculate the resolution for you, according to the paper size you've chosen. In most cases, you'll end up with the dreaded resolution overkill; head on over to page 621 for the details.

Figure 6-18:
Say you want to print this image and the largest paper size your printer can take is 8" × 10". A peek in the Image Size dialog box reveals that if you tried to print it at its current resolution, you'd need a huge piece of paper—one larger than 41" × 27". Even worse, at the image's current resolution of 72 ppi, that massive print would look crummy. But don't panic: You can use the settings in this dialog box to change the resolution so your image prints at a more manageable size.

Here's how to use the Resample Image checkbox to resize your image for printing without sacrificing quality:

1. **Open a photo and then choose Image → Image Size to open the Image Size dialog box, or press ⌘-Option-I (Ctrl+Alt+I on a PC).**

   The image shown in Figure 6-18 weighs in at 3000 × 2000 pixels at a resolution of 72 ppi. If you wanted to print it, you'd need a ridiculously big piece of photo paper (over 41" × 27"). Luckily, those dimensions come way down once you increase the resolution. Remember, increasing resolution is very much like that brown sugar analogy introduced back on page 223: you're packing all those pixels much more tightly together, resulting in a much smaller image but one whose quality (that is, resolution) is much higher.

2. **Lock the image quality by turning off the Resample Image checkbox at the bottom of the dialog box.**

Take a look at Figure 6-19. Notice how the pixel dimension text boxes disappeared once the Resample Image option was turned off? Now, the only info you can change is the document's size and resolution, which affect how tightly the pixels are packed together. You can't change the *number* of pixels contained in your image, which means Photoshop isn't adding or deleting pixels. See how the tiny black line on the right side of the Document Size section now connects width, height, and resolution? That line means a change in one of these fields affects the other two.

Figure 6-19:
Turning off the Resample Image checkbox lets you lock your image's pixel dimensions to protect its quality. After you lock the dimensions, you can increase the resolution without worrying about how your image will print—it'll get smaller, sure, but it won't become blocky and pixelated. Think about it this way: As the resolution goes up, the size of the printed document goes down because Photoshop is packing the same number of pixels (3000 × 2000) more tightly together. At 300 ppi, for example, this image produces a print that's 10"×6.667". Compare that to the file's original settings of 72 ppi and 41.667"×27.778".

3. **Increase the resolution.**

The value you enter here depends mostly on which kind of printer you're using; see Table 6-1 for advice on some recommended resolution settings and then do some tests yourself to see which settings work best for you. If you know your printer does a respectable job printing at 300 ppi, enter that amount in the Resolution field and the document dimensions decrease to 10"×6.667", as Figure 6-19 illustrates. The pixel dimensions and file size, however, remain the same—the image is still 3000×2000 pixels and 17.2 MB. The only thing that changes is the resolution.

NOTE Popping into the Image Size dialog box is a handy way to learn which size print you can produce with the pixel dimensions you have to work with. If you know your printer does a decent job at 240 ppi, for example, type that amount into the resolution field and see which size print you can make. If it's a funky size, you can always crop the image to a specific, more common size as explained on page 209.

4. **Click OK when you're done.**

Now you can print your image and it'll look great (though you may need to do a tiny bit of trimming).

Did you notice how much the onscreen image changed when you tweaked the resolution? That's right: Not at all. That's part of the reason resolution is so confusing. The 72 ppi image looks just like the 300 ppi version because our eyes can't see pixels that small onscreen. The lesson here is that as long as you turn off the Resample Image checkbox, you can tweak image resolution till the cows come home and you won't alter the image quality—ever. Sure, you'll change the image's printed size, but you won't be adding or deleting pixels that weren't there in the first place.

Resizing for Email or the Web

It sounds crazy, but not everyone has a high-speed Internet connection...at least, not yet. Some poor souls are doomed to live with dial-up for the foreseeable future, and even wireless hot-spots don't exactly provide warp-speed Internet connections (especially when a lot of people are trying to use them). That's why it's important to decrease the file size of that monster photo from Debra's divorce party before emailing it to your pals—if you don't, it might take them forever to download it! The same goes for images you plan to post online: The smaller their file size, the faster they'll load in a Web browser. (You'll learn a lot more about posting images online in Chapter 17, but the info in this section will get you started.)

To make an image smaller, you have to decrease its pixel dimensions. This process is called downsampling (page 226), and you can go about it in a couple of ways. Read on to learn both methods.

TIP If you'd rather resize your image by entering a percentage instead of pixel dimensions, see page 661.

Using the "Save for Web & Devices" dialog box

If you want to see a preview of your new, smaller image and maybe experiment with different file formats (if you're torn between a JPEG and a PNG, say), you'll want to use the "Save for Web & Devices" dialog box. ("Devices" refers to portable gadgets like cellphones and smart phones.) This method is a great way to reduce file size while you monitor image quality. Here's how:

1. **Open a photo and then choose File → "Save for Web & Devices".**

   When the large dialog box shown in Figure 6-20 takes over your screen, you can choose from a variety of file formats and quality levels that Photoshop can use to make your image Web- or email-friendly. You can see up to four previews of what your image will look like in various formats before you commit to one, which is why the dialog box is so darn big.

Figure 6-20:
The quickest way to resize an image for emailing or posting on the Web is to head straight for the "Save for Web & Devices" dialog box. It lets you reduce the image's size and save it in a different format in one fell swoop, complete with up to four previews.

2. **In the upper-left part of the dialog box, click the 4-Up tab (circled in Figure 6-20) and then pick an appropriate file type from the format pop-up menu in the upper–right corner (also circled).**

   When you first pop open this dialog box, you'll see the 2-Up tab, which is fine if you don't want to do a lot of experimenting with format or quality. However, if you want to see the size and quality difference between the original image and, say, a JPEG at low, medium, and high quality, you'll need to activate extra preview windows. (As you learned on page 46, JPEG is the best choice for photos, and that's the format selected in the figure.)

3. **To keep the photo's quality relatively intact while you reduce the file size, choose High from the Compression Quality pop-up menu (also circled in Figure 6-20, upper right).**

   To make the file smaller, Photoshop throws away a few pixels and then compresses what's left. So if you set the quality level to High (which has a numeric equivalent of 60), Photoshop tosses out only a few pixels, and the quality won't suffer much. But if you choose a quality level of Low (numeric equivalent: 10), Photoshop throws away significantly more pixels and the result is a low-quality image. (See page 663 for a more detailed discussion on the JPEG format.)

4. **Reduce the image's size.**

   At the bottom right of the dialog box lies a section called Image Size. If you know the dimensions you want the image to be, enter the width or height. If you don't know what size you want and are just concerned with making the *file size* smaller, you can enter a percent reduction like 25 percent. (That's a good percentage if you're emailing an image captured on a 10-megapixel camera at a high-quality setting.)

5. **Choose a resample method.**

   In the dialog box's lower-right Image Size section, choose Bicubic Sharper from the Quality pop-up menu. This method (explained on page 225) works particularly well when you're zapping pixels (downsampling). Some folks say it even works great for enlargements—see the box on page 227. As you can see in the middle of Figure 6-20, the resulting file is 212 KB at a quality setting of 60. That's more than 300 percent smaller than the original 3.52 MB file!

6. **Click the Save button at the very bottom of the dialog box (not shown in Figure 6-20) and then give the file a new name so you don't overwrite the original.**

   TIP It's a good idea to run the Unsharp Mask filter after you downsample images because they tend to get blurry from the compression. See Chapter 11 for more on sharpening.

Using the Image Size dialog box

Choose this method when you need to make the file as small as possible—for example, if you're designing a Web banner ad that has to be 40 KB or less. By resizing your image (changing its pixel dimensions) using the Image Size dialog box first, and then using the "Save for Web & Devices" dialog box to produce the JPEG, you'll produce a smaller file than you would using the method you learned in the previous section (see Figure 6-21). Just follow these steps:

1. **Open a photo and choose Image → Image Size.**

   Up pops the Image Size dialog box (Figure 6-16).

2. **In the dialog box, make sure the Resample Image checkbox is turned on, and then choose Bicubic Sharper from the resample method pop-up menu.**

   Bicubic Sharper is your best bet for getting a high-quality image when you downsample, as explained on page 225.

3. **In the top portion of the dialog box, enter a new pixel dimension for either width or height.**

   If the Constrain Proportions checkbox is turned on, the other measurement changes automatically so that the image is resized proportionately. (If it's not turned on, you'll have to enter both width and height, which can potentially make your image too narrow or too stretched out if you don't maintain the image's original aspect ratio [page 209].)

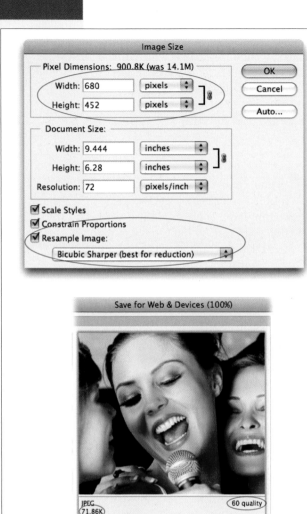

Figure 6-21:
Top: To reduce your image's file size, make sure the Resample Image checkbox is turned on and that Bicubic Sharper is selected in the resample method pop-up menu. At the top of the dialog box, enter the new pixel dimensions in either the Width or Height field (the other field changes automatically based on what you enter). Remember, the smaller the pixel dimensions, the smaller the file size. If you're designing an image for a Web site, you'll probably need to fit the image into a fixed set of dimensions. If you're emailing the image, shoot for 800 pixels or less in width.

Bottom: Once you've resized the image, you can use the "Save for Web & Devices" dialog box to select JPEG with a compression of 60. By taking the time to resize your image in the Image Size dialog box first, you'll produce a smaller file size in the end. As you can see here, the resulting file is a mere 71.86 KB.

In Figure 6-21, the new width is 680, which is also the width of the image in Figure 6-20. Notice how much smaller a file you can get using this method compared to using the "Save for Web & Devices" dialog box.

4. **Click OK to close the dialog box.**

The program pops you back into the main Photoshop window.

5. **Choose File → "Save for Web & Devices".**

That's right, you still need to enlist the help of *another* dialog box to finish up your compression work. In this new dialog box, choose JPEG at a compression quality of High, as explained in steps 2 and 3 on page 232.

6. Finally, click Save at the bottom of the dialog box and give your resized file a new name.

As Figure 6-20 shows, this method can strip a 3.52 MB file down to a mere 71.86 KB, which is substantially smaller than the 212 KB file created solely with the "Save for Web & Devices" dialog box on page 229.

Resizing Web Images for Print

Unfortunately, there will come a time when you need to print an image snatched from the Web. The problem is that Web images are usually fairly small so they'll load quickly in a Web browser, but that also means they contain precious few pixels for you to work with. Most of them are 72 ppi—a resolution so low that that the individual pixels are big enough to see when the images are printed—which means that, unless you like that blocky look, you *have* to increase the resolution before you print it. And, as you learned earlier in this chapter, when you bump up the resolution, you wind up with a print the size of a postage stamp. It's a lose-lose situation.

> **TIP** A good rule of thumb is that Web images print decently at about half the size they appear onscreen. So if you start with an image that's about 2" × 2" onscreen, it prints decently at 1" × 1".

For all those reasons, printing a Web image isn't ideal, but if that's the only image you've got, you have to make do. In that case, follow these steps to beef up its print quality:

1. **Save the image to your hard drive.**

   Find the image on the Web and Control-click (right-click on a PC) the image to summon your Web browser's shortcut menu and choose "Save Image to Desktop" (Save Image As or Save Picture As on a PC). Or you can choose Copy Image from the shortcut menu and paste the image right into a new Photoshop document.

   > **TIP** If you're on a Mac and want to save the image somewhere other than your desktop, press and hold the Option key while Control-clicking and the "Save Image to Desktop" menu option becomes Save Image As, so you can choose where to save it and give it a meaningful name (though some browsers, like the latest version of Firefox, give you this option automatically). On a PC, you automatically get a Save As option.

2. **Open the image in Photoshop and then open the Image Size dialog box by choosing Image → Image Size.**

   Photoshop displays the now-familiar dialog box shown in Figure 6-16.

3. **At the bottom of the dialog box, turn off the Resample Image checkbox, enter 150 in the Resolution field, and then click OK to close the dialog box.**

   A resolution of 150 ppi works okay if you're printing to an inkjet printer. The resulting print may not be frame-worthy, but, hey, it'll be identifiable.

4. **Back in the main Photoshop window, save the resulting file in TIFF format.**

   Choose File → Save As and choose TIFF from the Format pop-up menu, just like you learned in Chapter 2 (page 46). The photo is now primed and ready for popping into Word, InDesign, or any other word processing or page-layout program.

If the image is just too small after you follow these steps, visit the box on page 227 to learn about upsampling.

MESSAGE FROM THE LAWYERS

Thou Shalt Not Steal

This whole "snatching images from the Web" business opens a copyright can of worms. You're actually committing image theft if you download an image created by someone else and then use it in another format. That is, except in these situations:

- You've obtained express permission from the original photographer or artist (or other copyright holder).

- The image is clearly designated as being in the public domain.

- The image has been published under the Creative Commons license (*www.creativecommons.org*).

- You're using the image purely for personal reasons.

That said, if you're promoting a book raffle at your computer club and snatch cover art from the publishers' Web sites or you need a headshot to promote a speaker and you snag one from her Web site, the chances of finding the image police at your front door are slim.

Resizing Images for Presentations

You're probably thinking, "I thought this book was about Photoshop and here you are talking about *presentations*. What gives?" The fact is, you may be asked to prepare presentation graphics one day. If you are, the information in this section just might save your skin. Luckily, you don't have to worry about resolution; since your audience will view the images onscreen, it's the pixel dimensions that matter most.

Some folks claim to be more afraid of public speaking than they are of death. Standing before an expectant audience *can* be unnerving; obviously, you want everything to run smoothly and the graphics to look perfect. That's why it's smart to resize images before you stick them into Microsoft PowerPoint or Apple Keynote. Oversize images bloat the presentation's file size and cause it to run very slowly, or worse, crash. On the flip side, small images may look fine on your computer screen but terribly blocky when you project them on a larger screen.

The solution to both problems is to decide how big your images need to be and resize them *before* you import them into PowerPoint or Keynote. It's okay to resize images a little bit in those programs, but you don't want to put a dozen ginormous, 10 MB photos in your presentation. That's just asking for trouble.

If you want an image to fill a whole slide, find out the pixel dimensions of the projector you'll be presenting on (the slides should be that size, too). If you don't know, find out how big the slides are.

> **TIP** Most projectors have a resolution of 1024×768 pixels, although high-definition projectors, which have a resolution of 1280×720 pixels are becoming more common. If you've got no clue which kind of projector you'll be using, 1024×768 is a good bet. If you're really paranoid, go with 1280×720 just to be on the safe side. Honestly, though, these dimensions are so close that you probably won't see any difference either way.

Here's how to sniff out (and change) slide dimensions in the two most popular presentation programs:

- **Microsoft PowerPoint.** Choose File → Page Setup and look for the Width and Height fields. Now, here's where things get tricky. For some unknown reason, PowerPoint lists slide dimensions in inches instead of pixels. This peculiarity poses a challenge because, to ensure that your image fills the slide perfectly, you have to convert the inches to pixels. Luckily, Table 6-2 lists the most common conversions for you.

- **Apple Keynote.** Open the Inspector palette by clicking View → Show Inspector. Open the Document Inspector by clicking the icon on the far left of the Inspector palette (it looks like a piece of paper with a folded corner) and peek at the Slide Size pop-up menu at the bottom of the palette, which lists the slide dimensions in pixels. Those are your magic numbers. Back in Photoshop, grab the Crop tool, enter those numbers into the Options bar—leave the resolution blank because the image won't be printed—crop your image, and then save it as a JPEG or PNG (as discussed on pages 663-665).

Table 6-2. Slide size conversions

Pixel Dimensions	PC Slide Size	Mac Slide Size
800×600	8.33"×6.25"	11.11"×8.33"
1024×768	10.66"×8"	14.22"×10.66"
1280×720	13.33"×7.5"	17.77"×10"

Once you know the slide dimensions, hop on over to page 209 for step-by-step instructions on how to crop your image so that it'll fit perfectly on the slide.

> **NOTE** Because the Mac and Windows operating systems handle pixels a little differently (they're slightly bigger in Windows), you have to enter a resolution of 96 ppi when you resize images in Photoshop for use on a Windows machine. If you're designing presentation graphics on a Windows machine for use on a Mac, enter a resolution of 72 ppi instead. If you're designing graphics on a Mac for use on a Mac, you can leave the resolution field blank. Honest.

Resizing with Smart Objects

When you're designing a document—a poster, a magazine cover, or whatever—you'll probably do a fair amount of resizing before you get your page's layout just right. What if you shrink a photo down only to realize it worked better at its original size? Can you enlarge the image without lessening its quality? Negative, good buddy. That is, not unless it was opened as a Smart Object.

As you learned in Chapter 3 (page 115), Smart Objects are the best thing since sliced bread. They let you apply all kinds of transformations to the files they *reference*, including decreasing and then increasing their size—all without affecting the quality of that image as it appears in your document. Here's how to resize a Smart Object that contains an image:

- **To decrease the size of a Smart Object**, select the relevant layer in the Layers panel and choose Edit → Free Transform. Grab any of the resulting square handles and drag inward to reduce its size (remember to hold down the Shift key as you drag if you want to resize it proportionately). Let Photoshop know you're finished resizing by pressing Return (Enter on a PC).

    NOTE If you've used the Place command to open the Smart Object (as described on page 117), resizing handles appear automatically when the image appears in your document on its very own layer.

- **To increase the size of a Smart Object**, make sure you've got that layer selected in the Layers panel and then choose Edit → Free Transform. This time, drag outward with any of the resulting corner handles (again, while you hold down the Shift key if you want to preserve the image proportions). If you don't enlarge the image beyond its original pixel dimensions, the image quality remains pristine. Unfortunately, there's no quick and easy way to return the Smart Object to its original size if you forget what it was.

Automated Resizing with the Image Processor

As you'll learn in Chapter 18, you can record a series of steps into a replayable *action* that resizes and saves a batch of images en masse. But Photoshop has a niftier automatic resizing feature built in: It's called the Image Processor. This little program within a program (called a *script*) was developed specifically to change the file format and adjust the size of a lot of images—fast (see Figure 6-22). It can save you tons of time whenever you need to convert files to the JPEG, PDF, or TIFF format—it doesn't convert PNGs or GIFs.

TIP You can also access the Image Processor script within Adobe Bridge; see Appendix C.

Here's how to run the Image Processor script:

1. **Choose File → Scripts → Image Processor.**

    Photoshop opens the aptly named Image Processor dialog box.

Figure 6-22:
Russell Brown, Adobe's chief evangelist, developed the Image Processor a few years back. If you run this clever little script on a folder full of images, Photoshop automatically saves them in the format you choose or resizes them instantly–or both. It's amazingly cool. You can also access this dialog box within Bridge (see Appendix C).

2. **In the top section of the dialog box, tell Photoshop which images you want to run the Image Processor on.**

   Your options are to run it on the images you currently have open (Use Open Images) or run it on a folder of images (Select Folder). You can also choose to include all subfolders (if any exist) and to open the first image to be changed—just to make sure everything is okay—by turning on the appropriate checkbox(es).

3. **Pick where you want to save the images.**

   Feel free to save the images in the same folder they're currently in or click the radio button next to Select Folder and pick a new one. If you're sending the files somewhere new, turn on the "Keep folder structure" checkbox to make Photoshop organize the files the same way you had them. For example, if you're the ultra-organized type, you may store your images in a nested directory (a folder containing other folders). The main folder might be named by date and contain other folders such as Raw, Masters, Processed, Prints, and so on. If you turn on the "Keep folder structure" checkbox, Photoshop resizes and reformats the images, plops them into the new folder, and organizes them the same way you did originally.

4. **Enter the file type(s) you want Photoshop to save your files as and, if you want to resize them, enter a new size in pixels.**

   Here's where the real magic lies. You have three options:

   • Save the file as a **JPEG** and choose a quality setting (see page 232); you can also convert the color profile to sRGB (as page 670 describes, this is a good idea) if you wish.

   • Save as a **PSD** file and maximize the file's compatibility with other versions of Photoshop so you can open it with an earlier version of the program.

   • Save as a **TIFF**, with or without compression (see page 621, step 7).

   You can choose one option or all three! No matter what the original format, Photoshop converts your files to match the options you choose. You can also have Photoshop resize your files while it's at it; just turn on the "Resize to Fit" checkbox and enter a maximum pixel value for either width or height.

5. **In the Preferences section, you can enter custom settings if you want to.**

   Here's your opportunity to run an additional action. Just pick an action category from the first pop-up menu and then choose the action itself from the second pop-up menu. You can also include copyright information if you like. Unless your turn off the ICC profile checkbox, Photoshop automatically includes an ICC profile with your files (see the Note on page 630 for more on ICC profiles).

   TIP   You can save all of the settings you enter in the Image Processor dialog box as an XML file so you can use them again later or share them with someone else by clicking the Image Processor dialog box's Save button. Likewise, you can load an existing XML file by clicking the Load button.

6. **When you've got all the settings just right, click the Run button to make the Image Processor work its magic.**

   It may take Photoshop a while to run this script, depending on how many files you selected and how big they are. However, it certainly won't take as long as it would for you to do all this stuff yourself!

Resizing the Canvas

In addition to resizing images, you can also resize your canvas to give yourself room for more artistic goodness. As you learned on page xx, this extra room is called canvas space, and you can add it visually using the Crop tool (as shown on page 213, step 3) or manually by choosing Image → Resize → Canvas Size (Image → Canvas Size on a PC). The manual method lets you enter specific dimensions, as Figure 6-23 illustrates.

Figure 6-23:
Using the Canvas Size dialog box, you can increase canvas space by entering specific dimensions or a percentage change. Use the Anchor option (circled) to determine where the existing image lands within the newfound space. (If you don't select anything here, your image lands in the middle.)

The Canvas Size dialog box gives you the following options:

- **Current Size and New Size.** Ever informative, Photoshop lets you know how big the document is now and how big it will be once you click OK. These sections give you info on both file size and physical dimensions (width and height).

- **Width and Height.** When you enter width and height, Photoshop assumes you want to measure these new dimensions in pixels, but you can use the pop-up menus to change them to percent, inches, cm, mm, points, picas, or columns (change either the width or height setting and the other changes automatically).

- **Relative.** Turning on this option makes Photoshop add the existing image size to the new canvas size that you've specified. Otherwise, the new canvas size is exactly what you enter, regardless of whether the document already contains an image. If you know the exact size you want the canvas to be, leave this option turned off. If you're just trying to create some extra elbow room in which to work and you've already got an image in your document, turn it on.

- **Anchor.** Choose where you want Photoshop to put your existing image. When you click OK, it lands in whatever area you've chosen here. (If you don't choose anything, it ends up in the middle of the canvas.)

- **Canvas extension color.** If you want the new space to be a certain color, you can set that color here. If you don't pick a color—and the Background layer is locked (page 80)—Photoshop uses the color of your background color chip (page 22). If the Background layer is *unlocked*, the new space is the gray-and-white checkerboard pattern that indicates transparency (which is typically what you want).

If your image is in landscape orientation and needs to be portrait instead (or vice versa), you can rotate the canvas by choosing Image → Image Rotation → Flip Canvas Horizontal or Flip Canvas Vertical. Be careful when you use this command on a document that includes text—it may end up backwards!

The Content-Aware Scale Tool

Once in a blue moon, a software company adds a feature that works almost like magic. Adobe has done exactly that in Photoshop CS4 with *Content-Aware Scale* (affectionately known in nerdy circles as CAS). CAS examines what's in your image and intelligently adds or removes pixels from unimportant areas as you change the size of the overall image. The magic part? It knows enough to leave the important parts—people, for instance—unchanged. For example, think of Web pages you've used that resize themselves smoothly and fluidly as you make your browser window bigger or smaller. Now imagine doing the same thing with an image. With this new technology, Photoshop doesn't squash or stretch the whole image; instead, the program adds or deletes chunks of, say, that big ol' sky in the background or clumps of grass in the foreground, leaving the important bits—like the three frolicking friends—unscathed. A picture really is worth a thousand words when it comes to CAS so take a peek at Figure 6-24 to see what this new feature can do.

You can use CAS in all kinds of situations. For example, say you want to put your all-time favorite family picture in an 8"×10" frame but the aspect ratio (page 209) isn't quite right, the background isn't big enough, or the photo's subjects need to be a little bit closer together. In any of these circumstances, CAS can help. You can use it on layers and selections in RGB, CMYK, Lab, and Grayscale image modes (page 40) and at all bit depths (see the box on page 43); however, you can't use it on Adjustment layers, layer masks, channels, Smart Objects, 3-D layers, or Video layers.

When you're ready to take CAS for a spin, here's what to do:

> **NOTE**   To take CAS for a test drive using the images shown in this section, head to this book's Missing CD page at *www.missingmanuals.com* and download the file CAS.zip.

1. **Open an image and press Q to pop into Quick Mask mode.**

   Content-Aware Scaling isn't perfect, so you'll get better results if you help it out by masking the areas you want to protect. Quick Mask mode (page 162) is the fastest way to do that.

2. **Press B to grab the Brush tool and then set your foreground color chip to black.**

   Peek at the color chips at the bottom of the Tools panel. Press D to set them to the factory fresh black and white, then press X until black is perched happily on top.

3. **Mouse over to your image and paint the areas you want to protect.**

   When you start painting, you'll see the red overlay of Quick Mask Mode (see Figure 6-25, top). When everything you want to protect is covered with red (like the grass and the happy dude shown in Figure 6-25, top), press Q to exit Quick Mask Mode. You'll see marching ants appear around everything *except* those areas, which you'll fix in the next step (you learned all about marching ants and selections in Chapter 4).

Figure 6-24:
As you can see, CAS does an amazing job of resizing only the unimportant background in this image.

4. **Flip-flop your selection by pressing ⌘-Shift-I (Ctrl+Shft+I on a PC).**

   Since Photoshop selected everything *except* the area you painted in the previous step, you need to invert it. (You can also choose Select → Inverse.)

5. **Save your selection as an *alpha channel* (page 185).**

   As you learned in Chapter 5, alpha channels are a great way to save your selection. Open your Channels panel by choosing Window → Channels. When you save your selection as an alpha channel by clicking the little circle-within-a-square icon at the bottom of the Channels panel (circled in Figure 6-25, top), Photoshop adds a channel called Alpha 1 to the bottom of your Channels panel.

Figure 6-25:
Top: The areas you paint in Quick Mask mode turn red, as shown here. This mode is one of the fastest ways to make a selection, and you don't have to be that careful about the area you paint; anything you touch with the brush is protected. Once you exit Quick Mask mode and flip-flop your selection, click the "Save selection as channel" button at the bottom of the Channels panel (circled here).

Middle: Once you've activated the Content-Aware Scale tool, you can choose your protective alpha channel from the Protect pop-up menu in the Options bar (circled).

Bottom: Because you protected the tall grass and the man, Photoshop has left them alone and resized everything else.

6. **Tell Photoshop you want to resize your image by choosing Edit → Content-Aware Scale or pressing ⌘-Option-Shift-C (Ctrl+Alt+Shift+C on a PC).**

Photoshop puts white, square resizing handles all around your image; but don't grab any of the handles just yet!

7. **From the Options bar's Protect pop-up menu, choose Alpha 1 (Figure 6-25, middle).**

Choosing the alpha channel you've already created shows Photoshop which areas you want to protect. If your image contains people, you can preserve their skin tones by clicking the little stick-person icon to the right of the Protect menu.

If you want to make your image smaller or larger by a certain percentage, you can enter numbers in the W (width) and H (height) fields or in the Amount field. Most of the time, you won't mess with these size fields because it's easier to resize your image visually, as you'll do in the next step.

8. **Mouse over to your image, grab one of the resizing handles, and drag it toward the center of your image.**

    As you can see in Figure 6-25 (bottom), the image has been narrowed, but the tall grass and the happy dude remain unchanged. CAS resized only the unimportant parts of the image, and it did a great job.

Is this amazing technology? Yes. Is it still in its developmental phase? Heck, yes. Even so, it has many practical uses. For example, if you have to fit an image into a very small spot (like wedging a photo into a tight spot for a magazine article) you won't necessarily have to crop it. Just don't expect CAS to work on images that don't have plain backgrounds (like a portrait or other close-up image). Nevertheless, this exciting new tool will only get better in future versions of Photoshop.

Rotating, Distorting, and Other Creative Madness

Photoshop gives you lots of ways to rotate, distort, and otherwise skew images, all mighty useful techniques to have in your Photoshop bag of tricks. By rotating an image, you can add visual interest (see the Polaroid technique on page 211), convert vertical elements to horizontal ones (or vice versa), and straighten crooked items. Distorting comes in handy when you want an object or text to appear slanted or turned slightly on its side or if you want the object or text to fade into the distance with perspective.

This chapter has touched on rotation here and there; you've learned how to rotate a crop box (page 206), rotate an image with the Free Transform command (page 214), and rotate your whole canvas (page 241). In this section, you'll learn about simple rotations as well as more complex ones.

Simple Rotations

As you probably suspect, the Image Rotation command rotates images. Choose Image → Image Rotation to spin your whole document—layers and all—180 or 90 degrees (clockwise or counterclockwise) or by an arbitrary amount that you specify (see Figure 6-26). You can also flip the canvas (or layer) horizontally or vertically, as you learned on page 241.

The Transformers

Another way to resize and rotate (not to mention flip, skew, and distort) images is to use the Transform commands. These commands can help you make a single selected object or an entire layer bigger or smaller without altering the size of your document. If you hop up to the Edit menu, you'll see the Free Transform and Transform options about halfway down the list. Using the Free Transform Command, discussed later in this section, you can perform all the tasks listed on the Transform submenu (see Figure 6-27).

> **NOTE** If you're attempting to transform a shape or a whole path (see page 497), the Edit menu item changes to Transform Path. If you're trying to transform just *part* of a path, the menu item changes to Transform Points.

Selecting one of these commands summons a bounding box that looks and works just like a crop box (page 206), with tiny square handles on all four sides of the image. You can use Transform commands on objects you've selected (Chapter 4), on individual layers, or across many layers (to learn more about selecting layers, see page 75). The Transform commands resize the layer or selection but not the whole document (the only way you can resize the whole document is by changing the image size [page 223] or the canvas size [page 240]).

> **NOTE** You may find yourself wondering. "Why does Photoshop have both a Free Transform command *and* a Transform menu if I can use them to do the exact same things?" Good question! The only real difference between these two options is that choosing an item from the Transform menu locks you into performing just that particular task (using the Scale tool, for example), whereas the Free Transform command lets you perform any or all of the transformations at the same time (without having to press Return or Enter between transformations).

You're free to transform any objects you wish. Vectors, paths, Shape and Type layers, and Smart Objects are especially good candidates for transformation because they can all be resized without harming (pixelating) the image. But you don't want to enlarge raster images (page 48) very much because you have no control over resolution, resampling, or any of the other important stuff mentioned back on page 224.

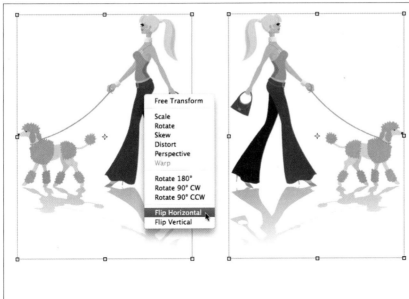

Figure 6-27:
When you activate one of the Transform commands by choosing it from the Edit menu (or activate all of them by choosing Free Transform), you'll get a bounding box surrounded by tiny, draggable handles.

Left: Another way to access all the options found in Edit → Transform is to Control-click (right-click on a PC) inside the bounding box to bring up the Free Transform command's shortcut menu, shown here.

Right: By choosing Flip Horizontal, you can make this girl and her poodle travel in the opposite direction.

To play it really safe, resize an image using the Transform commands only for the following reasons:

- To decrease the size of a selection on a single layer. (Page 161 has more info about transforming a selection without altering any pixels on that layer.)

- To decrease the size of everything on a single layer or multiple layers (see page 75 for details on selecting multiple layers).

- To increase the size of a vector, path, portion of a path, Shape layer, Type layer or Smart Object either on one layer or across several layers.

To use the Free Transform command, in the Layers panel, choose the layer you want to transform and then press ⌘-T (Ctrl+T on a PC) or choose Edit → Free Transform. Photoshop puts a bounding box around your image, complete with handles that let you apply any or all of the following transformations to your object (they're all illustrated in Figure 6-28):

- To **scale** (resize) an object, grab a corner handle and drag inward to decrease or outward to increase the size of the object. Press and hold the Shift key while you drag to resize proportionately (meaning the object won't get distorted, just resized). You can drag one handle at a time or press and hold the Option key (Alt on a PC) to scale from the center outward (meaning that all four sides of the bounding box move simultaneously).

TIP   If you summon the Free Transform command to resize something big, the transform handles may end up outside your document's edges (or margins), making them impossible to see, much less grab. To bring them back into view, choose View → "Fit to Screen" or press ⌘-0 (that's the number zero, not the letter O) or Ctrl+0 on a PC.

- To **rotate** an image, hover outside any corner handle. When your cursor turns into a curved, double-headed arrow, drag up or down in the direction you want the image to turn. If you drag far enough, you spin the image all the way back to where it started. To rotate in 15-degree increments, press and hold the Shift key while you drag.

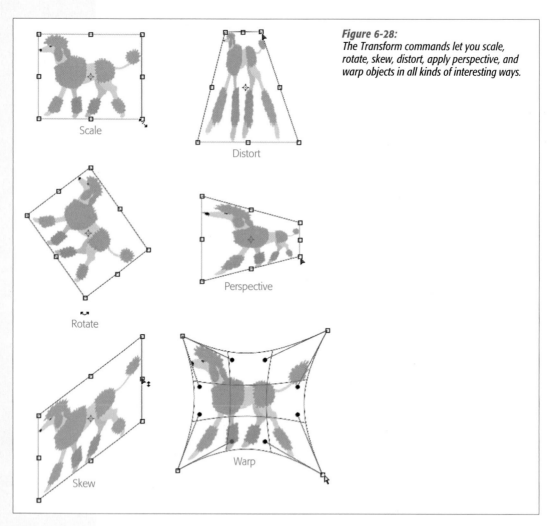

Figure 6-28:
The Transform commands let you scale, rotate, skew, distort, apply perspective, and warp objects in all kinds of interesting ways.

- To **skew** (slant) an object, press ⌘-Shift (Ctrl+Shift on a PC) and drag one of the side handles (your cursor turns into a double-headed arrow).

- To **distort** an image freely, press Option (Alt) while you drag any corner handle.

    NOTE   You can also reshape images with the Liquify filter. Flip to page 405 to learn how.

- To alter an object's **perspective**, press ⌘-Option-Shift (Ctrl+Alt+Shift) and drag any corner handle (your cursor turns gray). This maneuver gives the object a one-point perspective (in other words, a single vanishing point).

- To **warp** an image, click the "Switch Between Free Transform and Warp" button in the Options bar (page 250). Photoshop puts a warp mesh over your image so you can reshape it in any way you want. Drag any control point or line on the mesh to warp the image or choose a ready-made preset from the Warp pop-up menu at the far left of the Options bar. See page 550 for the scoop on warping text.

    TIP   The warp mesh grid can help you create the slickest page-curl effect you've ever seen. Head on over to page 163 to get the scoop.

- To **rotate or flip** your image, choose one of these preset options. Flip and Rotate are covered previously in this section. If you choose one of these little jewels, you won't get a bounding box; Photoshop just rotates or flips your image.

    NOTE   You can apply several transformations in a row if you like; just keep choosing different transformation types from the Transform menu or use the keyboard shortcuts listed above. To undo the last change you made without exiting the bounding box, press ⌘-Z (Ctrl+Z on a PC).

When you're finished with your transformation(s), press Return (Enter), double-click inside the bounding box, or click the checkmark icon at the far right of the Options bar to accept the transformation.

If you apply a transformation only to realize that it's not quite enough, you can repeat the transformation by choosing Edit → Transform → Again. You don't get a bounding box—instead, the same transformation is reapplied (for example, if you rotated the image by 90 degrees, it rotates another 90 degrees). If you're resizing raster images, try to transform the object only once: The more you transform a pixel-based image, the blurrier and more jagged it can become.

If you want more precise transformations than the ones you get by dragging handles around, you can use the Options bar to enter specific dimensions for scaling, rotating, and skewing (see the list beginning on page 238), as Figure 6-29 illustrates.

    TIP   All transformations are based on a tiny *reference point* that appears in the center of a transform box—it looks like a circle with crosshairs. You can drag it or set your own point by heading up to the Options bar and either clicking one of the reference point locator squares (shown in Figure 6-29) or entering exact X and Y coordinates.

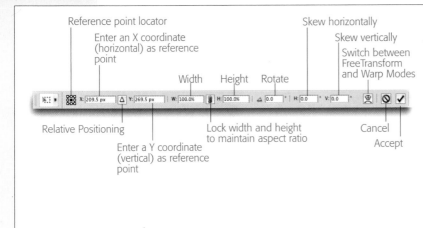

Reference point locator

Enter an X coordinate (horizontal) as reference point

Width   Height   Rotate

Skew horizontally

Skew vertically

Switch between FreeTransform and Warp Modes

Relative Positioning

Lock width and height to maintain aspect ratio

Enter a Y coordinate (vertical) as reference point

Cancel

Accept

Figure 6-29:
Instead of resizing by dragging handles, you can enter specific dimensions in the Options bar's W and H boxes (for width and height), as shown here, anytime you see a bounding box.

You can change the reference point (the point around which the transformation occurs) from dead center to a point on the bounding box by clicking one of the locator squares to highlight the corresponding handle on the bounding box. Folks who want a bit more precision can enter exact X and Y coordinates for the reference point so the reference point is relative to itself instead of the whole document.

TIP   To put the Free Transform bounding box at your beck and call anytime you select the Move tool (see Appendix E, online at *www.missingmanuals.com*), press V to activate the Move tool and then, in the Options bar, turn on the Show Transform Controls checkbox. (The only problem with this tactic is that you might end up resizing something when you don't mean to.)

Creating an image reflection

A great little trick you can perform with the Transform command is adding a simple image reflection (see Figure 6-30). Though this little technique takes a few steps, it's well worth the effort. Besides adding depth to an otherwise flat photo, a reflection can make an object appear as if it were shot on another surface altogether, like a table (handy for making product shots without a proper studio setup).

NOTE   To follow along, visit this book's Missing CD page at *www.missingmanuals.com* and download the practice file Reflection.jpg.

Figure 6-30:
Top: To add a reflection, duplicate the image layer (in this case, the balloon layer), flip it vertically with the Transform command, and then apply a gradient layer mask (page 265) to create the fade. Here you can see that a black-to-white, linear gradient (circled at top) did the trick. By dragging with the Gradient tool from the bottom of the document toward to the bottom edge of the photo (also circled), you can make the reflection appear to fade away.

Bottom: Here's what the image looks like after you place the final reflection on a black background and lower the opacity slightly to soften the effect. Adds a bit of visual interest, don't you think?

Here's how to create a simple reflection:

1. **Open a photo and duplicate the layer on which the photo lives (most likely, the Background layer).**

   Duplicate the layer by pressing ⌘-J (Ctrl+J on a PC). While you're at it, double-click the original Background layer so that it's editable, if you haven't done so already. Name the duplicate *Reflection*, just to keep your layers straight.

   TIP You can duplicate an item *while* you transform it by pressing ⌘-Option-T (Ctrl+Alt+T)—the transformation takes place on a duplicate item on a duplicate layer. Or you can press Option (Alt) while you choose Edit → Free Transform or Edit → Transform.

2. **Add some canvas space.**

   To make room at the bottom of the document for the reflection, you need to add some canvas space. Press C to select the Crop tool, draw a box around the image, and then drag the bottom handle down about two inches. Press Return (Enter on a PC) to accept the Crop. (Page 240 has more about adding canvas space in case you need a quick refresher.)

3. **Flip the reflection layer.**

   With the reflection layer selected, press ⌘-T (Ctrl+T on a PC) to summon the Free Transform command. Control-click (right-click) inside the bounding box and, from the resulting shortcut menu, choose Flip Vertical. When the layer is upside-down, press Return (Enter on a PC) or just double-click inside the bounding box to accept the transformation.

4. **Move the reflection below the other photo.**

   Press V to select the Move tool (see Appendix E, online at *www.missingmanuals. com*) and then hold down the Shift key while you drag the reflection toward the bottom of the document. Use the down arrow key to nudge the two layers slightly apart (they should *almost* touch, as Figure 6-30 shows).

   TIP Holding down the Shift key while you move a layer locks the layer into place horizontally or vertically, depending on the direction you're dragging. In this case, holding the Shift key ensures that the reflection lines up perfectly with the original photo.

5. **Add a gradient mask to fade the reflection.**

   Add a layer mask (page 105) to the reflection layer and then press G to select the Gradient tool (see Appendix E, online at *www.missingmanuals.com*). In the Options bar, click the tiny downward-pointing triangle next to the gradient preview to open the Gradient Picker. Choose Black to White from the pop-up menu and then choose Linear as the gradient type (both circled in Figure 6-30, top).

6. **Draw the gradient.**

Back in your document, press and hold the Shift key as you drag from the bottom of the image upward to roughly the height you'd like the reflection to be (circled in Figure 6-30, top). Holding down the Shift key locks the gradient vertically while you drag so it doesn't go from side-to-side. If you're not pleased with your first professional gradient dragging attempt, just give it another go; Photoshop keeps updating the mask as you drag.

7. **Add a new solid background.**

To add a new layer *below* the original layer (in other words, at the bottom of the layers stack), ⌘-click (Ctrl-click) the New Layer icon at the bottom of the Layers panel (page 76). Peek at the color chips at the bottom of the Tools panel and, if necessary, press D to set them to black and white and then press X until black hops on top. Fill the new layer with black by pressing Option-Delete (Alt+Backspace on a PC).

> **TIP**   By putting the new background on its own layer, you can experiment with the background color to see what looks best. While this example uses black, fuchsia may be more your style.

8. **Finally, soften the reflection by lowering its layer opacity to about 50 percent.**

This final step is really about personal preference: If you want your reflection to be very faint, lower the reflection layer's opacity to about 50 percent (you'll find the opacity slider at the top right of the Layers panel). If you want the original image to look like it's hovering above a mirror, go with an opacity of 75 percent or higher.

Now you've got yourself a professional-looking reflected image without all the hassle of setting up a reflective table. That's called working smarter, not harder!

Combining Images

One of the most rewarding projects you can tackle in Photoshop is combining images. Whether you're swapping skies, creating a complex collage, or building a panorama, this is where things start getting mighty fun. This chapter teaches you *all kinds* of techniques for mixing together images, from simply chopping a hole through one layer so you can see what's on the layer below it to a trick used by Photoshop heavyweights: mapping one image to the curves and contours of another.

Along the way, you'll learn how *layer blend modes* and *blending sliders* can help turn the images you have into the images you *want*. You'll also find out how to make Photoshop align and blend layers or stitch multiple images into one.

If you've got an older computer or limited space on your hard drive, you may want to combine images using the Clone Source panel so you don't have to bulk up your Layers panel (and your file size). This chapter walks you through that process, too. Finally, you'll get tips on combining illustrations and photos into unique pieces of art that marry the real and the imaginary. The techniques discussed in the following pages draw on *everything* you've learned so far—layers, selections, resizing, and so on—so get ready to put your new skills to work.

Cut It Out

The easiest way to combine two images is to start with the images on different layers in the same document and simply chop a hole through one layer so you can see what's on the layer below. It's not elegant, but it works. If you long to replace a dull window scene with something more fun, like the sunbathing dude shown in Figure 7-1, you can just cut a hole through the window so the new object fills the void.

Figure 7-1:
The simplest way to
combine images: Cut a
hole through one so you
can see the other. Once
you've selected the hole
(top left), you can delete
it and try out new vistas.

Here's how to get yourself a brand-new view:

> **NOTE**   To practice this combining maneuver yourself, visit this book's Missing CD page at *www. missingmanuals.com* and download the file View.zip.

1. **Open an image and double-click the Background layer to make it editable (page 80) if you haven't done so already.**

   Choose any picture you'd like to see *another* picture appear inside of: a window like the one shown in Figure 7-1, a picture frame, a friend's face, and so on.

2. **Select the area you want to delete.**

   To cut a hole in the image shown in Figure 7-1, you'd use the Rectangular Marquee tool since the window is square. Press M to grab the tool and draw a box just inside the window frame. (See page 127 for more on the Marquee tools; Chapter 4 has the full scoop on selection tools.)

3. **Use the Refine Edge dialog box to soften the selection's edges slightly.**

   Softening the edges makes the combined images blend better. After you make your selection, click the Refine Edge button on the Options bar and, in the dialog box that appears, use the sliders to smooth your selection by 1–2 pixels and feather it by 0.5–1 pixel. (See page 155 for more on using Refine Edge.)

TIP If your selection is larger or smaller than the area you want to cut, adjust the Contract/Expand slider near the bottom of the Refine Edge dialog box.

4. **Press Delete (Backspace on a PC) to cut the hole.**

   Once your selection is all set, you're ready to send it packin'. Peek in your Layers panel to make sure you're on the right layer before you perform this part of the surgery. Once you press Delete (Backspace), you see the transparent checkerboard pattern through the hole.

5. **Add other images to your document by copying and pasting from another file or by dragging them over from your Layers panel.**

   Here's where you add the image that you want to appear inside the original image. As you learned on page 85, you can copy and paste from other Photoshop documents or from other programs. Once you've copied the image, paste it into your Photoshop document and it'll land on its own layer. Or you can open the other image in Photoshop and then drag it from the Layers panel of one document into another document window (page 93). When you've got all the images added, position them *below* the original layer so you can see them *through* the hole in the original layer.

   Remember, as you learned in Chapter 3, whatever's at the top of the layers stack can hide what lies below. Cutting a hole inside the window frame in Figure 7-1 lets you see through to the image on the layer underneath. To see the whole image through the window frame, you may need to resize it by following the directions in the next step.

6. **Use the Move tool to position the glorious new vistas in your window frame.**

   Press V to grab the Move tool, select the layer you want to move and drag the layer into place. If you need to resize it so you can see all of it through the window frame, use Free Transform (page 245). Just press ⌘-T (Ctrl+T on a PC) and Shift-drag one of the corner handles inward to make the image smaller or outward to make it larger.

   NOTE You can make the image just a *hair* larger by using the Free Transform command, but if you increase it too much, it'll end up badly pixilated. In that case, you need to hunt for a different or bigger image to use instead.

7. **Preview the new vistas by turning your layers' visibility on or off.**

   For example, in Figure 7-1, you could compare dude vs. chick vs. plain beach. Click each layer's visibility eye to turn it on or off.

Pasting into a Selection

Instead of cutting a gaping hole through your window frame, you can combine two images by pasting a picture into a *selection* inside the window. When you use the *Paste Into* command, Photoshop puts the pasted image on its own layer *and* creates a layer mask for you, as Figure 7-2 illustrates. You see the new image only in the selected area; the rest is hidden by the layer mask. The best part? Paste Into is completely nondestructive.

Figure 7-2:
The Paste Into command tells Photoshop to create a layer mask that hides the outer bits of the pasted image so you can see it only through the selection. This image was created using Paste Into to place the couple inside a gaudy gold frame. Add a couple of well-placed layer styles (for example, drop and inner shadows) and the photo of the couple looks right at home in its new frame.

Here's how you can use Paste Into to combine two images without deleting any pixels:

1. **Open one image and select the area where you want the other image to appear.**

   As you learned in Chapter 4, it's wise to spend a few minutes looking at the area you want to select so you can pick the best tool for the job. For example, in Figure 7-2, the picture frame has a solid white interior. That means you can easily select it based on color. Press W to grab the Magic Wand (page 140) and click once in the white area to summon the marching ants.

2. **Use Refine Edge to soften the selection slightly.**

   Once you see the selection box's marching ants, click the Refine Edge button in the Options bar. The edges of Magic Wand selections tend to be a little rough, so you can use the Refine Edge dialog box to smooth them, as well as contract or expand them, if you need to.

3. **Open the image you want to put into the frame and copy it.**

   Press ⌘-A (Ctrl+A on a PC) to select the whole image and then copy it by pressing ⌘-C (Ctrl+C).

4. **Jump back to the frame document and choose Edit → Paste Into or press Shift-⌘-V (Shift+Ctrl+V).**

   Over in the Layers panel, Photoshop plops the pasted image onto its own layer, complete with a layer mask. In the document window, you see a portion of the pasted image peeking out at you through the frame.

5. **If necessary, resize the pasted photo and position it inside the frame.**

   If the photo is bigger than the frame (as in this example), you can make it smaller by using Free Transform. Press ⌘-T (Ctrl + T) and then Shift-drag one of the corner handles inward, as shown in Figure 7-3, to shrink the image proportionally. Next, position your mouse inside the bounding box; your cursor turns into an arrow that lets you drag the photo around inside the frame. When you're done adjusting the photo, press Return (Enter).

Figure 7-3:
If your photo is too big for the frame, resize it using Free Transform (page 245). Make sure to press and hold Shift as you drag so you don't squish or stretch the image!

TIP If the Free Transform bounding box hangs off the edges of your document, press ⌘-0 (Ctrl+0) to make Photoshop resize your document *just* enough so you can see all four corners of the box. This keyboard shortcut is worth memorizing 'cause you'll use it *all* the time.

6. **Lock the pasted photo and the mask together.**

   Once you get the photo sized and positioned just right, lock it to the layer mask (created in step 4) so everything stays in place. Over in the Layers panel, click the space between the layer and mask thumbnails. You'll see a little chain appear (you can see it in the highlighted layer in Figure 7-2). You're basically finished with this image-combining technique now, but you can add even more visual interest by rotating the frame, putting in a nice drop shadow and inner shadow, and giving it a new background. The next few steps explain how.

7. **Delete the white area around the frame.**

   The frame shown in Figure 7-2 originally appeared on a white background. To get rid of this background, select the frame layer in the Layers panel and double-click it to make it editable. Press W to grab the Magic Wand and click the white area outside the frame to select it. (If you've chosen a frame with all kinds of nooks and crannies around the edges, you can choose Select → Similar to make sure you've got all the little white areas selected.) Once you've got a good selection, use the Refine Edge dialog box to smooth the selection's edges. Press Delete to get rid of the white area for good.

8. **Use the Crop tool to make your canvas bigger.**

   You need some canvas space so you can rotate the frame and add a nice, fluffy drop shadow. The menu command for increasing Canvas size is discussed on page 240, but it's quicker to use the Crop tool. Press C to grab the Crop tool, and then drag to draw a box around your image. Option-drag (Alt-drag on a PC) one of the crop box's corner handles outward to make it bigger on all four sides, and then press Return (Enter). Ta-da! Now you've got all kinds of space to work.

9. **Select the frame and photo layers and rotate them with Free Transform.**

   In the Layer's panel, Shift-click to select both layers and then press ⌘-T (Ctrl+T) to summon Free Transform. Position your cursor outside the bounding box that appears and, when it turns into a curved double arrow, drag upward slightly to rotate the frame and photo. Press Return (Enter) when you've got them at an angle you like.

10. **Add an inner shadow to the photo layer.**

    To make the photo look like it's really *inside* the frame, you need an inner shadow. First, make sure that only the photo layer is selected in the Layers panel. Next, click the *fx* button at the bottom of the Layers panel and, from the drop-down menu, choose Inner Shadow. Tweak the settings in the Layer Style dialog box to your liking (layer styles are discussed on page 119) and click OK.

11. **Add a drop shadow to the frame layer.**

    To add a little depth, select the frame layer in the Layers panel, click the panel's *fx* button, and choose Drop Shadow. (See page 119 for the scoop on adding drop shadows.)

12. **Add a layer named *New Background* and fill it with color.**

To complete the design, you need a new background for the frame. Add a new layer by clicking the "Create a new layer" button at the bottom of the Layers panel (it looks like a piece of paper with a folded corner) and then click the foreground color chip at the bottom of the Tools panel. In the resulting Color Picker, select the color you want for the frame's background and then click OK. Fill the new layer with color by pressing Option-Delete (Alt+Backspace on a PC).

> **TIP**   If you mouse over to your image while the Color Picker is open, the cursor turns into a little eyedropper. Then just click anywhere in the image to select the color your cursor is over. Snatching a color that's already in your image is a great way to pick a new background color.

13. **Drag the New Background layer to the bottom of the layers stack.**

In your document window, the background appears behind your lovely framed image.

Whew! That was a lot of steps, but you're done. Now go find a place to hang your masterpiece.

Sky Swapping

You can also use the Paste Into technique described in the previous section to replace a bland sky with a more pleasing vista, as shown in Figure 7-4. Though, honestly, adding the layer mask yourself is just as easy as having Photoshop make it *for* you by using Paste Into (either way, you get the same result). Here's what you need to do:

1. **Open an image with an area that you want to replace (like the sky) and double-click its Background layer to make it editable (page 80).**

Photoshop won't let you add a layer mask to the Background layer unless you unlock it (which converts it to a normal layer that supports transparency). If you've worked with this particular image before, your layer may already be unlocked or named something else entirely. In that case, onward ho!

2. **Select the sky.**

You can use any of the bazillion techniques you learned about in Chapter 4. The channels method (discussed on page 190 and used to create the image shown in Figure 7-4) is a good one.

3. **Add a layer mask to hide the old sky.**

Once you've selected the sky, add a layer mask by clicking the circle-within-a-square button at the bottom of your Layers panel.

Figure 7-4:
Instead of deleting the
sky in the top image, you
can hide it with a layer
mask. Swapping skies
makes this rider's
accomplishment a bit
more impressive, don't
you think?

TIP   If the mask hides the *opposite* of what you want it to hide, open the Masks panel (new in Photoshop CS4; details on page 111) and click the Invert button at the bottom of the panel to flip-flop the mask. You can also use the other options in the panel to refine your mask. If you don't have CS4, you can get rid of the mask by going back one step in the History panel or by pressing ⌘-Z (Ctrl+Z). Next, choose Select → Inverse to flip-flop your selection and then add a layer mask.

4. **Open the image with the replacement sky and copy it.**

   Press ⌘-A (Ctrl+A on a PC) to select the whole image and then press ⌘-C (Ctrl+C) to copy it.

5. **In your other document (the one with the mask), paste the new sky onto its own layer by pressing ⌘-V (Ctrl+V).**

   If copying and pasting isn't your thing, arrange your workspace so you can see both open documents (page 63) and then drag the sky layer from the Layers panel into the other document's window (see page 93).

6. **Position the sky at the bottom of the layers stack.**

   In your Layers panel, drag the new sky to the bottom of the layers stack and you're done.

You just swapped your first sky! If you want to try out other skies, just paste or drag them into the document and position them below the layer with the layer mask. Hide the first new sky by clicking its visibility eye in the Layers panel.

Fading Images Together

So far, you've learned how to combine images with relatively hard edges like a rectangular head shot wedged into a frame. But if your soon-to-be combined images don't have such stark boundaries, you're better off using big, soft brushes to do your erasing or, better yet, hiding parts of your image with a layer mask (similar to what you just saw in the previous section). You can also use the Gradient tool to create a gradual transition from one image to another. This section explains all these methods.

Soft Erasers

Because you can set the Eraser tool to use a brush, you can use a soft brush to erase part of an image so you can see another image on the layer below, as shown in Figure 7-5. This technique gets the job done, but it's as destructive as cutting a hole—if you change your mind about how you want to combine the images, you have to start over. (See the next section for a nondestructive alternative.)

Figure 7-5:
Top: Use the Options bar's Mode pop-up menu to morph the Eraser into a brush. From the Brush menu, choose a big, soft brush (a 500-pixel brush was used here).

Bottom Left: Using a big, soft-edged brush (circled here) you can erase the left side of the helmet image (a dark gray background), allowing you to see through to the bike image on the layer below. The soft brush gives you a nice transition from one image to the other.

Bottom Right: A quick peek at the Layers panel reveals that half your original image is gone. Now you know why it makes sense to copy your original image!

Once you've wrangled the two images you want to combine into the same document (each on its own layer), follow these steps:

1. **Drag the image layer you want to partially erase to the top of the Layers panel.**

   The act of dragging the layer to the top of your layers stack should mean it's selected, but it doesn't hurt to make *triple* sure you're on the correct layer before you grab the Eraser tool. Triple-checking may sound obsessive, but when it comes to *erasing* your image, it's best to be sure.

   NOTE It's a good idea to duplicate the image layer you'll be erasing in case you don't like the results (press ⌘-J or Ctrl+J on a PC to duplicate the layer). If you turn its visibility eye off, it won't be in your way. (You can always turn it back on if you need it.)

2. **Grab the Eraser tool by pressing E and set it to Brush mode.**

   Head up to the Options bar and set the Mode pop-up menu to Brush. Then, from the Brush menu, choose a big soft brush (Figure 7-5, top). While you're up there, make sure the Opacity and Flow fields are both set to 100 percent (see Chapter 12 for more on brush options).

   TIP For an even *more* subtle fading effect, you can experiment with reducing the Eraser's opacity in the Options bar. That way, you can brush repeatedly over the area you want to erase for a more gradual effect.

3. **Mouse over to your image and erase the part of the image you don't want.**

   As shown in Figure 7-5 (middle), you can brush away the part of the image you want to erase (like the background to the left of the helmet). If you mess up or change your mind, use the History panel to go back a few brush strokes (page 25) or undo a step by pressing ⌘-Z (Ctr+Z on a PC).

4. **When you're finished, save your image as a Photoshop (PSD) file.**

   You've just erased your way to a very cool collage.

Soft Brushes and Layer Masks

A nondestructive alternative to using the Eraser tool is to paint on a layer mask with a big fluffy brush. That way you're merely *hiding* part of the image instead of deleting it. For example, let's say you want to really highlight—or completely fake—how fast the motorcyclist in Figure 7-6 is going. You can simulate a speeding effect by adding a bit of motion blur.

Here's how to fade one image into another softly by using a layer mask:

1. **Open your image and then duplicate the original layer by pressing ⌘-J (Ctrl+J on a PC).**

Figure 7-6:
Combining images isn't just about using different images; there's opportunity aplenty to combine different versions of the same image, as shown here.

Top: This freeze-frame version of the rider shows little evidence of his speed.

Bottom Right: The top layer shows a motion blurred version of the original image—perfect for combining with the original shot.

Bottom Left: Now the rider looks nice and speedy.

2. **Apply a pretty severe motion blur to the duplicate layer to make it look like your subject is going *really* fast.**

   Since the motion blur makes your *whole* image blurry, so it's hard to see the subject (in this case, the biker), you'll want to hide some of the blurry layer by adding a layer mask, as shown in Figure 7-6, bottom right.

3. **Position the blurry layer at the top of the layers stack and add a layer mask to it.**

   Drag the layer mask to the top of your Layers panel. Then, at the bottom of the panel, click the circle-within-a-square button to add a layer mask to the blurry layer.

4. **Press B to grab the Brush tool and pick a big, soft brush.**

   Up in the Options bar's Brush menu, choose a big (say, 500-pixel) soft-edge brush.

5. **Set the foreground color chip to black.**

   As you learned in Chapter 3 (page 105), in the realm of layer masks, painting with black *conceals*, which is exactly what you want to do here. Peek at the color chips at the bottom of your Tools panel and, if they're black and white, press X until black hops on top. If they're any other color, press D to reset them to black and white and then press X until black is on top.

6. **Mouse over to your image and paint the part of the blurry layer you want to hide.**

If your brush is big enough, you can get away with clicking a few times on the area you want to hide (like the biker in Figure 7-6). If you mess up and hide too much, press X to flip-flop your color chips (so that white is on top) and reveal that area again by painting with white.

7. **Save your image as a PSD file so you can go back and tweak it later on.**

Heck, after seeing or printing the final version, you may decide to add a little more motion blur. If that's the case, you can pop open this document, select the blurry layer, and run the Motion Blur filter again. You won't have to recreate the layer mask because it's still there. Whee!

Gradient Masks

All that soft-brush business aside, the way to create the smoothest fades of all between two images you're combining is to use a *gradient* (a soft, gradual transition from one color to another). The steps for combining two images using a gradient are basically the same as the soft-brush methods in that you're combining the images into one document and then adding a layer mask to the top layer. But instead of painting on the layer mask with a black or white brush, you'll use a black-to-white gradient for a seamless transition from one image to another, as shown in Figure 7-7.

Once you've put two images into one document (each on its own layer), take a spin through these steps:

1. **Drag the image you want on the top of your collage to the top of the Layers panel and then add a layer mask to it.**

In this example, you want the speedometer on top, so drag it to the top of your Layers panel. Add a layer mask to it by clicking the circle-within-a-square button at the bottom of the panel. The layer mask thumbnail appears in the Layers panel, but your document doesn't change because at this point the mask is empty.

2. **Press G to grab the Gradient tool and choose a black-to-white, linear gradient.**

In the Options bar, click the down-pointing triangle next to the gradient menu. Choose the black-to-white gradient from the pop-up list (third from left in the top row) and, in the row of gradient types, click the linear gradient button (it's circled in Figure 7-7, top).

3. **Mouse over to your image, click once where you want the fade to begin, and then drag slightly upward and to the right for one or two inches.**

As you drag, Photoshop draws a line that represents the width of the fade: The shorter the line (the distance you drag), the narrower the fade and the harsher the transition (it won't be a hard edge, but it'll be close). The longer the line, the wider the gradient and the softer the fade. As soon as you release your mouse,

Gradient type

Gradient menu

Figure 7-7:
Adding a black-to-white linear gradient to your layer mask is an easy and nondestructive way to blend images together gradually.

And, remember, you can rotate a layer to get the image in the right spot (here, the speedometer has been rotated slightly). The funky-looking layer in the middle of the Layers panel is a Black & White Adjustment layer, which you'll learn about in Chapter 8 (page 301).

Photoshop puts the gradient in the layer mask, which effectively fades your images together. If you're not happy with the gradient, just keep clicking and dragging until you get it right; Photoshop updates the mask automatically. Be sure to experiment with dragging different distances and at different angles. If you want to start over, click the mask thumbnail in your Layers panel and select the whole thing by pressing ⌘-A (Ctrl+A on a PC). Press Delete (Backspace) and you're back to square one.

4. **Save your document as a PSD file (page 46).**

   This file format preserves your layers so you can go back and edit the gradient mask later.

Not bad, eh? Incidentally, this technique is a *great* example of how to use your own imagery in conjunction with stock photos. Just think of the possibilities: A wedding photo faded into a bouquet of flowers, piano keys faded into a sheet of music, Captain Kirk faded into a shot of the Starship Enterprise, and so on.

Layer Blend Modes

Perched in the upper-left corner of your Layers panel is a pop-up menu that lists *blend modes*. You may have clicked it already and been startled by the number of items listed, which range from modes that darken everything to modes that lighten everything to modes that don't seem to do anything at all.

Blend modes control how pixels on different layers interact with each other. For example, when layers overlap, the top one can either block the bottom one completely or the layers can blend together in some way (these effects, and many more, are shown in Figure 7-8). You can control exactly *how* they blend together by using blend modes. As you might imagine, they're worth their weight in gold when you're combining images, whether you're combining an image with a copy of itself to produce a darker or lighter version (see page 109) or joining up lots of different images to create a collage (as shown in the figure on page 271).

This section covers how you can use blend modes to work with layers, but you can find other blend mode menus all over the place in Photoshop, including:

- In the Layer Styles dialog box, where you can add effects like drop shadows, glows, and so on (page 119).

- In some filters' dialog boxes (see Chapter 15).

- In the Edit → Fade dialog box, which you access after you run a filter (page 431) or applying any of the adjustments in the Image → Adjustments menu.

- In the Fill and Stroke dialog boxes (page 168).

- In the Options bar when you're using a tool you can paint with like the Brush, Healing Brush, Pencil, Eraser, Clone Stamp, History Brush, Eraser, Gradient, Blur, Dodge, and Burn tools.

- In the Calculations (page 199) and Apply Image (page 281) dialog boxes.

When you're dealing with blend modes, it's helpful to think of the colors on your layers as being made up of three parts:

- **Base.** This is the color you start out with, the one that's already in your image.

- **Blend.** This is the color you adding to the base color, whether it's in an image on another layer or one you're painting onto another layer with the Brush tool.

- **Result.** This is the color you get after mixing the base with a blend color, using one of the blend modes described in the next section.

To help you make a little sense of Photoshop's growing set of blend modes (and you'll need all the help you can get), they're divided into categories based on their *neutral color*—the color that causes *no* change in that particular mode. For example, some modes ignore white, some ignore black, and so on. This information doesn't mean a hill of beans to you just yet, but it'll start making sense as you learn more about the various modes in the next few pages. Read on for a quick tour of the blend mode menu.

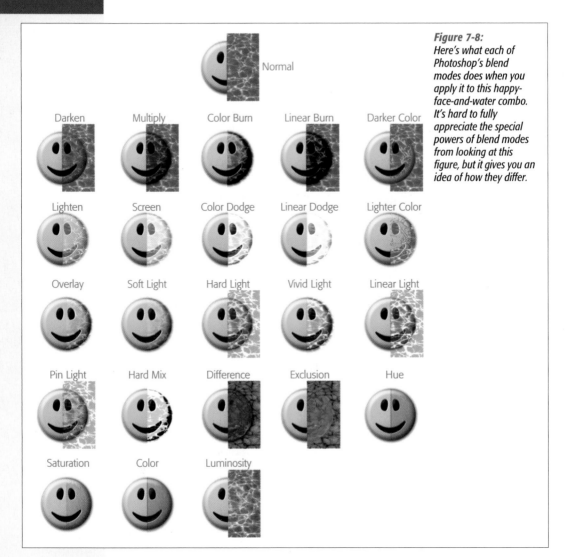

Figure 7-8:
Here's what each of Photoshop's blend modes does when you apply it to this happy-face-and-water combo. It's hard to fully appreciate the special powers of blend modes from looking at this figure, but it gives you an idea of how they differ.

Normal and Dissolve Blend Modes

You can find these two modes at the very top of the blend modes menu. Here's what they do:

- **Normal.** When you first use Photoshop, it's set to use this mode, which doesn't actually cause any blending at all. As Figure 7-8 shows, the pixels on the top layer totally block what lies below. Its keyboard shortcut is Shift-Option-N (Shift+Alt+N on a PC).

NOTE Photoshop CS4 includes lots of keyboard shortcuts you can use to change the current layer's blend mode. However, if you're using one of the painting tools listed on page 267, these shortcuts change the blend mode of that particular *tool* instead.

- **Dissolve.** This mode turns semitransparent pixels into a spray of dots (if you don't have any semitransparent pixels, your image won't change). Dissolve isn't very useful unless you want to make a drop shadow look coarse instead of soft (see Figure 7-9). Keyboard shortcut: Shift-Option-I (Shift+Alt+I on a PC).

Figure 7-9:
To create the spatter effect shown here, add a drop shadow with layer styles (page 119) and then, in the Layer Styles dialog box, change the shadow's blend mode to Dissolve. Photoshop changes the formerly see-through drop shadow into a spray of pixels.

Darken Blend Modes

The modes in this category have the power to darken, or *burn*, your image (see Chapter 9 [page 349] and Chapter 10 [page 414] for more on using the Burn tool). Simply put, when you apply these modes, the base and blend colors go to war and the darkest color wins. These modes are incredibly useful when you want to swap a light-colored background for something darker. The neutral color in this category is white, which means that white has no effect on the blend at all, and any white parts of your images will disappear.

- **Darken.** In this mode, Photoshop analyzes the base and blend colors and combines the darkest ones to create the result color. Any colors on the top layer that are darker than the colors on the layer below get to stay, and any lighter colors on the bottom layer disappear. Figure 7-10 has the details on using this mode to eliminate a white background with nary a selection tool. Keyboard shortcut: Shift-Option-K (Shift+Alt+K on a PC).

- **Multiply.** In Multiply mode, Photoshop multiplies the base color by the blend color. You can think of this mode like a double coat of ink since the result color will always be darker than the base. Multiply does a lot of cool things, including fixing images that are too light or overexposed (see page 109), removing white backgrounds (a technique sometimes called "knocking out"), or creating an *overprint* effect in which the graphic on the top layer looks like it's been printed on the layer below (like the fake tattoo shown in Figure 7-11). Keyboard shortcut: Shift-Option-M (Shift+Alt+M on a PC).

- **Color Burn.** This mode darkens your image by increasing the overall contrast. When you use it on 50 percent gray, Color Burn intensifies color on the layers below, which can beautify an ugly sky in a hurry (see Figure 7-12). You can also use it to colorize a grayscale image though the paint will be really dark and high contrast (it's better to use Hue mode, discussed on page 105). Keyboard shortcut: Shift-Option-B (Shift+Alt+B on a PC).

Figure 7-10:
By placing two images on separate layers, you can use Darken mode to zap a white background. Here, the top layer has a fairly dark sunburst and the bottom layer has a crazy guy on a white background. If you change the blend mode of the sunburst layer to Darken, the white background on the layer below seems to disappear.

Since parts of the crazy guy's face and hand are lighter than the sunburst—the sunburst wins the color war explained on page 269 and covers him up in those spots—you can hide those parts of the sunburst to keep him whole. Simply add a layer mask and paint with a Brush set to black (see page 105 for more on layer masks).

Figure 7-11:
By changing the blend mode of the tattoo layer to Multiply, its white background disappears so you can see through to the skin below. All you need to do now is put your name on the little banner across the heart!

Figure 7-12:
Ain't nothing like a dull sky to ruin a perfectly decent photo. Happily, you can whip the sky into shape by adding a layer to the top of your layers stack, filling it with 50 percent gray, and changing its blend mode to Color Burn. If the effect is too strong, you can lower the gray layer's opacity (as shown here). To apply the color change only to certain areas of your image, add a layer mask (page 105).

TIP   An easy way to fill a layer with 50 percent gray is to make a new layer, go to Edit → Fill, and then choose 50% Gray from the Use pop-up menu. Those Adobe programmers think of everything!

- **Linear Burn.** In this mode (which is actually a combination of Multiply and Color Burn), Photoshop darkens your image by decreasing brightness. Linear Burn produces the darkest colors of any Darken blend mode though with a bit more contrast than the others. It has a tendency to turn dark pixels solid black, which makes it ideal for grungy, textured collages like the one in Figure 7-13. Keyboard shortcut: Shift-Option-A (Shift+Alt+A on a PC).

- **Darker Color.** This mode compares the base and blend colors and keeps the darkest pixels. No blending going on here—the lighter colors just vanish.

NOTE   You may have noticed that Photoshop doesn't have a keyboard shortcut for Darker Color mode–that mode didn't come around until Photoshop CS3 when Adobe started running out of available keyboard shortcut combos. The same thing goes for Lighter Color mode.

Lighten Blend Modes

These modes, the opposite of the Darken modes, have the power to lighten, or *dodge*, your image (see Chapters 9 [page 349] and 10 [page 414] for more on using the Dodge tool). Black is the neutral color for this group; it disappears in all but one of the following modes:

Figure 7-13:
If you peek at this Layers panel, you can see the original image near the bottom followed by what's left of the face after adding a Threshold Adjustment layer (page 312). Popping in three pieces of art (circled) and changing their blend modes to Linear Burn created a collage. The opacity of the sunbeam and grunge texture was lowered to about 60 percent, and the sunbeam was positioned over the boy's eye. That's it!

- **Lighten.** In this mode, the lightest pixels win the war of colors. Photoshop compares all the colors and keeps either the base or the blend, whichever is lightest, and then combines them to produce the result color. Everything else is nixed (including black), which makes this mode perfect for removing a black background (see Figure 7-14). Keyboard shortcut: Shift-Option-G (Shift+Alt+G on a PC).

- **Screen.** In this mode, Photoshop multiplies the *opposite* of the blend and base colors, making everything a lot lighter as though a bottle of bleach was spilled on it. It's great for fixing images that are too dark or underexposed (like when your camera's flash doesn't fire; see page 109). Keyboard shortcut: Shift-Option-S (Shift+Alt+S on a PC).

- **Color Dodge.** This mode lightens your image by decreasing contrast. It has a tendency to turn light pixels solid white, and, unlike the other Lighten modes, it keeps black pixels, so the dark parts of your image don't change. You can use this mode with 50 percent gray to brighten your image—a great way to give hair some instant highlights (see Figure 7-15). Keyboard shortcut: Shift-Option-D (Shift+Alt+D on a PC).

- **Linear Dodge (Add).** This mode lightens your image by increasing brightness. It's a combo of Screen and Color Dodge modes, so it'll lighten your image more than any blend other mode. But since it tends to turn *all* light colors white, it can make your image look unnatural. Keyboard shortcut: Shift-Option-W (Shift+Alt+W on a PC).

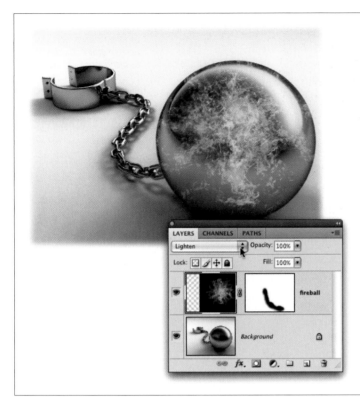

Figure 7-14:
To zap the black background of this fireball (top layer), change its blend mode to Lighten. Now the flames are visible only where they're lighter than the colors in the steel ball. (A layer mask was added to hide a few rogue flames underneath the ball.)

- **Lighter Color.** With this mode, Photoshop compares the base and blend colors and keeps only the lightest pixels. Unlike Lighten mode, it doesn't combine any colors; it just keeps the lightest ones. (See the Note on page 271 to learn why this mode has no keyboard shortcut.)

Lighting Blend Modes

In contrast to the Lighten and Darken modes, Lighting blend modes do a little darkening *and* a little lightening to increase the contrast of your image. They have a neutral color of 50 percent gray, which doesn't affect the result color; it just disappears.

- **Overlay.** In this mode, if the blend color is darker than 50 percent gray, Photoshop multiplies its color value with the base color. If it's lighter than 50 percent gray, Photoshop multiplies its color value with the inverse of the color (like it does in Screen mode). If the blend color is exactly 50 percent gray, Overlay has no effect on the result color at all. You can use this mode to increase contrast or to colorize a grayscale image. Keyboard shortcut: Shift-Option-O (Shift+Alt+O on a PC).

Figure 7-15:
By filling a layer with 50 percent gray and changing its blend mode to Color Dodge, you get instant hair highlights. Just add a layer mask to protect other parts of the image (like the face and background) from the highlighting.

- **Soft Light.** As the name suggests, this mode is the equivalent of shining a soft light on your image. It makes bright areas brighter (as if they were dodged) and dark areas darker (as if they were burned). If you paint with black in this mode, you'll darken the underlying image; if you paint with white, you'll lighten it. You can use this mode to add texture to an image or to make an image look like it's reflected in metal (see Figure 7-16). Seasoned Photoshop jockeys use Soft Light with the Dodge and Burn tools to retouch portraits (see Chapter 10, page 414). Keyboard shortcut: Shift-Option-F (Shift+Alt+F on a PC).

- **Hard Light.** This mode, which is equivalent to shining a harsh light on your image, combines Multiply and Screen modes: if the blend color is lighter than 50 percent gray, the image gets lighter (like Screen mode); if it's darker than 50 percent gray, the image gets darker (like Multiply). If you paint with black or white in this mode, you simply get black or white. If you *really* want to increase the level of detail in an image, you can use this mode in conjunction with the Emboss filter. Keyboard shortcut: Shift-Option-H (Shift+Alt+H on a PC).

Figure 7-16:
To create a quick reflection in a metal object, change the top layer's blend mode to Soft Light.

- **Vivid Light.** In this mode, Photoshop applies Color Burn to increase the contrast of colors darker than 50 percent gray and Color Dodge to decrease the contrast of colors lighter than 50 percent gray. Use Vivid Light to make an image pop or to add texture. Keyboard shortcut: Shift-Option-V (Shift+Alt+V on a PC).

- **Linear Light.** This mode combines the Linear Burn and Linear Dodge modes: It uses Linear Burn to decrease the brightness of colors darker than 50 percent gray and Linear Dodge to increase the brightness of colors lighter than 50 percent gray. Linear Light is great for adding texture to images, as shown in Figure 7-17. Keyboard shortcut: Shift-Option-J (Shift+Alt+J on a PC).

- **Pin Light.** This mode combines Lighten and Darken: if the blend color is *lighter* than 50 percent gray, it replaces areas of the base color darker than 50 percent gray with the blend color; pixels lighter than 50 percent gray don't change at all. But if the blend color is *darker* than 50 percent gray, Pin Light replaces lighter areas of the base color with the blend color and darker areas don't change. You'll rarely use this mode because it can produce odd results (or none at all), but feel free to experiment with it—especially with filters (see Chapter 15)—during fits of extreme boredom. Keyboard shortcut: Shift-Option-Z (Shift+Alt+Z on a PC).

- **Hard Mix.** This mode greatly reduces the range of colors in your image (an effect known as *posterizing*), so you end up with large blocks of super-bright colors like red, green, or blue. In this mode, Photoshop analyzes the sum of the RGB values found in the blend color and adds them to the base color.

Figure 7-17:
Want to turn a loved one to stone? No problem! Simply use the Quick Selection tool (page 137) to select the person's skin and then add a layer mask to a layer containing marble or stone (see the top layer). Change the marble layer's blend mode to Linear Light and you've got an instant statue.

For example, if the value of the red, green, or blue channel is 255, Photoshop adds that value to the base; and if the value is less than 255, Photoshop adds a value of 0. (See page 41 for more on color values.) You can reduce the effect of this mode by lowering the Fill setting at the top of your Layers panel (see page 87). You won't use Hard Mix very often, but it's fun for the occasional special effect, as you can see in Figure 7-18. Keyboard shortcut: Shift-Option-L (Shift+Alt+L on a PC).

Comparative Blend Modes

This category should really be called "psychedelic." Its two modes are similar, and they both produce freaky results that are useful only on Halloween or in grungy collages (discussed earlier in this chapter). However, as you'll soon find out, they can be *temporarily* useful. Black is the neutral color in both modes.

- **Difference.** This mode analyzes the brightness of both the base and the blend colors and subtracts the brightest pixels. If you use white as your blend color, Photoshop inverts (flip-flops) the base color, making the image look like a film negative. If you use black as your blend color, Photoshop doesn't change anything. You wouldn't want to use this mode on your image for keeps, but you can use it temporarily to locate the midtones in your image (see the box on page 373 for details). You can also use it to align two layers of the same image (if, say, they were shot at different exposures): just change the top layer to Difference mode and use your arrow keys to move the image until you no longer see the odd engraved look (when the images are perfectly aligned, the whole image turns dark gray). Keyboard shortcut: Shift-Option-E (Shift+Alt+E on a PC).

Figure 7-18:
In Hard Mix mode, Photoshop changes all the pixels to primary colors (see page 451), leaving you with solid blocks of bright, high-contrast color.

- **Exclusion.** This mode is similar to Difference but results in a little less contrast. Blending with white inverts the base color and blending with black doesn't do anything. You can also use Exclusion to align images; just follow the steps for aligning images with Difference mode. Keyboard shortcut: Shift-Option-X (Shift+Alt+X on a PC).

Hue Blend Modes

All the modes in this category relate to color and luminance (brightness) values (see page 452 for more on brightness). Depending on the colors in your image, Photoshop will apply one or two of these modes to the image (they don't have a neutral color like the other blend modes). Hue blend modes are extremely practical because you can use them to change, add, or intensify the colors in your image.

- **Hue.** This mode keeps the lightness and saturation (color intensity) values of the base color and adds the *hue* (another word for color) of the blend color. If you want to change the color of an object without changing how light or dark it is, use this mode (see page 333). However, Hue can't introduce a color that isn't already there to colorize grayscale images, so you have to use another mode (like Color, which is explained later in this list). Keyboard shortcut: Shift-Option-U (Shift+Alt+U on a PC).

- **Saturation.** This mode keeps the luminance and hue of the base color and picks up the saturation of the blend color. If you want to increase an image's color intensity, this mode can help you out (see Figure 7-19). You can also use Saturation to drain color from part of an image by painting that area black. Because black has no saturation value, it *desaturates* intersecting colors. Keyboard shortcut: Shift-Option-T (Shift+Alt+T on a PC).

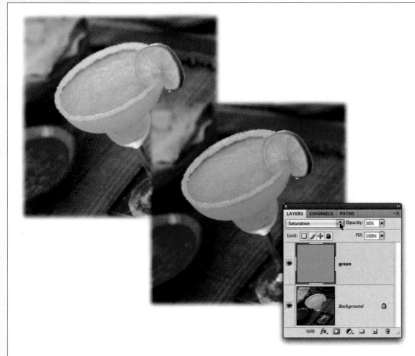

Figure 7-19:
If you've ever been to Texas, you know the margaritas there are much brighter than the one in the original image (left). To boost the color saturation, add a new layer filled with a color that has the saturation value you want (it doesn't matter which color) and then change its blend mode to Saturation. The image will take on only the the blend color's saturation value, not its hue.

- **Color.** In this mode, Photoshop keeps the luminance of the base color and picks up the hue and saturation of the blend color, which makes it handy when you're colorizing a grayscale image (see page 333). Keyboard shortcut: Shift-Option-C (Shift+Alt+C on a PC).

- **Luminosity.** This mode keeps the hue and saturation of the base color and picks up the luminance of the blend color. Use Luminosity when you're sharpening an image (see page 428). It's also super handy when you're using curves or levels Adjustment layers (see Chapter 9). Keyboard shortcut: Shift-Option-Y (Shift+Alt+Y on a PC).

Zapping Backgrounds with Blending Sliders

If the subject of your image is radically brighter or darker than its background, you'll want to sit up and pay attention to this section. While blend modes are

Pass Through Mode

When you create a layer group (page 98), Pass Through appears at the top of the blend mode pop-up menu. In this mode, Photoshop makes sure that any blend modes, blending slider settings (page 278), opacity settings, and fill settings you've applied to layers in the group trickle down to layers *below* the group.

Let's say you've created a layer group consisting of several image layers set to Linear Burn mode to create a grunge collage. Pass Through mode lets the Linear Burn effect trickle down to any background or text on layers below the group. If you don't want the blending to affect the layers below the group, change the layer group's blend mode to Normal.

pretty powerful in their own right (and several of them can pulverize a white or black background instantly), *another* set of blending options in the Layer Styles dialog box (page 119) can eat backgrounds for lunch—nondestructively!

Photoshop gives you a few different ways to open the Layer Styles dialog box (Figure 7-20). Once you've selected the layer you want to work with by clicking it, open the dialog box using one of the following methods:

- **Double-click its layer thumbnail** in your Layers panel.

- **Click the Layer Style pop-up menu.** If you click the little *fx* button at the bottom of the Layers panel, you can choose Blending Options.

- **Choose Layer → Layer Styles → Blending Options.**

   NOTE   The Blending sliders won't work on a locked Background layer; you have to double-click the layer first to make it editable.

At the bottom of the resulting dialog box are two pairs of sliders (they look like triangles): one set for the This Layer bar and another for the Underlying Layer bar, as shown in Figure 7-20 (top). Each slider lets you make parts of your image transparent based on the brightness value of the pixels. The left slider represents the shadows (blacks) contained in your image and the right one represents the highlights (whites). If you want to affect the currently active layer, then tweak the This Layer set (you'll learn about the Underlying Layer set in a moment).

For example, if the background of your currently active layer is black and the subject (or object in the foreground) is much brighter, you can hide the black part—which makes it transparent—by dragging the shadow slider (the one on the left) toward the middle until the background is hidden. If you want to hide a white background, you can drag the highlight slider (the one on the right) toward the middle until the white is completely hidden.

   NOTE   You can adjust these sliders anytime you want by summoning the Layer Styles dialog box.

Figure 7-20:
Top: You can use the blending sliders to make short work of removing solid-colored backgrounds. In this image, the black background has been hidden by dragging the shadow slider toward the middle. To soften the edges of the bits that remain, you can split the slider in half (as described lower on this page) and then drag its left half back to the left.

Bottom: Once you've hidden the hanging beads background, you can see through to the image on the layer below, which makes for a quickie collage.

To soften your subject's edges once you've hidden the background, you can make the edge pixels partially transparent by splitting the shadow or highlights slider in half. To soften the edge pixels after you've hidden a black background, Option-drag (Alt-drag on a PC) the left half of the shadows slider and drag it slightly back to the left (circled in Figure 7-20). Likewise, if you've hidden a white background, you can Option-drag (Alt-drag) the right half of the highlights slider slightly to the right to tell Photoshop to make pixels with that particular brightness value partially transparent.

You can perform this pixel-hiding magic on colors, too. Just pick the channel (see Chapter 5) you want to work with from the Blend If pop-up menu above the sliders, and that particular color appears in the slider instead of black and white.

The Underlying Layer sliders let you control the range of visible colors on layers *below* the currently active layer. As you drag the sliders, parts of the image on underlying layers appear *through* the pixels on the active layer as if you'd cut a hole out of it. If you drag the shadows slider toward the middle, you'll begin to see the darkest parts of the underlying image show through the active layer. If you drag the highlight slider toward the middle, you'll start to see the lightest parts of the underlying image.

As you can see in Figure 7-20, the blending sliders can do an amazing job of hiding backgrounds based on color. But if your *subject* contains some of the colors in the background, the blending sliders will zap those areas, too. In that case, you'll have to use a different method like another blend mode or a layer mask (discussed earlier in this chapter) to hide your background.

The Apply Image Command

This seldom-used command lets you combine two open images (as long as they're exactly the same size) and pick a blend mode and opacity at the same time. Although you can do the same thing using layer blend modes and opacity (as you learned in the previous pages), the Apply Image command lets you pick which *channel* Photoshop uses to do the blending, as shown in Figure 7-21. (See Chapter 5 for the lowdown on channels.)

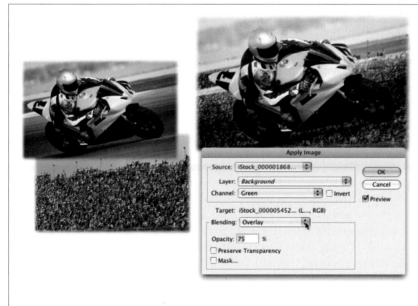

Figure 7-21:
Left: Apply Image lets you combine two same-sized images even if they're in different color modes like RGB, CMYK, Lab, and so on (page 40).

Right: By combining only the green channel from the crowd shot (the source image) with the motorcycle photo, you get all the details of the crowd shot but none of the color. The green channel usually contains more details than the other channels in RGB mode because digital cameras have twice as many green sensors as red or blue ones.

To use Apply Image on two RGB images, follow these steps:

1. **Open the source and target images.**

   The *source image* is the one you want to blend with another image; in Figure 7-21, the source image is the crowd shot. The *target image* is the one where Photoshop does the actual blending; in Figure 7-21, that's the photo of the motorcyclist.

2. **Duplicate the target image's Background layer.**

   Since the Apply Image command changes the pixels of the current layer, it's best to copy your image first so you can go back to the original or add a layer mask to reveal part of it. To duplicate the layer, press ⌘-J (Ctrl+J on a PC).

3. **Choose Image → Apply Image and pick the source image.**

   In the resulting dialog box (shown in Figure 7-21), choose the source image from the Source pop-up menu. If you don't see the image you want in the list, it means your source image isn't exactly the same size as your target image. In that case, press the Esc key and jump back to page 220 for the scoop on resizing. When you've got your images the same size, your source image appears on the list.

   NOTE   Page 223 tells you how to use the Image Size dialog box to find out an image's pixel dimensions.

4. **In the Apply Image dialog box, pick the layer and channel from the source image that you want to blend with your target image.**

   If your source image has more than one layer, you can specify which one you want to use in the Layer pop-up menu. The same goes for channels; you can use the composite channel (RGB) or one specific channel (red, green, or blue). Turn on the Invert checkbox if you want to reverse (flip-flop) the color info in the channel (turning what was light dark and what was dark light).

5. **Pick a blend mode and opacity.**

   The Apply Image dialog box's Blending pop-up menu lets you choose from the full range of blend modes (see the previous sections), plus two extras: Add and Subtract. In Add mode, the RGB color values of the source image's pixels are added to the target image's pixels *in the same location* (making colors brighter and more intense in those areas). In Subtract mode, the RGB color values are subtracted (making colors lighter and less intense). Pure white and pure black pixels remain unchanged in both modes.

   If you choose either Add or Subtract, Photoshop adds two more fields to the Apply Image dialog box: Scale and Offset. Scale makes Photoshop average the added or subtracted RGB color values by the number you enter here (in this case, a number between 1 and 2). For example, if you enter *2* in the Scale field, Photoshop divides the color values that it adds or subtracts by 2. The Offset field lets you alter the brightness of the resulting RGB color values by selecting from a scale of –255 (black) to 255 (white). You'll probably use Add only if you're working with two versions of the same image, maybe one that's too dark and one that's too light. And you'll probably never use Subtract unless you're going for a really funky, artsy effect.

6. **If you like, turn on the Preserve Transparency and Mask checkboxes.**

   The last two options in the dialog box are Preserve Transparency and Mask. Turn on Preserve Transparency if you've got any transparent pixels on the target layer that you want to *keep* transparent. Turn on the Mask checkbox to hide the source image from the lightest areas in your target layer (so you won't see the source image in those spots), and apply more of the source image to the darker areas.

7. **Click OK and enjoy your collage.**

Though you can blend only two images at a time, there's no rule against using Apply Image on the same target image with different source images to blend *several* images together. And because Photoshop literally applies one image to another when you run this command, you won't increase the number of layers in your target document. If you're concerned about file size (maybe you have limited hard drive space or a slow computer), this method produces a smaller file than it would if you combined all the images into one document and then changed the blend mode of each layer (or used layer masks).

You can also use Apply Image to combine channel information within the same document. For example, if you want to add more details to your image, you can choose the same document as both the source and the target image and then select the green channel from the pop-up menu. The result is similar to what you'd get if you copied and pasted the green channel into your Layers panel and then changed its blend mode and layer opacity to what you enter here in the Apply Image dialog box. The only difference is that using Apply Image doesn't increase the number of layers in your document.

Auto-Aligning Layers and Photomerge

If you've ever needed to combine a few group shots into one image where everybody is smiling and everybody's eyes are open, you'll appreciate Auto-Align Layers. Sure, you could manually align layers, but when you run this command, Photoshop does all the hard work for you by examining the selected layers and aligning them so identical areas overlap (see Figure 7-22).

> **NOTE**   The Auto-Align feature isn't magic; the angle and the distance from the subject in both shots need to be the same for it to work.

Figure 7-22:
Top: When you're trying to align multiple group shots, the Auto-Align Layers dialog box's Reposition option is your best bet.

Bottom: By combining the images into one document, you can place the layer with the guy who isn't smiling on top of the layer where the guy is smiling. After you run the Auto-Align Layers command, all you have to do is add a layer mask to the top layer so your smiling pal shows through!

Once you've gotten your images into the same document (on different layers), select at least two layers by Shift- or ⌘-clicking them (Ctrl-clicking on a PC), and then choose Edit → Auto-Align Layers (this menu item is grayed out unless you have at least two layers selected). In the resulting dialog box (Figure 7-22, top), you can choose from these alignment methods:

- **Auto.** If you're not sure which method will work best to align your images, let Photoshop decide for you. When you choose Auto, Photoshop picks either Perspective or Cylindrical, depending on which one it thinks will create the best composition. It usually does a good job aligning your images though you may notice some distortion (as explained in the next two bullet points).

- **Perspective.** When you choose this method, Photoshop adjusts the four corners of your layers and repositions, stretches, and skews each one so any overlapping areas match in perspective. The final image looks slightly warped—both ends are a little larger than the center of the image, as if they were closer to you. This method can also make one of your layers look like it's coming out of the screen toward you, which can be visually interesting.

  TIP   Photoshop picks its own *reference layer* (the layer it tries to align all the other layers with) unless you designate one yourself using the Lock All layer lock, discussed on page 96.

- **Cylindrical.** If you're combining several images into a panorama (see Figure 7-23, top), choose this option. Along with repositioning, stretching, and skewing your layers, Cylindrical helps get rid of any bow-tie lens distortion (where the subject looks like it's being pinched inward) by curving the images slightly (see Figure 7-23, middle).

- **Collage.** This method, brand spankin' new in Photoshop CS4, tells Photoshop to scale, rotate, and reposition the layers to align them with overlapping content, but it doesn't change their shape. Choose Collage if you don't want your images to become distorted in any way.

- **Spherical.** Like the Cylindrical method, Spherical repositions, stretches, and skews layers to match up overlapping areas. It also tries to correct barrel distortion (where the subject looks rounded) by making your panorama perfectly rectangular. This option is new in Photoshop CS4 (see Figure 7-23, bottom).

- **Reposition.** If you're aligning a group shot to hide a frown or closed eyes, choose this option. It won't stretch or skew your layers; it'll just reposition them so they line up.

The Auto-Align Layers dialog box also gives you two new ways to correct camera lens distortions. Turn on the Vignette Removal checkbox to get rid of darkened or soft edges caused by wide-angle lenses or turn on the Geometric Distortion checkbox to make Photoshop warp your image slightly to reduce the spherical look also caused by wide-angle lenses or being too close to your subject with a regular lens.

Once you've aligned your images, flip to page 288 to see how you can make Photoshop blend them together seamlessly using the Auto-Blend command.

Figure 7-23:

Top: If you want to stitch these forest images together, you can use the Auto-Align Layers command or Photomerge to get it done.

Middle: To compensate for bow-tie lens distortion, the Cylindrical alignment method curves your final image slightly (notice that the bottom and top edges of the image aren't straight).

Bottom: The Spherical method gives you a perfectly rectangular panorama.

Building Panoramas with Photomerge

Photoshop has an automatic photo-stitcher called Photomerge that gives you all the same options as the Auto-Align Layers dialog box, but you don't have to combine your images into the same document first—Photoshop does that for you. It's really helpful when you're merging images into a wide shot though Photoshop CS4, unlike previous versions, doesn't let you arrange your images into a panorama manually (see the box at the bottom of page 287).

To use Photomerge, choose File → Automate → Photomerge. In the resulting dialog box's Use pop-up menu (at the very top), tell Photoshop whether you want to use individual files or a whole folder. Click the Browse button to find the images on your hard drive, or, if you've already opened the documents, click the Add Open Files button. On the left side of the dialog box, you can pick an alignment method or leave it set to Auto and let Photoshop decide for you. If you want Photoshop to use layer masks to help cover up any seams, leave the Blend Images Together checkbox at the bottom of the dialog box turned on (turning on this

Shooting Panoramas

If you're taking photos specifically to make a big honkin' panorama, here are a few things to think about while you're snapping away:

- **Use a tripod.** A tripod or some other stabilizing surface (like your mate's shoulder) helps you take steadier shots. You don't want your panorama to be blurry, right?

- **Include an overlapping element in each shot.** If you're taking three shots, make sure you include some of what's in the first shot in the second and some of the second shot in the third. That way you have overlapping bits that Photoshop can use to align your images.

- **Keep the lighting (exposure) consistent.** Though Photomerge is pretty darn good at blending images, you're going to notice if you took one of your shots in the shade and the other in direct sunlight. If possible, keep your lighting constant.

- **Make sure the angles are the same.** Photoshop has one heck of a time matching up images shot at different angles, but mismatched shots can make for some interesting creative possibilities.

checkbox has the same effect as running the Auto-Blend command discussed on page 288). The Vignette Removal and Geometric Distortion checkboxes work the same way here as they do in the Auto-Align dialog box (see page 284).

When you've got all the settings the way you want them, click OK. Photoshop combines your images into a new document with each image on its own layer, rotated and positioned to fit with all the others. All you need to do is crop the image (page 206) to get rid of any transparent bits around the edges (or you can recreate that portion of the image by hand using the Clone Stamp tool; see page 288 for more on cloning).

Interacting with Photomerge

Dude, where's my interactive Photomerge dialog box? In the last version of Photoshop, I used it all the time to hand place images into a panorama!

The bad news is that the dialog box is gone; Adobe removed it from Photoshop CS4. The good news is that you can get it back if you're willing to jump through a few hoops.

Previous versions of Photoshop had an Interactive Layout option at the bottom of the Photomerge dialog box that opened a huge window where you could manually arrange images into a panorama. This wildly useful option

let you control exactly how Photoshop stitched your panorama together, and it let you create nonrectangular panoramas that went off in all directions instead of just left to right. Because the out-of-date programming code would have required all manner of reworking to get the dialog box to work in CS4, Adobe decided to nix it.

That said, the older version of Photomerge still works in CS4. If you want to get it back, you can install it as a plug-in from either the Adobe Photoshop CS4 DVD or Adobe's Web site, *www.adobe.com*. (Chapter 19 has the full story on plug-ins.)

Auto-Blending Layers

The Auto-Blend Layers command, which was designed to be used after the Auto-Align command (page 283), can help you blend images for a panorama or a collage or combine multiple exposures of the same image to create an extended *depth of field* (see below) so more of an object looks like it's in focus. When you use this command, Photoshop creates complex layer masks to blend your images, saving you a lot of hard work.

> **NOTE** You can use the Auto-Blend Layers command only when you're working in RGB or Grayscale mode (see page 40).

To get the best results, start with the Auto-Align Layers command and then choose Edit → Auto-Blend Layers. In the resulting dialog box, choose one of the following blending options:

- **Panorama.** Turn on this option to have Photoshop search for overlapping areas in your images to piece them together into a single image.

- **Stack Images.** If you've fired off several shots of an object with different parts in focus (known as different *depths of field*) and you want to combine those images into a single shot that looks like the *whole object* is in focus, choose this option. Let's say you shot a tiger—with a big zoom lens, of course—and the tiger was stretched out lengthwise and facing you. If you shot one image with his head in focus, another with the middle of his body in focus, and a third with his tail in focus, you can choose Stack Images to make Photoshop combine those three images into a single shot with the *whole* tiger in focus.

- **Seamless Tones and Colors.** Turn on this option to make Photoshop smooth any recognizable seams and color differences between your images during the blending process.

As mentioned earlier, this command has a ton of potential uses. One visually interesting possibility is to make a collage of two or more action shots to create a stop-motion effect. Figure 7-24 has the details.

> **TIP** You can also use the Auto-Blend Layers command to help you scan really big images. For example, if the image is too big to fit onto your scanner in one piece, scan different sections of it—being careful to create overlapping areas—and let Photoshop piece it together for you by first running the Auto-Align Layers command and then running Auto-Blend Layers.

Cloning Between Documents

All this combining-images-into-the-same-document business can cause your Layers panel to get long and unwieldy. And as you learned back in Chapter 3, loading a document with layers can increase its file size and even slow Photoshop down (especially if you've got an older computer or very little memory). Fortunately, if the images you want to combine use the same color mode (page 40), there's a solution.

Figure 7-24:
*You can use the Auto-
Blend Layers command
to create interesting
collages in mere seconds.
The best part is that
Photoshop does all the
masking for you, as
shown here in the Layers
panel.*

Figure 7-24:
*You can use the Auto-
Blend Layers command
to create interesting
collages in mere seconds.
The best part is that
Photoshop does all the
masking for you, as
shown here in the Layers
panel.*

Most folks think of the Clone Stamp tool as just for fun tricks like banishing blemishes (page 400) or giving someone a third eye, but it also has more important uses. To prevent your Layers panel from becoming overcrowded, use this tool to copy bits and pieces of an image from one open document to another. In Photoshop CS3, Adobe added a *Clone Source panel*—the clone source is the object you're copying—that lets you clone from up to five different sources whether or not they're in the same document.

Here's how to clone from one open image into another:

1. **Open the source (the image[s] you're cloning *from*) and the target (the image you're cloning *to*).**

   To choose clone sources in documents other than the current image, open the source document(s) (you can use more than one). Click the Arrange Documents button (page 63) to choose a preview method so you can see all your open documents or just click each document's tab to activate it (see Chapter 2, page 62, for more info on working with tabbed documents).

2. **Press S to grab the Clone Stamp tool (see Appendix E, online at *www.missingmanuals.com*) and then open the Clone Source panel.**

Choose Window → Clone Source or click the panel's icon in the panel dock. Full coverage of the Clone Source panel's many options starts on page 291.

3. **Set the clone source.**

Click the tab of the image you want to clone from (like the cats in Figure 7-25, top left). Then Option-click (Alt-click on a PC) the area you want to copy to set it as your clone source.

4. **Create a new layer.**

Unless you want to clone the new image on top of your original image (and you don't!), head back to your target document and add a new layer by clicking the "Create a new layer" button at the bottom of the Layers panel. That way, if you don't like the result, you can simply toss the new layer instead of having to start over.

5. **Paint to clone the item.**

As shown in Figure 7-25 (bottom left), Photoshop displays a preview of the image you're about to paint inside the brush cursor (this preview is new in CS4). If you don't want your clone source point to move as your brush cursor moves—because you want to create multiple instances of an object, for instance—turn off the Options bar's Aligned checkbox.

Figure 7-25:
Top: By cloning the kitties from one image onto the birdhouses in another image, you can create a mischievously cute collage.

Bottom: The new brush preview in CS4 is extremely helpful in positioning the cloned art (left). If you mess up and clone in a little too much (middle), grab the History brush (page 26) and paint to reveal that part of the original image (right). If you're cloning onto a new layer, you can also use the Eraser tool.

TIP   To change brush size and hardness, you can use the Options bar—or you can use CS4's new keyboard shortcuts: Press Ctrl-Option (Alt+right-click on a PC) and drag to the left or right to decrease or increase your brush size, respectively. Press Ctrl-Option-⌘ (Shift+Alt+right-click) and drag to the left or right to soften or harden your brush, respectively.

You need a pretty steady hand when you're working with the Clone Stamp tool because it's easy to clone too much and cover up parts of your image. You can solve that problem by first selecting a certain area to restrict your brush strokes to that part of the image. This technique is handy when you want to fill an area with another image, as shown in Figure 7-26.

Figure 7-26:
If you select the destination area first, you don't have to be as careful with your brush. As you can see here, the brush extends past the edges of these digital business dudes (circled), but Photoshop applies the Matrix-like background only within the selection.

You can also clone from one document to another by following the steps just described, but your clone target and destination will be in different images. If you want to get a little fancy and start doing things like pulling source points from *multiple* images and changing the angle of your cloned oblects, then you need to enlist the help of the Clone Source panel (Figure 7-27).

> **NOTE**   You can use the Frame Offset and Lock Frame options shown in Figure 7-27 (available only in Photoshop Extended) to clone content in video or animation frames.

In the Clone Source panel, you can tweak the following settings (all shown in Figure 7-27):

- **Offset.** Use this section of the Clone Source panel to move, resize, or rotate the object you're copying (the clone source). If you want to move your clone source, you can change its X and Y coordinates (measured in pixels) here. If you've got the Show Overlay checkbox (explained next) turned on, you see a preview of the source point on your image that moves as you tweak these settings. To clone the object at a different size, enter new percentages in the W and H fields (for width and height). To rotate your clone source—so the cloned item is turned—enter a number of degrees in the field next to the little triangle. To reset all these options, click the little curved arrow button.

Click to set other
open documents
as a clone source

Close panel

Panel menu

Clone Source
panel dock

Reset

Set position

Scale

Rotate

Figure 7-27:
*Assigning multiple clone sources
(page 291) is handy when you
want to clone items between open
documents or when you're trying
to create a complex scene from
different elements. For example, if
you're trying to remove a cow
that's standing in front of a fence,
one clone source can be the fence
and another can be the grass.
Once you've activated the Clone
Stamp tool, you can use the five
source buttons shown here to
switch quickly between different
source points without having to
reset them manually each time.
To set a source point, just Option-
click (Alt-click on a PC) the area
you want to clone. Your cursor
turns into a crosshair like the one
circled here.*

TIP   You can position your cursor above any of the field labels in the Offset section—X, Y, W, and
so on—to get the handy scrubby cursor (page 88). Drag left to decrease the setting and right to
increase it. You can Shift-drag to change it in larger increments or Option-drag (Alt-drag on a PC)
for smaller increments. If you're a fan of keyboard shortcuts, press Option-Shift-[(Alt+Shift+[on a
PC) to decrease your clone source's width and height proportionally and Option-Shift-]
(Alt+Shift+]) to increase them. To rotate your source, press Option-Shift-< (Alt+Shift+<) to rotate it
counterclockwise or Option-Shift-> (Alt+Shift+>) to rotate it clockwise.

- **Show Overlay.** With this checkbox turned on (it's on automatically), you see a
  preview of what you're about to paint *inside your brush cursor*. This handy feature, new in CS4, shows you exactly what the cloning looks like before you
  commit to it.

- **Opacity.** You can use this field to adjust the opacity of the overlay preview. To
  change the opacity of what you're *cloning* (your actual brushstrokes), you have
  to change the Opacity setting in the Options bar instead.

- **Clipped.** This checkbox restricts the preview overlay to the area inside your
  brush cursor. For Pete's sake, leave the Clipped checkbox turned on. If you
  don't, Photoshop previews the *entire* clone source image right underneath your
  cursor, which keeps you from seeing anything *except* the preview.

- **Auto Hide.** If you turn on this checkbox, the overlay preview disappears as soon
  as you click to start painting. It's a good idea to turn it on so you can see how
  much you've painted so far.

- **Invert.** Turning on this checkbox makes Photoshop invert the overlay preview so it looks like a film negative, which can be helpful if you're trying to align the cloned area with something that's already in your image

- **Blend Mode.** You can use this pop-up menu to change the blend mode of overlay preview. Your choices—Normal, Darken, Lighten, and Difference—are explained earlier in this chapter, starting on page 267. To change the blend mode of the *cloned pixels*, use the Mode pop-up menu in the Options bar instead.

Combining Vectors and Rasters

A fun trend in the design world is to combine vectors with rasters (page 48 explains the difference); in other words, to combine illustrations with photographs, a technique that provides an interesting look and lets you get creative. Because you can load vectors as Smart Objects (page 115) they remain infinitely resizable, letting you experiment with them as backgrounds, artful embellishments, and even ornamental photo frames.

As you can see in Figure 7-28, adding vectors to photos is a ton of fun. It's as if you're blending real images with imaginary ones. Even if you can't draw these little goodies yourself, stock image companies like Getty (*www.gettyimages.com*), iStockphoto (*www.istockphoto.com*), and others, sell affordable, vector-based images so you can still participate in the trend.

Figure 7-28:
A dash of vector art can spice up any photo.

You can add vector art to your images in a couple of ways:

- **Place it.** With a document open, choose File → Place and navigate to the vector file on your hard drive. Place This inserts the file as a Smart Object (page 115). Since you'll most likely need to resize the artwork, Photoshop considerately surrounds it with the Free Transform bounding box and resizing handles (page 245). Just Shift-drag any corner to make the art bigger or smaller. If you need to rotate it, place your mouse outside the bounding box and drag in the direction you want to rotate. Press Return (Enter on a PC) when you're finished.

- **Paste it.** If you're working in a vector-based program like Adobe Illustrator, you can copy artwork and paste it into your Photoshop document by choosing Edit → Paste or pressing ⌘-V (Ctrl+V on a PC). When you do, Photoshop displays the dialog box shown in Figure 7-29, asking how you want to paste it. If you choose Smart Object, you can resize the artwork as much as you want and never have to worry about losing quality (see page 115).

Figure 7-29:
When you paste a piece of vector art, Photoshop lets you choose how to paste it (left). If you choose Smart Object, the object appears in your document with helpful resizing handles, as shown here (right). It also carries the special Smart Object badge (circled) over in the Layers panel.

Framing a photo with an illustration is not only fun but incredibly flexible because you can continually resize the frame without starting over. Here's how to do it:

1. **Open the photo you want to frame and, if necessary, double-click the Background layer and give it another name to make it editable (page 80).**

   If your Background layer isn't locked, or if you've already worked with the photo and renamed this layer, you can skip this step.

2. **Create a new layer *below* the photo layer.**

You'll use this layer to make a brand-new background for your photo after you've made the frame. If you've got the photo layer selected in your Layers panel, you can ⌘-click (Ctrl-click on a PC) the panel's "Create a new layer" button to make Photoshop put the new layer *below* the one you're on.

3. **Fill the new layer with color.**

Try snatching a color from the image itself by pressing I to select the Eyedropper tool and then clicking on a color in your image (like the copper in the mermaid's hair in Figure 7-30). Since the new layer was automatically selected when you created it in the previous step, you can press Option-Delete (Alt+Backspace on a PC) to fill it with color.

4. **In your Layers panel, select the photo layer and then choose File → Place to import the illustration you want to use for the frame.**

Selecting the photo layer first ensures that Photoshop puts the Smart Object layer at the top of your layers stack. Navigate to the EPS (Encapsulated PostScript) or AI (Adobe Illustrator) file on your hard drive and then click the Place button.

5. **Resize the illustration.**

Conveniently, the illustration appears in your document with resizing handles around it, which you'll probably need to use to make it bigger or smaller. Grab a corner handle and drag until the frame is big enough to hold the photo. (To resize all four sides of the illustration at once, press and hold Shift-Option [Shift+Alt] as you drag a corner handle.) Click inside the bounding box to move it around. When it's just right, press Return (Enter).

6. **Load the illustration as a selection, as shown in Figure 7-30 (top).**

In your Layers panel, ⌘-click (Ctrl+click) the Smart Object's layer thumbnail to load it as a selection (you'll see marching ants). Then turn off the Smart Object's visibility eye; you won't need that layer again unless you want to resize it later.

7. **Select the photo layer and add a mask.**

Click the half-black/half-white circle at the bottom of the Layers panel to add a mask (make sure you're on the right layer first). Photoshop fills the mask with black around the shape of your selection to hide the edges of the photo. (As you'll remember from Chapter 3, when you're dealing with a layer mask, black conceals and white reveals.)

Figure 7-30:
This detailed illustration makes a gorgeous photo frame. After you place it as a Smart Object and resize it, just load it as a selection (top) and then add a mask to the photo layer (bottom).

8. **Use the Move Tool to position the photo and frame on your page.**

Press V to grab the Move tool and reposition the photo-and-frame layer. If you want to move the photo and mask independently, you've got to unlock them first. Click the tiny chain between the layer and mask thumbnails and then click the thumbnail of the bit you want to move (the photo or the mask). Use the Move tool to position the photo or mask and then click between them to lock them back together.

9. **Save your document as a PSD file.**

You're done! To resize the illustration, Ctrl-click (right-click on a PC) the mask thumbnail and choose Delete Layer Mask from the resulting shortcut menu. Then select the Smart Object layer and turn its visibility back on. Summon Free Transform by pressing ⌘-T (Ctrl+T) and use one of the corner handles to resize the illustration. Press Return (Enter) when you're finished and follow steps 6–8 again to load the illustration as a selection and add a layer mask. To give the frame a little depth, you can tack on a drop shadow using Layer Styles (page 119).

Mapping One Image onto Another

You can combine two images in an impressive way by wrapping one around the contours of another so the first image follows every nook and cranny of the second. To perform this feat, you need to create a *displacement map*—a grayscale image that

Photoshop uses to warp and bend one image to the curvature of another. Trying this technique on photos of friends and family is great fun. For example, you can take a circuit board and wrap it around a body or a face, as shown in Figure 7-31.

NOTE Want to follow along with the tutorial listed below? Visit this book's Missing CD page at *www.missingmanuals.com* and download the practice file Map.zip.

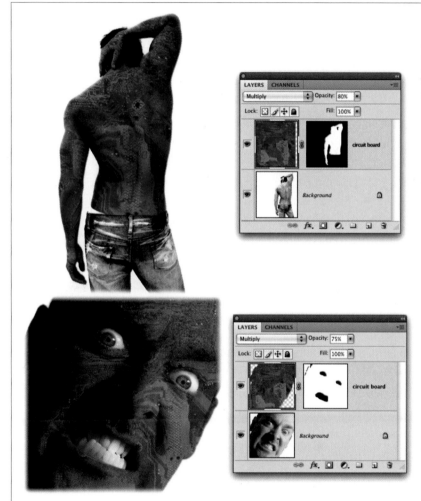

Figure 7-31:
With a displacement map, you can apply all kinds of wild textures to skin. (Know anyone who needs to be turned into a reptile?)

1. **Open the image you want to map another image onto and hunt down the channel with the greatest contrast.**

   To make the best displacement map possible, you need to find the channel with the highest contrast. If you're in RGB mode (and you probably are), you can cycle through your channels by pressing ⌘-3, 4, and 5 (Ctrl+3, 4, and 5 on a PC). Because digital cameras have so many more green sensors than red or blue ones, you'll most likely pick the green channel.

2. **Duplicate that channel and send it to a new document.**

   Open your Channels panel (page 174) by clicking its icon in the panel dock or by choosing Window → Channels. From the Channels panel menu, choose Duplicate Channel. In the resulting dialog box, choose New from the Destination pop-up menu and name it something memorable like *Map*. When you click OK, Photoshop opens the displacement map document that contains the grayscale channel you picked in step 1.

3. **Blur the displacement map slightly.**

   With the map document active, choose Filter → Blur → Gaussian Blur. Enter a value of 1–4 pixels (for low-resolution images, enter 1; for high resolution, enter 4) and then click OK. The goal here is to blur the image just a bit so the map is slightly smooth. (Page 591 has more on the Gaussian Blur filter.)

4. **Save the map.**

   Choose File → Save As and choose Photoshop from the Format pop-up menu at the bottom of the dialog box. Make sure the Alpha Channel option is turned on (it should be on automatically, but it doesn't hurt to check) and then click Save.

5. **Turn the composite channel back on.**

   When you cycled through the different channels in step 1, Photoshop temporarily turned off the composite channel (the one that shows your image in full color). Go back to the original face document (the one you opened in step 1) and turn all the channels back on by pressing ⌘-2 (Ctrl+2 on a PC).

6. **Select the face.**

   In the image shown at the bottom of Figure 7-31, it's simple to select the face because it's on a solid background. Grab the Magic Wand by pressing W, click once in the white area, and then Shift-click to select the other white parts until you have everything *except* the face selected.

7. **Invert your selection by pressing ⌘-Shift-I (Ctrl+Shift+I on a PC) or choosing Select → Inverse.**

   Photoshop flip-flops your selection so the face is surrounded by marching ants.

8. **Feather the edges of your selection slightly.**

   Click the Refine Edge button in your Options bar and feather your selection by 1 pixel. (See page 132 for more on feathering.)

9. **Save your selection by choosing Select → Save Selection.**

   Name it *Face* and then click OK. Get rid of the marching ants by pressing ⌘-D (Ctr+D) to deselect.

10. **Add the soon-to-be-a-map image to the face document.**

Pop open the image you want to map onto the face (like the circuit board in Figure 7-31, bottom), and either copy and paste the image into the face document or drag it from the Layers panel of one open document into the other.

11. **Choose Filter → Distort → Displace.**

In the resulting Displace dialog box, leave the factory settings alone and click OK. If you're not sure if the settings have ever been tampered with, press and hold the Option key (Alt on a PC) to change the Cancel button to Reset. Click it and you're back to the original settings.

12. **In the resulting Open dialog box, navigate to the Map document you saved a few moments ago and then click OK.**

If you peek at your document as you click OK, you'll see the circuit board shift to the contours of the face. It's extremely cool.

13. **Load the face selection.**

Choose Select → Load Selection → Face. You should see marching ants around the shape of the face (you can't see the actual face because it's behind the circuit board).

14. **Add a layer mask by clicking the circle-within-a-square button at the bottom of the Layers panel.**

Select the Brush tool by pressing B and, with black as your foreground color chip (page 22), paint over the guy's eyes and teeth to hide them, as shown in Figure 7-31 (bottom).

15. **Change the circuit board layer's blend mode to Multiply (page 269).**

You should see the face through the circuit board. If the circuit board is too dark, you can lower the opacity setting at the top of the Layers panel.

Congratulations! You've just mapped one image to the contours of another, one of the neatest Photoshop tricks ever.

Draining, Changing, and Adding Color

When you want to make a big difference with one simple change to your photo, you can't beat converting it from color to black and white. The Ansel Adams approach doesn't just evoke nostalgia; it puts the focus back on the subject in a powerful way. Going grayscale also lets you salvage an image that you can't color-correct, or beautify a subject whose teeth need heavy-duty whitening or whose skin needs fixing. Those problems all but disappear when you enter the realm of black and white.

But does that mean you should set your digital camera to shoot in black and white? Heck, no! It's *much* better to photograph in color and then drain the color in Photoshop. That way, you have a truckload of artistic options like bringing back just a touch of the original color for a partial color effect. And, speaking of color, Photoshop has several tools that let you change the color of anything, whether it's a car or the hair on your head. You can also breathe new life into vintage photographs by adding a dash of color.

This chapter teaches you how simple it is to drain, change, or add color to your photos. The following pages are packed with creative color techniques you'll use time and time again.

Draining Color

You've heard the saying, "You get what you pay for." In Photoshop, that saying translates to, "The quickest method ain't always the best." Some techniques just take a little extra time, and converting a color image to black and white is one of 'em—but it's well worth the effort.

To drive that point home, open a colorful image—download Dragon.jpg from this book's Missing CD page (*www.missingmanuals.com*) if you need a good sample—and then choose Image → Adjustments → Desaturate. (*Desaturate* is Photoshop's term for draining your image of all color.) Photoshop converts your image to black and white all right, but the results are less than inspiring (see Figure 8-1, top). You can also glance through your channels (page 176), select the one with the best contrast, and then choose Image → Mode → Grayscale. Photoshop keeps the channel you're on, tosses the rest, and gives you a black-and-white image. But unless you're using an old, pre-CS version of Photoshop, neither method is much good. Fortunately, the program has come a long way when it comes to black-and-white conversions, as you're about to find out.

Figure 8-1:

Top: True, the Desaturate command provides a one-step approach to black-and-white conversions, but you get a fairly lame dragon.

Bottom: A Black & White Adjustment layer, where you can introduce all kinds of contrast, is a much better option that lets you produce a properly menacing creature!

Black & White Adjustment Layers

Having made its debut back in Photoshop CS3, the Black & White Adjustment layer is hands down the easiest way to convert your color image into beautiful black and white. It couldn't be simpler to use, and, best of all, it's nondestructive. As Chapter 3 (page 71) explains, when you use Adjustment layers, Photoshop makes the changes on *another* layer (not on your original image), letting you tweak the opacity, toggle the visibility on or off, and so on. Though you'll learn about other kinds of Adjustment layers throughout this book, this section covers Black & White Adjustment layers, which let you create really nice black-and-white images in no time flat.

To convert your image to black and white, follow these steps:

1. **Pop open your soon-to-be-colorless image.**

   Since you're using an Adjustment layer, you don't need to bother double-clicking the Background layer to make it editable because you won't be messing with the original image.

2. **Create a Black & White Adjustment layer (see Figure 8-2).**

   In the panel dock on the right side of your screen, open the Adjustments panel (new in CS4). You can click its tab (see Figure 8-2) or, if you've collapsed the panels, you can click its icon (it's a half-black/half-white circle, just like the icon at the bottom of your Layers panel). If you don't see the icon, choose Window → Adjustments.

   Once you've got the panel open click the half-black/half-white rectangle (circled in Figure 8-2) to create a Black & White Adjustment layer. When you do that, Photoshop turns your image black and white and changes the Adjustments panel to display several sliders and other controls you can use to fine-tune your Adjustment layer (Figure 8-3).

   NOTE Photoshop gives you another way to add Adjustment layers: clicking the half-black/half-white circle at the bottom of your Layers panel. From the resulting pop-up menu, pick the kind of Adjustment layer you want to use. (In previous versions of Photoshop you saw a dialog box containing the same controls you see in CS4's Adjustments panel.)

Panel menu
Close panel

Switch panel to
expanded view

Apply
adjustment
to all layers

Figure 8-2:
New in CS4, the Adjustments panel gives you access to all the Adjustment layers and their presets (one-click, canned settings). Instead of having the dialog boxes of various adjustments open up atop your image as in previous versions of the program, you can make all your adjustments in this panel.

---

3. Move the Adjustments panel's various color sliders until you have a nice, contrasty black-and-white image.

Even though Photoshop has drained the color from your image, there's always room for improvement. Try dragging the various color sliders around to make your image look even better. Dragging to the right turns areas that previously were the color of that particular slider a lighter shade of gray; dragging to the left turns them a darker shade of gray. The pop-up menu at the top of the panel has a slew of canned settings—just click each one to see what it looks like applied to your image (unfortunately, you can't cycle through them with your arrow keys to get a preview). Some of the panel's other controls are shown in Figure 8-3, and the Tint checkbox is explained in the next section (page 304). When you're ready, click the Auto button to see what Photoshop thinks your grayscale image should look like.

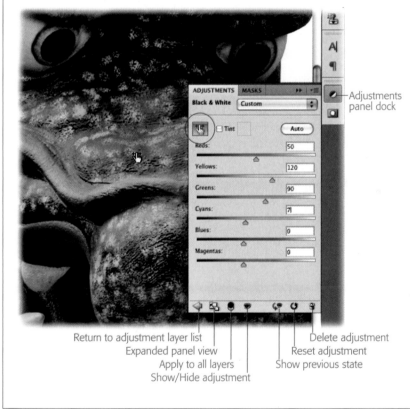

Adjustments panel dock

Return to adjustment layer list
Expanded panel view
Apply to all layers
Show/Hide adjustment

Delete adjustment
Reset adjustment
Show previous state

Figure 8-3:
Instead of adjusting a bunch of sliders, you can use the on-image adjustment button, which lets you tweak a certain range of colors by dragging on the image itself. Click the circled button at the top left of the Adjustments panel and then mouse over to your image (your cursor temporarily turns into an eyedropper, which lets you know you're about to sample a color). Next, drag the area you want to adjust to the left to make it darker or to the right to make it lighter. Your cursor turns into a pointing hand with an arrow on each side to indicate that you can drag from side to side to adjust that range of color. It's a handy way to edit your image visually instead of guessing which slider to tweak.

4. Close the Adjustments panel by clicking the dark gray bar at the top of the panel or by clicking the little double arrows at the top right to collapse it (shown in Figure 8-2).

5. Save your document as a PSD file (page 46).

If you want to change the Black & White Adjustment layer's settings later, just double-click the Adjustment layer in your Layers panel (its thumbnail is that familiar half-black/half-white circle icon) or select the layer and then open the Adjustments panel. If you print the image and then decide it needs more contrast, this little trick is a lifesaver.

Warp-speed tinting

You probably spotted the Tint checkbox lurking at the top of the Adjustments panel's Black & White settings (Figure 8-3). When you turn on this checkbox, Photoshop adds a brown tint (called a *sepia tone*) to your whole image as shown in Figure 8-4 (bottom right). If you want to choose a different color, click the colored square to the right of the checkbox to summon the Color Picker (page 457). This technique produces what's known as a *fake duotone*, the real ones are explained on page 315.

Figure 8-4:
Left: After you add a Black & White Adjustment layer to an image, you can add a sleek color overlay by turning on the Tint checkbox (circled).

Right: The original full-color image (top) is followed by a black-and-white version (middle) and a brown-tinted sepia version (bottom).

Channel Mixer Adjustment Layers

The Black & White Adjustment layers you read about in the previous section are the quickest, easiest way to drain images of their color, but if you're using Photoshop CS3, you don't have that tool. No need to panic; you can use the Channel Mixer instead. First, make sure you've got the Background layer selected in your Layers panel (or the image layer you want to work with), click the half-black/half-white circle at the bottom of the Layers panel, and then choose Channel Mixer from the resulting menu.

If you're in Photoshop CS3, turn on the Monochrome checkbox at the bottom of the dialog box that appears. If you're in CS4, your Adjustments panel opens and the Monochrome checkbox appears near the top of the panel. Tweak the Red, Green, and Blue sliders to your liking or pick one of the presets in the pop-up menu at the top of the dialog box (where the cursor is in Figure 8-5). If you want to darken or lighten your overall image, drag the Constant slider to the left or right (why it's not simply called the *Brightness* slider is anyone's guess).

Figure 8-5:
When you turn on the Monochrome checkbox, the Output Channel pop-up menu changes to Gray, letting you know you're mixing the channels to produce a grayscale image. (You won't see this menu in the Adjustments panel of CS4–it appears only in the Channel Mixer dialog box.) As you adjust the sliders, keep an eye on the Total percentage at the bottom (circled). If you keep it around 100 percent, you'll produce a grayscale version of your image with the same brightness as your original. If you go over or under 100 percent, a tiny gray warning triangle lets you know you're headed into the dreaded over- or underexposure zone. Luckily, as long as you've got the Preview checkbox in the upper-right corner of the dialog box turned on, you can peek back in your document to see what the image looks like.

The Lightness Channel

As you learned back on page 183, Lab mode gets its name from its three channels. The "L" in Lab mode stands for the Lightness channel where Photoshop stores all the light values and therefore the visible contours and details of your image. (The "a" and "b" stand for the a and b channels which store the color info.) This means that the Lightness channel makes for a lovely black-and-white version of your image (see Figure 8-6). To see what your Lightness channel looks like, open your image and choose Image → Mode → Lab Color. Over in the Channels panel (page 174), select the Lightness channel, tilt your head contemplatively, and see what you think. If you like the image, choose Image → Mode → Grayscale, and click Discard when Photoshop asks if it's okay to throw out your color information.

> **TIP** If you need to darken or lighten your new grayscale image, you can use the Screen and Multiply blend mode tricks mentioned back on page 109 or any of the adjustments explained in Chapter 9.

Preparing Grayscale Images for a Printing Press

If your color image is part of a document headed to a professional printing press (page 633) and you've been assigned the task of transforming it into a grayscale image, you need to take one additional step: To make it a real, live grayscale image, you have to change your document's color mode to Grayscale. (If your image is headed for an inkjet printer or destined for posting on the Web, you can stop reading this box now and skip to something more interesting.)

That's right, even though your image *looks* grayscale onscreen, it's still made from colors that have had their saturation values lowered to zero (saturation is the degree of color strength; see page 452). If you don't believe it, open your Channels panel by choosing Window → Channels and you'll find color channels peering back at you (what those channels *are* depend on which color mode you're working in).

If you don't change the mode to Grayscale and you send this image off to a printing press, your image prints with the colors found in your Channels panel instead of with black ink alone. While the result still looks like a grayscale image, it's actually made from color, which costs a lot more to print than grayscale because the press uses more colors.

To prepare a grayscale image for a printing press, start by using one of the methods in this chapter to make a grayscale

image. Otherwise, Photoshop makes it for you—with mediocre results like those you'd get using the Desaturate command discussed on page 301. Next, save your document as a PSD file by choosing File → Save As to preserve any Adjustment layers (like a Black & White Adjustment layer) you may have made when you created your grayscale image. Now you're ready to change the document mode to Grayscale by choosing Image → Mode → Grayscale.

Photoshop pops open a dialog box to let you know your document has other layers and asks what you'd like to do about them. To make Photoshop use the grayscale version of your image that you've created, click Flatten. (Clicking anything else causes Photoshop to convert the image to grayscale for you whether you like it or not.) In the next dialog box, click Discard to throw away all the color info in your document. You're left with a grayscale document that contains a single channel named Grayscale.

To save the image for use in a page-layout program like InDesign, choose File → Save As and then, from the Format pop-up menu near the bottom of the Save As dialog box, choose TIFF. Close the document by pressing ⌘-W (Ctrl+W on a PC). In the resulting dialog box, click Don't Save to make sure you don't overwrite your original layered Photoshop file

Going Grayscale in Camera Raw

If you're shooting photos in the Raw format, you may as well use the Camera Raw plug-in (page 53) to convert images to grayscale. It's easy to use and it does a nice job with these conversions. To open a Raw image, just double-click its file icon and it opens in Camera Raw automatically. If you're using Adobe Bridge (Appendix C) to peruse your images, you can double-click its thumbnail or Ctrl-click (right-click on a PC) the image and choose "Open in Camera Raw" from the shortcut menu.

> **TIP** In Photoshop CS3 and CS4, you can open JPEGs and TIFFs (page 46) in Camera Raw, too. Choose File → Open and navigate to the file on your hard drive. In the Format pop-up menu at the bottom of the Open dialog box (Open As on a PC), choose Camera Raw and then click Open. See Chapter 9 for more on editing in Camera Raw.

Figure 8-6:
Because the Lightness channel holds all your image's details but none of the color, it makes a nice black-and-white version of your image all by itself.

Once you've opened your image in Camera Raw, follow these steps to convert it to a gorgeous grayscale image:

1. **In the Camera Raw window, open the HSL/Grayscale panel.**

   To open the panel, click the button circled in Figure 8-7, top, and then turn on the panel's "Convert to Grayscale" checkbox. A set of color sliders appears on the right side of the Camera Raw window. To lighten a specific color, drag the slider to the right. To darken it, drag the slider to the left.

2. **Open the Basic panel and adjust the Exposure slider to fine-tune your grayscale image.**

   To get back to the Basic panel that greeted you when you first opened Camera Raw, click the button that's circled in Figure 8-7, bottom. To brighten your image, drag the Exposure slider slightly to the right until you see just a few red areas in your image. (If you don't see any red, click the "Highlight clipping" triangle labeled in Figure 8-7, bottom.) The red is Camera Raw's way of telling you that you're *clipping* or *blowing out* an image, which means you're losing details in your image's highlights.

3. **Drag the Recovery slider to the right to bring back details in the highlights.**

   You can use the Recovery slider to get back some of the details that disappeared when you increased the exposure. Just drag the Recovery slider to the right until all (or most) of the red goes away.

4. **Drag the Blacks slider a tiny bit to the right to make the shadows in your image a little darker.**

   If you see blue areas appear on your image, don't worry—it's just a warning that you're losing details in the shadows. (If you don't see any blue, click the "Shadow clipping" triangle labeled in Figure 8-7, bottom.) Losing a few details in your shadows isn't as critical as losing details in the highlights because, hey, shadows are mostly black, anyway. If your shadows *do* contain important details, you can skip adjusting this slider. Only one more slider adjustment to go!

CHAPTER 8: DRAINING, CHANGING, AND ADDING COLOR

Figure 8-7:
Top: In the Camera Raw window, click the HSL/Grayscale button (circled) to see the "Convert to Grayscale" option.

Bottom: Back in the Basic panel (click the circled button to get to it), Camera Raw warns you if your exposure adjustments are overexposing your image's highlights by marking those areas in red. (Photo pros use the term "blown out" for overexposed areas.)

5. **Drag the Clarity slider to the right to boost contrast.**

   By doing some serious behind-the-scenes voodoo, this slider increases the contrast in the midtones (the grays) of your image, giving it extra oomph. Most images look better if you increase the Clarity setting to at least 30.

6. **When you're finished, click Done to close the Camera Window or click Open Image to proceed to Photoshop.**

You've got yourself a lovely grayscale version of your image with lots of details. At this point, you may want to jump ahead to Chapter 11 to learn about sharpening your image.

Partial Color Effect

One of most creative ways to accentuate part of an image is to colorize that area and make everything else black and white. You can do that easily by using a Black & White or a Channel Mixer Adjustment layer (page 301 and page 304, respectively) to convert your image to black and white and then adding a layer mask (page 105) to hide the conversion in the parts that you want to retain their color. This technique is a wonderfully nondestructive way to add creativity to your image.

As luck would have it, *all* Adjustment layers come with a mask; the mask (which starts out empty) automatically appears in your Layers panel to the right of the Adjustment layer's thumbnail, as you can see in Figure 8-8, right. So just pick whichever conversion method you like best to make your image black and white and then follow these steps:

1. **In the Layers panel, click the Adjustment layer's mask thumbnail.**

   Photoshop puts a tiny black outline (circled in Figure 8-8) around the mask thumbnail as soon as you click it to let you know it's active.

   TIP   If the thumbnails in your Layers panel are *really* small, you may not see the black outline around the mask thumbnail. Thankfully, you can make the thumbnails bigger by choosing Panel Options from the Layers panel menu. Choose the biggest thumbnail size and click OK. *Now* you should be able to see the thumbnail without squinting.

Figure 8-8:
All Adjustment layers come with a layer mask that lets you hide that adjustment from certain areas. By painting with black (the brush cursor is circled here on the left) to mask certain areas from the Black & White Adjustment layer, you can hide the adjustment and bring back the color. Just make sure you've got the mask selected before you start painting—or you'll add a nice coat of black paint to your original image.

2. **Press B to grab the Brush tool and set your foreground color chip to black; then hide part of the Adjustment layer by painting it.**

Remember the layer mask rhyme "Black conceals and white reveals"? When you're about to work with a mask, take a moment to think about what you want to do: To *hide* parts of the Adjustment layer, you need to paint with black. Find the color chips at the bottom of your Tools panel and press X until black pops on top. Then mouse over to your image and press B to grab the Brush tool, When you start painting, the original color appears, as shown in Figure 8-8. If you reveal too much of the color, don't panic; just swap color chips by pressing X so that white is on top and then repaint that area to reveal the adjustment. (When you're working with masks, it's helpful to keep a finger poised over the X key.)

TIP   To make sure you're painting only what you want to colorize, you can zoom in on your image by pressing ⌘-+ (Ctrl-+ on a PC) or zoom out by pressing ⌘ (Ctrl) and the minus key [–]. When you're zoomed in, you can toss your image from side to side with the Hand tool–very helpful if you need to view a different portion of your image. To grab the Hand tool, just press the space bar and drag, or choose the Hand tool (page 59) from the top of your screen. (For more tips on viewing your images at close range, see page 55.)

3. **When you're finished painting the mask, save the document as a PSD file.**

Saving your document as a PSD file makes Photoshop keep all your layers; that way you can go back and edit the mask later.

To see a quick before-and-after preview of your image, mouse over to the Layers panel and turn off the Adjustment layer's visibility eye.

Fading Color to Black and White

You can use a technique similar to the one you learned in the previous section to create a soft fade from full color to black and white (Figure 8-9). After you've made your image black and white using either a Black & White or a Channel Mixer Adjustment layer, follow these steps:

NOTE   Want to follow along? Visit this book's Missing CD page at *www.missingmanuals.com* and download the practice file Facepaint.jpg.

1. **Over in the Layers panel, select the Adjustment layer's mask thumbnail (circled back in Figure 8-8, right).**

2. **Press G to fire up the Gradient tool and, in the Options bar, choose the black-to-white linear gradient.**

In the Options bar, open the Gradient Preset picker by clicking the down arrow next to the large gradient preview (it's the third item from the left) and click the "Black, White" gradient thumbnail (circled in Figure 8-9, top left) to choose the

Figure 8-9:
By using a black-to-white gradient in a layer mask, you can create a beautiful faded-color effect. The farther you drag with the gradient cursor (which looks like a crosshair though it's hard to see here), the softer and wider the transition from color to black and white. As you can see here, this technique can produce stunning results.

black-to-white linear gradient. You can hover over each gradient preview to see its name. (If your foreground and background color chips are set to black and white, you can also choose the "Foreground to Background" gradient, which appears first in the preview list.) To the right of the Gradient Preset picker, find the first gradient style (Linear Gradient) and make sure it's turned on (it should be selected unless you've changed gradient styles recently). You can also hover your cursor over each gradient style button to see its name.

3. **Mouse over to your document and click where you want the color to start fading out and then drag in any direction for an inch or two.**

The beauty of using a mask for this technique is that if you're unhappy with your first gradient dragging attempt, you can have another go at it...and another and another until you get it right as Photoshop just keeps updating the mask. Try dragging from corner to corner or top to bottom and see what you get. Depending on your image, one gradient angle may look better than another. For this particular image, a horizontal gradient works just fine.

4. **When you're finished, save your document as a PSD file and marvel at your handiwork.**

> **TIP**   If you start editing a mask and then decide you want to clear it out and start over, just press ⌘-A (Ctrl+A on a PC) to select everything you've done so far and then press Delete (Backspace). Photoshop deletes your changes so your mask is empty again.

High-Contrast Black and White

The highest contrast black-and-white images are *just* black and white, with no shades of gray, like the one in Figure 8-10, right. It's a striking yet versatile effect that gives your image an edgy look. In Photoshop, you can create this effect with a Threshold Adjustment layer. This adjustment lets you specify a brightness threshold in which all the lighter-colored pixels become pure white while the darker pixels become pure black. More simply put, Photoshop turns your shadows black and your highlights white.

> **TIP**   If you've ever wanted to create Andy Warhol–style pop art portraits, applying a Threshold Adjustment layer to your image is the first half of the technique. You'll learn the second half later in this chapter on page 334.

Before you get started, it's worth noting that this technique works better if your subject is on a solid white or other light-colored background, If it is, the background disappears when you make the adjustment. If the background is dark, you may have to clean up with a white brush.

> **NOTE**   To practice the following technique at home, download the image Girl.jpg from this book's Missing CD page (*www.missingmanuals.com*).

Here's how to use a Threshold Adjustment layer to make a pure black-and-white image:

1. **Pop open a photo and duplicate its Background layer by pressing ⌘-J (Ctrl+J on a PC).**

If you don't expect you'll need to do any darkening with the Burn tool (because your image has lots of shadows), you can skip this step. If you like, turn off the original layer's visibility.

Figure 8-10:
Left: Threshold Adjustment layers make shadows pure black and highlights pure white. If you want to use one on an image of a face that doesn't have many shadows around the cheeks, nose, or lips, you'll end up with a solid white face that's pretty creepy. The fix is to grab the Burn tool (page 414) and do some darkening on the image layer either before or after you add the Threshold Adjustment layer (it's easier to do it afterward because you can see what you're doing). If you darken too much, you can always switch to the Dodge tool (page 414) to lighten that area back up.

Right: You can't get any contrastier than this, baby! As you can see, the effect is eye-catching.

2. **Create a Threshold Adjustment layer.**

   In your Adjustments panel, click the Threshold icon, which looks like a rectangle with a couple of diagonal black stripes across it. When you do that, Photoshop displays a histogram (page 363) with a slider in the Adjustments panel. Drag the slider slightly to the right until you get a nice level of detail in your image. (If you drag too far, you'll make your image solid black.)

   TIP If you have trouble remembering what all the icons in the Adjustments panel are for, just hover above each one to make Photoshop display its name at the top of the panel.

3. **If necessary, press O to grab the Burn tool, select the image layer, and touch up your image.**

   The lady shown in Figure 8-10 has pale skin, so you need to darken her lips, nose, and cheeks with the Burn tool (page 414) so her features don't get lost. If parts of the image get too dark, switch to the Dodge tool (page 414) and lighten them. You're basically finished at this point, but with a couple more steps you can put your high-contrast face on a bright red background for a Che Guevara look, as shown in Figure 8-11.

Figure 8-11:
By adding a layer of solid color, you can create another popular look.

4. **Merge (page 103) the face layer and the Adjustment layer onto a *new* layer.**

   In the Layers panel, Shift-click to select both layers. Open the Layers panel menu (page 72), and then press and hold the Option key (Alt on a PC) while you click the Merge Layers menu item. When you hold down this modifier key, Photoshop adds a *new* layer to the top of your Layers panel that contains a merged version of the face and threshold layers. (If you don't see that new layer, press ⌘-Z [Ctrl+Z on a PC] and have another go at it. Make sure to press Option [Alt] *before* you choose Merge Layers.)

5. **Select the new layer and soften it slightly with a Gaussian Blur filter.**

   The high-contrast version of the image is a little too sharp (too many hard edges), but you can easily soften it up with a blur filter. In the Layers panel, select the merged layer and choose Filter → Blur → Gaussian Blur (page 591 explains this filter). Enter a pixel value of .5–1.5 depending on the pixel dimensions of your image (use a lower number for smaller images and a higher number for bigger images) and then click OK.

6. **Create a new layer for the red background.**

   Click the "Create a new layer" button at the bottom of your Layers panel and, in the resulting dialog box, name it *Red* and then click OK. Photoshop adds the new layer to the top of your layer stack.

7. **Fill the new layer with red.**

   At the bottom of the Tools panel, click the foreground color chip, pick red from the resulting Color Picker, and then click OK. Press Option-Delete (Alt+Backspace on a PC) and Photoshop fills the layer with red.

8. **Change the red layer's blend mode to Darken.**

   Use the pop-up menu at the top of your Layers panel to change the red layer's blend mode to Darken. As you learned on page 269, blend modes in the darken category tell Photoshop to look at the colors on the active layer and the layers below it and keep the darkest colors. In this case, those colors are black and red, so you end up with the black face on a red background. Pretty neat, huh?

9. **Save your document as a PSD file and rejoice at your creativity.**

The High-Key Effect

Another nifty black-and-white effect is known as *high key*. In the real world, you can create a high-key effect by aiming *tons* of lights at your subject (or, in this case, victim) and shooting a picture. This gives you a high-contrast image (though not quite as high-contrast as the technique explained in the previous section) where the shadows are shades of gray and everything else is almost pure white. Mosey on over to page 181 for the scoop.

Delicious Duotones

There are a couple of big reasons you may be interested in learning to create duotones like those showcased in this section: to save on professional printing costs and to create some *seriously* high-end looking black-and-white prints like the ones on display in Figure 8-12. (Hint: They actually use a bit of color.) To understand what's going on, you first need a quick primer on duotones (they're covered in more detail in Chapter 16) and a *brief* excursion back into some of the color mode nitty-gritty you learned about in Chapter 5.

Duotone refers to an image that's made from two colors (black is usually one of them). Photoshop's Duotone mode lets you add special colors to genuine grayscale images. (See the box on page 306 for the full story on what qualifies as true grayscale.) If you add one color to a true grayscale image, you get a duotone. If you add another color, you get a *tritone* (grayscale plus two colors), and if you add one more you get a *quadtone* (grayscale plus three colors). For the purposes of this discussion and as far as Photoshop is concerned, duotones include tritones and quadtones (as confusing as that may sound).

As you learned back in Chapter 5, printing presses use CMYK ink that prints on four separate plates, which correspond to the four channels in CMYK mode. A duotone or tritone has fewer channels, so it prints on fewer plates—grayscale plus one or two special inks (for duotone and tritone, respectively)—and *that* reduces your printing costs. So if your document is headed for a printing press, making a duotone is an affordable way to produce a striking, one-of-a-kind image. (See page 645 for the scoop on preparing duotone images for print.)

Click to save a preset

Figure 8-12:
Top: At first glance, you might mistake this image for a black and white, but it's actually made from black, gray, and yellow.

Bottom: You wouldn't know it just by looking, but this image is made from four colors.

Another reason to love duotones is that, because they're used so much in professional printing, Adobe has spent beaucoup bucks concocting color combinations that produce some of the most amazing images you've ever seen—and you can access these color combos only in Duotone mode. In fact, most (if not all) award-winning black-and-white photos hanging in galleries aren't black and whites at all—they're duo-, tri-, and quadtones with subtle color tints that give them extra depth and richness (see Figure 8-12).

Even if your image *isn't* headed for a professional printer, you want to get your paws on Photoshop's built-in color combos. You can get at them by popping into and then back out of Duotone mode. Here's how:

1. **Convert your image to black and white using one of the methods described in this chapter and then save your document as a PSD file.**

   It doesn't matter which method you use; just don't let Photoshop do the conversion for you because you'll end up with a drab grayscale image like the one you saw back on page 301.

2. **Change your image's mode to Grayscale and let Photoshop flatten the file.**

   Choose Image → Mode → Grayscale and, when Photoshop asks if you want to flatten or preserve your layers, take a deep breath and click Flatten. Then, when it asks if you want to discard your color information, steel yourself and click Discard.

3. **Trot back up to the menu bar and choose Image → Mode → Duotone.**

   Now you're ready to pick out one of those built-in duotone color combos, so you need to pop into Duotone mode to get to them.

4. **At the top of the Duotone Options dialog box that appears, choose the color combination you want.**

   Photoshop has *hundreds* of duo-, tri-, and quadtones in the Preset menu. (You could spend a whole evening looking through all the options.) When you choose one of these settings, Photoshop flips the dialog box's Type pop-up menu to the appropriate option. If you'd rather have a go at mixing colors yourself, choose Duotone, Tritone, or Quadtone from the Type menu and then click the little color wells below the menu to pick your inks (remember, Duotone mode thinks you're sending your files to a professional printing press that uses ink).

   If you want to save the combination you create, click the button to the right of the Preset menu (see Figure 8-12, top) and give your combo a name to make Photoshop add it to the Preset menu. Click OK when you're finished to close the Duotone Options dialog box. (Page 645 has more on creating custom duotone combos and the printing concerns that go along with them.)

5. **Go back to the color mode you were working in by choosing Image → Mode → RGB.**

   Because Duotone mode is a special document mode for printing (it's not meant for editing), you don't want to hang around there. When you go back to RGB mode, you won't notice anything different—except the awesome new color of your image.

That's it! You've just snatched your first color combo from Duotone mode. It's like bank-robbing for Photoshop jockeys.

Changing Color

Photoshop is the ultimate recolorizing tool because it gives you the power to put a fresh coat of paint on *anything*. You can repaint your car, change the color of your cabinets, or recolor your hair. You can also create cartoonish pop art (page 328) or reverse the color in your image (page 330). The next few pages describe all that and more.

Hue/Saturation Adjustment Layers

If you're experimenting with color, start by creating a Hue/Saturation Adjustment layer, which offers you a friendly set of sliders that let you change either the overall color of your image or a specific range of colors (see page 321). Because you're working with an Adjustment layer, any color changes take place on another layer, leaving your original image unharmed. And since a layer mask automatically tags along with the Adjustment layer, you can use it to hide the color change from certain parts of your image.

If you select an object or specific area of your image before creating a Hue/Saturation Adjustment layer, you can change the color in just that one spot by following these steps:

1. **Open an image and create a selection using one of the techniques discussed in Chapter 4.**

   For example, if you want to change the color of your car, you could use the Quick Selection tool to select just the car. Once it's surrounded by marching ants, you're ready for the next step.

2. **Create a Hue/Saturation Adjustment layer.**

   To do so, open the Adjustments panel and click the Hue/Saturation icon, which looks like three rectangles stacked on top of each other. Photoshop fills your Adjustments panel with the three sliders shown Figure 8-13, top.

3. **To change the color of your selection—like the car shown in Figure 8-13— drag the Hue slider to the left or right.**

   Hue is just a color geek's way of saying "color" (for example, red, blue, palish yellow, whatever). If you know exactly which color you want the car to be (say, purple) you can drag the triangular slider until it reaches purple on the rainbow-colored slider beneath the word "Hue". As you drag the slider, the color of the selected area changes. If you watch closely, you can see one of the rainbow-colored bars at the bottom of the Adjustments panel change, too. The top rainbow bar shows you the color in your original image and the bottom one shows you what you're changing that color *to*. In Figure 8-13, you can see the turquoise of the original Corvette at the far left of the top bar and the purple it's been changed to at the far right of the bar below it. It's helpful to think of these rainbow-colored bars as flattened-out color wheels (flip ahead to page 451 in Chapter 12 to see a real live color wheel).

   NOTE   This color-changing trick works only on colored areas; anything that's black, white, or gray remains unchanged.

4. **To adjust the color's intensity, drag the Saturation slider to the left or right.**

   If you want to decrease the intensity, drag this slider to the left (if you drag it all the way to the left, you'll completely desaturate the image, making it grayscale).

Original color   New color

Figure 8-13:
Top: To change the colors in your image, grab the triangle-shaped Hue slider and drag it in either direction. If you hover your cursor above the rainbow-colored Hue slider, it turns into a scrubby cursor (circled), which you can drag to the left or right. The scrubby cursor does the same thing as the triangular sliders, but it's a bit easier to control.

Bottom: If you select an object (like the car chassis in this figure) before you add a Hue/Saturation Adjustment layer, Photoshop automatically fills the mask (circled) with your selection, limiting the color change to that area.

To increase the intensity, drag the slider to the right (if you drag it too far to the right, your colors become so vivid you'll need sunglasses). To get an idea of what this adjustment does, look closely at the color slider beneath the word "Saturation" in Figure 8-13, top, which ranges from gray on the left to a vivid red on the right.

5. **To adjust the color's brightness, drag the Lightness slider to the left or right.**

   Lightness is what civilians call "brightness"; think of it as the amount of light shining on your color. Drag this slider to the left to darken the color or to the right to lighten it.

6. **When you're finished, save your image as a PSD file.**

Back in your Layers panel, notice how Photoshop filled in the Adjustment layer mask based on the area you selected before it added the Adjustment layer (Figure 8-13, bottom). If you don't make a selection before you create the Adjustment layer, the mask stays empty—meaning the color change affects your whole image.

If you save your document as a PSD file, you can go back and edit your color changes anytime you want by double-clicking the Hue/Saturation Adjustment layer in the Layers panel, which is extremely handy if you're recoloring an object for a nitpicky person (even if that person is you!).

There are a few other settings lurking in the Adjustments panel for Hue/Saturation Adjustment layers:

- **On-image adjustment button.** New in Photoshop CS4, this button lets you choose a range of colors to adjust and then change the saturation of those colors by clicking directly on your image instead of using the sliders. In the top left of the Adjustments panel, click the on-image adjustment button (it looks like a pointing hand with a double-headed arrow) and then mouse over to your image (your cursor turns into an eyedropper). Click the color in your image that you want to change to make Photoshop select the appropriate color channel for you from the Edit pop-up menu (described later in this list). Drag to the left to decrease the saturation, making the color less intense, or to the right to increase the saturation, making the color more vivid.

- **Preset menu.** This pop-up menu (which lives at the top of the panel) lets you choose from a few canned settings called presets. Once you start tweaking the sliders, the menu changes to Custom as shown in Figure 8-13, top.

- **Edit pop-up menu.** This menu, which doesn't have a label, lets you choose the color channels you want to adjust. When you first use Photoshop, it's set to Master, which means you're changing the composite channel and affecting all the colors in your image. If you want to target a specific color channel, choose it from this menu so any changes you make affect only the colors in that channel. Let's say you've got an image with too much red in it (a common problem in photos of people). You can choose the red channel from this menu and then drag the saturation slider to the left to desaturate just the reds without affecting the other colors (a great way to zap color casts that you can't get rid of any other way). If you don't know which color channel to pick, use the on-image adjustment button described earlier in this list to click a color in your image and let Photoshop pick the channel for you. Once you've selected the color, you can use the sliders like you normally would.

- **Eyedroppers.** The eyedroppers toward the bottom of the panel also let you pick the colors in your image that you want to change. You'll see these guys in action in the next section.

• **Colorize checkbox.** This checkbox lets you use the Hue slider to add color to an image that doesn't have any, like a black-and-white image.

Targeting a specific range of colors

When you add a Hue/Saturation Adjustment layer, Photoshop assumes you want to change all the colors in your image, which is why the Edit pop-up menu just mentioned is set to Master. If you want Photoshop to change just the reds, yellows, greens, or whatever, choose them from the Edit pop-up menu first. To narrow your focus even *more*, you can use the new on-image adjustment button along with the eyedroppers near the bottom of the Adjustments panel to target very specific *ranges* of color for your adjustments.

Let's say you're thinking about changing your hair color. If it's fairly light, you can do your experimenting in Photoshop rather than on your head. Follow these steps to take a trip to the virtual salon:

> **TIP** It's much easier to change the color of light- to medium-colored pixels than really dark ones.

1. **Open your image and leave the Background layer locked.**

   If you're experimenting on an image that you've worked with before, this layer may be named something besides Background.

2. **Add a Hue/Saturation Adjustment layer as described in the previous section.**

3. **Use the on-image adjustment button to choose the range of colors you want to adjust.**

   Click the on-image adjustment button (the hand with the two arrows poking out of it), mouse over to your image, and then click the colors you want to change (for example, click the hair). Photoshop picks the appropriate color channel in the Edit pop-up menu (in Figure 8-14, top, this menu is set to Reds).

4. **Edit the range of colors using the eyedroppers.**

   Once you click a color in the previous step, Photoshop marks that color range with a small gray bar that appears in the white area between the two rainbow-colored bars at the bottom of the Adjustments panel (circled in Figure 8-14, top). To edit that range, use the + and − eyedroppers near the bottom of the panel to add or subtract colors from the targeted range. To expand the range to catch all the hair colors, grab the eyedropper with a + sign, mouse over to your image, and click another part of the hair (you'll see the little gray bar get a little wider). To narrow the range of hair colors, use the eyedropper with a − sign to subtract the colors you don't want.

   As usual, Photoshop gives you several ways to do the same thing. You can also edit the color range by dragging the tiny sliders on the gray bar, which, you may have noticed, is two different shades of gray. The dark gray part in the middle represents the hues that change completely once you make adjustments; to see those hues, just look at the rainbow-colored bars directly above and below the gray one. The lighter gray parts on either end of the gray bar represent hues that *partially* change. If you want to narrow the range of colors, drag the little half triangles inward toward the middle of the gray bar. To widen the range, drag them outward.

TIP If the gray bar representing your targeted color range gets split across the left and right ends of the rainbow bars, press ⌘ (Ctrl on a PC) and drag the pieces to the left or right until the range indicator is in one solid bar again.

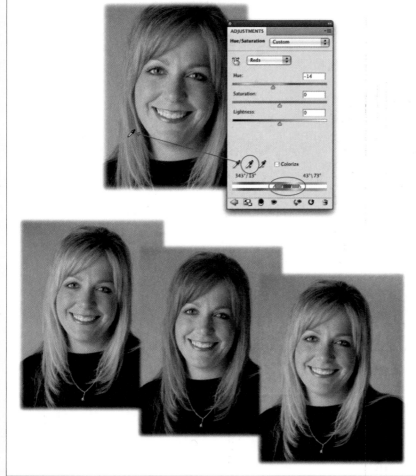

Figure 8-14:
Top: Instead of changing all the colors in your image, you can use the on-image adjustment button and the eyedropper tools to target a certain color range instead. When you click the on-image adjustment button, the Edit pop-up menu near the top of the Adjustments panel changes to reflect the color channel (page 178) of the part of the image you clicked (in this case, Red), and the color range is indicated by the gray bar toward the bottom of the panel (circled here).

Bottom: If you duplicate the Adjustment layer using one of the methods described on page 82, you can experiment with all kinds of hair colors before you head to the salon.

5. **Recolor your hair by tweaking the Hue, Saturation, and Lightness sliders as discussed in the previous section.**

Photoshop reflects your changes in real time, so you can watch as your hair changes from green to blue to magenta. Good times!

6. **If necessary, use the Adjustment layer's mask to hide the color change from other parts of your image.**

When you start moving the Hue, Saturation, and Lightness sliders, you may notice that your hair isn't the *only* thing that changes color. If your skin color is similar to your hair color, parts of your skin may change color, too. In that case, you can use the Adjustment layer's mask to keep your skin from getting a makeover. Just select the mask thumbnail in your Layers panel, press B to grab the Brush tool, and set your foreground color chip to black (press X if you need to flip-flop color chips). Then mouse over to your image and paint the parts of your skin that resemble your hair to hide them from the adjustment. If you hide too much, flip-flop your color chips by pressing X and paint that area white. To create the images shown in Figure 8-14, bottom, black paint was added to the mask to hide the color change from her face.

TIP If you want to go back and edit your Hue/Saturation Adjustment layer later, you have to remember to change the Edit pop-up menu first. While Photoshop remembers all the changes you made with the sliders, it can't remember which color channel you used, so it resets the menu to Master every time you double-click the Hue/Saturation Adjustment layer. Bummer.

Hue Blend Mode

Another easy way to repaint an object is to put the paint on another layer and change the paint layer's blend mode to Hue. As you learned in Chapter 7, blend modes control how color on one layer interacts with color on another. (Page 277 explains how the Hue blend mode works.)

NOTE This technique is especially fun to use with a graphics tablet if you have one!

To give this method a spin, open an image and create a new layer using one of the techniques listed on page 76. In the pop-up menu at the top of the Layers panel, change the new layer's blend mode to Hue (it's at the bottom of the list). Press B to grab the Brush tool, click the foreground color chip, and then pick a color from the resulting Color Picker. Then, with the new layer selected, start painting over the object as shown in Figure 8-15.

If you end up changing too much color, you can press and hold E to switch temporarily to the Eraser tool. Or you can prevent the problem by adding a layer mask (page 105) to the paint layer and hide the areas you want to leave unchanged with black paint.

Replacing Color

Remember the Color Range command you learned about in Chapter 4 (page 143)? You can use a similar command—Replace Color—to select one color and replace it with another. This command works really well if the color you want to change is fairly consistent and concentrated in one area, like the car chassis in Figure 8-16.

Figure 8-15:
The goal here is to repaint this red motorcycle blue. If the area you want to repaint has a lot of black, white, and gray around it (like this bike), you can paint right over those areas and they won't change a bit (note the brush cursor circled here). That's because, in Hue blend mode, the new paint affects only areas that contain color.

It's also a little easier to choose a paint color from the friendly Color Picker than to mix the color yourself using a bunch of sliders.

When you choose Image → Adjustments → Replace Color, you see the Replace Color dialog box shown in Figure 8-16. Grab the Eyedropper tool to tell Photoshop which color you want to change—that color appears in the Color square in the Selection area toward the top right of the dialog box. In the Replacement area toward the bottom of the dialog box, click the color square above the word "Result" to choose a new color from the Color Picker. When you click OK, the new color appears in the square. If you need to make further adjustments to the color, you can use the Hue, Saturation, and Lightness sliders (also in the Replacement area).

> **NOTE** Because the Replace Color command doesn't use an Adjustment layer, it affects your original image. So be sure to copy your image layer before you use this command.

Figure 8-16:
You can use the Eyedropper tools to add to or subtract from the range of colors you want to change. Click the Result color swatch at the bottom right of the dialog box to open the Color Picker and choose a replacement color.

Selective Color Adjustment Layers

Selective Color Adjustment layers are gloriously useful because they let you make a single color in your image brighter or darker, which is helpful when you need to make your whites whiter or your blacks blacker. You can also use them to shift one color to another, but that technique can be a bit challenging if you don't know anything about color theory (that is, why certain colors mix to create other colors).

To add a Selective Color Adjustment layer to your image, click the Selective Color icon in the Adjustments panel (it looks like a square divided into four triangles). From the Colors pop-up menu at the top of the Adjustments panel, choose the color closest to the one you want to change. For example, if you want to change the color of the bike and the matching leathers shown in Figure 8-17, choose Reds. Next, you can use the Cyan, Magenta, Yellow, and Black color sliders to change that color to something else entirely. Don't let it throw you that these sliders represent the CMYK color mode, because they work just fine on RGB images.

You can drag each slider to determine exactly how the color you've chosen in the pop-up menu changes. If you drag a slider to the left, you shift the color *away* from the color shown above that particular slider. For example, if you choose Red from the pop-up menu and then drag the yellow slider all the way to the left, you drain all the yellow out of the reds, making them look hot pink (as shown in Figure 8-17). If you drag a slider to the right, you shift the color in the pop-up menu toward the color *opposite* of that particular slider's color. And how would you know what the opposite of say, cyan, is? By learning how to read a color wheel, that's how. Luckily, you can flip over to page 450 for a short and sweet lesson on color wheels to get you started.

Figure 8-17:
With a well-placed Selective Color Adjustment layer, you can change the red bike and matching leathers to hot pink in seconds. Just hover above one of the sliders in the Adjustments panel until your cursor turns into a handy scrubby cursor and then drag left and right.

Matching Colors

The Match Color command makes the colors in one image resemble those in another. It's a huge time-saver when you're working with several images in a magazine spread or book and need to make the color somewhat consistent (see Figure 8-18). Since this command isn't available as an Adjustment layer, be sure to duplicate your image layer first by pressing ⌘-J (Ctrl+J on a PC).

To get started, open two images: the one whose color you're trying to match (the *source*) and the one whose color you want to change (the *target*). Click within the target document to activate it and then choose Image → Adjustments → Match Color. In the resulting dialog box, Photoshop automatically picks the current document as the target (which is why you activated it first). Next, tell Photoshop the name of the source document by choosing it from the Source pop-up menu toward the bottom of the dialog box (you'll see a thumbnail preview of the image at the bottom right).

If the source has several layers, you can choose the one you want from the Layer pop-up menu or choose Merged if the source image contains Adjustment layers; if it's got only one layer, Photoshop chooses that layer automatically.

If you want to confine your match to specific spots in the source and target images, create selections in each document before you open the Match Color dialog box. If the Match color dialog box detects an active selection, it lets you turn on the "Use Selection in Source to Calculate Colors" and "Use Selection in Target to Calculate Color" checkboxes, both of which can be helpful when you're trying to match colors in two different images—skin tones, for example.

Figure 8-18:
The Match Color dialog box lets you copy the colors from a source image (the golden landscape where the arrow is pointing) onto a target (the top motorcycle image). The result? The golden-hued motorcycle (bottom). Full details for the Match Color process start on page 325. Use the Luminance (lightness) and Color Intensity (saturation) sliders to make the colors match a little better. Adjust the Fade slider to use more or less of the source document's original color. If your target image has a bit of a color cast, turn on the Neutralize checkbox to make Photoshop try to get rid of it for you.

TIP If you've got a source color that you might want to use on *other* images in the future, you can save your Match Color settings as a preset. When you get everything just right, click the Save Statistics button at the bottom of the dialog box and then give your preset a name. The next time you want to use those settings, you won't have to open the source image–just open the Match Color dialog box, click the Load Statistics button, and navigate to your preset. Sweet!

Photo Filter Adjustment Layers

To adjust the colors in an image gently, use a *Photo Filter Adjustment layer*. For example, you can quickly warm your image with golden tones like those in the "after" photo in Figure 8-19. The effect is fairly subtle, making your image look like it's been tinted with a color rather than having its color changed completely.

To get started, just choose the layer from the Adjustments panel (its icon looks like a camera with a circle above it). In the resulting Filter pop-up menu, choose from a list of 20 presets that range from warming and cooling filters to shades of red, violet, and so on. If you want to choose your own color instead, turn on the Color option and click the square color swatch to its right. Choose a color from the resulting Color Picker and click OK. You can use the panel's Density slider to soften or strengthen the effect (just pretend the slider is called "intensity" if the "Density" label confuses you) and keep the Preserve Luminosity checkbox turned on to keep Photoshop from lightening or darkening your image.

Figure 8-19:
A Photo Filter Adjustment layer is really handy when you've combined images whose color doesn't quite match or when you want to add a warming tone to an image as shown here.

TIP You can also use a Photo Filter Adjustment layer to reduce a color cast. For example, if your image has a strong blue cast, you can introduce a little orange with a Photo Filter to neutralize the cast (orange is opposite blue on the color wheel). If your image has a yellow cast, use purple to even it out. Flip to Chapter 12 to learn all about the color wheel (page 450).

Adjustment Layer Blend Modes

When you're introducing or shifting colors with Adjustment layers, experiment with changing their blend modes, too. (See page 267 for more on blend modes.) For example:

- The **Hue** blend mode alters the color of your image but doesn't change the brightness (how dark or light it is) or saturation (how intense the colors are). This mode is useful when you want to change an object's color as described on page 323.

- **Color** blend mode changes the color and saturation of your image but leaves the brightness alone, which is handy when you're adding color to an image (page 332).

- **Luminosity** blend mode changes the image's brightness but not its color or saturation, which is helpful when you need to lighten or darken an image.

If you want to change the blend mode *before* you add the Adjustment layer—so you can actually see what the adjustment looks like as you're making it—Option-click (Alt-click on a PC) the half-black/half-white circle at the bottom of the Layers panel. Photoshop opens the New Layer dialog box so you can change the blend mode of the Adjustment layer you're about to add.

Posterizing: Your Ticket to Cartoon Art

You'll use this adjustment only once in a blue moon, but if you need to make your image look like a cartoon, the Posterize Adjustment layer is perfect. In the Adjustments panel, click the Posterize icon (the striped gray one) to make Photoshop analyze your image's colors and throw out the majority of them, leaving you with big ol' blocks of solid color. On some images, posterizing has interesting results as the examples in Figure 8-20 illustrate. On other images, not so much.

Inverting Colors

Graphic designers, this one's for you! If you need to reverse the colors in your image—turning orange to blue, yellow to purple, and so on—you can add an Invert Adjustment layer. To find out the reverse (or opposite) of a color, you need to use a color wheel; head on over to page 450 for details.

If you're a photographer, you'll use this adjustment even *less* often than Posterize because it turns most images into a negative (which might be useful on Halloween). That said, if you've got an image of a black silhouette that you want to make white, this Adjustment layer can do it with just one click (see Figure 8-21). To add an Invert adjustment, open your Adjustments panel and click the icon that shows two smaller squares with shapes inside them.

Figure 8-20:
Posterizing doesn't work very well on portraits, but on images with relatively solid colors, like those shown at left, the results are pretty nifty, as you can see in the right-hand images.

Adding Color

There will be times when you want to add color that wasn't originally part of your image, and Photoshop gives you lots of ways to do that. The techniques in this section will serve you well whether you're colorizing a black-and-white image or painting on an existing color image or an empty canvas.

Variations

If you want to add a quick color tint to a black-and-white image, use the Variations command. It's not available as an Adjustment layer, so, to be safe, duplicate your image layer first by pressing ⌘-J (Ctrl+J on a PC).

Choose Image → Adjustments → Variations, and in the center of the honkin' big dialog box that appears (Figure 8-22), you see a slew of previews surrounding your original image. Each preview has one of the six basic colors added to it: green, yellow, red, magenta, blue, and cyan. To add a blue tint to your image, for example, click the More Blue preview and Photoshop applies its effect to your current pick in the center of the dialog box. If you want to add even more blue, click the blue preview again (the clicks are cumulative). Over on the right side of the dialog box, you can click the Lighter or Darker preview to lighten or darken your current pick (these clicks are cumulative too, so if you want the tint to be even lighter or darker, keep clicking away).

Figure 8-21:
The Invert Adjustment layer turns black into white, blue into orange, and so on. For graphic designers, this is an incredibly useful trick. The images on the left are the originals.

The options at the top of the dialog box let you choose what to change: the shadows, the midtones, the highlights, or just the saturation levels. If you want to colorize a black-and-white image, leave this option set to midtones because the majority of what you *have* in a grayscale image is midtones. Beneath those options lies a slider that you can use to change the intensity of the color tint (don't let the oddly chosen slider labels—Fine and Coarse—fool you). Drag the slider to the left toward Fine to lower the intensity or to the right toward Coarse to increase the intensity.

Figure 8-22:
If you like choosing from a bunch of previews better than tweaking sliders, Variations is for you!

TIP Flip over to page 345 to learn how fix an image with a color cast using Variations. It doesn't do a *great* job, but it's a relatively easy alternative to the more complicated methods you'll learn about later in that chapter. Honestly, the only thing the Variations command does *really* well is add a color tint to a black-and-white image.

Color Balance Adjustment Layers

You can think of Color Balance as an Adjustment layer version of Variations but with sliders instead of image previews (see Figure 8-23). When you add a Color Balance Adjustment layer, you can shift the colors in your image toward one side or the other of the color wheel (page 450). Or, if you're working with a black-and-white image, you can use it to add a color tint. You can add a Color Balance Adjustment layer to your image by clicking its icon in the Adjustments panel (it looks like a set of scales—get it?).

Figure 8-23:
If you don't mind using sliders, a Color Balance Adjustment layer is more flexible than the Variations command if only because you can double-click the Adjustment layer and edit it again later.

Colorizing Images

If you want to scan some vintage photos, Photoshop can help you give them a little color. Colorizing a black-and-white (or true grayscale) photo *seems* straightforward—just grab a brush and paint the image. Unfortunately, while you succeed in adding color, you also cover up all the details, as shown in Figure 8-24, left.

Figure 8-24:
Unless you change the blend mode of the paint layer, the paint covers up all the details of this girl's cute little dress (left). Once you set the blend mode to Color (right), the details come shining through.

TIP   Before you colorize a black-and-white image, choose Image → Mode and make sure your document is set to RGB Color. If it's in Grayscale mode, Photoshop won't let you add any color no matter how hard you try.

Fortunately, you can use blend modes to add color while keeping your image's details intact. Here's how:

1. **Add a new layer for the paint.**

   Since you don't want to mess up your original image by painting directly on it, you need to add a new layer. Click the "Create a new layer" button at the bottom of the Layers panel, name the layer *pink paint*, and then position it above the photo layer in your layers stack.

2. **Set the paint layer's blend mode to Color.**

   Select the new layer and then use the pop-up menu at the top of the Layers panel to change the blend mode (page 267). As explained in the box on page 328, this mode not only keeps the brightness of the gray tones in your photo, it adds the hue and saturation values from the pink paint, letting the details of the image show through the paint.

3. **Grab the Brush tool and set it to whatever color you want to paint the dress.**

   Press B to activate the Brush tool. Then, in the Tools panel, click the foreground color chip, pick a nice pastel color from the Color Picker, and then click OK.

4. **Paint the part of the image that you want to colorize.**

   Be sure to paint only the areas you want to colorize. Since the paint layer is on top, there's nothing to mask any parts you don't want colored. If you need to, zoom in and out of your image using the keyboard shortcuts explained in the Tip on page 310.

5. **Use the Eraser tool to fix any mistakes.**

   Press and hold E to switch temporarily to the Eraser tool to fix your mistakes and then let go of the key to switch back to the Brush tool.

6. **When everything looks good, save your document as a PSD file.**

   Saving the document in PSD format lets you go back and change the paint later. For example, after you print the colorized photo you might decide to change the little girl's dress to yellow instead of pink. If you've saved the document with all its layers intact (as a PSD file lets you do), you can load the paint layer as a selection by ⌘-clicking (Alt-clicking on a PC) the layer's thumbnail and then using a Hue/Saturation Adjustment layer to change the color (page 318). That's a heck of a lot quicker than repainting the dress! But don't tell anyone—let 'em think it took you hours and hours.

Just think how much fun you can have using this technique with a graphics tablet and the new Rotate View option in CS4 (page 61)! Even if you paint the color using the Brush tool, you can create a selection and then use the Fill command (page 168) to fill a particular area with paint or fill a whole layer with paint and then erase or hide certain areas with a layer mask (page 105).

Adding Solid Blocks of Color

Remember the high-contrast face earlier in this chapter (page 312)? With just a little modification and a few well-placed blocks of color, you can turn that face into an Andy Warhol–style portrait like the one in Figure 8-25.

> **NOTE**   If you downloaded the practice image file for the high-contrast face tutorial back on page 312, you can use that edited image for the maneuver described in the following list.

Figure 8-25:
You can create all kinds of interesting art by adding your own color to images.

Once you've used a Threshold adjustment to make a high-contrast face using steps 1–3 on page 312, follow these steps:

1. **Merge the Threshold Adjustment layer with the photo layer.**

   To add bunches of color blocks to the image, you need to isolate the black parts of the face on their own layer. First, merge the Threshold and face layers so you can select all the black bits at one time. Over in the Layers panel, click the Threshold Adjustment layer and then choose Merge Down (page 103) from the Layers panel menu. Now you should have a *single* face layer instead of two: the Threshold Adjustment layer and the photo layer.

2. **Select all the black areas in the merged face layer you created in the previous step.**

   Grab the Magic Wand tool (page 140), click one black area, and then choose Select → Similar to make Photoshop select *all* the black bits (you could select them yourself, but Shift-clicking each black area with the Magic Wand could take days!).

3. **Jump the selection onto its own layer.**

   To isolate the selected black parts onto their own layer, press ⌘-J (Ctrl+J on a PC). Then double-click the layer's name in your Layers panel and rename it *face*. (Since you're about to add a bunch of layers, it's helpful to give each one a descriptive name.) Turn the the original photo layer's visibility off because you won't need it anymore. Now you're ready to start painting!

4. **Add a new layer below the face layer.**

   Click the "Create a new layer" button at the bottom of your Layers panel and name the new layer *skin*. Make sure this layer is *below* the Face layer.

5. **Grab the Polygonal Lasso tool (page 151) and draw a selection around the woman's face and shoulders (see Figure 8-26, top left).**

   Since the Polygonal Lasso tool uses straight lines, it's perfect for creating blocks of color. Just click once where you want the selection to start and then click again each time you need to change angles. Don't worry about being precise; the point is to make it blocky. When you're finished, close your selection by hovering over the starting point. When you see a tiny circle (it looks like a degree mark) next to your cursor, click once to complete your selection.

6. **Fill your selection with color.**

   Click the foreground color chip at the bottom of the Tools panel and pick a nice peachy color for the woman's skin and then click OK. Fill the selection with color by pressing Option-Delete (Alt+Backspace on a PC) and then get rid of the marching ants by pressing ⌘-D (Ctrl+D) to deselect.

7. **Add another new layer above the skin layer but below the face layer and name it *lips*.**

   Repeat steps 5 and 6 to give her some hot-pink lipstick. Remember, you want to make the color areas blocky, so don't be afraid to make your selection go outside of her lips.

   TIP   Instead of changing the color of the blocks, you can change their opacity by using the setting at the top of the Layers panel (see page 87).

8. **Keep adding new layers and repeating steps 5 and 6 to give her some eye shadow add color to the iris of each eye.**

   When you're all done, your Layers panel should look something like the one in Figure 8-26.

9. **Add another new layer, fill it with a bright color, and make it your new background.**

   Drag this layer below the skin layer so it becomes the new background of the whole piece of art you're building.

Figure 8-26:
If you want to make five more versions of this portrait, select all the layers that make up this version and stuff them into a group by choosing "New Group from Layers" from the Layers panel menu (see page 98 for more on layer groups). This not only helps you keep track of each version, it also makes creating additional versions easier: Simply duplicate the layer group instead of each individual layer.

And because you wisely placed each block of color on its own layer, changing those colors is as simple as loading a layer as a selection. Just ⌘-click (Ctrl-click on a PC) its thumbnail, and fill it with a new color. Because your duplicated layers are all sitting on top of each other, you can toggle the visibility of each group off or on while you're changing colors. Once you've created several versions of the portrait, you can increase your canvas size (page 240) and then use the Move tool to position the layer groups next to each other, as Figure 8-25 illustrates.

Congratulations—you've just finished your first Warhol-style portrait! The really fun thing about this technique is how creative it lets you be (not to mention that you're using almost every skill you've learned in the preceding chapters). Oh, sure, you *could* seek out Warhol's pop-style art online and use the same colors he did, but what fun is that? By using your own vision, you're creating something unique. Also, try experimenting with people who have light-colored hair. If the model for this portrait were blonde, you could color her hair, too. The possibilities are endless!

Gradient Map Adjustment Layers

If you need to turn a mediocre sunrise photo into something spectacular, use a Gradient Map Adjustment layer. Rather than letting you add one color to your image like the Photo Filter Adjustment layer (page 327), a Gradient Map Adjustment layer lets you add as many colors as you want. Behind the scenes, Photoshop turns your image black and white and then maps the shadows (blacks) to one end of the gradient and the highlights (whites) to the other. To reverse those colors, turn on the Reverse option in your Adjustments panel (see Figure 8-27).

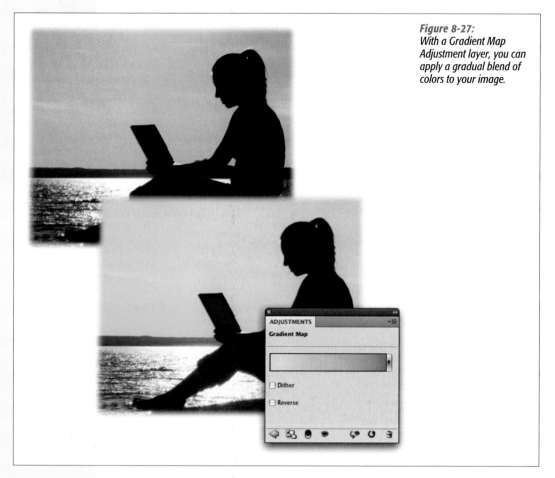

Figure 8-27:
With a Gradient Map Adjustment layer, you can apply a gradual blend of colors to your image.

To add a Gradient Map Adjustment layer, follow these steps:

1. **Open your image, set your color chips to black and white by pressing D, and then add a Gradient Map Adjustment layer.**

   Because the Gradient Map Adjustment layer you're about to add uses your foreground and background color chips, it's less startling to set them back to factory-fresh black and white first. Next, open the Adjustments panel and click the Gradient icon, which looks like a vertical white-to-black fade. Photoshop applies a black-to-white gradient so your image looks like it's grayscale and changes the panel so you see options for tweaking the new gradient.

TIP   Adding a Gradient Map Adjustment layer generates a pretty amazing black-and-white version of your image. If you want to get more creative with this technique, use the Gradient Editor (discussed later in this section) to create a black-to-gray-to-white gradient, which adds depth to your black-and-white image.

2. **In the Adjustments panel, click the gradient preview to open the Gradient Editor.**

   In the resulting dialog box, you can choose a preset gradient (best for newcomers) or make one of your own by following the next couple of steps (which requires a bit of patience and practice). You can load even more ready-made gradients by clicking the tiny right arrow circled in Figure 8-28.

Figure 8-28:
The Gradient Editor lets you choose from tons of existing gradients or create your own by editing any of the existing presets and adding color stops.

3. **Edit the gradient's color stops to create a yellow-to-orange-to-red gradient.**

   In the middle of the Gradient Editor dialog box, you see little colored squares called *color stops* (see Figure 8-28) that you can drag around to control the width of the color fade. When you click a color stop, its color appears in the Color field (also called a *color well*) at the bottom of the dialog box. If you want to change the color, click the color well to make Photoshop open the Color Picker so you can choose something else. If you click *between* existing color stops, you'll add a new stop. You can also drag the tiny white diamonds beneath the gradient left and right to determine where one color stops and another one starts.

   TIP   If you create the perfect sunset gradient, you can save it by clicking the Save button and then giving it a name. Photoshop adds it to the preset previews, giving you easy access to it in the future.

4. **In your Layers panel, change the Gradient Map Adjustment layer's blend mode to Color.**

   To keep the Gradient Map from changing your image's lightness (which you probably know by now is the same as brightness), change the pop-up menu at the top of the Layers panel to Color. That way, the gradient affects only the image's color values and not its lightness values (the box on page 329 has more on Color blend mode).

   TIP   If you want to keep any part of your image from being affected by the Gradient Map, click the Adjustment layer's mask thumbnail, grab the Brush tool, and then paint those areas with black.

You're all finished! Nothing like a beautiful sunset, is there?

Correcting Color and Lighting

Most digital photographs could stand to have their colors and lighting adjusted. When you think about all the variables that come into play when you're capturing images, it's a wonder any photos turn out halfway decent. You're dependent on Mother Nature or the quality of artificial lighting, and, even then, it's easy to over- or underexpose an image. You need a good camera that can snap the shot before you miss it, a high-quality lens, and so on. Even if the stars are aligned and you get all that right, the camera itself may introduce a *color cast*, making your image look like it's overdosed on one particular color.

All these variables mean you need to spend some time correcting both the color and the lighting of your images. Not to worry: You've got an arsenal of tools at your disposal in Photoshop and its trusty sidekick, Camera Raw. In this chapter, you'll learn how to use all the automatic fixer-uppers (and there's a slew of 'em) like Auto Color, Variations, and so on. Then, you'll dive headfirst into a pair of professional-level adjustments, Levels and Curves. Next, you'll explore the glorious realm of Camera Raw for the easiest adjustments in the West, and, finally, you'll learn some tricks for saving truly troubled images.

Quick Fixer-Uppers

Before you dive headfirst into the muddy waters of manual adjustments using Levels (page 363) and Curves (page 379), it's worth trying to make Photoshop do some of this stuff automatically. As luck would have it, Photoshop has lots of auto fixer-uppers, but you need to do a wee bit of setup to make them work better.

A Word on Workflow

Every adjustment you make can reduce the quality of your image a bit, so the order in which you work—known among those in the biz as *workflow*—is important. Because some techniques are more destructive than others (like sharpening), it's wise to save those techniques for last. Here's a quick cheat sheet to follow when it comes to adjustment order:

1. Import pictures using Adobe Bridge (see Appendix C) or another program.

2. Have Bridge save copies of your images to an external hard drive and then burn your originals to a DVD for off-site safe-keeping. This process (also covered in Appendix C) is one of the big benefits of using Bridge.

3. View your photos, rate the best ones, and mark the bad ones as rejected (see—you guessed it—Appendix C).

4. Crop, resize, and (if necessary) straighten your image. There's no point in fixing pixels you're not going to keep! See Chapter 6 for the scoop.

5. Fix whatever you can in Camera Raw (white balance, exposure, contrast, and so on). As you'll learn later in this chapter, corrections are a *breeze* in Camera Raw, and you can use it to fix TIFFs and JPEGs, too.

6. Fix the remaining problems in Photoshop (like reducing wrinkles, enhancing eyes, correcting colors, and so on) using Adjustment layers, duplicate layers, and layer masks as described in this chapter

7. Apply special effects like fancy edges, head swapping, filters, and so on.

8. Sharpen your image using the techniques you'll learn in Chapter 11.

9. Print the image (Chapter 16) or save it for the Web (Chapter 17).

If you make your adjustments in this order, you'll end up with the sharpest, highest-quality image possible.

NOTE   While you may get satisfactory results using combinations of the following adjustments, they're nothing compared to what you can do if you master Levels or, better yet, Curves (both adjustments are covered later in this chapter). In other words, use the methods in this section only while you're learning or as down-and-dirty quick fixes.

Setting Target Colors

Photoshop needs some guidance before it can fix the colors and lighting in your image. You can tell it what you want those colors to look like by setting targets for the three categories of color in any image:

- **Shadows** are created when light is blocked (you knew that). Rarely jet black, shadows can be different colors depending on how much light is blocked.

- **Highlights** represent the lightest or brightest parts of your image where the light is at full strength. When an image is overexposed, the highlights are described as *blown out*.

- **Midtones** are tonal values that fall between the darkest shadows and lightest highlights. By enhancing midtones, you can increase the contrast and the details in your image.

Setting target colors is a bit of a pain, but if you do it only once and save the settings, you can run these auto-fixers on any image and know your target colors are set correctly (see Figure 9-1).

Figure 9-1:
In the Auto Color Correction Options dialog box (now that's a mouthful!), you can adjust several settings to help Photoshop do a better job correcting your images. Anytime you use an auto-correction method like the ones covered in this section or make a manual adjustment using either Levels or Curves, Photoshop refers to the target colors you set here.

Follow these steps to set Photoshop's target shadow, midtone, and highlight colors:

1. **Click either the Levels or Curves icon in your Adjustments panel—it doesn't matter which one.**

   Open the Adjustments panel by clicking its panel icon dock on the right side of your screen or by choosing Window → Adjustments. The Levels icon looks like fire with three triangles under it, and the Curves icon looks like a graph with an S-curve on it. When you click either one, Photoshop changes the Adjustments panel to show options related to Layers or Curves.

2. **Open the Auto Color Correction Options dialog box.**

   In the Adjustments panel, Option-click (Alt-click on a PC) the Auto button to open the dialog box.

3. **Choose the Find Dark & Light Colors algorithm.**

   The Algorithms menu at the top of the Auto Color Correction Options dialog box has three options. Straight from the factory, the algorithm (set of instructions for Photoshop) is set to Enhance Per Channel Contrast, which makes Photoshop adjust the red, green, and blue channels individually—the highlights get a little lighter, and the shadows get a little darker. You get more noticeable results with this algorithm than with the other two options, but your colors may shift. The Auto Tone adjustment (page 348) uses this algorithm.

   If you don't want your colors to shift, you can choose Enhance Monochromatic Contrast to make Photoshop apply the exact same amount of lightening and darkening to each channel. The Auto Contrast adjustment (page 349) uses this algorithm.

Perhaps the best algorithm of all is Find Dark & Light Colors, which locates the average lightest and darkest pixels and then uses them to increase the contrast. The Auto Color adjustment uses this algorithm.

4. **Turn on the Snap Neutral Midtones checkbox.**

   At the bottom of the Algorithms section, turn on the Snap Neutral Midtones checkbox. This setting makes Photoshop hunt for a nearly neutral color—one that has the same level of brightness in all color channels—and then adjust it so that it really *is* neutral. It works like a charm for fixing color casts. (The Auto Color adjustment—page 345—uses this setting.)

5. **Set a target shadow color.**

   In the Target Colors & Clipping section of the dialog box, click the black rectangle labeled Shadows to set a target shadow color. In the resulting Color Picker, enter *10* in the R, G, and B fields (you'll work in RGB mode most of the time). Ten is a good choice because, on the 0–255 brightness scale (see the box on page 378), 10 is a dark gray. Once you start using the auto fixers, this setting gives you nice dark shadows that aren't so black you can't see details. Click OK when you're finished to close the Color Picker.

6. **Make sure the Clip field next to the black rectangle is set to 0.10 percent.**

   Clipping is the term Photoshop uses when it turns a light pixel pure white or a dark pixel pure black, stripping the pixel of all its details. Setting this field to 0.10 percent means Photoshop won't clip your image's pixels much more than your camera did.

   NOTE   As you might imagine, clipping is more worrisome in your image's highlights, which usually contain important details, than in the shadows.

7. **Set your target midtone color.**

   Click the gray rectangle labeled Midtones to set your target midtone color. In the Color Picker, enter *133* in the R, G, and B fields to get a nice charcoal gray just a touch lighter than 50 percent. Click OK to close the Color Picker.

8. **Set a target highlight color.**

   Click the white Highlights rectangle to set a target highlight color. When the Color Picker opens, enter *245* in the R, G, and B fields so your highlights are pale gray instead of pure, blinding white.

9. **Turn on the "Save as defaults" checkbox.**

   Since the settings listed here are good for almost every color correction, you can turn on the "Save as defaults" setting. That way you don't have to reset all this stuff every time you use one of the auto correctors or a Levels or Curves adjustment (both discussed later in this chapter).

10. **Close the Adjustments panel and throw away the Adjustment layer.**

To close the Adjustments panel, click the dark gray bar at the top of the panel. Since you created the Adjustment layer just to get at the target color settings, you can throw it away by selecting it in your Layers panel and pressing Delete (Backspace on a PC).

Once you've set your target colors, you're ready to start using the correction methods discussed in the next few sections.

> **TIP** A handy way to remove distractions from your screen so you can focus on fixing your image's colors is to go up to the Application bar at the top of your screen (new in Photoshop CS4; see page 12), click the Screen Mode icon, and choose Full Screen Mode With Menu Bar. You can also press the F key repeatedly to cycle through the screen modes.

Fixing Color

If your image looks flat (like it has no contrast) or has a noticeable color cast, give the following methods a spin. If your image is in pretty good shape to begin with, the following tools can fix your color in no time flat:

- **Auto Color.** If your image has a noticeable color cast (everything looks a little green, say), the Auto Color command can help. When you run it, Photoshop hunts down the shadows, highlights, and midtones in your image and changes their color values to the target colors you set earlier. You can also use this command to tone down oversaturated images, where all the colors look too intense. To run it, choose Image → Auto Color or press Shift-⌘-B (Shift+Ctrl+B on a PC). This command works only on images that are in RGB mode, so if the menu item is gray, choose Image → Mode → RGB Color.

> **TIP** You can run Auto Color nondestructively as an Adjustment layer by following steps 1–2 in the previous section. If you'd kept the Adjustment layer hanging around when you finished setting your target colors, you would have *applied* the Auto Color adjustment to your image.

- **Variations.** Besides using a Variations adjustment to add color to black-and-white images (page 330), you can also use it to fix color (see Figure 9-2). Choose Image → Adjustments → Variations and then click one of the six previews—More Green, More Yellow, and so on—that represent various changes in color balance, contrast, and saturation (your current pick appears in the middle). Your clicks have a cumulative effect: Each time you click the More Red preview, for example, Photoshop adds more red to your image. As you click the previews, Photoshop updates all the images. To adjust the brightness, click either the lighter or darker preview on the right side of the dialog box as many times as you need to get the lighting you want.

Figure 9-2:
A Variations adjustment is a very visual way to fix your image though it works only on 8-bit images (see the box on page 43). Click one of the six color previews on the left side of the dialog box as a starting point and then use the Fine to Coarse slider to change the intensity of the adjustment (Fine lowers the intensity and Coarse increases it, which makes you wonder why the slider isn't named Intensity instead). Moving the slider one tick mark doubles the strength of the adjustment.

If you choose Shadows or Highlights and then turn on the Show Clipping checkbox, Photoshop indicates the clipped areas of your image (page 341) with funky neon colors (which won't show up in the printed version of the image).

TIP Since you can't use Variations as an Adjustment layer (meaning it'll affect your original image), it's a darn good idea to duplicate your original layer before you apply this adjustment by pressing ⌘-J (Ctrl+J on a PC). Alternatively, you can select the image layer and then choose Filter → Convert for Smart Filters so the adjustment runs on its own layer instead. See page 588 for more on Smart Filters.

• **Color Balance.** This adjustment changes the overall mixture of colors in your image or selection by shifting the highlights, midtones, and shadows to opposite sides of the color wheel (see Chapter 12, page 450, for a quick lesson on color theory). It's also handy for adding color to a black-and-white image (Chapter 8, page 332) or for fixing a problem area (like a dull sky) fast.

The only drawback to Color Balance is that you have to know *which* color you want to shift your image *toward* (which is why color theory comes in handy). That said, Photoshop gives you sliders to adjust, making Color Balance fairly easy to play with (see Figure 9-3). Because it's available as an Adjustment layer, it's nondestructive and you can use the layer mask that tags along with it to limit the adjustment to certain parts of your image (see page 105 for more on masks). Photoshop gives you lots of ways to summon the Color Balance controls:

- Choose Color Balance from the Adjustments panel (click the button that looks like a scale).

- Click the half-black/half-white circle at the bottom of your Layers panel and choose Color Balance from the pop-up menu.

- Choose Image → Adjustments → Color Balance or press ⌘-B (Ctrl+B on a PC) to make Photoshop apply Color Balance to the currently active layer (your original image) without creating an Adjustment layer.

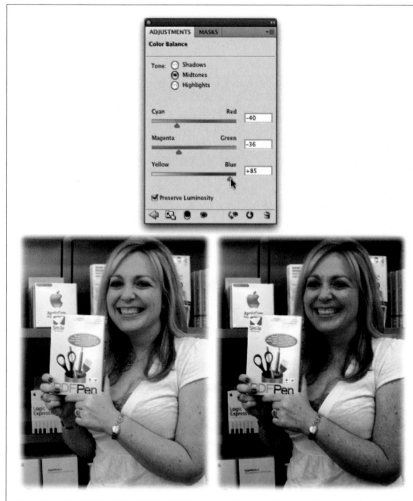

Figure 9-3:
A Color Balance Adjustment layer can zap a color cast instantly. Dragging the top and bottom sliders toward Cyan and Blue and the middle slider toward Magenta to introduce a little red gets rid of the nasty yellow cast shown at left. (Incidentally, PDFPen is a really handy program that lets you fill in and sign PDF forms. If you use a Mac, visit www.smileonmymac.com to learn more about it.)

TIP To preserve your image's brightness values, be sure to leave the Adjustments panel's Preserve Luminosity checkbox turned on.

• **Photo Filter.** To add a tint to your image, you can add a Photo Filter Adjustment layer to warm up your images with a golden tint or cool them off with a bluish tint. If your image has a color cast, you can neutralize it by adding the opposite color (again, a little color theory comes in handy here). Though it's much safer to run Photo Filter as an Adjustment layer, you can also run it (gasp) directly on your image by choosing Image → Adjustments → Photo Filter. See page 327 for more about Photo Filter.

TIP You don't have to apply these adjustments to your whole image. If you make a selection ahead of time, the adjustment affects only the selected area. And if the adjustment is available as an Adjustment layer, you can use the included layer mask to keep the layer from affecting areas that don't need adjusting. For adjustments that *aren't* available as Adjustment layers, you can duplicate your original layer, run the adjustment on it, and then add a layer mask (page 105).

POWER USERS' CLINIC

Fixing Colored Edge Fringe

If you see a slight blue or purple fringe loitering around the edges of near-black objects in your image, you've got a dreaded *edge halo* (page 158). They're especially noticeable when the object is on a white background. For example, if you take a picture of a white clock face, you may see a purplish or bluish tinge around the edges of the numbers and hands. Fortunately, you can use the Gaussian Blur filter to get rid of the tinge, though there's a trick to it. Flip to page 591 for the step-by-step scoop.

Fixing Lighting

Unless you're carting around your own light kit with your camera, you're totally dependent on ambient light, which is less than perfect on a good day. Nevertheless, Photoshop has several tools that can help fix almost any lighting problem you might have:

• **Auto Tone.** This adjustment brightens your image, adding a bit more contrast (in previous versions of Photoshop, it was called Auto Levels). Auto Tone resets both the black and the white pixels to the target values you set earlier in this chapter—see page 341. (It's essentially the same as clicking the Auto button in either a Levels or Curves adjustment—or at least it was until you changed the algorithm back on page 341!) If your image needs a *little* lighting boost, this adjustment can get it done. You can apply it to the current layer by pressing Shift-⌘-L (Shift+Ctrl+L on a PC).

Better yet, you can run Auto Tone as an Adjustment layer. Click the Levels or Curves button in the Adjustments panel—or click the half-black/half-white circle button at the bottom of your Layers panel and choose Levels or Curves—and then Option-click (Alt-click) the Auto button. Choose the Enhance Per Channel Contrast algorithm and then click OK.

- **Auto Contrast.** This adjustment is an automatic version of the Brightness/Contrast adjustment discussed at the bottom of this page. It increases the contrast in your image by lightening and darkening pixels. It doesn't adjust channels individually, so if your image has a color cast, it'll still have one after you make this adjustment. And if your image is flat to begin with, it'll still be flat afterwards. But if you have a decent amount of contrast, this adjustment can boost it a little. To run Auto Contrast on the current layer, press Option-Shift-⌘-L (Alt+Shift+Ctrl+L on a PC).

  To run it as an Adjustment layer, click the Adjustments panel's Levels button or click the half-black/half-white circle at the bottom of the Layers panel and choose Levels. In the dialog box that opens, Option-click (Alt-click) the Auto button. Choose the Enhance Monochromatic Contrast algorithm and then click OK.

- **Shadows/Highlights.** If you need to lighten the shadows or darken the highlights in your image quickly, this tool can do an *amazing* job in no time flat. It's discussed in detail on page 350.

- **Equalize.** This adjustment evens out your pixels' brightness by turning the lightest pixels white (or the color you've set as your target white—see page 341) and the darkest ones black (or your target black). It's handy when some areas of your photo are decently lit. It's not available as an Adjustment layer, so you'll definitely want to duplicate your original layer by pressing ⌘-J (Ctrl+J on a PC) before you run this adjustment. To apply it, choose Image → Adjustments → Equalize.

  Be careful when you run Equalize, as it can make your image look washed out by lightening it too much. But if you keep your wits and immediately choose Edit → Fade, you can lessen its effect by choosing Luminosity from the Blending pop-up menu (so it affects only the lightness values, not the color values) and lowering the opacity to about 50 percent, as shown in Figure 9-4.

- **Dodge and Burn tools.** These tools can be useful when you need to lighten or darken certain areas of your image by hand, and in CS4 they've both been re-designed so that they aren't as harmful to your image (especially skin tones). For example, you can use the Burn tool to selectively brighten a boring sky and the Dodge tool to lighten overly dark shadows. But unless you duplicate your original layer first, there's no way to use these tools nondestructively. Luckily, there's a trick that lets you use the Brush tool so it behaves just like the Dodge and Burn tools. Flip over to Chapter 10 (page 414) for the scoop.

  TIP You can also adjust lighting using filters. See Chapter 15, page 590, for details.

Brightness/Contrast Adjustment layers

These Adjustment layers do exactly what you'd think: They brighten your image or increase the contrast in it—or both. In days of old, these adjustments didn't work worth a darn because they adjusted your whole image by the same amount, which

Figure 9-4:
Top: Here's the original image (left) and the equalized version (right). As you can see, the lighting in the image on the right has been evened out, but it's also completely washed out.

Bottom: After reducing the adjustment with the Edit → Fade command, the results are more visually pleasing.

usually resulted in nice-looking shadows but blown-out highlights. Thankfully, Brightness/Contrast got a much-needed overhaul in Photoshop CS3 and now it's a useful tool, especially on black-and-white images. (Just be sure to leave its Use Legacy checkbox turned off, or it'll behave as it did in pre-CS3 days!)

You can choose Brightness/Contrast from your Adjustments panel (its button looks like a sun) or by clicking the half-black/half-white circle at the bottom of your Layers panel and choosing Brightness/Contrast from the pop-up menu. In your Adjustments panel, drag the Brightness slider to the left to darken your image or to the right to brighten it as shown in Figure 9-5. If you want to increase your image's contrast, drag the Contrast slider to the right. To decrease it, drag the slider to the left and watch as your image becomes flatter than a pancake (tonally speaking!).

Shadows/Highlights adjustments

The most useful of all the quick-fix adjustments is Shadows/Highlights. If your camera's flash didn't fire and your subject is way too dark, this command can bring your photo back to life by analyzing each pixel in your image and then adjusting it according to the lightness values of neighboring pixels. This is a big deal because even the much lauded Levels and Curves adjust lightness values *equally* among all pixels, whether they need it or not.

Figure 9-5:
The revamped Brightness/Contrast Adjustment layers do a much better job of adjusting the lighting in your image than they used to. But since the brightening focuses mainly on the highlights (it leaves the shadows alone for the most part), you need to be careful that they don't get too light. For a quick lighting fix, though, this adjustment does a fantastic job.

You can apply this adjustment by choosing Image → Adjustments → Shadows/Highlights, but because it's destructive, you may want to duplicate your image layer first (or better yet, convert it for Smart Filters as described in the steps below). At first you'll see just two sliders in the dialog box that appears: Shadows and Highlights. Because Photoshop assumes you want to lighten the shadows—and you usually do—it automatically sets the Shadows slider to 50 percent, which is way too much (it leaves the Highlights slider set to 0 percent). If you lower the Shadows slider to 20 percent, you see some details in the shadows, but your whole image starts to look flat, and skin tones can turn unattractively pink. To get the most out of this adjustment, you need to turn on the Show More Options checkbox at the bottom of the dialog box. The following numbered list explains all your options.

Here's how to lighten overly dark shadows in your image using a Shadows/Highlights adjustment:

1. **Select the image layer and choose Filter → "Convert for Smart Filters".**

   Since the Shadows/Highlights adjustment is destructive (it's not available as an Adjustment layer), it'll affect your original image. To use it nondestructively, you can either duplicate the layer first by pressing ⌘-J (Ctrl+J on a PC) or convert it for Smart Filters. The second method forces Photoshop to make the adjustment on a separate layer as if you had run a Smart Filter (see page 588). Both methods let you hide parts of your image with a mask though the Smart Filter method won't bloat your file size as much as duplicating the layer.

2. **Choose Image → Adjustments → Shadows/Highlights.**

   In the Shadows/Highlights dialog box that appears, turn on the Show More Options checkbox (circled in Figure 9-6) so you can see all the settings.

Click to edit mask

Double-click to
reopen dialog box

Figure 9-6:
Left: Here's an image before (top) and after (bottom) using the Shadows/Highlights adjustment.

Right: Turning on Show More Options (circled) gives you a slew of sliders. When you click OK to close the dialog box, you'll see the adjustment happen on its own layer (shown here at bottom right). By painting with black within the mask that comes from running Shadows/Highlights as a Smart Filter, you can protect certain parts of the image from the effect.

3. **Lower the Shadows section's Amount slider to between 20 percent and 30 percent.**

   That's really as high as you want to go, or you'll start to see noise (graininess) in your image.

4. **Leave the Shadows section's Tonal Width slider set to 50 percent.**

   This slider lets you control which shadows Photoshop adjusts. If you lower this number, the program changes only the darkest shadows; if you raise it, Photoshop changes a wider range of shadows. Though the factory setting of 50 percent usually works just fine, you may want to lower it if your image looks super grainy.

5. **Increase the Shadows section's Radius slider to between 250 and 300 pixels.**

   Since the Shadows/Highlights adjustment works by looking at the brightness values of neighboring pixels, you can use this setting to determine how big that neighborhood is. Pump this baby way up to make Photoshop analyze more pixels.

   TIP   If your shadows are okay but your highlights need darkening, apply these same settings to the Highlight portion of the dialog box instead of the Shadows portion (they work the same way). Just be sure to set the Shadows section's Amount slider to 0 percent to turn that section off if you don't need to use it.

6. **In the Adjustments section at the southern end of the dialog box, set the Color Correction field to 0.**

   Lowering this setting keeps Photoshop from shifting your colors and introducing funky pinks in skin tones.

7. **Leave the Adjustments section's Midtone Contrast setting at 0.**

   Photoshop makes dark pixels a little darker and light pixels a little lighter to increase contrast. Since the whole point of a Shadows/Highlights adjustment is usually to lighten shadows, increasing this setting pretty much cancels out what you're trying to accomplish. To avoid that conflict, leave this slider set to 0.

8. **In the Adjustments section, leave the Black Clip and White Clip fields set to .01 percent.**

   Leaving the Black Clip and White Clip fields set to .01 percent keeps your light and dark pixels from getting clipped (forced to pure white or black). Page 341 has the full story on clipping.

9. **Click the Save As Defaults button.**

   Photoshop saves your settings so you don't have to reset everything the next time you use this adjustment.

10. **Click OK to close the Shadows/Highlights dialog box.**

    Over in the Layers panel, you'll see a new layer called Smart Filters above the Shadows/Highlights adjustment (see Figure 9-6). This lets you know that Photoshop ran the adjustment as a Smart Filter instead of applying it to your original image.

11. **If necessary, hide the adjustment by painting within the mask that results from making a Smart Filter.**

    When you click the Smart Filters thumbnail to select it, Photoshop puts a tiny black border around it. Press B to grab the Brush tool, Press D to set your color chips to black and white, and then press X until black hops on top. Mouse over to your image and paint the areas that you don't want adjusted. Pretty cool huh? You can think of this technique as Smart Shadows.

12. **For a quick before-and-after comparison, turn the Smart Filters layer's visibility eye on and off.**

As Figure 9-6 shows, this adjustment does a bang-up job of lightening shadows without introducing a funky color cast. To get even *better* results, you can run the Shadows/Highlights adjustment on the Lightness channel in Lab mode. It sounds really difficult, but it's not. Just follow these steps:

1. **Duplicate your original layer by pressing ⌘-J (Ctrl+J on a PC).**

   For reasons known only to the Lords of Adobe, you can't run the Shadows/
   Highlights adjustment on one channel if your original layer has been converted
   to a Smart Object to run the adjustment as a Smart Filter. So to keep this
   adjustment from running in Super Destructo mode, you've got to duplicate the
   layer first. Bummer!

2. **Switch to Lab mode temporarily.**

   Choose Image → Mode → Lab Color. (It doesn't matter whether you were originally in RGB or CMYK mode; as you know from Chapter 2, page 40, you'll *usually* be in RGB mode.) When Photoshop asks if you want to flatten layers, click
   Don't Flatten. If you've got any Smart Objects in your document, it'll also ask if
   you want to rasterize them; in that case, click Don't Rasterize.

3. **Select the Lightness channel.**

   Open your Channels panel by choosing Window → Channels and click once to
   select the Lightness channel. As you learned back in Chapter 5 (page 183), one
   of the great things about Lab mode is that it separates your image's light info
   from its color info. Since you want to lighten the shadows without shifting
   color, you can run the Shadows/Highlights adjustment on the Lightness channel, which makes the adjustment work *noticeably* better.

4. **Choose Image → Adjustments → Shadows/Highlights.**

   Turn on the Show More Options checkbox and enter the settings suggested in
   the previous list (page 341): Shadows Amount 20 percent; Shadows Tonal
   Width 50 percent; Shadows Radius 275 pixels. Click OK when you're finished.

5. **Switch back to RGB (or CMYK) mode.**

   Choose Image → Mode → RGB (or CMYK) to go back to the color mode you
   started out in.

6. **To see before and after versions of your image, turn the duplicate layer's
   visibility off and on.**

Sure, this method takes two extra steps, but the results are well worth it. And
remember, if you need to adjust the highlights instead of the shadows, you can use
the same magic numbers in the Highlights section—just be sure to set the Shadows
section Amount slider to zero.

Correcting Images in Camera Raw

As you learned in Chapter 2, Camera Raw is a powerful plug-in that lets you correct the color and lighting of images shot in Raw format, as well as JPEGs and
TIFFs. Since most of the settings in Camera Raw are slider-based, it's hands down
the easiest place to fix your images (that's why this section comes before the ones
covering Levels and Curves, which are, truth be told, 100 times more confusing).

Fixing Lighting with Blend Modes

If your image is *still* too dark or too light after you run a Shadows/Highlights adjustment, you can fix it with blend modes. The technique is described in step-by-step glory back on page 109, but it's so important that it deserves a mention here:

To darken your image, duplicate the original layer and change the duplicate's blend mode to Multiply using the pop-up menu at the top of the Layers panel. Next, add a layer mask to the duplicate layer by clicking the circle-within-a-square icon at the bottom of the Layers panel.

Then paint with a black brush to hide the darkened bits from areas that don't need darkening.

To lighten your image, duplicate the original layer and change the duplicate layer's blend mode to Screen. Then add a layer mask and hide the *light* bits if you need to.

If your image needs to be darker or lighter still, you can duplicate the *duplicate* layer. To reduce the effect of the darkened or lightened layer, lower its opacity using the field at the top of your Layers panel.

The adjustments you make in Camera Raw are also nondestructive; instead of applying them to your image, Camera Raw keeps track of them in a list it stores within the image or in a file called *Sidecar XMP* (could that name be more cryptic?) so you can undo anything you've done in Camera Raw whenever you want.

> **TIP**   You can zoom in/out of the Camera Raw preview window just like you can in Photoshop (press ⌘-+/– or Ctrl-+/– on a PC). To move around within your image, press and hold the space bar as you drag with your mouse. You can see a preview of your image by turning on the Preview option at the top right of the window or by pressing the P key.

The Camera Raw plug-in is covered in several different places throughout this book. Here's a handy cheat sheet:

- Learning more about the Raw format (page 53)
- Opening files in Camera Raw (page 54)
- Cropping and straightening in Camera Raw (page 217)
- Going grayscale in Camera Raw (page 306)
- Editing multiple files in Camera Raw (see the box on page 390, later in this chapter)
- Removing dust spots in Camera Raw (page 395)
- Fixing red eye with Camera Raw (page 421)
- Sharpening in Camera Raw (page 443)

In this section, you'll learn how to use various sliders in Camera Raw to fix both color and lighting, plus you'll pick up some tricks to make your images leap off the page with color. And when you're finished adjusting your image in Camera Raw, you can use the buttons at the bottom of the Camera Raw window to do the following:

- Click **Save Images** to convert, rename, or relocate your file(s)—or any combination of those options—so you don't overwrite the original(s).

- Click **Open Images** to apply the changes you've made and open the image in Photoshop. You can also Shift-click to open it as a Smart Object (page 115) in Photoshop.

- Click **Cancel** to bail out of Camera Raw without saving or applying your changes.

- Click **Done** to apply the changes (which you can edit the next time you open the image in Camera Raw) and exit the Camera Raw window.

If you use Camera Raw's adjustments in the order they're presented in this section (which is also the order they appear in the Camera Raw window—how handy!), you'll be amazed at the results.

Changing White Balance

When you set the white balance, you're telling Camera Raw which color the light in your image *should be*. As you might suspect, changing the light's color changes *all* the colors in your image, as shown in Figure 9-7. Because each light source gives off its own special color cast—whether it's a light bulb (Tungsten), fluorescent light, a cloudy sky, and so on—most digital cameras let you adjust the white balance based on the current source (though you may have to dig out your owner's manual to find where that setting lives).

> **NOTE**   Want to follow along? Visit this book's Missing CD page at *www.missingmanuals.com* and download the practice file Armadillo.zip.

One of the big advantages of shooting in Raw format is that if you get the white balance wrong in your camera, you can always reset it using Camera Raw. For example, if you're shooting in an office using a white balance of Fluorescent and then walk outside and shoot in the courtyard, the light's color will be off in the outdoor images. Another advantage is that Raw files store more color info than JPEGs because they're not compressed (which is why Raw files are so much bigger). The point is that if you *can* shoot in Raw, you *should*.

> **NOTE**   Raw files are like raw cookie ingredients. Before you mix and roll cookie dough into balls and bake it, you've got all kinds of flexibility. You can change the ingredients, add nuts or chocolate chips, and form the cookies into interesting shapes. A JPEG, on the other hand, is like a *baked* cookie; there's very little you can do to it because it's already cooked. Sure you can add a topping or two, but it's much less flexible than the raw ingredients.

In Camera Raw, you can change the white balance by using the presets in the White Balance pop-up menu in the Basic tab. Or you can set it manually (and maybe more accurately) using Camera Raw's White Balance tool (see Figure 9-8). Press I to grab the tool (which looks like an eyedropper) and then mouse over to your image and click an area that *should be* white or light gray. Just keep clickin' till the image looks right, and then adjust the Temperature and Tint sliders until you get the color you want.

Figure 9-7:
Here's an image with each of Camera Raw's White Balance presets applied to it. As you can see, changing the white balance makes a big difference! Cycling through the list of presets is a great way to experiment with color because it's so darned easy and it opens your eyes to more color possibilities. After all, this color-correction mumbo jumbo is purely subjective; the color that's closest to the original may not always look the best or suit your taste. It's all about what looks best to you!

Figure 9-8:
When you're using the White Balance tool, be careful not to click a white reflection, like the one on the Lone Star bottle shown here. For more accurate color, click an area that's really supposed to be white (or light gray), like this armadillo's underbelly. If you can't seem to get the color quite right, tweak the Temperature slider; dragging it to the right warms up your image and dragging it to the left cools it off. Use the Tint slider to adjust the balance of green and magenta.

NOTE   You can't reset the white balance of JPEGs or TIFFs because those file formats have already been processed a bit by the camera or scanner that captured them, but you can still adjust the file's Temperature and Tint.

Fixing Exposure

The next group of sliders in Camera Raw's Basic tab lets you adjust your image's *exposure* and *contrast* (the difference between light and dark pixels). Exposure is determined by how much light your camera's sensor captures. As you learned on page 342, your image consists of three categories of color: highlights, midtones, and shadows. Problems can arise in one of those categories or all three; luckily, you can fix them all right here in Camera Raw as the following list explains. If you're not up to fiddling with these six sliders, you can make Camera Raw adjust the image for you by clicking the word Auto above the Exposure slider. But you'll get better results if you adjust the following settings by hand:

NOTE   If you'd like to follow along, visit this book's Missing CD page at *www.missingmanuals. com* and download the practice file Keywest.zip.

- **Exposure.** Drag this slider to the right to lighten your image or to the left to darken it. Be careful not to drag it *too* far either way or you'll start to lose details. For that reason, it's a good idea to turn on Camera Raw's clipping warnings (they look like triangles and are shown at the top right in Figure 9-9) so you can see if you're destroying details. (Press U to turn on the shadow clipping warning and O—that's the letter o, not the number zero—to turn on the highlight clipping warning.) It's okay to lose a few details because you can bring them back with the very next setting.

  TIP   If you're not a fan of the highlight clipping warnings and don't want to see them all the time, you can *temporarily* see clipped highlights by Option-dragging (Alt-dragging on a PC) the Exposure slider to the right. Your image preview turns black and the clipped areas appear in bright colors as you drag.

- **Recovery.** This aptly named slider recovers lost details in overexposed highlights. If you drag it to the right, you can make the red clipping warnings in your image disappear and get some details back in those areas. If you can't get rid of all the red, drag the Exposure slider a little ways to the left.

- **Fill Light.** This setting is like a digital fill flash (an additional flash that you aim at the shadows when you're taking a photo): it lightens the shadowy areas of your image but leaves the highlights alone. Don't get carried away with this adjustment: If you lighten the shadows too much, you'll end up with an image *so* evenly lit that it looks boring and flat.

Shadow clipping · Highlight clipping

Figure 9-9:
When you turn on the highlight clipping warning by clicking its icon (top right), areas that are losing details—like this woman's hand and her glass—turn bright red. The farther you drag the Exposure slider to the right, the more red areas you see. Don't let this worry you too much because the Recovery slider can bring back most (if not all) of the lost details.

A little known fact is that both clipping warnings appear black if no pixels are being clipped; however, if the shadow clipping triangle turns blue or the highlight clipping triangle turns red, some clipping has occurred.

- **Blacks.** To darken your image's shadows, drag this slider *slightly* to the right. You'll get a bit of a contrast boost, too, though it's best not to go much past 6 (if at all). If you do, the details in your shadowy areas disappear into a big ol' black hole. You can turn on the shadow clipping warning by clicking the triangle at the top left of the histogram (also shown in Figure 9-9) or pressing U. From then on, Camera Raw highlights any clipped areas in blue.

TIP To temporarily see clipped shadows (while leaving the shadow clipping warning off), Option-drag (Alt-drag on a PC) the Blacks slider to the right. Your image preview turns white, and the clipped areas appear in bright colors as you drag.

- **Brightness.** You can use this slider to adjust the midtones in your image. If you darkened the image by dragging the Exposure setting to the left, you can drag this one to the right to brighten it back up.

- **Contrast.** Drag this slider to the right to increase your image's contrast (the difference between light and dark pixels) or to the left to decrease it. Increasing contrast makes the light pixels in your image lighter and the dark pixels darker.

Making Colors Pop

If you want to intensify the colors in your image, give the next three sliders in Camera Raw's Basic tab a tug:

- **Clarity.** This slider boosts contrast in the midtones, increasing the depth so your image looks clearer. You'd be hard pressed to find an image that wouldn't benefit from dragging this slider almost all the way to the right.

- **Vibrance.** Use this slider to intensify colors without altering skin tones (it has more of an effect on brighter colors and less on light colors, like skin tones). If you've got people in your image, this is the adjustment to use (see Figure 9-10).

- **Saturation.** Intensifies *all* the colors in your image, including skin tones. Don't use it on people pictures unless you like fluorescent skin.

Figure 9-10:
As you can see, Camera Raw can greatly improve the color and light in your image. The original, underexposed image is on top and the end result is on the bottom. That's an impressive result from just dragging a few sliders back and forth!

TIP To reset *any* slider in Camera Raw back to its original setting, simply double-click the slider.

Camera Raw's Adjustment Brush

New in Camera Raw 5 (the version that comes with CS4) is the Adjustment Brush, which lets you selectively adjust certain areas of your images by painting them (see Figure 9-11). When you select the Adjustment Brush by pressing K, you see a whole host of adjustments appear on the right side of the Camera Raw window. They're the same adjustments you've learned about so far, along with an extra one called Color that lets you paint a color tint onto your image.

Figure 9-11:
See the dotted line around the brush cursor? It indicates the feather amount, which softens the edge of your adjustment to make it blend in with the rest of the image. The solid line indicates the brush size, and the crosshair lets you know where you're applying the adjustment. The Flow slider (near the bottom of the window on the right) controls the strength of the adjustment, and the Density slider (just below it) controls the transparency of your brushstroke (think of it as the brush's opacity).

To use the Adjustment brush, choose the type of adjustment you want to make using the sliders on the right, mouse over to your image, and then paint to apply the adjustment. A little green pushpin appears to mark the area you adjusted though on a PC it looks more white than green (press V to show or hide the pins). Behind the scenes, Camera Raw creates a mask that hides the rest of your image so you can continue to tweak the adjustment sliders even after you've finished painting. Camera Raw updates the area you painted to reflect those changes.

You can click the little + and − signs on either end of the adjustment sliders to strengthen or lessen the adjustment (respectively) by a preset amount (.5 on Exposure, whose scale ranges from −4 to +4, and 25 on all the other sliders, which range from −100 to +100). If you want to see the mask, turn on the Show Mask checkbox near the bottom of the window (or press Y). You can change the color of the mask's overlay by clicking the little white square to the right of the Show Mask checkbox and then choosing a new color from the resulting Color Picker. Turn on the Auto Mask checkbox to limit your adjustment to brushstrokes that fall on similar-colored areas.

To undo part of the mask, turn on the Erase radio button near the top of the window and then paint that area of your image to remove the adjustment. Likewise, to add to the mask, turn on the Add radio button and then paint your image. To apply a new adjustment to an existing mask, turn on the New radio button. To select the mask, click the pushpin. And if you want to delete the mask, click its pushpin and then press Delete (Backspace on a PC).

Camera Raw's Graduated Filters

Also new in Camera Raw 5 is the Graduated Filter tool, which lets you apply adjustments much like a real graduated filter you screw onto the end of your camera lens (the filter is a thin piece of glass that fades from gray to white so it darkens overly bright parts of the scene you're shooting). When you select this tool by clicking its button at the top of the Camera Raw window (it's circled in Figure 9-12) or by pressing G, you get the same set of adjustments you do with the Adjustment Brush. The difference is that, with the Graduated Filter tool, you apply them by dragging rather than painting, as shown in Figure 9-12. This adjustment is great for fixing overexposed skies because Photoshop gradually applies it across the full width or height of your image in the direction you drag.

Behind the scenes, this tool creates a gradient mask (page 265), which restricts the adjustment to specific parts of your image. You can continue to make adjustments using the sliders at the right of the window even after you've used the tool, and use the little + and − signs on either end of the sliders to strengthen or lessen the adjustment, respectively. To draw a perfectly vertical or horizontal mask, press and hold the Shift key as you drag.

More Fun with Camera Raw

As you can see, the Camera Raw plug-in is crazy powerful and each new version is bursting with new features. You can use it to adjust Curves (page 379), softly darken the edges of your image (called *vignetting*; see page 590 to learn how to add a dark vignette with a filter in Photoshop), and much more. Camera Raw deserves a whole book all to itself, and there are plenty of 'em out there. When you're ready to learn more, pick up *Getting Started with Camera Raw, Second Edition* by Ben Long (Peachpit Press, 2008), a great guide for beginners. Or check out *Real World Camera Raw with Adobe Photoshop CS4* (Peachpit Press, 2008) by Jeff Schewe and Bruce Fraser. If you'd rather learn by watching a video, check out Ben Willmore's *Mastering Camera Raw* DVD (*www.digitalmastery.com*).

Figure 9-12:
You can use the new Graduated Filter tool to darken and intensify this sky gradually. The horizontal dotted line that runs through the green dot represents the start of the mask, and the similar line running through the red dot represents the end. To delete the mask, click the red dot and then press Delete (Backspace on a PC). To move the midpoint of the mask (where the adjustment begins to fade), drag the dotted line.

Using Levels

The adjustments you've seen so far are okay for when you're starting out with Photoshop and they're darn handy when you're pressed for time. But to become a real pixel wrangler, you've got to kick it up a notch and learn to use *Levels* and *Curves*. With a single Levels adjustment, you can fix lighting problems, increase contrast, and—in some cases—balance the color in your image. (If you've got *serious* color problems, you need to use Curves; skip ahead to page 379 to learn how.) Levels adjustments change the intensity levels—hence the tool's name—of your shadows, midtones, and highlights. They're a very visual and intuitive way to improve your images. And because they're available as an Adjustment layer (yay!), they're nondestructive and won't harm your original image.

In this section, you'll learn how to use Levels adjustments in a few different ways so you can pick the one you like best. But, first, you need to get up close and personal with the mighty *histogram*, your secret decoder ring for interpreting problems in your image.

Histograms: Mountains of Information

A histogram (Figure 9-13) is a visual representation—a collection of bar graphs, to be specific—of the info contained in your image. Once you learn how to read it, you'll gain an immensely valuable understanding of why your image looks the way it does. More importantly, you'll learn how to tweak the histogram itself or, more commonly, other tools—all of which lets you use the histogram's changing readout to monitor the vibrancy of your image. It sounds complicated, but once you watch it in action, you'll see it's actually pretty straightforward…and tremendously powerful.

Photoshop automatically displays an editable histogram when you create either a Levels (page 363) or Curves (page 379) Adjustment layer. You can also summon one any time by choosing Window → Histogram to open the Histogram panel shown in Figure 9-13.

Panel menu
Close panel
Panel dock

Uncached refresh

Cached data warning

Figure 9-13:
Photoshop gives you three different ways to view the histogram (each of which is listed in the Histogram panel menu): the Expanded View (top), the honkin' big All Channels View (bottom), and Compact View (not shown).

In All Channels View (bottom), you can see your image's individual channels in their respective colors by choosing "Show Channels in Color" from the panel menu. (In this figure, the channels appear in black.) You can also control how the histogram looks by using the Channel pop-up menu at the top of the Histogram panel. Choosing RGB turns the histogram black (top), and choosing Colors puts it in full color (bottom). You can choose the other options (Red, Green, and Blue) to see info in just those channels.

The cached data warning triangle (labeled) means that the histogram's info isn't based on the current version of your image (the cache is part of your computer's memory). You'll see this warning periodically when you're editing large files (it's Photoshop's way of redrawing the histogram more quickly). Just click the triangle to make Photoshop update the histogram; clicking the Uncached Refresh button at the top right does the same thing.

The histogram looks like a mountain range, which is a perfectly fine way to think about what you're looking at (more on that metaphor in a moment). Its width represents your image's *tonal range*—the range of colors between the darkest and lightest pixels—on a scale of 0 to 255. Pure black (0) is on the far left and pure white (255) is on the far right. All told, the histogram measures 256 values. If that number sounds familiar, it should: it's the same 256-value range you learned about back in Chapter 2 (page 41), which represents the minute gradations between a total absence of light (black) and full-on illumination (white). The histogram's height at any particular spot represents how many pixels are at that particular level of brightness. Using the mountain analogy, a noticeable cluster of tall and wide mountains means that particular brightness range makes up a good chunk of your image. Short or super-skinny mountains mean that brightness range doesn't appear much. And a big, flat prairie means there are few or no pixels in that range. A glance at the histogram, in other words, can tell you whether you've got a good balance of light and dark pixels, whether the shadows or highlights are getting clipped (page 341), whether the image is over- or underexposed (see Figure 9-14), and whether it's been adjusted before.

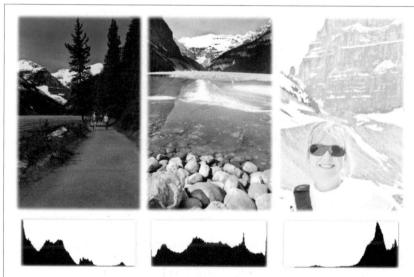

Figure 9-14:
The histograms in the bottom row can help tell you if an image is underexposed (left), if it's got a good balance of color (middle), or if it's overexposed (right).

NOTE   The histogram's width is also referred to as the image's *dynamic range*. You'll learn more about it in the High Dynamic Range (HDR) section later in this chapter (see the box on page 387).

Here are a few tips for understanding your histogram:

- An extremely jagged mountain range means your color info is unbalanced. Your image may contain a decent amount of some colors but very little of others.

- A narrow mountain range means you've got a narrow tonal range and little difference between the darkest and lightest pixels. Your whole image probably looks rather flat and lacks both details and contrast.

- If you see a sharp spike at the left of the histogram, your shadows have probably been clipped (by the camera or scanner). If the spike is at the right end of the histogram, your highlights may have been clipped instead.

- If your mountain range is bunched up against the left side (toward black, aka 0) with a vast prairie on the right, your image is underexposed (too dark); see Figure 9-14, left.

- If your mountain range is snug against the right side (toward white, aka 255) with a vast prairie on the left, your image is overexposed (too light); see Figure 9-14, right.

- An image that has a good balance of light and dark colors has a wide mountain range—one that spans the entire width of the histogram—that's fairly tall and pretty uniform in height. Basically, you want your histograms to look like the older, eroded Appalachians (Figure 9-14, middle) instead of the newer, super-jagged peaks of the Himalayas (Figure 9-14, right).

- If your histogram looks like a comb—with a bunch of gaps between spikes—it's either a really lousy scan or the image was adjusted at some point in the past. (Anytime you shift the brightness values of pixels, you introduce gaps.)

All this histogram and correction business is subjective; if your histogram looks terrible but the image looks great to you, that's fine—in the end, that's all that matters.

Thankfully, you can fix a lot of the problems listed above using the correction methods discussed in this chapter. You can smooth the height of the histogram's mountains to balance color and widen the mountain range to expand your tonal range and increase contrast. And by keeping the Histogram panel open, you can see before and after histograms of any adjustment whose dialog box has a preview checkbox (Shadows/Highlights, Color Balance, Variations, and so on). If you choose RGB from the Channel pop-up menu at the top of the Histogram panel, you see the original histogram in light gray and the new one in black.

If the whole histogram concept is clear as mud, don't fret; it'll make more sense once you start using Levels. If you've got a little free time, you can use the Dodge and Burn tools to help you understand the relationship between what you see in your image and how the histogram looks. With an image and the Histogram panel open, use the Dodge and Burn tools on different areas of your image (be sure to set the tools' Exposure fields to about 20 percent). Use the Dodge tool to lighten dark areas and see how the histogram changes, and then use the Burn tool to darken light areas and see how that affects it. With a little experimentation, you can get a clearer idea of what your histograms are telling you.

> **TIP** Many digital cameras can also show you a histogram (though you may have to root through your owner's manual to learn how to turn it on). Once you get comfy with histograms, you can use them to see whether the shot you're about to take will have good exposure.

Histogram Statistics

If you choose Expanded View or All Channels View from the Histogram panel menu, you'll see a bunch of cryptic info below the histogram. The most useful thing that appears is the Source pop-up menu, which lets you see the histogram of your entire image, a selected layer, or an *adjustment composite.* If your document contains Adjustment layers, that last option displays a histogram based on the selected Adjustment layer and all the layers below it. See page 71 for more info on Adjustment layers.

The stuff that appears below the Source menu is pretty heady, but here's the gist of what each item means:

- **Mean** represents the average intensity value of the pixels in your image.

- **Standard Deviation** (abbreviated as Std. Dev.) shows how widely the intensity values vary.

- **Median** is the midpoint of the intensity values.

- **Pixels** tells you how many pixels Photoshop analyzed to generate the histogram.

- **Cache Level** shows the current image cache Photoshop used to make the histogram. When this number is higher than 1, Photoshop is basing the histogram on a representative sampling of pixels in your image rather than on all of them. You can click the Uncached Refresh button (shown in Figure 9-13) to make the program redraw the histogram based on the actual image.

If you position your cursor over the histogram (or drag across part of it), you also see values for the following:

- **Level** displays the intensity level of the area beneath your cursor.

- **Count** shows the total number of pixels that are at the intensity level beneath your cursor.

- **Percentile** indicates the cumulative number of pixels at or below the level beneath your cursor, expressed as a percentage of all the pixels in your image.

Math geeks, bless their hearts, love this kind of stuff.

The Levels Sliders

Now that you know how to read your histogram, you're ready to make a Levels adjustment, which lets you use a set of three sliders to reshape and expand the information in your histogram. You can create a Levels Adjustment layer by clicking the Levels button in the Adjustments panel (it looks like a tiny histogram) or by clicking the half-black/half-white circle at the bottom of your Layers panel and choosing Levels from the resulting list. Either way, Photoshop displays a black histogram in your Adjustments panel, as shown in Figure 9-15.

> **NOTE**   You can also add a Levels adjustment by pressing ⌘-L (Ctrl+L on a PC) or by choosing Image → Adjustments → Levels though in both cases the adjustment happens on your original image instead of on an Adjustment layer. Yikes!

As shown in Figure 9-15, the black slider at the far left of the histogram represents the shadows in your image. It starts out at 0, the numeric value for pure black. The white slider on the far right, which represents highlights, starts out at 255—pure white. To give your image the greatest tonal range and contrast, move the shadows and highlights sliders so they point to wherever your histogram's values begin to slope upward (at the foot of your mountains, so to speak).

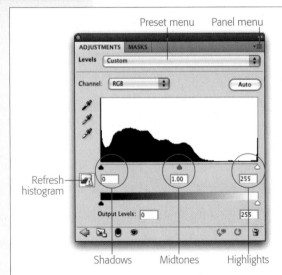

Preset menu   Panel menu

Figure 9-15:
The simplest way to apply a Levels adjustment is by using the Input Levels sliders circled here. You'll also find a slew of presets in the Levels pop-up menu at the very top of the panel. Feel free to give them a spin to see what they do and how they change your histogram.

Refresh histogram

Shadows   Midtones   Highlights

In other words, if there's a gap between the shadows slider and the beginning of the histogram, drag that slider to the right. If there's a gap between the right end of the histogram and the highlights slider, drag the slider to the left. Figure 9-16 should make all this repositioning stuff crystal clear.

When you move the sliders, Photoshop adjusts the tonal values in your image accordingly. For example, if you drag the highlights slider inward to 183, Photoshop changes all the pixels in your image that were originally at 183 or higher to 255 (pure white). Translation: They get brighter (see Figure 9-16). Similarly, if you move the shadows slider inward to 7, Photoshop darkens all the pixels with a brightness level of 7 or lower to 0 (pure black). The pixel levels in between get redistributed, too, boosting your image's overall contrast by increasing its tonal range (widening your mountain range).

The gray slider in the middle (midtones) lets you brighten or darken the image by changing the intensity of the middle range of grays (check out the box on page 378 to learn why you're dealing with grays instead of color). Drag it to the left to lighten your image or to the right to darken it. Because the gray slider focuses on the midtones, it won't make your highlights too light or your shadows too dark—unless you go hog wild and drag it all the way left or right!

TIP   If you hold down the Option key (Alt on a PC) as you drag the shadows or highlights sliders, you can see which parts of your image you're forcing to pure black or white. When you Option-drag (Alt-drag) the shadows slider to the right, your image turns completely white. The darkest parts of the image begin to reappear as you drag, first in black and then in other colors. If you Option-drag (Alt-drag) the highlights slider to the left, the opposite happens: Your image turns completely black, and the lightest parts are the first ones to reappear, first in white and then in color. Option-dragging is a great way to tell if you're dragging the sliders too far because whatever areas are visible while you Option-drag (Alt-drag) are the areas that will be pure black or pure white. It's also a great trick for finding the lightest highlights and darkest shadows as the next section explains.

Figure 9-16:

Left: Near the top of the Histogram panel is the Channel pop-up menu, which lets you view and adjust the composite channel (page 174) or each channel individually. If each channel's histogram differs, it's worth adjusting each one separately. If the histograms are almost identical, you can get away with adjusting only the composite channel. Here you see the composite and color channel histograms for an RGB image. Since the gaps on the right side vary quite a bit, you should adjust each channel separately. Be careful not to drag the sliders too far in, or you'll make parts of your image pure black or pure white (or the colors you set as your black and white targets back on page 341).

Right: Here you can see the before (top) and after (bottom) versions of the image, along with the new composite channel histogram. Notice how the mountain range has become, overall, flatter and much wider; that means the image's tonal range has expanded. You can tell this image has been adjusted from its original state because the new histogram looks like a comb: lots of vertical lines with gaps in between.

Output levels

The black-and-white bar near the bottom of the Adjustments panel (shown in Figure 9-15) includes a couple of sliders you can use to control the color of the black pixels and white pixels in your image. Drag the black slider to the right to lighten the pure black pixels or the white slider to the left to dim the white pixels. These adjustments used to be crucial if you were sending grayscale images to a commercial press because the printing process was notorious for making highlights too light and shadows too dark. Nowadays, if you use good-quality color profiles (page 617), these adjustments aren't such a big deal, but knowing how to change the way your blacks and whites look when they're printed is still useful if you can't trust your printer to print highlights and shadows properly.

The Levels Eyedroppers

Another way to adjust Levels is to use the eyedroppers on the left side of the Adjustments panel (see Figure 9-15). Instead of dragging the sliders directly below the histogram, you can use the eyedroppers to sample pixels that should be black (the darkest shadows that contain details), those that should be white (the lightest highlights that contain details), or neutral gray (midtones). If you use this method, Photoshop adjusts the sliders for you. The only problem is that it can be darn tough to figure out which pixels to sample, but you can use a couple of tricks to solve this problem, as you'll learn shortly.

With an image open, follow these steps:

1. **Grab the Eyedropper tool and change the Sample Size pop-up menu to "3 by 3 Average".**

    Press I to activate the Eyedropper tool. Because you're about to use the eyedroppers to reset your black and white points, you need to change the way the tool measures color (the eyedroppers in Levels and Curves adjustments use the main Eyedropper tool's settings). In the Options bar, the Sample Size pop-up menu is automatically set to Point Sample, which means the Eyedropper samples exactly one pixel when you click with it. By changing the sample size to "3 by 3 Average", you tell Photoshop to average several pixels around the spot where you click, which is much better for color-correcting.

    TIP If you have the Eyedropper or Color Sampler tool (page 363) selected, you can open a Sample Size shortcut menu by Ctrl-clicking (right-clicking on a PC) anywhere in your image. If you're working with extremely high-resolution files, the pixels are so tiny and so tightly packed that you may want to increase the sample size to, say, 51 by 51 or higher. See page 221 in Chapter 6 for more on resolution.

2. **Create a Levels Adjustment layer.**

    Click the half-black/half-white circle at the bottom of your Layers panel and choose Levels from the pop-up menu that appears. Photoshop adds an Adjustment layer to your Layers panel and opens the Adjustments panel.

3. **In the Adjustments panel, click the black eyedropper.**

   The left side of the Adjustments panel sports three eyedroppers. The black one resets your image's black point (shadows), the gray one resets the gray point (midtones), and the white one resets the white point (highlights). Simple enough!

4. **Mouse over to your image and click an area that *should be* black.**

   Though in most cases, it's pretty obvious which parts of your image should be black, sometimes it's hard to tell, and you need to consider a few things before you click. First, you want to pick an area near your image's focal point (the spot you want your viewer to focus on). For example, if you're correcting a portrait, find a dark shadow near your subject's face. Second, try to pick an area with some details in it instead of one that's pure black; if it's pure black, there's probably nothing there!

   If you need help figuring out where the darkest pixels in your image live, hold down the Option key (Alt on a PC) as you drag the Adjustments panel's shadows slider (see Figure 9-15) to the right. At first, your image turns completely white, but as you continue to drag, Photoshop displays color in some areas (see Figure 9-17). The first colored area that appears is the darkest spot in your image. Make a mental note of that spot and then drag the shadows slider all the way back to the left. Mouse over to your image and then click that spot with the black eyedropper.

   TIP   You can also use the Info panel to see the value of the dark pixels in your image so you can pick one that's not pure black (which is zero). Skip to the next section (page 363) for details.

   When you click, you'll probably see the colors in your image shift a bit. If you don't like the results, click somewhere else to set a *new* black point or undo your click by pressing ⌘-Z (Crl+Z on a PC).

   NOTE   If you'd like to play around with the image shown in Figure 9-17, you can download the file Bridge.jpg from this book's Missing CD page at *www.missingmanuals.com*.

5. **In the Adjustments panel, click the white eyedropper and then click an area in your image that should be white.**

   The same rules apply when it comes to choosing a new white point as choosing a black one: Try to pick an area that's close to the focal point and not pure white (because a pure white one doesn't have any details). You also don't want to pick a reflection from a light source as your white point because it's not a true white. You can use the same Option-drag (Alt-drag on a PC) trick to find the lightest highlights, though this time your image turns completely black. As you drag the highlight slider to the left, the first areas that appear in color are what you're after.

Figure 9-17:
Top: Here's a trick you can use to find the darkest and lightest pixels in your image: In the Adjustments panel, Option-drag (Alt-drag on a PC) the shadows slider (remember, that's the one on the left) to the right. The first areas to appear in your image are the darkest. Likewise, when you Option-drag (Alt-drag) the highlights slider to the left, the first colors to appear are the lightest. Just don't forget to drag the sliders back where they were when you're done!

Bottom: As you can see, a little Levels adjusting can go a long way toward improving your image's color and contrast.

6. **Select the gray eyedropper and then click an area that should be neutral gray, meaning the pixels are about 50 percent gray and have nearly equal color values.**

   Unfortunately, the Option-drag (Alt-drag) trick doesn't work on midtones, but if you're willing to jump through a few hoops, you can track down your neutral gray. The box on page 373 has the details.

7. **To see before and after versions of your image, turn off the Levels Adjustment layer's visibility.**

   In the Layers panel, click the visibility eye to the left of the Levels Adjustment layer to turn it off and see whether your adjustment made a difference.

Good Gray Hunting

Alas, if you're looking for a neutral gray to click with the gray Levels or Curves eyedropper and nothing in your image is gray, there's no quick trick for finding a good gray. Some images don't even *have* any neutral grays.

One way to look for them is to open the Info panel (Figure 9-18) and then hover over areas that appear gray with the Eyedropper tool (see Appendix E, online at *www.missingmanuals.com*) and look for nearly equal RGB values (like R: 222, G: 222, B: 224, for example). When you find matching RGB values, you've found a neutral gray.

The Info panel method works just fine if you've got a few extra hours to spend mousing around your image checking pixel values. But if you're pressed for time, here's a foolproof way to hunt them down—if they actually exist in your image. Photoshop guru Dave Cross (*www.davecross.blogspot.com*) came up with this technique—and he's graciously given permission to include it here for your reading enjoyment. With the image you want to search open, follow these steps:

1. Create a new layer by clicking the "Create a new layer" button at the bottom of the Layers panel. Make sure this layer sits *above* the image layer.

2. Fill the new layer with gray by choosing Edit → Fill, and then choose 50 percent Gray from the Use pop-up menu and click OK.

3. Use the pop-up menu at the top of your Layers panel to switch the gray layer's blend mode from Normal to Difference (page 276). Your photo looks really funky, but don't panic; this layer won't live long.

4. Create a Threshold Adjustment layer by clicking the half-black/half-white circle at the bottom of your Layers panel and choosing Threshold from the resulting list.

5. In the Adjustments panel, drag the Threshold slider all the way to the left until the image turns solid white and then slowly drag it back to the right. The first areas that appear black are your neutral grays. As soon as you see a good-sized black spot, stop dragging.

6. Mark the spot with the Color Sampler tool (see Appendix E, online at *www.missingmanuals.com*): Press Shift-I to activate the tool (it looks like an eyedropper with a tiny circle above it), and then click once in the black spot. A tiny circle with the number 1 next to it appears where you clicked. Feel free to mark more than one spot if you'd like; the Color Sampler tool lets you set up to four markers.

7. Delete both the Threshold adjustment layer and the gray layer (you don't need them anymore). Shift-click to select them both and then press Delete (Backspace on a PC).

That's it! With the neutral gray point marked, you don't have to wonder where to click with the gray eyedropper in a Levels or Curves adjustment. To delete the marker once you've set your gray point, grab the Color Sampler tool, mouse over the marker, and Option-click (Alt-click) it. Your cursor turns into the tiniest, cutest pair of scissors you've ever seen.

Correcting by the Numbers

Ever heard the phrase, "Numbers don't lie"? That old adage applies to color-correcting in Photoshop, too: Using numbers helps you take the guesswork out of it. Instead of relying on what looks good to your naked (and possibly sleepy) eye, you can use the pixels' color values to balance your image's color perfectly.

To see pixels' color values, you need to open the Info panel (page 24) by choosing Window → Info. Once you open this panel, which shows you all kinds of info about the pixels in your image, you can mouse over your image with any tool to see (in the left-hand quadrant of the panel) a numeric value for the particular pixel your cursor is hovering over (see Figure 9-18). For RGB images (page 178), you'll see a value for R, G, and B. If you're in CMYK mode (page 180), you see C, M, Y, and K values; in Lab mode you get L, a, b; and so on. (You also see C, M, Y, and K values in the right-hand quadrant when you're in RGB mode, but that's just Photoshop being overly informative.)

In RGB mode (which is where you spend the majority of your time), these values correspond to the 0–255 scale you learned about earlier in this chapter and in Chapter 2 (page 41). Depending on the color of the area you hover your cursor over, the numbers may lean more toward one channel than the others. For example, when you hover over a pixel in a sky, your B (blue) value spikes higher than the R or G (red or green) values. When you hover over reddish skin, the R value is higher than the B or G values.

Figure 9-18:
The Info panel has four quadrants that you can change to display values in other color modes. Click one of the little eyedroppers (circled) to summon this pop-up menu and then click the color mode you want to see info for. If you happen upon a gray area with (nearly) equal RGB values like the ones shown here, congratulations— you've found a neutral gray!

This info is useful in several situations:

• You can use it to figure out what's causing a color cast. For example, if you're hovering over a white cat and the blue value is really high, you have a problem in the blue channel. If the green value is off the charts, then that's where the problem is.

- The Info panel can help you find the darkest and lightest pixels when you're making a Levels (page 363) or Curves (page 379) adjustment. As you learned in the previous pages, you don't want to choose shadows or highlights that are pure black or pure white because they lack details. If you hover over the area you're considering, you can see if it's really pure black (0) or pure white (255).

TIP If you're mousing around a shadowy area and the numeric values in the Info panel keep changing, that means there are details lurking in that spot. If you lighten the shadows (page 342), you may be able to bring them out.

- Monitoring these values can keep you from overadjusting your image and losing details. For example, since you know that 0 means pure black and 255 means pure white, you can take care that pixels in the important parts of your image don't reach those values when you're making an adjustment. You can use the Color Sampler tool, along with the Info panel, to monitor the original and adjusted values of up to four sample points by following these steps.

Here's how to correct an image in RGB mode by the numbers:

1. **Open the Info panel by choosing Window → Info or pressing F8.**

   As you hover your cursor over various parts of your image, watch how the Info panel's numbers change to reflect the pixel underneath your cursor.

2. **Grab the Color Sampler tool and make sure the Sample Size is set to "3 by 3 Average".**

   Press I to activate the Eyedropper tool and then press Shift-I to switch to the Color Sampler tool (it lives in the same toolset). Take a peek in the Options bar and make sure the Sample Size pop-menu is set to "3 by 3 Average".

3. **Create a Levels Adjustment layer.**

   Click the half-black/half-white circle at the bottom of your Layers panel and choose Levels, or click the Levels button in your Adjustments panel. Technically, you don't *have* to create this layer just yet, but if you've already got a Levels adjustment open, you can use the Option-drag (Alt-drag on a PC) trick (page 363) to help you find the highlights and shadows points in the next two steps.

4. **Mark the lightest highlight in your image.**

   Following the guidelines explained in the previous section (starting on page 370), locate the lightest highlight and click it once with the Color Sampler tool. Photoshop adds a marker like the ones shown in Figure 9-19 to your image.

TIP Strictly speaking, you don't have to choose the Color Sampler tool to set sample point markers. If you're using the Eyedropper tool, you can Shift-click to set a marker and Option-Shift-click (Alt-Shift-click on a PC) the marker to delete it.

Figure 9-19:
Top: By setting sample point markers (circled), you can monitor the value of your pixels before and during an adjustment (in your Info panel, the two values are separated by a slash).

Bottom: As you can see in these before (left) and after (right) versions, making adjustments based on the Info panel's data took care of the blue color cast and improved the contrast.

5. **Mark the darkest shadow in your image.**

   Again, use the criteria described on page 363 to choose a shadow point and then click once to mark it (you'll see a little 2 next to the mark, as shown in Figure 9-19).

6. **Using the Levels histogram, adjust each channel's highlight value.**

   Your goal in fixing the highlights is to make all three channels' values match the *optimal* highlight value, which—as you know from the very beginning of this chapter (step 8 on page 341)—is 245. To balance your channels' highlight values, you have to adjust the highlight in *each* channel. Over in your Adjustments panel, use the Channel pop-up menu to pick a channel and, while watching the numbers in the Info panel, drag the highlights slider (Figure 9-15, page 363) to the left until it reaches 245, or just type *245* into the slider's text field. Repeat this step for the other channels. When all three channels' highlight values are nearly or exactly equal, you've got yourself a balanced image (well, in the highlights at least!).

7. **Adjust each channel's shadow value.**

   Use the same process to balance your shadows: Choose each channel in your Adjustments panel and drag the shadows slider inward until it reaches 10, or type *10* into the slider's text field.

8. **Adjust your image's midtones, if necessary.**

   You don't always have to adjust your midtones since your image may look just fine the way it is (though you may not realize how much better it *could* look!). In your Adjustments panel, select the composite channel (RGB) and drag the gray slider to the left to lighten your image, or to the right to darken it.

9. **Take a peek at the "before" version of your image by turning off the Levels Adjustment layer's visibility.**

   In your Layers panel, click the Levels Adjustment layer's visibility eye to hide that layer so you can see what a difference your changes have made.

If you need to go back and make further adjustments, just double-click the Adjustment layer in your Layers panel. As you can see in Figure 9-19, this technique makes a big difference.

> **TIP** When you're using the Info panel it can help to rearrange the various panels in your workspace. If you really dig having the Info and Histogram panels open—and you will once you get used to using them—you can create a custom workspace so they automatically open and appear wherever you'd like. Flip back to page 15 to find out how.

Color-Correcting Skin

You're not limited to monitoring the Info panel's values of highlights and shadows; you can slap sample points anywhere you want. If you're correcting a people picture, you most certainly want to monitor the values of skin tones. While you won't find any magic target values that work for *every* skin type, here are a few tips that can help you make sure your skin tones at least look human, which is (hopefully!) your goal:

- When you're color-correcting photos of women, place sample points on your subjects' necks if you can. Women don't typically put makeup on their necks, so you get a more accurate reading of the woman's *real* skin tone based on her neck than you would on, say, her cheek.

- Skin tones should have red values greater than their green values and green values greater than their blue values. This rule is easy to remember because that's the order of the letters in RGB. (To learn about switching between CMYK and RGB modes, see Chapter 16.)

- The difference between the red and green values in skin should be about double the difference between the green and blue value. For example, if the difference between the red and green values is 60, the difference between the green and blue values should be around 30.

- The fairer a person's complexion, the closer the RGB values should be to each other.

- The darker someone's complexion, the lower the blue value in their skin should be.

By following these guidelines, you should end up with nicely balanced skin colors in your images. And if you'd like to use a color swatch as a reference, you can find skin tone color charts lurking on the Web. An oldie but goodie is Bruce Beard's skin tone and hair color chart, available from *www.retouchpro.com/pages/colors.html*.

FREQUENTLY ASKED QUESTION

There Is No Color

What's all this talk about black, white, and gray? I'm trying to fix color!

Consider this concept: There *is* no color in Photoshop, so you can't use the program to *fix* color.

After you clean off the coffee you just splurted on your screen, take a moment to think about the channel information you learned about in Chapter 5. Remember how Photoshop displays it all in grayscale (page 175)? That's because the information really *is* grayscale; that is, until it hits your monitor. All color is created by output devices like your monitor, printer, and professional printing presses (which you'll learn more about in Chapter 16). Your computer (and the programs on it like Photoshop), your digital camera, and your scanner are all digital devices; all they really understand are *bits*, which represent either zero or one (see the box on page 43). When you send these bits to an output device, the device assigns color values to that information.

If you can wrap your brain around this mind-bending concept, a few things start to make sense. For example:

- **Why it's so hard to match what you see onscreen to what you print.** When you realize that the output device is responsible for how the bits are translated into color, you understand why it's such a nightmare getting colors to match across devices that work differently (like LCD and CRT monitors) or that use different inks (like inkjet printers and printing presses). Chapter 16 has more about *color management,* the science behind matching colors.

- **Why color-correction tools like Levels and Curves (page 379) focus on white, gray, and black values.** Once you realize that you're working with grayscale info, it makes sense that, to change a grayscale image, you have to change what Photoshop thinks should be black, neutral gray, or white (or change the intensity or brightness values) to alter the image. Shades of gray are all that matters when you're correcting in Photoshop.

- **Why the histogram measures color intensity (brightness) on a scale from 0 to 255.** A typical RGB image has 256 shades of gray, which correspond to brightness values of 0 percent to 100 percent gray. You see this 0–255 scale in the Info panel when you hover over pixels in an RGB image (page 178). Each pixel has a value ranging from 0–255 for each channel.

All this talk of grayscale can sound pretty abstract since we see in color, not grayscale. But what it boils down to is that your *real* goal in color-correcting images is to get the *grayscale* information right. Once you do, your output device has a much better chance of getting the colors right. Now go refill that coffee cup!

Working with Curves

The last stop on the Color Correction Express is Curves, the most powerful (and fear-inducing) adjustment in all of Photoshop. The basic idea is that, by curving a diagonal line on a grid, you change the brightness of the pixels in your image. Instead of the three main adjustment sliders you get with Levels (shadows, highlights, and midtones), Curves give you up to *16* adjustments. But that's not as scary as it sounds. If you arrived here relatively unscathed after getting through the section on Levels (page 363), you already know a *ton* about using Curves. For example:

- You can use Curves as an Adjustment layer so that it's nondestructive (whee!), which means you can also use the included layer mask to restrict the adjustment to certain areas of your image. And in Photoshop CS4, the Curves grid shows up in the sparkling new Adjustments panel, just like Levels.

- A Curves adjustment uses a histogram (page 363) and the same 256 shades of grayscale you saw in Levels (see the box on page 378). It also has the same shadows and highlights sliders (though no midtones slider), and it harbors the same trio of eyedroppers for resetting the black, white, and midtone points (page 363). So far so good!

- You can Option-drag (Alt-drag on a PC) the shadows and highlights sliders to find the darkest and lightest areas of your image, just like you learned on page 363.

- You can use Curves to correct your image using the Info panel and the Color Sampler tool, and you can type target values into the Input field. To summon the Input field (shown in Figure 9-20), click a point on the curve. If you haven't added any points yet (which you'll learn about shortly), you can click either the shadows or highlights slider beneath the grid to activate the corresponding *curve point* at the tip of the diagonal line.

- You can use the pop-up menu at the top of the Adjustments panel to the left of the Auto button (shown in Figure 9-20) to adjust individual channels with Curves, just like with Levels.

- You'll find a ton of presets in the pop-up menu at the top of the Adjustments panel, some of which are quite useful (also shown in Figure 9-20). It's worth taking them for a spin just to see how they affect both the curve and your image.

To create a Curves Adjustment layer, click the Curves button in the Adjustments panel (it looks like a grid with an S curve on it) or click the half-black/half-white circle at the bottom of the Layers panel and choose Curves. Your Adjustments panel pops open to reveal a grid with a diagonal line running from the bottom-left corner to the top-right corner (see Figure 9-20).

> **NOTE** To try your hand at the Curves adjustments described in this section, download the image Hiking.jpg shown in Figure 9-21 from this book's Missing CD page at *www.missingmanuals.com*.

Preset menu

Pick a channel to adjust

Point's new value (output bar)

Curve

Adjustment point added to the curve

Point's original value (input bar)

Figure 9-20:
Photoshop's Curves tool is incredibly flexible—and that's what scares most folks: They don't know when, how, or why to add adjustment points or in which direction to move them. Fear not: You'll learn everything you need to know about this powerful tool in the following pages.

Once you learn how to add a point to the curve (which isn't actually curved yet—it's still a straight line), you can use the grayscale bars on the left side and bottom of the grid to figure out which direction you need to drag the point. You can follow a point down the grid to see its original brightness value (on the input bar) and you can follow it to the left to see its new brightness value (on the output bar). After you click a point on the curve, those numeric values also appear in the Output and Input fields below the curve.

The diagonal line in the middle—which is the actual *curve* even though it starts out straight—represents the original brightness values (tonal range) of your image. To adjust your image's brightness values, you can place up to 14 points along the diagonal line. (You can't delete the original points at either end of the curve, though you can adjust them like any other point.)

Add a point to the curve by clicking the line itself or by using Photoshop CS4's new on-image button and clicking your image (Figure 9-21 explains how that maneuver works). Each point you place on the line corresponds to a brightness value in the horizontal black-to-white gradient bar below the grid (called the *input bar*). The direction you drag a point determines whether the brightness of pixels in that tonal range increases or decreases: Drag *upward* to *increase* brightness or *downward* to *decrease* it. (Even if nothing else about Curves makes sense, that part certainly does!)

Ben Willmore (*www.digitalmastery.com*) compares Curves adjustment points to a row of dimmer switches, which makes perfect sense if you think about how a dimmer switch works. Just as turning up a dimmer switch gradually turns on the light, raising a point on the curve gradually makes your image brighter and lighter. Likewise, just as lowering a dimmer switch gradually turns off the light, lowering a point on the curve makes your image darker. It's a great analogy because the adjustments you make in Curves are as gradual as using a dimmer switch; you generally don't have to move a point very far to introduce a big change. As you move a point, the diagonal line curves in the direction you drag, and you can see its new brightness level represented on the out put bar (the vertical gradient bar on the grid's left side), as shown in Figure 9-21, bottom.

Click to activate on-image adjustment

The bar on the bottom shows the point's brightness range

Clicking sets an adjustment point on the curve

While holding down your mouse button, drag up or down to adjust the curve

The bar on the left shows the new brightness range

Figure 9-21:
Top: In Photoshop CS4, Curves got a lot easier to use because the new on-image adjustment tool (circled, left) lets you add and move adjustment points by dragging in your image. Just click the button that looks like a pointing hand (circled, top) to activate this tool and then hover your cursor over the area you want to change (your cursor turns into an eyedropper). A white preview circle appears on the curve (circled, right) that corresponds to the tonal value of the pixels you're hovering above. When you're ready to add a point to the curve, click once.

Bottom: To darken overly light gray pixels, drag downward (your cursor turns into a hand with an up-and-down arrow, circled). As you drag, the curve bends in the direction you're dragging, as shown here. Notice that the Input field's value is lower (meaning darker) than it was originally: 201 vs. 213.

TIP Instead of dragging the adjustment points around, you can nudge them with the up and down arrow keys on your keyboard. It's easier to make precise adjustments this way, and it keeps you from accidentally changing contrast (discussed in the next section) by dragging the point to the left or right. Use the up arrow to brighten and the down arrow to darken your image.

The grid behind the curve is merely a visual aid to help you move points around and to determine which part of the tonal range you're affecting. Out of the box, it's set to a 25 percent quarter-tone grid, which means the shadows, midtones, and highlights are split into four equal parts: The left-hand column represents the darkest shadows, the middle two columns represent the midtones, and the far-right column represents the lightest highlights. If you change it to a 10 percent grid by Option-clicking (Alt-clicking on a PC) the grid, Photoshop displays a grid with smaller squares and 10 rows and columns. If you want to change it back, Option-click (Alt-click) the grid again. In the Curves Display Options dialog box (shown in Figure 9-22), you can switch between these two grid options by clicking the button that looks like a tiny grid.

Figure 9-22:
You can access the Curves Display Options dialog box by choosing (naturally) Curves Display Options from the Adjustments panel menu. These options also appear at the bottom of the Curves dialog box, which you can open by pressing ⌘-M (Ctrl+M on a PC). But be careful: If you apply a regular Curves adjustment (instead of using a Curves Adjustment layer), Photoshop alters your original image.

Here's a run-down of the other settings in the Curves Display Options dialog box:

- **Show Amount of.** Unless you change it, the Light option is selected, which means your image's shadows correspond to the bottom-left corner of the Curves grid and its highlights to the top-right corner. You can turn on the "Pigment/Ink %" option to show ink percentages on the input and output bars instead of the 0–255 brightness scale. Usually, though, you'll want to leave it set to Light.

- **Show.** This menu has several options that are all turned on to start with:

  — **Channel Overlays** lets you see a separate curve for each channel in your document. If you're new to Curves and find a panel riddled with colorful diagonal lines both distracting and alarming, you can turn this checkbox off.

  — **Histogram** determines whether Photoshop displays a light-gray version of your image's histogram behind the grid. If you find the histogram distracting, turn this setting off.

  — **Baseline** tells Photoshop to display the original curve as a straight line, which is a great way to know at a glance, "Dude! That's the original curve!"

  — **Intersection Line** makes Photoshop display horizontal and vertical "helper" lines when you drag a point to help you align it properly (which isn't really necessary if you use arrow keys to nudge points instead of dragging them).

Changing Contrast

The angle of the curve controls contrast. If you steepen it, you can increase the contrast in your image; if you flatten it, you can decrease contrast (see Figure 9-23). Just select an adjustment point by clicking it and then use the left or right arrow key to nudge it one way or the other.

Figure 9-23:
Top: A steeper curve gives your image more contrast; you can see the original diagonal line in the background and the adjusted, steeper curve in the foreground. In fact, you can start with one of the contrast presets in the Curves pop-up menu at the top of the Adjustments panel and then use the on-image control (page 379) to add additional points and nudge them as necessary.

Bottom: To keep the trees in the foreground from getting too dark, you can keep the adjustment from affecting that area by painting the Curves Adjustment layer's mask with a black brush.

Another way to increase contrast is to make a subtle S curve, as shown in Figure 9-24 (top right). Here's how: Darken your shadows slightly by clicking to add an adjustment point to the lower-left grid intersection and then use the down arrow to nudge by 2–3 notches. Next, lighten your highlights by adding a point to the top-right grid intersection, and then nudge it up by the same amount. Finally, lighten the midtones by adding a point to the very center of the grid and then nudge it slightly upward.

If the effect is a little too strong, you can always lower the opacity of the Curves Adjustment layer using the pop-up menu at the top of the Layers panel. If you inadvertently intensify a color while you're making a Curves adjustment, you can tweak that particular channel. Choose the appropriate channel from the pop-up menu directly above the grid and then click the on-image adjustment button at the top-left of the panel. Then click the color in your image that you want to adjust and use your down arrow key to neutralize it, as shown in Figure 9-24 (bottom right).

Figure 9-24:
You can create as many Curves Adjustment layers as you want in a document. For example, the image on the left definitely needs a contrast boost. You can create one Adjustment layer for the magic contrast-inducing S curve (top right), and then add another one to neutralize the suddenly sky-high red in the skin tones. If you choose the red channel from the pop-up menu above the grid, you can use the on-image control button to select the too-intense red and then use your down arrow key to nudge it back down to earth (bottom right).

Remember that you can also change the blend mode of any Adjustment layer (see page 329). To preserve the color in your image, you can change a Curves Adjustment layer's blend mode to Luminosity so the adjustment affects only the image's lightness values and not its color balance. This is a great way to avoid color shifts.

In the end, getting good at using Curves simply takes practice. But as long as you use an Adjustment layer, you'll never harm your original image. Heck, if you're feeling really frisky, click the Pencil button in the panel's lower left and draw your *own* curve by hand. If you go that route, you can click the "Smooth the curve values" button, which activates beneath the Pencil to smooth the line you drew. To go back to adding points to adjust the curve, click the button above the Pencil called "Edit points to modify the curve". When you're ready to learn more, check out Taz Tally's training video *Photoshop: Color Correction* (*www.lynda.com*).

> **TIP**   If you create a really useful or incredibly funky Curve, you can save it for use later by choosing "Save Curves Preset" from the Adjustments panel menu. (You can save a favorite Levels adjustment in the same way.) From then on, it'll show up in the preset pop-up menu at the top of the panel.

Keyboard Curves

If you're a fan of keyboard shortcuts and keyboard/mouse combinations, dog-ear this page right now—or better yet, print a copy of the shortcuts from this book's Missing CD page (*www.missingmanuals.com*)—because there are a slew of 'em that you can use with Curves:

- To cycle through your document's channels (starting with the composite channel), press Option-2, 3, 4, 5, 6 (Alt+2, 3, 4, 5, 6 on a PC). In CS3, press ⌘-1, 2, 3, 4, 5 (Ctrl+1, 2, 3, 4, 5).

- To show clipped shadows and highlights, Option-drag (Alt-drag) the panel's shadows or highlights sliders, or click the shadows or highlights eyedropper and then press and hold Option (Alt) as you hover your cursor over the image.

- To switch from 25 percent to 10 percent grid (page 379), Option-click (Alt-click) the grid.

- To cycle forward (left to right) through curve points, press =. (In Photoshop CS3, the keyboard shortcut is ⌘-Tab [Ctrl+Tab].)

- To cycle backward through curve points, press – (that's the minus sign). (In CS3, the shortcut is Shift-⌘-Tab [Shift+Ctrl+Tab].)

- To deselect the selected point(s), press ⌘-D (Ctrl+D).

- To select multiple points, Shift-click the points.

- To delete a single point, select it and press Delete (Backspace), drag it off the grid, or ⌘-click (Ctrl-click) it.

- To nudge the selected point one unit in the standard Curves dialog box (two units in the Adjustments panel), press one of the arrow keys.

- To nudge the selected point 10 units in the standard Curves dialog box (16 units in the Adjustments panel), press and hold Shift and then use the arrow keys.

Regular Curves dialog box only:

- To open the Curves dialog box, press ⌘-M (Ctr+M).

- To open a Curve dialog box with the settings you used previously, press Option-⌘-M (Alt+Ctrl+M).

- To reset all settings, Option-click (Alt-click) the Cancel button.

- To cycle through the Curves dialog box's buttons, fields, and lists, press Tab on a PC. When you have a checkbox selected, you can press the space bar to turn it on or off. If you select the Preset field, you can cycle through the presets by using the arrow keys on your keyboard. Likewise, if the Channel pop-up menu is selected, you can cycle through the channels with the arrow keys. And if one of the labels like Output or Input contains an underlined character, you can press the corresponding key to select it. For example, instead of pressing the Options button to open it, you can tab to Options and then press the letter T.

- New in CS4, you can open the Auto Color Options by Option-clicking (Alt-clicking) the Auto button in the Adjustments panel.

And here are a couple of shortcuts you can use only after you click the on-image adjustment button (shown in Figure 9-21):

- To add a point to all channels simultaneously, Shift-⌘-click (Shift-Ctrl-click) your image.

- To delete a point on the curve, ⌘-click (Ctrl-click) an area of the image with the same Input/Output levels as the point you want to delete. When a preview circle appears around the point, (circled in Figure 9-21), you're clear to click.

Making Colors Pop

Once you've corrected your image's color and lighting, you can have some serious fun by boosting or intensifying its colors, too. You've already learned how to do that in Camera Raw with the Clarity, Vibrance, and Saturation adjustments. In Photoshop, you can adjust two out of those three—sadly, there's no Clarity adjustment…yet!

Intensifying Colors

You can use a Vibrance Adjustment layer (new in Photoshop CS4) to intensify your image's colors. This kind of layer has less of an effect on intense colors (because they're *already* highly saturated) than on lighter tones—yet it manages to leave skin tones relatively unchanged. You can also use a Vibrance Adjustment layer to tweak your image's saturation (it includes a regular ol' Saturation slider), but when you do, Photoshop applies the change evenly to the whole image no matter how intense the colors are and with no regard for skin tones. So if you've got people in your picture, you're better off increasing the Adjustment layer's Vibrance slider and leaving the Saturation slider alone. Figure 9-25 has the scoop.

> **TIP** Since a layer mask tags along with every Adjustment layer, you can always use the Brush tool set to black to protect certain areas from the adjustment (just be sure you have the Adjustment layer's mask selected before you start painting). You can also use the Layers panel's Opacity field to lower the Adjustment layer's opacity and lessen its effect.

Adjusting Hue/Saturation

If you want to make a *specific* color pop, you can use a Hue/Saturation Adjustment layer to boost one color channel's contrast. It's a simple and nondestructive way to accentuate a certain range of colors.

To create a Hue/Saturation Adjustment layer, click its icon in the Adjustments panel (it looks like three gradient bars, and it's to the right of the Vibrance icon) or click the half-black/half-white circle at the bottom of your Layers panel and choose Hue/Saturation. Choose the color you want to intensify from the pop-up menu near the top of the Adjustments panel (which is set to Master until you change it) and then drag the Saturation slider to the right. Be careful not to go hog wild or your color enters the dreaded Neon Realm. You should be fine with a 10 percent to 15 percent saturation increase. Good times!

Adding Lab Pop

Another way to make your colors really jump off the page is to creatively blend color channels while you're in Lab mode (page 183). It's incredibly easy and the results can be amazing. With your image open in Photoshop, follow these steps:

1. **Duplicate your original layer by pressing ⌘-J (Ctrl+J on a PC).**

2. **Pop into Lab mode.**

   Choose Image → Mode → Lab Color. When Photoshop asks if you want to merge layers, tell it no thanks by clicking the Don't Merge button.

POWER USERS' CLINIC

Three Exposures Merged into One: High Dynamic Range Images

Once you get used to peeking at your histograms (page 363), you'll notice that very few images exploit the full range of brightness values from light to dark. More often than not you'll have more info on one end of the histogram than the other, meaning the highlights *or* shadows look really good, but rarely both. That's because digital cameras can collect only so much data in a single shot. If you've got a scene with both light and dark areas—like a beach with dark rocks at sunset—you have to choose which area to expose for: the rocks or the sky. To capture more info, you can shoot multiple takes of the same shot at different exposures and then combine them later in Photoshop into what's known as a High Dynamic Range (HDR) image.

First, dig out your camera's owner's manual and hunt for a feature called *auto-bracketing* (which lets your camera take a series of shots with different settings). Tell your camera how many shots to take (three or more) and how many f-stops to put in between each one (pick two if you have the choice). For example, for three shots, you'd have one at normal exposure, one that's two f-stops lighter than normal, and one that's two f-stops darker than normal. After you've taken a few series shots with these settings you can upload them to your computer (see Appendix C to learn how to upload using Bridge).

In Photoshop, choose File → Automate → "Merge to HDR" and navigate to where the images live on your hard drive. Photoshop combines the images into one document and auto-aligns them on separate layers (page 283). When it's finished (depending on your computer, this process can take a while), you see the "Merge to HDR" dialog box. From the Bit Depth pop-up menu at the top right, choose 32 Bit/Channel and then click OK.

Next, you need to compress all the extra info into a regular 16-bit image by *tone mapping* (mapping one set of colors to another). You can do that in Photoshop or with third-party software like Photomatix (*www.hdrsoft.com*),

which is quite a bit simpler and faster. If you want to stick with Photoshop, choose Image → Mode → 16 Bits/Channel. In the resulting HDR Conversion dialog box, pick a conversion method:

- **Highlight Compression** makes the brightest part of your image white, even if it's *brighter* than white in the 32-bit file. Pick this method if you want to see details in your image's highlights without messing with the overall image contrast.

- **Exposure and Gamma** lets you adjust the image's exposure to make the highlights brighter or the shadows darker. Drag the Exposure slider to the right to brighten the highlights, and use the Gamma slider to set the comparative brightness difference (across the series of shots) between shadows and the highlights. Drag it to the left to darken the shadows or to the right to brighten them.

- **Equalize Histogram** gives you a peek at what your blended image looks like. It doesn't work quite as well as the other methods because it doesn't have as many options, and it tends to make the darkest shadows black.

- **Local Adaption** lets you apply a Curve to your HDR image right there in the HDR Conversion dialog box. Choose this option if you've mastered Curves (page 379).

Click OK when you're finished and admire your new HDR image. You should be warned that once you go HDR, you may not come back! The conversion process takes time, but it can produce the most stunning (albeit unrealistis!) images you've ever seen. To learn more, check out Ben Willmore's *HDR Mastery* DVD at *www.digitalmastery. com*.

Figure 9-25:
To create a Vibrance Adjustment layer, click its button in the Adjustments panel (it looks like V-shaped triangle) or click the half-black/half-white circle at the bottom of the Layers panel and choose Vibrance. Unlike a regular saturation adjustment, a Vibrance Adjustment layer won't completely destroy skin tones, even if you boost its Vibrance slider to 100 percent, as shown here.

3. **Choose Image → Apply Image.**

   If you're dealing with a multi-layered document, choose the layer you want to adjust from (you guessed it) the Layer pop-up menu.

4. **In the Apply Image dialog box, change the Blending pop-up menu to Soft Light.**

   As you learned on page 267, this blend mode makes bright areas brighter and dark areas a little darker; it also helps make your colors pop off the page.

5. **In the Channel pop-up menu, pick the channel that makes your image look best.**

   As you choose different channels, take a peek at your image to see how it changes. Remember, this kind of color adjustment is *purely* subjective; there's no right or wrong channel to pick, and the channel that looks the best to you in this image may not look best on another image. Figure 9-26 shows you what this effect looks like using each channel.

6. **If necessary, lower the channel's opacity.**

   If the effect is too intense, you can lower the channel's opacity by entering a new number in the Opacity field. Click OK to close the Apply Image dialog box.

7. **Switch back to RGB mode.**

   Choose Image → Mode → RGB. If Photoshop asks whether you want to merge layers, say no.

You're done! Put your sunglasses on and smile as you enjoy your image's brilliant new colors. You can toggle the duplicate layer's visibility eye on and off to see before and after views.

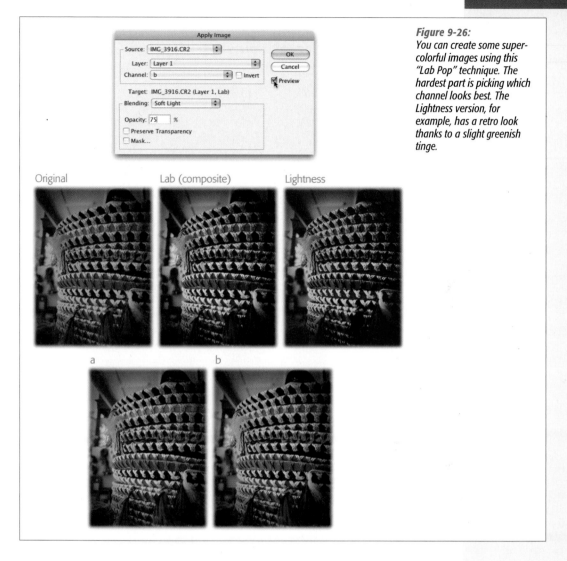

Figure 9-26:
*You can create some super-
colorful images using this
"Lab Pop" technique. The
hardest part is picking which
channel looks best. The
Lightness version, for
example, has a retro look
thanks to a slight greenish
tinge.*

Rescuing the Unfixables

Sadly, even with all the tricks you've learned in this chapter, you can't fix *every*
image. If you run into what seems to be an unfixable photo and you're desperate to
salvage it, try one of these techniques:

- **Use the Lab Pop technique** described on page 386 and use the Lightness channel to create unique, retro-style color.

- **Create an overexposed, high-key effect** (see page 181).

- **Convert it to grayscale.** By draining the color from your image, your color
problems have no choice but to vanish (Chapter 8, beginning on page 300).

Processing Multiple Files

At this point, you've probably realized how time consuming all this image-correction business can be. That's why it's important to know how to save time by correcting more than one image with a single adjustment. Happily, there are several ways to do it:

- **Open multiple files in Camera Raw.** If you're using Camera Raw, you can adjust several files at once by opening them all together, and then clicking the Select All button at the top left of the Camera Raw window. From that point on, Camera Raw applies anything you do to one image to all the others, too (see page 218).

- **Drag and drop Adjustment layers.** If you've (wisely) corrected your image by using Adjustment layers, you can drag and drop them into other open images. That way, you can quickly fix a bunch of images from the same shoot that have similar lighting. Even if you have to tweak the adjustment a tiny bit, it's faster than hunting for highlights, shadows, and midtones in *each* photo.

- **Record repetitive tasks with actions.** While you can't record every aspect of color-correcting because it's unique to each image (or at most applies only to images taken during a single photo shoot), you can automate the little things you do over and over—like duplicating the original layer and adding an Adjustment layer—using *actions*.

Creating a single action that performs those two steps can save you a couple of clicks. You can also automate finishing touches like making color pop (Lab Pop on page 386, for example), record an action for the sharpening techniques in Chapter 11, and so on. See Chapter 18 for more action goodness.

- **Use Adobe Bridge to copy and paste Camera Raw settings**. If you're working on photos from the same shoot that have similar lighting and you don't want to (or can't) open them all at once, you can adjust one and then copy and paste the Camera Raw settings using Bridge. See Appendix C for the lowdown.

- **Use Adobe Bridge to rename a bunch of files at once.** Okay, so this one has nothing to do with correcting your images, but it can still save you some time! If you like renaming your processed files—before correcting them—and then saving them in a different location than your originals (a wise move), you can have Bridge do that for you for an *entire folder* of images. Appendix C shows you how.

- Add a color tint using a Black & White or Photo Filter Adjustment layer (Chapter 8, page 301 or 327, respectively).

- Turn it into a duotone (page 315).

- Use a Threshold adjustment to create a pure black-and-white image (page 312).

- Use a combination of filters to turn your image into a pencil sketch (page 604).

- Use a plug-in like LucisArt to create a super high-contrast, grungy look (page 721).

The Beauty Salon: Photoshopping People

It's certainly no secret that the beautiful models gracing the covers of magazines have been Photoshopped within an inch of their lives. They've had the digital equivalent of every plastic surgery you can imagine, and then some: Skin smoothing, blemish banishing, tummy tucking—they get it all.

This chapter will teach you all those tricks and more, but that doesn't mean you should use every technique on every photo. It's easy to get carried away with this kind of stuff, and with great editing skills comes great responsibility. The challenge is to retouch your subjects enough to *enhance* their appearance without making them look fake. For example, if you're tempted to remove a wrinkle completely, soften it instead. If you'd like to hack off 30 pounds, be content with 5 or 10.

All that aside, there's nothing wrong with a little vanity, and it's darn comforting to know you can zap a zit, whiten teeth, and fix red eye whenever you want (you'll never want to let photos of yourself out into the wild until you've spent some quality time with them). By the time you're finished with this chapter, you'll be able to fix shiny spots, remove unsightly bulges, and enhance eyes with the best of 'em. In other words, you're about to become the most popular picture-fixer-upper in your *entire* social network.

> **NOTE**   For a fascinating profile of one of today's leading Photoshop-using, model-enhancing gurus, check out this *New Yorker* article: *www.newyorker.com/reporting/2008/05/12/080512fa_fact_collins*.

The Great Healers

Some of the simplest retouching you can do is to remove dark circles and bags under eyes, as well as other blemishes. In days of old, you were stuck with cloning (copying) one area of skin onto another, which never *really* looked quite right; texture and tonal (color) differences always made the fix stick out like a sore thumb. Now, Photoshop has a set of tools *specifically* for retouching skin. Instead of grafting skin by cloning, these tools blend two patches of skin together so the texture and tones actually match (see Figure 10-1).

> **NOTE** The first three tools covered in this section (Spot Healing Brush, Healing Brush, and Patch) are all in the same toolset. Press J to activate it and then, if necessary, click the toolset's icon in the Tools panel (what the icon looks like depends on which tool is active) to choose the tool you want. You can also cycle through them by pressing Shift-J until you get to the tool you want.

Figure 10-1:
Top: Photoshop's magical healing tools.

Bottom: As you can see here, a lot of moles—and an eyebrow ring—have completely disappeared. With a few clicks here and a few drags there, you can clean up a photo without making it look obviously retouched. A few of the guy's lighter freckles are still hanging around and the bags under his eyes aren't completely gone; they're just lightened so they're not distracting to the viewer.

The Spot Healing Brush

This tool's cursor is a round brush—perfect for fixing round problem areas like pimples, moles, and so on. It's literally a one-click fixer-upper. You don't even have to drag (though you can if you want). When you click a spot with this tool,

Photoshop looks at the pixels just *outside* the edge of your cursor and blends them with the pixels *inside* your cursor. It's great for retouching people, fixing dust and specks in old photos, and removing anything that's roundish. You can also drag with this tool to remove, say, power lines on a relatively solid background (like a sky) or to fix scratches in old photos.

To use the Spot Healing Brush, grab it from the Tools panel by pressing J (it looks like a band-aid with a circle behind it). Hover your cursor over the blemish and adjust your brush cursor's size so it's slightly larger than the area you want to fix (see Figure 10-2). You can change brush size by using the Brush picker at the top left of the Options bar or by using the left and right bracket keys on your keyboard: press the left bracket key ([) to go down in size, and the right bracket key (]) to go up.

Figure 10-2:
The key to success with the Spot Healing Brush is to make your cursor a little bit larger than the area you want to fix.

TIP   In Photoshop CS4, you can also resize your brush by Ctrl-Option-dragging (Alt+right-click+dragging on a PC) to the left or right.

In the Options bar, in addition to the pop-up menus for changing tool presets, you can tweak these settings:

• **Mode.** This field lists some of the blend modes discussed back in Chapter 7 starting on page 267: Multiply, Screen, Darken, Lighten, Color, and Luminosity, as well as a new one: Replace. Unique to the Healing brushes (both Spot and Healing), Replace is handy if you're using a soft-edged brush because it preserves some of the texture and details around the brush's edges. Normal mode usually works just fine.

• **Type.** This setting controls which pixels Photoshop looks at when it heals things. You've got two options:

— **Proximity Match.** Photoshop comes from the factory with this option selected, which tells the program to use pixels just outside the edge of your cursor to fix the blemish.

— **Create Texture.** Choose this option if the blemish you want to fix is surrounded by tons of details. Instead of looking at pixels outside the edge of your cursor, Photoshop tries to recreate the texture by looking at the pixels *inside* your cursor.

• **Sample All Layers.** Turn on this option if you want to sample pixel info from all layers instead of just the one you're on. Sample All Layers also lets you do the healing on another layer instead of on your original image. Just create a new layer *above* the photo layer and make sure the new layer is active. That way, when you click to fix the spot, the fix happens on the new layer. This technique builds a lot of flexibility into your document because, if you decide you've done too much healing, you can erase those specific areas from the new healing layer or lower the layer opacity of that layer to soften the effect.

The Healing Brush

This tool also blends two areas of skin together, but you have to tell it where to find the skin that looks good. This process, called *setting a sample point*, is how you let Photoshop know which portion of skin—or fur, or whatever—you want it to *sample* (or blend with). To set a point sample, activate the Healing Brush tool by pressing J (or press Shift-J to cycle through the healing tools) and then Option-click (Alt-click on a PC) an unblemished area of skin to set the sample point. Then mouse over to the bad skin and brush it away. This tool works really well on wrinkles, scratches, and so on, and you can make the healing happen on its own layer, as explained in Figure 10-3. And new in Photoshop CS4, you get a live preview of the sample skin right inside your brush cursor, as shown in Figure 10-3.

> **TIP** Anytime you set a sample point, try choosing a spot that's as *near* to the problem skin as possible so the texture and color match better. For example, you wouldn't want to repair skin on Aunt Edna's nose with skin from her neck.

When you activate the Healing Brush tool, the Options bar gives you the following options:

• **Mode.** You get the same set of blend modes for the Healing Brush as you do with the Spot Healing Brush (page 392). Both tools work really well in Normal mode, so you probably don't need to change this setting.

Fixing Spots in Camera Raw

If you find yourself using the Spot Healing Brush repeatedly to fix a pesky speck that appears in the exact same place in every photo you take, you've got dust on your camera's sensor. You'll want to take your camera to a trustworthy shop and have them clean the sensor, or do it yourself with a bit of bravery and the right tools. But fixing the camera doesn't fix the photos you've already taken. Fortunately, you can make Camera Raw zap those spots automatically. Here's how:

1. **Open all the problem images in Camera Raw (see page 54 in Chapter 2).**

2. **In Camera Raw, press B to grab the Spot Removal Brush, click the offending spot, and then drag to resize your cursor.** Clicking makes the brush cursor appear (it's a red-and-white circle) and dragging resizes it. If you click once, you create a super tiny brush, so it's better to drag until the brush is big enough to see. You can also use the Radius slider on the right side of the Camera Raw window to change the brush size. The goal is to make the brush size slightly bigger than the spot itself.

3. **Set your sample point.** When you release the mouse button, Camera Raw displays a green–and–white circle near where you clicked, and the pesky spot should vanish. The green-and-white circle (which is connected to the red-and-white circle by a black-and-white line) marks the *sample point*

Camera Raw is using to the fix the spot. Camera Raw usually does a good job of selecting a sample point, but if you want to move it to another area that better matches the problem spot, hover your cursor inside the green-and-white circle and, when a four-headed arrow appears next to your cursor, drag it somewhere else. If you need to fix several specks, repeat this step for each one until they're all gone. Now you're ready to apply the fix to the other images you have open.

4. **Select all your open images and then click the Synchronize button to apply the changes you just made to them, too.** In the Camera Raw window's top-left corner, click the Select All button and then click the Synchronize button below it. In the resulting dialog box, choose Spot Removal from the Synchronize pop-up menu.

5. **Click OK to close the Synchronize dialog box, and then click the Done button at the bottom of the Camera Raw window to store your changes.** If you have hundreds of images open, you probably don't want to click the Open button. That'll pop 'em *all* open in Photoshop, which could send both your computer and Photoshop into a deep freeze. (Eek!) *Now*, aren't you glad pressing Return (Enter on a PC) in Camera Raw automatically triggers the Done command instead of Open?

- **Source.** You can use a sample (which you choose by Option-clicking [Alt-clicking on a PC]) as your source or you can use a pattern. Photoshop assumes you want to use a sample, but if you turn on the Pattern option, you can pick from the pop-up menu to its right. Healing from a pattern is useful if you don't have enough area in your image to heal *from*. For example, if you're using the Healing Brush to remove graffiti from a wall, you can create a new pattern from part of the wall texture and save it as a reusable pattern.

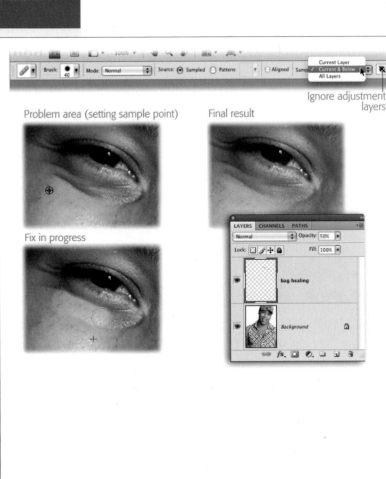

Problem area (setting sample point)

Final result

Fix in progress

Ignore adjustment layers

Figure 10-3:
Top: In the Options bar, set the Sample pop-up menu to Current & Below so you can make the healing happen on a new layer that you've created and placed above the image layer. If you want to sample from all the layers in your document, choose All Layers from the pop-up menu. If you've got some Adjustment layers that you used to alter color hanging around, you can have Photoshop ignore them by turning on the "Ignore Adjustment layers" checkbox to the right of the Sample pop-up menu.

Bottom Left: When you press the Option key (Alt on a PC), your cursor turns into a target so you can click to set a sample point (top). As you start painting over the bad skin, you see a little crosshair marking your sample point (right) that moves along with your brush (in most cases, keeping the two areas together improves your chances of matching the texture and tone).

Bottom Right: By healing on another layer, you can reduce the effect of the healing by lowering that layer's opacity. Here it's set to 50 percent.

TIP You can also sample from another open document as long as both images are in the same color mode. Just hop over to the other document, Option-click (Alt-click) to set a sample point, and then click back in your original document to do the healing (use the Arrange Documents menu in CS4's new Application bar to position both document windows so you can see them [see page 63]). This technique is handy when you want to snatch texture from one image and apply it to another. That way, you let the Healing Brush do the heavy lifting of blending the texture with existing pixels.

- **Aligned.** Turn on this checkbox to keep your sample point aligned with your cursor, even if you release your mouse button and move to another area. By contrast, when this setting is *off*, Photoshop uses the original sample point each time you start to paint even if you move your cursor far away. So if your healing requires several brushstrokes, it's helpful to turn this setting on.

- **Sample.** This pop-up menu lets you choose which layers you want to sample from. To make the healing happen on a separate layer, create a new layer above the one you want to fix and then choose Current & Below. You can also sample from all visible layers by choosing All Layers. If you pick All Layers, you can make Photoshop ignore Adjustment layers by clicking the button of the same name, labeled in Figure 10-3, top.

Here's how to use the Healing Brush:

1. **Add a new layer *above* the layer you want to fix.**

   Click the "Create a new layer" button at the bottom of your Layers panel, and name it something like *Healing*. Make sure it's above the layer you're fixing and that it's selected.

2. **Choose the Healing Brush from the Tools panel.**

   Press J to activate the Healing Brush, whose icon looks like an itty-bitty Band-aid.

3. **In the Options bar, set the Sample pop-up menu to Current & Below.**

   This setting lets you sample pixels from the layer below the current one so the healing happens on the new layer you just created. In other words, you're essentially telling Photoshop: "Create a sample from the current layer and any other layers that lie below it, but make the fixes happen on the layer I'm currently on." This process gives you a ton of flexibility. You can lower the layer's opacity to lessen the healing's strength, change the layer's blend mode, or toss it in the trash if you decide you don't like it.

4. **Mouse over to your document and set a sample point by Option-clicking (Alt-clicking on a PC).**

   Photoshop has no clue where the good skin lives, so you have to tell it by setting a sample point. Option-click (Alt-click) an area of good skin that's similar in texture to the bad skin. It's okay if the sample skin is on the other cheek so long as the texture is the same. As soon as you set the sample point, you're ready to start healing.

5. **Click (or drag across) the area you want to fix.**

   Mouse over to the problem area and click it or drag to paint it away. You'll see a tiny crosshair marking the sample point as you drag. You also see a preview of the sample area inside your cursor as you paint. If you're fixing a small area, like the bags beneath this guy's eyes, you're probably okay with setting just one sample point. If you're fixing a larger area, you may need to set a new sample point every few brushstrokes to match the tone and texture of what you're fixing.

The Patch Tool

The Patch tool may become one of your favorite Photoshop tools because it's so easy to use and does an amazing job. It works like the Healing Brush in that you need to set a sample point, but it's often better than the Healing Brush for fixing big areas like dark circles or bags beneath tired eyes. It's also handy for removing piercings, tattoos, and shiny or shadowy spots. For the Patch tool to work on shines and shadows, you need a patch of good skin the same size as the bad skin or you'll have to patch one small area at a time. In that case, a better option is to use the Clone Tool, described in the next section (page 400).

> **NOTE** With the Patch tool, you can't make the healing happen on another layer like you can with the Spot and Healing brushes (the Patch tool can't sample from other layers), so it's a good idea to duplicate your original layer first by pressing ⌘-J (Ctrl+J on a PC). That way you're not harming your original image.

Grab the Patch tool from the Tools panel, mouse over to your image, and drag to draw an outline around the area you want to fix (marching ants appear when you let go of your mouse button). Next, click anywhere inside the selected area and hold down your mouse button as you reposition the selection outline so it's over a *good* patch of skin (see Figure 10-4, top right). You get a live preview of the good skin in your selection area as you drag (this preview is new in CS4). When you let go of your mouse button, Photoshop blends the two areas.

> **TIP** To drag perfectly vertically or horizontally, hold down Shift as you drag.

The Options bar gives you the following settings for the Patch tool:

> **TIP** If you need to adjust your selection while you're drawing it, use the buttons near the left end of the Options bar to add to or subtract from your selection or to create one from two intersecting areas. Better yet, use these keyboard shortcuts: Shift-drag to add to your selection, Option-drag (Alt-drag on a PC) to subtract from it, and Option-Shift-drag (Alt+Shift-drag) to select an intersecting area.

- **Patch.** This setting has two options:

  — **Source.** Out of the box, Photoshop takes the texture from the good skin and tries to match it with the color and lighting of the area just outside your original selection. To produce unnoticeable patches, leave this radio button turned on.

  — **Destination.** If you'd rather select the good skin first and *then* drag it atop the bad skin, turn on this radio button.

- **Transparent.** Turn on this checkbox if you want to copy an area's texture but not its content. For example, if you're working with a brick wall, you could use this option to copy the texture of the super grungy bricks onto those that look newer, without duplicating the grungy bricks in their entirety. This setting works best when you use it in conjunction with the next setting.

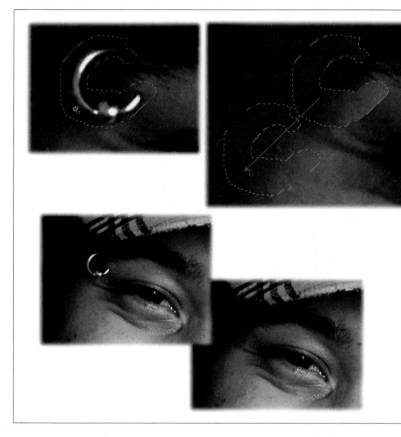

Figure 10-4:
If you need to get rid of a new piercing before the parents see it, the Patch tool can get it done fast.

Top: The Patch tool lets you draw an outline of the offending area freehand (left). Once you see marching ants, click inside the selection and drag it to a good patch of skin and then release your mouse button (right).

Bottom: Problem solved! The Patch tool can help you keep your piercing secret for a little while longer.

- **Use Pattern.** If you want to apply a pattern to the area you've selected with the Patch tool, click this button and then choose a pattern from the pop-up menu next to it. You'll rarely use this option, because instead of merely making Photoshop copy and blend pixels from one area to another, it adds the pattern you picked from the pop-up menu to the selected area. That said, it can be useful if you're trying to add texture to an area that doesn't have any.

As soon as you apply a patch, check to see if the effect is too strong (like in Figure 10-5, top right) because you've got exactly *one* chance to fade it. Before you use any other tool or create adjustment layers, choose Edit → Fade Patch Selection. Position the resulting dialog box so you can see your image and use the dialog box's slider or Opacity field to tweak the opacity until the patch looks more realistic. Click OK when you're finished.

> **TIP**   It's a little known fact that you can actually select the area you want to patch *before* choosing the Patch tool. That way, you can use any selection method you want (see Chapter 4) instead of drawing the selection freehand. You can also draw straight lines with the Patch tool by Option-clicking (Alt-clicking on a PC).

Figure 10-5:
Top: Here's what this woman's dark circles look like before (left) and after (right) using the Patch tool. As you can see, the result is too blurry.

Bottom: With the Fade dialog box, you can lower the patch's opacity to lessen the effect. If you want to hide the marching ants while you decide how much to fade the patch (which can make it easier to see how well the patch blends into the surrounding skin), press ⌘-H (Ctrl+H on a PC); press it again to bring 'em back.

Zapping Shines and Shadows

Shiny spots, (or *hot spots*, as some folks call them) are truly evil. They can ruin a perfectly good photo by making your subject look like a big ol' sweat ball. That's okay if the person just finished a marathon—glistening is certainly expected—but not if she's sitting for a portrait. Fortunately, the Clone Stamp tool can get rid of shiny spots and unsightly shadows in a hurry. It works by copying pixels from one area of the image to another (see Figure 10-6).

> **NOTE** Be careful not to erase *all* the shine and *all* the shadows in your images; you want to leave a little bit hanging around so the photo looks real. The goal is to remove just enough shine and shadows that viewers aren't distracted by them.

Here's how to reduce shine and shadows with the Clone Stamp tool:

1. **Open your photo and create a new layer named** *Shine.*

   Make sure this layer is *above* the image layer you want to fix. Remember, by doing your skin-fixing on another layer, you're protecting the original image and giving yourself the option of reducing the strength of the fix by reducing the layer's opacity.

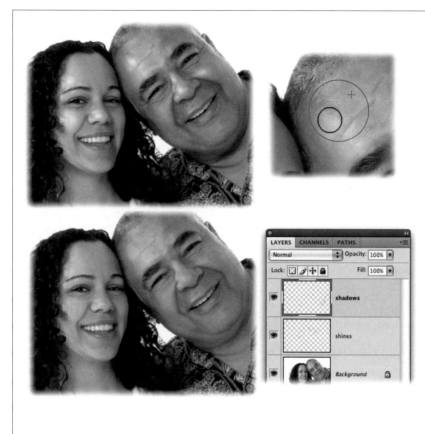

Figure 10-6:
Top: This photo would be worth framing if the subjects weren't so shiny (left). To fix that problem, grab the Clone Stamp tool and set your sample point as close to the shiny area as possible to match tone and texture (right). Be careful not to let your sample point (the crosshair) go into the shiny area itself, or you'll replicate the shine.

Bottom: Now you can print that photo with pride. No more shiny spots! The shadows on their faces and necks have also been lightened. And by setting the Sample pop-up menu to All Layers (see page 402, step 5), you haven't harmed your original image. Toggle the visibility of the layers you just added off and on for a quick before-and-after comparison.

2. **Grab the Clone Stamp tool from the Tools panel.**

   Press S to activate the Clone Stamp tool, which looks like a rubber stamp (in fact, that's what it used to be called: the Rubber Stamp tool).

3. **In the Options bar, choose a soft-edge brush and change the blend mode to Darken.**

   Choosing Darken from the Mode pop-up menu makes Photoshop darken any areas lighter than the sample point to darken the shiny area.

4. **Also in the Options bar, lower the Opacity setting to 20–30 percent.**

   If you leave the tool's opacity at 100 percent, you'll perform a full-on skin graft, and the retouching will be painfully obvious. Lowering the opacity lets you fix the area little by little; the more you paint, the more skin gets cloned (or copied).

5. **Set the Sample pop-up menu to All Layers.**

   To make the cloning (copying) happen on another layer, you have to tell Photoshop to sample other layers. Now you're all set to start cloning.

6. **Create a sample point for the first shiny part.**

   Mouse over to your document and Option-click (Alt-click on a PC) some non-shiny skin. Make sure this sample point is as close to the shiny skin as possible so it'll match.

7. **Drag to paint away the shiny skin.**

   As you drag, you see a little crosshair representing your sample point. Keep a close eye on it because if it heads into a shiny patch, you'll paint a shine with a shine. If that happens, don't panic; just set another sample point by following step 6 again. When you've fixed one shiny spot, mouse over to another and repeat steps 6 and 7.

8. **Create another new layer and name it *Shadows*.**

   Click the "Create a new layer" button at the bottom of your Layers panel, give the layer a name in the resulting dialog box, and then click OK. You'll use this layer for the fixes you make to the shadowed regions.

9. **In the Options bar, change the Mode setting to Lighten.**

   With this setting, the tool lightens only areas that are darker than the sample point. This technique works wonders for shadowy double chins and deep crevices—pretty much any problem area that's too dark.

10. **Set a new sample point and paint the shadow away.**

    Option-click (Alt-click) to set your sample point as close to the shadowy area as possible and drag to make it go bye-bye. Repeat steps 9 and 10 until you've taken care of all the shadow problems.

11. **Save your document as a PSD file.**

    That way, you can go back and change your fixes later.

Print that baby out and slap it into the nearest frame!

Whitening Teeth

If you've ever enjoyed a big cup of coffee or a Texas-sized glass of red wine and then had your picture taken, you'll want to bookmark this page. Stained teeth are even more embarrassing than shiny spots, but they're easy to fix (see Figure 10-7). The hardest part of whitening teeth is selecting the little buggers in the first place, but that step got easier when Adobe added the Quick Selection tool in Photoshop CS3.

Figure 10-7:
Once you select the teeth (top), you can fix them with a Hue/Saturation Adjustment layer (bottom left). That way, the fixing happens on its own layer so you're not harming the original image (bottom right).

Here's how to make those pearly whites, well, white:

1. **Open your image and zoom in so you can see the teeth.**

   Press ⌘ and the + key (Ctrl and the + key on a PC) to zoom in on your document. Press ⌘ (Ctrl) and the – key to zoom out.

2. **Open a duplicate of your image and leave it at close to actual size.**

   Choose Window → Arrange → "New window for [your document's name]". Since it's so doggone easy to overwhiten teeth, it's helpful to keep an eye on a copy of the same image at roughly the size you plan to print it. The cool part is that Photoshop reflects what you do in one window in the other window—in real time—because it's the same document.

   It's good to get into the habit of opening a duplicate in a new window when you're doing detail work because it keeps you from getting carried away with fixing individual pixels while you're zoomed in. Nine times out of ten, when the image is at normal size, your teeny-tiny changes are barely noticeable, if you can see them at all. This duplicate window trick helps you see what kind of effect your changes have at actual size.

3. **Select the teeth.**

   You can use any selection method you learned in Chapter 4. Since the teeth are basically white, one good option is the Quick Selection tool (page 137) to paint across them, and then pop into Quick Mask mode (page 162) to refine your selection.

4. **Add a Hue/Saturation Adjustment layer.**

   Click the half-black/half-white circle at the bottom of the Layers panel and choose Hue/Saturation from the resulting list.

5. **Lower the Adjustment layer's saturation and increase its lightness.**

   In the Adjustments panel, drag the Saturation slider to the left and the Lightness slider to the right. Keep an eye on both document windows to make sure you don't make the person's teeth unnaturally white.

6. **Open your Masks panel by choosing Window → Masks and then soften your selection's edges by dragging the Feather slider slightly to the right (one pixel should be fine).**

   NOTE   If you don't have Photoshop CS4, you'll need to do your feathering after you make the selection in step 3 by Ctrl-clicking (right-clicking on a PC) and choosing Feather from the resulting shortcut menu. A feather amount of one pixel should do the trick.

7. **Save your document as a PSD file.**

   If you decide you want to tweak the teeth again later, just open the file again, double-click the Adjustment layer, and fiddle with the sliders to your heart's content.

This method is sufficient to whip most teeth into shape. But if you encounter a set with a serious yellow cast, there's one extra step you can take: In the Hue/Saturation adjustments panel, choose Yellows from the pop-up menu near the top of the panel and then drag the Saturation slider slightly to the left.

TIP   You can use the technique described in the list above to whiten eyes, too, but you don't have to reduce the saturation since increasing the lightness should do the trick.

Super Slimmers

Photoshop CS4 has a bunch of tools you can use to do some serious slimming so you can fix flabby chins and paunchy waistlines and instantly shave off five pounds. Tools of the body-sculpting trade include the Pinch and Liquify filters, the Clone Stamp tool, and more, all explained in this section. Read on!

Fixing Flabby Chins

You can suck the life out of a flabby chin with the Pinch filter. It sounds gross, but it makes a *huge* difference and takes mere seconds. All you have to do is make a rough selection—the Lasso tool (page 151) works well—that includes the flab and some of the surrounding details, as shown in Figure 10-8 (bottom left). Then choose Filter → Distort → Pinch and, in the resulting dialog box, enter *20* in the Amount field, and then click OK. If you need to pinch it a little more, press ⌘-F (Ctrl+F on a PC) to run the filter again. Easy, huh?

Figure 10-8:
Top: If you click in the Pinch filter's dialog box preview window and hold down your mouse button, Photoshop shows you the prepinched version of your image. You can drag to move the image around (your cursor turns into a little hand). You can also use the + and – buttons below the preview window to zoom into or out of your image.

Bottom: A fix like this one will earn you loyal clients for life!

TIP   As you'll learn in this chapter, filters are destructive (they change your image's pixels). But you can protect your original image if you duplicate the image layer first by pressing ⌘-J (Ctrl+J on a PC). Or flip over to page 588 to get the scoop on Smart Filters.

Liquifying Bulges

Drastic bulges call for drastic action, and the Liquify filter is as drastic as it gets in Photoshop. It lets you push, pull, and pucker pixels any which way you want. You can use it to get your waistline under control, add a smile, enlarge lips, and so on (see Figure 10-9).

Figure 10-9:
If you use the Liquify filter's Push Left tool, you can eliminate any bulge you want. If only this trick worked in real life!

NOTE Give the following maneuver a try yourself. Visit this book's Missing CD page (*www. missingmanuals.com*) and download the practice file Lovehandles.jpg.

Here's how to do some serious bulge busting:

1. **Pop open your photo and duplicate the image layer.**

   To protect your original pixels, duplicate the image (Background) layer by pressing ⌘-J (Ctrl+J on a PC). That way, if you get carried away and create a lumpy mess or an alien, waiflike creature, you can trash this layer and start over.

2. **Choose Filter → Liquify.**

   Photoshop opens the humongous Liquify dialog box, which may take over your whole screen.

3. **Grab the Push Left tool and increase your brush size.**

   The Liquify dialog box has a small toolbar on its left side. Grab the Push Left tool by clicking its icon in the toolbar (it looks like a checkered column of pixels poked by a left-facing arrow—it's selected in Figure 10-9). You can also press O to select the tool (that's the letter *o*, not the number zero). Though you can use the Tool Options section on the right side of the dialog box to pick a bigger brush, it's simpler to press the right bracket key (]) to increase brush size or the left bracket key ([) to decrease it.

   NOTE The Ctrl-Option-drag (Alt+right-click+drag on a PC) keyboard shortcut that lets you resize your brush in CS4 does *not* work in the Liquify dialog box.

4. **Mouse over to the bulge on the right side of the body and drag *upward*.**

   If you need to, move your image around in the preview window by pressing the space bar and dragging with your mouse. Once you've got a good view of the bulge you're getting rid of, position your cursor so the crosshair touches the background and the edge of the brush touches the bulge where it starts down at the waistband. Push the bulge back toward the torso by dragging *upward*. If you think that's weird, you're not alone; nobody knows why this process scoots pixels to the left, but it does.

5. **Move to the left side of the body and drag *downward*.**

   Press the space bar and drag to move to the other side of your image. This time, position your cursor at the *top* of the bulge and then drag *down* to nudge the pixels to the right. Again, why this tool works this way is a mystery.

6. **Click OK when you're finished.**

   TIP   To undo a single nudge, press ⌘-Z (Ctrl+Z on a PC). To undo *everything* you've done with the Liquify filter without closing the Liquify dialog box, press Option (Alt) and the Cancel button changes to read Reset. Click it to get the original image back. You can also use the Reconstruct tool discussed below.

You make all the tools in the Liquify dialog box work by holding down your mouse button or by dragging. Figure 10-10 gives you an idea of what the other tools can do.

Here are the other tools in the Liquify dialog box:

- **Forward Warp.** Use this tool to push pixels forward (ahead of your cursor in the direction you're dragging) or Shift-drag with it to push pixels in a straight line. Forward Warp is another great bulge-buster, and you can also use it to make your subjects smile whether they want to or not. Its keyboard shortcut is W.

- **Reconstruct.** Think of this one as an undo brush. If you want to restore your pixels to their original state, paint over them with this tool. Keyboard shortcut: R.

- **Twirl Clockwise.** If you want to spin your pixels clockwise as if they were going down a drain, grab this tool. You can click and hold or drag with this tool. Option-drag (Alt-drag on a PC) to make the pixels rotate counterclockwise. Keyboard shortcut: C.

- **Pucker.** This tool collapses pixels in on themselves like the Pinch filter (page 405). You can use it to make a tummy or thigh look smaller or shrink a flabby chin, a large nose, and so on. To make it have the opposite effect, press Option (Alt) so that it acts like the Bloat tool. Keyboard shortcut: S.

- **Bloat.** Use Bloat to enlarge pixels from the center out. If you're considering collagen injections to fluff up your lips, try this tool first. It's also useful for opening up squinty eyes. Keyboard shortcut: B.

Original | Forward warp | Twirl

Pucker | Bulge | Mirror | Turbulence

Figure 10-10:
Here's a sampling of what the Liquify tools can do for you (or to you). Picasso and Salvador Dali would have loved Turbulence.

- **Mirror.** This tool copies pixels from one spot to another and reverses them to create a reflection. Keyboard shortcut: M.

- **Turbulence.** To stir and scramble your pixels in random ways, use Turbulence. It can come in handy if you're trying to create realistic-looking fire or clouds. Keyboard shortcut: T.

- **Freeze Mask.** To protect an area from any of the Liquify filter's other tools, paint over it with this tool and you'll see the red overlay of Quick Mask (page 162). It's similar to painting with black in a layer mask (page 105). Keyboard shortcut: F.

- **Thaw Mask.** To release pixels you've protected with the Freeze Mask, paint across them with this tool to make the red overlay disappear. It's the equivalent of painting with white in a layer mask (page 105). Keyboard shortcut: D.

- **Hand.** This Hand tool is the same one that you get by pressing the space bar or clicking the hand icon in the Application bar (page 12). You can use it to move around your image when you're zoomed in. Keyboard shortcut: H.

- **Zoom.** You can use this tool to zoom in and out of your document though it's quicker to press ⌘ (Ctrl on a PC) and the + or – key instead. Keyboard shortcut: Z.

Slimming with the Free Transform

A couple of years ago, Hewlett-Packard came out with a "slimming camera" that they promised would make you look 10 pounds slimmer in every picture. Behind the scenes, the camera's software was squishing the sides of your image inward (reducing its width), making you appear slightly thinner. You can do the exact same thing with Photoshop's Free Transform tool, as shown in Figure 10-11.

Figure 10-11:
Hey, squirrels need slimming. too! If you're slimming a photo while you're working in public, be sure to look over both shoulders first. You don't want to reveal this kind of retouching secret to just anyone.

Here's how to lose five pounds instantly:

1. **Pop open the soon-to-be-slimmer photo and double-click the Background layer to make it editable.**

   If your layer isn't locked (page 80), you can skip the double-clicking.

2. **Summon Free Transform.**

   When you press ⌘-T (Ctrl+T on a PC), Photoshop puts a bounding box around your whole image. Grab the little square handle in the middle of the right or left edge of your photo (it doesn't matter which). Drag the handle inward while keeping an eye on the Option's bars W field. You want to make your image between 5 and 8 percent narrower (so the W value is 92–95 percent); if you narrow it any more than that, your image will look stretched out. (You can also type a new width into the W field.) When you've got the width just right, release your mouse button and press Return (Enter) to accept the transform.

3. **Crop the image to get rid of the newly transparent area.**

   Grab the Crop tool by pressing C, draw a box around your image to nip that extra quarter inch or so off the side, and then press Return (Enter).

This simple retouch is absolutely impossible to spot—if you keep it between 5 and 8 percent, that is. Anything more and your subject will look decidedly smooshed.

Selective Slimming

Instead of using Free Transform to squish the whole image, you can use it to squish only a certain part. Just create a selection and then summon Free Transform by pressing ⌘-T (Ctr+T on a PC). Figure 10-12 has the details.

Skin Softeners

Your skin is your body's largest organ though not everyone gives it the respect it deserves. We sometimes forget to use sunblock, moisturizer, and so on. This section teaches you how to make skin look like it's *really* well cared for. You'll learn how to make it look soft and glowing, and even how to reduce lines and wrinkles, all without spending tons of money on anti-aging creams.

Selective Blur

One of the fastest ways to smooth skin is to give it a good dose of the Gaussian Blur filter (it's named for the gentleman who invented this blur method, Carl Gauss). This filter is often the only skin fixer you need, and it's faster than the Healing brushes you learned about earlier in this chapter. The beauty of this filter is that you can run it on a separate layer, lower its layer's opacity, and use a layer mask to apply it only where you need it (see Figure 10-13).

Figure 10-12:
Top: If you create a selection first, you can use Free Transform to shrink just the selected area. You may need to go back and use the Healing Brush to blend certain areas after you're finished.

Bottom: This before-and-after shot shows quite a difference, no?

TIP   You can also use this technique to create a "shallow depth of field" effect in which the background is blurry and your subject is in focus.

To soften skin, follow these steps:

1. **Duplicate the Background layer.**

   Press ⌘-J (Ctrl+J on a PC) to duplicate the Background layer. If you want to use a layer mask to keep certain parts of your subject from getting blurred (like her eyes, hair, and so on), you need to run the filter on another layer. You can also adjust the intensity of the blur effect by lowering this layer's opacity, which you'll do in step 6.

2. **With the duplicate layer selected, choose Filter → Blur → Gaussian Blur.**

   In the resulting dialog box, adjust the Radius slider until your image is severely blurred (a radius of 8 was used to create Figure 10-13). Don't worry if you start to lose details; you can use the layer's opacity to lessen the effect in a minute.

Figure 10-13:
Just like Robitussin and duct tape, the Gaussian Blur filter can darn near fix anything. As this image shows, it made this woman's skin look nice and smooth by lessening the intensity of her freckles without removing them completely.

TIP   If you click in the Gaussian Blur dialog box's preview window and hold down your mouse button, Photoshop shows you the unblurred version of your image. You can drag to move the image around.

3. **Add a layer mask filled with black.**

    As you've learned, in the realm of layer masks, black conceals and white reveals. Since you need to keep the majority of the image unblurred so folks can tell it's a face, save yourself some time by starting out with a black mask. Make sure the blurry layer is selected and then add a black-filled layer mask by Option-clicking (Alt-clicking) the circle-within-a-square button at the bottom of your Layers panel. Photoshop masks the whole layer, hiding all the extra blur from your image.

4. **Press B to grab the Brush tool and set your foreground color chip to white.**

    Peek at the color chips at the bottom of your Tools panel. Press D to set the chips to black and white and then press X until white hops on top.

5. **With a fairly large, soft-edged brush, paint part of the skin you want to blur.**

    Painting with white reveals the blurry layer. Be sure to avoid your subject's eyes, lips, nostrils, and hair. If you reveal too much of the blur layer, press X to flip-flop color chips and paint that area with black.

6. Lower the opacity of the blurry layer to around 75 percent.

At the top of your Layers panel, change the Opacity field's setting to about 75 percent or until the skin looks pretty natural.

Easy Glamour Glow

A quick way to add an ethereal glow to skin is to use the Diffuse Glow filter. As with Gaussian Blur, you want to create a special layer to run this filter on. Building on the skin-softening technique you learned about in the previous section, you can merge the original layer and the blur layer you created into a single layer that you'll run the filter on (this technique is called *stamping*).

Just Shift-click to select the two layers in your Layers panel and, while you press Option (Alt on a PC), choose Merge Layers from the Layers panel menu. Photoshop merges the two layers into one and puts the merged layer at the top of your Layers panel. When you choose Filter → Distort → Diffuse Glow, up pops the giant Diffuse Glow dialog box shown in Figure 10-14, top.

Figure 10-14:
Top: This filter adds a serious amount of grain to your image, so grab the Graininess slider and drag it all the way to the left. Set the Glow Amount to about 5 and leave the Clear Amount set to 15. Click OK when you're finished.

Bottom: Back in your Layers panel, change the glow layer's blend mode to Luminosity so you're shifting only the image's lightness value, not its color, and reduce the layer's opacity to about 75 percent.

Softening Wrinkles with Faux Dodge and Burn

You've already seen a couple of tools that can reduce wrinkles: the Healing Brush (page 394) and the Clone Stamp tool (page 400). Another option is to slightly lighten or darken the wrinkled area so the wrinkling isn't so severe.

You could reach for the Dodge and Burn tools to perform this task; after all, they're designed to lighten and darken pixels (respectively). These tools hail from the days when photographers developed their own film, disappearing mysteriously into a broom closet with an amber light and emerging hours later with dilated pupils and reeking of pungent chemicals. Without diving too deeply into what goes on in darkrooms, a photo is created by projecting an image onto special paper. During this process, if you block some of the light by holding an object in front of the light source, the resulting image will be lightened or *dodged* in the area that was exposed to less light. If you *increase* the amount of light that hits a certain area, that part of the image will be darkened or *burned*.

> **NOTE** The Dodge tool's icon looks like a lollipop because you could theoretically block light from hitting your developing image by holding something in front of it that looks like a circle on a stick. The Burn tool's icon looks like a hand because you could use your hand to cover the areas that you want to keep lighter while you let light through your curled fingers. The icons are a bit of a stretch, but they make more sense when you know how the tools originated.

In Photoshop, you've got a fair amount of control over how the Dodge and Burn tools work. They each have a Range pop-up menu that lets you choose which pixels get altered—shadows, midtones, or highlights. You can also control the strength of the tools' effects by adjusting the Exposure setting, which works kind of like opacity. But it's important to remember that these tools are darn destructive (even though both tools were redesigned for CS4 so they don't completely destroy skin tones when you use them). You can't make them work on a layer other than your original image unless you duplicate your image, and both of them can change the color of pixels, which might make your image look worse than it did before you started messing with it. Finally, it's a pain to have to keep trotting up to the Options bar to adjust the Range and Exposure settings. That being said, they can certainly lighten and darken parts of your image though you need to duplicate the layer first so you're not affecting the original image. Also, be sure to lower the Options bar's Exposure setting before you use them.

A better solution is to use the Brush tool so it *behaves* like the Dodge and Burn tools. By filling a layer with 50 percent gray and changing its blend mode to Soft Light (page 274), you can do exactly that (see Figure 10-15).

> **TIP** This technique isn't just good for softening wrinkles. It's a great way to lighten or darken *any* part of your image though it's especially helpful on portraits.

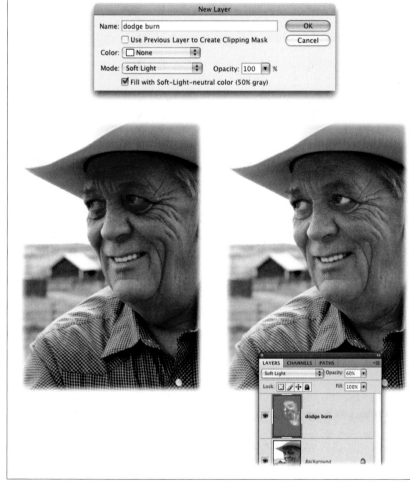

Figure 10-15:
Top: A quick way to create a layer you can use for your faux dodging and burning is to use the New Layer dialog box; press ⌘-Shift-N (Ctrl+Shift+N on a PC) to call it up. Set the Mode menu to Soft Light and then turn on the "Fill with Soft-Light-neutral color (50% gray)" checkbox and click OK.

Bottom: When you use faux dodge and burn, your subject retains his character but his wrinkles aren't so distracting. Notice how much brighter his eyes are, too. The whites were dodged and the darker rim of color around the outer edge of each iris was burned.

Here's how to do some faux dodging and burning:

1. **Open your image and, in your Layers panel, Option-click (Alt-click on a PC) the "Create a new layer" button.**

   In the resulting dialog box, name your new layer *Dodge Burn*, choose Soft Light from the Mode pop-up menu, turn on the "Fill with Soft-Light-neutral color (50% gray)" checkbox, and then click OK. Sure, you could create a new layer, use the Edit → Fill command to fill it with gray, and then change its Mode setting, but this way is faster.

2. **Press B to grab the Brush tool and set its opacity to 10–20 percent.**

   To touch up your image gradually, lower the brush's opacity to something between 10 and 20 percent. Yes, it'll take longer to retouch your image, but you can dodge and burn little by little, which is better than doing too much at once.

3. **Set your foreground color chip to white for dodging.**

Take a peek at the color chips at the bottom of your Tools panel. Press D to set them to black and white, then press X to flip-flop them so white's on top.

4. **Mouse over to your image and paint across the dark wrinkles.**

To lighten just the shadowy parts of the wrinkles, you need to use a small brush (or else you'll lighten areas that don't need to be lightened). It's also helpful to zoom *way* into your image when you're doing detailed work like this. You can zoom in or out by pressing ⌘ (Ctrl on a PC) and the + or – key. Photoshop CS4 gives you a new pixel-grid view when you zoom in more than 500 percent (see page 56).

5. **Swap color chips so that your foreground color is black and then paint light areas that you need to burn (darken).**

If the wrinkles are so deep that they cause highlights, you can darken those a little. In Figure 10-15 the edge of each iris was also darkened to make the man's eyes look brighter.

6. **Lower the Dodge Burn layer's opacity slightly.**

If you've overdone the changes a bit, you can lower the layer's opacity.

7. **Save your document as a PSD file in case you ever need to go back and alter it.**

Show-Stopping Eyes

One of the simplest yet most impressive eye-enhancing techniques is waiting for you over in Chapter 11. Just as you can selectively blur an image, you can also selectively sharpen it. Hop on over to page 437 to see how to use sharpening to make eyes really pop. Here in this section you'll learn how to enhance and whiten eyes, fix red eye a bazillion different ways, and get the scoop on fixing your furry friends' eyes.

Enhancing Eyes

A quick and painless way to make eyes stand out and look sultry is to lighten them by changing their blend mode to Screen. This technique enhances the iris *and* brightens the white bits at the same time, as Figure 10-16 shows. To achieve this effect without duplicating the original layer (which increases your file's size), you can use an empty Adjustment layer.

Here's how to quickly enhance eyes:

1. **Pop open a photo and add an empty Adjustment layer.**

Click the half-black/half-white circle at the bottom of the Layers panel and choose Levels from the menu. When the Adjustments panel opens, click the double arrows at its top right or the dark gray bar at the top of the panel to close it (you don't need to actually make a levels adjustment).

Figure 10-16:
If you use an empty Adjustment layer set to Screen mode, you can add a whole new dimension to your subject's eyes. (The original image is at left and the adjusted image is on the right.) The cool thing about this technique is that it enhances the iris and the white part simultaneously.

2. **Set the Adjustment layer's blend mode to Screen.**

   At the top left of the Layers panel, use the pop-up menu to change the blend mode to Screen. When you do, Photoshop makes your whole photo *way* too light, but don't panic—you'll fix it in the next step.

3. **Fill the Adjustment layer's mask with black.**

   Peek in your Layers panel and make sure the Adjustment layer's mask is selected (it should have a tiny black outline around it). To hide the over-lightening from the last step, choose Edit → Fill, pick Black from the Use pop-up menu, and then click OK.

4. **Grab the Brush tool and set the foreground color chip to white.**

   Press B to grab the Brush tool and then glance at the color chips at the bottom of the Tools panel. If white's on top, you're good to go. If it's not, press D to set the chips to black and white and then press X until white is on top. Now you're ready to paint a hole through the mask so the lightening will show through only on your subject's eyes.

5. **Paint the eye area.**

   Mouse over to your image and paint the eyeballs. If you mess up, just press X to flip-flop the color chips and paint with black.

6. **Duplicate the Adjustment layer.**

   Once you've got the mask just right, you can intensify the effect by duplicating the Adjustment layer. Press ⌘-J (Ctrl+J on a PC) to duplicate the layer and lower the duplicate's opacity to about 50 percent.

7. Save the image as a PSD file.

Ta-da! This technique makes a galactic difference, and your subject's eyes will pop off the page.

Fixing Red Eye

One of the most annoying things about taking photos with a flash is the creepy red eyes it can give your subjects. Photoshop's Red Eye tool does a good job on most cases of red eye though sometimes you'll encounter a really stubborn case that just refuses to go away. That's why it's good to have a few tricks up your sleeve, including stealing pupils from another channel, using the Color Replacement tool, creating a Hue/Saturation Adjustment layer, or fixing 'em in Camera Raw. This section explains all those options.

The Red Eye tool

Oh, man, if only all of Photoshop's tools were as easy to use as this one! The Red Eye tool is part of the Healing Brush toolset (it looks like an eye with a plus sign next to it). Just grab the tool, mouse over to your document, and draw a box around the eye, as shown in Figure 10-17, top. As soon as you let go of your mouse button, Photoshop hunts for the red inside the box and makes it black. That's all there is to it!

Figure 10-17:
Contrary to what you might think, it's better to draw a box around the whole eyeball rather than just around the pupil. For some odd reason, the smaller the box, the less effective the Red Eye tool is.

WORKAROUND WORKSHOP

Stealing Pupils from Channels

Why bother with all this red-eye fixing mumbo jumbo when you've got perfectly good black pupils in your Channels panel? Since Photoshop doesn't display channels in color, the pupils aren't red. There's certainly no law saying you can't pop into your image's channels and snatch the pupils from there.

Here's how to do it:

1. Open your Channels panel by clicking its icon in the panel dock (page 17) or by choosing Window → Channels. Then stroll through the channels by clicking each one or by pressing ⌘-3, 4, 5 (Ctrl+3, 4, 5) to find the channel where the pupils are darkest (it's most likely the Green channel). If you happen to be in CMYK mode, you've got one extra channel to look at, which you can see by pressing ⌘-6 (Ctrl+6).

2. Grab the Elliptical Marquee tool (page 127) and draw a selection that's slightly larger than the pupil in one eye. Then press and hold the Shift key to draw a selection around the other pupil.

3. Ctrl-click (right-click) in one of the selections (it doesn't matter which one) and choose Feather from the resulting shortcut menu. In the next dialog box, enter *1* in the Feather Radius field and then click OK.

4. Copy the pupils by pressing ⌘-C (Ctrl+C on a PC) and turn the composite channel (page 172) back on by pressing ⌘-2 (Ctrl-2).

5. Open your Layers panel and create a new layer for the pupils: Click the "Create a new layer" button at the bottom of the panel, name the layer *New Pupils,* and then place it above the photo layer.

6. Paste the pupils onto the new layer. Press ⌘-V (Ctrl+V) to paste the pupils. Poof—you're done! Your subject should look much less demonic now.

The Color Replacement tool

Another option for getting rid of super-stubborn red eye is the Color Replacement tool. If you choose black as your foreground color chip, you can use this tool to replace the red with black. But because this tool is destructive (and because there's no way of knowing what kind of job it'll do), it's best to select the eyes and jump them onto their own layer first.

Here's what you do:

1. **Select the eyes and copy them onto another layer.**

   Using the Lasso tool (page 151), draw a rough selection around each eye (grab the whole eye, not just the pupil) and then press ⌘-J (Ctrl+J on a PC) to jump the eyes onto their own layer. That way, if this technique goes south, you can toss this layer and start over.

2. **Select the Color Replacement tool from the Tools panel.**

   It's hiding within the Brush toolset, and it looks like a brush with a tiny curved arrow pointing to a black square (the square is supposed to represent your foreground color chip). You can press Shift-B repeatedly to cycle through the toolset.

3. **Set your foreground color chip to black.**

Press D to set your color chips to black and white, and then press X until black hops on top. You can also set the new color by Option-clicking (Alt-clicking on a PC) an eyelash or other black part of the eye.

4. **In the Options bar, set the Mode field to Hue, the Limits field to Contiguous, and the Tolerance field to around 30 percent.**

Choosing the Hue blend mode means you're replacing color without altering its brightness (for more on blend modes, see page 267). The Contiguous setting means that you want Photoshop to replace only the red pixels that are clustered in one spot and not separated by other colors. The Tolerance setting determines how picky the tool is: lower numbers make the tool pickier; higher numbers result in a color-replacing free-for-all.

5. **Paint the red away.**

You'll want to use a small brush for this maneuver. Press the left bracket key ([) to cycle down in brush size, and the right bracket key (]) to cycle up. Or in CS4, Ctrl-Option-drag (Alt+right-click+drag on a PC) to the left or right to decrease or increase your brush size. When you've got a size that looks good, mouse over to the pupils and paint over the red, being careful to touch *only* the red with your cursor's crosshair.

6. **When you're finished painting, use the Eraser tool or a layer mask to clean up the area just outside the pupil, if necessary.**

If you end up with a little black outside the pupil, you can use the Eraser tool (see Appendix E, online at *www.missingmanuals.com*) to fix it because you'll be erasing to the original layer below. Press E to select the Eraser and carefully paint away any extra black pixels. You can also add a layer mask to the eye layer and paint with black to hide the excess black.

7. **Save your document as a PSD file and call it a day.**

Hue/Saturation Adjustment layers

Yet another option for fixing red eye is to zap the red with a Hue/Saturation Adjustment layer, which you learned about in Chapter 8. Select the red eyes with the Lasso tool, click the half-black/half-white circle at the bottom of your Layers panel, and then choose Hue/Saturation from the pop-up menu. When the Adjustments panel opens, adjust the sliders until the red eye leaves the building.

The Sponge tool

As a *last* resort, you can use the Sponge tool to desaturate (remove) color from the pupils. The Sponge tool looks—not surprisingly—like a sponge, and it's part of the Dodge toolset. Though you can use it to desaturate *or* saturate an image, it's set to desaturate (which is what you want when you're zapping red eye) until you change it. After you grab the Sponge tool, head up to the Options bar and change the Flow field to 100 percent or you'll be painting for days (it's set at 50 percent originally). Finally, mouse over to your image and paint over the red area repeatedly until it turns almost black. This technique takes a while, but it's guaranteed to work…eventually.

Fixing red eye in Camera Raw

Camera Raw's Red Eye Removal tool looks and works the same as Photoshop's. It's handy to have this ability in Camera Raw because, if you're shooting in Raw format and you don't *need* to do any other editing in Photoshop, you don't have switch programs just to fix red eye. After you open an image in Camera Raw (see page 53), press E to grab the Red Eye Removal tool. Then simply draw a box around the eyeball, as shown in Figure 10-18, and let go of your mouse button.

Figure 10-18:
When you're finished using the Red Eye tool in Camera Raw, you'll see a black-and-white circle around the pupil, letting you know that Raw made the red-eye fix. Just switch to another tool and the box disappears. Click Done to save your changes and close the Camera Raw window.

Fixing Animal White Eye

Okay, *technically* animals aren't people—though to some folks (this author included) they might as well be. Our furry friends have a version of red eye, too; it's called white eye, and it can ruin their photos, too. Actually, white eye is more challenging to fix than red eye because there aren't any pixels in the eye left to work with—the pupils turn solid white. The Red Eye tool won't work because the pupils aren't red, and the Color Replacement tool won't work because there's no color to replace. The solution is to select the pupil and fill it with black, and then add a couple of well-placed glints (tiny light reflections) to make the new pupils look real (see Figure 10-19).

Figure 10-19:
By selecting the blown-out pupils (top), adding some black paint, and topping it off with two flicks of a white brush to add a glint, you've transformed Miss Abbey from devil dog to angel in minutes.

Here's how to fix your furry friend's eyes:

1. **Open the image and select the white pupils.**

   Since you're selecting by color, you can use either the Magic Wand or the Quick Selection tool: Just click one pupil and then Shift-click the other. You can also select them with the Elliptical Marquee: Draw a selection around the first pupil and then press and hold Shift while you draw a circle around the second pupil. While you're holding the mouse button down, you can press and hold the space bar to move the selection around as you're drawing it.

2. **Feather the selection with Refine Edge.**

Once you've got marching ants, click the Refine Edge button in the Options bar and make sure the resulting dialog box's Feather field is set to one pixel and the Smooth field is set to one (otherwise the edges will be too soft). For good measure, you might expand your selection by 10 to 20 percent or so by dragging the Contract/Expand slider to the right (that way, you make sure to get all the white bits). When you're finished tweaking your selection, click OK.

NOTE Remember, the settings in the Refine Edge dialog box are sticky—they reflect the last settings you used. So take a second to make sure they're all set to zero except for the ones mentioned here.

3. **Create a new layer named *New Pupils*.**

Click the "Create a new layer" button at the bottom of the Layers panel and give it a name. Make sure it's at the top of the layers stack.

4. **Fill the selection with black.**

To recreate the lost pupil, press D to set your color chips to black and white and then press X until black is on top. Next, press Option-Delete (Alt+Backspace on a PC) to fill your selection with black. If the color doesn't seem to reach the edges of your selection (which can happen if you feathered or smoothed your edges a little too much in step 2), fill it again by pressing Option-Delete (Alt+Backspace). Once you've filled the pupils with color, you can get rid of the marching ants by pressing ⌘-D (Ctrl+D) to deselect.

5. **Create another new layer and name it *Glint*.**

You'll want to soften the glints you're about to create by lowering layer opacity, so you need to put the glints on their own layer.

6. **Grab the Brush tool and set your foreground color chip to white.**

Press X to flip-flop color chips and, with a very small brush (10 pixels or so), click once in the left eye to add a glint to mimic the way light reflects off eyes (every eye has one). Next, click in the *exact* same spot in the right eye to add a sister glint. Then lower the glint layer's opacity to about 75 percent.

7. **Save your document as a PSD file.**

Pat yourself on the back for salvaging such a great shot of your pet.

The Art of Sharpening

You know the saying "Last but not least"? Well, that definitely applies to *sharpening*—a digital attempt to improve your image's focus—since it's generally the last thing you do before sending your precious images off to the printer. Sharpening is *muy importante*: It brings out details and makes your image really pop. But it's also one of the least understood processes in Photoshop. In addition to teaching you *how* to sharpen, this chapter also gives you some guidelines about *when* and *how much* sharpening to apply, so you're not just guessing.

In case you're wondering *which* of your photos need sharpening, the answer is pretty much all of 'em. If your image came from a digital camera or a scanner, it needs sharpening. But why? In his comprehensive book on sharpening, *Real World Image Sharpening with Adobe Photoshop CS2* (Peachpit Press, 2006), the late Bruce Fraser explains that images get softened (their pixels lose their hard edges) when cameras and scanners capture light and turn it into pixels. Then, those images get softened even *more* when they're printed. Even if you create an image from scratch in Photoshop, the same deterioration occurs if you shrink it. To combat all these problems, you need to spend a little quality sharpening time with your images.

While Photoshop is pretty darned good at sharpening, it's not magic—it can't take an out-of-focus image and make it *tack sharp* (photographer slang for super-duper sharp, derived from the phrase "sharp as a tack"). One of the few ways you can produce guaranteed perfectly focused photos is to shoot using a tripod (to keep your camera stable) and a remote (so you don't move your camera when you press the shutter button). The program doesn't have a magical "make my blurry picture sharp" button, though maybe Photoshop CS25 will. What Photoshop *can* do is take an in-focus image and make it nice and crisp. But before you start sharpening, it's important to understand how the whole process works.

NOTE You can save a slightly blurry image by running the Emboss filter on it. Flip to page 606 for the super-secret scoop.

What Is Sharpening?

Sharpening an image is similar to sharpening a kitchen knife. In both instances, you're refining (emphasizing) the edges. On a knife, it's easy to identify the edge. In a digital image, it's a little more challenging: the edges are the areas where different-colored pixels meet (see Figure 11-1).

Unsharpened

Oversharpened

Figure 11-1:
Left: You can easily spot the edges in this image because its contrast is pretty high.

Right: In this before-and-after closeup of the Chihuahua's antlers— who does that to their pet?—see how the edges are emphasized after some overzealous sharpening (bottom)? The weird white glow around the antlers is the dreaded sharpening halo.

When you sharpen an image—whether in Photoshop, Camera Raw (page 53), or a darkroom—you exaggerate the edges in the image by increasing their contrast. Where two colors meet, you make the light pixels a little lighter and the dark pixels a little darker. Though it may sound similar to increasing the overall contrast of your image, it's not. When you run one of Photoshop's sharpen filters, the program analyzes your image and increases the contrast *only* in spots it thinks are edges (and you have some control over what Photoshop considers an edge, as you'll learn later on).

Sharpening is a bit of an art: If you don't sharpen enough (or at all), your image looks unnaturally soft and slightly blurred; if you sharpen too much, you get a nasty *sharpening halo*, a white gap between light and dark pixels as shown in Figure 11-1 (bottom right). But if you sharpen just the right amount, no one will notice the sharpening—they'll just know that your image looks *really good*.

One of the downsides to sharpening is that it also emphasizes any kind of noise—graininess or color speckles—in your image. The only way around that problem is to get rid of the noise *before* you sharpen, or at least have a go at reducing it (see the box on page 427 for tips).

Now that you know what sharpening does, you're reading to give it a whirl in Photoshop. The next few pages focus on basic sharpening techniques; more advanced methods are discussed later in this chapter.

Basic Sharpening

After you've retouched your image (Chapters 8, 9, and 10) and resized it (Chapter 6), it's time to sharpen. If you've ever peeked in the Filter menu at the top of your screen, you've probably noticed a whole set of filters devoted to sharpening. They include:

- **Sharpen, Sharpen Edges, Sharpen More.** When you run any one of these filters, you leave the sharpening up to Photoshop (scary!). Each filter analyzes your image, tries to find the edges, and creates a relatively narrow sharpening halo (see Figure 11-1, bottom). However, none of these filters gives you an ounce of control, which is why you should forget they're even there and stick with the next two filters instead.

- **Smart Sharpen.** When you see three little dots next to a menu item, it means there's a dialog box headed your way (and when it comes to sharpening, that's good!). Luckily, this filter—which made its debut in Photoshop CS2—has those dots. Smart Sharpen lets you control how much sharpening happens in your image's shadows and highlights and lets you pick which kind of mathematical voodoo Photoshop uses to do the sharpening. This filter is discussed in detail on page 432.

- **Unsharp Mask.** This filter has been the gold standard sharpening method for years because, until the Smart Sharpen filter came along in Photoshop CS2, Unsharp Mask was the only one that gave you dialog box–level control over how it worked. Most folks still prefer this method because it's easy to use and quick (it runs faster than the Smart Sharpen filter). Page 428 has the scoop.

No matter which filter you choose, sharpening is a destructive process, so it's a good idea to protect your image by following these guidelines:

- **Resize your image first.** Make sharpening your last step before you print an image or post it on the Web—in other words, after you've retouched and resized it. Because pixel size depends on an image's resolution (page 221) and sharpening has different effects on different-sized pixels, it's important to sharpen the image after you make it the size you want.

UP TO SPEED

Keeping the Noise Down

It's best to reduce or get rid of any noise in your image before you sharpen it, or you'll end up sharpening the noise along with the edges. Photoshop gives you a variety of noise-reducing filters; they're discussed starting on page 599. All of them work by *reducing* the amount of contrast between different-colored pixels. (This process is exactly the *opposite* of sharpening, which is why removing noise also reduces sharpness!) The aptly named Reduce Noise filter is the best of the bunch because it gives far more control than the others.

Because all filters run on the currently active layer (meaning they affect your original image), be sure to duplicate your image layer by pressing ⌘-J (Ctrl+J on a PC) before you run this filter. Then, with the duplicate layer selected in the Layers panel, choose Filter → Noise → Reduce Noise (you'll learn another nondestructive way to run filters over in Chapter 15—see page 588). In the resulting dialog box, you can adjust the following settings:

- **Strength.** If you've got a lot of *grayscale noise*—luminance or brightness noise that looks like grains or splotches—or color noise that looks like little specks of color in your image, you can increase this setting to make Photoshop reduce it in every color channel. This setting ranges from 1 to 10 (it's set to 6 unless you change it).

- **Preserve Details.** You can increase this setting to protect the detailed areas of your image, but if you do, Photoshop can't reduce as much grayscale noise. For best results, tweak this setting along with the Strength setting and find a balance between the two.

- **Reduce Color Noise.** If you've got colored specks in your image, try increasing this setting to make Photoshop erase even more of the little buggers.

- **Sharpen Details.** Because every noise-reducing filter blurs your overall image, this option lets you bring back some of the sharpness. But resist the urge to use it and use one of the other sharpening methods described in this chapter instead.

- **Remove JPEG Artifacts.** If you're dealing with an image that's gotten blocky because it was saved as a low-quality JPEG, turn on this checkbox and Photoshop tries to reduce that Lego look.

- **Advanced.** This setting lets you tweak each color channel individually (for more on channels, see Chapter 5). So if the noise is in just one or two color channels (noise is notoriously bad in the blue channel), turn on this option and tweak each channel's settings individually. (Because Reduce Noise can make your image blurry, it's better to adjust as few channels as possible.)

Once you're finished modifying these settings, press OK to run the filter and then toggle the duplicate layer's visibility off and on (page 78) to see how much effect the filter really had. (Seeing the whole image gives you a better idea than looking at the preview in the filter's dialog box.) You can also add a layer mask (page 105) to restrict the filter's effects to certain parts of the image if you need to (though you get a mask automatically if you use Smart Filters—see page 588).

And if you determine that the filter didn't help one darn bit, run—don't walk!—over to Chapter 19 to find a third-party, noise-reduction plug-in that can. Or, if buying a plug-in isn't in your budget, flip to page 200 to learn how to sharpen individual channels.

You may now proceed with sharpening your image.

- **Get rid of any noise first.** If you see any funky color speckles or grains that shouldn't be in your image, get rid of them *before* you sharpen or they'll look even worse. The box on page 427 tells you how.

- **Sharpen your image on a duplicate layer or run it as a Smart Filter.** Before you run a sharpening filter, select the image layer and duplicate it by pressing ⌘-J (Ctrl+J on a PC). That way, you can toggle the sharpened layer's visibility on and off (page 78) to see before and after versions of your image. You can also restrict the sharpening to certain areas of your image by adding a layer mask (page 105) to the sharpened layer and reduce the opacity of the sharpened layer (page 87). Page 435 has tips for dealing with a multi-layered file. Better yet, convert your image layer for Smart Filters so Photoshop does the sharpening on its own layer *and* includes a layer mask for you; page 588, has the details.

- **Change the sharpening layer's blend mode to Luminosity.** Because you're about to make Photoshop lighten and darken a whole lot of pixels, you risk having the colors in your image shift. However, if you change the sharpening layer's blend mode to Luminosity, it affects only the brightness of the pixels, not their color.

> **TIP** Sharpening on a duplicate layer and changing that layer's blend mode to Luminosity does virtually the same thing as changing the color mode to Lab (page 183) and then sharpening the Lightness channel, and it's a whole lot faster!

- **Sharpen your image slightly multiple times.** It's better to apply too little sharpening and run the sharpening filter *again* than to apply too much sharpening all at once. Sharpening your image gradually gives you more control. Just use your History panel or press ⌘-Z (Ctrl+Z on a PC) to undo the last sharpen if you go a little too far.

In the following pages, you'll learn various ways to sharpen, starting with the most popular method: the Unsharp Mask filter.

Sharpening with the Unsharp Mask

This filter is the favored sharpening method of the pros, but its name is rather confusing—it sounds like it does just the opposite of sharpen. The odd name came from a technique used in darkrooms, which involves using a *blurred* ("unsharp") version of an image to produce a *sharper* one. In Photoshop, the Unsharp Mask filter studies each pixel, looks at the contrast of nearby pixels, and decides whether they're different enough to be considered an edge (you control how picky the filter is using the Threshold setting, shown in Figure 11-2 and discussed below). If the answer is yes, Photoshop alters the pixel to increase the contrast of that edge. The basic process is simple: Photoshop lightens the light pixels and darkens the dark pixels.

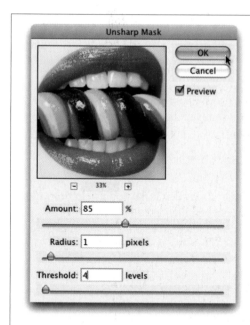

Figure 11-2:
Before the Smart Sharpen filter came along, Unsharp Mask was the only sharpening method that gave you any level of control. Because it's so quick and easy to use, it's still the preferred method today. To bail out of the Unsharp Mask dialog box (shown here) without doing anything, click the Cancel button or press Esc.

NOTE   The Unsharp Mask filter's effects look a little stronger onscreen than they do when you print the image. That's because the pixels on your screen are *much* bigger than the ones your printer prints. So to get a printed image that's nice and crisp, make your onscreen image look a little *too* sharp.

Here are the settings you can adjust in the Unsharp Mask dialog box:

- **Amount.** This setting, which controls the sharpening intensity, ranges from 1 percent to 500 percent. The higher the setting, the lighter Photoshop makes the light pixels and the darker it makes the dark pixels. If you set it to 500 percent, Photoshop makes all the light pixels near edges pure white and all the dark ones pure black, giving your image a sharpening halo you can see from outer space. For best results, keep this setting between 50 percent and 150 percent (you can find other magic numbers on page 430).

- **Radius.** This setting controls the width of the sharpening halo or, rather, how many pixels on either side of the edge pixels Photoshop analyzes and changes. This setting alters your sharpening preview thumbnail (shown in Figure 11-2), so it's a good idea to change it first. Typically, when you increase this setting, you need to reduce the Amount setting to avoid creating a Grand Canyon–sized sharpening halo. For best results, never set the Radius higher than 4.

- **Threshold.** This setting lets you control how different neighboring pixels have to be before Photoshop considers them an edge. Oddly enough, this setting works the opposite of how you might expect: Setting it to 0 sharpens *every* pixel in your image! For best results, keep this setting between 3 and 20 (it ranges from 0 to 255).

Here's how to use the Unsharp Mask filter:

1. **Duplicate your image layer and set the duplicate layer's blend mode to Luminosity.**

   This filter is destructive, so be sure to run it on a duplicate layer. Over in your Layers panel, select the layer you want to sharpen and then press ⌘-J (Ctrl+J on a PC) to duplicate it. Make sure the duplicate layer is selected and then, using the pop-up menu at the top of the Layers panel, change its blend mode to Luminosity.

2. **Choose Filter → Sharpen → Unsharp Mask.**

   In the resulting dialog box (see Figure 11-2), tweak the settings to your liking. In the next few pages, you'll find some recommended values that you can memorize for later use, but, for right now, just adjust the settings so the image in the preview thumbnail looks good to you.

   TIP Anytime you see a preview thumbnail in a dialog box (like the one shown in Figure 11-2), you can click it and hold your mouse button to see a before version of your image (in this case, the unsharpened version). You can also drag to move the preview around or click the little + and – buttons below the preview to zoom in or out.

3. **Click OK when you're finished to close the dialog box.**

Sit back and marvel at your new Photoshop sharpening prowess.

How much to sharpen?

Some images need more sharpening than others. For example, you don't need to sharpen a portrait as much as you do a photo of Times Square because they have different amounts of detail (the Times Square photo is super busy). If you sharpen the portrait too much, you see pores and blemishes with enough details to haunt your next power nap.

Photoshop guru Scott Kelby came up with some especially effective values to use in the Unsharp Mask dialog box and published them in *The Adobe Photoshop CS3 Book for Digital Photographers* (New Riders Press, 2007). With his blessing, here they are:

- **Sharpening soft stuff.** If you're sharpening images of flowers, puppies, babies and other soft, fluffy subjects (stuff that often blends into its background), you don't want to apply much sharpening at all. For extremely soft sharpening, try setting the Amount to 150 percent, the Radius to 1, and the Threshold to 10.

- **Sharpening portraits.** While close-up portraits need a bit more sharpening than the items mentioned above, you don't want to sharpen them as much as something hard like a building with lots of straight lines and angles. To sharpen portraits enough to make their subject's eyes stand out, try setting the Amount to 75 percent, the Radius to 2, and the Threshold to 3.

- **Sharpening objects, landscapes, and animals.** This stuff tends to be a little harder and contain more details (sharp angles, fur, and so on) than portraits, so it needs a moderate amount of sharpening. Try setting the Amount to 120 percent, the Radius to 1, and the Threshold to 3.

  NOTE These numbers are merely guidelines—they're not absolute rules. Experiment with your own images and printer to see which settings give *you* the best results.

- **Maximum sharpening.** For photos of cars or of buildings (which are chock full of hard lines, angles, and details) or for photos that are a little out of focus, try entering an Amount of 65 percent, a Radius of 4, and a Threshold of 3.

- **Sharpening anything.** For everyday sharpening, regardless of what's in your image, enter an Amount of 85 percent, a Radius of 1, and a Threshold of 4, and then call it a day.

- **Sharpening for the Web.** If you've resized an image so that it's small enough to post on the Web (see page 231), it needs lots of sharpening because downsizing makes an image softer. Set the Amount to 200 percent, the Radius to 3, and the Threshold to 0.

POWER USERS' CLINIC

Fading Filters

You may feel that this chapter is jumping the gun a little bit by covering sharpening filters because there's a *whole chapter* on filters headed your way (Chapter 15). However, some of the things you can do with filters—like fading a filter you've applied—are too dad-gummed useful to wait until then!

If you run a filter—it doesn't matter which one—and the effect is a little too strong, you can lower the filter's opacity to lessen its effect and to change its blend mode (page 267). But Photoshop only lets you do this right after you run the filter, so you don't want to miss your chance. (If you didn't duplicate the original layer before running the filter, this fix is the only thing that can save you.)

After you run the filter and before you do *anything* else, head up to the Edit menu and choose "Fade [name of the last filter you ran]". (If you click another button or select another tool, the Fade option is grayed out and you're out of luck.) In the resulting Fade dialog box, enter a percentage in the Opacity field to let Photoshop know how much you want to fade the filter. For example, if you think the filter is twice as strong as you need, enter *50* to reduce its effect by half. (If you click OK and then change your mind, you can select Edit → "Fade [name of filter]" again and enter a new number. The Edit menu's Fade option remains clickable until you run another command or use another tool.)

The Fade dialog box also has a Mode pop-up menu that lets you change the filter's blend mode to adjust how the sharpened pixels blend in with the original ones. Changing this setting to Luminosity has the same effect as running the filter on a duplicate layer and setting that layer's blend mode to Luminosity. The drawback to *not* running the filter on a duplicate layer is that you have only this one chance to lessen the effects of the filter; if you print the image and then decide you need less sharpening, you're out of luck.

When you press OK, Photoshop lessens the filter's effect by the percent you entered.

- **More Accurate.** If you turn on this checkbox, Photoshop thinks long and hard before it does its sharpening. With this setting turned on, you'll get more precise results though the sharpening won't be as strong. Since turning on this option makes the filter take longer to run, you'll want to leave it off if you have a slow computer or if you're working with a huge file. If you buy a new computer every time you upgrade your copy of Photoshop, on the other hand, you can turn it on and leave it on.

If you turn on the Advanced radio button at the top of the dialog box, Photoshop adds three tabs to the settings section. Besides the options just listed, which appear on the Sharpen tab, you get Shadow and Highlight tabs, as shown in Figure 11-5. These last two tabs, which have the same settings, let you control the following:

- **Fade Amount.** This field lets you reduce the amount of sharpening Photoshop applies to your image's highlights or shadows, depending on which tab you're on. So, for example, if you enter *100* in the Sharpen tab's Amount field but want Photoshop to do a bit less sharpening in the shadows, click the Shadow tab and enter a Fade Amount of 25 percent or so. If you want *no* sharpening to happen in the shadows, enter 100 percent. (This setting is similar to the Fade command you learned about in the box on page 431.)

Figure 11-5:
If you turn on the Smart Sharpen filter's advanced options, you can adjust how much sharpening takes place in both the shadows (left) and the highlights (right). You don't get this kind of control with the Unsharp Mask filter.

- **Tonal Width.** This setting lets you control which highlights and shadows Photoshop sharpens. It starts out at 50 percent, meaning the shadows get sharpened evenly throughout their tonal range. If you enter a lower number, Photoshop sharpens only the lightest highlights or the darkest shadows (depending on which tab you're on); if you enter a higher number, Photoshop sharpens all the highlights or all the shadows. Unless you've increased the Fade Amount, this setting doesn't do a darn thing.

NOTE If you pop into Advanced mode and tweak the Highlight and Shadow tabs' settings and then go *back* into Basic mode, the changes you made in Advanced mode *still* affect the filter, so it's a good idea to reset all the Smart Sharpen settings by Option-clicking (Alt on a PC) the Cancel button to change it to Reset (clicking the Reset button takes you back to Basic mode). Or, when you switch into Advanced mode, make a mental note to *stay there*.

- **Radius.** Radius lets you control how many pixels Photoshop analyzes to figure out whether it thinks a pixel is in a highlight or a shadow. In other words, this setting controls how wide an area Photoshop sharpens in either highlights or shadows (depending on which tab you clicked). Like the Tonal Width setting, this setting doesn't do anything unless you adjust the Fade Amount first.

TIP   See the tiny disk and trash can icons in the Smart Sharpen dialog box to the right of the Settings pop-up menu? These buttons let you save or throw away custom settings. If you click the disk button to save your current settings and give 'em a name, Photoshop adds them to the Settings pop-up menu. If you want to throw a custom setting away, choose it from the Settings pop-up menu and then click the trash can button.

FREQUENTLY ASKED QUESTION

Sharpening with the History Brush

Can I use the History Brush to sharpen my image?

The answer is yes—but you really shouldn't.

Photoshop captures the last several things you do—unless you change the setting in Preferences (page 24), it memorizes the last 20—and lets you undo or redo them by painting with the History Brush (see page 26). So instead of sharpening on another layer, you can sharpen the image and then set the History Brush's source to the sharpened state and your image to the state *before* you sharpened it. Then you can grab the History Brush and selectively paint the sharpening onto your image.

However, this procedure is risky because:

- Once you close your document, the memorized history is gone. Poof. Buh-bye. If you print the image and later decide you've oversharpened, you're out of luck.

- If Photoshop crashes while you're painting with the History Brush, you're hosed.

The list goes on, but the bottom line is that sharpening with the History Brush is destructive editing; you're affecting original pixels, and that's *always* a bad idea. A much better solution is the method this chapter recommends: Sharpen on a separate layer so you can add a layer mask or lower that layer's opacity if you need to, or use Smart Filters as described on page 588.

That being said, if you've got a super-small hard drive you may not be able to work with large Photoshop documents. And if your image is already big, it'll only get bigger as you add layers. If that's the case, sharpen with the History Brush, but proceed with caution.

Sharpening Layered Files

When you run a sharpening filter, it affects only the current layer—there's no way to make it affect *all* the layers in your document. So what happens if your image is on more than one layer? (You've combined several images [Chapter 7] and added several Adjustment layers [page 71], say.) The solution is to *merge* all those layers into a brand-new one you can sharpen (as shown in Figure 11-6).

Figure 11-6:
If you need to sharpen a multi-layered document, first combine all the layers into a single layer you can sharpen by Option-clicking Merge Visible.

Here's how:

1. **Open a layered file and select the topmost layer.**

   Since the sharpening layer needs to be *on top of* your layers stack, select the top layer so the new sharpening layer ends up exactly where you want it (see Figure 11-6, left).

2. **Make sure you've turned on the visibility eyes (page 78) of the layers you want to merge.**

3. **Open the Layers panel menu by clicking the upper-right part of the Layers panel (circled in Figure 11-6, left) and then Option-click (Alt-click on a PC) the Merge Visible option.**

   If you simply clicked Merge Visible, Photoshop would compact all your layers into one. But by Option-clicking (Alt-clicking) the Merge Visible option, you tell Photoshop to compact all your layers onto a completely *new* layer at the top of your layers stack (circled in Figure 11-6, right). You can also press ⌘+Shift+Option+E (Ctrl+Shift+Alt+E) to do the same thing.

Now you can sharpen the new layer using any of the methods described in the previous pages.

> **TIP** When you have a multi-layer file, it's a good idea to name your layers so you know what's what. Just double-click the new layer's name and type in a descriptive name like *Sharpen*.

Sharpening Part of an Image

Sometimes, you need to sharpen only a portion of an image. If you've followed the advice sprinkled throughout this chapter—sharpening on a duplicate layer or merging several layers into a sharpen layer—you're more than halfway there. You just need to add and edit a layer mask.

For example, one of the most useful portrait retouching techniques you'll ever learn is to accentuate your subject's eyes and lips, as shown in Figure 11-7.

Figure 11-7:
Left: When you sharpen a duplicate layer, you can add a layer mask and sharpen only certain areas of the image. Here you can see what a difference the eye and lip sharpening makes (check out, for example, the details visible on the girl's sharpened lips).

Right: You can also lessen the intensity of the sharpening by lowering the sharpening layer's opacity.

Here's how to sharpen only certain areas, leaving the rest of your image unscathed:

1. **Create a duplicate layer to use for sharpening.**

    If you're dealing with a single-layer file, select the original layer and then press ⌘-J (Ctrl+J on a PC) to duplicate it. If you've got a multi-layer file, combine your layers into a single sharpening layer as explained in the previous section (page 426). Double-click the new layer's name and rename it *Sharpen*.

2. **With the new layer selected, choose Filter → Sharpen → Unsharp Mask.**

    Enter an Amount of 120 percent, a Radius of 2, and a Threshold of 3. These numbers are rather arbitrary; the goal is to severely oversharpen your image so you can scale back the effect.

3. **Run the Unsharp Mask filter two more times.**

Have a little faith, will ya? You'll reduce this extreme oversharpening in a minute. To run the filter again, press ⌘-F (Ctrl+F on a PC) or choose Filter → Unsharp Mask (the last filter you ran always shows up at the top of the Filter menu).

4. **Add a solid black layer mask to the sharpened layer.**

At the bottom of your Layers panel, Option-click (Alt-click on a PC) the circle-within-a-square icon to add a layer mask filled with black, which hides the sharpened layer. (Recall from page 105 that, in the realm of layer masks, black conceals.)

5. **Grab the Brush tool and set your foreground color chip to white.**

Press B to activate the Brush tool and take a peek at the bottom of the Tools panel. If the foreground color chip (page 22) is white, you're good to go. If it's not, press D to return the color chips to the factory setting of black and white and then press X to flip-flop the chips.

6. **Mouse over to your image and paint your subject's irises.**

When you're doing detail work like this, it's helpful to zoom in on the image by pressing ⌘-+ (Ctrl-+ on a PC) a few times. You also need to adjust your brush size: Press the left bracket key ([) to make your brush smaller and the right bracket key (]) to make it bigger. Be sure to paint only the iris of each eye. If you mess up and reveal too much of the sharpening layer, don't panic. Just press X to flip-flop color chips so you're painting with black and then paint over that area to hide the sharpening.

TIP In Photoshop CS4, you can drag to change your brush size by holding Ctrl-Option as you drag left or right with your mouse. (On a PC, Alt+right-click and drag.)

7. **When you're finished painting the eyes and you're still zoomed in, hold the space bar and drag to move the image so you can see your subject's lips and reveal the sharpening in that area, as well.**

Painting over your subject's lips is like adding a bit of digital lip gloss. You'll probably want to increase your brush size a bit.

8. **Lower the Sharpen layer's opacity until you get a realistic effect.**

At the top of the Layers panel, change the Opacity field to approximately 50 percent to lessen the effect of the sharpening you applied in step 3.

9. **Save the image as a PSD file.**

With this method, you're not harming the original pixels, and you can alter the layer's opacity to make the effect look real instead of otherworldly. Saving the document as a PSD file (page 46) lets you go back and edit the layer mask or change the sharpened layer's opacity, which is a great option if you print the image and think, "If only it was just a *hair* sharper…".

The Sharpen Tool

What's all this talk about sharpening with filters? Why can't I use the Sharpen tool instead?

Just because Photoshop has a certain tool doesn't mean you should use it. While it seems like a no-brainer that the Sharpen tool would be your best bet for sharpening (it's specifically designed for that, right?), you can actually get better results using other methods. That said, since this book covers *all* of Photoshop, here's a quick primer on how it works.

The Sharpen Tool is part of the Blur toolset. When you click its icon (it looks like a triangle) and mouse over to your image, you see a familiar brush cursor. With the Sharpen tool, you can paint across areas you want to sharpen and, well, that's it. (You don't get nearly as much control with this tool as you do with the sharpen filters discussed so far in this chapter.) Up in the Options bar, you can adjust the following settings:

- **Brush.** This menu lets you pick brush size and type (big or small, hard or soft).

- **Mode.** In this pop-up menu, you can change the tool's blend mode from Normal to Darken, Lighten, Hue, Saturation, Color, or Luminosity.

- **Strength.** This field is automatically set at 50 percent. But unless you want to oversharpen your image, lower this setting to 25 percent or less before you use it. That way, you apply reasonable amounts of sharpening and can continue to brush over areas to apply more.

- **Sample All Layers.** Photoshop assumes you want to sharpen only the current layer. If you want to sharpen *all* the layers in your document, turn on this checkbox.

As you might imagine, using this tool can be a time-suck of epic proportions because you're sharpening with a brush *by hand*, so it's best to use it only on small areas.

Advanced Sharpening Techniques

Now that you understand the basics of sharpening, it's time to delve into the realm of advanced sharpening. Consider yourself warned that this is pro-level stuff and not for the faint of heart. (Basically, these methods involve many more steps than the techniques you've learned so far.) In this section, you'll learn how to create a detailed edge mask, create a new high-contrast channel, and sharpen using the High Pass filter. Read on, brave warrior!

> **NOTE** This book doesn't cover *every* sharpening technique; if it did, it'd be too heavy to lift! Instead, it covers the most practical and frequently used methods. If you want to learn more, pick up a copy of *Real World Image Sharpening with Adobe Photoshop CS2* (Peachpit Press, 2006), by Bruce Fraser. The book is a couple of years old, but it teaches you everything you ever wanted to know about the art of sharpening.

Creating an Edge Mask

An *edge mask* is simply a layer mask that accentuates the edges in your image. (Pop back to page 425 for a refresher on what "edges" means in this context.) The mask itself, which you apply to the layer you want to sharpen, is black except for a white outline of your image that makes the sharpening appear only in the edges (because, once again, in the land of the layer mask, black conceals and white reveals). However, instead of drawing such a mask yourself (that would take days!), you can have Photoshop create one for you by using the (rather lengthy) method described in the following list. It takes a little time, but it's well worth the effort:

1. **Find the channel with the greatest contrast and duplicate it.**

   As you learned back in Chapter 5, your image's color info is stored in individual layers called channels. To create an edge mask, you need to find the channel with the greatest contrast (which channel that is depends on your image). To do that, open the Channels panel (page 174) and cycle through them—if you're in RGB mode—by pressing ⌘-3, 4, and 5 (Ctrl+3, 4, and 5 on a PC). (If you're in CMYK mode, you've got one more channel to look at so add ⌘-6 [Ctrl-6] to that list.) To leave your original image intact, you need to keep your channels intact, so that means creating your edge mask on a *duplicate* of the highest-contrast channel. To duplicate the channel, Ctrl-click (right-click on a PC) the appropriate channel in the Channels panel and then choose Duplicate from the shortcut menu that appears. In the resulting dialog box, name the channel *Mask*. (Or you can create a brand-new, even higher-contrast channel by using the Calculations adjustment or Channel Mixer. See the box on page 444 for the scoop.)

   NOTE If you'd like to work with the image used in this example, you can download the file Building.jpg from this book's Missing CD page at *www.missingmanuals.com*.

2. **With the Mask channel selected in the Channels panel, choose Filter → Stylize → Find Edges.**

   You don't get a dialog box when you run this filter; it's an all-or-nothing kind of deal. Photoshop instantly makes your image look like a drawing (see page 604 to learn more about this filter), with the edges shown in dark gray and black. This is the exact *opposite* of what you want, but you'll fix that in the next step.

3. **Invert the Mask channel by choosing Image → Adjustments → Invert.**

   Photoshop flip-flops the info in the Mask channel so the image's edges are white instead of black (see Figure 11-8). That way, when you copy the Mask channel and paste it into a layer mask on the sharpened layer, the sharpening is revealed only along the edges; the black areas hide the sharpening from the rest of your image.

4. **Increase the Mask channel's contrast with a Levels (page 363) or Curves (page 379) Adjustment layer.**

   To really accentuate the edges in your image, you can add extra contrast to the Mask channel with a Levels adjustment. Choose Image → Adjustments → Levels and then adjust the gray slider to get the most contrast (see page 363 for more on Levels). The black areas of the Mask channel don't get sharpened; only the light gray and white areas do. Press OK when you're finished to close the dialog box.

Figure 11-8:
Left: When you first run the Find Edges filter, your image looks like a pencil sketch as shown here. (To see the original photo, check out Figure 11-9, left.) The edges of the image are black, which is the opposite of what you want.

Right: After you invert the Mask channel, your edges turn white and everything else turns black, which is exactly what you want. That way, when you paste this channel into a layer mask, the sharpening shows through only in the white areas.

5. **Blur the Mask channel *slightly* with the Gaussian Blur filter.**

   To avoid harsh sharpening halos (page 425), you can blur the Mask channel a little by choosing Filter → Blur → Gaussian Blur. Enter a radius between 0.5 and 3 to soften the edges of your mask a little. (Use a lower number for low-resolution images and a higher number for high-resolution images.)

6. **Select everything in the Mask channel and then copy it to your computer's memory.**

   Since you're already in the Channels panel, copy the Mask channel (you don't need it just yet, but you will in a minute). Select the whole thing by pressing ⌘-A (Ctrl+A on a PC) and then copy it by pressing ⌘-C (Ctrl+C on a PC).

7. **Throw the Mask channel away and deselect to get rid of the marching ants.**

   To delete the Mask channel now that you've copied it, either drag it down to the tiny trash can at the bottom of the Channels panel, or Ctrl-click (right-click on a PC) it and then choose Delete from the resulting pop-up menu. Get rid of the marching ants by pressing ⌘-D (Ctrl+D on a PC).

8. **Back in your Layers panel, duplicate the layer you want to sharpen (or combine several layers to create a new one as described in the previous section [page 435]) and add a layer mask to the duplicate.**

   Select the layer you want to sharpen and duplicate it by pressing ⌘-J (Ctrl+J on a PC). Then add a layer mask to it by clicking the circle-within-a-square-icon at the bottom of your Layers panel.

9. **In your Layers panel, Option-click (Alt-click on a PC) the layer mask's thumbnail.**

   To paste the Mask channel you painstakingly created into the layer mask, you need to be inside the layer mask. When you Option-click (Alt-click) the layer mask's thumbnail, your entire document turns white because the mask is empty. (If you don't see solid white, you're not in the mask.)

10. **Paste the Mask channel you copied in step 6 into the layer mask.**

    Once you're in the layer mask, press ⌘-V (Ctrl+V on a PC) to paste the Mask channel into it. You should see the black-and-white Mask channel that you created in steps 1–5.

11. **Click the image's layer thumbnail, and then choose Filter → Sharpen → Unsharp Mask.**

    To see your image again, click the image layer's thumbnail to the left of the layer mask. Next, head up to the Filter menu and choose Sharpen → Unsharp Mask.

12. **Press OK to run the Unsharp Mask filter and then lower the sharpened layer's opacity if you need to (see Figure 11-9).**

    When you press OK, Photoshop runs the sharpening filter. If the sharpening looks too strong, you can lower the sharpened layer's opacity in your Layers panel. You may not need to lower it, but it's sure nice to have the option.

Whew! That was a lot of work, but your image should look light years better, as shown in Figure 11-9. You can toggle the sharpened layer's visibility off and on to see what a difference the edge sharpening made. Thanks to the edge mask, only the building's details got sharpened, leaving areas like the sky untouched (which all but eliminates sharpening-induced noise).

Sharpening with the High Pass Filter

When you're dealing with a fairly flat image like the one shown in Figure 11-10, give this sharpening method a spin. It's quick and it lets you add a bit more depth to your image by increasing contrast in the midtones (the colors in your image that aren't the lightest or darkest). It involves using the High Pass filter, which essentially keeps the highest-contrast edges in your image (the ones with the biggest difference between colors) and makes everything else gray.

First, create a duplicate layer for sharpening just like you've done in the previous pages. Then change its blend mode to Overlay as shown in Figure 11-11, top. (As explained on page 273, Overlay mode can brighten or darken your image, which increases contrast.) Next, choose Filter → Other → High Pass and enter a Radius between 0.5 and 3 (Figure 11-11, bottom). That's it! Check out your image to see if you like it, and turn off the sharpening layer's visibility to see what the original image looked like.

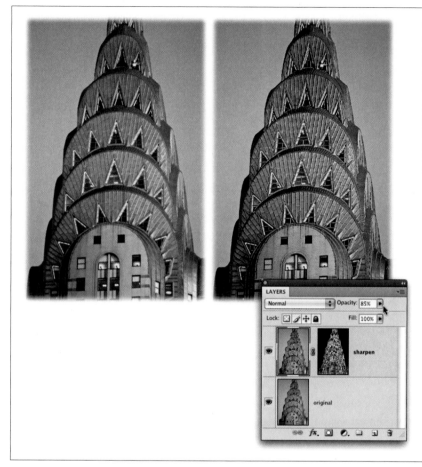

Figure 11-9:
Left: The original,
unsharpened photo of
the Chrysler Building in
New York City looks
rather flat.

Right: Sharpening the
same photo with an edge
mask (visible in the
Layers panel) confines
the sharpening to the
image's details.

Sharpening in Camera Raw

Camera Raw's sharpening capabilities have improved greatly in the last couple of versions of the plug-in (starting with Camera Raw 4.1, which was released after Photoshop CS3), and its controls now rival the sharpening you can produce in Photoshop. Sharpening in Camera Raw even affects your image's luminosity (lightness or brightness values) and leaves the color alone.

But *should* you use Camera Raw for your sharpening? The answer is yes—*if* you're not going to edit the image much in Photoshop. The answer is no if you *are* going to do a lot of editing in Photoshop, in which case, you should save the sharpening for your very last step (after retouching and resizing) and use one of the methods described earlier in this chapter instead. It's that simple.

You *don't* want to sharpen in both programs—at least, not the whole image. Sharpening in Camera Raw is a global process, meaning it affects your entire image (though you can wield a little control using Camera Raw 5's new Adjustment Brush,

Creating a High-Contrast Edge Mask

If you're trying to create an edge mask (page 439) but your color channels don't have much contrast, you can always create a *new* channel with contrast a-plenty. If creating a new channel sounds hard, don't panic; it's easier than you think. There are two ways to go about it:

- **The Calculations adjustment** can combine two channels for you. After strolling through your channels to see which ones have the most contrast (let's say they're the Red and Green channels), head up to the Image menu and choose Calculations. In the resulting dialog box, tell Photoshop which channels you want to combine by choosing the Red channel from the Source 1 section's Channel pop-up menu and Green from the same pop-up menu in the Source 2 section. From the Blending pop-up menu near the bottom of the dialog box, pick one of the blend modes in the Overlay category like Soft Light (Chapter 7 describes all these blend modes in detail, beginning

on page 267). When you press OK, Photoshop creates a brand-new channel you can tweak into a high-contrast edge mask. *Now* you're ready to proceed with step 2 back on page 439. (Since this channel is totally new, you don't have to duplicate it like you did in step 1.) To learn more about the Calculations adjustment, flip back to page 190.

- **The Channel Mixer** doesn't really create another channel; instead, it lets you create a grayscale (black-and-white) version of your image that you can use as if it were a channel. Duplicate your image layer and then choose Image → Adjustments → Channel Mixer. Turn on the Monochrome checkbox at the bottom left of the dialog box and then tweak the various sliders. When you get some really good contrast, press OK. Next, start with step 2 on page 439 and run the Find Edges filter in the Layers panel instead of the Channels panel (the steps are exactly the same).

discussed later in this section). It's also a somewhat automatic process: your image gets sharpened the minute you open it in Camera Raw (unless you turn off automatic sharpening as described in the next section). If you let Camera Raw sharpen your image, you'll need to practice selective sharpening (described on page 437) once the image is in Photoshop to avoid oversharpening and introducing halos.

Global Sharpening

You can sharpen in Camera Raw by first opening your image (page 54) and then clicking the tiny Detail icon circled in Figure 11-12. If you don't want any global sharpening, drag the Amount slider to zero (from the factory, it's set to 25). If you *do* want to sharpen your image, mosey on down to the lower-left corner of the Camera Raw dialog box and change the view percentage to 100 percent so you can see the effect of the changes you make to the Detail settings (otherwise it looks like your sharpening is having no effect on the image). Then, tweak the following settings to your liking:

- **Amount.** This setting works just like Unsharp Mask dialog box's Amount slider (page 429); it controls the intensity of the sharpening. Setting it to 0 means no sharpening, no how; setting it to 150 means tons of sharpening (which is way too much). Try setting it to 40 and toggling the Preview checkbox at the top of the Camera Raw window off and on to see if it makes a difference (be sure you're zoomed in to 100 percent, though!).

Figure 11-10:
Top: The original image with no sharpening is pretty flat and lacks contrast in the details.

Bottom: If you sharpen this image with the High Pass filter, you can give it some depth. Notice how many more details appear around the crown, face, and torch.

- **Radius.** This slider controls the size of the details that Camera Raw sharpens. If you're sharpening a photo with lots of fine details, leave it at 1. If your photo doesn't have many details, you can pump it up to 1.5, or if you're feeling wild and crazy, *maybe* 2.

- **Detail.** This slider lets you control the level of detail Camera Raw brings out (how much it emphasizes the edges). Pump this setting way up (to 90 or so) if you've got an image with tons of details and textures (like a rocky landscape, a closeup of a tree, or a fancy-schmancy building). This slider ranges from 0 to 100; for most images, you can keep it around 40 or so (but be sure to experiment to see what looks good to you).

Figure 11-11:
Top: After you create a duplicate layer for sharpening, change its blend mode to Overlay as shown here.

Bottom: The Radius setting controls the width of the sharpening halo (page 425) that the High Pass filter creates, so you'll want to keep this setting pretty low.

- **Masking.** If you increase this setting, Camera Raw reduces the amount of sharpening it applies to areas that aren't edges. It's sort of like using a layer mask on a sharpened layer in Photoshop, except that it's automatic, so you can't really control where the sharpening is hidden. Nevertheless, it's worth experimenting with. If you set it to 0, Camera Raw sharpens everything; at 100, it sharpens only the edges.

- **Luminance.** This setting makes Camera Raw try to decrease the amount of grayscale noise (see the box on page 427) in your image. Make sure you're zoomed into your image to at least 100 percent and then drag the slider to the right to reduce the grains or splotches in your image.

- **Color.** If your image has a lot of color noise (funky color specks), which can happen if you shoot in really low light, move this slider to the right to make Camera Raw try to remove the specks.

Figure 11-12:
If you don't want Camera Raw to sharpen your images automatically, you can make it stop. Click the Detail icon (circled, left) and then drag the Amount slider to zero. Open the Camera Raw menu (circled, right) and choose Save New Camera Raw Defaults as shown here.

TIP   To see what's *really* going on with any of Camera Raw's sharpening options, hold the Option key (Alt on a PC) as you drag the individual sliders (it works only if you're zoomed in to 100 percent or more). Your image goes grayscale, letting you see which areas Camera Raw is adjusting (though it's tough to see *anything* when you're tweaking Radius). The most useful setting is Masking—if you hold the Option (Alt) key while you tweak it, you see what looks like an edge mask (page 439) that shows you exactly which parts of your image are being sharpened and which are being hidden by the mask.

Selective Sharpening in Camera Raw

As you learned in Chapter 9 (page 361), Camera Raw 5 sports a new Adjustment Brush that lets you paint slider-based adjustments directly onto your image. Behind the scenes, Camera Raw builds a mask to hide the adjustments from the rest of your image. Great, but how does the Adjustment Brush relate to sharpening, you ask? The Sharpness slider lets you increase or decrease the amount of sharpening you've set in the Detail tab—here's the good part—in the areas you paint with the Adjustment Brush. Sure, the sharpening still affects your whole image, but using the Adjustment Brush gives you a little more control over how much sharpening Camera Raw applies where, as shown in Figure 11-13. The Sharpness slider ranges from –100 to +100.

Figure 11-13:
If you've applied a round of sharpening to your whole image by adjusting the Detail tab's settings, you can apply even more sharpening to specific areas like this girl's headband. Press K to grab the Adjustment Brush, increase the Sharpness slider (circled here), and then paint the headband. If you want to decrease the sharpening in a specific area, drag the Sharpness slider to the left into negative numbers.

Painting in Photoshop

Many artists who learned to sketch and paint using pencils, oils, and brushes have come to love the creativity that the digital realm affords. Heck, the biggest advantage is that there aren't any brushes to clean or paints to mix! And you can't beat the infinitely forgiving undo command. Most important, as you can see in Figure 12-1, there's no limit to the kind of artwork you can create in Photoshop.

If you're a traditional artist, the techniques covered in this chapter will set you on the path of electronic creativity. You'll learn how to use Photoshop's color tools and built-in brushes to create a painting from start to finish, in full step-by-step detail. You'll also discover how to load additional brushes, customize the ones Photoshop provides, and create new brushes of your very own.

If you're a graphic designer or photographer, there's a ton of info here for you, too. Just take a minute to think about how much time you spend with brushes when you're working in Photoshop. Whether retouching an image with one of the healing brushes (page 392), painting on a layer mask to hide an adjustment (page 105), or duplicating objects in your image using the Clone Stamp tool (page 288)—all of those things (and more) involve either the Brush tool itself or a tool that uses a brush cursor. For that reason, learning how to work with and customize brushes is extremely important. Plus you'll learn all kinds of other fun (and useful) stuff like the basics of color theory, how to use Photoshop's various tools to choose the colors you work with (including the new Kuler panel from which you can snatch whole color schemes!), and how to give your photos a painted edge.

Since painting is all about using color, that's where your journey begins.

Figure 12-1:
This beautiful painting by Melissa Findley was created entirely in Photoshop. You can see more of her artwork at www.WickedFae.com.

Color Theory: The Basics

Color can evoke emotion, capture attention, and send a message. That's why choosing the *right* color is so important. It may also explain why picking colors that go well together can be an exercise in frustration. Some colors pair up nicely, some don't, and who the heck knows why.

The great thing about using Photoshop is that you don't actually need to know *why* certain colors go together. Instead, thanks to a circular diagram called a *color wheel*, you can easily identify which colors live in sweet visual harmony. A color wheel won't turn you into the next Matisse, but for most mortals it's the tool of choice for deciding which colors to use in their projects.

Before you take the color wheel for a spin, you need to understand a few basic color concepts. Consider this section *Color Theory: The Missing Manual*:

- A **color scheme (or color palette)** refers to the group of colors you'll use in your project or painting. Just take a look at any book cover, magazine ad, or Web site and you'll see that it's made from a certain set of colors (usually between three and five colors, plus white or black). The designer usually picks a main color (like blue) and then chooses the other colors according to how they look together and the feeling they evoke when they're viewed as a group. There's a whole science behind picking colors based on what they mean to us humans and how they make us feel. For example, have you ever pondered why hospitals are bathed in pale blue or green? It's because researchers have found that those colors have a soothing effect. If this type of thing interests you, pick up a copy of *Color: Messages and Meanings* by Leatrice Eiseman (Hand Press Books, 2006).

• A **color wheel** is a tool that helps you pick colors that look good together. Without diving too deeply into the science of color relationships let's just say that all colors are related because they're derivatives of one another. The color wheel, which dates back to the 17th century, arranges visible colors on a round diagram according to their relationships. It's based on the three basic colors: yellow, blue, and red—known as *primary colors*—from which all other colors spring. By mixing equal amounts of the primary colors, you get a second set of colors called—surprise—*secondary colors*. As you might suspect, mixing equal parts of the secondary colors gives you a third set of colors called *tertiary colors*. Together, all these colors form the color wheel shown in Figure 12-2.

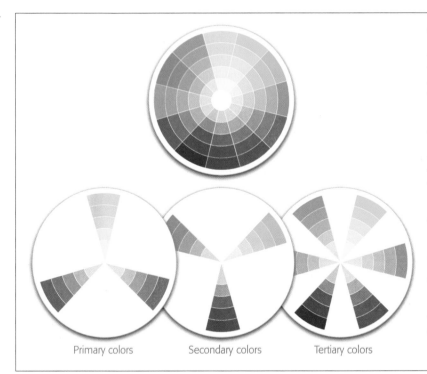

Primary colors   Secondary colors   Tertiary colors

Figure 12-2:
Top: You can pick up your own color wheel at the local art supply store or you can order one online from the Color Wheel Company at www. colorwheelco.com. It may not look exactly like the one shown here (it might have more colors), but it'll be similar. Once you learn a few rules about which colors go best together (described in the next section), you can easily use a color wheel to pick visually pleasing color schemes.

Bottom: Here's the same color wheel with a few of the color wedges hidden so you can see the primary, secondary, and tertiary colors by themselves.

NOTE   Photoshop CS4 has a built-in color wheel inside the new Kuler panel, a color scheme generator discussed in detail later in this chapter.

You'll also run into three different terms to describe color: hue, saturation, and brightness (you've seen them here and there throughout this book). Together, they form all the glorious colors the human eye can perceive:

- **Hue** can mean a few different things, but for the purposes of this discussion, you can think of it as another word for "color," as in red, blue, lime green, or cotton-candy pink. So when you see it in a Photoshop dialog box, just substitute the word *color* in your mind.

- **Saturation** describes a color's strength or intensity. For example, a highly saturated hue has a vivid, intense color. A less saturated hue looks dull and gray. Think vibrancy and you'll have this one down pat.

- **Brightness (or lightness)**, which is usually measured in terms of percent, determines how light or dark a color appears. You can think of brightness as the amount of light shining on an object, ranging from white (100 percent) to black (0 percent). For example, if you shine an incredibly powerful flashlight on an apple, the apple looks almost white (100 percent lightness). When the flashlight is off, you've got no light, so the apple appears almost black (0 percent lightness).

Selecting a Color Scheme

As mentioned earlier, if you're picking a color scheme for your project, you usually begin by choosing a main (or *base*) color. This main color can come from a piece of art that you're starting with (like a logo or photo) or it can be a color that you want to build your design around. Once you know the main color, you can use a few simple rules to find other colors that go well with it. In this section, you'll learn how to use a color wheel to pick a color scheme using four popular *color scheme harmonies* (color combinations proven by color experts to go well together). But don't worry. You'll also learn where to find tools to automate the process in case picking a color manually isn't your cup of tea.

Using a Color Wheel

Let's say you've gotten your hot little hands on a color wheel. Great! Now, what the heck do you do with it? For starters, you need to pick the main color you want your color scheme to revolve around and then plot its location on the color wheel. Once you've done that, you can use one of the following color scheme harmonies to help you pick other colors that go well with it. (To see what these color schemes look like, skip ahead to Figure 12-4.)

- **Monochromatic** schemes use colors from the same wedge of colors on the color wheel.

- **Analogous** schemes use colors from the wedges on both sides of the main color.

- **Complementary** schemes use colors from the wedge directly across from the main color.

- **Split complementary** schemes use colors from the wedges on either side of the main color's complement.

> **NOTE**   This list isn't comprehensive; it includes only the four most common color scheme harmonies. If you want to learn more, grab a copy of *Color Index* (Turtleback, 2002) by Jim Krause.

To use a color wheel to pick a color scheme, follow these steps:

1. **Open an image and choose a main color to start with.**

   Every project starts with something, whether it's a photo, a company logo, or a piece of art. Give it a good long stare and decide on a main color to use for your color scheme. Let's say you want to add color to the design shown in Figure 12-3. Since there's quite a bit of blue in the image, you could easily start there and designate one of the blues as your main color.

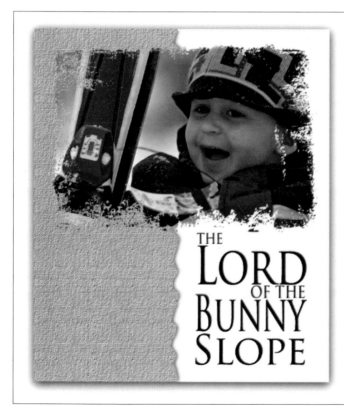

Figure 12-3:
Instead of racking your brain trying to pick colors for the text and background of this greeting card, it's much easier to start with a color that's already in your design. In this case, you could start with one of the blues in the photo.

2. **Once you've picked a color, identify its general location on the color wheel.**

   If you've got an actual color wheel in your hand, you can locate the main color on the wheel simply by looking at it.

3. Locate other colors that go with the main color by using one of the color scheme harmonies described earlier in this section and shown in Figure 12-4.

If you choose your other colors from the related color wedges, you can be sure they'll look good when you use them together.

Using the Kuler Panel

New in Photoshop CS4, *Kuler* is an amazingly useful, community-driven color scheme generator. It began life a couple of years ago as a Web application, and it's never been accessible in Photoshop until now. If you're not a fan of the color wheel, you don't have one handy, or you just need some fresh new color scheme ideas, you can choose from many *themes*—Kuler's name for color schemes—that folks in the Kuler community have created. You can pop open the panel by choosing Window → Extensions → Kuler (see Figure 12-5).

> **NOTE** In order for the Kuler panel to download the latest and greatest themes from the Kuler online community, you need to be connected to the Internet.

At the very top of the Kuler panel you'll see three buttons:

- **About.** If you want to get to know—or get involved with—the online Kuler community, this button will transport you to the Kuler Web site. If you create a free account, you can upload your own themes, rate other people's themes, post to the forums, and so on.

- **Browse.** If you want to browse themes that other people have created, you can search for themes by entering a descriptive word ("rustic," "nature," "corporate," and so on), creator, theme name, or *hex number* in the search field (see the box on page 673 to learn about hex numbers). Or just use the scroll bar to see what's there. The pop-up menus at the top of the panel let you sort themes by their ratings, when they were uploaded, and so on.

  To use a particular theme—that is, to import its colors into Photoshop—select it and click the "Add selected theme to Swatches" button shown in Figure 12-5 (the Swatches panel is discussed on page 460). You can also click the little triangle that appears at the right of the scheme when it's selected and choose "Add to Swatches Panel" from the pop-up menu (see Figure 12-5, left).

- **Create.** Use the controls in this area (Figure 12-5, right) to cook up your own themes. Start by picking a color scheme (page 452) from the Select Rule pop-up menu—choices include analogous, monochromatic, triad, complementary, and so on—and then click the white-rimmed circle on the color wheel and drag it to the color you want to base your theme on (your main color, in other words). You'll see little bars sprout out from your original color choice that follow the rule you picked earlier. The other colors will move around, too, as you move the base color. You can drag the base color's white circle inward or outward, left or right, up or down until you find the color you want. The middle square color swatch beneath the wheel shows the resulting base color.

Figure 12-4:
There are tons of color scheme harmonies out there (you'll need to study up on color theory to learn about them all), but you can think of the ones shown here and described on page 650 as the Fantastic Four. The red box marks the main color's location; each color wedge used in the color schemes is highlighted (the other wedges are faded out). Here you can see what the design looks like using monochromatic (top left), analogous (top right), complementary (bottom left), and split complementary (bottom right) color schemes.

Figure 12-5:
Left: Use the Browse tab to check out themes created by members of the Kuler online community.

Right: You can use the color wheel in the Create tab to make your own themes.

Once you find the right color, you can change its lightness value by using the brightness slider on the right (drag it up to make the base color lighter or down to make it darker). To change another color in your theme, select it by clicking its square swatch below the color wheel. You'll see the corresponding circle on the wheel highlighted in white (or you can click the circle itself to highlight it). Once the circle is highlighted, you can drag it to another area on the wheel to change the color or use the slider on the right to adjust its brightness. When you're happy with your theme, click the Save Theme button at the bottom left of the panel to save it and then click the button to its right to load it into your Swatches panel (page 460). If you want to share your theme with the world, click the Upload button and Photoshop sends you to the Kuler Web site.

TIP   For easier access to the Kuler panel, drag its tab into the Color and Swatches panel group so you don't have to trot up to the Window menu every time you want to use the panel. If your Color and Swatches panel group looks too crowded, drag the Styles tab out of the panel—you won't use it much (if ever) anyhow. See page 17 for more on working with panels.

Other Color Scheme Generating Tools

If you don't have Photoshop CS4 and this whole color-picking business feels overwhelming, never fear; helper applications a-plenty are lurking around the Web. Most work just like Kuler: You pick a base color and a color-scheme rule, and the software generates the rest of the scheme for you based on the rule you chose. Helpful Web sites include:

- **Color Scheme Generator 2.** Free Web-based version only. (*www.wellstyled.com/tools/colorscheme2*).

- **Color Schemer.** Free Web-based version or $50 download; versions for both Mac and Windows (*www.colorschemer.com*).

- **GenoPal.** $50 download, Mac and Windows versions (*www.genometri.com/color*).

- **Painter's Picker** replaces Photoshop's Color Picker (see the next section) with a *real* color wheel. If you've got a background in graphic design, it may be your soul mate. $20 download, Mac only (*www.oldjewelsoftware.com/products/ppicker*).

Choosing Individual Colors

Once you decide on the colors you want to use, the next step is to summon the colors in Photoshop. As you learned in Chapter 1 (page 22), you can use the color chips at the bottom of the Tools panel to choose colors quickly. But, as with most things in Photoshop, you've got plenty of choices, including the Color Picker, the Eyedropper tool, and the Color and Swatches panels. They're all discussed in this section.

The Color Picker

To pick the color you want to paint with, click the foreground color chip at the bottom of the Tools panel to open the *Color Picker* (Figure 12-6). The Color Picker is a fine tool for picking colors, and it's probably the one you'll use most often (especially while you're learning). If you're not trying to summon a specific color value, pick a color by selecting it in the big, square *color field* on the left side of the dialog box; use the color slider to the right of the field to pick a different range of colors. The color you pick shows up in the smaller square swatch at the upper right of the box. Close the Color Picker dialog box and your foreground color chip changes to match the color you chose.

If you need to pick a *specific* color, you can enter its color values in the HSB (hue, saturation, brightness), RGB (red, green, blue), hex number (page 673), Lab (page 183), or CMYK (cyan, magenta, yellow, black) fields. As you learned back in Chapter 2, each color mode identifies colors with specific numeric values. As you click within the color spectrum on the left side of the dialog box, you'll see those values change to reflect the currently selected color. If you want to use a color that already exists in your Photoshop document, just mouse away from the Color Picker and your cursor turns into an eyedropper. When you click the color you want to snatch, it appears in the topmost color swatch in the Color Picker. Sweet!

Click within the spectrum to choose color

Figure 12-6:
Use the Color Picker to tell Photoshop which color you want to use with a particular tool. If you see a tiny gray triangle with an exclamation point (shown in Figure 12-7) beside one of the color swatches, that means the color can't be reproduced with CMYK ink (see Chapter 16 for more info on printing images). A little 3D cube beside the swatch (circled) means the color isn't Web safe (the box on page 665 explains what that warning means and why it's not such a big deal anymore).

NOTE   Once you become accustomed to working with colors and seeing their numeric values, you may begin to visualize the color from the values alone. But if you really want to understand how colors mix to make other colors, you need to study color theory. One great starting point, in addition to some of the books suggested earlier, is *www.avivadirectory.com/color*, which has a huge list of useful color-related links.

The Eyedropper Tool

When you're developing a color scheme, you may want to start by grabbing colors that already exist in your image. The Eyedropper tool is perfect for that job. Grab it by pressing I, mouse over to your image, and then click once to make your foreground color chip match the color your cursor is hovering over. If you want to use the Eyedropper tool to set your *background* color chip, Option-click (Alt-click on a PC) in your image instead.

> **TIP**   When you're painting with the Brush tool and want to pick up a color from your image, you can Option-click (Alt-click) to switch temporarily to the Eyedropper tool. See page 673 to learn how to snatch color from a document or Web page *outside* Photoshop.

Loading Color Libraries

Sometimes, you need to be very precise about your color picking. Maybe a client has given you specific colors to match or you're creating a piece of art that needs to mesh with another designer's work. Enter Photoshop's many built-in *color libraries,* which feature specialized color collections. Figure 12-7 shows you how to get started with them.

The most popular library is the Pantone Matching System (PMS), which lets designers keep colors consistent across projects (it's used on professional printing presses). Each PMS color has a number corresponding to a very specific ink mixture that lets professional printers reproduce the color with the same results every time. That said, to use *true* PMS colors you have to create a spot channel (see page 637). If you pick a color from a color library without using spot channels, Photoshop picks the nearest RGB or CMYK equivalent (depending on which color mode you're in).

Figure 12-7:
Click the Color Libraries button at the top right of the Color Picker to open this dialog box (you can also load libraries using the Swatches panel, discussed in the next section). Choose a library from the Book pop-up menu at the top and then use the slider (or your up and down arrow keys) to move through the list. Once you've found the color you want, click it once to make it your foreground color chip. Then click the Picker button to go back to the Color Picker or click OK to close the dialog box.

TIP If you're in the Color Libraries dialog box and you know the name of the color you want (for example, Pantone 375), you can enter a shorthand version of its name using the number keys on your keyboard. Typing a number feels weird because there's no text field to enter it in, but if you type 375, you'll see a lovely light green swatch appear in the list on your left. You must trust in the Force!

The Swatches Panel

The built-in color libraries are actually just custom collections of swatches. If you want to save a certain group of colors that you've created yourself—or snatched from Kuler (page 454)—you can store them in the Swatches panel (see Figure 12-8). Think of this panel as a holding pen for frequently used colors; it lets you store an ever-growing inventory of colors, each of which you can summon easily with a quick click.

TIP Both the Color Picker and Kuler have buttons for adding a selected color to your Swatches panel so you can easily find that same color later.

To open the panel, choose Windows → Swatches. To use a swatch as your foreground color chip, just click it (Figure 12-8, bottom right).

Figure 12-8:
Top: If you need quick access to one of Photoshop's built-in color libraries, you can load it into your Swatches panel by choosing it from the bottom of the panel menu (circled).

Bottom Left: Photoshop then asks if you want replace the swatches you already have with these new ones.

Bottom Right: If you choose Append, the new swatches appear at the bottom of your Swatches panel, where they remain at your fingertips for as long as you need them. If you've gone hog wild and loaded a ton of colors into the Swatches panel, you can clean it out by choosing Reset Swatches from the panel menu (top) to make Photoshop restore the factory-fresh swatch set.

Here's how to manage your Swatches panel like a pro:

- **To create a new swatch that's the same color as your current foreground color,** hover over an empty area of the panel. When your cursor turns into a little paint bucket, click to add the new swatch. Photoshop displays a dialog box where you can give your swatch a descriptive name.

- **Use the Preset Manager to arrange your swatches.** Since Photoshop lets you load additional swatches only at the end of the list, you may want to use the Preset Manager to rearrange them by project, client, and so on. Flip back to page 35 for the details.

- **To make a swatch's color your foreground color** (page 22), simply click the swatch.

- **To make a swatch's color your background color** (page 22), ⌘-click (Ctrl-click on a PC) the swatch.

- **To delete a swatch,** Option-click (Alt-click) it.

The downside of using the Swatches panel is that there's no way to open a certain set of swatches in its own panel—they're always intermingled with the other swatches in the Swatches panel. You can keep them all together using the Preset Manager as discussed on page 34, or you can make your own swatch layer in the document where you're using those colors. Just create a new layer and use the Brush tool to add little blobs of color from your project or color scheme. Lock the layer so you can't accidentally paint on it (see page 96 for more on locking layers) and then use the Eyedropper tool to sample colors from it when you need them. You can keep the swatch layer out of the way by turning off its visibility (page 78).

The Color Panel

Photoshop has yet another place where you can choose colors: the Color panel (Figure 12-9). It's a lot smaller than the Color Picker and, since it's a panel, it won't pop open a dialog box that covers up your image. To open the panel, choose Window → Color. You'll see the color values of your foreground or background color chips on the left side of the panel (just click the appropriate swatch to select it). You can use the sliders at the bottom of the panel to adjust the colors of the current color chip. If you want to pick a new color, click within the spectrum bar at the bottom of the panel (your cursor turns into an eyedropper).

(Re)Introducing the Brush Tool

You've already used the Brush tool for all kinds of things in previous chapters: editing layer masks (page 111), creating a selection (pages 137 and 162), colorizing grayscale images (page 333), and so on. In this section you're going to learn how to *paint* with it. But first you need to understand a bit more about how this tool works. Grab the Brush tool by pressing B or by clicking its icon in the Tools panel (see Figure 12-10).

Figure 12-9:
Though the Color panel stays nicely tucked out of the way in your panel dock (page 17), it's much smaller than the Color Picker, making it a little tough to see. If your eyesight is good, you'll probably enjoy using it because it takes up so much less space. It's also customizable; you can use the Color panel menu to control what it displays. In this example, the sliders are set to RGB and the spectrum bar at the bottom is set to Grayscale.

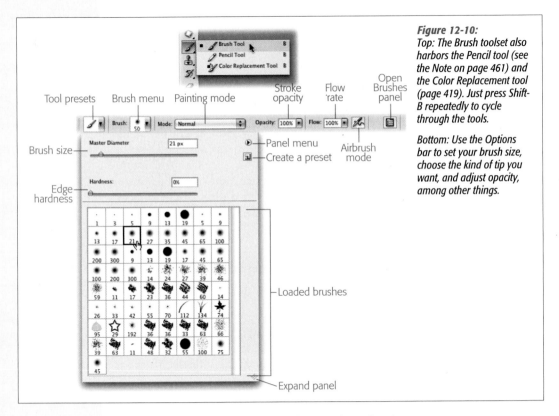

Figure 12-10:
Top: The Brush toolset also harbors the Pencil tool (see the Note on page 461) and the Color Replacement tool (page 419). Just press Shift-B repeatedly to cycle through the tools.

Bottom: Use the Options bar to set your brush size, choose the kind of tip you want, and adjust opacity, among other things.

If you peek in the Options bar, you'll see a slew of settings:

- **Tool presets.** Use this pop-up menu to access brush settings you've previously saved.

- **Brush menu.** Photoshop has a ton of built-in brushes, and you can use this pop-up menu to access and manage them (page 472). You can also use it to control brush size and edge hardness and to save your settings as a preset (page 488). Think of it as a mini version of the full-fledged Brushes panel (page 476).

- **Mode.** This pop-up menu contains all the blend modes (page 267) you've seen so far, along with two new ones: Behind and Clear. Behind mode makes the pixels you're painting appear *behind* the pixels already on that layer (which is essentially the same, though not quite as safe, as painting on a new layer below it). Clear mode makes the pixels you paint transparent.

- **Opacity.** This setting controls how transparent your brushstrokes are; you'll use it a lot since it lets you change the appearance of the paint you're applying. For example, you can start out by painting with bright green at 100 percent opacity and then keep lowering the opacity to produce lighter and lighter shades of green.

- **Flow.** To control the flow of paint to the brush or, rather, the rate at which the color is applied, use this setting. If you paint by dragging across an area, the paint builds up in that spot. Set Flow to a low number for less paint and a high number for more paint.

- **Airbrush.** Click this button to make your brush work like a can of spray paint, as Figure 12-11 explains.

- **Brushes panel.** This magnificent beast lets you customize your brushes in ways you've never imagined. It's covered later in this chapter, starting on page 476.

Once you've adjusted these settings, you can paint with the brush by mousing over to your image and dragging. Your cursor reflects the size and shape of your brush (most of the time it's round like in Figure 12-11, top, unless you've chosen one of the textured or more creative brushes discussed later). If you mouse over a dark part of your image, the ring representing your cursor turns white; if you mouse over a light area, it turns black.

Figure 12-11:
Top: In Airbrush mode, the Brush tool works like a can of spray paint. If you drag, you keep applying more paint (left) than you do in regular mode or with a single click (right).

Bottom: Here you can see the difference between a soft-edged brush (top), which has very soft, semitransparent pixels around the edge, and a hard-edged brush (bottom).

TIP   To paint a straight horizontal or vertical line (or one that's at a 45-degree angle) with the Brush tool, click once where you want the line to start and then Shift-click where you want it to end.

Controlling the Brush Cursor's Appearance

Straight from the factory, your brush cursor reflects the size and shape of whatever brush you've chosen, but you can change your cursor using Photoshop's preferences as shown in Figure 12-12. Most of the time you'll want to stick with either the Normal Brush Tip or the Full Size Brush Tip setting because they let you have a more natural painting experience (the Normal Brush Tip is slightly smaller than your actual brushstroke). The Precise version of the cursor is a crosshair so small it's almost impossible to see, and the Standard option is even less useful because it makes your cursor match the Brush tool's icon (neither option gives you any indication of your brush size).

Figure 12-12:
Choose Photoshop →
Preferences → Cursors
(Edit → Preferences →
Cursors on a PC) to
control how Photoshop
displays your brush's
cursor. The settings in the
Painting Cursors section
let you adjust what the
Brush tool's cursor looks
like while the ones in the
Other Cursors section let
you choose between the
standard tool-shaped
version or a precise
(crosshair) version for
tools like the Eyedropper,
Patch, and Eraser. If you
want to see a crosshair in
the middle of your cursor
so you know exactly
where it's centered, turn
on the "Show Crosshair
in Brush Tip" checkbox.
The color swatch in the
Brush Preview section
shows which color you
see when you use the
new drag-to-resize
keyboard shortcut
explained on page 478.

TIP   If your brush cursor suddenly turns into a microscopic dot inside a crosshair, check your keyboard to see if Caps Lock is turned on. Pressing Caps Lock lets you switch between the precise cursor (the crosshair) and the cursor you're currently using, which could be useful when you're zoomed in and painting tiny details. (Turning on Caps Lock is a *fantastic* trick to play on your coworkers; just make sure you 'fess up before they reinstall the program!)

Painting from Scratch

Now you're ready for the really good stuff: actually painting in Photoshop. Not only is it fun, but it's a great way to get used to the Brush tool.

One thing to remember about painting is that different people use different techniques. Some folks start by drawing a sketch while others dive right into painting. People even have different ways of creating sketches: Some draw pencil sketches on paper, scan them into their computer, and paint over them while others sketch right in Photoshop. And some folks use graphics tablets (which make painting a lot easier and more natural) while others fare quite well with a mouse. The following steps are very basic explain how most folks paint from scratch, but, in the end, it's all about what works for you, so feel free to adapt these steps to suit your style.

> **TIP**   In Photoshop CS4, you can rotate your canvas so it's at a more natural angle while you're painting. See page 61 for the scoop.

Turn on some music, think about what you want to draw, and follow these steps:

1. **Create a new document by pressing ⌘-N (Ctrl+N on a PC), give it a white background, and save it.**

   The question of which size canvas and which resolution to work with depends on what you want to do with your painting. If you've got a new computer with a lot of memory, you may as well make it big enough to print just in case it turns out really well: 3600×5400 pixels at a resolution of 300 ppi is a good choice. If you're going to post it on the Web or view it only onscreen (or if you have a slow computer), make it 1200×1800 at a resolution of 72 ppi instead. It's a good idea to make your document at least 1200 pixels wide or high (it doesn't matter which); that way, you'll have enough pixel info to show details when you zoom in to work on tiny stuff. If your document is less than 1200 pixels in one direction, it'll look really blocky when you zoom in. And since the steps ahead are a bit long and involved, protect your hard work by saving the document as a PSD file now by choosing File → Save As.

2. **Create a new layer and name it Sketch.**

   It's usually best to start with a rough sketch though you certainly don't have to. You can draw the sketch on paper and scan it into Photoshop (see the box on page 472 for the scoop on isolating a sketch onto its own layer) or sketch it with the Brush tool, as explained in the following steps. To add a layer to your document, click the "Create a new layer" button at the bottom of the Layers panel (see Chapter 3 for more on layers), or press Shift-⌘-N (Shift+Ctrl+N on a PC).

3. **Press B to grab the Brush tool.**

   Hop up to the Options bar and pick a fairly small, round, hard-edged brush using the Brush preset panel (Figure 12-10, bottom). Then set your foreground color chip to a dark gray (the color of real pencil lead).

4. **Sketch your drawing.**

With the Sketch layer selected, mouse over to your document and draw a rough sketch of what you want to paint like the one shown in Figure 12-13. Don't worry about fine lines or getting things perfect; you can add details later.

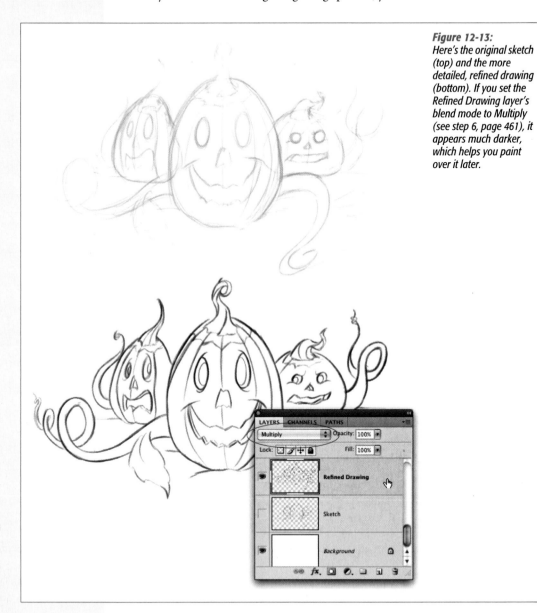

Figure 12-13:
Here's the original sketch (top) and the more detailed, refined drawing (bottom). If you set the Refined Drawing layer's blend mode to Multiply (see step 6, page 461), it appears much darker, which helps you paint over it later.

NOTE   Technically, you could use the Pencil tool to draw your sketch, but the Brush tool is *far* more flexible and produces nice, soft-edged lines instead of the hard, jagged edges you get with the Pencil tool. The only redeeming feature of the Pencil tool is its Auto Erase option that lets you erase previous strokes by drawing over them a second time (which is mainly just cool to watch).

5. **Lower the Sketch layer's opacity to about 40 percent.**

   At the top of the Layers panel, lower the opacity of the sketch until it looks kind of ghostly. You'll use this sketch to help you create a more detailed drawing in the next step.

6. **Create a new layer named Refined Drawing.**

   Press Shift-⌘-N (Shift+Ctrl+N on a PC) to add another new layer, name it *Refined Drawing*, and then click OK. Use the pop-up menu at the top of the Layers panel to change the layer's blend mode to Multiply (Figure 12-13, bottom) to make it appear darker, so it's easier to paint over later.

   This new layer helps you fine-tune your sketch—think of this layer as a piece of tracing paper you've placed on top of the original sketch. The Sketch layer underneath acts like a guide to help you draw more precise and intricate details on the Refined Drawing layer.

7. **Refine the drawing until you're happy with it.**

   By refining your sketch on another layer, you're protecting the original. If you need to erase some of your brushstrokes, hold the E key to switch temporarily to the Eraser tool. Once you're satisfied with the refined drawing, turn off the original sketch layer's visibility by clicking its visibility eye.

8. **Create another new layer named Blue Background and drag it below the Refined Drawing layer.**

   If you build the background of your painting before you paint the drawing, you create a strong color foundation on which to build your painting. That way, you can bind the painting together using the background color(s).

9. **Fill the background layer with whatever you want your dominant background color to be.**

   Over in the Tools panel, click the foreground color chip and pick a fairly dark blue from the Color Picker and then fill the Blue Background layer with that color by pressing Option-Delete (Alt-Backspace on a PC). Alternatively, you can choose Edit → Fill and then pick Other from the Use pop-up menu to access the Color Picker. Click OK twice to fill the layer—once to close the Color Picker and again to close the Fill dialog box.

10. **In the Options bar, grab a large, round, textured brush and lower its opacity to 25 percent.**

    You're getting ready to add even more paint to the Blue Background layer. Why? So you can keep the pumpkins and vines from looking flat by using textured brushes or brushes with rough edges (like the speckled spatter brushes).

As you can see, Photoshop paintings are a lot of work, but they can be very rewarding. By creating every aspect of your painting on a separate layer, you build the image gradually so you don't destroy any one part if you mess up. Okay, who needs a nap?

> **TIP** If you want to practice painting this sketch, you can download the file named Pumpkins.psd from the Missing CD page at *www.missingmanuals.com*.

FREQUENTLY ASKED QUESTION

Isolating a Scanned Sketch

Help! I scanned my sketch, but it's got a white background! How do I get rid of it?

If you go the pencil-and-paper route rather than drawing your sketch in Photoshop, you'll end up with a white background when you bring the scanned image into Photoshop. Luckily, you can get rid of it quickly by using channels.

Flip back to Chapter 5 (page 190) for the scoop on using channels to create a selection. Once you've got marching ants around your sketch, open the Layers panel and create a new layer for the sketch. Fill your selection with the color of your choice by choosing Edit → Fill. Poof! That's all there is to it. Now you've got an inked outline of your sketch, ready for you to fill with paint.

Loading More Built-in Brushes

For all the built-in brushes you see in the Brush preset menu (Figure 12-10), there are hundreds more lying in wait right inside Photoshop—you just have to load them. More brushes means more creativity at your fingertips for stuff like digital paintings, applying a painted edge to a photo (discussed in the following list), adding a sparkle (page 474), or aging a photo so it looks torn and tattered (page 491).

Here's how to load more brushes *and* give your photo a painted edge (if you want skip the technique and go straight to loading brushes, see steps 6–7):

1. **Open a photo and double-click its Background layer to make it editable.**

   This technique involves adding a layer mask, which means you have to unlock the Background layer first (or Photoshop won't let you add the mask). In the resulting dialog box, give the layer a new name if you like and then click OK.

2. **Create a new layer at the bottom of your layers stack.**

   At the bottom of the Layers panel, ⌘-click (Ctrl-click on a PC) the "Create a new layer" button.

3. **Fill the new layer with white (or any other solid color).**

   In a few steps, you're going to hide the edges of your image with a layer mask. If you kept the layer you added in the previous step as is, you'd see through to a transparent checkerboard pattern that makes your edges tough to see. A white background (or other high-contrast solid color) works much better. Choose Edit → Fill and, in the resulting dialog box, pick White from the Use pop-up menu and then click OK.

4. **Press M to grab the Rectangular Marquee tool and draw a selection box around your image about a quarter of an inch inside the edges of your image.**

You'll paint the edges outside this selection box in step 9.

5. **Select the image layer and add a layer mask to it.**

Over in the Layers panel, select the image layer (the one you started out with in step 1) and then click the circle-within-a-square icon to add a layer mask. When you do, Photoshop hides the edges of your photo outside the selection you made in the previous step.

6. **Press B to grab the Brush tool, and then open the Brush menu in the Options bar.**

Head up to the Options bar at the top of your screen and click the down-pointing triangle to the right of the brush preview to see all your brushes (circled in Figure 12-17, top).

7. **Choose Faux Finish Brushes from the Brush fly-out menu.**

Click the tiny right-facing arrow at the top right of the Brush menu (it's circled in Figure 12-17, top). In the resulting fly-out menu, you'll see options for setting the size of your brush previews, loading and saving brushes, and so on. Toward the middle of the menu you'll find lots of new brushes organized into categories like Assorted Brushes, Basic Brushes, and so on. Scroll down until you see Faux Finish Brushes and click it. Photoshop asks if you want to replace your current brushes with the new ones. Instead of clicking OK, click Append so Photoshop adds them to the bottom of the list (after the ones you've already got).

TIP   If you load a new brush set and want to get back to the set you had when you first started using the program, choose Reset Brushes from the fly-out menu shown in Figure 12-17, top.

8. **Pick one of the new brushes.**

Scroll down the Brush menu until you see "Rolled Rag – Terry 120 pixels" (it's circled in Figure 12-17, bottom) and click it. Then mouse over to your document and you'll see the funky, squarish brush cursor circled in Figure 12-18.

9. **With black as your foreground color chip and the layer mask selected, paint along the edges of your image to create a unique border.**

Peek at the color chips at the bottom of your Tools panel and press X until black hops on top. With the layer mask selected, paint over the edges of your photo as shown in Figure 12-18. If you paint over too much of your image, press X to swap color chips so that white is on top and then paint the areas you want to reveal.

10. **Save your image as a PSD file.**

If you decide to go back and edit the painted edges, just select the layer mask, grab the Brush tool and have a ball.

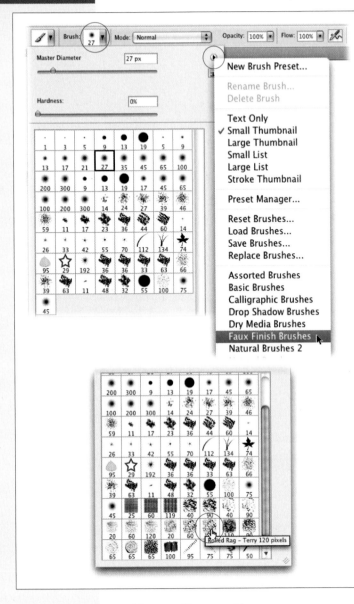

Figure 12-17:
Top: Once you've opened the Brush menu, you can click the tiny right-facing triangle (circled here) to open its fly-out menu. You'll see a long list of menu items that include loading, saving, and resetting brushes (along with several options for controlling the size of your brush previews). Toward the middle, you'll see a variety of brush categories (your list may differ slightly from the one you see here).

Bottom: Once you've selected a new category of brushes to load (like Faux Finish Brushes), they'll appear at the bottom of your Brush menu as shown here. For this particular technique, the Rolled Rag brush (circled) works quite well.

Making an object sparkle

Another fun use for interesting brushes is to make an object look like it's sparkling. Just follow steps 6–7 in the previous list but instead of loading the Faux Finish Brushes, load the Assorted Brushes. Once the new brushes have loaded in your Brush menu, scroll down the list of brush previews and you'll see a couple of crosshatch brushes that make a perfect sparkle if you rotate them (see Figure 12-19).

Figure 12-18:
Top: Be careful to make short brushstrokes or you'll create an edge that looks like a repeating pattern of your brush shape. Just keep brushing back and forth until you get an interesting look.

Bottom: If you use a layer mask to create the technique, your original image remains unharmed as shown here in the Layers panel.

Click one of the crosshatch brushes to select it, click your foreground color chip at the bottom of the Tools panel, and then pick a nice gold from the resulting Color Picker. Over in the Layers panel, create a new layer for each sparkle, so you can rotate each layer individually.

With the first new layer selected (it should be at the top of the Layers panel), click once on your image to add a sparkle. Add another new layer and click again to add another sparkle. Finally, rotate the sparkle using Free Transform by pressing ⌘-T or Ctrl+T on a PC. (Page 245 has the lowdown on Free Transform.) Press Return (Enter) when you're finished rotating and then Shift-click to select both sparkle layers in the Layers panel. Press V to grab the Move tool and drag the sparkle into place.

> **TIP** New in Photoshop CS4, you can hold the V key to switch temporarily to the Move tool. When you let go of the key, you switch back to whatever tool you were using before.

Painted photo edges and sparkles are two of an infinite number of visually interesting techniques you can create using the extra brushes that come with Photoshop. Look through the various brush sets and see if some of the unusual shapes inspire you!

Figure 12-19:
Top: The Assorted category's crosshatch brushes, like the one circled here, are perfect for making an object in your image sparkle.

Bottom: The beauty of creating each sparkle on its own layer is that you can move them around, spin 'em, and control their intensity with the layers' opacity settings.

Customizing Brushes

Once you get really comfortable with the Brush tool, you can experiment with changing the way it behaves. Maybe you'd like to change the spacing between brush marks in a single stroke, have the brush apply a texture, or whatever. The Brushes panel (see Figure 12-20) gives you an amazing amount of control over your brushes. To open the panel, go to Window → Brushes.

The following sections explain in detail the various settings you can tweak in the Brushes panel, but here's the basic procedure for customizing brushes: In the upper-left side of the Brush panel, click the words Brush Presets. Then, in the upper-right part of the panel, choose the brush you want to edit by clicking it. Finally, turn on the checkboxes on the panel's left side and tweak the various settings. (The preview window at the bottom of the panel shows you how your changes affect the brush in real time.) Simple, huh?

> **NOTE** In the Brushes panel, the numbers beneath each brush represent that brush's size in pixels.

The next few sections explain the ways you can customize your brush, and Photoshop gives you a ton of options. They're divided into the categories listed on the left side of the panel; when you click the checkbox next to a category's name, Photoshop displays the options for that category on the right side of the panel. Once you've got a brush's settings in a particular category just right, click the little padlock icon to the right of that category's name to lock those settings.

The Joy of Painter

If you got a charge out of creating a painting from scratch (page 465), you may enjoy using a program called Painter (*www.corel.com/painter*) as a companion program to Photoshop. For years, Painter has been revered by fine artists, commercial designers, and entertainment artists who work on everything from special effects to character and set design. Painter is designed by artists for artists: it's the digital equivalent of a traditional art studio. It works on both Macs and PCs, and it costs $100 for the junior version (called Essentials) and $419 for the full version. If you want to get really serious about digital painting, it's a must have. Here's a sampling of what you can do with it:

- The program shows you the bristles of each brush and how they splay onto your canvas, just like brushes in the real world.

- You can control how fast the paint dries, where the wind is coming from, and how many bristles are in your brush.

- You can create color swatches from an image, layer, or from its mixer pad, allowing you to have custom swatch sets for different projects.

- You can actually blend paints in Painter using a mixer pad just as if you were mixing two colors of wet paint together.

- The program lets you specify the kind of (virtual) paper you're drawing on and whether your brush picks up that texture. You can also create custom brush- and paper-texture palettes (think panels in Photoshop).

- Painter automatically saves the settings you use for each individual brush, so you don't have to keep resetting them. For example, if you tweak one brush, switch to another brush, and then go back to the *first* brush, Painter remembers the settings you used for that first brush (unlike Photoshop, which resets the original brush completely unless you saved it as a preset).

You can save layered PSD files from Painter that you can open in Photoshop for more fine-tuning like color correcting (Chapter 9) and sharpening (Chapter 11). You can also work the other way around and open PSD files directly in Painter.

For true bliss, invest in a Wacom graphics tablet while you're at it (*www.wacom.com*) and you may never leave your studio again. A graphics tablet is an electronic pad that you can draw on with a special pen (known as a *stylus*). A graphics tablet lets you control brush size and opacity by varying the amount of pressure you apply to the tablet with the pen. Combined with Photoshop CS4's new Rotate View feature (page 61), a tablet gives you a truly natural painting experience—without all the mess!

NOTE In the following pages you'll learn a million ways to customize your brushes (okay, maybe not that many, but a whole lot). While it'd be great to list an example of what each one is best suited for, there's just not enough room in this book. You can use a brush to paint literally anything in Photoshop, so how you use the following options is based more on your personal preference and experimentation than on a specific formula. You'll find that the majority of these settings are geared toward introducing random behavior into your brushstrokes so they don't look quite so perfect.

Panel menu
Close panel

Figure 12-20:
The Brushes panel gives you oodles of options for changing the way your brushes behave. If you master these controls, you can make some super cool brushes that make your brushstrokes look more real and less perfect. Start by selecting one of the brush presets (a brush that's built into Photoshop) displayed in the upper-right part of the panel.

Panel dock

Create new brush   Delete brush
from current settings

Brush Tip Shape

The settings in this category affect (surprise!) how the tip of your brush is shaped, which determines how your brushstrokes look. Once you've selected a brush tip from the list of presets on the upper-right part of the panel, you can control the following characteristics:

- **Diameter.** This setting controls the size of the brush. You can also change brush size by going to the Options bar and clicking the down-pointing triangle next to the Brush menu and then adjusting the Master Diameter slider. In Photoshop CS4, you can resize your brush by Ctrl-Option-dragging (Alt+right-click+dragging on a PC). Dragging to the left decreases your brush size and dragging to the right increases it.

- **Use Sample Size.** If you're dealing with a brush that you've customized, clicking this button makes Photoshop return the brush back to its original size.

- **Flip X.** Turning on this checkbox flips the brush tip horizontally. For example, if your brush is shaped like a curved line that points to the right, turning on this checkbox will make it point to the left instead. If the brush is symmetrical, you won't notice any change.

- **Flip Y.** This checkbox flips the brush vertically. If your brush tip is a leaf that points up, for example, this setting will make it point down.

- **Angle.** If you're working with an irregular-shaped or elliptical brush, this setting lets you change its angle, which is great for making a chiseled stroke (imagine an ellipse tilted to one side or the other, similar to calligraphy). You can either enter a number in the Angle box or drag the right-facing arrow in the window to the right (the diagram looks like a crosshair).

- **Roundness.** Use this setting to control the shape of your brush, from perfectly round to elliptical. You can also click the black dots on the crosshair image and drag up or down to change this setting.

- **Hardness.** This slider controls the edges of your brush, from 0 percent (very soft) to 100 percent (hard). The harder the brush's edges, the cleaner your lines. Softer edges give you an airbrushed look. (You can't adjust this setting on custom brushes you've made from images. Bummer!)

- **Spacing.** This slider lets you control the amount of space between brush marks when you make a stroke. The lower the percentage, the closer together the brush marks will be, creating a more solid, cleaner line. Higher percentages make gaps between the brush marks, which is excellent for scatter brushes. If you turn off the Spacing checkbox, Photoshop bases the spacing on how quickly you move your mouse while you paint: Drag slowly for narrow spacing and quickly for wider spacing.

Shape Dynamics

The settings in this category let you make brushes that create natural, realistic-looking brushstrokes made from a series of brush marks rather than solid, perfect-looking brushstrokes.

- **Size Jitter and Control.** These settings determine how much the size of the brush marks varies (see Figure 12-21). When you're painting with a real brush, the strokes aren't perfectly uniform (you'd be hard pressed to make two identical strokes). With this setting, you can specify how much jitter you want the brush to have by entering a percentage or dragging the slider, or you can turn it off altogether by choosing Off from the Control pop-up menu. The Fade setting makes each stroke taper off (like it ran out of paint) within the number of steps you enter in the text box that appears. Setting the Control menu to Pen Pressure makes your stroke taper off at the beginning and end of the mark *if* you're using a graphics tablet. If you have a high-end pen tablet like an Intuos or Cintiq (*www.wacom.com*), you can choose the Stylus Wheel or Pen Tilt setting for other variations (like being able to tilt your brush by tilting your pen).

  NOTE Some of the settings in the Shape Dynamics category may not work for you. For example, Pen Pressure doesn't work with a mouse, so if you choose it from the Control menu, you'll see a tiny triangular warning symbol next to it if you don't have a graphics tablet attached to your computer.

Figure 12-21:
The jitter control lets you introduce a bit of random variation to the brush marks in your stroke. Here's an example of a brushstroke with no jitter (left) and a brushstroke with jitter turned on (right).

- **Minimum Diameter.** This setting controls how small the brush can get. It's helpful on custom brushes when you don't want them to get too small and on round or elliptical brushes when you don't want them to get too thin.

- **Tilt Scale.** This setting is available only if you have a graphics tablet (otherwise it's grayed out); it lets you resize a brush by tilting your stylus.

- **Angle Jitter and Control.** These settings determine how much the angle of the brush marks vary within a single stroke. It's automatically set to 0 percent, but if you want a lot of variation in the angle of your brushstrokes, set it higher. Use the Control pop-up menu to choose from settings like Off, Fade, Pen Pressure, Pen Tilt, Stylus Wheel, and Rotation, discussed earlier under Size Jitter and Control. Also included are Rotation, which rotates the brush marks; Initial Direction, which bases the brush-mark angle on the way you *initially* drag your mouse when you start the brushstroke; and Direction, which bases the brush-mark angle on the direction of the brushstroke. Adjusting the Angle Jitter slider on sampled brushes (custom brushes you've made from images, see page 488) can turn a flat, repetitive brushstroke into a richly textured one.

- **Roundness Jitter and Control.** This setting lets you control how much the roundness of your brushstrokes varies. The Control menu includes Off, Fade, Pen Pressure, Pen Tilt, Stylus Wheel, and Rotation options, as well as Minimum Roundness, which lets you specify a minimum percentage of roundness for your brush (it indicates the ratio between your brush's width and height).

- **Flip X Jitter and Flip Y Jitter.** These options let you flip the jitter on its x- or y-axis (or both), much like you can flip the shape of the brush.

Scattering

Turn on this category's checkbox when you want to make the spacing between your brush marks a bit random as if your brushstroke were splattered onto the canvas instead of applied evenly as shown in Figure 12-22.

Figure 12-22:
When you use it with a layer mask, a Scatter brush lets you break a photo into pieces as shown here. To create this effect, select a brush from the Square Brushes category, turn on Scatter and set it to 60 percent, and then, in the Brush Tip Shape category, set the Spacing to 25 percent.

Choose from the following settings:

- **Scatter and Control.** Unless you change this setting, all your brush marks will follow the line of your stroke. The Scatter slider distributes the brush marks above and below the center of the stroke line, giving them a random look. Turn on the Both Axes checkbox to make Photoshop scatter to the right and left, too.

- **Count.** This setting controls the quantity of marks applied at each spacing interval, which you set using the Spacing setting in the Brush Tip Shape category. Increasing this setting's percentage makes a scatter brush denser; lowering it will thin out the brush.

- **Count Jitter and Control.** Use these settings to control how random the number (quantity) of marks is. If you're using a graphics tablet, set the Control pop-up menu to Pen Pressure and the brush marks will thin out at the beginning and end of your stroke but be dense in the middle.

Texture

These options let you apply a repeating pattern to your brushstroke, which makes it look textured. Photoshop comes with a ton of ready-to-use patterns—though you have to load most of them as explained in Figure 12-23—and you can also add your own.

- **Invert.** Since texture in Photoshop doesn't literally mean that some parts of your image stick up farther than others (that innovation has to wait till CS15), the program bases texture on the colors in a pattern. It considers dark areas "lower" than lighter ones, which makes sense because, in the real world, the parts of a textured surface that protrude receive more light than lower areas, which are darker because they're filled with shadows. Also as in real life, when you paint over a textured part of your document, the lighter (higher) areas get more paint than darker (lower) ones since the hairs on your virtual brush have a hard time reaching down into those low areas. But if you turn on this checkbox, Photoshop reverses the high and low points of the texture, so light areas are low points that don't get very much paint and dark areas are the high points that get lots of paint.

- **Scale.** This slider lets you adjust the size of the pattern. Drag it to the left to make the pattern smaller or to the right to make it bigger.

- **Texture Each Tip.** This checkbox applies the texture to each brush mark *within* the stroke, rather than the *whole* stroke, which results in a more textured look (and slightly less chance of creating a painfully obvious repeating pattern). You have to turn this option on to use the Depth setting discussed later in this list.

- **Mode.** Use this pop-up menu to pick a blend mode for Photoshop to use to apply the pattern to the brushstroke (see page 267 in Chapter 7 for more on blend modes).

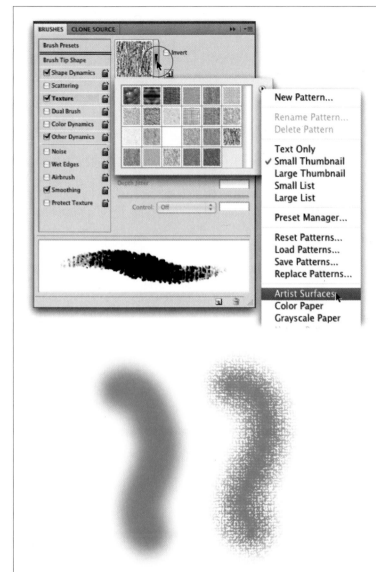

Figure 12-23:
Top: Click the down arrow beside the texture preview (circled) to open the Texture preset menu. You can click the right arrow in the menu's upper-right corner to display the list shown here and load even more textures.

Bottom: Here you can see the difference between a brushstroke with no texture (left) and one with the texture setting turned on (right). The only drawback to using a pattern texture is that you risk of making the repeating pattern in your image identifiable. If that happens, try using a Dual Brush tip instead (see page 484).

- **Depth.** This slider controls how deeply the paint seeps into the texture by increasing the contrast of the colors in the texture. Changing the Depth to a high percentage means the low points of the texture won't get any paint and entering a low percentage means all the areas get the same amount of paint, which reduces the contrast so much you can't see the texture.

- **Minimum Depth.** This slider lets you set the minimum depth that paint can seep into the texture.

• **Depth Jitter and Control.** These settings let you introduce randomness into how the depth varies when the Texture Each Tip checkbox is turned on. To decrease the amount of depth jitter, drag the slider to the left; to increase it, drag the slider to the right. In the Control pop-up menu, you can choose from Off, Fade, Pen Pressure, Pen Tilt, Stylus Wheel, and Rotation (discussed on page 479).

Dual Brush

These options let you combine two brush tips to introduce more texture and randomness into a brushstroke or to give texture to a brush that doesn't have any (see Figure 12-24). Photoshop applies the second brush's texture to the brushstroke of the first brush wherever the two strokes overlap (brush tips of differing shapes will overlap in different places). Pick your first brush in the Brush Tip Shape category by clicking one of the presets and then adjusting its options. Click the Dual Brush category and follow the same process to choose your second brush.

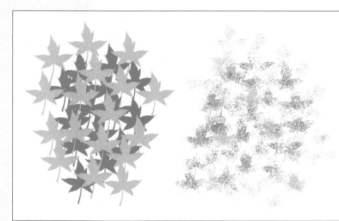

Figure 12-24:
If you want to introduce texture to a brush that doesn't have any, like the leaf brush shown here (left), you can combine it with a textured brush tip (right).

In the Dual Brush category you have these options (and they all apply to the second brush tip you selected):

• **Mode.** Lets you set the blend mode Photoshop uses to combine your brush marks.

• **Diameter.** Controls the size of the second brush tip.

• **Spacing.** Controls the distance between the dual tip's brush marks in a stroke.

• **Scatter.** Lets you control how the brush marks are distributed throughout the stroke.

• **Count.** Use this setting to specify the number of brush marks at each spacing interval.

Color Dynamics

These settings let you control how the paint color varies throughout a brush-stroke—another way to introduce a bit of variety into your brushstrokes so they don't look so uniform (see Figure 12-25).

Figure 12-25:
The Color Dynamics settings let you make a single brushstroke look like it's made from more than one color. If you don't have Color Dynamics turned on and your foreground color chip set to green, your brushstroke will look like the one on the left. But if you turn on Color Dynamics and set your background color chip to yellow, you can use the Foreground/Background Jitter slider to create a brushstroke that randomly combines those two colors (middle). And if you turn on the Hue Jitter setting, you can introduce all kinds of funky colors to your brushstroke (right).

- **Foreground/Background Jitter and Control.** These settings let you control how the paint alternates between the foreground and background colors throughout a stroke. In the Control pop-up menu, you can choose from Off, Fade, Pen Pressure, Pen Tilt, Stylus Wheel, and Rotation (described on page 479).

- **Hue Jitter.** Lets you control color variation in your brushstroke; a higher setting introduces all kinds of funky color flecks into your brushstroke. Figure 12-25, right, shows this setting in action. Drag the slider to the right to introduce more color flecks and drag it to the left to introduce fewer.

- **Saturation Jitter.** Increasing this setting makes Photoshop vary the saturation of the color throughout the stroke.

- **Brightness Jitter.** Use this setting to vary the brightness of the color throughout the stroke.

- **Purity.** This setting increases (if you set it to a positive percentage) or decreases (if you set it to a negative percentage) the color's saturation.

Other Dynamics

These settings change how much paint Photoshop lays down with each brush-stroke (see Figure 12-26). Both controls override the Opacity and Flow settings in the Options bar, so if you tweak them you may find that the Options bar's settings don't seem to work. For example, if you set your Opacity Jitter to 60 percent, that's the most opaque your brush can be, even if you set it to 100 percent Opacity in the Options bar. You've been warned!

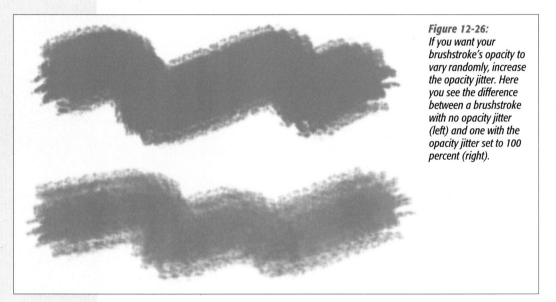

Figure 12-26:
If you want your brushstroke's opacity to vary randomly, increase the opacity jitter. Here you see the difference between a brushstroke with no opacity jitter (left) and one with the opacity jitter set to 100 percent (right).

Here are your options:

- **Opacity Jitter and Control. These settings** control how transparent the paint is throughout the brushstroke. Setting the Opacity Jitter slider to a higher percentage makes the stroke more see-through (see Figure 12-26, right). In the Control pop-up menu, your choices are Off, Fade, Pen Pressure, Pen Tilt, and Stylus Wheel (page 479).

- **Flow Jitter and Control.** These settings let you specify how much paint the brush lays down throughout the brushstroke. A higher percentage means the flow varies more and a lower percentage means the flow varies less. The Control menu gives you the same options as in the Opacity Jitter bullet point.

Noise

Turn on this checkbox to make Photoshop apply a dose of random, grainy texture to your brush tip (if you're using a dual brush tip, the program applies it to both tips). You can use it to introduce more texture and randomness to your brush-strokes. For some reason, the noise isn't as noticeable with hard-edge brushes as it is with soft-edge brushes (maybe because the noise is just more visible in the gray edge pixels you get with a soft-edge brush).

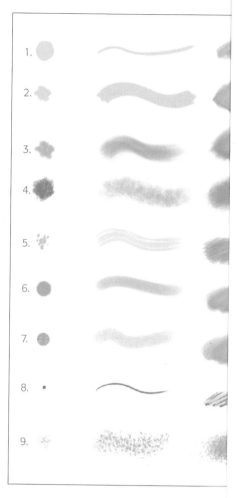

The first step is to create the *paint dab*—
tip—you want to turn into a custom brus
a paint dab in a variety of ways, from the
premise is to create a new 300×300–pix
brushes at various opacity settings to creat
it—the more irregular and messy the dab,
To turn the dab into a brush that you can
using black and gray paint at 100 percent
setting). When you paint with the brush la
ate opaque color and the gray areas will be

> **TIP** If you want to practice making a custo
> Figure 12-28, download the file *DotsBrush.p.*
> *missingmanuals.com.*

Wet Edges

Turning on this checkbox makes the center of your brushstrokes look transparent,
so the paint looks like it's building up along the edges of your brushstroke (similar
to painting with watercolors).

Airbrush

Turn on this checkbox to make your brush behave like a can of spray paint. It has
the same effect as clicking the Airbrush button in the Options bar (page 461).

Smoothing

If you want your brushstrokes to look smoother than they were when you painted
them, turn this option on. It's especially helpful if you don't have a very steady
hand, which can make your brushstrokes look jagged.

Protect Texture

This option lets you apply the same texture pattern and size to all your brush presets (the built-ins) that have a texture. So, for example, you could use this option
to make it look like you're painting on the same surface with a variety of brushes
without actually having to turn on the Texture category for each brush. You can
think of it as a global texture option, much like setting the global light direction of
a drop shadow layer style across several layers in the same document (see page 119
for more on layer styles).

Suggested Brush Customizations

With so many settings, it can be confusing to figure out which brushes really need
changing. You'll find that the presets are really handy, and with just a few tweaks
here and there, they can become indispensable. Figure 12-27 shows a sample of
some extremely useful yet simple customizations. If you like what you see, check
out Table 12-1 to learn about specific settings.

Table 12-1. Suggested brush customizations

Brush number in Figure 12-22	Description	Opacity[a]	Spacing[b]	Shape Dynamics	Other Dynamics	Uses
1	Round, hard-edged brush	25%	0%	Size Jitter = Pen Pressure		Shading, blocking in color, sketching
2, 3	Rough-edged brush	25%	0%	None	With (2) or without (3) Flow Jitter = Pen Pressure	Shading, adding texture, making hair

Table 12-1. Suggested brush cus

Brush number in Figure 12-22	Description
4	Rough brush (custom)c
5	Small dot brush (custom)
6	Round, rough-edged brush
7	Textured round brush
8	Textured round brush
9	Scattered spot brush (custom)

a Adjust this setting in the Options bar.
b Set this in the Brush Tip Shape categor
c Meaning a custom made brush you ma

Defining a New Br

For some seriously creativ
out of anything—a stroke
an image that you've scar
Some folks call brushes th
ple part of a pattern, obje
have to select the pattern,

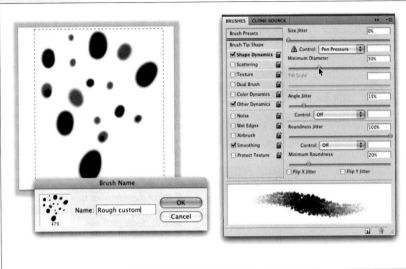

Figure 12-28:
Left: You can create this paint dab by starting with one of the small, soft-edge brush presets. Set your foreground color chip to black and paint a few dots and then switch to some percentage of gray and paint a few more. Just make sure that your Opacity setting in the Options bar is set to 100 percent.

Right: If you make a few changes in the Brushes panels, you can create an extremely useful texture and shading brush.

Once you've created your brush dab, follow these steps to turn it into a brush:

1. **Use the Rectangular Marquee to select the paint dab.**

   To define a brush, you have to select the object first. Press M (or Shift-M) to grab the Rectangular Marquee and draw a selection around the dab (Figure 12-28, left).

2. **Choose Edit → Define Brush Preset.**

   In the resulting dialog box (Figure 12-28, left), give your brush a name and then click OK.

3. **Open a new document (it can be any size) and press B to grab the Brush tool.**

   Press ⌘-N (Ctrl+N on a PC) to open a new document so you can test drive your new brush.

4. **In the Options bar, select your new brush from the Brush menu and then open the Brushes panel.**

   Once you've selected your new brush, click the button at the far right of the Options bar to open the Brushes panel (or click its panel dock icon on the right side of your screen or choose Window → Brushes).

   TIP   Alternatively, you can open the Brushes panel first, click Brush Presets, and then select your new brush from there.

5. **In the Brushes panel, click the Brush Tip Shape category.**

   To create a brush similar to number four in Figure 12-27, change the diameter to 100 pixels, the angle to 70 degrees, and the spacing to 1 percent. If you have a graphics tablet, click the Other Dynamics category and set Opacity Jitter and Flow Jitter to Pen Pressure.

6. **If you have a graphics tablet, click the Shape Dynamics category.**

   Set Size Jitter to Pen Pressure and Minimum diameter to 30 percent (Figure 12-28, right). If you don't have a graphics tablet, try entering a Size Jitter of 25 percent instead (you just won't be able to change it by applying more or less pressure with your pen).

7. **Turn on the Smoothing checkbox.**

   As explained on page 487, this setting makes your brushstrokes smoother than if you're actually drawing them, so they look less jagged.

8. **Save your brush again.**

   Click the "Create new brush" button at the bottom right of the Brushes panel (it looks like a piece of paper with a folded corner). If you don't save the brush again, you lose the settings you just changed. In the resulting dialog box, give it the same name that you did in step 2.

Not only have you created a brush that's great for textures in digital paintings, but you can also use it to make some interesting grunge effects when you're editing photos. The ability to make your own brushes gives you a ton of control when you're applying textures. Who knew?

> **TIP**   If you want to share your new brush with the masses, choose Save Brushes from either the Brush menu's fly-out menu (Figure 12-17) or the Brushes panel menu. Give it a name and then hop on over to the Adobe Studio Exchange site (*www.adobe.com/cfusion/exchange*) and upload your file to achieve Photoshop fame.

Installing New Brushes

You're not alone when it comes to creating new brushes. Folks love sharing their creations, and once they've made a really cool brush, they're usually happy to share it with the masses. That's why all manner of free brushes are available on the Web; one of the best resources is the Adobe Studio Exchange site (*www.adobe.com/ cfusion/exchange*). Click the site's Photoshop link and then choose Brushes from the category list on the right side of the page (you can find all manner of actions, custom shapes, gradients, and so on here, too). You can even download a brush set that'll make your image look like it was printed on torn paper as shown in Figure 12-29. Once you've downloaded the brush set to your hard drive, choose

Load Brushes from the Brush menu's fly-out menu (or from the Brush panel menu) and navigate to where the brush set lives (look for a file named Paper_ Damage.abr) and then click Load. Your new brushes appear in the Brush menu, ready for you to use.

Figure 12-29:
At the Adobe Studio Exchange site, you can download some amazing brushes and share your own creations (top left). After you download and install the Paper Damage brush set (top right), you can use it's brushes to age a photo (bottom).

In this image, each damaging brushstroke was painted in white on its own layer to control the layer's opacity and to protect the original image.

The streaks in Figure 12-29 were made by setting the foreground and background chips to white and brown and then choosing Filter → Render Cloud followed by Filter → Blur Motion → Blur. Next, the streak layer's blend mode was changed to Hard Light. With a few clicks of the funky Paper Damage brushes, the photo looks ancient!

The Art History Brush

Adobe would have you believe that you can use the Art History Brush to turn a photo into a painting, but the darn thing doesn't work very well (as painfully evidenced in the figure below). It's similar to the History Brush (page 26) in that you can select a snapshot of your image (a previous version saved at a particular time) to work from, which is why it's in the same toolset. That said, take this tool for a spin and decide for yourself whether it deserves a spot in your regular tool rotation. Here's how:

1. Grab the Art History Brush by pressing Y.

   Adding the Shift key lets you cycle through all the tools in a toolset. So, if pressing Y selected the History Brush, simply press Shift-Y to select the Art History Brush instead.

2. In the History panel, pick a snapshot or history state (page 25).

   Open the History panel by choosing Window → History and then choose a state by clicking the left column beside the state or snapshot you want to work with.

3. Pick a small, soft-edged brush from the Options bar's Brush menu.

   You can also set the tool's blend mode and opacity in the Options bar just like you can with the Brush tool. And you can use the new keyboard shortcut Ctrl-Option-drag (Alt+right-click+drag on a PC) to resize your brush on the fly—drag left to make your brush smaller and right to make it bigger.

4. In the Options bar, choose Tight Short from the Style menu.

   You'll find 10 different painting styles in this pop-up menu, including Tight Short, Loose Medium, Loose Long, and so on. Anything with the word "tight" in the name works a little better than the others because it keeps the brushstrokes closer together.

5. Change the Options bar's Area field to 50 pixels.

   This setting controls the area covered by the artsy (and totally destructive) brushstrokes you create as you brush across your image. Enter a large number for more strokes or a smaller number for fewer strokes. If you have any hope of recognizing the object you're painting, keep this number relatively low (less than 40 percent).

6. Make sure the Tolerance field is set to 0 percent.

   A low tolerance lets you paint strokes anywhere you want. A high tolerance limits them to areas that differ from the color in the snapshot or history state you picked in step 2.

7. Mouse over to your image and paint it.

   As you brush over your image, your clear and recognizable photo will be replaced with random, supposedly artistic swaths of paint transforming your image into madness and mayhem. Undo command, anyone?

Drawing with the Vector Tools

If your first thought when someone mentions drawing is, "But I can't even draw a straight line!", don't worry: You *can* draw in Photoshop. To draw a straight line, just grab the Line tool (it's one of the shape tools—see page 509) and drag from one spot to another. Or, as you learned in the previous chapter, grab the Brush tool, click in one spot, and then Shift-click another spot. It's that simple. The program also includes all kinds of built-in shapes like circles, rectangles, and lines that are incredibly easy to use.

But what about creating more sophisticated drawings and illustrations? The good news is, you don't have to worry about drawing *anything* freehand, whether it's a line or a curvy shape. Instead, the vector drawing tools you'll learn about in this chapter let you set down a series of *points;* Photoshop then creates *paths* in between those points to form the outline of your shape. Unlike the things you draw by hand with the Brush tool or a real-world pencil, these vector objects are infinitely tweakable: You can move points and adjust the paths to create any shape you want so you can make complex (yet flexible) works of art from scratch, as Figure 13-1 shows.

If you're tempted to bail from this chapter because you're not an artist, hold your horses—you can use the vector drawing tools in a variety of other ways. For example:

- Once you get the hang of these tools, you can use them to add elements to your images that don't exist and can't be photographed, like the ornamental shapes and embellishments shown on page 293.

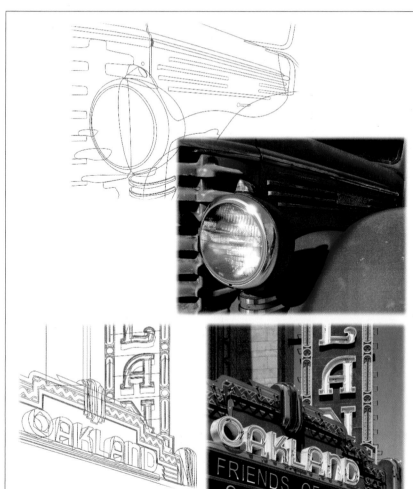

Figure 13-1:
Top: Here you can see the paths that make up the basic shapes of this digital painting by Bert Monroy called "Red Truck." You read that correctly: it's not a photograph—Bert drew every detail by hand. He created the basic shapes using the Pen tool, and then filled in the details with the Brush tool. Instead of a mouse, he used a Wacom interactive pen display (a monitor you can draw directly on; see www.wacom.com/cintiq).

Bottom: This wire-frame drawing (called "Oakland" and also by Bert) is even more complex. If you look closely, you can make out the shapes he created with the Pen tool to make the neon tubes and the sockets that the tubes go into. Now that's something to aspire to! You can see more of Bert's work at www.bertmonroy.com.

- You can use the drawing tools to create precise selections that you can't make any other way. In fact, the Pen tool is a favorite of seasoned Photoshop jockeys because of its selection prowess (see page 521).

- You can use the shape tools to mask (hide) parts of your image (see page 527). Because they're vector based, they're a lot more flexible than the regular ol' layer masks you learned about back on page 105.

Learning to draw with Photoshop's vector tools takes time and patience because they work *very* differently than any other tool you've used so far. But taking the time to master them sets you on the path to becoming a true Photoshop guru.

Before you dive into using the tools themselves, though, you need a quick tour of the different drawing modes you can use. Take a deep breath and read on!

Photoshop's Drawing Modes

In the real world, the word *drawing* implies that you're sketching lines and shapes by hand. But in Photoshop and in this book, drawing refers to creating objects using Photoshop's vector tools: the Pen tool and the various shape tools. Drawing with these tools is more like drafting (think technical drawings such as blueprints) because you're creating precise outlines of shapes instead of the varying lines of a sketch or painting.

> **NOTE**   Here's a way to make sense of the difference between Photoshop's painting tools and its vector drawing tools: If Van Gogh or Michaelangelo had used Photoshop, they would have liked the Brush tool because of its similarity to real-world paintbrushes. However, artists like Matisse, Mondrian, and Picasso would have favored the vector drawing tools because their painting styles are more precise and angular and depend on creating smooth, clean geometric shapes and lines.

Photoshop has three different drawing tool modes (see Figure 13-2); each one determines the kind of drawings you create. Here's what each mode does:

Figure 13-2:
When you press P to grab the Pen tool, you see three buttons for different drawing modes on the left end of the Options bar. The third option (Fill pixels) is grayed out here because you can only use it with shape tools (page 509).

- **Shape layers.** When you're in this mode and you make your first click with any vector drawing tool, Photoshop creates a new Shape layer (page 509) for the shape you're drawing. When you finish drawing the shape, Photoshop automatically fills it with your foreground color (page 22). Drawing in this mode is like using a pair of scissors to cut shapes out of a piece of construction paper in that these shapes hide content on any layers below them.

Shape layers mode works with the Pen tool and the shape tools. It's great for creating geometric shapes filled with color that you can use in your design or overlay onto your image (like the embellishments shown on page 293). You can also use this mode to add a symbol or logo to a product in your image (see page 509). Photoshop comes with a slew of built-in shapes to choose from, though you can also create your own (page 513) and download shapes from the Internet. As you learned back in Chapter 6, you can also use the shape tools to create selections. (See page 134, for example, to learn how to round the edges of your photo using the Rounded Rectangle tool.)

- **Paths,** as you learned earlier, are made up of *points*, which you'll find out more about in the next section. Path mode doesn't create a new Shape layer or fill the path with color. When you're in this mode, Photoshop turns whatever you draw into an empty outline. Use this mode when you want to use the Pen tool to make selections (page 521) or create a clipping path (page 524). You can also fill paths with color (page 519) and give them a stroke (page 517), but Photoshop doesn't automatically create a new layer when you use the Pen tool in Path mode; you have to create a new layer first *and then* add the fill or stroke. The paths you create in this mode live in the Paths panel, which you'll learn about on page 506.

- **Fill pixels.** This mode works only with the shape tools (page 509). Normally when you use one of these tools, Photoshop plops you into Shape layers drawing mode and fills the vector shape with your foreground color. But in Fill pixels mode, Photoshop creates a *pixel*-based layer instead (it still fills the shape with your foreground color). This is handy if you need to edit the shape using tools that don't work with vectors, like filters, painting tools, and so on. That said, you could just as easily rasterize a Shape layer (see page 103) *and then* use those tools. So unless you know *for sure* that you'll never need to change the shape of the object you're drawing, you probably won't use this mode very often.

The drawing process is the same no matter which mode you choose: You pick the Pen tool or one of the shape tools, choose a drawing mode, draw the shape, edit the shape, and then save it for future use. In the following sections you'll learn how to do all that and more.

Now that you have a bird's eye view of the process, it's time to dig into drawing with the Pen tool.

Drawing Paths with the Pen Tool

The Pen tool made its debut in Adobe Illustrator way back in the '80s and offered people precision and control the likes of which they'd never seen. The only problem was that the tool was (and still is) *darn* hard to use. It was met with all kinds of resistance from the artistic community because it didn't conform to the way folks were used to working with digital graphics (not to mention pens and pencils). Instead of clicking and dragging to draw a line, when you use the Pen tool, you create *anchor points* and *control handles*, which are collectively referred to as *vector paths* or *Bezier Curves* (named for their inventor). The handles aren't actually part of the line; they're little levers you use to control each line segment's shape. Figure 13-3 shows what all this looks like.

As you learned back in Chapter 2 (page 48), you can edit and resize vectors without losing quality. For example, you can adjust an object's points and paths (see Figure 13-3, bottom) to tweak its shape and then use Free Transform (page 245) to resize, rotate, distort, warp, or flip your object. When it's just right, you can fill the shape with color (page 519), trace its outline with one of the painting tools (page 517), or load it as a selection to use with a layer mask (page 527).

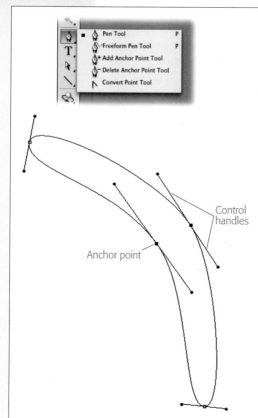

Figure 13-3:
Top: The mighty Pen tool lives near the middle of the Tools panel.

Bottom: This boomerang shape is made from a series of points and paths. The points mark the beginning and end of each line segment; in Photoshop-ese, a line segment is called a path. To change a path's shape, you can drag the points, adjust the control handles, and add or subtract points.

Control handles

Anchor point

With the Pen tool, you have to click twice to create a line: The first click sets the starting anchor point of the line, the second click adds the ending anchor point, and Photoshop adds the path in between. It's kind of like digital connect-the-dots: each time you add a new point, a path appears.

You use two different kinds of anchor points to tell Photoshop whether you want a curved or straight path:

- **Smooth.** Use these anchor points when you want your path to curve. If you click to set an anchor point and then drag in any direction—before releasing your mouse button—the Pen tool creates a *control handle* that you can drag to make the very next path curve. (The direction you drag is extremely important, as you're about to learn.) When you click to make the second anchor point, Photoshop creates the actual path—a curved line between the two points.

- **Corner.** Use these anchor points when you want to draw a straight line. Simply click *without* dragging to set a point, and you don't get any control handles; instead, the Pen tool creates points connected by straight paths. To draw perfectly horizontal or vertical lines, press and hold the Shift key while you click to set more points. This limits the Pen tool to drawing straight lines at angles that are multiples of 45 degrees (45, 90, and so on), which is great when you want to draw geometric shapes.

Once you have, well, *a handle* on points and handles, you can make any shape you want. In the following pages you'll learn how to create both straight and curved paths.

Drawing Straight Paths

It's easy to create straight paths. Here's how:

1. **Press P to grab the Pen tool.**

   The Pen tool lives above the big T in the Tools panel, and its icon looks like a fountain pen.

2. **Choose Paths mode (page 497) in the Options bar.**

   The Paths mode button (shown in Figure 13-2) looks like a fountain pen in a box with little square corners. While you could use Shape layers mode for this exercise, in that mode, Photoshop starts filling your path with color as soon as you start drawing it, which gets confusing (and these techniques are hard enough as it is!). So to see only the path itself—with no fill color—work in Paths mode.

3. **Mouse over to your document and click once to create your first anchor point.**

   Photoshop puts a tiny black square where you clicked, as shown in Figure 13-4, top.

First click   *Second click*

Figure 13-4:
Each time you click, Photoshop adds another anchor point to your line, and connects each point with paths that form your shape. If you want to start a new path instead of add to an existing one, just tap the Esc key and then click somewhere else in your image.

4. **Move your cursor to the right of the first anchor point and click to create a second anchor point.**

   Photoshop adds a straight line that connects the two points.

5. **Move your cursor down an inch or so and click to create another anchor point.**

   Photoshop continues to connect the points with paths after you place each point. If you want to create a perfectly horizontal or vertical line, press and hold the Shift key as you click to add another anchor point. (You can also use this trick to create lines at 45-degree angles.)

6. **When you're finished drawing your lines, press the Esc key or ⌘-click (Ctrl-click on a PC) elsewhere in your document.**

   The anchor points of the lines you've just drawn disappear and you see a thin gray line representing the path you just drew.

7. **If you want to move an anchor point to change the angle of your line, grab the Direct Selection tool by pressing Shift-A until the white arrow appears in the Tools panel.**

   The Direct Selection tool's icon looks like a white arrow, and it lives in the toolset just below the big T in the Text tool (see Figure 13-4, bottom). You'll learn more about the Direct Selection tool when you start editing paths on page 513.

8. **Drag one of your line's anchor points.**

   As long as you hold your mouse button down, you can move the point wherever you want. When you get it positioned just right, simply release the mouse button.

Congratulations! You've just drawn your first path with the Pen tool. Enjoy your success because it gets harder from here on out.

Drawing Curved Paths

Drawing curves with the Pen tool is more complicated because you have to use the control handles mentioned on page 497 to tell Photoshop how big you want the curve to be and in what direction you want it to go. Here's what you do:

> **NOTE**   It's next to *impossible* to get a sense of how the control handles work just by reading about them. So if you're near a computer, turn it on and fire up Photoshop so you can follow along. Better yet, visit this book's Missing CD page at *www.missingmanuals.com* and download the file Curve.tif so you can practice drawing the curves shown in Figure 13-5.

1. **With the Pen tool selected, click your document to set your first anchor point and—without letting go of your mouse button—drag to the left or right to make the point's control handles appear.**

   The control handles pop out from the point you created, and one of the handles sticks to your cursor. These handles indicate the direction your path will take; if you drag to the right, for example, your path will curve right when you add your next anchor point. If you drag left, your path will curve left. For this exercize, drag upward and to the right about half an inch. Once you've extended the control handles that half inch, release your mouse button (see Figure 13-5, top).

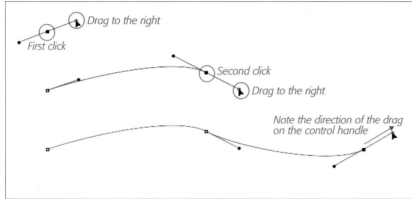

Figure 13-5:
The direction you drag the
control handle determines
the direction of the next
path you draw. You can
watch the path between
two points twist and bend
as you drag the handle.
And notice that the two
opposing handles are
connected and they move
in tandem. If you pull a
handle longer, the curve
gets bigger.

2. About two inches to the right of the first point, click to add a second point and, while holding your mouse button down, drag the new handle downward and to the right half an inch, and then release your mouse button.

   In step 1, you pulled the first handle upward and the curve obediently bent upward. By dragging this second control handle downward your next curve will head downward (see Figure 13-5, middle).

3. Create a third point by clicking and dragging upward and to the right.

   The path that appears when you click to add this third point curves downward because you pulled the control handle downward in the previous step. Drag the third point's control handle upward and slightly to the right to make the curve shown in Figure 13-5, bottom.

4. When you're finished, press the Esc key to let Photoshop know you're done drawing your path.

   You can also ⌘-click (Ctrl-click on a PC) elsewhere in your document.

You've just drawn your first curved path! With practice, you'll get the hang of using the control handles to determine the direction and size of your curves. However, as you may have guessed, the drawing process gets even more complicated from here.

Converting Anchor Points

As you learned on page 497, there are two kinds of anchor points in Photoshop: smooth and corner. To draw complicated paths, you need to know how to switch between smooth points and corner points so you can create curves within a single path that go in the same direction. (Take a peek ahead at Figure 13-7, bottom, to see what this looks like.) To do that, you start by creating a series of curves, and then convert some of the smooth points to corner points. Here's how:

1. **With the Pen tool active, click and hold with your mouse button to create your first point, and then drag the control handle up and away from the anchor point to set the direction of your next curve (Figure 13-6, top left).**

   Release your mouse button when you're ready to make your next anchor point.

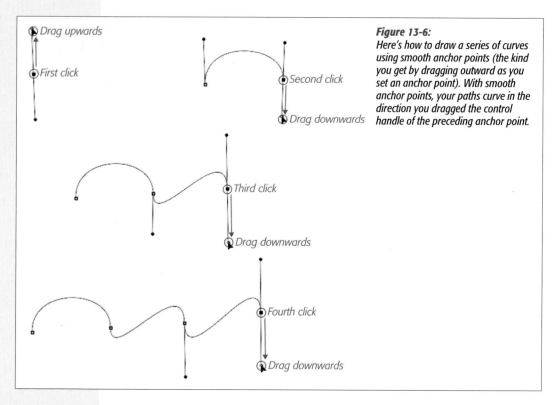

Drag upwards

First click

Second click

Drag downwards

Third click

Drag downwards

Fourth click

Drag downwards

Figure 13-6:
Here's how to draw a series of curves using smooth anchor points (the kind you get by dragging outward as you set an anchor point). With smooth anchor points, your paths curve in the direction you dragged the control handle of the preceding anchor point.

NOTE To practice drawing these paths yourself, visit this book's Missing CD page at *www.missingmanuals.com* and download the file *ComboPath.tif*.

2. **Click to set your second point to the right of the first, and then drag downward (Figure 13-6, top right).**

   When your path has the curve you want, release your mouse button.

3. **Click and drag downward to create a third point (Figure 13-6, middle).**

4. **Click and drag downward once again to create a fourth point (Figure 13-6, bottom).**

5. **Head over to the Tools panel and grab the Convert Point tool (Figure 13-3).**

   The Convert Point tool is tucked away inside the Pen toolset (its icon looks like a caret symbol or upside-down V). Just click and hold on the Pen tool to see the rest of the toolset, or press Shift-P to cycle through the tools.

6. **Click and drag the bottom control handle that's attached to your third anchor point (see Figure 13-7, top) and drag it up so it's close to the opposite control handle on the same anchor point.**

The Convert Point tool "breaks" the bottom control handle away from its partner so that it can move all by itself. This converts the anchor point from a smooth point to a corner point, and changes your path from a smooth curve to a sharp angle. Once you break your control handles apart, they behave much like the hands of a clock and you can move them independently to adjust the angle and curve of your path.

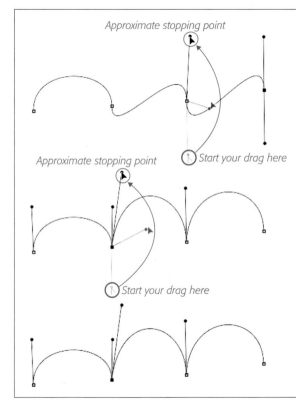

Approximate stopping point

Approximate stopping point

①Start your drag here

①Start your drag here

Figure 13-7:
Once you convert smooth anchor points into corner ones, you can adjust each control handle separately to create a series of curves that bend in the same direction, as shown here.

If you move both parts of your control handle so they're on top of each other, you only see one handle (like the third anchor point shown at the middle and bottom), just as you only see one hand of a clock at noon, when the hour and minute hand overlap. If that happens, grab the Direct Selection tool and drag one of the handles out of the way so you can see them both.

7. **Use the Direct Selection tool to grab your path's second point from the left.**

Unfortunately, you can't select points with the Convert Point tool, so to see the second anchor point's control handles, you have to use the Direct Selection tool. You can use Photoshop CS4's new spring-loaded tools function to temporarily grab the Direct Selection tool—just press and hold A, click the point, and then release the A key. As soon as you select the anchor point, its control handles appear.

TIP   ⌘-clicking (Ctrl-clicking on a PC) changes the Convert Point tool to the Direct Selection tool temporarily, saving you a trip to the Tools panel.

8. Grab the Convert Point tool (or release the A key), grab the bottom control handle that just appeared, and drag it upward next to its partner (see Figure 13-7, middle).

When you're finished, you should have a series of curves that all bend in the same direction (see Figure 13-7, bottom).

UP TO SPEED

Drawing with a French Curve

This Bezier curve business is darn tough to wrap your brain around. But if you've taken any kind of art class—even if it was as far back as middle school—there's a real-world counterpart that makes the curved paths you draw with the Pen tool a little easier to understand.

Drawing with Photoshop's Pen tool is similar to using a brush, pencil, or art knife with a set of *French curves*—plastic stencils that folks use as guides to create flowing, curved lines. French curves have some of the same limitations as the Pen tool. For example, the main challenge when using French curves is picking the stencil that will give you the longest sweep (or arc) possible. It's often necessary to switch stencils or change its position to follow a particular sweep.

With the Pen tool, you can take a similar approach: Try creating the longest possible distance between two points to keep your paths as simple—that is, with as few anchor points—as possible. The more points in your path, the longer Photoshop takes to draw the path. This is especially important when you want to turn the path into a *clipping path* (see page 524) that you can use in a page-layout program like Adobe InDesign or QuarkXPress. Those other programs have to translate and draw your path too, so keeping them as simple as possible helps you avoid problems down the road.

Path Drawing Tips

Here are a few things to keep in mind when you're drawing curved paths with the Pen tool:

- **Exaggerating Curves.** If you want to create an exaggerated curve or one that curves back on itself, you need to drag one side of the control handle in the opposite direction that you drew the path (see Figure 13-8, left). Also, keep in mind that it's the *length* of the handle that determines the height or depth of the curve. (You lengthen a control handle by dragging it farther in any direction.) Figure 13-8, right, shows the affect of different handle lengths on two similar paths.

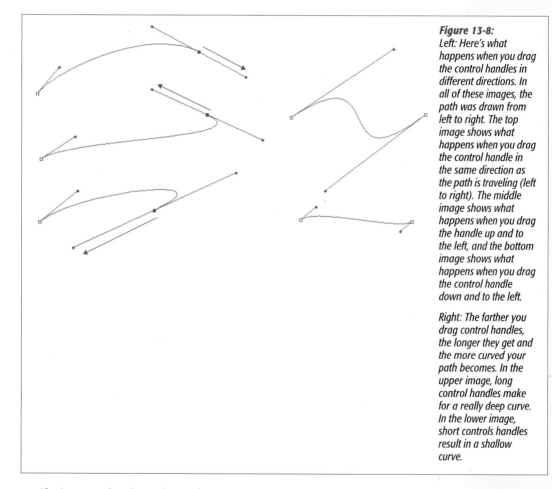

Figure 13-8:
Left: Here's what happens when you drag the control handles in different directions. In all of these images, the path was drawn from left to right. The top image shows what happens when you drag the control handle in the same direction as the path is traveling (left to right). The middle image shows what happens when you drag the handle up and to the left, and the bottom image shows what happens when you drag the control handle down and to the left.

Right: The farther you drag control handles, the longer they get and the more curved your path becomes. In the upper image, long control handles make for a really deep curve. In the lower image, short controls handles result in a shallow curve.

- **Closing a Path.** The paths you've seen so far have all been left open, meaning the starting and ending anchor points aren't connected. If you want to make an arc, for example, you *want* to leave your path open. To create an open path, just press the Esc key after you create the last anchor point, ⌘-click (Ctrl-click on a PC) somewhere else on your screen, or select another tool from your Tools panel. But if you want to fill your path with color, you need to close it to create a *closed shape,* where the two ends of the path are connected. To create a closed path, add your last anchor point and then hover your cursor over the path's starting anchor point (a tiny circle that looks like a degree symbol appears next to your cursor). Once you see the tiny circle, click the starting anchor point and Photoshop adds a straight path that joins the two points and closes the shape.

- **Adding control handles.** If you want to add a control handle to an anchor point that doesn't have one—like the starting or ending anchor point of a straight line—grab the Pen tool and Option-click (Alt-click on a PC) the anchor point. You'll see a tiny, upside-down V (called a *caret*) appear next to your cursor. Keep holding your mouse button down and drag outward to create a *new* control handle that you can adjust to any angle you want, as shown in Figure 13-9. If you Option-click (Alt-click) an anchor point that already has handles, you'll just grab that point's handles instead of adding new ones.

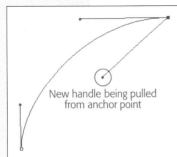

New handle being pulled
from anchor point

Figure 13-9:
If you need to change the direction of a curve, you have to create a control handle that you can drag in a new direction, as shown here. When you drag the new control handle away from the path, you get a curve that heads in the direction you're dragging. But if you Option-click (Alt-click on a PC) the control handle and drag toward the path, you'll create a corner point that changes the direction of the curve. This gives you independent control over each of the point's control handles, as you learned on page 497.

TIP   You can adjust the length of control handles by ⌘-dragging (Alt-dragging on a PC) the path itself. This trick changes the depth of the curve as you drag. If the anchor point at the other end of the path segment doesn't have control handles, you'll end up with an angled corner at the far end of the path segment. You can move anchor points that don't have control handles by ⌘-dragging (Ctrl-dragging on a PC). These tricks make it easy to edit your paths while you're drawing them.

Saving Paths

After all your hard work creating a path, it's a good idea to save the path so you can use it later and edit it. Or you might want to use the path with other objects in your image, like when you're using a path as a vector mask, as explained on page 527. Since paths are vector-based, they don't take up much memory and won't increase your file size much at all, so feel free to save as many paths as you want.

As you're drawing a path, Photoshop stores it in the Paths panel as a temporary *work path* (see Figure 13-10) and displays it in your document as a thin gray line. If you want to hide the path's outline—so you don't accidentally edit or move it—just press Return (Enter on a PC). To create multiple paths in a single document, you have to save the first path you create, or Photoshop adds the next path to the original. To work with your paths, open the Paths panel by choosing Window → Paths (see Figure 13-10).

Drawing with the Freeform Pen Tool

Lurking in the Pen toolset is the *Freeform Pen* tool, which lets you draw simply by dragging (kind of like how you draw with a real pen) instead of clicking to add points and tugging on control handles. Once you've used it to draw a path, you can edit that path using any of the techniques discussed in this chapter. If you're comfortable working with a graphics tablet (see the box on page 477), the Freeform Pen tool may be the way to go. For precise shapes, however, you'll probably be better off sticking with the Pen Tool.

When you're using the Freeform Pen tool, you can turn on the Options bar's Magnetic checkbox to turn it into the *Magnetic Pen* tool, which lets you create a path by clicking and then moving your cursor around the edge of the shape you want to select, trace, or mask (like you do with the Magnetic Lasso tool, page 151). (When you turn on the Magnetic checkbox, Photoshop puts a tiny horseshoe magnet next to your cursor.) The downside is that this tool sometimes produces more points than you can shake a stick at, which means you have to go back and do some point pruning (page 513).

To change the Magnetic Pen tool's settings, in the Options bar, click the down-pointing triangle to the left of the Magnetic checkbox. The resulting menu lets you change the following settings:

- **Width.** This setting determines how close to an edge your cursor has to be before Photoshop selects the edge, like the Magic Wand's tolerance setting (page 140). You can enter a value from 1 to 256 pixels.

- **Contrast.** This setting tells the tool how much contrast there has to be between pixels before it considers an area an edge and plunks down points. You can enter a percentage between 1 and 100; use a higher value for objects that don't have much contrast.

- **Frequency.** This setting lets you control how many points the Magnetic Pen tool adds. Enter a value between 0 and 100; the higher the number, the more points it adds.

- **Pen pressure.** If you're using a graphics tablet and pressure-sensitive stylus (see the box on page 477), turn on this checkbox.

When you're ready to start drawing, click once to set the starting point and then simply trace the outline of the object with your cursor. If the tool starts to go astray and adds points in the wrong spot, just click to add a point of your own. If you want to delete a point the tool created, hover above the point and press Delete (Backspace on a PC). When you've got an outline around your shape, move your cursor over your starting point (a little circle appears next to your cursor) and then click once. That's it!

Figure 13-10:
The Paths panel works pretty much like any other panel. Photoshop highlights the current path. If you want to delete a path, select it and then press Delete (Backspace on a PC) or drag it onto the trash can at the bottom of the panel. As with layers, you can change your paths' stacking order, double-click to rename them, and so on.

Changing the stacking order is a good way to keep related paths together; unfortunately, you can't group paths to organize them like you can with layers (see page 98).

Labels on figure:
Fill path with foreground color
Stroke path with brush
Load path as selection
Make work path from selection
New path
Delete path

Menu items: Save Path... / Duplicate Path... / Delete Path / Make Work Path... / Make Selection... / Fill Path... / Stroke Path... / Clipping Path... / Panel Options... / Close / Close Tab Group

NOTE Miraculously, Photoshop keeps an unsaved work path in your document even if you close the file and don't open it for a year. The catch is you can only have *one* unsaved work path in a document at a time. If you want to add to that work path, simply select it in your Paths panel and start drawing. Don't forget to select it, because if you start drawing *without* selecting the work path first, your original path goes the way of the Dodo. To be safe, you're really better off saving your path if you think you'll want to re-use it.

Photoshop gives you several ways to save a path:

- **Choose Shape layers mode** (page 496) before you start drawing and Photoshop stores your path on its own layer. Don't forget to name the layer so you can keep track of your different paths.

- **Save the path before you draw it** by clicking the "Create new path" button at the bottom of the Paths panel (it looks like a piece of paper with a folded corner). Photoshop will name it Path 1, but you can double-click its name to rename it.

- **Save the path after you draw it** by choosing Save Path from the Paths panel menu.

- **Save the path as a custom shape** (page 512) that you can access through the Options bar's Custom Shape menu. You can save as many paths as you want (they won't bloat the size of your file), so go ahead and have a path-saving party so you can reuse them again later.

- **Save the path as a *clipping path*** (see page 524) that you can use to *isolate* an object (hide its background) in a page-layout program like QuarkXpress or InDesign. If you plan on working with your image in older versions of these programs—which don't understand layered Photoshop documents—this is your best bet.

Drawing with the Shape Tools

Photoshop has a pretty good selection of built-in, vector-based shapes, which are perfect for adding artistic embellishments or using as vector masks (discussed later in this chapter). They include a rectangle, a rounded rectangle (great for making round-edged selections; see page 134), an ellipse, a polygon, a line, and a gazillion custom shapes (see page 512). These preset goodies are huge timesavers because they save you from having to draw something that already exists. Since these preset shapes are made from paths, you can also use the techniques described later in this chapter to morph them into anything you want.

The shape tools work in all three drawing modes (see page 496). This section focuses on the first mode, Shape layers. Just like any other kind of layer, you can stroke, fill, and add layer styles (page 119) to Shape layers, and load them as selections.

For example, let's say you want to create a starburst shape to draw a viewer's attention to some important text (Figure 13-11). There's no sense drawing the starburst from scratch because Photoshop comes with one. And since the shapes are all vector-based, they're resizable, rotatable, and colorable. If you need to make the shape bigger, for example, just select the Shape layer, press ⌘-T (Ctrl+T on a PC) to summon Free Transform, and then use the little handles to make it as big as you want.

Figure 13-11:
You can save time and energy by using Photoshop's built-in shapes. Unless you tell the program otherwise (page 497), it puts each shape on its own Shape layer (circled here). You can resize and rotate the shape using Free Transform (both the Shape and Type layers are selected here so they'll rotate together). You can change your shape's color by double-clicking its layer thumbnail, or gussy it up even more by adding a layer style (see page 119).

Using the Shape Tools

The shape tools couldn't be easier to use: If you can move your mouse diagonally, you can draw a shape. Each shape (rectangle, rounded rectangle, and so on) has its own Options bar settings (Figure 13-12 shows the Line tool, which Photoshop considers a shape). These settings let you create shapes that are certain sizes or have certain proportions, specify the number of sides in a polygon, indent the sides to make a star, and so on.

Figure 13-12:
One of the most commonly used shapes is the Line tool. When you select it, you can use its options (shown here) to add arrowheads to either end of the line—or both ends.

TIP   To draw a symmetrical shape (like a perfect square or circle), press and hold the Shift key as you drag with a shape tool and Photoshop keeps the shape's sides the same size. To draw a shape from the center out, press and hold Option (Alt on a PC) as you drag.

All the shape tools work pretty much the same way. Here's how to use the Line tool:

1. **Grab the Line tool from the Tools panel.**

   The Line tool lives in the shape toolset near the bottom of the Tools panel. If you've never used the shape tools before, the Rectangle tool is probably on top. Click it and hold down your mouse button to choose the Line tool from the resulting fly-out menu, or cycle through the various shape tools by pressing Shift-U repeatedly.

   NOTE   Don't forget to set your drawing mode to Shape layers in the Options bar *before* you draw with the Line tool. If you've used any other drawing mode (page 496), the Options bar will still be set to that previous mode.

2. **In the Options bar, open the shape options menu and add an arrowhead.**

   Click the down-pointing triangle that's circled in Figure 13-12 and turn on the Start or End checkbox (or both). If you like, specify a size for the arrowhead(s) by entering percentages in the Width and Length fields (the factory setting of 500% times the line weight usually works fine). To curve the sides of your arrowhead inward, enter a percentage in the Concavity field.

3. **Enter a width for the line.**

In the Options bar's Weight field, enter a width for your line in pixels.

4. **Pick a line color.**

Click the Color box at the far right of the Options bar to summon the Color Picker (page 457); choose a color and then click OK. If you don't pick a color, Photoshop uses your foreground color (page 22).

5. **Mouse over to your document and click where you want the line to start, and then drag and release your mouse button where you want the line to end.**

Photoshop creates a new Shape layer in your Layers panel. It has a large colored box and a mask area. If your line isn't quite at the angle you wanted or it's not long enough, summon Free Transform by pressing ⌘-T (Ctrl+T on a PC) and then use the resizing handles to rotate the line or make it longer (be careful, though: Your arrowhead might get squished or stretched in the process).

6. **Just for fun. change the line's color by double-clicking the Shape layer thumbnail in your Layers panel and choosing a different color from the resulting Color Picker.**

Click OK when you're finished and your line turns the new color.

> **NOTE**   If you don't like how your line turned out, you don't have to start over—just grab the Direct Selection tool (page 515) and move the line's anchor points until you get the look you want.

For practice, you can try using the Rectangle or Ellipse tool the same way. And remember, once you've created a shape you can modify it in many ways:

- Grab the Direct Selection tool and move the shape's anchor points or alter the points' control handles.
- Use the Pen tool to add or subtract points. You'll learn more about editing paths on page 513.
- Change the shape's color by double-clicking the Shape layer's thumbnail.
- Use Free Transform to resize, distort, or rotate the shape (page 245).
- Use layer styles to add special effects to your Shape layer (page 119).

You can do all kinds of wonderful things with Shapes layers, so it's worth taking the time to experiment with the shape tools.

Drawing Multiple Shapes on One Layer

Each time you draw with a shape tool in Shape layers mode (page 496), Photoshop adds a new Shape layer to your document. If you want to keep drawing on the *same* Shape layer instead, use the Options bar's Add, Subtract, Intersect, and Exclude buttons, shown in Figure 13-12. Flip ahead to page 515 for details on how these options work.

TIP   You can move shapes independently even if they live on the same layer. To do that, grab the Path Selection tool from the Tools panel (the black arrow—see page 515), click to select the shape, and then drag it wherever you want. Or instead of dragging, use the arrow keys on your keyboard to nudge it one pixel at a time (add the Shift key to nudge it 10 pixels at a time).

Using Custom Shapes

To find the really useful shapes that come with Photoshop, you have to do a bit of hunting. Grab the Custom Shape tool (which looks vaguely like a starfish) from the Tools panel—it's in the same toolset as all the other shape tools. Then head up to the Options bar and open the Custom Shape picker by clicking the down-pointing triangle shown in Figure 13-13.

Figure 13-13:
If you create a shape with the Pen tool, you can save it by choosing Save Shapes from the menu shown here (click the circled button to open it). Give your shape a name and it appears in your list of presets. You can also do the same thing by creating a shape, selecting its layer in the Layers panel, and then choosing Edit → Define Custom Shapes.

As soon as the menu opens, click the little right-facing arrow circled in Figure 13-13. In the resulting menu, choose All. A dialog box pops up asking if you want to replace the current shapes; click OK. Now you can see a preview of *all* the built-in shapes right there in the Custom Shape menu (why Photoshop doesn't load these shapes automatically is a mystery). You can also use this menu to change the size of the previews or display them as a text-only list.

You draw with these shapes just as you did with the Line tool (page 510) except that instead of dragging horizontally or vertically, drag *diagonally* to create the shape. You can also press and hold the Shift key to make the perfectly proportional so it looks like the little icon you selected in the shape presets menu. You can modify the shape by filling them with colors and applying layer styles, and customize them by using the Direct Selection tool to tweak its anchor points and control handles (page 514).

The *real* power of using custom shapes, however, lies in defining your own, which can save you tons of time. For example, if you have a piece of vector art that you need to use over and over, you can save it as a custom shape. Choose File → Place to import the art into Photoshop (page 117), and then load it as a selection by ⌘-clicking (Ctrl-clicking on a PC) its layer thumbnail. Next, save it as a path by opening the Paths panel and choosing "Make Work Path" from the Paths panel menu. Finally, choose Edit → Define Custom Shape and, in the resulting dialog box, give your new shape a name and press OK.

From that point on, your custom shape appears in the Options bar's shapes menu any time you're using the Custom Shape tool. To draw the shape you added, just select it from the shapes menu then drag in your document. The only drawback is that the artwork can only be one solid color because Shape layers can only contain one color.

Editing Paths

All this talk about setting points, dragging handles, and creating shapes can sound a bit intimidating. But it's important to remember that the Pen and shape tools are very forgiving—if you don't get your path right the first time, you can always edit it by adding, deleting, and repositioning points and dragging their control handles. The trick lies in knowing *which* tool to use to make the changes you want. This section explains all your options.

Adding, Deleting, and Converting Points

At first, you may have a wee bit of trouble drawing paths that look exactly like you want (surprise!). But don't stress; just add more points, move them around, and adjust the curves until you get the shape you want. You'll need fewer and fewer points as you get more comfortable using the vector drawing tools. If you've had yourself a point party, you can delete the extra ones. Adding and deleting points is really easy since the Pen tool figures out what you want to do depending upon what your cursor is hovering over. For example:

- **To add a point,** grab the Add Points tool (shown on page 497) from the pen toolset (it looks like the Pen tool's icon with a plus sign next to it). When you see a tiny plus sign appear next to your cursor, you can click an existing path to create a new point. You can also just grab the Pen tool, hover your cursor over an existing path (but avoid hovering over any anchor points) and your cursor turns into the Add Points tool automatically. Click anywhere on the path to set new anchor points.

- **To delete a point,** open the pen toolset and grab the Delete Points tool (it looks like the Pen tool though with a tiny minus sign). Or grab the Pen tool and then place your cursor over an existing point, and a tiny minus sign appear next to your cursor to let you know that your cursor has turned into the Delete Points tool (shown on page 497). Either way, click once to get rid of that point.

- **To convert a point from a smooth point to a corner point** (or vice versa), use the Convert Point tool nested in the pen toolset (see the exercise on page 497). To quickly change to this tool while you're using the Pen tool, press the Option key (Alt on a PC) and place your cursor over an anchor point. (Photoshop puts a tiny, upside-down V next to your cursor to let you know that it's swapped to the Convert Point tool.) Click to make Photoshop change the point from one type of anchor point to the other.

- **To add a segment to a path,** put your cursor over the ending anchor point of an open path (shown on page 513) and then click or click and drag to continue drawing. (A tiny forward slash appears next to your cursor.)

- **To join the ends of two open paths,** grab the Pen tool, click one path's endpoint and then hover your cursor over one of the other path's endpoints. When a tiny circle with a line on either side of it appears next to your cursor (it looks almost like a chain link), click to connect the two paths.

Selecting and Moving Paths

Because Photoshop's paths are made up of multiple line segments or individual shapes, you can select, move, reshape, copy, or delete parts of your path—or the whole thing—using the Direct Selection tool and the Path Selection tool. These tools share a toolset near the middle of the Tools panel (both their icons are arrows). To select them, click the arrow icon in the Tools panel or press A (or Shift-A to switch between the tools).

The Path Selection tool turns your cursor into a *black* arrow and lets you select a whole path (Figure 13-14, bottom right) so you can do things like move, resize, or rotate the whole thing. The Direct Selection tool turns your cursor into a *white* arrow and lets you select specific points in a path or individual line segments and apply changes only to them, leaving the rest of the path alone (see Figure 13-14, bottom left).

> **TIP** You can make the Direct Selection tool act like the *Path* Selection tool by pressing Option (Alt on a PC). You can also select multiple points by drawing a box around them by dragging with either the Direct Selection or Path Selection tool.

Once you've selected a path or part of a path, you can:

- **Copy it** by Option-dragging (Alt-dragging on a PC) it to another location. This is handy if you're making a pattern or want to add a bunch of objects to your document. Add the Shift key to copy in a straight line (the copies will all be on the same layer).

- **Delete a segment** by pressing Delete (Backspace on a PC). If you've got a point selected, you can delete the whole path by pressing Delete (Backspace) twice.

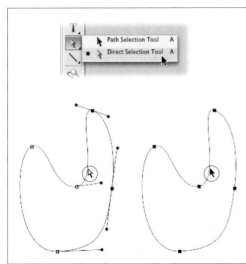

Figure 13-14:
Top: To move points and paths around, grab them with the Direct Selection and Path Selection tool, respectively.

Bottom Left: Use the Direct Selection tool to choose specific points. Two points on this path are selected (the selected points are black).

Bottom Right: Use the Path Selection tool to select a whole path (notice how all the points are black).

- **Align it** using Photoshop's alignment tools (page 71). Use the Path Selection tool to select two or more paths and Photoshop displays alignment tools in the Options bar.

- **Combine it with another path.** If you want to combine two or more paths, select them and then click the Options bar's Combine button.

- **Resize it.** Turn on the Options bar's "Show Bounding Box" checkbox and Photoshop adds a bounding box around the path you selected, complete with resizing handles you can drag. Or summon Free Transform by pressing ⌘-T (Ctrl+T on a PC).

- **Change its intersect mode.** In the Options bar between the Show Bounding Box checkbox and the Combine button are four buttons that let you intersect shapes (closed paths) in a variety of ways. The modes, which are described in the next section, let you combine your paths to make new shapes.

- **Change it** (fill it with color or add a stroke to it, for example) without affecting the whole path, as shown in Figure 13-15. By selecting certain segments, you can fill them with color or give them a stroke (you'll learn how on pages 517 and 519).

Making Paths Intersect

You can use the Options bar to change the *intersect mode* of two or more paths. These modes let you combine shapes in a variety of ways. Here are your options:

- **Add to shape area.** Use this mode to add one shape to another. The combined shapes merge into one, and Photoshop deletes the paths in the shapes' overlapping areas (see Figure 13-16). Its button looks like two overlapping squares that blend together in the middle.

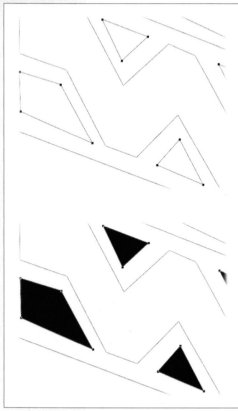

Figure 13-15:
Top: Here's a closeup of the painting shown in bottom, with certain paths selected (notice the black anchor points around the selected shapes).

Bottom: By selecting specific paths, you tell Photoshop to apply any changes you make only to those paths. Here, the selected paths were filled with dark blue.

Figure 13-16:
Left: The first piece in this flower was drawn in "Create new shape layer" mode (page 510), but the rest of the parts were drawn in "Add to shape area" mode (page 515) so that everything stayed on one layer. Drawing all your shapes on a single layer lets you combine the parts together into a single shape.

Right: Use the Path Selection tool to grab all the shapes in the flower, and then click the Options bar's Combine button. Photoshop joins all the selected paths together to make a single shape.

- **Subtract from shape area.** This mode cuts out the area where two shapes overlap (see Figure 13-17). Its button icon looks like a white square overlapping a gray square.

Figure 13-17:

Left: While in "Add shape to area" mode, draw a circle in the flower's center.

Right: With the new circle selected, head up to the Options bar and click "Subtract from shape area" button, which looks like a white square overlapping a gray square. When you do, Photoshop knocks the center out of the flower.

- **Intersect shape areas.** Use this mode to get rid of the areas of your shapes that *don't* overlap, as shown in Figure 13-18. Its button icon looks like two hollow squares with a dark area where they overlap.

Figure 13-18:

Left: To hide the top and bottom of the flower, grab the Pen tool and pop to the Options bar and click the "Intersect shape area" button. Next, grab the Rectangle tool and drag over the flower to hide everything that falls outside of the square's edges.

Right: Want to see your work without lines and handles? You can hide the shape outlines and handles by tapping the Return key (Enter on a PC); press Return (Enter) again to bring 'em back.

- **Exclude overlapping shape areas.** This mode hides the areas where your shapes overlap (see Figure 13-19). Its button looks like two overlapping grey squares that are transparent where they intersect.

Adding a Stroke to a Path

After you create a path with the Pen tool, you can add a *stroke* (outline) to it using any of the painting tools. This is handy when you're trying to draw a long, smooth, flowing line like the one in Figure 13-20 (right). Try drawing that Z freehand using the Brush tool—it's *really* hard to create such a perfect Z shape. But with the Pen tool, you can draw the path first, edit it (if necessary) using the techniques described in the previous sections, and *then* add the fancy red stroke using your favorite brush (see Chapter 12 for more on brushes).

Figure 13-19:
Left: You can hide all of the flower except its tips by excluding overlapping areas. Start by trotting up to the Options bar and clicking the "Exclude overlapping shape areas" button. Now grab the Rounded Rectangle tool and drag over the flower to hide the parts that overlap your rectangle. (Since the circle in the center of the flower was already hidden, it flips back to its original color.)

Right: Press Return (Enter on a PC) to hide your shape outlines so you can see what your finished piece looks like.

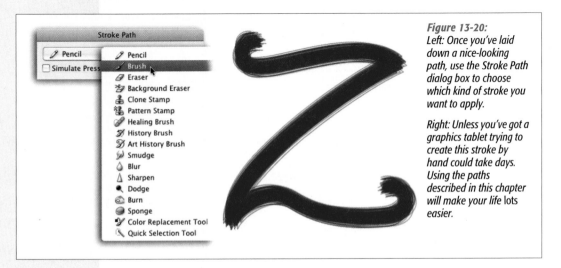

Figure 13-20:
Left: Once you've laid down a nice-looking path, use the Stroke Path dialog box to choose which kind of stroke you want to apply.

Right: Unless you've got a graphics tablet trying to create this stroke by hand could take days. Using the paths described in this chapter will make your life lots easier.

NOTE When you add color to a path with either a fill or stroke the color appears on the current layer. So it's a good idea to take a peek in your Layers panel and make sure you're on the right layer first.

Once you've created a path, open your Layers panel and add a new layer by clicking the "Create a new layer" button at the bottom of the panel. With the new layer selected, you can add a stroke to a path in a couple of ways:

• **Choose Stroke Path from the Paths panel menu.** In the resulting dialog box (Figure 13-20, left), pick the tool you want to use for the stroke. The drawback to this method is that the stroke picks up whatever settings you last applied to that tool (you don't get a chance to change them). For example, if you set the Brush tool to a certain blend mode or lowered its opacity, your stroke uses that blend mode or opacity.

TIP   You can open the Stroke Path dialog box by Option-clicking (Alt-clicking on a PC) the Stroke Path button at the bottom of your Paths panel (it looks like a hollow circle), or by Option-dragging (Alt-dragging) the path in the Paths panel onto the Stroke Path button.

- **Activate the tool you want to use to stroke the path,** adjust its settings in the Options bar, and *then* click the Stroke Path button at the bottom of your Paths panel. This method helps you avoid having to undo the stroke because the tool's settings are all screwy.

Filling a Path

Before you fill a path, take a moment to consider whether it's an open or closed path. As described on page 499, the starting and ending anchor points of an open path don't meet. Since you can't really fill a shape that's not closed, if you try to fill an open shape, Photoshop *imagines* a straight line that connects the starting point to the ending point, and then fills all the closed areas created by that imaginary line. This can lead to some rather strange results, as shown in Figure 13-21, top. When you fill a closed path—one where the starting and ending points *do* meet—Photoshop fills the whole shape just like you'd expect (see Figure 13-21, bottom).

After you draw a path, create a new layer for the fill color, and then choose from the following methods:

- **Choose Fill Path from the Paths panel menu.** Photoshop opens the Fill Path dialog box, where you can choose what you want to fill the shape with (see Figure 13-22). This is handy if you want to fill the shape with a pattern or use a specific blend mode (page 267).

- **Click the "Fill Path with foreground color" button** at the bottom left of your Paths panel (it looks like a circle filled with gray) and Photoshop uses your foreground color (page 22) as the fill color (you don't get a dialog box with this method). Selecting the path in the Paths panel and then dragging it onto this button does the same thing.

- **Option-click (Alt-click on a PC) the Fill Path button** to summon the Fill Path dialog box (Figure 13-22). You can do the same thing by selecting the path in your Paths panel and then Option-dragging (Alt-dragging) it onto the Fill Path button.

The Fill Path dialog box (Figure 13-22) is divided into three sections:

- **Contents.** The Use pop-up menu lets you select whether you want to fill the path with your foreground or background color, a gradient, or a pattern (you can choose a pattern from the Custom Pattern pop-up menu). Choose Color to summon the Color Picker. If you choose History, Photoshop fills the path with the currently selected History state or a snapshot of the image in a previously saved state (see page 25).

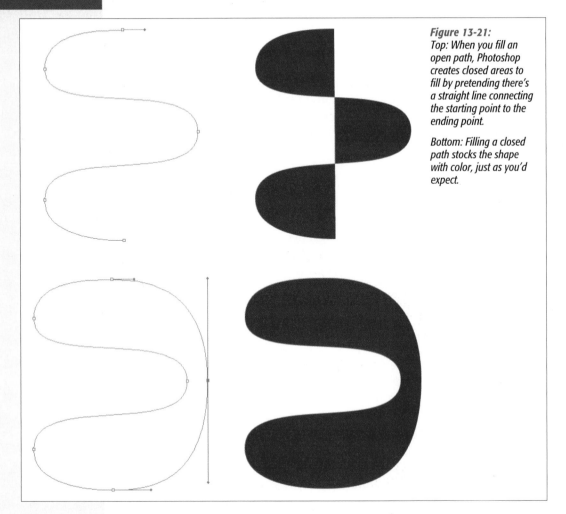

Figure 13-21:
Top: When you fill an open path, Photoshop creates closed areas to fill by pretending there's a straight line connecting the starting point to the ending point.

Bottom: Filling a closed path stocks the shape with color, just as you'd expect.

- **Blending.** Use the Mode pop-up menu to change the fill's blend mode (see page 267), and the Opacity field lets you change the fill's opacity. Turn on the Preserve Transparency checkbox if you're filling a path on a layer that's partially transparent so Photoshop only fills the part that's *not* transparent.

- **Rendering.** If you want to make the fill's edges soft and slightly transparent, enter a number in the Feather Radius field (this setting works like Feather slider in the Refine Edge dialog box; see page 155). The higher the number, the softer the edge. Leave the Anti-alias checkbox turned on to make Photoshop smooth the fill's edges by adding a slight blur. If you turn it off, your fill's edges will be hard and look blocky in curved areas.

Figure 13-22:
You can use this dialog box to tell Photoshop exactly what you want to fill the path with, and change the fill's blend mode or feather its edges. To open the Color Picker, choose Color from the Use pop-up menu.

Making Selections and Masks with Paths

As you learned in Chapter 4, Photoshop is loaded with selection tools. However, when you're trying to select something *really* detailed, like the column section shown in Figure 13-23, none of the regular selection tools can help. That's because the shape is complex and there's very little contrast between the area being selected and the surrounding pixels.

Luckily, you can use the Pen tool to draw a path that follows the contours of any shape you want to select (Figure 13-23, bottom), no matter how intricate it is. The beauty of this method is that the Pen tool is so forgiving—if you don't get it right the first time, you can edit the path. When you've got the path in place, you can load it as a selection and proceed merrily on your way, doing whatever you want with the selected object.

To load a path as a selection, first create the path with the Pen tool and then choose one of these methods:

- **Choose Make Selection from the Paths panel menu.** This summons the dialog box shown in Figure 13-24, where you can adjust settings like the selection's feather amount and whether you want Photoshop to apply anti-aliasing. In the Operation section, you can choose to create a new selection, add to or subtract from an existing one, or create a selection from the intersection of this one and an existing one.

- **Click the "Load path as a selection" button** at the bottom of the Paths panel (it looks like a tiny dotted circle). This method lets you bypass the Make Selection dialog box. Photoshop applies the settings you used the last time you used the Make Selection dialog box (like feather radius). If you haven't yet used that dialog box, Photoshop sets the Feather Radius to zero, leaves anti-aliasing turned on, and creates a brand-new selection when a selection tool is active.

Figure 13-23:
*The lack of contrast in
this image makes it
nearly impossible to
select just part of the
façade (top). But with
the Pen tool, you can
draw a path around the
section you want by
hand (bottom).*

Figure 13-24:
*The Make Selection dialog box lets you feather the selection, tell
Photoshop to apply anti-aliasing to the selection's edges, or
combine it with an existing selection (discussed on the next
page).*

- **Option-click the "Load path as a selection" button** at the bottom of the Paths panel. When you do, Photoshop opens the Make Selection dialog box.

- **Drag the path in the Paths panel onto the "Load path as a selection" button.** This method bypasses the Make Selection dialog box and applies the settings you used last time.

- ⌘-click (Alt-click on a PC) the path's thumbnail in the Paths panel. You won't get a Make Selection dialog box this way, either; the program simply applies the last settings you used.

> **TIP** If you're a fan of keyboard shortcuts, you can load your path as a *new* selection by pressing ⌘-Return (Alt-Enter on a PC); add your path to an *existing* selection by pressing ⌘-Shift-Return (Ctrl+Shift+Enter); *subtract* your path from an existing selection by pressing ⌘-Option-Return (Ctrl+Alt+Enter); or *intersect* your path with an existing selection by pressing ⌘-Shift-Option-Return (Ctrl+Shift+Alt+Enter).

At the bottom of the Make Selection dialog box there lies a section called Operation (Figure 13-24). If you don't have any active selections, Photoshop assumes you want to make a new selection and doesn't let you choose any of the other options. But if you already have an active selection, you can make the selected path interact with it in different ways:

- **Add to Selection** adds the path's shape and attributes (like feather radius, fill color, stroke thickness, and so on) to the selection.

- **Subtract from Selection** subtracts the path's shape and attributes from the selection.

- **Intersect with Selection** selects only the area where the path and the selection overlap.

Making a Path from a Selection

You can also do the opposite and create a path from an existing selection. This is helpful if you need to alter a selection you made with another tool. For example, you can start out with a selection you made with the Rectangular Marquee tool, turn it into a path, and then tweak it with the Pen tool. Here's what you need to do: With an active selection, click the "Make work path from selection" button at the bottom of the Paths panel (it looks like a circle with lines extending from either side). Then, using the path-editing techniques you learned earlier in this chapter, edit away. To transform the path back into a selection, just use one of the options listed in the previous section.

> **NOTE** Beware! The paths that Photoshop creates when you turn a selection into a path aren't always terribly sharp. Pixel selections—especially those created by the Magic Wand—can create bumpy paths that have too many points. If you select an area that needs to be smoothed, open the Paths panel menu and choose Make Work Path. In the resulting dialog box, you can adjust the Tolerance setting to smooth out the pixels. The higher the tolerance, the smoother the resulting path will be. But if you set the tolerance too high (anything over 5), you'll start to lose details.

Making a Clipping Path

If you want to isolate an object from its background to use it in a page-layout program like QuarkXPress or Adobe InDesign, you need to create a *clipping path*. A clipping path is like a written description of your selection that those programs can understand even if they can't handle PSD files, layers, and transparency. You still send the entire document to the page layout program, but the clipping path specifies which *portion* of your image to display.

For example, Figure 13-25 shows a cup that's been isolated from its background in Photoshop using a clipping path and then placed on a blue background in a page-layout program. The page-layout program understands the clipping path that travels along with the file, and uses it to hide the cup's original background.

Figure 13-25:
Top: Use a clipping path to isolate this cup from its background in a way that older page-layout software can understand.

Bottom: Here's the cup after it was placed on a totally different background in a page-layout program.

NOTE Both Adobe InDesign CS4 and QuarkXPress 8 *can* read layered Photoshop files with transparency, and recognize paths saved in TIFF files. So if you're using the latest versions of those programs, you don't need to worry about clipping paths. But if you're dealing with an older version, mastering clipping paths can make you the office hero.

To create a clipping path around an image like the cup in Figure 13-26, follow these steps:

1. **Draw a closed path around the cup with the Pen tool.**

   Press P to grab the Pen tool and start by drawing a path around the outside edge of the cup, using the techniques discussed earlier in this chapter. Zoom in nice and close when drawing the path (page 55); see Figure 13-26, top. When you're done, make sure you click the starting point to close the path.

   TIP   When you're trying to isolate an object from its background, it's a good idea to draw the path about 1 or 2 pixels *inside* the object's edge just to make sure that none of the background sticks around. This way, you're more likely to avoid jagged or muddy edges where bits of the background show through your selection.

2. **Draw a second path inside the cup's handle.**

   To knock out the area inside the handle, click the Options bar's "Exclude overlapping path areas" button so the second path cuts a hole through the first (see Figure 13-26, bottom). Be sure to close this second path by clicking its starting point.

3. **Save the paths.**

   Photoshop won't let you make a clipping path until you save your path. Over in the Paths panel, select the work path (page 506) and drag it onto the "Create new path" button at the bottom of the panel, or choose Save Path from the Paths panel menu. In the dialog box that appears, give your path a descriptive name like *Cup outline*.

4. **Turn your path into a clipping path.**

   From the Paths panel menu, choose Clipping Path. In the resulting dialog box (Figure 13-27), choose the path's name from the Path pop-up menu. The Flatness field controls how accurately printers will follow your path. A lower number means the printer pays attention to more points on your path (so the print is more accurate), and a higher number means it pays attention to fewer points (so the print is less accurate). Some printers can't handle paths with lots of points, so setting this field to a higher number reduces your path's complexity and helps make things easier on your printer. For now, though, just leave this field blank and click OK. In the Paths panel, your path's name now looks like a hollow outline to let you know that it's a clipping path.

   TIP   If you get a call from your printing company complaining that your file caused a printing error, you may need to redo the clipping path and increase the Flatness setting to 4 or 5. This cuts the printer a little slack as far as how precisely it has to follow the clipping path.

Figure 13-26:
*You can see the path as it
travels along the edge of
the cup (top left), and
continues until the entire
cup is surrounded (top
right). To omit the space
inside the handle, draw a
second path around the
inside of the handle
(bottom).*

5. **Save your document as an EPS or TIFF file.**

   Choose File → Save As and pick EPS or TIFF from the Format pop-up menu. If
   you're paranoid about print quality, pick EPS to ensure the best results; because
   EPS format is based on the same language PostScript printers use, it tends to
   print a little more crisply.

Figure 13-27:
Top: Pick your path from the pop-up menu at the top of the Clipping Path dialog box.

Bottom: Once Photoshop has converted your path into a clipping path, it displays the path thumbnail's name in hollow text in your Paths panel.

You've now got yourself a perfectly selected and isolated cup, ready to be beamed up into the nearest page-layout program.

> **TIP** Some stock photography comes with clipping masks or paths, which save you a *ton* of work if you need to place that object on another background. The next time you download a stock image, open it in Photoshop and then take a peek in your Paths panel to see if there's a path or a clipping mask. If there is, you can load it as a selection by ⌘-clicking (Ctrl-clicking on a PC) it and then use it in a mask. Sweet!

Using Vector Masks

Photoshop gives you two ways to make *vector masks* with paths: by using Shape layers or by using the path outlines themselves. These masking methods are quick and easy, and you're absolutely gonna love their flexibility (vectors are infinitely resizable and editable, remember?). That said, it's worth noting a couple of things about using Shape layers as vector masks. First, they work just like the pixel-based masks you learned about in Chapter 3: They can hide any underlying layer content that's *beyond* the shape's edges. Second, because a vector mask is made from vector-based paths, they give you much smoother edges than pixel masks.

Masking with Shape layers

Technically speaking, a Shape layer is one that's filled with color using a vector mask. It only lets the fill color show *through* the shape. That means you can use a Shape layer to mask *other* layers, whether they're pixel- or vector-based, as shown in Figure 13-28. Here's how:

1. **Open an image and double-click its Background layer to make it editable.**

   Since you need to place the Shape layer beneath the image layer, you have to unlock the Background layer or Photoshop won't let you place anything below it. (If you've worked with the photo before and you've already unlocked the Background layer, you can skip this step.)

Figure 13-28:
Left: Here you see an oval drawn with the Ellipse tool (the Ellipse shape tool, not the Elliptical Marquee tool).

Right: By placing he Shape layer below the photo, you can then clip the two layers together so the photo is only visible through the shape.

2. **Using one of the shape tools, draw a shape on your photo.**

   Any shape tool will work, though for this example, press Shift-U to cycle through the shape tools until you've got the Ellipse tool selected. Then mouse over to your image and draw an oval. Don't worry about the fill color because it'll disappear in the next couple of steps.

3. **In the Layers panel, drag the image layer *above* the Shape layer.**

   To use a Shape layer as a mask, it has be below the image layer.

4. **With the Shape layer active, choose Layer → Create Clipping Mask.**

   Photoshop clips the image layer to the Shape layer that lies below. In your Layers panel, the image layer thumbnail scoots over to the right and you see a down-pointing arrow letting you know that it's attached to the layer below. You can do the same thing by hovering your cursor between the line that separates the two layers in the Layers panel and pressing Option (Alt on a PC); when your cursor changes to two intersecting circles, click once.

5. **Since the edges of the image layer are now hidden by the Shape layer, you might want to create a new solid-colored background by adding a new layer to the bottom of your layers stack and filling it with color, but this step is purely optional.**

The wonderful thing about this kind of mask is that you can activate the Shape layer and modify it using Free Transform (page 245). You can also edit the anchor points that make up shape's path using the techniques described on page 514. Photoshop instantly reflects any changes you make in your document because the image layer is bound to (clipped through) the Shape layer.

You can also mask more than one layer with a Shape layer. Just arrange your layers so the soon-to-be-a-mask Shape layer is *below* the other layers. Next, ⌘-click (Ctrl-click) to select the layers you want to mask—don't select the Shape layer—and then, from the Layers menu (or Layers panel menu), choose Create Clipping Mask; you can also press ⌘-option-G or Ctrl+Alt+G on a PC. Either way, Photoshop clips all the selected layers to Shape layer.

Creating a vector mask from a path

You can also create a vector mask from a path outline. It works just like the regular ol' layer masks you learned about back in Chapter 3 and adds a mask thumbnail to the currently active layer. (If your Background layer is locked, you'll need to double-click it before adding the vector mask.) The difference is that since it's vector-based, you can edit it all you want and its edges stay nice and sharp.

Here's how to make a vector mask from a path:

1. Grab the Pen tool by pressing P and, in the Options bar, select the Path drawing mode.

2. Draw a path using the method described on page 497.

3. Open the Paths panel by choosing Window → Paths and then select the new path by clicking it.

4. Back in your Layers panel, select the layer you want to add the mask to and then create the mask by ⌘-clicking (Ctrl-clicking on a PC) the "Add a layer mask" button at the bottom of the panel.

   Photoshop adds a vector mask to your layer.

   TIP In Photoshop CS4, you can also create a vector mask by choosing Window → Masks to open the Masks panel, and then clicking the "Add a vector mask" button in the panel's top-right corner. (See page 111 for more on the Masks panel)

If you decide you need to edit the vector mask, just select its thumbnail in the Layers panel and use the Path Selection tool to activate the anchor points and control handles. Sweet!

Creating Artistic Text

Text has the power to make or break your design and Photoshop has a veritable smorgasbord of text creation and formatting options. But just because you *can* do something doesn't mean you *should*. The act of creating text is something of an art form (called *typography*), though it's all too easy to get carried away with decorating rather than creating legible prose.

Keep in mind that Photoshop isn't always the right place to be wordsmithing in the first place. The box on page 532 gives you some pointers to help decide whether to hunt and peck in another program altogether. Nevertheless, Photoshop has plenty of tools that, when used tastefully, can help create beautiful type. Some of these tools are easy to find, while others are hidden so deep in the program that you'd need a treasure map to find 'em. This chapter will guide you in the right direction, but more importantly, you'll learn when and how to use each tool. You'll also pick up quite a lot about the art of type in the process.

Typography 101

People have been creating and arranging symbols for thousands of years. In the early days of print, text and symbol wrangling was handled by exacting craftsmen called typesetters, who lovingly hammered letterforms into metal plates that were then physically set onto printing presses (hence the phrase, *setting type*). With the advent of desktop publishing, however, everyone *and* their Cocker Spaniel started creating text. This has been both good and bad: It's great that you can zap up your own yard sale signs, invitations, and posters; but, as you might suspect, the quality of typography has suffered since most folks lack professional training. Figure 14-1 shows examples of good and bad typography.

Figure 14-1:
Left: When formatted well, type can become a beautiful and powerful form of art.

Right: Done badly, type can be garish and difficult to read. The combination of Comic Sans (a truly horrible typeface) and multiple layer styles (page 119) renders this innocent text completely hideous.

Some of the most frequent typographic offenses include:

- **Overusing decorative fonts (page 535) and using too many fonts per design.** Just because you have a ton of wacky fonts doesn't mean you should use them—especially not all in the same document.

- **Setting whole sentences in capital letters.** This makes the text hard to read and tends to imply that you're YELLING.

- **Underlining text that isn't a hyperlink.** Thanks to the Internet, when folks see an underlined word, they assume it's a hyperlink. Find another way to make your text stand out, such as bolding or italicizing.

- **Centering large bodies of text.** It's best to reserve centered text for formal announcements; you'll learn why in the figure on page 568.

- **Misusing straight and smart (curly) quotation marks and apostrophes.** Use the straight ones to indicate units of measurement (feet and inches) and curly ones for everything else. Photoshop can take care of this for you by turning on the Smart Quotes feature shown on page 537.

- **Misusing (or not using) hyphens, en dashes, and em dashes.**

  - **Hyphens** are for combining two words (like "pixel-jockey") and for line breaks (when a word gets split across two lines of text).

  - **En dashes** are slightly longer than hyphens and are a good substitute for the word *to*, as in "Chapters 1–4" or "8:00 a.m.–5:00 p.m." On a Mac, you can create an en dash by typing Option-Hyphen (on a PC, press and hold Alt and type the numbers 0150).

  - **Em dashes** are the longest of the bunch and imply an abrupt change—like this!—or a halt in thought or speech. Use them instead of a comma or period, when the former is too weak and the latter too strong. To create an Em dash on a Mac, press Shift-Option-Hyphen (press Alt and hold and type the numbers 0151).

- **Improperly spaced ellipses (…).** An ellipse indicates an omission, interruption, or hesitation in thought, as in, "But…but…you promised!" Instead of typing three periods (which can get broken between lines), let your computer create the dots for you. On a Mac, it's Option-; (press Alt and type the numbers 0133).

There are more offenses, to be sure, but this isn't *Typography: The Missing Manual* (now there's an idea!). Nonetheless, the guidelines listed above will serve you well throughout the rest of this chapter, if not your entire career.

FREQUENTLY ASKED QUESTION

Photoshop and Text

When should I use Photoshop for text?

There's a time and place for everything, and that includes Photoshop text. Though each new version of the program boasts new and improved text formatting capabilities, it's just not made for handling big hunks of text. This book, for instance, was written in Microsoft Word, *not* Photoshop.

Here are a couple of rules of thumb that can help you figure out when to use Photoshop for text:

- **Avoid using Photoshop if you're sending the piece to a professional printer.** It's much better to use page layout software like Adobe InDesign or QuarkXPress because both programs produce *vector* text (each character is described mathematically as a series of curves and lines—see Chapter 13 for details), which will print nice and crisp.

Though Photoshop text starts out as editable vectors, it can get *rasterized* (converted to dots) when the file is flattened (page 104) and exported, making it look fuzzy when printed. The fix is to save the Photoshop file in EPS or PDF format (see page 620) so the letterforms remain vector (though they won't remain editable). You could also convert the text into a *shape*, as discussed on page 585.

- **Use Photoshop if the text is part of the image itself.** For example, if you want to make a photo visible through the text (as shown on page 583) or give it an artistic treatment like a texture (see page 578), then Photoshop is the way to go. Just save the file as an EPS or PDF before sending it to a commercial printer to ensure it will print smoothly.

Of course, if Photoshop is the only program you've got, then you have no choice. May the force be with you.

The Face of Type

At the heart of typography lies the *letterform,* the specific shape of various letters or characters. In the digital realm, letterforms are called *typefaces* or *fonts*. Technically, a typeface is the overall shape of the letterforms and a font is the specific design, size, style, and weight (but people use the terms interchangeably). For example, the text you're reading right now is Times, a typeface, while Times 14-point, bold is a *font*—the latter being more descriptive.

> **NOTE**   Just to keep you on your toes, you may also see the term "font family" used to describe typefaces.

Common typeface formats

Typefaces come in various formats that determine how and what kind of information gets stored in each font file and ultimately, how they print. There are only three formats you need to worry about in Photoshop: PostScript, TrueType, and OpenType. If the piece *is* headed for a professional printer, the kind of typeface you pick can make a big difference in print quality. Here's some info that can help you decide which one to choose:

TIP   If you've already created some Photoshop text, you can discover what font format you've used by taking a peek at the Font Family menu—the pop-up menu showing the font's name—in the Options bar (shown on page 554) or the Character panel (page 556), as explained in Figure 14-2.

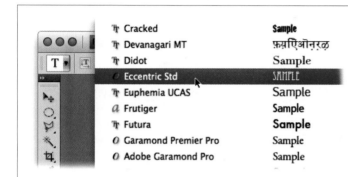

Figure 14-2:
In the Font Family menu, you'll spot a symbol to the left of each font name denoting its format. A lowercase a means it's a PostScript font, TT stands for TrueType, and an O indicates OpenType.

- **PostScript.** Most graphic design pros consider this format the safest and most reliable for printing because it's been around for years. This format creates vector text, wherein characters are made up of curves and lines, so you can resize them infinitely without losing quality. Each PostScript typeface consists of two files containing two sets of characters: one that gets displayed onscreen (called *screen* or *bitmap* because screens display bits or dots) and another that gets printed (called *outlines* because it contains an outline drawing of each character, though it's also commonly referred to as the *printer* file). This format produces high quality text when printed on PostScript devices like laser printers and professional printing presses. The downside is that the two files can get separated or (gasp!) lost. (If you lose the screen file, you can't see the font onscreen; if you lose the outline, you can't print it.) People who install and manage fonts manually (see the box on page 536) occasionally run into these kinds of problems.

- **TrueType.** Developed jointly by Apple and Microsoft, TrueType is the most common typeface format on computers today. It's what you'll find in both the Mac and Windows operating systems (though they're different versions so they won't look the same). Both the screen and outline information are stored in a single file, so they're more difficult to separate and lose than PostScript fonts. Though they rival the quality of PostScript, and their usage in the design community has increased, many professional printers still prefer PostScript because of its longtime reliability.

- **OpenType**. This font format, created by Microsoft and Adobe, is the new kid on the block. Like TrueType, OpenType fonts store the screen and outline information together in one file. They work well and look the same on both Macs and Windows computers (which is helpful), plus they can store more than 65,000 different *glyphs* (a unique graphical representation of a letter, number, punctuation mark, or pictographic symbol) in one font file. This makes them ideal for decorative and pictorial languages like Asian and Middle-Eastern, and for other fancy typographic goodness like ligatures and stylistic alternates (page 564). As with most things, change takes time, so a lot of printers don't yet support this format. But because it's so versatile, someday OpenType will rule the typographic world.

NOTE If you're designing a piece that'll be posted online, typeface format doesn't matter because the text isn't headed for a printer. If you're printing to a non-postscript device like an ink-jet printer, *anti-aliasing* matters more than typeface format—see page 555 for details.

Typeface categories

Font foundries, the purveyors of fonts, crank out new typefaces daily. Depending who you ask, there are between 50,000–150,000 known fonts in the wild. No wonder it's tough to choose! Luckily, there are a few basic principles for choosing a typeface that's appropriate to your message—one that will reinforce, rather than distract from it. Figure 14-3 shows you an example of the following typeface categories:

Serif
Sans serif
Slab serif
Decorative, Display
Scripts

Figure 14-3:
Different situations call for different typefaces. It'd be silly to print a newspaper in a decorative font—it'd be nearly impossible to read. And no one will come to your tea party if they're put off by the big, bold letterforms of a display font, which seem to say, "Come to my party or else!"

- **Serif.** These typefaces have little lines (*serifs*) extending from the main stroke that resemble tiny feet, like the ones at the top and bottom of this T. The main strokes vary from thick to thin, and the serifs actually help lead the eye from one character to the next. Serifs are great for large bodies of text like books (you're reading a serif font now), newspapers, or magazines where legibility is paramount. However, they're not so good for large bodies of *online* text (the next bullet point explains why). Examples include Times New Roman, Garamond, and Minion.

- **Sans serif.** Typefaces lacking the aforementioned feet are called *sans serif* ("sans" means "without"). They're perfect for headlines, subheads, and surprisingly enough, online body copy. Because their main strokes are uniform—they don't vary from thick to thin—they display well at small sizes, so they're ideal for Web use. Examples include Arial, Helvetica, and Futura.

- **Slab serif.** These guys have uniform main strokes, thick serifs, and often appear bolded. Use them when you want to attract attention, or when printing body copy under less than optimal conditions (cheap paper, cheap printer, or fax machine). Examples include Bookman, Courier, and Rockwell.

- **Decorative, Display.** This group includes all kinds of distinctive, eye-catching fonts, from the big and bold, to the swirly, to letters made out of bunnies. Though gloriously unusual, they're harder to read due to the extra ornamentation or stroke thickness. Use them sparingly and on small blocks of text (or perhaps on a single word). Examples include Impact, Party, and Stencil.

- **Scripts.** Casual scripts are designed to look as though they were drawn (quickly) by hand. Formal scripts have carefully crafted strokes that actually join the letters together, like cursive handwriting. Use casual scripts for small blocks of text (again, because they're a little harder to read), and reserve formal scripts for fancy announcements (weddings, graduations, and so on). Examples include Brush Script, Freestyle, and Edwardian.

Font styles

Most typefaces contain myriad *styles* (variations) like bold, semi-bold, italic, condensed, and so on. When these styles are included in the typeface itself (meaning they were designed by the typeface creator), they're called *native* or *built-in styles*. To view all native styles for a particular typeface, use the font styles pop-up menu (which sits to the right of the Font Family menu) in the Options bar (page 554) or in the Character panel (page 556). Just click a style to select it.

If the typeface doesn't contain a bold or italic version, Photoshop can fake it for you. Just select a font from the Font Family menu then head over to the Character panel and click the bold or italic button (the bold button has a capital T on it, and the italic button has a slanted *T*). Photoshop will do its best to tilt the characters or make them thicker, creating what's known as a *simulated* or *faux style*. These faux styles often look fine onscreen but terrible when printed, as the printer has no outline file (drawing) to go by. Whether it's font styles, shoes, or handbags, real is *always* better than fake.

Managing Fonts

Unless you never, ever, work with text in your Photoshop documents, you've had to make font choices now and then. Odds are good that you've also added fonts to your computer, which means you've got more than a handful floating about.

Installing fonts manually can be dangerous, as you'll eventually run into *font conflicts*—when you have two or more font formats with the same name—or worse, damaged fonts (fonts that get corrupted and don't work properly). Either scenario can wreak all manner of havoc on the performance of both your computer and Photoshop, and can make them crash. If you think this is scary, you're right; and, if you've got a ton of fonts, it's a matter of *when* you'll run into a conflict, not *if*.

The solution, dear grasshopper, is to invest in font management software. These programs serve as a localized repository for all your fonts, instead of having them scattered throughout your hard drive. They can turn fonts on or off (so you don't have to scroll through a mile-long font list), and let you organize them in a multitude of ways such as by favorites, project or client, and so on.

There are some free font management programs flitting around on the Web, but when it comes to working with professional programs like Adobe Creative Suite, it's worth paying for one. Both Extensis (*www.extensis.com*) and Insider Software (*www.insidersoftware.com*) have great offerings for Macs and PCs that are loaded with features designed to make your font life easier and more importantly, headache free.

Extensis offers Suitcase Fusion for the Mac and Suitcase for Windows XP and Vista for $100. Insider Software has a cross-platform offering called FontAgent Pro, which is also $100. Both programs have similar features: They track and manage the fonts you add to your computer as well as system fonts (the ones that came with your computer), which is a real bonus if you have third-party fonts with the same names as your system fonts. They also activate fonts when you need them and perform basic checks when you add new ones to make sure they're not damaged. This alone could save your hide because damaged fonts are notorious for causing Photoshop crashes and printing problems.

FontAgent Pro also has one special feature that Suitcase doesn't: Auto font activation in Photoshop. That means if Photoshop encounters a missing font when opening a document (see the box on page 542), FontAgent Pro will activate it on the fly, without you having to lift a finger. How cool is that?!

Previewing fonts

Choosing a font is 100 times easier if you can actually *see* what it looks like. Photoshop is happy to show you an example of each font in the Font Family menu (page 554), but you've got to tell it that you want to see them. On a Mac, choose Photoshop → Preferences → Type, or Edit → Preferences → Type in Windows. Turn on the Font Preview Size checkbox, and then pick a preview size from the pop-up menu as shown in Figure 14-4 (Large is a good choice), and then click OK. Both the Options bar and Character palette's font family menus will now display the word "sample" in the actual typeface to the right of the font's name, making it a heck of lot easier to choose one. To turn the previews off, just pop open the Type preferences as described above and turn off the Font Preview Size checkbox.

> **NOTE** Font previews can make Photoshop feel sluggish. If you have thousands of active typefaces, a slow computer, or very little memory (RAM), you might want to keep them turned off.

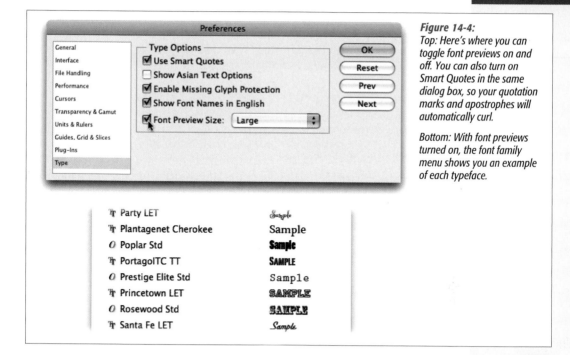

Figure 14-4:

Top: Here's where you can toggle font previews on and off. You can also turn on Smart Quotes in the same dialog box, so your quotation marks and apostrophes will automatically curl.

Bottom: With font previews turned on, the font family menu shows you an example of each typeface.

GEM IN THE ROUGH

Scrolling for Typefaces

Have you ever grown weary of scrolling through all available typefaces? Even with font previews turned on, you'll still probably try out several typefaces before you find one that's just right. The process usually goes like this: Select the text, mouse over to the Options bar or Character palette's font family menu and choose a typeface, and then deselect or hide the text selection (page 540) to see how it looks in your document. If you don't like it, you reselect the text, trot back to the font family menu and select another, then deselect or hide, and so on. A font management utility lets you preview typefaces quickly

and easily (see the box on page 536); but if you don't have one, this kind of manual typeface trolling is a royal pain.

Here's a better method: The next time you need to pick a typeface, highlight the text in your document, and then click the font family menu in the Options bar or in the Character panel. Click the name of a typeface and then use your up and down arrows on your keyboard to cycle through the list. The selected text changes as you scroll through the list, saving you loads of mouse-travel time. Nice!

Creating and Editing Text

You can create all kinds of text in Photoshop: from plain ol' horizontal to up-and-down vertical. You can even lay down text that flows around or inside a shape. However, no matter what kind of text you create, it lives on a special layer called a *Type layer.* You can do anything to a Type layer that you would to any other layer (see Chapter 3): adjust its opacity, change its blend mode, apply layer styles, and so on. (Type layers are labeled with a big fat T in the Layers panel so they're easy to spot.) Photoshop automatically names each new Type layer with the first few words you type, though like any other layer, you can double-click its name in the Layers panel to give it a more meaningful name.

> **TIP** You can change the orientation of your text—whether it flows from left to right or top to bottom—at any time. Just click the Option bar's Orientation button—it looks like a capital T with tiny downward and right-facing arrows—to switch from one direction to the other (see page 554). To create text that flows backwards (from right to left or bottom to top), see page 544.

To create a new Type layer, select either the Horizontal or Vertical Type tool from the Tools panel as shown in Figure 14-5. Click once in the document where you want your text to start and let the hunting and pecking begin. When you're finished typing, press Enter (not Return!) or click the black checkmark at the far right of the Options bar to let Photoshop know you're done (you can also just select another tool from the Tools panel).

> **NOTE** There's a freaky glitch involving the Type tool in Photoshop CS4. When you first select the tool and then click your document, nothing happens—you have to click *again* for Photoshop to create a Type layer. The glitch only happens when you first activate the Type tool; if you've been using the tool for a while, switch to another layer, then click your document again, Photoshop makes a new Type layer straight away. Hopefully, Adobe can fix this annoying bug in one of their updates to the program. But for now, be aware that you may have to click *twice* before Photoshop creates a Type layer.

Horizontal

V
e
r
t
i
c
a
l

Figure 14-5:
Left: Click the big T in the Tools panel to reveal all your Type tool options: the Horizontal and Vertical Type tools, and the Horizontal and Vertical Type Mask tools (discussed on page 544).

Right: Use the Horizontal Type tool to create text that flows from left to right in a straight line. Use the Vertical Type tool to create text that flows up and down from top to bottom, as in a column.

Point Text vs. Paragraph Text

Chances are, most of the text you'll create in Photoshop will be *point text*, which starts at a certain spot (or point) and continues along a single line. To create point text just click in a document and start typing. If you type a bunch of text and want it to wrap to the next line, you'll have to press Return (Enter on a PC) to force the line to break (Photoshop is quite content to let text dangle off the edge of your document). If you want Photoshop to automatically wrap text to the next line, you'll need to create *paragraph text* instead.

> **NOTE** Photoshop refers to these two kinds of text as point and paragraph, but you might hear people call them *character* and *area text*, respectively.

Think of paragraph text as a text box, wherein Photoshop is happy to make your prose flow from line to line all by itself. To create paragraph text, you can drag with the Type tool to draw a box or Option-click (Alt-click on a PC) your document (with the Type tool active) and enter the desired width and height into the resulting dialog box, shown in Figure 14-6, left. (Photoshop assumes these measurements will be in points, though you can type another unit of measurement such as *in* for inches or *px* for pixels.) Click OK to dismiss the dialog box and Photoshop places a dashed box in your document, with the upper-left corner in the spot where you originally clicked (as shown in Figure 14-6, right). If the box isn't the right size, press Esc and have another go at it, or simply adjust the size of the box by dragging the tiny white resizing handles strategically placed around its edges.

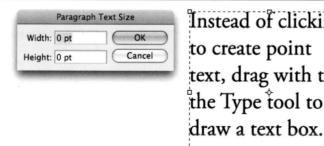

Figure 14-6:
Left: To create a multi-line text box, Option-click (Alt-click on a PC) in your document and enter the dimensions you want.

Right: You can also click and drag with the Vertical or Horizontal Type tools to draw the box manually, as shown here. To resize a text box, select the Type layer, click in the box, and drag any of the resulting white square handles, like the one circled here.

When the text box is all set, just start typing. As your text hits the edge of the box, Photoshop will add line breaks—and hyphenate words. You can resize the text box now, too, just make sure the Type layer is selected in the Layers panel. Click anywhere in the text box and drag any of the resulting handles. The size of the *text* won't change, but the size of the text box will; and just like magic, the text will reflow automatically to fit inside the newly sized box. (If you want to change the size of the text itself, flip to page 542.) Using paragraph text instead of point text gives you some extra formatting options in the Paragraph panel, like justification. See page 567 for the details.

TIP   Photoshop can convert point text to paragraph text (or vice versa) on the fly. Just select the appropriate text layer in the Layers panel and choose Layer → Type → "Convert to Point Text", or "Convert to Paragraph Text". You can also Ctrl-click (right-click on a PC) the text itself and choose the same items from the resulting shortcut menu.

Moving Text

If you start typing and then decide it's not in the right spot, no problem—moving text is easy. Just grab your mouse and move the cursor *away* from the text (about an inch or so), until the cursor turns into a tiny arrow (just as if you'd grabbed the Move tool). Then drag the text to a new position and continue typing. Another way to move text while typing is to press and hold ⌘ (Ctrl on a PC), place your cursor inside the resulting box, and then drag it to a new location.

If you've already finished typing the text, you can still move it. Just make sure the appropriate Type layer is selected over in the Layers panel, press V to grab the Move tool, and then drag the Type layer to a new position. If dragging isn't your bag, grab the Move tool and nudge it into position by tapping the arrow keys on your keyboard.

Selecting Text

Chances are, the Photoshop text you create won't be perfect right off the bat; it'll need to be massaged, manipulated, and played with (and honestly, that's half the fun). To tweak your text, you'll need to first select the appropriate Type layer in the Layers panel (it'll be highlighted, as shown in Figure 14-7, top), and then select the text *itself*. When text is selected, you'll see a black (or blue) background appear behind the characters (which will now appear white or orange), as shown in Figure 14-7, middle.

NOTE   Selecting text is totally different from *loading* text as a selection, wherein marching ants surround the characters as shown in Figure 14-7, bottom. To load text as a selection, simply ⌘-click (Ctrl-click on a PC) the Type layer's thumbnail.

What's the difference, you ask? Selecting text lets you edit the characters (to fix a typo, for example), whereas loading text as a selection lets you apply effects to the *shape* of characters, such as adding a stroke (page 573), altering other graphics in the shape of the characters (page 544), or creating another piece of art out of them altogether (page 583).

You've got several ways to select text:

- **To select a character,** click within the text and, once the cursor turns into a blinking I-beam, drag across the character(s).

- **To select a word,** click within the text and then double-click the word.

- **To select a whole line,** click within the text and then triple-click anywhere in the line you want to select.

- **To select a paragraph,** click within the paragraph and then quadruple-click (that's four quick clicks).

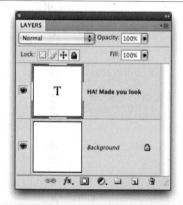

Figure 14-7:

Top: To alter text in Photoshop, you've got to select the Type layer on which it lives. Once selected, the Type layer gets highlighted, as shown here.

Middle: When you select the text itself, a black (or blue) background appears. (Photoshop temporarily makes the text white or orange so you can see it.) You can hide this black background by pressing ⌘-H (Ctrl+H on a PC).

Bottom: Here's what text looks like when it's been loaded as a selection. Notice how the edges of the letters look blurry? That's because each letter is surrounded by marching ants.

There is no escape;

you have been selected!

There is no escape;

you have been selected!

- **To select the entire layer,** in the Layers panel, double-click the Type layer thumbnail or, in your document, click within the text and then click five times really fast.

TIP   When you've got a Type layer selected and the Type tool is active, Ctrl-click (right-click on a PC) anywhere in your document to see a shortcut menu with all kinds of useful options for working with text. These include Edit Text (see "selecting" page 540), Check Spelling (page 553), Find & Replace (page 552), Rasterize (page 543), "Create Work Path" or "Convert to Shape" (page 585), and more.

- **To select multiple Type layers,** in the Layers panel, Shift- or ⌘-click (Ctrl-click on a PC) the name—*not* the thumbnail—of each layer you want to select.

TIP   To edit several Type layers at once, first select them in the Layers panel and make sure the Type tool is active. Then make your changes using either the Options bar or the Character panel and they'll apply to all the selected layers in one fell swoop, which can be a huge timesaver. (Find & Replace is another great tool for multi-layer changes—see page 552.)

FREQUENTLY ASKED QUESTION

Type Warnings

Sometimes when I open a document, I see a little yellow or gray triangle on the Type layer in the Layers panel. What the heck does that mean?

One day you're bound to open a Photoshop document only to be met with a *type warning*. They come in two flavors, and show up in the Layers panel as a tiny yellow or gray triangular warning symbol on the Type layer's thumbnail:

- A **yellow warning symbol** means you're missing a font. You'll see this icon if you open a document that uses a font that isn't installed on your machine (though you'll likely see an error message *before* the document actually opens that lets you cancel opening the document, or proceed). If you don't need to edit the text, you've got nothing to worry about—just do what you need to do and then save the file. If you *do* edit the text, Photoshop will substitute something else for the missing

font (the substitution is permanent, even if you send the file back to its creator who actually *has* the original font). If it's important to keep the original font, you'll have to close the document, quit Photoshop (unless you're running font management software, as discussed in the box on page 536), install the font, re-launch Photoshop, and then re-open the document.

- A **gray warning symbol** means that the document you've opened was created in a different version of Photoshop and that the text may get reflowed if you edit it (that doesn't mean it *will* get reflowed). Because each new version of Photoshop contains new type features, text created in an earlier version might get spaced or hyphenated differently in the new version. In that case, Photoshop marks the affected Type layer with a little gray warning symbol. Now you know.

- **To select all the Type layers in a document,** select one Type layer then choose Select → Similar Layers. This is handy if your Layers panel has grown unwieldy and contains a bazillion Type layers.

TIP   The black background that appears behind text to show that it's selected can be distracting, and make it hard to see your image. Toggle it off and on by pressing ⌘-H (Ctrl+H on a PC).

Resizing Text

Photoshop lets you create everything from nano-sized text that you'd need an electron microscope to read, to ginormous letters fit for the side of a building. You can resize text by creating a selection using any of the methods described above, and then altering the point size in either the Options bar (page 554) or the Character panel (page 556). But where's the fun in that?

Unless you know the exact size your type needs to be, you may be better off resizing it visually, either while typing or afterward. If it's the latter, select a Type layer from the Layers panel and click inside the line of text (or the text box) so you see an I-beam cursor blinking within the text (if you're typing, you should already see this cursor). Press and hold ⌘ (Ctrl on a PC) to make Photoshop display resizing handles around the text. Drag any handle to resize the text, as shown in

Beware of Rasterizing Text

No matter what kind of text you create in Photoshop—whether it's horizontal, upside down, inside a shape, or what have you—it's begins life as *vector type* (as long as you're using Photoshop 6 or later). With vector type, each character is made up of curves and lines, rather than pixels. (See page 48 for a detailed discussion of raster vs. vector files.)

This is great news because it means that the text is editable and fully *scalable,* so you can make it bigger or smaller without worrying that it'll be blurry when printed. However, some cool effects require you to rasterize the text (convert it to pixels), like running filters (though there is a workaround, see page 582), distorting, and applying perspective, to name a few. If you try to do any of these things to a Type layer, you'll be met with an error message asking your permission to proceed with rasterization.

The bad news is that some things in Photoshop *automatically rasterize* text, so that it becomes completely un-vectored, un-editable, and pretty much un-resizable. Sure, you can shrink raster text without much quality loss, but making it bigger will bring about disastrously jagged results.

Photoshop automatically rasterizes text when you:

- Merge a Type layer with another layer(s) (see page 103).

- Flatten a file (see page 104).

- Save a file as any format other than PSD or TIF (see page 46).

- Send a file to a non-PostScript (inkjet) printer (see Chapter 16).

If you save a file in EPS, PDF, or DCS format (see page 46 to learn all about your file format options), Photoshop preserves the text by converting it into vector outlines, which is pretty much the same thing as converting it into a shape (see page 585). You won't be able to edit it anymore, but it'll look nice and crisp when printed because it's still a true vector. Watch out though, if you open *any* of these file types again in Photoshop, the program will automatically rasterize the text.

All that being said, if you truly wish to rasterize text, it's a good idea to duplicate the layer first (as described on page 82) just in case you want to edit it later. Once you've duplicated the layer, you can rasterize either the copy or the original by choosing Layer → Type → Rasterize.

Figure 14-8, left (press and hold the Shift key while dragging to resize the text proportionately—meaning the relationship between the width and the height stays the same). The point size displayed in both the Options bar and Character panel will change as you drag.

> **TIP** If you're a keyboard shortcut fan, you can increase the font size of selected text in 2-point increments by pressing Shift-⌘->, and decrease it by pressing Shift-⌘-< (use Shift+Ctrl+> and Shift+Ctrl+< on a PC). To increase or decrease in *10-point* increments, add the Option key (Alt on a PC) to those key combinations.

You can also use Free Transform to resize text. With a Type layer selected—not the *text* itself, just the Type layer—summon the Free Transform tool by pressing ⌘-T (Ctrl+T on a PC). Up pops a now familiar resizing box (complete with little white handles) around the text. Drag one of the handles in any direction to resize the text. (You won't see the point size change as you drag because that only happens

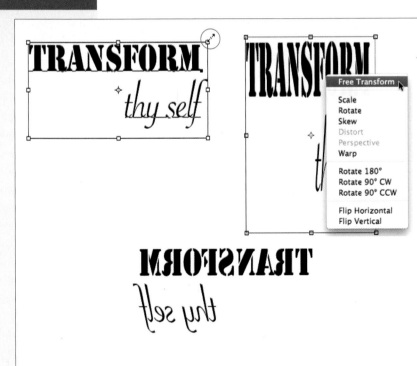

Figure 14-8:
Left: You can resize text visually while typing by pressing ⌘ (Ctrl on a PC) and then dragging one of the resizing handles circled here.

Right: You can also resize text using Free Transform. After you've summoned the tool by pressing ⌘-T (Ctrl+T on a PC), Ctrl-clicking (right-clicking) in the transform box will bring up this shortcut menu, which offers a slew of other text-altering options.

Bottom: If you've ever wanted text to flow backwards, Free Transform can make it so. Just open the shortcut menu as described above, and then choose Flip Horizontal (or Flip Vertical for upside-down text).

when the Type tool is active.) Again, hold the Shift key to resize the text proportionately. For more options, Ctrl-click (right-click) in the transform box for a handy shortcut menu (see Figure 14-8, right).

Creating a Hollow Text Selection

Sometimes you don't really need the letters *themselves* to create the effect you're after, you just need a *selection* of them instead (or rather, their outline). Enter the Type Mask, a wonderful tool hidden in the Type tool's flyout menu (shown on page 537). Instead of creating a Type layer, the Type Mask tool creates an empty text *selection*, which you can use on other layers, like one that contains an image.

With the Type Mask tool, it'll look like you're creating normal text, but once you're finished typing, marching ants will surround the edges of the characters, creating a hollow selection in the shape of text—no new Type layer gets created. Think of a type mask as one of those plastic stencils you used as a kid to draw perfectly formed letters and numbers—the letters are hollow so you can see through them to the layer below.

TROUBLESHOOTING MOMENT

Adding Type Layers

There are lots of benefits to creating different pieces of text on their own Type layer. As you learned in Chapter 3, you can edit anything that lives on its own layer independently from everything else, letting you change blend modes, opacity, and so on, without messing with other layers. So, if you're creating a poster publicizing Woodstock IV, for example, it's a good idea to put the (obligatory) psychedelic heading on one layer, and the details of the concert on layers of their own.

Creating your first Type layer's easy: As explained on page 537, simply click the big T in the Tools panel to activate the Type tool and then click in the document to add the new Type layer. However, it can be challenging to create *additional* Type layers while the Type tool is selected because when you click, Photoshop insists on selecting the *existing* Type layer nearest to where you clicked. Likewise, if you hover your cursor close to an existing path (page 497), Photoshop assumes you want to create type on a path (see page 548) and promptly attaches the text to it.

The fix for both situations is to press and hold the Shift key while you click a blank area of the document. This forces Photoshop to create a brand new, bright and shiny Type layer. Now, take back all those bad things you said about the Type tool.

NOTE Sure, you could just use the regular Type tools to create text and then load it as a selection by ⌘-clicking (Ctrl-clicking on a PC) the Type layer thumbnail. But the Type Mask tool *creates the selection for you*, sparing you that extra step.

The Type Mask tools open a boatload of graphic design possibilities because they let you affect other graphical elements (other layers) through the shape of the text, as shown in Figure 14-9. The Type Mask tool comes in two flavors: One for creating horizontal text and one for creating vertical text. They both merely create a selection of whatever you type without creating a new layer. You can treat the text selection as you would any other selection: move it around, use it to create a layer mask (page 105), wear it as a hat (kidding), save it to use later (see page 166), or turn it into an editable path (page 585).

One of the many neat effects you can create with the Type Mask tool is a text-shaped photo fade; a unique look that'd make an eye-catching magazine ad. Here's how:

1. **Open a photo and grab the Horizontal Type Mask tool.**

    To activate the tool, click the big T in the Tools panel, and then click the Horizontal Type Mask tool in the flyout menu (you can also press Shift-T repeatedly to cycle through all the tools in the Type toolset). You don't need to bother duplicating the background layer because this technique is 100% non-destructive, meaning the original pixels will remain untouched (as described in Chapter 3).

2. **Choose a typeface from the Font Family menu.**

    Be sure to choose a thick, fat typeface so the selection area will be fairly big (thin or script typefaces won't work). Arial Black or Impact work well for this technique.

Figure 14-9:
*Top: When the Type
Mask tool is active,
clicking in a document
causes a red overlay or
mask to appear (see
page 162 for more on
this particular mask). As
you type, the letters are
revealed through the
mask. The text remains
editable (and resizable)
until you accept the mask
by clicking the black
checkmark at the far
right of the Options bar,
or by pressing Enter.*

*Middle: Once you accept
the mask, you'll see a
selection of the text
appear, indicated by the
little army of marching
ants surrounding the
characters, as shown
here. (In real life, they
actually move.)*

*Bottom: After you inverse
the selection (page 126),
the area behind the text
gets selected, letting you
change the background
of your design in the
shape of the text. Here,
the text selection was
used in conjunction with
an adjustment layer on a
photo of pizza. As you
can see, all manner of
graphic design goodness
is possible with this
technique.*

3. **Click anywhere in the document and type your text.**

   You'll notice that the text appears hollow (you can see through to the photo, as shown in Figure 14-9, top), while the background takes on the red cast of Quick Mask Mode (page 162). That's because this really *is* Quick Mask Mode—clicking anywhere in the document with the Type Mask tool automatically activates it.

4. **Format the text to your liking.**

   If you don't like the typeface, change it by selecting the text (page 540) and making a new choice from the Font Family menu. You can reposition the text by moving your cursor away from it about an inch and then dragging with the resulting arrow cursor. You can also move the text by pressing ⌘ (Ctrl on a PC) and clicking inside the resulting box and then dragging it or nudging it with your keyboard's arrow keys. Drag any of the square handles to resize the text (remember to hold the Shift key to resize it proportionately).

5. **Convert the mask to a selection.**

   When the text looks just right, click the black checkmark at the far right of the Options bar to accept the mask, or just press the Enter key (*not* Return). This creates a selection of the text (so you see marching ants) and gets rid of the red overlay, as shown in Figure 14-9, middle.

   NOTE   If you decide to edit or reformat the text after accepting the mask, you have to start over. You'll need to get rid of the existing selection first by pressing ⌘-D (Ctrl+D on a PC) to deselect; then you can grab the Type Mask tool and retype the text.

6. **Inverse the selection.**

   In order to fade the area of the photo around the letters, you need to flip-flop the selection. Choose Select → Inverse to select everything *except* the letters. Now you can adjust the background of the photo while leaving the letter area alone.

7. **Create a Hue/Saturation adjustment layer (page 318) and use it to desaturate (page 301) and lighten the part of the photo in the selection area.**

   Over in the Layers panel (page 72), click the "Create New Fill or Adjustment Layer" button (the half-black/half-white circle) and choose Hue/Saturation from the pop-up menu. Using an adjustment layer lets you do the desaturating and lightening on another layer, instead of on the original image. That way, the original photo remains unchanged.

   In the Adjustments panel that opens, drain most of the photo's color by lowering the saturation to –65. Next, drag the Lightness slider to +60 to screen back (lighten) the photo, making the text more legible.

NOTE Since you had an active selection before creating the adjustment layer, Photoshop plopped the selection into the adjustment layer's mask for you (see page 71 for more on adjustment layers and their masks). This ensures that only the selection area will be affected by the changes you make here.

You're done! Figure 14-9 (bottom) shows the final result: clear, photo-filled text with a faded background.

Creating Type on a Path

Photoshop lets you bend text to your every whim, and one of the coolest tricks you can do is make text march around a shape. The key is to use the Type tool on a pre-existing path (either open or closed—see page 513), drawn with the Pen tool or created with a vector shape such as the Rectangle, Rounded Rectangle, Ellipse, Polygon, or Custom Shape tools (Figure 14-10). (See Chapter 13 for a detailed discussion of paths and vector shape tools.) When you attach text to a path, both the text and the path remain editable, so you can reformat the text or reshape the path anytime.

TIP Heck, you can even turn text *into* a path or a vector outline (think shapes). This lets you rotate individual letters and create cool intersecting effects. Grab a beverage and head on over to page 585 for the details.

Here's how to attach text to a custom shape:

1. **Create a path.**

   Using either the Pen tool or one of the vector shapes mentioned above, create a path for the text to follow. Figure 14-10 shows a snail drawn with the Custom Shape tool (see page 512 to learn how to load other built-in shapes).

   NOTE The direction you draw the shape (or path) determines the direction the text flows. For example, draw the shape from left to right and the text will flow normally; draw it from right to left and the text will appear backwards and upside down.

2. **Attach text to the path.**

   Grab the Horizontal Type tool (click the big T in the Tools panel) and then hover your cursor above the path (or the shape's edge). You'll see a wavy line appear beneath the I-beam cursor (see Figure 14-10, top). This is the Type tool's way of telling you that it recognizes the path you're about to attach the text to. Click once and then start typing.

3. **Align or reposition the text on the path.**

   You can use any of the alignment buttons in the Options bar (page 554) or Character panel (page 556) to align the text on the path.

Figure 14-10:
Top: With the Type tool active, hover your cursor above any path and a little wavy line will appear at the bottom of the cursor. That's Photoshop's way of saying "permission granted" for creating type on a path.

Middle: Slide the type along the path by dragging with the Path Selection Tool (the black arrow that lives below the Type tool in the Tools panel). A tiny black arrow appears next to the cursor facing either left or right, depending on which end of the text you're hovering near (here it's facing right). The start point of the text is marked with a tiny x, and the end point is marked with a dot (both circled).

Bottom: To give your text a little breathing room, adjust the baseline shift (page 561) over in the Character panel (page 556). This will scoot the text away from the path it's attached to. You can also increase tracking if the letters start crashing into each other.

You can also slide it back and forth along the path, or flip it from the top of the path to the bottom, using the Path Selection tool—just click the black arrow below the Type tool in the Tools panel to select it (see page 515 for more). Hover your I-beam cursor over the starting point of the text (which is marked with an x—see Figure 14-10, middle). When a tiny, right-facing arrow appears next to your cursor, drag to the left or right to move the text. (The little arrow points to the left if you hover your mouse over the end of the text, which is marked with a black dot.) To flip the text to the opposite side of the path—in this example, that means putting it inside the snail shell rather than on top— drag your cursor below the path (toward the bottom of the shape).

What's really happening here is that Photoshop is adjusting the start and end points of the text. You can move the start point by single clicking the path with the left-arrowed cursor. Likewise, you can move the end point by hovering at the end of the text and clicking with the right-arrowed cursor. (If the text is center aligned, you'll likely see a double-arrowed cursor.)

NOTE If your text disappears, that means the space between the start and end points is too small to house the text. In that case, adjust one of the points or reformat the text to make it fit.

Type on a path can be formatted like any other text. Just switch back to the Type tool (or double-click the Type layer thumbnail in the Layers panel) and then make a selection using one of the techniques described on page 540.

TIP You may need to adjust tracking (page 559) over in the Character panel to keep letters from colliding in tight spaces. To make the text sit above or below the path (instead of directly on it, see Figure 14-10, bottom), you can adjust the baseline shift as described on page 561.

Filling a Shape with Text

Placing text inside a shape is even simpler that placing it on an object's edge, and it's a fun little exercise in type design. First, create a closed shape with the Pen or one of the shape tools as discussed above, and then grab the Horizontal Type tool. Hover your cursor inside the shape and when it turns into an I-beam surrounded by tiny dots (shown in Figure 14-11, top), just click and type your text. Easy, huh?

When you're finished typing, you can format the text using any of the options discussed on page 553 and beyond (you'll likely need to change its color in order to actually *see* it). Centered alignment (page 556) is especially useful for this technique, because you can use it to push the text away from the edges of the object (see Figure 14-11, bottom). Otherwise, you can give the text a little more space using the Indent Left and Indent Right Margin controls over in the Paragraph panel (page 567).

Warping Text

Another way to create text that follows a shape is to use the Create Warped text command. Be forewarned, though, that this option distorts the *shape* of the letters (so they might not be very legible when you're done), whereas type on a path only alters the baseline and orientation (direction).

The Create Warped Text button appears in the Options bar only when a Type tool is active. Unlike placing type on a path or inside an object, to warp text, you have to create the text first and *then* click the Warp button. Pick one of the 15 canned settings in the Warp Text dialog box's Style pop-up menu (Figure 14-12). You can customize the style by tweaking the Bend, Horizontal, and Vertical Distortion sliders.

TIP Make sure the Warp dialog box isn't covering up your text. Photoshop applies all your changes in real time, so you'll want to be sure and watch.

Figure 14-11:
Top: Once your cursor is surrounded by tiny dots, just click inside the object and start typing to add your text.

Bottom: Using a centered alignment helps push the text away from the object's edges.

When
moving
to a new
home, always
put the cat in
through a window
instead of the
door. That way it
won't leave.
-Author Unknown

NOTE   To produce some seriously demented text, try warping type you've placed on a path or inside a shape. It won't be readable, but it'll sure look cool!

If you don't like the result, just press Option (Alt on a PC) and the Cancel button will change to Reset. Click it to snuff out any changes you've made so far (click Cancel to exit the dialog box completely). Once you've got your text looking good and warped, click OK.

As long as you don't rasterize the Type layer (see the box on page 543), you can change the warp settings at any time. Just select the Type layer, grab the Type tool, and click the Warp button to see the warp settings you used previously.

Figure 14-12:
*You can create super-
funky text by using the
Create Warped Text
command. Among the
many styles are Bulge,
Arch, and Shell Lower
(all shown here).
Depending on what
you're creating, this
technique could be just
the ticket or complete
cheese. Use this tool
sparingly, because it
could easily go either
way.*

TIP   You'll get an error dialog box if you try to warp text that's been faux bolded (see page 535).
However, Photoshop will let you warp faux italic text with nary a squawk.

Using Find and Replace

No matter what kind of text you set, at some point you might need to exchange a
word, phrase, or character for something else. It's usually easy enough to make
such fixes manually, but if there's a fair amount of text in your document, you can
reach for the "Find and Replace" command instead. For example, suppose you're
working on a full-page ad for a sports-drink company and they've just changed the
name of their flagship product from Dr. Bob's Thirst Remedy to Quenchtastic
4000. In that situation, you can save yourself lots of time by using the "Find and
Replace" feature. Photoshop will seek out the offending word or phrase and
replace it with whatever you want.

Choose Edit → "Find and Replace Text" to summon the dialog box shown in
Figure 14-13 (you don't even need to have the Type tool active or a Type layer
selected). Enter the offending word or phrase in the Find What field and its
replacement in the Change To field. Use the checkboxes to tell Photoshop whether

you want it to search through all the Type layers in your document; look only for instances that match the case (capitalization) of what you've typed; search from a specific point in a Type layer forward (this one's only available if you have the Type tool active and the cursor blinking at a point within the text); look for whole words only; or any combination of these options.

Figure 14-13:
Hopefully you'll never set enough Photoshop text to need the "Find and Replace Text" feature, but it can come in handy in a pinch.

WORD TO THE WISE

Thou Shalt Spell Check

Few mistakes are as embarrassing (or avoidable) for a graphic artist as a misspelled word. Most software comes with a built-in spellchecker—and Photoshop's no exception. There's little excuse for the common typo (*wordos,* on the other hand—real words in the wrong place—are another story). And let's face it: The people who create copy can rarely spot their own mistakes, either because they've been staring at it for too long or they're rushing to meet a deadline. In those situations, using a spellchecker is essential.

To check spelling in Photoshop, choose Edit → Check Spelling. In the resulting dialog box, Photoshop will scour the document (layer by layer), alerting you to words it considers suspect. It dutifully offers a list of suggestions that you can ignore or accept, changing just one instance or all of them. If it encounters an unknown word that is oft-used and correctly spelled, just click the Add button and Photoshop assimilates the word into its dictionary.

The lesson here is that whether you're typing five words or five paragraphs, take time to run the spellchecker—you'll be glad you did.

Formatting Text

Now that you've learned all about the different *kinds* of Photoshop text, it's time to dig into how to format it. Photoshop CS4 lets you control text within an inch of its life! Beyond the basics of typeface, size, and color, you can adjust the softness of the letters' edges, the space between each letter, the space between lines of text, and so on.

The most commonly used settings live in the Options bar, while the more advanced typographic goodies are nestled snuggly inside the Character and Paragraph panels. But no matter where the settings live, if they control text, you'll learn about them in the following pages. Read on!

Formatting with the Options Bar

When you have the Type tool active, the Options bar (Figure 14-14) offers basic text-tweakers such as font family (typeface), style, size, anti-aliasing (see page 555), alignment, and color. (The Character panel, discussed on page 556, offers all these settings and more.)

> **NOTE**   Remember, any changes you make in the Options bar *remain* until you change them back. If you suddenly find that your text isn't behaving like you expect, chances are there's a setting in the Options bar that needs changing.

Figure 14-14:
You'll see these formatting choices in the Options bar anytime the Type tool is active. A handy way to change any numeric setting (like font size) is to hover your cursor over the field's label until you see a double-arrowed scrubby cursor (circled). Simply drag to the left or right to decrease or increase that setting without using the field's drop-down menu (or your keyboard).

You can apply formatting either before or after you create text:

- **Before you type.** If you know exactly what font, style, and size you want to use before you start hammering out text, this is the way to go. Press T to select the Type tool and then head up to the Options bar or the Character panel to pick your settings.

- **After you type.** This is the more common method, since it's easier to see how formatting choices affect *existing* text than try to imagine how it might look. With the Type tool active, select the text you want to format using one of the methods described on page 540, and then use the Options bar or Character panel to change the formatting however you wish.

From left to right, the Options bar gives you control over the following:

- **Type Tool Preset picker.** Out of the box, this tool performs the fairly useless service of letting you quickly summon horizontal type in either the Myriad or Minion typeface in a variety of sizes. Thankfully, with just a little bit of work, you can create your own presets—a fantastic idea if you use the same formatting over and over again.

Start by formatting the text exactly the way you want it and make sure the Type layer is selected (you don't have to select the text itself). Then click the triangle next to the Tool Preset picker and choose New Tool Preset from the pop-up list. Enter a meaningful name in the resulting box, and then click OK. Photoshop memorizes how you formatted the text so it can apply that formatting automatically the next time around. Just grab the Type tool, select your style from the Tool Preset picker, click in your document and start typing.

- **Text orientation.** There's no need to decide if you want horizontal (left to right) or vertical (top to bottom) text before you type: pushing this little button will flip the whole Type layer on the fly. You don't have to select any text first.

- **Font family.** This menu lists every typeface currently installed on your machine. If you want to see a preview of what each font will looks, flip over to page 536.

- **Font style.** Here's where you can choose a native style (page 535) for the typeface you selected, such as light, bold, condensed, and so on.

- **Font size.** Enter a point size for your text in this field, or hover above the field label and use the scrubby cursor shown in Figure 14-14 to change the size. Though text size is typically stated in points, you can change the unit of measurement to pixels or millimeters by choosing Photoshop → Preferences → Units & Rulers (PC: Edit → Preferences → Units & Rulers).

TIP If you need to create *super* large text, Photoshop will put up a fight. When you type a number greater than 1296 into the Font size field, you'll see an error message asking you to enter a number between 1 and 1296. This is an odd little quirk of Photoshop's, but if you're sneaky, you can work around this limitation by resizing your text with the Free Transform tool (page 245): Enter 1296 into the size field and then choose Edit → Transform → Scale. Drag the resizing handles that appear to make the text really honkin' big and then press Return (Enter on a PC) to accept the transform. Then double-click the Type layer thumbnail to select the text, hop back up to the Option's bars Font size field, and enter the text size of your dreams. For some unknown reason, once the text size surpasses 1296 points (which it did when you resized it), Photoshop stops squawking and lets you change that number to anything you want.

- **Anti-aliasing.** Anti-aliasing was mentioned way back in Chapter 4 as a method for smoothing the edges of a selection (page 127). Similarly, this option can also smooth text, helping you avoid the dreaded jagged edges so common when printing to an inkjet printer or when posting on the Web.

Your choices here are None, Sharp, Crisp, Strong, and Smooth. Each setting has a different effect on various text sizes, so you might have to do a little experimenting. Use None on extremely small text to make it clean and sharp (especially super-small text destined for the Web), and use Strong or Smooth for larger text to keep it from looking jagged when it's printed (especially if it's headed for an inkjet printer).

- **Alignment.** These three buttons make text appear flush left, centered, or flush right, within a single line of text or a text box. To align a single line of text on a Type layer that contains many lines, press T to activate the Type tool, click within that line, and then press one of the alignment buttons. To center everything on a Type layer, double-click the Type layer thumbnail in the Layers panel, and then click an alignment button. (Unless you specifically apply a different alignment, Photoshop automatically left-aligns text.)

   TIP   You can also use keyboard shortcuts to align text. To left align, select some text and press ⌘-Shift-L (Ctrl+Shift+L on a PC). For center alignment, press ⌘-Shift-C (Ctrl+Shift+C), and for right alignment, press ⌘-Shift-R (Ctrl+Shift+R).

- **Text color.** You can set text color by selecting your text and then clicking the little colored swatch on the Options bar, which shows the current text color. (There's a similar button on the Character panel that does the same thing.) You can also set text color before you type by clicking the foreground or background color chip (page 22).

   To recolor the text with the foreground color chip, select the text using one of the methods described on page 540, and then press Option-Delete (Alt+Delete on a PC). To use the background color chip, press ⌘-Delete (Ctrl+Delete).

   NOTE   When choosing a text color, resist the urge to go hog wild. Bear in mind that black text on a white background is the easiest to read, as is any dark colored text on a light background. The key is contrast—it's really hard to read text that's similar in color to its background. However, if you're adding text to a dark background, you risk the danger of introducing *too* much contrast. For example, a single line of pure white text on a black background is quite legible, but a large block of white text on a black background—especially on the Web—is eye-numbing. In that situation, you'd be better off using light gray text instead, because the contrast won't be quite so high.

- **Create Warped text.** You can use this option to curve and distort text in all manner of exciting ways, as explained on page 550. The button itself is easy to spot; it has a capital T perched atop a curved line.

- **Character panel.** Click this little button to pop open the Character and Paragraph panels for even more text formatting goodness, as explained in the next two sections. (Click it again to hide them.)

The Character Panel

You've probably noticed the Character and Paragraph panel icons lurking near the right side of your screen in the panel dock (see page 17 for more on the panel dock)—they look like a capital A and a paragraph symbol, respectively. If you don't see them in the panel dock, choose Window → Character (or Window → Paragraph) and Photoshop adds both panels to the dock for you. (It assumes that if you're using one, you'll soon be using the other, which is a pretty safe bet.) Read on for a detailed discussion of each.

The Character panel, shown in Figure 14-15, has enough formatting options to please the most discerning typesetter. It includes all the settings found in the Options bar, plus it lets you control the space in and around individual characters, where they sit on a line, the height of the line, and more. The Character panel also holds the key to unlocking some amazing OpenType features discussed earlier in this chapter on page 534. Mastering this panel can help you turn ordinary type into a work of art.

NOTE   Like the Options bar, any changes made in the Character panel remain in effect until you change them back. So, if you play with leading (page 557) on Monday and then add text to a brand new document on Tuesday, the leading may look a bit off. Either use the leading pop-up menu to change it back to Auto or go the Character panel menu (see Figure 14-15) and choose Reset Character, which reverts *all* the Character panel's settings back to normal.

Figure 14-15:
Behold the mighty Character panel! Here you'll find controls for tracking, kerning, adjusting text's baseline, and more. You can control every bit of horizontal and vertical space in and around the letters in your document from this panel. Hover your cursor above any numeric field label to summon the ever-handy scrubby cursor (shown in Figure 14-14), and drag left or right to decrease or increase the values.

If you (understandably) forget what some of these settings do, just hover your cursor over any of the field labels and a handy balloon will appear letting you know what that setting does.

NOTE   To close the Character panel, click the two right-facing arrows in the upper-right corner of the panel, and Photoshop will slide it shut. To get it back, just click the A button on the panel dock or choose Window → Character.

A lesson in leading

If you've ever added extra carriage returns between lines of text to create space, or wondered how designers make lines of type appear all squashed together, you've encountered *leading*. Leading (rhymes with "bedding") controls the amount of blank space between lines of type. The term originated back in the days when type was set by hand onto printing presses, and lead strips of various thicknesses were used to create space between lines. Learning to control leading is a useful design skill, and happily, Photoshop gives you complete control over it as shown in Figure 14-16.

Figure 14-16:
Attention Goldilocks: The leading on the left is too little, the leading on the right is too much, but the leading in the middle—set to Auto—is just right (for this situation, anyway; auto leading isn't perfect for every project). As you can see, leading can make a design statement; ask yourself which one your typography needs to make.

Leading is measured in points just like text, though it *includes* the point size of the text itself. Leading that's equal to the point size of text is called *solid leading*, and it will create lines of text that almost touch (spacing that falls in between what's shown in the left and middle of Figure 14-16). Photoshop's leading is set to Auto (unless you change it), which is approximately 120 percent of the text's point size (see Figure 14-16, middle). For example, 10-point type has an auto leading of 12 points.

In the Character panel, the leading control (labeled with two As stacked on top of each other) lives directly beneath the font style pop-up menu. You can adjust the leading of several lines of text at once or one line at a time.

To adjust the leading of multiple lines of text on the same layer, select the offending Type layer in the Layers panel (there's no need to highlight the text), and then choose a point size from the leading pop-up menu, or type directly into the text field. (Better yet, hover your cursor above the field's label and use the handy scrubby cursor.) If you want to adjust the leading of a single line of text on a Type layer that contains many, select the text first (highlight it) and then change the leading.

> **TIP** You can also use keyboard shortcuts to change leading. Select the text and then press and hold Option (Alt on a PC) and tap the up or down arrow keys to change the leading in increments of 2 points; add ⌘ (Ctrl) to change it in increments of 10 points. To set leading back to auto, press Shift-Option-⌘-A (Shift+Alt+Ctrl+A).

Learning to kern

To *kern* means to adjust the amount of space between letters according to how much room each letter needs. Poorly kerned (or unkerned) text looks funky and can be distracting to the reader, as you can see in Figure 14-17, top. A lack of kerning is perhaps the biggest clue that text has been set non-professionally (nothing exposes a typographical novice faster!). Admittedly, the problem is more noticeable with less expensive—or free—typefaces (like Frolicking Ferrets), scripts, and decoratives (especially fonts that mimic handwriting, like the one in the figure).

Figure 14-17:
Top: Here's some text borrowed from a BMW motorcycle ad in a naked, unkerned state. Notice how several of the letters appear too close together? The punctuation is even worse—it's practically in a different Zip code.

Bottom: After a little kerning, the text looks normal instead of helter-skelter, so readers can focus on what the copy says instead of the weird spacing. (Get it? My hairstylist is my motorcycle helmet? Oh, nevermind.)

Over in the Character panel, the kerning button is marked by the letters AV and two arrows pointing in opposite directions. The numbers in the kerning pop-up menu range from positive to negative; positive values increase space, and negative values decrease space. Kerning values are measured in 1/1000 em; an *em* is a relative measurement based on the point size of the type. For example, if the type size is 12-point, 1 em equals 12 points. Since you can create type of various sizes, this measurement ensures that your kerning is always based on the type size you're currently working with.

> **NOTE** Though Photoshop tries to kern text automatically, it's best to do it manually as described here. For more information on auto vs. manual kerning, see the box on page 560.

Because the amount of space each letter needs (on either side) differs—a *W* requires more space than an *I*, for example—you'll want to kern each space individually. Press T to grab the Type tool and position the cursor into the first problem area you spot. In Figure 14-17, that's between the *a* and *v* of *have*—they're way too close together. To widen the space, pick a positive value from the kerning pop-up menu or drag the scrubby cursor gently to the right (you can also type a value into the kerning field). If you want to narrow the space, pick a negative value or drag the scrubby cursor to the left.

> **TIP** There's a keyboard shortcut for changing kerning, though you need to place your cursor between the letters you want to adjust. Press and hold Option (Alt on a PC) while tapping the left or right arrow key to change the kerning in increments of 20. Add the ⌘ key (Ctrl) to change it in increments of 100.

Track it out

If you want to change the spacing between *all* letters in a word by the same amount, you'll need to adjust *tracking*. This adjustment is great for when you're trying to make text fit into a small area. Also, vast amounts of tracking, as shown in

Auto vs. Manual Kerning

Ever the helpful soul, Photoshop tries to kern text for you. Perched high atop the kerning pop-up menu in the Character panel, you'll find two auto-kerning methods: Metrics and Optical.

Metrics kerning is the most common and it's where Photoshop adjusts the space between letters according to their *kern pairs*—the amount of spacing between letter pairs (like *Tr*, *To*, *Ta*, and so on) that the designer specified when creating the typeface. Photoshop applies metrics kerning automatically anytime you create or import text (unless you've changed it in this menu).

However, some typefaces contain little or no information regarding kern pairs, but you're not going to know it until you start typing. So, if the kerning looks really bad, Adobe recommends that you manually switch to optical, where Photoshop adjusts the space according to character shape instead. Optical kerning is also helpful when you use more than one font (or font size) in a single word.

The best method of all, though, is to kern text manually as described on page 559. It takes more time, but the results are worth it.

the word "conference" in Figure 14-18, can be a useful design trick. Like kerning, tracking is measured in 1/1000 em. To make an adjustment, you must first select the word(s) you want to track and then trot over to the Character panel and look for the setting marked with an AV with a double-headed arrow beneath it. Pick a value from the pop-up menu, enter it manually, or use the scrubby cursor (circled in Figure 14-14).

TIP As you might suspect, there's a keyboard shortcut for this one too. To adjust tracking in increments of 10, select some text and then press and hold Option (Alt on a PC) while tapping the left or right arrow key. Add the ⌘ key (Ctrl) to change tracking in increments of 100.

Figure 14-18:
Tracking is a great way to make a word fit into a small space, or fill a big space. In this example, the word conference has been "tracked out" to stretch from the g in digital to the last a in camera. Because the large amount of space between the letters is uniform and obviously deliberate, it becomes a useful design element (and it's also one of the few ways all caps text looks good—the extra space makes it easier to read).

Doin' the baseline shift

The *baseline* of text is an invisible line on which letters sit. Changing it can make a character appear higher or lower than other characters on the same line (see Figure 14-19). This is called *baseline shift*, and you can think of it as an exaggerated super- or subscript control (as in dollar signs and degree symbols). Remember the section way back on page 548 about type on a path? Baseline shift was used to scoot the text above the path. It's also helpful when you want to create fractions, initial caps (shown in Figure 14-19), or manually adjust characters in a decorative typeface.

Figure 14-19:
Notice how the big, fancy D appears lower than the rest of the word? That's because its baseline shift has been decreased to −30 points.

To adjust the baseline of a character, word, or phrase, select the text you want to tweak and then head to the Character panel (if you don't select anything, the adjustment will be applied to the next thing you type). Use the baseline shift setting (it's marked with a big A and little a) to move the text up or down by picking a positive or negative value (respectively) from the pop-up menu, by entering a value manually, or by using your little scrubby-cursor.

> **TIP**   Once you've selected the text, press Shift-Option (Shift+Alt on a PC) while tapping either the up or down arrow on your keyboard to shift the baseline in increments of 2 points. Add the ⌘ key (Ctrl) to shift it in increments of 10 points.

Other character options

The Character panel is chock full of other formatting controls. Just remember that, to apply any of the formatting discussed in this section, you first have to select the text.

As shown in Figure 14-15, the Character panel is where you can turn on faux styles (page 535), like bold and italic (they're not built into the typeface, but faked by Photoshop instead). Feel free to use faux styles if you're creating a piece for online use or at-home printing. That said, it's best to stay away from the faux stuff if the work is bound for a professional printer, as they can cause *unexpected* results.

Problems include jagged text (due to rasterization); characters that refuse to print (which will cause Photoshop to substitute another font); or a PostScript error, which can halt printing altogether.

Among the other styles offered for your formatting pleasure are underline (which places a line under the type), and strikethrough (which places a line *through* the type).

> **TIP** The keyboard shortcut for bolding text (after it's selected) is Shift-⌘-B (Shift+Ctrl+B on a PC), for italicizing it's Shift-⌘-I (Shift+Ctrl+I), for underlining it's Shift-⌘-U (Shift+Ctrl+U), and for adding a strikethrough it's ⌘-Shift-Ctrl-? (Ctrl+Shift+?). Whew!

The other options in the Character panel are:

- **Horizontal/Vertical Scale.** These two settings (which stretch or shrink text horizontally or vertically) have the power to squish, cram, and spread type to within an inch of its life, rendering it utterly unreadable and unrecognizable. Use these options at your own risk! If you're trying to save space, a better solution is to adjust kerning or tracking (or both). If you're trying to fill space, increase the type size or tracking instead.

> **TIP** If you've played around with the scale of your text, you can instantly get it back to normal with the flick of a keyboard shortcut. Reset the vertical scale to 100% by selecting your text and pressing Shift-Option-⌘-X (Shift+Alt+Ctrl+X on a PC). Likewise, you can reset the horizontal scale to 100 percent by pressing Shift-⌘-X (Shift+Ctrl+X).

- **All Caps/Small Caps.** If you need to switch lowercase text to uppercase, just select the text and press the All Caps button (marked with TT). But keep in mind that, unless you're creating a small amount of text, and perhaps tracking it out as shown in Figure 14-18, using all caps is a bad idea. They're extremely hard to read because the words all take on the same blocky shape. Besides, they tend to insinuate screaming (LIKE THIS), and that's not very reader friendly. The Small Caps button (marked with a bit T and a smaller T) isn't much better as it creates smaller versions of the same, hard-to-read all caps. The keyboard shortcut for all caps is Shift-⌘-K (Shift+Ctrl+K on a PC); for small caps, it's Shift-⌘-H (Shift+Ctrl+H).

> **NOTE** The Small Caps style is faux (simulated) on anything other than an OpenType typeface (page 534). That means it can sure put a hitch in the giddyup of a professional print job.

- **Super and Subscript.** The Superscript and Subscript buttons cause the baseline and point size of the selected character(s) to change. (If you don't have any text selected, the next character you type, will be superscript or subscript.) Superscript increases the baseline shift so the character sits above other text in the same line (great for dollar signs and degree symbols), while subscript decreases the baseline shift so the character sits below other text (perfect for footnotes and scientific or mathematical text).

TIP The keyboard shortcut for superscript (which you can use after first selecting text) is ⌘-Shift-plus (Ctrl+Shift+plus on a PC). For subscript, press ⌘-Shift-Option-plus (Ctrl+Shift+Alt+plus).

- **Language.** The language pop-up menu at the bottom of the Character panel won't translate text for you; it merely means that Photoshop will adjust spell checks and hyphenation to suit the language selected. The 40 or so choices include everything from Bulgarian to Ukrainian. (See the box on page 553 to learn about spell checking.)

- **Anti-Aliasing.** The Character panel's anti-aliasing control (in the lower-right corner of the panel) works just like the anti-aliasing control on the Options bar, described on page 556.

But wait—that's not all! The Character panel has *even more* settings hidden in its menu. You can read all about 'em in the next few pages.

Orienting text

The Character panel is jam-packed with formatting options, and even though Adobe managed to cram an astonishing amount of stuff into this one panel, they couldn't fit everything. The solution was to stuff the remaining features into a menu tucked away in the upper-right corner of the Character panel (circled in Figure 14-20). When you open it, Photoshop unveils a long list of options that you won't use all that often, but they occasionally come in handy.

Figure 14-20:
To open the Character panel menu, click the button circled here. This menu also unlocks the secret typographic extras of OpenType typefaces (shown here in its expanded view), which are discussed in the following pages.

The first couple of options determine how text is oriented (the direction in which it's headed):

- **Change Text Orientation.** This menu item lets you switch horizontally-aligned text to vertical, and vice versa. Just select the Type layer you want to swap, not the text itself.

- **Standard Vertical Roman Alignment.** This is a fun one, though it only works on vertical type. Instead of the letters flowing from top to bottom, perched atop each other, they'll flow from left to right as if they were turned on their side. (Picture the word "Vertical" back in Figure 14-5, laid down on its side.) Another way to create this effect is to use the Free Transform tool (page 245) to spin the type around 90 degrees.

Ligatures and other fancy flourishes

These goodies are reserved for OpenType typefaces only (PostScripts and True-Types need not apply). As discussed on page 534, this format lets font designers include alternative character designs and all manner of glyphs into a typeface. Some have alternate *ligatures* (two or more characters that have been designed into one for better flow—like an *fi* or *fl* combination), fancy flourishes, a whole set of ornaments, and more. These embellishments are perfect for creating fancy initial caps, formatting numbers, and for adding a bit of typographic pizzazz, as shown in Figure 14-21.

Figure 14-21:
The top line of text is in standard Adobe Garamond. The middle line was created using Ordinals, which is usually used for numbers, but it creates an interesting typographic effect. The last line was made with Stylistic Alternates.

Choose OpenType from the Character panel menu and the extras will be revealed to you in yet another menu (shown in Figure 14-20). Be aware, though, that some OpenType fonts have extras and some don't; if one of the menu items is grayed out, that means it doesn't exist in that particular typeface. Here's a quick rundown of what you might encounter in the OpenType menu:

- **Standard Ligatures** are alternate character designs for certain letter combinations that tend to touch—like *fi, fl, ff, ffi,* and *ffl.*

- **Contextual Alternates** substitutes certain letterforms for others that join together more fluidly. This option is common on script typefaces because it makes the letters look like cursive handwriting.

- **Discretionary Ligatures** are replacements for letter pairs like *ct, st, ft*. They tend to have a bit more flourish than their standard ligature counterparts.

- **Swash** will substitute a standard character for one with an exaggerated stroke (think calligraphy).

- **Oldstyle** prompts Photoshop to use a shorter set of numerals than normal; some even sit below the baseline (page 561).

- **Stylistic Alternates** are characters that have extra bits of decoration here and there, as shown at the bottom of Figure 14-21. They're for your visual pleasure only (and, of course, that of the font designer).

- **Titling** calls to action a special set of all capitals designed to be used at large sizes, for things like titles (hence the name).

- **Ornaments** are symbols or pictographs (like WingDings).

- **Ordinals** decreases the size of letters appearing next to numbers and increases their baseline shift, so they look like this: 2nd, 3rd, 4th, and so on.

- **Fractions** will convert a number-slash-number combination (like this: 1/2) into a real fraction (like this: ½).

To apply the special OpenType features to existing text, create a selection using one of the methods described on page 540 and then select an item from the Open-Type menu (which you can find in the Character panel menu). If you don't make a text selection, the feature will be applied to the next character you type.

Fractional widths

Also in the Character panel menu, the *fractional widths* command rounds character widths to the nearest part of a pixel, instead of the normal whole pixel. This setting is automatically turned on because it usually tightens text spacing, making it more visually pleasing (like kerning, discussed on page 558). However, Adobe recommends turning this option off if you're working with anything smaller than 20-point text because the tighter spacing can make small text hard to read. Once it's turned off, Photoshop uses whole pixel spacing, which gives each character a bit more breathing room and keeps them from running into each other.

> **NOTE** You can't apply the Fractional Widths setting to individual characters; it's an all-or-nothing, "everything on the Type layer is affected" kind of thing. To use whole-pixel increments for the entire document, choose System Layout (explained next) from the Character panel menu.

System Layout

The *System Layout* option will revert your text to the way your particular operating system displays it—similar to what you might see in TextEdit on a Mac or WordPad on a PC. It switches character widths to whole pixels (as discussed in the previous section) and turns off anti-aliasing (page 553). This is a good option to use when designing text for the Web, because the bit of extra space and letter sharpness makes super small text a little easier to read.

No Break

When it comes to hyphenation, some words are meant to be broken and some aren't (as shown in Figure 14-22). To prevent such a typographical gaffe from happening to you, select the word(s) you want to keep together and select *No Break* from the Character panel menu. This forces Photoshop to reflow the text so the word doesn't end up sliced in two. For more on hyphenation, see page 569.

In MotoGP,
Rossi is a leg-
end.

Angry wife is
jailed for mans-
laughter.

Figure 14-22:
This is what happens when good hyphenation goes bad. As you can see, some words just aren't meant to be broken. The fix is to highlight the offending word and choose No Break from the Character panel menu.

Reset Character

If you've gone a bit overboard with formatting and want to return the formatted text to its original glory, select the text and choose *Reset Character* from the Character panel menu. If you don't have an active text selection, the newly restored character settings will affect the next thing you type.

Close and Close Tab Group

Close and *Close Tab Group* are new in Photoshop CS4. Choose Close to make the currently active panel disappear (like the Character panel), or Close Tab Group to make a whole group of related panels disappear (both the Character and Paragraph panels, for example). See Chapter 1 for more on panels and docks.

The Paragraph Panel

The Paragraph panel, shown in Figure 14-23, doesn't have anywhere *near* the number of options as the Character panel, though that doesn't make them any less important. Paragraph formatting options control alignment, hyphenation, justification, indentation, and spacing. Read on for a full discussion of each.

Figure 14-23:
You can apply the formatting options found in the Paragraph panel to one or more paragraphs of text.

Not one to be left out, the Paragraph panel also has a menu containing features that just wouldn't fit anywhere else. This menu is shown in Figure 14-24 and discussed in the following pages.

Figure 14-24:
You can access the Paragraph panel menu by clicking the button in the upper-right corner of the panel (circled).

NOTE   Just like the Character panel, any changes you make in the Paragraph panel remain until you change them back. If you want to restore the settings (or your text) to their original form, choose Reset Paragraph from the Paragraph panel menu (shown in Figure 14-24).

Aligning text

Alignment gives readers' eyes a hard edge to follow as they read through text, with the edge itself forming an invisible line that connects items on a page. The basic alignment types are left, center, and right, and picking the correct one for your document can make it look stronger, cleaner, and more dramatic. So which alignment should you choose? It depends on what you're going for. Here are a few guidelines for your consideration:

- **Use left alignment on big blocks of text.** Newspapers, books, and magazines (which should not be created in Photoshop) usually stick with left alignment because it's the easiest to read. Unless you tell it otherwise, Photoshop will left-align everything.

- **Use centered alignment for formal situations.** There's a reason the copy in every graduation and wedding announcement you've ever seen is centered—it conveys a feeling of formality and elegance. So unless you live on Pennsylvania Avenue, resist the urge to center the copy on your next yard sale flyer.

- **Use right alignment for small blocks of text or numbers.** Right alignment can make text stand out because it's out of the norm, and therefore draws attention. Bear in mind, though, that it's harder to read than left alignment, meaning you'll want to save it for relatively small chunks of text (don't right align your next novel). However, it's great for using on lists of numbers because it makes the decimals points (or commas) line up perfectly.

TIP   With vertical type, these options align the text based on a vertical line instead of a horizontal one. So instead of left, center, or right, the alignment becomes top, center, or bottom.

You can align text on a single layer (or even a single line on a layer) or across multiple Type layers:

- **Aligning text on a single Type layer or on multiple Type layers.** Feel free to use different alignments on lines of text on the same Type layer if you'd like. First, activate the Type tool and the Type layer you want to work on. If you want to align a single line of text, click anywhere within that line and then press the appropriate alignment button in the Options bar or in the Paragraph panel. To align all the text on that layer, select it using one of the methods described on page 540, and then click the appropriate alignment button. To align the text on several Type layers, select the layers by Shift- or ⌘-clicking (Ctrl-clicking on a PC) to the right of the layers' thumbnails and then clicking one of the alignment buttons.

- **Aligning the Type layers themselves.** If you need to align the left edge of text across several layers, you use a whole different set of alignment tools. Select the offending layers as described in the previous bullet point, and then press V to grab the Move tool (which makes sense because in this case, the Type layers themselves will move) and poof!—a whole slew of alignment tools appears in the Options bar. Click the one you want to apply, and the selected layers dutifully jump to the left, right, or center. These alignment tools are covered more fully in Chapter 3 on page 91.

Hyphenation and Justification

Known to page-layout pros as H&J, these controls work together to spread paragraph text so that both the left and right edges are perfectly straight, or *justified*. (The text in most magazines, newspapers, and books—including this one—is justified.) They also determine how the words are sliced and diced (*hyphenated*) in order to make them fit within a text box, or to make the margins perfectly straight.

> **NOTE** Hyphenation and justification work only on paragraph text, not point text. (See page 539 to learn the difference.)

Hyphenation is automatically turned on, though you can turn it off using the checkbox at the bottom of the Paragraph panel, or by selecting the text and pressing ⌘-Shift-Option-H (Ctrl+Shift+Alt+H on a PC). However, you have to turn on justification manually by selecting one of the following options:

- **Justified, last line left.** This setting spreads text so that the left and right edges are perfectly straight (even on both sides, like the text in this book), with the last line of the paragraph left aligned (meaning it doesn't reach across to the right margin, like the figure captions in this book). The keyboard shortcut for this kind of justification is to select your text and then press Shift-⌘-J (Shift+Ctrl+J on a PC).

- **Justified, last line centered.** This is the same as the previous setting, but with the last line center aligned instead.

- **Justified, last line right.** Same again, but with the last line right aligned.

> **TIP** Justification is affected by which *composition method* you've chosen. See the box on page 571 for more info.

- **Blocked.** With this setting turned on, the left and right edges of text are perfectly straight, but the last line is spread out to span the entire width of the paragraph. The results usually don't look very good (the last line tends to look really sprawled out), but once in awhile some rebellious designer manages to pull it off, as shown in Figure 14-25.

> **NOTE** If you're working with vertical text, the justification options become justify last top, centered, and bottom.

Figure 14-25:
If you want to truly tax your text, use blocked justification. This forces all the lines of text to line up vertically, even the last one. It's really hard to make blocked text look good, though the folks at QuotableCards.com managed it quite nicely in this magnet design.

It's unlikely you'll ever need to adjust the H&J options, and if you do, that's a sign you should be creating your text in another program (see the box on page 532). Nevertheless, you *can* customize hyphenation and justification through the Paragraph panel menu (see Figure 14-24). For the scoop on adjusting these settings, see Figure 14-26.

> **TIP** If you don't want a word or phrase to get hyphenated, use the No Break option over in the Character panel menu (see page 566).

Indenting text

It should be clear by now that Photoshop is no word processor, so don't go rooting around expecting any serious margin controls. However, you do have *some* say in how much space Photoshop puts between the text and the left or right edge of a single line (for point text) or the boundaries of a text box (for paragraph text). You can find the following options in the middle of the Paragraph panel (shown in Figure 14-23):

- **Indent Left Margin and Indent Right Margin.** These options will scoot a line of text to the left or the right by the number of points you enter here.

POWER USERS' CLINIC

Photoshop's Composition Methods

"Great artists steal," or at least that's what Picasso and Steve Jobs say, and the folks at Adobe clearly agree: Deep within the Paragraph panel menu (Figure 14-24) you'll find a couple of options snatched unabashedly from Adobe's page-layout software, InDesign.

Displaying text is a complicated matter. To determine how paragraph text is displayed, Photoshop takes into consideration word spacing, letter spacing, glyph spacing, and any hyphenation options you've set. With that information, it uses a complex formula to determine how lines of text are spaced (and broken, if necessary) in order to fit them within the text box you've created. This is called *composition*, and you have two composition methods to choose from:

- Choose **Single-Line** if you're dealing with just one line of text, or if you want to hand-craft the spacing between letters and lines with kerning or by inserting manual line breaks (carriage returns). With this method, Photoshop composes each line individually, no matter how many lines your paragraph contains.

- Choose **Every-Line** if you're dealing with more than one line of text. Choosing this method tells Photoshop to compose the paragraph as a whole. The program tries to arrange lines in such a way that it can avoid nasty line breaks. This method generally creates more visually pleasing text, in part because it makes Photoshop avoid hyphenation whenever possible. Photoshop uses this method automatically, unless you tell it otherwise.

- **Indent First Line.** This option indents only the first line of the paragraph. If you need to create a *hanging indent*—where all lines of a paragraph are indented *except* the first—you can do that here. (However, this is yet another indicator that you should be using page layout software instead.) To create a hanging indent, enter a positive number (like 10) for the left indent and a negative number (like –10) for the first line indent.

- **Roman Hanging Punctuation.** This totally awesome feature is tucked away in the Paragraph panel menu (circled in Figure 14-24). You can use it to make the punctuation appear *outside* the text margin, while the letters themselves remain perfectly aligned, as shown in Figure 14-27. (You don't need to select any text before applying this setting.)

"To enjoy the
flavor of life
take big
bites."

Robert Heinlein

Figure 14-27:
The Roman Hanging Punctuation setting moves punctuation (in this case, the initial quotation mark) outside the margin, leaving the text perfectly aligned. Magnet designers love this one!

Space Before and After

Take a peek at the headers and subheads in this book. Notice how there's more space above them than below? This kind of spacing makes it easy for you to tell—even at a glance—that the paragraph following the header is related. That's because the spacing itself is a visual clue: Information that *is* related should appear closer together than information that's *not* related. (In design circles, this is known as the rule of *proximity*.) Proper spacing makes it a lot easier for people to read a document quickly (or even just scan it) and understand how it's organized.

To adjust the spacing of information in your document, you could take the easy way out and add a few extra carriage returns; though, chances are good that you'll introduce too much—or too little—space. Instead, use the Paragraph panel's Space Before and Space After options, which let you control spacing right down to the point (oh glorious control, let us bow before thee!). To do that, select a Type layer and grab the Type tool by pressing T. Click anywhere in the offending line (don't select it, just click it), and then head to the Paragraph panel and enter an amount (in points) into the Space Before or Space After field, or both. (You can also use the little scrubby cursor as discussed previously.)

Special Text Effects

You can spice up Photoshop text in a variety of ways, by adding strokes, drop shadows, textures, and more. You can even take a photo and place it *inside* of text. The great thing is that you can perform all these techniques without rasterizing the text, so it remains fully and gloriously editable. Read on to learn all kinds of neat ways to add a little something special to your text.

> **TIP**   Perhaps the easiest special effect of all is creating partially opaque or *ghosted* text. All you have to do is lower the Type layer's opacity in the Layers panel, as explained on page 87. That's it!

Stroked Text

One of the easiest ways to enhance text is to give it an outline, making it really stand out. Photoshop calls this outline a *stroke*, and it's simple to add using the layer styles menu you learned about back in Chapter 3 (page 119). The following steps explain how to add a plain black stroke, as shown at the top of Figure 14-28.

Figure 14-28:
Here are a few ways of stroking text with a layer style. The great thing is that no matter what kind of stroke you create, you can edit it by double-clicking the newly added stroke style layer over in the Layers panel.

Top: The classic thick, black, outside stroke.

Middle: By changing the Stroke Type to Gradient and the Style to Shape Burst, you can introduce more than one color to the stroke, which gives it a bit of flair. This gradient stroke was made with the Silver preset from the Metal set (see page 573 for more on loading gradients).

Bottom: By using the Gradient Editor (page 330) to create a custom solid gradient, you can make multi-stroked text, as explained in the next section.

NOTE You might be tempted to choose Edit → Stroke instead of following the steps below. Don't. To use the Edit menu's Stroke command, you have to rasterize the text first (in fact, the Stroke menu item will be grayed out if a Type layer—which is vector-based—is selected). Using Layers Styles is a much more flexible way to outline text because your text remains editable.

1. **Add some text.**

   Press T to grab the Type tool and type a word. Be sure to choose a fairly weighty typeface like Futura bold or Cooper (the words in Figure 14-28 are in Cooper). If the letterforms are too thin, the stroke can overpower them.

2. **Choose Stroke from the Layer Styles menu at the bottom of the Layers panel.**

   Photoshop will pop open the Layer Styles dialog box and display the many options for adding a stroke to your text.

3. **Enter a stroke width.**

   In the size field, enter a pixel width (or use the Size slider). Use a lower number for a thin stroke and a larger number for something more substantial (in Figure 14-28, top, the size was set to 8).

4. **Pick Outside from the Position menu.**

   Using a stroke position of Outside works well for text as it causes the stroke to appear on the *outside* of the character (as opposed to the inside where it takes up more space, or straddling the character's edge, as is the case with a Center position). Leave the blend mode set to normal and the opacity at 100 percent.

5. **Choose Color from the Fill Type pop-up menu.**

   Photoshop assumes you want to fill the stroke with color (as opposed to a gradient, as explained in the next section) and it automatically chooses black. To create a standard black stroke, as shown at the top of Figure 14-28, leave this setting alone. If you want to pick something else, click the little color swatch and choose something else from the resulting Color Picker.

6. **When you're finished, click OK to close the Layer Style dialog box and admire your newly stroked text.**

You can edit the new stroke at any time by double-clicking the new stroke style layer in the Layers panel.

TIP To produce hollow text, apply a Stroke layer style and then lower the Type layer's Fill opacity (page 87) to 0%. The stroke will still be visible, but everything *inside* the stroke will vanish.

The rare multi-stroked text effect

If you want to *really* make your text stand out—like in a comic book situation—try giving it more than one stroke, like the Shazam example shown at the bottom of Figure 14-28. This technique is rewarding, but requires a few more steps than the plain ol' single-stroked version in the previous section. Begin with steps 1 and 2 for creating stroked text, and then proceed as follows:

1. **In the Layer Style dialog box, set the fill type to Gradient and the Style menu to Shape Burst, as shown in Figure 14-29, top.**

   Using a gradient stroke lets you add a multi-colored stroke to the text, though you'll need to do some gradient editing first. Choosing Shape Burst as the gradient style makes the gradient stroke appear on the *outside* of the text only. You don't have to select a gradient style before editing the gradient; doing so just lets you see what you're creating.

2. **Open the Gradient Editor (page 330) and choose a new a gradient.**

   To open the Gradient Editor, shown in Figure 14-29, bottom, click the rectangular gradient preview. In the resulting dialog box, click once to use one of the handy preset swatches that appear at the top (see page 330 for more on loading and editing gradients). Figure 14-28, middle, shows a silver gradient from the Metal set.

   If you want to get really creative, proceed to the next step. If not, skip to step 4.

3. **Choose Solid as the Gradient Type and edit the individual color stops.**

   To edit one of the gradient colors, click the tiny color stop (circled in Figure 14-29) and then click the color well that appears below it (or just double-click the color stop itself). Move the color stops around by dragging or by entering a number in the position field. You can create the illusion of space between the color strokes by introducing white into the gradient, as shown in Figure 14-29.

4. **When the preview looks good, click OK in the Gradient Editor, and then click OK again to close the Layer Style dialog box.**

Pretty nifty, 'eh? Once again, if you want to edit the stroke, just double-click the stroke style layer in the Layers panel.

Classic Metal Text

When it comes to text effects, the oldest and most classic (and perhaps overused) effect is that of shiny metal, as shown in Figure 14-30. This book just wouldn't be complete without showing you how it's done.

In days of old, this kind of effect wasn't very forgiving; if you didn't get it right the first time, you had little choice but to start over. Now the whole thing can be done with layer styles, leaving the Type layer intact so you can experiment with typefaces and sizes after you're finished. The most complicated part is editing the gradient, as you'll see in the following steps.

1. **Create some text with the Type tool.**

   It's best to pick a nice, thick font so the letterforms have enough surface area to really show off the metal effect. The example in Figure 14-30 was made using the typeface Capitals, set to 130 points.

Figure 14-29:
These are the settings that were used on the Starship Enterprise…er, sorry…that were used to create the multicolored strokes around Shazam in Figure 14-28.

Top: Once you get the hang of editing gradients, you can simulate space between the color strokes by creating a solid gradient that goes from black to white (or whatever your document's background color is) to green and then back to white. Note that the color appearing closest to the text (white in this case) is the last color in the gradient preview shown here.

Bottom: To make your gradient match this one, you'll need to create six color stops. Place two at the 25% mark (black with white on top), two at 50% (white with green on top), and two more at 75% (green with white on top). As shown here, you'll only see three color stops when you're finished because the other three will be directly underneath them.

Click to open Gradient Editor

Color stop
Color well
Controls loacation
of color stop

2. **Add a Gradient Overlay via the Layer Styles menu.**

   To create the look of shiny metal, you need to add a blending of colors atop the text; a gradient overlay is just the ticket. Click the tiny *fx* button at the bottom of the Layers panel and choose Gradient Overlay from the pop-up menu.

3. **Edit the gradient.**

   Click the gradient preview and, in the Gradient Editor, edit the color stops so that they resemble what's shown at the bottom of Figure 14-30. (If you're feeling frisky, you can experiment with adding more stops.) Don't close the Layer Styles dialog box just yet.

4. **Add a gradient stroke.**

   Click the Stroke checkbox on the left side of the Layer Styles dialog box and choose Gradient from the Fill Type pop-up menu.

Figure 14-30:
Top: This bright and shiny look is comprised of two Type layers and four well-placed layer styles—that's it! The best part is that the text remains editable so you can play around with typefaces, text size, and layer styles for hours (or until the snacks run out).

Bottom: The hardest part of creating metal text is editing the gradient. But as long as your color stops resemble these, you're golden—or, more appropriately, chromed.

5. **Load the Metals gradient set.**

   From the Presets menu, choose Metals and click the swatch named Silver (hover above any swatch to see its name). For more on loading gradients, see page 330.

6. **Apply a bevel and emboss to the stroke.**

   Click the "Bevel and Emboss" checkbox on the left side of the Layer Styles dialog box and choose Stroke Emboss from the Style pop-up menu.

7. **Change the Technique pop-up to Chisel Hard.**

   This setting really makes the edges of the text look more like steel. Increase the depth to about 350 percent and change the Gloss Contour to Ring Double (it looks like two steep hills). *Now* you can close the Layer Styles dialog box.

8. **Adjust the kerning of the text, if necessary (to learn about kerning, see page 558).**

   The next step involves duplicating the Type layer to create yet another stroke, so you'll want to get the text just right before proceeding. If there's too much space between the letters, you should fix that now.

9. **Duplicate the Type layer and drag it below the original.**

   Press ⌘-J (Ctrl+J on a PC) to duplicate the Type layer with all the layer styles attached. In the Layers panel, drag the duplicate layer (with its entourage of styles) below the original Type layer.

10. **Remove all the formatting except the Stroke layer style from the duplicated layer.**

    With the duplicate layer selected in the Layers panel, drag both the gradient overlay and the bevel and emboss layer styles to the trashcan at the bottom right of the Layers panel.

11. **Change the Stroke layer style to solid black.**

    In the Layers panel, double-click the duplicate layer's Stroke layer style and in the resulting Layer Styles dialog box, choose Color from the Fill pop-up menu. Make sure the color is set to black (it will be unless you've changed it).

12. **Adjust the size and opacity of the stroke.**

    You don't want this final stroke to be so big that it takes away from the beautifully shiny metal text. Reducing the opacity also helps it remain subtle. In Figure 14-30, the stroke size was set to 8 with an opacity of 70 percent.

13. **When everything looks good, click OK to send the Layer Style dialog box on its merry way.**

Voilà—you've got yourself some shiny, metallic text. But just because you know how to do this doesn't mean you *should*; you are hereby given permission to use this technique twice a year—at most.

Texturizing Type

Design trends come and go, but the distressed, tattered look has been popular for a long time. You can spot it everywhere: in movie posters, magazine ads, book and album covers. Admittedly, it looks pretty darn good when applied to text. After all, text doesn't always have to look new, does it?

As with most effects, Photoshop gives you all kinds of ways to create a textured look. You can use a photo for the texture, run a filter (or several), or hide portions of the text using a layer mask and then paint it back with an artistic brush. Depending on your situation, one of these methods will work better for you than the rest (or at the very least, one will be faster). That's why all of them are covered in the following pages.

> **NOTE** Adding a layer mask to a Type layer opens up all manner of creative possibilities, some of which appear in the following pages (there are just too darn many to include them all). However, one simple text masking trick is a classic text fade. Simply add a layer mask to an existing Type layer and use the Gradient tool to fill it with a black-to-white gradient. The resulting text will appear to fade softly out of sight. See page 265 for more fun with gradient masks.

Texture from a photo

You can come up with some really unique effects by grabbing texture from a photo and applying it to text through a layer mask. And the great thing about this technique is that it's completely non-destructive: the Type layer remains editable. Start with an extremely busy photo—one with lots of hard lines and angles, like a picture of wood, leaves, or an interesting piece of architecture. In the steps below, you'll use the Threshold adjustment (page 312) to morph the photo into a high contrast texture primed for plopping into the nearest layer mask, as shown in Figure 14-31.

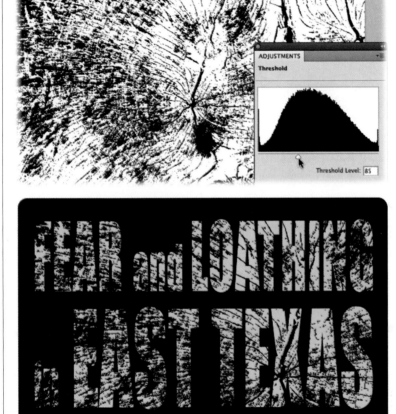

Figure 14-31:
Top: You can create a texture from any photo by using a Threshold adjustment (the more lines the photo contains, the better). Areas in shadow will become black and the highlights will become white.

Bottom: Here's what the wood texture looks like after it's been copied into the layer mask of a Type layer. Imagine the possibilities!

Here's how to texturize your text using a photo:

1. **Add some hefty text to your document.**

   Use a thick font (like Impact), and set the font size to something high (try 107 point). This will ensure you have plenty of surface area to texturize.

2. **Open a photo and convert it to a high-contrast, black-and-white image using a Threshold adjustment.**

   Choose Image → Adjustments → Threshold. Drag the Threshold Level slider almost all the way to the left. The highlights in the image turn completely white, and the shadows turn black. These black areas will become the texture, so bear in mind that too much texture (black) will render the text unreadable.

3. **Create a selection of the black areas and then copy them.**

   When you want to create a selection based on color, reach for the Magic Wand (page 140). Press W to activate the Magic Wand and then click inside one of the black areas. Select the rest of the black areas by choosing Select → Similar. (You can also Ctrl-click [right-click on a PC] inside the selection area and choose Similar from the shortcut menu that appears.) Copy the selection by pressing ⌘-C (Ctrl+C).

4. **Add a layer mask to the Type layer, and then open the mask.**

   Give the Type layer a layer mask by clicking the circle-within-a-square icon at the bottom of the Layers panel (see page 105 for more on layer masks). Next, open the mask by Option-clicking (Alt-clicking on a PC) the mask's thumbnail in the Layers panel. Your document should go completely white because the mask is empty.

5. **Paste the texture into the mask and, if necessary, reposition the text, mask, or both with the Move tool.**

   Once you're in the layer mask, press ⌘-V (Ctrl+V on a PC) to paste the new texture into the mask. Feel free to resize the texture using Free Transform (page 245) or move it around with the Move tool.

6. **Deselect the texture and exit the layer mask.**

   Banish the marching ants by pressing ⌘-D (Ctrl+D on a PC). Or if you'd rather use the menu system, choose Select → Deselect. To see the finished product, exit the layer mask by clicking the Type layer thumbnail (to the left of the layer mask).

   TIP   Photoshop assumes that if you want to move a layer mask, you'll want to move whatever it's attached to as well, though this may not always be the case. If, for example, you want to move the text independent of the mask, or vice versa, you have to unlink them first. Just click the little chain icon that lives between the type and layer mask thumbnails in the Layers panel, and the chain will vanish. Next, activate the Move tool and then click the thumbnail of whatever you want to reposition—either the image or its mask—and drag it into place. To lock them back together, click between their thumbnails in the Layers panel and the chain icon will reappear.

Texture from a brush

Another way to texturize text is by painting on a layer mask with the Brush tool. Photoshop has some amazingly funky-shaped brushes so you might as well make good use of them! With this method, you can be a little more particular about exactly where the texture goes since you'll be painting it by hand, as shown in Figure 14-32.

Figure 14-32:
By using some of Photoshop's more creative brushes, you can paint a unique texture onto your text using a layer mask (circled here). The brush cursor even takes on the shape of the brush, as you can see on the left side (it looks like a bunch of black squiggles). As with most type effects, you'll want to start out with a weighty typeface so you can actually see the texture you've so painstakingly applied (Poplar Std at 134 and 236 points was used here).

Go ahead and add some big, thick text to your document, and then proceed with the following steps:

1. **Add a layer mask to the Type layer.**

   Select the Type layer and add a layer mask by clicking the circle-within-a-square icon at the bottom of the Layers panel. This mask will let you hide bits of the text, instead of deleting it.

2. **Select the Brush tool and choose one of its more artistic manifestations like Spatter or Chalk.**

   Press B to select the Brush tool and then open the Brush Preset picker in the Options bar, or open the Brushes panel by clicking its panel dock (see Chapter 1 for more on panels). Scroll through the brush previews and select one of the more irregular, splotchy-type brushes. (Photoshop has a ton of built-in brushes. You can learn more about loading them on page 472.)

3. **Increase the brush size till it's 100 pixels or so.**

Making the brush size fairly big will help you see the brush edge more clearly when you begin to paint, so you'll know exactly what kind of texture you're painting where. While the Brush tool is active, you can press the right bracket key (]) repeatedly to increase brush size, or the left bracket key ([) to decrease it. This is an important keyboard shortcut to memorize, because this particular technique looks better if you vary the brush size quite a bit.

4. **Make sure your foreground color chip is set to black and the mask thumbnail is selected, then mouse over to your document and start clicking on the text to apply the texture (clicking works better than dragging).**

As you learned on page 105, painting with black within a layer mask conceals (hides) whatever is on that layer, while painting with white reveals. To hide portions of the text in the shape of the brush, you'll need to paint with black. Take a peek at the color chips at the bottom of the Tools panel (page 22) and make sure black is on top. If it's not, press X to flip-flop the color chips.

If you hide too much of the text, press X to swap color chips so that white is on top, and then click to paint that area back in. (You'll do a lot of swapping color chips when editing masks, as explained on page 111.)

The best part of this technique is that by using a layer mask, you haven't harmed the text. If you don't like the effect, just delete the layer mask (page 113) and you're back where you started.

Texture from filters

Running a filter on text is among the fastest ways to give it extra character. As with the previous two techniques, this method involves using a layer mask, though this time you need to create a selection of the text *before* adding the mask.

Add some chunky text to your document and, in the Layers panel, ⌘-click (Ctrl-click on a PC) the Type layer thumbnail to load the text as a selection. Once you see marching ants, add a layer mask to the Type layer as described in step 1 in the previous technique (page 581). Then head to the Filter menu and choose Distort → Ocean Ripple. (Other filters that work well include the Artistic and Distort sets, along with Sketch → Torn Edges.) In the resulting dialog box, tweak the filter's settings so that the text edges look fairly tattered in the handy preview window. Figure 14-33 shows the results of changing the Ripple Size to 8 and Ripple Magnitude to 4, and then running the filter 3 times. Press OK to dismiss the Filter dialog box and admire your newly distressed text.

> **TIP**   If you want to rerun the last filter you used, Photoshop will do it for you with the Last Filter command. Just press ⌘-F (Ctrl+F on a PC), and Photoshop will use the exact same settings you used last time (don't expect a dialog box though). This trick works until you quit Photoshop.

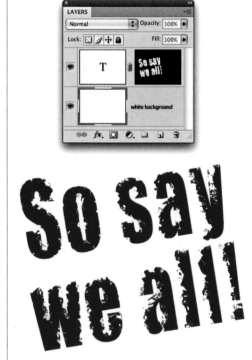

Figure 14-33:
Top: By loading the text as a selection before adding the layer mask, the mask takes on the shape of the letters, giving you a safe place to run the filter (otherwise, you'd have to rasterize the Type layer before running the filter).

Bottom: As you can see from the Layers panel, the Type layer remains unscathed after applying this technique, so you can still change the text color or resize it even after you're done. To change the color, double-click the Type layer and click the color swatch in either the Options bar or Character panel, as described on page 556. Resize the text by using one of the methods described on page 542.

Placing a Photo Inside Text

Ever wonder how designers place an image inside text? It takes *years* of practice. (Just kidding!) They do it by creating a *clipping mask* (see the box on page 114), which takes about five seconds. All you need is a photo, a Type layer, and the secret layer stacking order. To create the effect shown in Figure 14-34, follow these steps:

Figure 14-34:
Placing a photo inside text is one of the easiest text tricks to perform, though it looks really complicated. Be sure to pick a nice, thick typeface like Impact (shown here). That way a good chunk of the photo can be seen through the letters. For even more fun, use layer styles to add a stroke or drop shadow to the Type layer, as shown here.

1. **Open a photo and make it editable.**

   By default, Photoshop tries to protect you from yourself by locking the Background layer. Just double-click it to make it editable, and give it another name if you'd like. You have to do this in order to change the layer stacking order in the next few steps.

2. **Create some text.**

   Press T to grab the Type tool and add some text to your document. It doesn't matter what color the text is (as long as you're able to see it while you're typing); what matters is that you pick a really big, thick font. Figure 14-34 was made using Impact—a display font—at 95 points. Short words work better than longer ones (they're easier to read), and you may want to use all caps so more of the photo shows through.

3. **Drag the Type layer below the image layer.**

   Over in the Layers panel, drag the Type layer *below* the image layer. If the Type layer is *above* the photo layer, this technique won't work.

4. **Clip the photo layer to the Type layer.**

   With the photo layer selected, choose Layer → Create Clipping Mask, or press and hold Option (Alt on a PC) while hovering your cursor over the dividing line between the two layers in the Layers panel. (When the cursor turns into two intersecting circles, click once.) The thumbnail of the photo layer will scoot to the right and a tiny downward pointing arrow will appear to let you know that it's clipped (masked) to the Type layer directly below. You should now see the photo peeking through the text.

5. **Add a new layer at the bottom of the layer stack and fill it with color.**

   Rather than stare into the checkerboard of a transparent document, add a colorful background instead (in Figure 14-34, the background's sage green). Create a brand new layer and position it at the bottom of the layers stack. To make sure the background goes well with the photo, select the Eyedropper from the Tools panel and click within the photo to snatch a color. Next, fill the background layer with the new color by choosing Edit → Fill, or by pressing Option-Delete (Alt+Backspace on a PC).

6. **Use the Move tool to reposition either the photo or the text (see the Tip on page 580 to learn how to move the layer independently of its mask, or vice versa).**

   You're basically done at this point, but feel free to play around with text formatting, layer styles, different typefaces, or just sit back and admire your handiwork.

   NOTE   Another neat Photoshop trick is to place text *behind* an object. This technique, in all its step-by-step glory, is detailed on page 107.

Converting Type to a Shape or Path

Last but certainly not least, Photoshop lets you do all kinds of cool things with text that has been converted into a vector shape or path (for more on shapes and paths, see Chapter 13). Though the converted text is uneditable, what used to be the Type layer is morphed into a resizable, distortable piece of art or editable path that you can do all kinds of interesting things to.

To convert text into a shape or path, just select the Type layer in the Layers panel and then choose Layer → Type → Create Work Path or "Convert to Shape". This miraculous transformation lets you:

- **Edit the letterforms themselves.** Want to add an extra flourish here and a swoosh there? Create a work path from the text and then use the Path Selection tool (page 515) to twist and pull the letters any which way you'd like.

- **Apply distort and perspective with Free Transform.** You may have noticed that the Free Transform tool's distort and perspective options are grayed out when a Type layer is active; but they're ready for action on a shape layer. If you've ever wanted to create text that fades into the distance in proper perspective, here's your chance.

- **Rotate individual letters.** Instead of creating each letter on its own layer and rotating them individually, you can convert the word into a shape layer first, and then use the Path Selection tool (page 515) to grab one letter at a time and rotate it with Free Transform, as shown in Figure 14-35. Graphic designers love doing this kind of thing.

- **Creating intersecting or intertwining text.** Once you've converted text to a shape, you have the full arsenal of shape commands at your disposal, including the ever-useful Exclude Overlapping Shape Areas option, shown in Figure 14-35. (For more on shape commands, see page 515.)

- **Scale to infinity—and beyond!** Because the shape is a vector, you don't have to worry about jagged edges. So after you've created one of the coolio techniques in this list, feel free to resize it using Free Transform without fear of losing quality.

- **Enjoy stress-free printing.** That's right: You can send the file off to a professional printer (or to an inkjet printer, for that matter) without a care in the world. By converting text to a shape, you don't have to worry about including the original fonts or how the text will print.

More Typographic Resources

This book is by no means the end-all-be-all on typography and typefaces. If you want to learn more about finding, identifying, and buying fonts, crack open a nice bottle of wine and check out some of the following resources:

Figure 14-35:
This effect was created by converting text (Arial Black) into a shape and then spinning each letter individually with the Free Transform tool. (Don't forget to press Return—Enter on a PC—when you're done rotating each letter.)

For added fun, you can use the Path Selection tool to move each letter so that they overlap just a touch. Use the tool again to select all the letters and choose Exclude Overlapping Shape Areas from the Options bar. This causes the color to disappear from the overlapping areas (as shown here), letting the white background show through.

- *The Non-Designer's Type Book,* **Second Edition,** by Robin Williams (Peachpit Press, 2005). This book is an easy read and well worth the time. You'll learn more than you ever wanted to know about typography.

- *www.Helveticafilm.com.* Visit this site for a feature-length film about typography and graphic design made in celebration of the Helvetica typeface's 50th birthday in 2007. It's fascinating!

- *www.fonts.com.* Hands down the Internet's number one resource for all things font-related.

- *www.myfonts.com.* Another great resource, this site features a font identification service. Just send them an image of the text and they'll tell you what the closest matching font is. How cool is that?!

- *www.fontshop.com.* More than just a font shop, these guys offer typeface format conversions, plus they'll create custom fonts for specific needs.

- *www.identifont.com.* This site will help you identify fonts by filling out a fairly simple questionnaire.

- *www.lucasfonts.com* and *www.vllg.com/fonts/.* These are two popular online font foundries that have more fonts than you could ever imagine.

The Wide World of Filters

Filters apply special effects to your images. They're both incredibly useful and out-rageously fun. You can run them on image layers, masks, channels, shapes, and even Type layers. The list of special effects you can create by applying filters once, twice, or even ten times is a mile long. There are a slew of the little buggers too, each with its own special brand of pixel wrangling. As of this writing, Photoshop sports 13 different filter categories, each of which includes anywhere from 2 to 15 filters! You've already seen a few filters in action like the ones used for sharpening (Chapter 11), blurring (Chapter 10, page 410), adding texture to type (Chapter 14, page 582), and mapping one image to the contours of another (Chapter 7, page 296). But that's just a tiny sliver of what's available.

In this chapter you'll be immersed in the world of filters and discover how you can use them to:

- Transform your image with painterly effects (page 591).

- Create a shallow depth-of-field effect (page 592).

- Fix funky edge halos or color fringes (page 591).

- Add artistic edge effects to your images (page 595).

- Make a portrait pop with a dark-edge vignette (page 590).

- Add texture (page 590 and page 608).

- Create additional lighting (page 590).

- Conjure up fake snow (page 590).

- Rescue a slightly out-of-focus image (page 607).

- Turn a photo into a pencil sketch (page 605).

- Tighten or expand a layer mask (page 610).

But before you start plowing through the Filter menu, you need to know how to use filters in ways that won't harm your original images. That means learning to use Smart Filters. Onward, ho!

> **NOTE** If the Filter has three dots after its name, it comes with a dialog box that lets you tweak various settings. If it doesn't, the sucker just runs—you've been warned!

The Joy of Smart Filters

Filters, by their very nature, are destructive—they move, mangle, distress, and distort pixels like you can't believe, and they always run on the currently active layer (or active selection). Back in the pre-Photoshop CS3 days, the only way to protect your image—and give yourself *any* level of editing flexibility—was to duplicate the layer first and run the filter on that copy. At least then you could lower the filter's strength by reducing layer opacity (page 87) or hide the filter from parts of the image with a layer mask. However, as you know from Chapter 3, duplicating layers can bloat your document's file size and make Photoshop feel like a sloth (especially if you've got a slow computer).

Then along came Photoshop CS3 and the introduction of *Smart Filters* (enter monks chanting in unison here). If you convert a layer into a Smart Object (page 116) before you modify it, you can make the filter run on its *own* layer, complete with blend mode (page 267) and opacity control (page 87). It even comes with a layer mask.

Smart Filters are, indeed, the best thing since sliced bread, but a few filters—Extract (page 149), Liquify (page 405), Vanishing Point (page 609), and Lens Blur (page 592)—will run only on regular image layers (those that haven't been converted to Smart Objects). If that's the case, just duplicate your image layer and run the filter on the copy. Smart Filters are also picky about which color mode your image is in (they won't work in Lab color mode, for instance); however, since you'll spend most of your time in RGB mode, anyway, that isn't a huge deal.

When Smart Filters *are* an option, they're the only way to roll, and creating them couldn't be easier: All you have to do is open your image, select the layer you want to work on, and choose Filter → "Convert for Smart Filters". You'll get a friendly message letting you know that Photoshop is about to turn your layer into a Smart Object, to which you should reply with a resounding OK. (You'll probably want to turn on the "Don't show again" checkbox to eliminate future message clutter.)

Over in the Layers panel, the image layer now carries the special badge of a Smart Object at the bottom right of its thumbnail, and the next filter you run appears on its own layer (see Figure 15-1). You can run as many filters on the image layer as you want by choosing them from the Filter menu; they'll just continue to stack up in your Layers panel. If you need to rearrange their stacking order, say, to keep one from covering up another, you can drag them up or down in the Layers panel.

Figure 15-1:
Top: Smart Filters occupy their very own layer, complete with a layer mask as shown here. (The layer to which the filter is applied is highlighted in blue.) Once you've run a filter, the image layer displays both a Smart Object badge and a Filter Effects icon.

Bottom: Double-clicking the Blending Options icon opens a dialog box that lets you lower the filter's opacity and change its blend mode (left). When you change the blend mode to Luminosity, the Plastic Wrap filter affects only the lighter areas of the superhero's cape. You can use the built-in mask to hide the effects of the filter from certain areas—like his face and the bricks—as shown here (right).

TIP If you can't use a Smart Filter and you forgot to duplicate your image layer, you can lessen the strength and change the blend mode of the filter by using the Edit → Fade command. But you have to run the command before you do anything else, or the command won't be available. Flip back to Chapter 11 and see the box on page 431 for the full scoop.

If you want to apply the same filters to another layer, you can copy them from one layer to another by Option-dragging (Alt-dragging on a PC) the Smart Filter layer. To get rid of 'em entirely, drag them to the trash can icon at the bottom right of your Layers panel.

> **NOTE**   While you can delete a garden-variety layer by selecting it and pressing Delete (Backspace on a PC), you can't do that with Smart Filters (or Layer Styles for that matter). You have to drag them to the trash or click the trash can icon and then click OK in the resulting "Are you sure?" dialog box.

A Filters Tour

With so many filters to choose from, it can be tough to get a handle on what they all do. That's why several filters—those in the Artistic, Brush Strokes, Distort, Sketch, Stylize, and Texture categories—summon a large dialog box called the Filter Gallery (see Figure 15-2). On the left you'll see a nice big preview of your image (zoom in or out by using the + and − buttons underneath it), a list of *all* the filters in these categories in the middle, and the specific settings associated with each filter on the right.

Once the Filter Gallery dialog box is open, you can go through the whole list of filters by clicking each one and then tweaking its settings; your image preview will update immediately. You can even select additional filters while you're in the dialog box by clicking the "New effect layer" button at the bottom right (Photoshop shows each filter as a list right above the buttons). You can also delete individual filters you've added by clicking the tiny trash can icon at the bottom right.

Choose zoom level
Zoom in/out of preview

Create new effects layer
Delete effects layer

Figure 15-2:
Several filters automatically open Photoshop's Filter Gallery though you can open it yourself by choosing Filter → Filter Gallery. This big dialog box makes it easy to zip through most filters to get a quick idea of what they do. With the right music and snacks, filter browsing can make for an entertaining evening!

Here you can see what the Poster Edges filter looks like on a superhero wannabe. Even with no adjustments to the factory settings, the effect gives you a neat, cartoonish look.

NOTE   Not all filters appear in the Filter Gallery dialog box, so don't let that throw you. You can choose the others straight from the Filters menu.

Throughout this chapter, you'll find some helpful ideas of how to use at least one filter in each filter category (think of it as a greatest hits tour). Since a complete listing of every filter would swell this book to Yellow-Pages proportions, feel free to check this book's Web site, *www.missingmanuals.com*, for more ideas and techniques (they'll be added periodically). Grab your favorite beverage, sit back in your chair, and read on.

TIP   If you want to rerun the last filter you used with the same settings, press ⌘-F (Ctrl+F on PC). You can also click the Filter menu; the last filter shows up as the first item on the list. To summon the filter's dialog box, you can press ⌘-Option-F (Ctrl+Alt+F).

Artistic

If you want to make your image *resemble* a painting or a cartoon, turn to the filters in this category. Their special purpose is to mimic real-world artistic effects created with brushes, pencils, and palette knives though they can also give your image a very artsy look. If you're just looking for a quick artistic touch, these filters can get the job done.

For example, if you want to soften an image and make it look like it's painted, try running the Paint Daubs filter to introduce brush strokes and then running the Underpainting filter to give the image a little texture (as if it were painted on a real canvas). But if you really want to make your image look like a painting, you need to use these filters along with the painting techniques you covered in Chapter 12 (or paint the image from scratch).

Figure 15-1 shows the effects of Plastic Wrap, which makes your image look shiny—as if it were covered in actual plastic (it's also great for making an object look glossy or slimy). Figure 15-2 shows the Poster Edges filter, which makes the edges of your image black and gives the whole thing a cartoonish look (for more on posterizing, see page 329).

Blur

You've seen various blur filters in action already, including the Gaussian Blur to smooth skin (page 410) and the Motion blur to simulate motion (page 262). They're worth their weight in gold when you need to soften pixels for better blending, but you can also use a blur filter to zap edge halos or eliminate a color fringe—that slight blue or purplish collar loitering around the edges of near-black objects in your image (see Figure 15-3, left).

The color fringe problem is especially common in photos taken using cheap wide-angle lenses; it also rears its ugly head when you shoot something really dark on a light background. The image may look okay at a glance, but a closer inspection often reveals some serious bluish or purplish fringing (*artifacts*) around the dark objects. Here's how you can fix it with a good dose of the Gaussian Blur filter:

Figure 15-3:
At a zoom level of 200 percent, you can see the weird color fringe around the 8 (left); running the Gaussian Blur filter removes it completely (right).

1. **Open the blurred image and select the layer you want to work with.**

2. **Choose Filter → "Convert to Smart Filters".**

3. **Choose Filter → Blur → Gaussian Blur.**

   In the resulting Gaussian Blur dialog box, enter a Radius of five to seven pixels and then press OK (this setting controls how much blurring is applied to your image). Depending on the pixel dimensions of your image, you may need to experiment with this value (increase it for larger images or reduce it for smaller ones).

4. **Change the filter Blending Options to Color.**

   Double-click the Blending Options icon next to the Gaussian Blur layer and change the Mode pop-up menu to Color. As you learned in Chapters 7 and 8, the Color blend mode affects only hue, and since your goal is to blur the *colored* pixels (as opposed to the black ones), this blend mode works perfectly.

5. **Adjust the Opacity setting to 96 percent.**

   This high setting keeps the blur from looking too obvious.

6. **Click OK when you're finished.**

   A quick zoom-in reveals that the pesky color fringing is gone as shown in Figure 15-3, right.

Lens Blur

Another handy filter in the Blur category is Lens Blur. It's perfect for creating beautifully blurred backgrounds…after you've taken a photo. In fact, you can use it to mimic a popular tilt-lens called the Lensbaby (*www.lensbaby.com*), which is a bendable lens—if you can imagine—that lets you control which part of the picture is in focus. Once you get the angle just right, you can lock the lens into place and snap the shot. It's a great way to draw the viewer's eye to your subject, but at $200 or more, it's not exactly an impulse buy.

You wouldn't want to use the following technique on every picture you take, but it can certainly enhance a select few, especially those with distracting backgrounds:

1. **Open your image and locate the Channels panel.**

   Open the Channels panel by clicking its panel dock or by choosing Windows → Channels. To tell Photoshop which part of your image you want to blur and which part should stay in focus, you need to create a selection that the Lens Blur filter can use. An easy way to do that is by making an alpha channel (page 185), which you'll do in the next step.

2. **Create a new alpha channel.**

   Click the New Channel icon at the bottom of the Channels panel. At the top of the panel, click the visibility eye next to the RGB channel (also called the composite channel—see page 174). Your entire image takes on the Quick Mask mode's red overlay (page 162), which lets you create your selection by using a big soft, fluffy brush. Don't panic; the red overlay is temporary, so your image won't end up pink.

3. **Grab the Brush tool and set your foreground color chip to white.**

   Your goal here is to edit the Quick Mask so that the area you want to remain in focus doesn't have any red on it (any areas that you *do* leave red become blurry once you finish the technique). Make sure your color chips are set to black and white (just press D if they're not), and press X until white is on top (if it's already on top, you don't have to press X).

4. **Choose a big, soft brush and lower its opacity to 50 percent.**

   Hop up to the Options bar and, from the Brush menu, choose a nice soft brush (fuzzy edges rather than hard) that's fairly big (around 200 pixels, or even a bit larger). To create a subtle transition from sharp to blurry pixels, lower the brush opacity to 50 percent.

   TIP   In Photoshop CS4, you can resize your brush by Option-Ctrl-dragging (Alt+right-click+dragging on a PC) to the left to make it smaller or to the right to make it bigger.

5. **Paint across the areas you want to remain in focus.**

   In Figure 15-4, for example, paint across the boy's face. As you paint, the photo starts to show through just a little, but, since you lowered the opacity of your brush, you need to keep painting over the same area to achieve 100 percent focus. Remember: Anything that's red will be blurry when you're done, and the rest of the image will remain sharp. To create a perfectly sharp area, lower your brush size and paint over that area until all the red is gone. If you mess up and bring back too much of the photo, press X to flip-flop the color chips and paint that area with black to make it blurry again.

Figure 15-4:
Top: When you first run the Lens Blur filter, it does the exact opposite of what you want—it blurs what's supposed to be sharp, and vice versa. To fix it, just turn on Invert.

Bottom: This effect not only draws the viewer's eye, it can also make a building look like a miniature.

6. **Turn off the alpha channel's visibility eye and select the RGB layer.**

There's no need to leave the alpha channel turned on, so go ahead and hide it by clicking its visibility eye. Next, click the RGB layer so you can see the full-color version of your image again.

7. **Open the Layers panel and duplicate the original layer.**

   Since Lens Blur isn't available as a Smart Filter, the only way to protect your original image is to duplicate the layer and then run the filter on the duplicate. To open the Layers panel, click the Layers tab in your panel dock on the right side of the screen (page 17) or choose Window → Layers. Click to select the image layer and duplicate it by pressing ⌘-J (Ctrl+J on a PC).

8. **With the duplicate layer selected, choose Filter → Blur → Lens Blur.**

9. **In the resulting Lens Blur dialog box, change the Depth Map source to Alpha 1.**

   Use the dialog box to tell the filter about your alpha channel by selecting it from the Depth Map pop-up menu. Unless you gave it a different name, it goes by Alpha 1.

10. **Turn on Invert.**

    Initially, the blurry and sharp areas will be flip-flopped from what you created in the alpha channel. Turning on the Invert checkbox will fix things, as shown in Figure 15-4.

11. **Adjust the Radius slider until you get the right amount of blur.**

    This slider lets you determine just *how* blurry the background gets. If you're working on a really big image (for example, one from your digital camera), it may take Photoshop a few seconds to update the preview window, so be patient. Also, be sure to release your mouse button so Photoshop can generate a new preview.

12. **Click OK when you're finished.**

    Since you used an alpha channel to create the effect, you can change the results. If you don't like how your image looks, just toss the duplicate Background layer, pop open your Channels panel, grab your Brush tool, and edit the alpha channel. Then repeat steps 6–12 to run the filter again.

    TIP   If you want to add a little noise to the blurry bits to make your image look less perfect, you can adjust the Noise Amount slider at the bottom right of the Lens Blur dialog box. Turn on Gaussian Distribution and Monochromatic and then click OK.

Brush Strokes

There are a slew of filters in this category and, like the Artistic set, they're geared toward recreating traditional fine-art effects. If you want to add interesting edge treatments to your images, these filters work especially well when you use them with a layer mask (see Figure 15-5). Among the most useful filters for these kinds of edge effects are Spatter and Sprayed Strokes (choose Filter → Brush Strokes → Spatter or Sprayed Strokes).

Figure 15-5:
If you draw a selection around your image (top) and then add a layer mask (bottom), you can run a filter on the mask itself, which makes for some really nice edge effects (all without harming your original image). Tack on a well-placed inner shadow for an even more interesting look.

NOTE   A couple of other filters that work well with this technique are Glass, Ocean Ripple, Twirl (Filter → Distort → Glass, Ocean Ripple, or Twirl), and Torn Edges (Filter → Sketch → Torn Edges).

When you're ready to spice up the edges of your image, take this technique for a spin:

1. **Open a photo and double-click the Background layer to make it editable.**

   Since you'll run the filter on a layer mask, you don't need to use Smart Filters.

2. **Grab the Rectangular Marquee tool and draw a box where you want the frame to appear.**

   For best results, draw your box at least a quarter of an inch in from the edges of your photo as shown in Figure 15-5, top. (The filter will run outside your selection, on the edges of your image.)

3. **Add a layer mask.**

   At the bottom of the Layers panel, click the circle-within-a-square icon to add a layer mask to the part of your image where you'll apply the filter.

4. **With the layer mask selected, choose Filter → Brush Strokes → Spatter.**

   In the resulting Filter Gallery dialog box, increase the Spray Radius to 20 and the Smoothness to 8.

5. **Click OK.**

   If you want to soften the edges just a bit, you can run an additional filter. Choose Filter → Blur → Gaussian Blur, adjust the blur radius until you get the look you want, and then click OK.

Because the layer mask hides the edges of your image, you'll see the checkerboard transparency pattern (see the box on page 44). To add a new background, add a layer of solid color *beneath* the image layer by ⌘-clicking (Ctrl-clicking on a PC) the "Create a new layer" icon at the bottom of the Layers panel and then choosing Edit → Fill. Choose Color from the Use pop-up menu, pick a color from the resulting Color Picker, and then click OK. Photoshop fills the new layer with the color you selected. As a final touch, add an inner shadow or drop shadow to the image layer using layer styles (page 119).

> **TIP**   If you want to reposition either the photo or the frame, you have to unlock the layer from the mask by clicking the little chain icon between the layer and mask thumbnails in the Layers panel. Then click the thumbnail of the layer or mask you want to move and reposition it with the Move tool (see Appendix E, online at *www.missingmanuals.com*). To lock them together again, just click between the two thumbnails to make the little chain icon reappear.

Distort

The filters in this category distort and reshape your image. It includes all kinds of goodies like the Displace filter, which lets you apply one image to the contours of another (page 296); the Pinch filter, which is great for shrinking double chins (page 405); and the Glass, Ocean Ripple, and Twirl filters, which work well as edge effects.

But the real gem here is the Lens Correction filter. Not only can you use it to fix all kinds of geometric weirdness you might get from your camera lens (like the spherical look caused by wide-angle lenses), you can also use it to add a dark-edge vignette effect that can beautifully frame a portrait (see Figure 15-6).

Figure 15-6:
As you can see from this before (top) and after (bottom) photo, even a little thing like softly darkening the edges can make a huge difference. Notice how the darker edges draw your eyes more quickly to the pint-sized superhero. This technique is also handy to use with a sepia tone (page 304) to produce an aged photo look.

Here's how to add a dark-edge vignette effect quickly:

1. **Pop open a portrait and choose Filter → "Convert for Smart Filters".**

   Flip back to page 588 for a refresher on Smart Filters.

2. **Choose Filter → Distort → Lens Correction.**

Photoshop opens the very large Lens Correction dialog box. You may want to turn off the Show Grid options at the bottom so you can get a better look at what you're doing.

3. **Adjust the Vignette amount.**

On the right side of the dialog box, grab the Vignette section's Amount slider and drag it all the way left; Photoshop will softly darken the edges of the image. To darken the edges even more, grab the Midpoint slider and drag it slightly left to about 35 (see Figure 15-6).

4. **Click OK.**

See how fast that was? If, after admiring your handiwork, you decide the effect is a little too dark, mouse over to the Layers panel, double-click the icon to the right of the Smart Filter to open the Blending Options dialog box, and then lower the opacity slightly. In most cases, though, full strength looks just fine.

Noise

The filters in this category let you add or remove noise (graininess or color speckles). If you're working on an extremely noisy image or restoring an old photo, these filters can come in really handy. For example, if you've scanned an old photo that has scratches in it, you can run the Dust & Scratches filter and Photoshop will scour your image for irregular pixels and blur them to smooth that area. More than likely, you'll use the Reduce Noise filter most often because it can help reduce noise in the dark areas (shadows) of images shot in low light. See the box on page 427 for the scoop.

Sometimes, you may need to *add* noise to an image, as odd as that may sound. For example, if you're working with a portrait that's been corrected within an inch of its life and it looks *too* perfect (as if it were airbrushed), you can use the Add Noise filter to introduce some random speckles to make it look more realistic.

Pixelate

You probably won't use the Pixelate filters often, but once in awhile they're useful for applying funky blurs and textures to your image as shown in Figure 15-7. For example, the Crystallize filter makes your image look like it's behind a textured shower door. If you're aiming for the newspaper image look (think lots of tiny, visible dots) try experimenting with the Halftone filter.

Render

These filters generate cloud patterns, introduce lens-flair effects, and add lighting to your images. Two in particular—Clouds and Difference Clouds—are great for creating all kinds of backgrounds, like the splotchy-colored ones you see in portrait studios, for example. These filters mix your foreground and background colors into what looks like soft, fluffy clouds. The more times you apply each filter,

Figure 15-7:
If you want to distress an image with random streaks and strokes, check out the Mezzotint filter (Filter → Pixelate → Mezzotint). In this example, medium strokes were applied (right), and the Blending Options were changed to Soft Light at 50 percent opacity.

the more clouds you get (Difference Clouds gives you clouds with higher contrast). If you use them with a Motion blur filter (applied after the Cloud filter), you can create some terrific streaks to make an image look older than it really is.

Another useful filter in this category is Lighting Effects (Figure 15-8). If you didn't get your subject lit right in the studio, there's a good chance you can fix it here. This filter, which works only with RGB images, gives you three light types (think light sources) to choose from including Omni (shines light in all directions like a lightbulb), Directional (shines light from a distance like the sun), and Spotlight (shines light in a beam like a flashlight).

Once you've chosen the type of light from the Light Type pop-up menu toward the top of the dialog box, you can adjust its strength with the Intensity slider (drag it to the left to weaken the light or to the right to make it stronger). If you want to change the color of the light, click the color square to the right of the Intensity slider and pick a color from the resulting Color Picker. For example, instead of adding a stark white light to a portrait, you could change it to light peach or yellow to give your subject a slightly warm glow. If you've chosen Spotlight, you can also adjust the width of the light beam with the Focus slider; drag it to the left to make the light narrower and to the right to make it wider (Figure 15-8 shows a fairly wide spotlight).

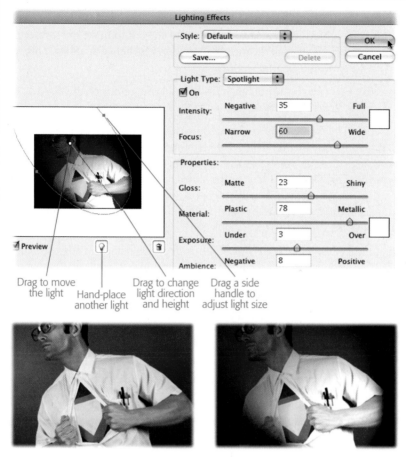

Figure 15-8:
Top: You can use the little lightbulb (labeled) to add additional light sources or drag existing lights to the trash can icon to delete them. You can also duplicate a light by Option-dragging it (Alt-dragging on a PC).

Bottom: As you can see in the right-hand photo, a well-placed spotlight can put the viewer's attention exactly where you want it.

Drag to move the light

Hand-place another light

Drag to change light direction and height

Drag a side handle to adjust light size

TIP   If you want to change the direction of the light without altering the height, ⌘-drag (Ctrl-drag on a PC) the handle at the end of the line.

The Lighting Effects dialog box is a little complex, though you can find some excellent presets in the Styles pop-up menu at the very top. Once you've chosen a style, you can tweak the Light Type settings as mentioned earlier, along with the following Properties:

- **Gloss.** Use this setting to control how reflective you want the light surface in your image to be. For example, if you shine light onto a plain old piece of paper, it won't reflect very much. But if you shine it onto a glossy piece of paper, the reflection is much greater. Drag this slider to the left to decrease reflection and to the right to increase it.

- **Material.** This setting lets you change the surface the light is reflecting on. For example, a plastic surface reflects the light's color while a metallic surface reflects your subject's color. Drag the slider to the left to make the surface plastic or to the right to make it metallic (anything in between affects both your light's color and your subject's color).

- **Exposure.** You can control the amount of available light with this setting. Drag the slider to the left to decrease light or to the right to increase it.

- **Ambience.** This setting lets you tone down the light source you've been painstakingly creating in this dialog box by mixing in more light from another source (as if the sun were also shining in the room or you had turned on an overhead light). Drag the slider to the left to remove the additional light source or to the right to mix in more light from it. You can change the light's color by clicking the color square to the right of the slider. Just choose a color from the resulting Color Picker and then click OK.

For even more creative fun, give your lighting depth by using the Texture Channel option at the bottom of the dialog box. This option lets you tell Photoshop to shine your light through a grayscale image (referred to as a *bump map*). Turn on the White Is High checkbox to make the white parts of your grayscale image appear raised (so they take on a shine as if they're taller than other areas). You can control how much they're raised by using the Height slider (drag it to the left to decrease height or to the right to increase it). If you want the dark parts to appear raised instead, leave this checkbox turned off. To get the grayscale image, use one of the existing color channels in your image (red, green, or blue) or a previously created alpha channel (page 185).

> **TIP** Click the Save button near the top of the dialog box to save a light source that you want to use again later as a preset. Give your custom light source a memorable name and then click OK to add it to the bottom of the Style pop-up menu.

Sketch

If you want to add a bit of texture to your images, this category is the one to reach for. Here you'll find a variety of filter-driven pens, crayons, paper, and so on that give your images a hand-drawn look. The Graphic Pen filter is perfect for adding realistic snow, as shown in Figure 15-9.

Here's how to use the Graphic Pen filter to add some realistic-looking flurries:

1. **Open a snowless photo and create a new layer filled with black.**

   As you learned back in Chapter 7 (page 267), blend modes have various neutral colors that disappear when that particular blend mode is used. If you run the Graphic Pen filter on a solid black layer, you can use a blend mode to make the black disappear, leaving you with the streaks made by the filter (which look like snow). Click the "Create a new layer" icon at the bottom of the Layers panel and drag it above the image layer if you need to. Fill it with black by choosing Edit → Fill and picking Black from the Use pop-up menu, and then clicking OK.

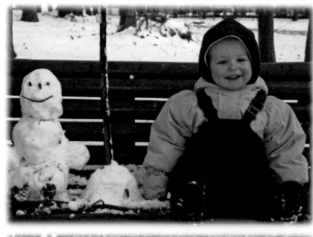

Figure 15-9:
Meet the Graphic Pen filter. To create a visually pleasing snowfall that doesn't completely bury your subject, lower the filter's Stroke Length setting to somewhere around 5 and increase the Light/Dark Balance setting to around 90. A too-high Stroke Length and a too-low Light/Dark Balance leave your subject stuck in what looks like a blizzard of sleet.

2. **With the black layer selected, choose Filter → "Convert for Smart Filters".**

   To make the Graphic Pen filter run on its own layer, you have to convert it for Smart Filters first (page 588).

3. **Change the blend mode of the black layer to Screen (see Figure 15-9, circled).**

   As you learned back in Chapter 7 (page 271), the Screen blend mode lightens the underlying photo and completely ignores black, which means the snowlike streaks you create in the next step will lighten the photo and the black will disappear.

4. **Choose Filter → Sketch → Graphic Pen.**

Photoshop opens the Filter Gallery dialog box set to the Graphic Pen filter. Since it generates random streaks in the direction and length you choose, it's perfect for making fake snow.

5. **On the right side of the dialog box, change the Stroke Direction pop-up menu to Vertical.**

This setting makes the snow fall straight down.

6. **Enter a Stroke Length of 5 and Light/Dark Balance of 90.**

Think of Stroke Length as flake size; lowering it to around 5 creates fairly small flakes. Think of Light/Dark Balance as the amount or heaviness of the snowfall. Set it to 60 for a blizzard or a higher number (like 90) for light snow. Click OK when you're finished to close the Filter Gallery dialog box.

7. **Choose Filter → Blur → Gaussian Blur and, in the resulting Gaussian Blur dialog box, enter a Radius of 1.5.**

To soften the snowflakes (so they don't have hard edges), you need to blur them slightly.

8. **Click OK when you're finished.**

The beauty of creating artificial snow using a Smart Filter is that you can control the opacity—if the effect is too strong, just double-click the icon to the right of the Graphic Pen Smart Filter and lower the opacity in the Blending Options dialog box. If it looks terrible, you can trash the filter and start over. It's lots of fun to add snow to *completely* inappropriate photos, too!

Stylize

This category is also artistic, but you can create a painted look with more contrast than you can with the Artistic filters. One filter in this category, discussed a little later in this section, can save an out-of-focus image. Several of the filters found here enhance the edges in your image, and Find Edges does such a good job that you can use it to create a pencil-sketch effect. It's a great technique to have in your bag of tricks because it can single-handedly save an image with color problems that can't be fixed by anything you learned back in Chapter 9. As a bonus, you create an image with a totally different look and feel from the original as shown in Figure 15-10.

Here's how to use Find Edges to convert a photo into a pencil sketch:

1. **Pop open a photo and create a Black & White Adjustment layer.**

The first step toward a pencil sketch is to get rid of the color, which you can do easily with a Black & White Adjustment layer (page 301). Click the half-black/half-white circle at the bottom of your Layers panel and choose Black & White (in Photoshop CS4, you can also create the Adjustment layer straight from the new Adjustments panel). Adjust the various color sliders in your Adjustments panel until you're happy with the contrast in your image.

Figure 15-10:
As you can see, this technique can evoke a completely different feel from the original, and it can do wonders to rescue an image with lousy color. The lighter color of the pencil sketch brings out a ton of detail that you couldn't see before because the photo's original color was so dark and saturated.

2. **Select the image layer and choose Filter → "Convert for Smart Filters".**

   Once again, to make the filter run on its own layer, you have to convert it for Smart Filters first. Besides protecting your original image, Smart Filters let you change the filter's blend mode and opacity (which you'll do in a couple of steps) .

3. **Choose Filter → Stylize → Find Edges.**

   You won't get a dialog box with this filter; it just runs. Don't panic when your image turns into a freaky-looking outline because you'll reduce the filter's strength in a second.

4. **Open the Blending Options for the Find Edges filter.**

   In your Layers panel, double-click the little icon to the right of the Find Edges Smart Filter to open the Blending Options dialog box.

5. **In the resulting dialog box, change the blend mode to Hard Mix and lower the opacity to about 85 percent.**

   As you change these settings, keep an eye on how your image looks back in your document (move the Blending Options dialog box out of the way if you need to).

As you learned in Chapter 7 (page 273), the blend modes in the Overlay category increase your image's contrast, which is great if you're trying to make a pencil sketch (and you are). You may need to experiment with other Overlay blend modes when you're trying out this technique on your own because some work better than others (depending on the colors in your image). The Opacity setting also varies according to how much contrast you had in the original though a setting between 75 and 85 percent usually works just fine. Click OK to close the Blending Options dialog box.

6. **Choose Filter → Blur → Gaussian Blur and, in the resulting dialog box, enter a Radius of *2*.**

   Your image should start resembling a pencil sketch at this point though you'll want to soften it by blurring it slightly. A Radius of 2 usually works well, but, again, you'll have to experiment with this setting. Click OK to close the Gaussian Blur dialog box.

7. **Open the Blending Options for the Gaussian Blur Smart Filter.**

   In your Layers panel, double-click the icon to the right of the Gaussian Blur layer to open the Blending Options dialog box.

8. **Change the blend mode to Lighten.**

   When you change the blend mode to Lighten, the Gaussian Blur filter blurs only the light pixels in your image. That way, you preserve the detail of the darker pixels (the edges you accentuated with the Find Edges filter).

9. **Click OK to close the Blending Options dialog box.**

   At this point you're finished, but if your sketch looks too dark, you can try placing it atop a white background and then lowering its opacity. Click the "Create a new layer" icon at the bottom of your Layers panel. Fill the new layer with white by choosing Edit → Fill and clicking White in the Use pop-up menu. If your original image layer is a locked Background layer, double-click it to make it editable (if you don't unlock the Background layer, Photoshop won't let you place any other layers beneath it). Drag the new solid white layer *below* your original image layer. Make sure the original image layer is selected and then lower its layer opacity to about 85 percent (see page 87 for more on layer opacity). That'll soften your sketch right up.

   TIP   For a watercolor look, select the Black & White Adjustment layer and then lower its opacity slightly to let some of the original color show back through.

Emboss

Although no magic fixer-upper can make an out-of-focus image look like it's in focus, the Emboss filter comes close. Technically it's not really *fixing* the image and making it sharp, it's merely bringing out the edges that are already there, making the image *look* sharper than it was as shown in Figure 15-11.

Figure 15-11:
The Emboss filter won't save a completely out-of-focus image, but it can sure take one that's only slightly blurry (top) and make it look sharper (bottom).

Samantha and Sylvester say hello!

Here's how to do it:

1. **Open the out-of-focus image and choose Filter → "Convert for Smart Filters".**

   Smart Filters makes the filter run on its own layer and lets you fiddle with filter-blending options and opacity.

2. **Choose Filter → Stylize → Emboss.**

   In the resulting dialog box, leave the angle, height, and amount settings as they are—that's right, don't touch 'em. Your image will look gray, and the edges of your subject will be brightly colored (as shown in Figure 15-11), but that's exactly what you want. In the next couple of steps you'll change the blend mode to make the gray parts disappear.

3. **Open the Emboss filter's Blending Options.**

   Over in your Layers panel, double-click the tiny icon to the right of the Emboss layer.

4. **In the resulting dialog box, change the blend mode to Hard Light.**

   As you learned on page 273, the blend modes in the Overlay category add contrast to your image *and* they ignore gray. Since the Emboss filter turned your image gray and gave it brightly colored edges, changing the blend mode to Hard Light makes the gray vanish, leaving *only* the edges visible so they stand out more and appear sharper than they really are. Who knew?

5. **Click OK to close the Blending Options dialog box.**

That's all there is to it. Well, aside from grinning triumphantly because you fixed your image. Sweet!

Texture

As you might suspect, the filters in this category add texture to your image, which can help give it some depth and visual interest as shown in Figure 15-12. You can access them through the Filter Gallery (page 590) to get an idea of what you can create. For example, if you want to spice up the background in an image you can add a texture to just that area by creating a selection first.

The technique is very simple: Just open an image and choose Filter → "Convert for Smart Filters" like you've done in the last several pages. Select the area behind your subject using any of the techniques in Chapter 4. Next, choose Filter → Texture and pick one of the six options: Craquelure, Grain, Mosaic Tiles, Patchwork, Stained Glass, and Texturizer. Adjust their various sliders in the Filter Gallery dialog box and then click OK.

Figure 15-12:
If you select the dark green rays with the Quick Selection tool before you run the Craquelure filter (Filter → Texture → Craquelure), you can make the filter's effects visible on just those areas. As you can see here, Photoshop filled in the Smart Filter mask for you. Remember from Chapter 3: When you're dealing with layer masks, black conceals and white reveals (see page 105 for a refresher on layer masks).

TIP   The Texturizer filter actually lets you load your *own* images so you can use them as a texture (see page 579 for an example of this filter used with text).

Video

As the name suggests, the two filters in this category deal strictly with individual frames extracted from videos. De-Interlace smoothes moving images and NTSC Colors restricts the color palette to colors that TVs can display. See the box on page 74 in Chapter 3 for more on Video layers.

Other

Since these filters don't really fit into any *other* category, they get their own. Custom, for example, lets you design your own custom filters to manipulate an image's brightness. As you learned on page 442, you can use the High Pass filter to sharpen images. Maximum and Minimum have a more practical use—you can use them to shrink or enlarge a layer mask (pages 105 and 158). For example, if you select an object, add a layer mask, and then place it atop *another* image, you may find some stray pixels left around the edges from the original background. To eliminate those stray pixels, you can use the Minimum filter to shrink the mask (see Figure 15-13).

Digimarc

The Digimarc filter lets you add a nearly invisible watermark to your images to protect them from being stolen and used without your permission (a problem inherent with images posted online). Page 685, has the scoop.

Browse Filters Online

Since filters are basically little programs that run inside Photoshop, they're easy to install (see the instructions on page 149). When you choose the Browse Filters Online option in the Filter menu, you'll be transported to Adobe's Web site where you can choose from loads of third-party plug-ins.

Vanishing Point

This filter appears last because it behaves nothing like *any* of the filters you've read about so far.

Over your illustrious Photoshop career, there will be times when you need to edit an object so it appears in proper perspective (meaning the object you're editing seems to get smaller as it disappears into the distance). Here are a few situations in which you'll likely run into perspective problems:

- If you need to affix a graphic or text onto any kind of surface that's not flat, like an image of a book cover, a cereal box, or a DVD case that's positioned sideways.

- If you need to clone an object on the side of a wall or on top of a table.

- If you want to make a building or other structure look taller than it really is.

Figure 15-13:
Top: Here you can see the original image before the background was hidden by the layer mask.

Bottom Left: If you run the Maximum filter on the layer mask, you can expand it. Notice how a wee bit of the original background now appears around the hero's edges.

Bottom Right: The Minimum filter does the exact opposite—it shrinks a layer mask—a great way to snip away leftover edge pixels.

This kind of editing is a real challenge because Photoshop sees everything as flat, with no perspective at all. The fix is to use the Vanishing Point filter to draw *perspective planes*—a mesh grid that you can use in your editing—*before* you start painting or cloning. Once you've drawn the grid, you can do your editing *inside* the Vanishing Point dialog box. While you're there, you can create a selection, copy and paste an image or text, or use the Clone Stamp or Brush tool, all in perfect perspective.

Here's how to paste one image on top of another, in proper perspective:

1. **Select and copy the image you want to paste (for example, the cartoon superhero in Figure 15-14).**

   Open the image, select it using one of the techniques in Chapter 4, and then press ⌘-C (Ctrl+C on a PC).

2. **Open the image you want to add the *copied* image to and create a new layer.**

   You can't run the Vanishing Point as a Smart Filter, which means it runs on the currently active layer. To run the filter nondestructively, you either have to duplicate your image layer or add a *new* layer to work with, depending on what you're going to do. For example, if you're going to use the Brush or Clone Stamp tool, you need to duplicate your image layer by pressing ⌘-J (Ctrl+J on a PC).

   However, if you're pasting another object *into* your document—as you are in this example—you need to create a new layer for the pasted object to land on. Click the "Create a new layer" button at the bottom of the Layers panel. Since the new layer is transparent, you can see through it to the layer below—your original image layer—which you'll use to draw your perspective plane in step 4.

3. **Choose Filter → Vanishing Point.**

   Photoshop opens the *huge* Vanishing Point filter dialog box (you can also open it by pressing ⌘-Option-V [Ctrl+Alt+V on a PC]).

4. **Use the Create Plane tool to draw your perspective plane.**

   Happily, the Create Plane tool is automatically activated as soon as the Vanishing Point dialog box opens (it looks like a + sign with a tiny grid behind it). Just click once on your image to set the first corner point of your plane. Mouse over to the next corner point and click it, mouse to the third corner point, and then click again to close the grid. If you have trouble seeing where to click to add your corner points, you can zoom into your image by holding the X key (as soon as you let go, the image goes back to its normal viewing percentage). As you draw the plane, Photoshop places a blue mesh grid over the area as shown in Figure 15-14.

5. **Use the Edit Plane tool to position and tweak the grid.**

   Once you've drawn the grid, the Edit Plane tool automatically activates, letting you move a point by dragging it (the tool looks like an arrow with a tiny grid behind it). If you need to move the whole grid, click within it and then drag it to another position.

   TIP   If you need to draw more than one perspective plane in your image (say, if you have two similar buildings to work on), you can copy a plane to another area by Option-dragging (Alt-dragging on a PC). If you're working with an object with more than one side and you need to make the grid wrap around it (like a book cover and its spine), you can ⌘-drag (Ctrl-drag) one of the mesh points (it doesn't matter which one) to tear off another plane that you can position at an angle.

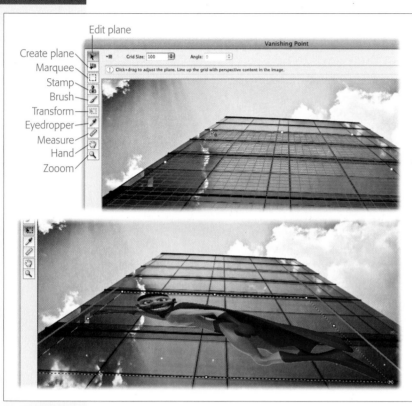

Edit plane

Create plane
Marquee
Stamp
Brush
Transform
Eyedropper
Measure
Hand
Zooom

Vanishing Point

Grid Size: 100   Angle: 0

Click+drag to adjust the plane. Line up the grid with perspective content in the image.

Figure 15-14:
When you get the grid placed and sized just right, it turns one of three colors: red, yellow, or blue. A red grid means you've drawn an impossible perspective, so grab the Edit Plane tool (it looks like an arrow with a grid behind it) from the left side of the dialog box and resize your grid by dragging one or more of the corner points to another position. A yellow grid means your perspective is possible though unlikely. You can continue to edit the plane or keep it as is. A blue grid means you've drawn the plane in proper perspective. You can also use the Grid Size slider at the top of the dialog box to resize the grid mesh to fit your object.

6. **Paste the object you copied back in step 1 and drag it on top of the plane.**

   Press ⌘-V (Ctrl+V on a PC) to paste your image into the Vanishing Point dialog box. At first, your image appears flat (not in perspective) and surrounded by a black-and-white selection box, but when you drag the image on top of your plane, it twists and distorts to conform to the perspective you've drawn.

7. **If you need to resize the image you just pasted, press T to summon a resizable bounding box.**

   Photoshop puts a bounding box around your image. To resize it proportionately, hold the Shift key as you drag one of the corner handles inward to make it smaller. If your object is bigger than the perspective plane, you can't *see* the handles because they extend beyond the edges of mesh grid. In that case, click in the center of the image and move it in one direction or another until you can see one of the handles and then drag the handle inward to make the object small enough so you can see them all. When you're finished resizing it, *don't* do anything else: If you press Return (Enter) when you finish resizing, you'll close the Vanishing Point dialog box before you're ready. If you need to move the pasted image, you can click inside it and then drag it to another position. When you're finished, click OK to close the Vanishing Point dialog box.

8. **Change the blend mode of the pasted image layer to Soft Light.**

Back in your Layers panel, you can make the colors of the superhero (the pasted image) blend better with the colors of the building by changing the blend mode to Soft Light, as shown in Figure 15-15.

Figure 15-15:
As you learned back on page 267, the Soft Light blend mode is great for creating reflections.

TIP   Interestingly, you've got *multiple* undos when you're in the Vanishing Point dialog box—just keep pressing ⌘-Z (Ctrl+Z on a PC) and Photoshop keeps undoing the last thing you did.

Other tools in the Vanishing Point dialog box include:

• **Marquee** lets you draw a selection (in perspective) to duplicate an area inside the plane you've drawn (if, say, you want to make a building taller, you can duplicate the top few floors). Or you can use the Marquee tool to restrict the Stamp or Brush tools (discussed later in this list) to a specific area of your image. Your selection can be smaller than the plane itself, and you can use the options at the top of the dialog box to feather the selection so its edges will be soft. Or, if you're moving the selected pixels to another area in your image, you can change their opacity.

TIP   To select the entire plane, double-click the mesh grid with the Marquee tool.

If you're copying the selection to another area, you can use the Heal pop-up menu to determine how the selection area blends with the area you're dragging it to. Your options include Luminance (the selected pixels are blended with the lightness values of surrounding pixels), On (the selected pixels are blended with the pixel color values that you're dragging the selection onto), or Off (no pixels are blended).

The Move Mode pop-up menu lets you specify how the selection behaves. For example, you can choose Source to *fill* the selection with the pixels you move your mouse over (you can also ⌘-drag or Ctrl-drag the selection). The selection itself won't move, but it will become filled with the pixels you hover above with your mouse. Use this option when you want to remove an object like a window or door by copying other pixels on top of it. Destination *selects* the area you move the selection to. The selection itself moves, but no pixels are copied. Choose this option when you want to copy a selection that can be resized using the Transform tool (discussed below) to make it *float*. For example, if you've removed a window using Destination mode, you can copy the selection and then move it into place to remove even more windows. You can also press ⌘-Shift-T (Ctrl+Shift+T on a PC) to duplicate your last duplicating move (helpful when you've got a bunch of windows to zap).

- **Stamp** works just like the regular Clone Stamp tool and lets you clone (copy) pixels from one area to another by painting while you use the perspective of the plane you've drawn. This tool comes in handy when you're extending an object or a building's height.

- **Brush** lets you apply paint with perspective. If you choose Luminance in the Heal pop-up menu, the new paint takes on the lightness values of the underlying pixels. Set the brush's color by clicking the color well toward the top right of the Vanishing Point dialog box.

- **Transform** will resize a floating selection (one that you've pasted) though it's quicker to press T to activate the Transform tool. Don't press Return (Enter) when you finish resizing or you'll close the Vanishing Point dialog box. At the top of the Vanishing Point dialog box, you can turn on the Flip option to flip your selection horizontally. Flop does the same thing, but vertically.

- **Eyedropper** will snatch a color from the image so you can use it with the Brush tool.

- **Measure** shows up in the Extended version of Photoshop, and lets you measure the distance and angle of items in a plane. Architects, interior designers, and scientists love this kind of stuff.

- **Hand** allows you to move around within your image while you're zoomed in. Just click the hand and then drag with your mouse to move around within your image.

- **Zoom** lets you zoom in and out of your image. You can also press ⌘ and the + or – minus key (Ctrl and + or – on a PC) or pick a magnification percentage at the bottom left of the Vanishing Point dialog box.

Photoshop and Print

Getting your prints to match what you see on screen is one of the biggest challenges you'll face when dealing with digital images. As you learned in the box on page 378, your image files are actually filled with grayscale information—it's the monitor and printer's job to give them color. And with the sheer volume of monitors, printers, inks, and papers, producing consistent color is a *nightmare*. That's why you hear so many folks screaming, "But my print doesn't match what I see on my screen!" Unless you prepare your monitor and files properly, it's *impossible* to make them match.

Thankfully, there's a solution, though it lies in understanding *why* this stuff happens to begin with. Unfortunately that means learning about things like color modes, gamuts, and color profiles. It's dense stuff, to be sure, but it's not rocket science. The main concepts are (fairly) straightforward, and if you've got the strength to make it through this chapter (an energy drink might help), you can create consistent, predictable high-quality prints.

The Challenge of WYSIWYG Printing

WYSIWYG, as you may know, is an acronym for "What You See Is What You Get." For image-editing buffs, it describes that elusive goal of getting your prints to match what you see on your screen. When you think about the different ways colors are produced by monitors versus printers, the problem starts to make sense.

A monitor's surface is made from glass or some other transparent material, and, as you learned in Chapter 5, it produces colors with phosphors, LCD elements, or other light-emitting technology. In contrast, printers use a combination of opaque paper, reflected light, and CMYK ink. (Remember, that's short for cyan, magenta, yellow, and black.) To add even more excitement, some printers use additional colors like light cyan, light magenta, several varieties of black, and so on. Given these two completely different approaches, it's a miracle that the images on your monitor look *remotely* similar to the ones you print. And because there are a bazillion different monitors and printers on the market—each using different printing technologies—you'll see a big difference in how your images look simply because of the monitor or printer you're using at that time. Heck, even changing the paper in your printer makes a big difference in how your images print.

The only way to achieve consistent printing results is to know which printer your image is headed for, which color mode (page 40) that printer wants your image to be in, which *range* of color that printer can reproduce on paper, and which paper you're using. Whew! Once you get that info, you have to communicate it to Photoshop. This section describes how you can make all that happen.

Understanding Color Gamuts and Profiles

As a first step toward WYSIWYG printing, remember from Chapter 5 (page 178) that, in most cases, your image starts life in RGB color mode when you capture and view it and eventually ends up being converted to some version of CMYK when it's printed (as you'll learn later, the printer can convert the modes or you can do it manually). Your next step is to understand a little more about how those two color modes differ. Enter the concept of *color gamut*.

Color gamut refers to the range of colors a given device can reproduce (flip back to Chapter 5 for more on how color works). An RGB monitor, for example, can reproduce one range of colors and a CMYK printer can reproduce another (and no printer on the planet can produce a color range as wide as your eyes can see). While the color ranges of monitors and printers frequently overlap, they're rarely identical. Your printer's color gamut depends on the specific combination of printing technologies you're using, which include:

- **Colorants (color-producing substances).** The printers you're likely to encounter include inkjet and laser printers, commercial offset presses, and digital presses. Some printers, like commercial offset presses, use pigment-based inks to produce color. Others, like inkjets, use dye-based inks, and still others, like laser printers and digital presses (which are like fancy laser printers), use toners.

- **Dot pattern.** All these printers use a pattern of dots (also known as *halftone dots*) to reproduce your images. They employ a wide range of dot patterns, but circles and diamonds are the most common shapes.

- **Paper types.** Each printer can also use a wide range of paper. For example, you can print on plain paper, matte, or super high-quality glossy paper (quick tip: You'll get a *much* higher-quality print using glossy paper). If you want your inkjet printer to reproduce its full gamut of color, you need to use a specially coated paper made to work with dye-based inks.

To account for all these variations, you have to use *color profiles* to tell Photoshop exactly which colorants and papers you want to print with. Color profiles contain detailed info about the printer's color gamut and, in some cases, the paper you're using. Photoshop includes a variety of all-purpose, rather generic, profiles, but you can also get profiles from the printer and paper manufacturers. Throughout this chapter, you'll learn how to use profiles both to proof (review) and to print your images on commonly used printers like inkjets, commercial printing presses, and digital presses.

Finding and installing color profiles

Most of the time, you can download color profiles right from the printer or paper manufacturer's Web site. However, you can also get custom profiles from professional printing companies; they're usually quite happy to share them with you if you ask for them. Installing a profile once you've got it is a snap. For example, you can follow the steps below to download and install a color profile for an Epson R2400 printer:

1. Visit the Epson Web site (*www.epson.com*) and choose your geographic area from the map.

2. Click the Drivers & Support → Printers link and choose Inkjet from the list of printers.

3. Click the link for your printer type (like inkjet) and, in the resulting right-hand list, click the link for your particular printer model.

   For this example, locate the Epson Stylus Photo R2400 printer as shown in Figure 16-1 (top).

4. At the top of the resulting Web page, click the "Drivers and Downloads" link.

5. In the special note paragraph near the top of the next Web page, click the "Premium ICC Profiles for Stylus Photo R2400" link.

6. On the resulting profiles page, scroll down until you find the right paper type and then click the link for your operating system (Mac or Win) to access the paper profiles for your printer.

7. The download should begin as soon as you click the operating system link in the previous step.

   If the installation program doesn't launch automatically after your computer's done downloading the profile, you can trigger it by double-clicking the installer (the VISE icon shown in Figure 16-1, bottom) that appears on your desktop or in your downloads folder.

8. Once the installer opens, click the Install button.

   You'll see a progress bar allowing you to watch the installation's progress. The process may vary depending on your operating system, but the results will be the same—you'll install the paper-specific profiles for Epson's whole range of glossy papers.

Figure 16-1:
Top: Not every printer or paper manufacturer's Web site will look the same though they'll have similar options (you may have to hunt for 'em!).

Bottom: If the installation doesn't begin automatically, you may have to double-click the installer.

Congratulations! You've just installed paper-specific color profiles for the glossy range of Epson papers. For other profiles, you can repeat this same download and installation process. Once you've installed the profiles, you can access them through Photoshop's Print dialog box.

Calibrating Your Monitor

Now that you understand how to tell Photoshop which kind of printer and paper you're going to use, you need to make sure your monitor is displaying color accurately. Rather than using the built-in calibration program that came with your computer, you need to calibrate your monitor using an external measuring device like a *colorimeter* or *spectrophotometer*—hand-sized gadgets that clamp onto your monitor and measure the color it displays. The calibration process involves adjusting your monitor so that it displays a series of colors and images *consistently*. Having a calibrated monitor also lets you preview how images and colors will print (a process called *soft-proofing*, discussed later in this chapter).

Profiles Aren't Created Equal

Even more shocking, some profiles are just plain wrong!

Photoshop offers many built-in profiles (like "Adobe RGB 1998") that include general color mode info, along with slightly more specific though still generic profiles (like "US Sheetfed Coated v2") that contain gamut information for printing on a standard sheetfed printing press using standard inks and coated paper. If your printing conditions are indeed standard, you may get decent results by using this profile.

You can also use paper-specific profiles, commonly referred to as *paper profiles*, created by manufacturers like Epson, who make paper profiles to match almost every kind of paper they sell: glossy, luster, matte, and so on. The more closely a profile matches your printing conditions,

the more accurate and useful it is. You'll find that high-quality profiles like the Epson paper profiles provide invaluable help with proofing and printing.

When you're out paper shopping, it's wise to confirm that the paper manufacturer does indeed have paper profiles that match your printer and ink (and be wary of buying paper from companies that don't!).

You'll also want to test the profiles by actually printing with them. If you've been printing with other paper and profiles, print some test images using the same image for both sets of papers and profiles and then compare your results. You'll probably find that some paper manufacturer's profiles are better then others.

The good news is that you can buy a calibration system for under $100 though the more sophisticated devices will set you back a lot more. There's certainly no harm in starting with an affordable model like the Pantone Huey (*www.pantone.com/huey*), but if you want to *truly* trust the colors your monitor is showing you, you'll need to spend more. Other good options are the Spyder (*www.spyder.datacolor.com*), which runs about $250 and the ColorMunki (*www.xrite.com*), which costs $500.

Another step toward making your monitor display your images as they'll look when they're printed is telling Photoshop exactly which color profile you want to use while you're working on the image (referred to as your "color working space"). Choose Edit → Color Settings and, in the resulting dialog box, choose a built-in profile from the RGB and CMYK pop-up menus in the Working Spaces section. If you spend a lot of time editing images from digital cameras, choose "Adobe RGB 1998" from the RGB pop-up menu. If you're preparing images for the Web, leave this option set to sRGB. If you routinely edit CMYK images, pick a profile from the CMYK pop-up menu that most closely describes the kind of press your images will be printed on.

Printer-Friendly Resizing and File Formats

Besides making sure your images are in the right color mode, installing the right color profiles for your printer and paper, and calibrating your monitor—are you exhausted yet?—you need to make sure your image's size matches the size you want to print. For example, if you want to print your image at 5"×7", it should really be 5"×7" (as opposed to, say, taking a 6"×8" image and cramming it into that smaller format). You also need to make sure your image has sufficient resolution (see the table on page 228 for resolution guidelines). Finally, you need to save your image in a file format that works well with your printer.

Printers can accept a wide range of file formats, including PSD (Photoshop) files, as well as TIFF, EPS, PDF, and even JPEG formats. But don't worry; choosing the format isn't as hard as you might think. Once you've saved your master file as a PSD file (see the box on page 47 in Chapter 2), choose File → Save As and pick one of the following formats:

- **TIFF.** This format has long been considered the print-safe gold standard (and for that reason, almost any program can work with TIFF files). A TIFF file doesn't involve any kind of automatic compression, so the quality remains as good as that of your original file. And if your image will be used in another program and you don't know what that program is—you might, for instance, be the graphics guru whose work will be used in a book or magazine—save it as a TIFF.

> **TIP**   If you have to email or upload a TIFF, be sure to create and send a .zip archive of the file first because TIFFs are notorious for becoming corrupted during the transfer process. On a Mac, Ctrl-click the file's icon and choose Create Archive from the resulting shortcut menu. On a PC, you can zip the file using an application like WinZip, available at *www.winzip.com*.

- **PDF.** This format is becoming more popular by the minute. While it's capable of compressing your files, it doesn't do so automatically, which makes it perfect for printing (plus it preserves the smooth edges of vectors). In fact, if you need to transfer your file via the Internet before you print it, PDF (short for "portable document format") is a better choice than TIFF because the format was designed to be used on the Internet. With a PDF file, you've got a much better chance that your file will arrive at its destination uncorrupted than you do with a TIFF.

- **EPS.** If you've created a multi-tonal image (page 645) or one with spot colors (page 637), you can use the EPS format (long the native format for vectors, it stands for Encapsulated PostScript). However, PDF files can *also* handle multi-tonal and images with spot colors, and you'll find that saving a file is in PDF format is simpler than saving it in EPS format. For that reason, go with PDF format unless someone—like a prepress manager at your printing company—specifically requests an EPS file. (And if she does, ask her tactfully if she's heard about PDFs!). Look for more on this topic on page 622.

Resizing and Saving as a TIFF

Here's an example of how to prepare your image for a high-quality print even if you don't know exactly which resolution you need or which program will be used to print your image:

1. **With your image open, summon the Image Size dialog box.**

   Choose Image → Image Size (or press ⌘-Option-I or Ctrl+Alt+I on a PC). See page 223 in Chapter 6 for a full introduction to this important dialog box.

2. **At the bottom of the dialog box, turn off the Resample Image checkbox.**

This prevents you from changing the pixel info in your image—and therefore changing its quality.

3. **In the middle of the dialog box, set the document width and height to the size you want to make your print (for example, 10" × 10").**

Don't worry about changing the resolution for this exercise because you'll save the file at its maximum resolution (Photoshop changes it automatically as soon as you enter the width and height). If you're sending the file to a professional printer and your resolution is between 300 and 450 ppi, you can sleep well knowing it'll print nicely. If the resolution is lower than that, see page 227 for a workaround. Click OK to close the Image Size dialog box.

4. **Save the file in the TIFF format.**

Choose File → Save As and, in the resulting dialog box, choose TIFF from the Format pop-up menu in the dialog box. You can also open the Save As dialog box by pressing ⌘-Shift-S (Ctrl+Shift+ S).

5. **At the bottom of the dialog box, turn off the Layers and Alpha Channels checkboxes.**

Turning these options off forces Photoshop to save a new, simplified version of your image that you can print while preserving your original, fully editable file.

6. **At the top of the dialog box, select a destination for the new file and give it a name.**

You may want to develop your own naming system for print files. A name like "AlaskaLight_10x10_Print_CMYK.tif" specifies the file's dimensions, its designation as a print file, and its color mode (see Figure 16-2, left). If you know you'll need to convert your RGB image to CMYK later, add CMYK to the name here (you'll learn more about when to leave your image in RGB color mode and when to convert to CMYK later in this chapter). Click Save to close the Save As dialog box.

7. **In the TIFF Options dialog box's Image Compression section, choose None.**

This option prevents Photoshop from compressing your image, keeping the quality as high as possible. Leave the Pixel Order as Interleaved and turn on the IBM PC radio button under Byte Order to make the file compatible with Windows computers (a Mac can read either one). Leave the "Discard Layers and Save a Copy" option at the very bottom of the dialog box turned on (see Figure 16-2, right).

8. **Click OK.**

Following these steps lets you create an uncompressed, simplified, print-ready copy of your image at the right print size without harming your original file. You can print the TIFF image straight from Photoshop or hand it off to a page-layout program like Adobe InDesign.

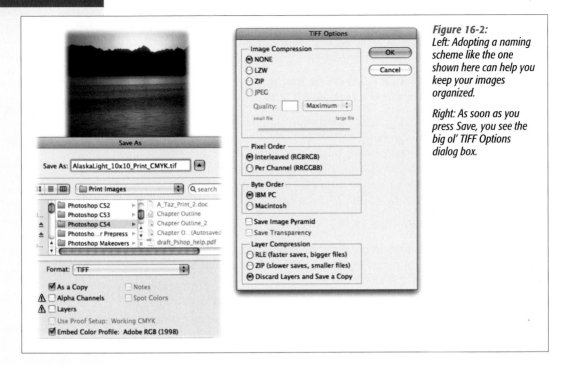

Figure 16-2:
Left: Adopting a naming scheme like the one shown here can help you keep your images organized.

Right: As soon as you press Save, you see the big ol' TIFF Options dialog box.

NOTE You can print multi-layer PSD files and place them in page-layout software like Adobe InDesign and QuarkXPress (InDesign actually prefers PSD files). So why bother saving a simplified TIFF? If you don't know which program your image will be used in (and you can't find out), you're safer with a TIFF.

Resizing and Saving as a PDF File

Another high-quality image file format option is PDF. In fact, PDF can be used to save some of the most complex images you'll ever create like those with spot colors (page 637) or multi-tonal images (page 645) that historically required EPS format or its print-specific variation, DCS (Desktop Color Separations) format (page 642). As mentioned earlier, creating a PDF file is usually easier than making an EPS file, and PDF files are safer to transfer over the Internet.

You can use the following steps to both resize and save your image as a PDF file:

1. **Open your Photoshop document and duplicate the image.**

   Since this technique involves lowering the resolution, it's safer to do it on a *copy* of your image rather than on the original. Choose Image → Duplicate and name the new image something like "Alaska Light_5x5_300", which is a handy way of embedding info about the file's size and resolution in its file name.

2. **Open the Image Size dialog box, turn off the Resample Image checkbox, and resize the image.**

   Choose Image → Image Size (or press ⌘-Option-I or Crtl+Alt+ I on a PC) and turn off the Resample Image option at the bottom of the dialog box. Change the width and height if you need to. For example, the image shown in Figure 16-3 started at 9"×9"; now it's 5"×5". If you made these changes yourself, you'd see that they caused the resolution to balloon from 348 ppi to 691 ppi (see Figure 16-3). The next step shows you how to lower that number to a more reasonable level (see page 227 for a discussion of resolution overkill).

3. **At the bottom of the Image Size dialog box, turn the Resample Image checkbox back on and lower the resolution to 300 ppi.**

   To change image resolution, you have to turn the Resample Image checkbox back on. Enter *300* into the resolution field.

4. **Choose "Bicubic Sharper (best for reduction)" from the resample method pop-up menu at the bottom of the dialog box.**

   Choosing this method makes Photoshop reduce the softening (blurring) that results from making your image smaller. (See page 220 for more about resampling.) Click OK to close the Image Size dialog box.

   TIP   You may also want to apply a round of sharpening after you resize and resample an image to help maintain its sharpness (an amount between 50 percent and 75 percent should do the trick). See Chapter 11 for the scoop on sharpening.

5. **Save your document by choosing File → Save As.**

   Since you're working on a duplicate copy of the image that hasn't yet been saved, choosing File → Save will also summon the Save As dialog box (⌘-S or Ctrl+S).

6. **In the Format pop-up menu, choose Photoshop PDF and then turn off the Layers and Alpha Channels checkboxes.**

   Turning off these checkboxes forces Photoshop to duplicate your image, creating a new, simplified PDF print version and preserving the original layered Photoshop file at the same time.

7. **Give your file a name and tell Photoshop where to save it.**

   When you click the Save button, the Save Adobe PDF dialog box appears.

8. **On the left side of the dialog box, choose General and make sure the Compatibility pop-up menu on the right-hand side is set to "Acrobat 5 (PDF 1.4)" as shown in Figure 16-4.**

   If you want to edit your PDF in Photoshop later, you can also turn on the Preserve Photoshop Editing Capabilities checkbox. If you intend to open and edit it in a previous version of Photoshop, leave this option turned off.

Figure 16-3:
Top: Anything over 450 ppi is resolution overkill, so aim for something closer to 300 ppi. Notice that the pixel dimensions shrink from 3456 × 3456 to 1500 × 1500 and that the file size decreases from 34.2 MB to 6.44 MB, a much more manageable size. If you need to email the file, it transfers much faster. Heck, even if you don't need to email it, it prints faster on your own printer thanks to its svelter file size.

Bottom: This naming scheme reveals at a glance the size and resolution of this file.

9. **Click the Compression category on the left and, from the Options pop-up menu in the middle of the dialog box, choose Do Not Downsample and then set the Compression pop-up menu to None.**

These options let you retain all your original pixel info so you can create a high-quality print. If you want to reduce the file size without losing much of the image's quality, you can choose "Zip 8 bit" or JPEG Maximum Quality from the Compression and Image Quality pop-up menus (respectively). A maximum-quality JPEG is a great choice when you're sending an image to a service bureau or print company that provides a Web site for transferring customer files.

Figure 16-4:
The Save Adobe PDF dialog box has a slew of options, and you can go through them all by selecting each category (shown here, left).

10. Click the Output category and pick No Conversion from the Color Conversion pop-up menu.

    This option will retain all the original color info in your image.

11. **Save these settings as a preset so you can use them again later.**

    Before you click the Save PDF button, ask yourself if you'll ever want to use these settings again. If the answer is yes (and it probably will be), click the Save Preset button in the lower-left corner of the dialog box (Figure 16-5). Give your preset a descriptive name like *Print Image PDF* and then click Save.

12. **Click the Save PDF button when you're finished.**

    You can place your PDF file in an Adobe InDesign document or send it to somebody via the Internet. Unlike TIFF or EPS files, which usually need to be encased in a protective .zip or .sit archive (a compressed document container), PDF files are Internet compatible and safe.

Printing on an Inkjet Printer

If you're a photographer, you probably use an inkjet printer. Most likely it's an expanded gamut inkjet printer—one that uses six to eight inks, rather than the

Figure 16-5:
If you save your settings as a preset, you can access them in the PDF Presets pop-up menu at the top of the Save Adobe PDF dialog box. You can save as many presets as you want, which can be a huge timesaver.

standard four (they're really dyes, but most folks call them inks). The most common combination of expanded gamut ink includes the four standard process colors—cyan, magenta, yellow and black (CMYK)—plus light cyan and light magenta. You may also have a choice of black inks, like glossy or photo black, matte black, light black, and even light *light* black (seriously!).

NOTE Inkjet printers are more common than dye-sublimation or color laser printers, so they're the focus of this section, but you can use printer and paper profiles no matter what kind of printer you use.

Nearly all expanded gamut inkjet printers can convert your RGB images to CMYK (plus any additional inks they may have). For the best results (and the brightest colors), you should let the printer convert the color mode for you.

If you've already converted your RGB image to CMYK, don't panic—many of these printers can print a regular, four-color CMYK file too. However, some print your image using CMYK inks and others convert your image into *another* color mode, like Lab (see page 183) and *then* convert your image to its own so-called CMYK-Plus mode before it prints. The latter option can be scary because anytime you do massive color-mode shuffling (RGB → CMYK → Lab → CMYK-Plus), you

FREQUENTLY ASKED QUESTION

Why Not Print JPEGs?

Hey, what do you have against JPEGs? It seems like a decent enough file format.

You may be wondering why you shouldn't save and print your images in JPEG format. That's a legitimate question because, after all, JPEG is the format used by most digital cameras. The problem occurs once you start editing, resaving, and printing your images as JPEGs.

When you save your images as a JPEG, they're automatically compressed using a system known as *lossy compression*—the amount of info in your image is reduced (some of it is thrown out or lost), which lowers image quality. The amount of compression, and the resulting loss of info and quality, varies from one JPEG to another (you can set the level of compression yourself as discussed on page 659). However, when you *resave* a JPEG without changing its format to something else like PSD or TIFF, you apply yet *another* round of compression, and *that's* when everything goes to heck in a handbasket.

Here's what you should do instead:

- If possible, set your digital camera to capture your images in an uncompressed format like TIFF or Raw to prevent any initial compression and resulting loss of info and quality. Raw is the most flexible format as you learned on page 53, so choose that option if you can (not all cameras can save images in Raw format; consult your owner's manual to see if yours can).

- Save any JPEGs you receive in TIFF or PSD format to prevent them from getting any worse.

To speed up this file conversion, you can use actions (Chapter 18) and/or the Image Processor script (Chapter 6, page 238) to quickly and automatically convert several images from one format to another.

If you have no choice but to use JPEG because the image is large or your computer doesn't have much memory, use only the highest quality and lowest compression settings to maintain the best quality possible.

---

can lose your brightest and most saturated colors. And some colors may change altogether—for example, blue becomes purple—which is *not* good! That's why it's better to print an RGB image instead.

To print a high-quality image with an expanded gamut printer, just follow these steps:

1. **Prepare your image for printing by cropping, editing, and resizing it.**

   Make sure you've color corrected (Chapter 9), cropped, and resized the image and set the resolution to between 200 ppi–450 ppi (Chapter 6). If you forget to crop your image to the exact dimensions you want, your printer may crop it for you. It's also a good idea to double-check the Image Size dialog box to confirm that your document dimensions and resolution are correct (open it by pressing ⌘-Option-I or Ctrl+Alt+I on a PC).

2. **Choose File → Print to summon the Print dialog box, shown in Figure 16-6 (top).**

3. **Select your printer from the Printer pop-up menu at the top of the dialog box.**

   For this example, choose Epson Stylus Photo R2400.

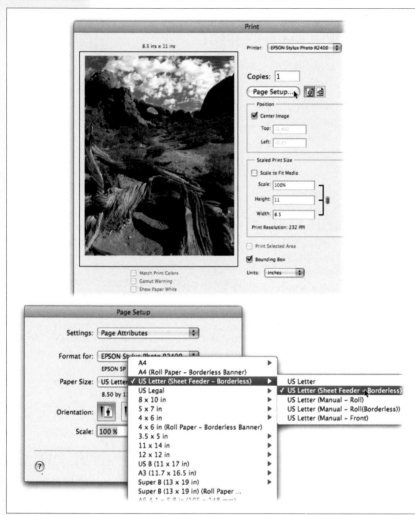

4. **Click the Page Setup button.**

   Most folks miss this super critical setting (see Figure 16-6, top).

5. **In the Page Setup dialog box, choose your printer from the "Format for" pop-up menu.**

6. **From the Paper Size pop-up menu, choose your *exact* paper dimensions.**

   If you're printing borderless, be sure to move over one more submenu and choose a borderless version of the paper dimension you picked (see Figure 16-6, bottom). If you don't pick an option that includes the word *borderless*, your image will print with a border, anyway. Next, check your paper orientation for either portrait or landscape and be sure the scale is set to 100 percent (so your image prints at full size).

7. **Click OK to close the Page Setup dialog box.**

   In the Print dialog box, peek at the preview window on the left side and make sure your image fills the whole window. If you wisely cropped your image to your exact print dimensions, it should fill the preview area perfectly.

8. **In the Position section of the Print dialog box, turn on the Center Image checkbox (see Figure 16-6, top).**

   If for some reason you *didn't* crop your image first, you can use this setting to print a certain portion of your image instead of the whole thing.

9. **Make sure Scaled Print Size is set to 100 percent.**

   This setting, along with the Position setting mentioned earlier, can be used to control which part of your image prints if you didn't crop it first. However, just because you *can* scale (resize) your image while it's being printed doesn't mean you *should*; besides preventing you from sharpening your image after you make it smaller, scaling it through the Print dialog box makes it take longer to print.

10. **Choose Color Management from the pop-up menu at the top right of the Print dialog box and turn on the Document option (see Figure 16-7).**

    Color management is the process of making the colors produced by the devices you work with every day—your digital camera, monitor, and printer—match as closely as possible by referencing specific color profiles. Choosing Document rather than Proof means you intend this print to be final rather than a simulation used for proofing (you'll learn more about the proofing function later in this chapter).

11. **In the Color Handling pop-up menu near the top of the dialog box, choose Photoshop Manages Color.**

    This setting controls whether Photoshop or the printer converts the color mode from RGB to CMYK-Plus. It's certainly worth experimenting with both though you'll likely find that controlling the conversion through Photoshop gives you higher quality and more consistent results *if* you're using paper-specific profiles.

    Heed the warning note, "Remember to disable color management in the printer dialog box." Most printers are configured to apply *some* kind of color management profile to your printing, which can conflict with the color management you're trying to apply through Photoshop (usually with unsavory results). In the next Print dialog box discussed in step 16, you should see an option to disable printer color management. Since there's no standard for that setting, you'll need to hunt for a setting labeled "color management," or "color options".

Figure 16-7:
Here you can see the second column of the big ol' Print dialog box that lets you determine exactly who controls your document's color management.

12. **From the Printer Profile pop-up menu, choose the paper-based profile that matches the paper and print settings you're using to convert your image from RGB to CMYK-Plus mode.**

Click the Printer Profile menu and scroll down the long list of profiles (it'll get longer each time you install new ones). For example, the Epson profile begins with SPR2400, and the name of the paper and a print setup condition is included in the name. For example, if you're printing on Epson's Premium Luster Paper with a Best Photo condition, choose "SPR2400 Premluster BstPhoto.icc."

NOTE The extension (.icc) refers to the industry standard color profile format created by the International Color Consortium (ICC).

13. **In the Rendering Intent pop-up menu, choose Perceptual and turn on the Black Point Compensation checkbox.**

These options help maintain the tonal value relationships in your image and make sure that the black shadows in your original RGB image are also black in the final CMYK-Plus version (which preserves contrast).

14. Underneath the preview window in the Print dialog box, turn on the Match Print Colors and Show Paper White options to view an onscreen proof (also called a *soft proof*).

    You can ask Photoshop to show you a proof of any colors in your image that are *out of gamut* (meaning they're unprintable) for the printer and paper you've selected. Photoshop simulates onscreen what your printed image will look like (see page 649 for more).

15. Turn on the Gamut Warning checkbox to make any out-of-gamut pixels appear gray in the preview area of your Print dialog box.

    When you're printing to expanded gamut printers, you'll find far fewer out-of-gamut colors than you would with a standard CMYK printing press. You'll also find Photoshop CS4's soft-proofing accuracy to be significantly improved over previous versions of the program. But none of this means diddly unless you've calibrated your monitor so you see reliable results (see page 618).

POWER USERS' CLINIC

Printing Vectors and 16-bit Images

If your image contains vectors or 16-bit images (page 43), yet another set of printing options you need to worry about is hiding on the right side of the Print dialog box. Choose Output from the pop-up menu at the top right and you'll see the following options:

- **Include Vector Data.** If your image contains vector artwork (Chapter 13) or Type layers (Chapter 14), you need to print them with a Post-Script printer (like *some* laser and inkjet printers). If you're printing to a non-PostScript printer (like *most* inkjets), you should rasterize (page 103) your vectors first so you can see how they'll look *before* you actually print them. If your printer *is* a Post-Script printer, you can preserve the wonderfully crisp edges of your vectors by turning on this option.

If it's grayed out, your image doesn't include any vector info so you don't have to worry about it.

If you have no idea whether your printer can support PostScript, check your owner's manual. Another option is to print a specification or diagnostic page that lists which technologies the printer works with.

- **Send 16-bit Data.** If your image contains 16-bit pixel info, Photoshop CS4 lets you print all 16 bits of it; that is, if your printer can handle it (the option is grayed out if it can't). To make sure the extra info is sent to your printer, turn on this option.

---

16. Check your settings in the Print dialog box one last time and, if they're okay, click the Print button to access yet *another* Print dialog box—this time for the printer itself (see Figure 16-8).

    This Print dialog box controls the printer (in this case, an Epson printer).

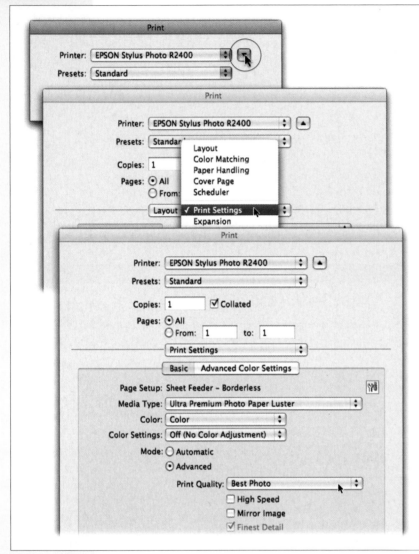

Figure 16-8:
If your Printer's dialog box is really small (top), click the triangle to the right of the Printer pop-up menu (circled here) to see the expanded version where you can access the printer controls (another setting that most folks miss).

Your own dialog boxes may look a little different, depending on your operating system and printer, but you should find all these settings lurking somewhere nearby.

17. **From the pop-up menu in the middle of the dialog box, choose Print Settings.**

Again, the wording of your dialog box may vary slightly or you may not have this option at all—instead you may just *see* the settings listed below:

Borderless. Make sure that your Page Setup is set to Sheetfed Borderless (sometimes the Page Setup options from Photoshop get lost in the shuffle of dialog boxes, so it's a good idea to check them again). If it's not, roll your eyes, sigh deeply, click Cancel, and repeat steps 5–7.

Media Type. Choose the paper you're printing on, like Ultra Premium Photo Paper Luster (now that's a mouthful!).

Color. Make sure you've chosen to print in color or all this color-management and profile stuff has been for nothing.

Color Settings. Make sure these settings are turned off so the printer doesn't adjust the color. This setting—another one that most folks miss—is crucial because if you don't turn it off, it conflicts with the color-management settings and profiles you've assigned in Photoshop.

Mode. Click Advanced and be sure Print Quality is set to Best Photo (or something similar, like World's Best Photo). You may also find the Quality setting hiding in the Media Type options mentioned earlier in this step.

High Speed. If you *have* this option, which lets your printer's *print head* (the bit that applies the ink to the paper) to print while it's moving in *both* directions (forward and backward), turn it off initially. Sure, it can double your printing speed, but your image may not look as good. If you want, you can fire off a couple of test prints with High Speed turned on and off. Be sure to look closely at your image's details to see the difference.

18. **Click the Print button.**

   After *all* that hard work, trudging through dialog box after dialog box, you see the fruit of your labors in the form of a gloriously accurate, high-quality print. Yippee!

Printing on a Commercial Offset Press

If you prepare artwork for magazines, product packaging, newspapers, and so on using a commercial offset printing press, you've got *loads* more to worry about than if you're sending your image to an inkjet printer. Unlike printing to an inkjet printer, where your images gets converted from RGB to CMYK during the printing process, a commercial offset press usually requires you to convert your image to CMYK *before* it's printed. In this section, you'll learn the very specific steps you need to follow to preserve your image's color while you convert it to CMYK. But before you dive too deeply into color-mode conversion, you need to understand a bit more about how offset presses work.

> **NOTE** Inkjet printers spray their ink from a print head directly onto a page. An offset press, however, transfers, or *offsets*, ink from an image on a plate onto a rubber blanket and then onto a page—which is why commercial printing presses are called "offset presses."

Commercial offset presses are huge, noisy, ink-filled metal beasts. As you learned back in Chapter 5 (page 180), they split your image's four CMYK channels into individual color separations, which are loaded onto big cylinders aligned so that all four colors are printed, one on top of another, to form your final image. If the cylinders aren't aligned properly, you'll see faint traces of one or more colors peeking outside the edges of your image, making it look blurry (this blurriness is called being "out of registration").

Instead of the dyes used by inkjet printers, commercial offset presses use two types of ink: process and spot. Process inks include cyan, magenta, yellow, and black (CMYK), and they're printed as overlapping patterns of halftone dots (Figure 16-9, left) that let you economically reproduce the wide range of colors found in continuous-tone images like photos (Figure 16-9, right).

> **NOTE**   Why are the *halftone* dots called "halftones"? Because they simulate a solid color (continuous tone) or a graduated screen on a page based on how close or far apart each dot is. It's a clever visual trick that lets designers make a single color look like a wide range of shades or blend multiple colors to simulate other colors.

Figure 16-9:
Left: If you look closely at an image printed on a press, you can see the dots it's made from. The next time you pick up a magazine or newspaper, stick it right up to your nose and you'll see 'em.

Right: Images that contain a wide range of smooth colors are called continuous-tone images, like this beautiful photo by Taz Tally (www. taztallyphotography. com).

Spot inks, on the other hand, are used to match a very *specific* color requirement (like a color in a corporate logo—the official UPS brown, for example), and they're printed on a *separate* cylinder on the press. More spot colors mean more cylinders, which means more separations, which translates into higher printing costs. Since it's easy to get hit with unexpected costs when you're sending out a print job, you need to make *darn* sure you know exactly how many colors it'll take to print your image (most print jobs involving color photos use only the four process colors). You'll learn all about spot colors later in this chapter.

Finally, unlike sending an image straight from Photoshop to your inkjet printer, you'll *rarely* (if ever) send a single image to an offset press. Instead, you place your image in a page-layout document (like one made with Adobe InDesign) that contains other images, along with text (also referred to in geek circles as *copy*), and *that's* what you send to the printing company. You need to make sure your images have the right print dimensions and resolution (discussed earlier on page 619) and that they're in the right color mode *before* you place your image in InDesign. The following pages will show you how to do that as painlessly as possible.

Converting RGB Images to CMYK Using Built-In Profiles

First and foremost, you need to know who's handling the conversion from RGB to CMYK. Historically, printing companies have requested (required!) you to convert it yourself though this is *slowly* changing, particularly with the increased use of digital presses (see page 654).

If you have no idea whether you're supposed to convert the RGB to CMYK yourself or if you want to know whether the printing company has a custom profile you can use for the conversion, *pick up the phone*. Communication is paramount in situations like this because if your print job hits the press at 2:00 a.m., it'll be *your* phone that rings if there's a problem. And this is one phone call you're better off making than receiving.

If you have to convert the color mode yourself, it's important to choose the proper CMYK color printer and paper profile. You can do it in a couple of ways, but the following steps will lead you down a simple and foolproof path:

1. **Open your RGB image and duplicate it.**

   Choose Image → Duplicate to create a new copy of your image to *guarantee* that you won't accidentally save over your original RGB image.

2. **Name your new image and save it as a TIFF file.**

   Choose File → Save or press ⌘-S (Ctrl+S on a PC) and then give it a name. It's a good idea to include the file's color mode in the name so you can see at a glance which mode it's in. Choose TIFF from the Format pop-up menu at the bottom of the Save dialog box and then click Save.

3. **Choose Edit → "Convert to Profile".**

   In the Conversion Options section of the dialog box (see Figure 16-10), set the Engine menu to "Adobe (ACE)" and the Intent menu to Perceptual. Turn on the Use Black Point Compensation checkbox.

4. **From the Destination Space's Profile pop-up menu (Figure 16-10), choose a profile that reflects the type of ink, press, and paper your printing company will use to print your image.**

   You can think of this menu as a printer profile menu. If you can't find a custom profile (see the next section), hunt for a profile that matches the ink, press, and paper for your current print job. If your image is being printed in North America on a sheetfed printing press using coated paper stock, for example, you can pick the tried-and-true "U.S. Sheetfed Coated v2" profile. A newer commercial sheetfed profile that also might work is "Coated GRACoL 2006". But before you guess, *ask* your printing company which profile it wants you to use.

5. **Click OK to complete the color conversion process and save your image.**

   Press ⌘-S (Ctrl+S) to save your image in the new color mode.

Figure 16-10:
Don't panic when you see the Profile pop-up menu. These super funky names are simply the various color profiles you can use to convert RGB to CMYK. As you learned at the beginning of this chapter, there are a bazillion printers, papers, and colorants (inks, dyes, toners) out there, so this long list merely reflects that diversity.

After you save your CMYK image, you're ready to place it in your page-layout document. Because you wisely duplicated your image in step 1, you've still got the original, full-color RGB image to go back to if you ever need to edit it. Sweet!

Custom RGB to CMYK Profile Conversions

If your printing company has painstakingly created its own custom color profile, you're much better off using it than one of the built-ins. The process is similar to the one explained in the previous section, but you need to *install* the custom profile before you can use it. Once you've got it, follow these steps to put it to use:

1. **Locate the appropriate profile folder on your hard drive.**

   Figuring out where to store the profile is your biggest challenge since different operating systems *and* different versions of Photoshop store profiles in different places. On a Mac running OS X 10.5, you can find the main color profiles folder here: *User/Your Home Directory/Library/Application Support/Adobe/Color/Profiles.* If you have a Windows computer, look in *Users\Profiles and Windows\System32\ Spool\Drivers\Color.* You can always search for a folder named *profiles,* or better yet, call your printing company and ask them where the folder is.

   NOTE If your computer uses Windows, you can use the Color Management Control Panel to add and remove profiles.

2. **Copy the custom profile to the Profiles folder.**

   In Figure 16-11, you'll see a profile named "MwHwkCC98_28#txt_CMYK_o_ PCG.icc". The name indicates that this profile was made using a 28-pound Mohawk text stock paper. Printing companies that have embraced color management have CMYK color profiles for a *variety* of paper stocks, so be sure you load the one for the paper you're printing on by dragging the file into the folder.

Figure 16-11:

Top: The toughest part of using a custom profile is figuring out where the heck to put it! Fortunately, on a Mac, the folder is named Profiles (shown here).

Bottom: If you're using a custom profile, the printing company may also want you to change other settings in the Print dialog box. For example, they might have you select Relative Colorimetric rather than Perceptual from the Intent menu. But you won't know unless you ask 'em.

3. **Open your image, duplicate it, and save it as a TIFF file.**

   To duplicate your image, choose Image → Duplicate and then choose File → Save or press ⌘-S (Ctrl+S on a PC) and give the copy a name. Pick TIFF from the Format pop-up menu at the bottom of the Save dialog box and then click Save.

4. **Choose Edit → "Convert to Profile" and, in the resulting dialog box, choose your new profile from the Profile pop-up menu.**

   If you don't see the right profile in the list, you may need to restart Photoshop. In that case, press ⌘-Q (Ctrl+Q) to quit the program and then double-click your image to relaunch it.

5. **Change the Conversion Options settings if you need to.**

   Ask the printing company if you need to adjust any settings in the Conversion Options section.

6. **To save your image, click OK and press ⌘-S (Ctrl+S).**

   You've just completed your first custom CMYK conversion. That wasn't so bad, was it?

Using Spot Color

As mentioned earlier, commercial printing presses sometimes use special pre-mixed custom inks called *spot colors*. If you're a graphic designer working in *pre-press* (the department that preps files for printing), the info that lies ahead is really important. If you're a photographer or Web designer, save your brainpower and skip this part. Really.

Photoshop wizard Ben Willmore (*www.DigitalMastery.com*) has come up with a great analogy to explain spot colors. Remember the box of crayons you used as a kid? A small box had 8 basic colors like blue, orange, and yellow. And then there was the big box of 64—with a sharpener on the back!—that had special colors like cornflower, melon, and thistle. No matter how hard you tried, you couldn't reproduce the special colors with a box of 8 crayons. Back in Photoshop, you can think of those special colors as spot colors and the box of 8 crayons as the CMYK color mode.

Because of the impurity and variety of CMYK inks, they can't produce all the colors you see in RGB mode (just like you can't reproduce, say, cornflower from those original 8 crayons). If you happen to be tooling around in the Color Picker (page 457) and choose a color that *can't* be produced in CMYK, Photoshop places a little yellow warning triangle next to it (see Figure 16-12). This triangle is known as an out-of-gamut warning (gamut, as you learned earlier, means the full range of colors). If you click the triangle (or the tiny square color swatch below it), Photoshop will change your color to the closest possible match that *can* be printed with CMYK inks.

Figure 16-12:
Top: If you pick a color that can't be produced with CMYK ink, a little warning triangle appears next to the color swatch (circled). Click the triangle or the tiny square of color below it to make Photoshop pick the next best color.

Bottom: In most cases, you can't see any difference between the original color and the new one, but if you check your cursor's location in the color field (circled), you can see that Photoshop moved it slightly.

In some cases, the closest color match will be close enough, but spot color ink comes in handy in certain situations, like when you need:

- **To reduce printing costs.** As you learned earlier, the more colors you use, the more cylinders and separations you need and the more money the job will cost you. If you print an image in black and one or two spot colors, you can *reduce* your printing costs because you'll be using two or three separations instead of four. This technique is commonly used with line art (illustrations or outline drawings like those in a coloring book), though you can also use it on a photo (see page 633).

- **To ensure color accuracy.** If your paycheck depends on color accuracy, you *have* to use spot color ink. For example, if UPS hires you to design a flyer for their company party, you want to make sure that *your* version of brown matches their *official* brown. Unless you use a spot color (which is consistent because it's premixed), your brown will be printed using a mix of CMYK inks and may end up looking maroon.

- **To use specialty inks.** If you want to add a bit of pizzazz to your printed image, you can use specialty inks like metallics or a varnish that looks glossy when it's printed. You can also add a vibrant spot color to a particular area to make that part stand out. However, if you use specialty inks on a CMYK document, you're *adding* color separations to your job, which will increase the cost.

The most popular brand of spot color ink is Pantone (*www.pantone.com*), and before you can use it, you have to create a special channel for it called a *spot channel*. Each spot color you use needs its very own spot channel. See Chapter 5 for more info on channels.

> **NOTE** You'll also hear Pantone colors referred to as *PMS* colors, which stands for "Pantone Matching System".

Let's say you're preparing the cover photo for the next issue of *Cutting Horse* magazine, and, to cut down on printing costs, the magazine has decided to use a grayscale image with one spot color for visual interest. (That way, they're paying for two separations instead of four.) Your mission is to make the horse's bridle Pantone Red. No problemo! Just make a selection of the bridle and then create a spot channel for the special ink (see Figure 16-13).

Here's how to add a spot channel:

1. **Use one of the methods described in Chapter 4 to select the area you want to colorize.**

   If you're lucky enough to start with the full-color version of the photo, you can easily select the horse's bridle by using Color Range (page 143). See page 300 for the scoop on converting a color image to black and white and page 306 for changing your image's color mode to Grayscale.

Figure 16-13:
Top: Once you've selected the area you need to colorize, you can add a new spot channel by opening the Channels panel menu (circled, top).

Bottom: Click the little color swatch (circled) in the New Spot Channel dialog box to open the Color Libraries. The new ink you choose will be added to your selection automatically.

2. From the Channels panel menu (see Figure 16-13, top), choose New Spot Channel.

   In the resulting dialog box, open Photoshop's Color Libraries to pick which spot color you want to use. You can also add a new spot channel by ⌘-clicking (Ctrl-clicking on a PC) the New Channel icon at the bottom of the Channels panel.

3. Click the color swatch to open the Select spot color dialog box and then click Color Libraries. In the resulting dialog box, choose a spot color (see Figure 16-13, bottom).

   From the pop-up menu at the top of the Color Libraries dialog box, choose a color book (if you're preparing a photo for a magazine, pick "Pantone solid coated" because magazines print on glossy paper). If you know the number of the ink you want (like 032), you can enter it by typing the numbers or just dragging the triangles along the vertical scroll bar to find the one you want (you can also use the arrow keys to move through the list of ink swatches). Click the color's swatch to select it and then click OK to close the Color Libraries dialog box.

4. **Back in the New Spot Channel dialog box, leave Solidity at 0 percent and click OK to close the dialog box.**

You can think of Solidity as ink opacity though it affects only the onscreen image and not the print. Depending on the image you're working with, increasing the ink opacity so it appears solid and not see-through may be helpful (it's a personal preference). When you click OK, you'll see a new spot channel appear in the Channels panel as shown in Figure 16-14.

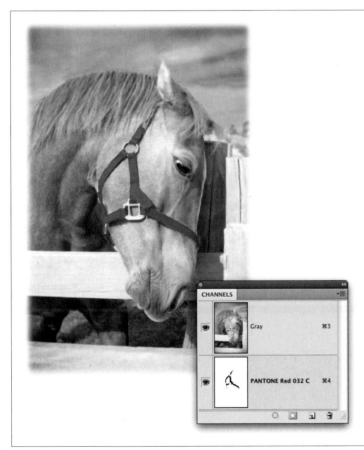

Figure 16-14:
Here's the final cover shot for your magazine. If you peek into the Channels panel, you can see the total number of channels (and thus separations) is two. If you send this Photoshop grayscale document straight to InDesign, that program adds a new color swatch for the spot color, and makes sure that the new color prints on top of the black (also called overprinting).

Editing a spot channel

Once you've created a spot channel, you can change the ink color by double-clicking it in your Channels panel. You can also add or remove color by painting with the Brush tool (or by using any other selection tool and filling it with color, as described on page 168). Since channel information is shown in grayscale, you can edit a spot channel just like a layer mask (page 105)—by painting with black, white, or shades of gray.

- **To add color at 100 percent opacity,** grab the Brush tool by pressing B and set your foreground color chip to black. Mouse over to your image and begin to paint.

- **To remove color at 100 percent opacity,** set your foreground color chip to white before you begin to paint.

- **To add or remove color at any other opacity,** set your foreground color chip to a shade of gray before you paint.

Saving a document with spot channels

To keep your spot channels intact, you need to save the document in a format that works with spot channels: DCS format, a PSD file, or a PDF file. So which one do you pick? It depends on what you're going to do with the file.

If you're the hired Photoshop gun and you'll be handing the file off to someone else for further fluffing, save it as a PSD file, get your motor runnin', and head out on the highway (insert guitar riff here). If you're importing the image into InDesign, you'll also want to save your image as a PSD file.

If you're using the file in QuarkXPress, you need to save it as a DCS 2.0 or a PDF file (see page 643). DCS is a special file format that lets you save color separations if your image will be printed on a printing press. To save your document as a DCS file, make sure your document is in either Grayscale or CMYK color mode (page 40), choose File → Save As, and pick Photoshop DCS 2.0 from the Format pop-up menu. When you click Save, you'll see the DCS 2.0 Format dialog box (see Figure 16-15) where you can fine-tune the following settings:

Figure 16-15:
Here you see the DCS 2.0 Format dialog box. DCS 2.0 is one of three formats you can use to save your spot channels intact. though DCS files can be read by most page-layout programs, you may find that using a PDF is easier as discussed on page 643.

- **Preview.** This setting controls which kind of image preview you see in your page-layout software. If your image is headed for a Macintosh and you want a 256-color preview, choose "Macintosh (8 bits/pixel)" or "Macintosh (JPEG)" (the second choice gives you a slightly nicer preview). If it's headed for a Windows computer, choose "TIFF (8 bits/pixel)". See the box on page 43 to learn what the term "8 bits" is all about.

- **DCS.** You'll want to leave this one set at "Single File DCS, No Composite" so Photoshop doesn't generate all kinds of files that only the printing press peeps know what to do with.

- **Encoding.** This menu lets you control how the print information is encoded (stored) in your file. If you're on a Macintosh, choose Binary. If you're on a Windows computer, choose ASCII or, for a more compact file, pick ASCII85.

  NOTE In case you're wondering, *ASCII* stands for "American Standard Code for Information Interchange", and ASCII85 is the newest version. ASCII was developed as a way to convert binary (computer) information into text. This stuff is great bar-bet trivia.

Leave the remaining options at the bottom of the dialog box (Halftone Screen, Transfer Function, and Interpolation) turned off and then click OK. You're ready to import the DCS file into QuarkXPress. Party on!

WORKAROUND WORKSHOP

Printing Spot Channel Proofs

Since spot channels are used only by commercial printing presses, getting them to print on your *own* printer for proofing can be…exciting. The solution is to pop into RGB mode temporarily and merge the spot channels.

To safeguard your original document, save it and open a copy by choosing Image → Duplicate. Choose Image → Mode → RGB and then, in your Channels panel, Shift-click to select each spot channel you've created. Open the Channels panel menu and choose Merge Spot Channel.

When Photoshop asks if it's okay to flatten the layers, click OK. Each spot channel is instantly swallowed up by the closest matching RGB equivalent.

At this point, you can fire it off to your printer without a fuss. The colors won't be *exact*, but you'll get a decent approximation of what your image will look like when you finish editing it. When you've finished printing, you can toss the temporary RGB document and continue editing the original.

Saving Spot Colors in PDF Format

While DSC 2.0 has long been the standard format for saving documents with spot colors, PDF format is simpler. To see for yourself, follow these steps:

1. **Open an image with a spot color and press ⌘-Shift-S (Ctrl+Shift+ S on a PC) or choose File → Save As.**

   Figure 16-16 shows a file named "Autumn Art_CMYK" that contains the Digital Gypsies logo with an assigned spot color of 810C (the C indicates the coated version of the color).

Figure 16-16:
Left: You might consider adding the spot color name (like Pantone 810C) to your document name to help maintain color-naming consistency as you move your image from one program to another (for example, from Photoshop to InDesign).

Right: If you think you might use these settings again, click the Save Preset button (not shown in this figure; it's at the bottom left) before you click the Save PDF button. Give your preset a name (like "Print Image PDF") so you can access it again later from the Adobe PDF Preset pop-up menu at the top left of the dialog box. It'll come in handy when you learn about duotones later in this chapter.

2. **Choose PDF from the Format pop-up menu.**

   If your document has layers, turn off the Layers checkbox to flatten the image.

3. **Turn on the Spot Colors checkbox.**

   Turning on this checkbox ensures that Photoshop includes your spot colors in your image, along with process colors.

4. **Rename your image to indicate it harbors a spot color.**

   For example, rename the image "Autumn Art_CMYK_Spot" and then click Save to summon the Save Adobe PDF dialog box.

5. **In the General section, choose Acrobat 5 (PDF 1.4) from the Compatibility pop-up menu.**

6. **In the Compression section, choose Do Not Downsample and pick Maximum Quality JPEG or None from the Compression pop-up menu.**

   Picking either compression option *should* leave you with a high-quality image because "Maximum Quality JPEG" essentially leaves your images uncompressed. If you aren't comfortable using a compression format that can reduce your image's quality, choose "None" instead.

7. In the Output section, check to make sure the Color Conversion pop-up menu is set to No Conversion.

8. Click Save PDF.

   You're now free to send this PDF file off to the page-layout program of your choice.

If you save the settings you entered as a preset, this method is much faster than saving your file as a DCS 2.0. However, be sure to ask your printing company if they'll accept a PDF file with spot colors. Some companies using older equipment may not be familiar with PDFs or may not be able to use them just yet (change is hard, you know!).

Printing Duotone (Multi-Tonal) Images

One of the advantages of printing with a commercial printer is that you can print duotones and other multi-tonal images (see the box below) by adding a second ink to your grayscale images. You can add a spot color, another gray ink, or even process colors—great news if you want to colorize a grayscale image, add some tonal depth and richness, or both. Either way, you can create some amazingly beautiful effects as discussed back in Chapter 8 (page 315). However, it's really easy to add *too* much ink, which makes your image way too dark once it's printed. If that happens, you lose details in the shadows and your contrast goes down the tubes.

UP TO SPEED

Defining Duotones

The term *duotone* generally refers to grayscale images that have had additional inks added to them: Technically, if you add one ink, it's a duotone; two inks make it a tritone; and three inks make it a quadtone, so the correct *general* term is multi-tonal images. But most folks use the term duotone to describe all these alternatives, which can get confusing.

So why add other inks to grayscale images to begin with? You can do it for a couple of reasons. Some folks use duotones to add color to an image inexpensively—as you learned on page 639, reducing the number of colors in your image can mean a cheaper print job. However, duotone (or multi-tone) aficionados will tell you the additional inks add tonal range and depth to an image (and they're right!). In fact, you can add a second gray ink to enhance tonality without adding any color at all.

The two keys to creating high-quality duotones are:

- Start with a high-quality grayscale image with a good tonal range and high contrast.

- Substitute your second ink for part of the original black ink—rather than just adding it (see page 633) to prevent your image from becoming too dark and flat because it's drowning in ink.

With a bit of practice, you'll gain confidence in creating duotones and you'll enjoy doing it. However, it's always a good idea to plan extra time in your production schedule to print some tests. Since you can't trust your monitor or proof your own nonprocess duotones (see page 649), a test print is worth its weight in gold.

To produce a truly amazing duotone or multi-tone image, you need to start out with a good quality grayscale image—one that has high contrast and isn't overly dark to begin with. Once you've settled on a good image, convert it to Grayscale mode (page 306) and then follow these steps:

1. **Duplicate your image.**

   Choose Image → Duplicate and then give the copy a name. To get a bit more descriptive with your image name, consider incorporating the word *duotone* like "Red Mtn_Duotone CMYK".

2. **Choose Image → Mode → Duotone.**

   If this option is grayed out, you're not in Grayscale mode. In that case, choose Grayscale mode first and then switch to Duotone. If the Duotone dialog box opens, notice that the Duotone dialog box reports your image to be a mono-tone image made from nothing but black ink.

3. **Click the Curve icon to the left of the Black Ink (see Figure 16-17).**

   Clicking this icon opens the Duotone Curve window where you can peek at how the ink will be applied in your image. For this particular ink, you have a straight 45-degree curve from the highlight to shadow areas, and it's being applied at 100 percent. Click OK to close the Duotone Curve window.

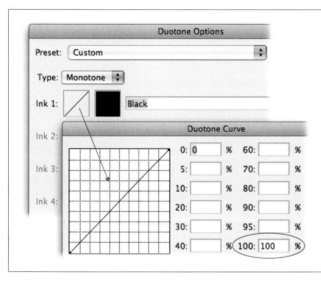

Figure 16-17:
The Duotone Curves are just like the Curves you learned about back in Chapter 9 (page 379) though here they let you know how much ink is being applied to the shadows, midtones, and highlights of your image. The percentages tell you how much ink is being added.

4. **Choose Duotone from the Type pop-up menu.**

   This menu gives you a choice of various types of multi-tonal images. If you choose duotone, you see two inks activate in the dialog box (choosing tritone shows you three inks, and so on). However—and this is key—both inks have straight, 45-degree highlight-to-shadow curve lines, which means they print with the same amount of ink in the same color range. That's *not* good! If you click on the "Ink 2:" color swatch and load a new color, you'll add too much ink for the image to print decently. So instead of editing the Duotone Curves yourself, use one of the many presets as described in the next step.

5. **Click the Preset pop-up menu and choose one of the Duotone presets from the list (see Figure 16-18).**

Feel free to experiment with the wide variety of choices in the Preset menu. Some of the selections, like the true duotones, offer anywhere from one to four options, which represent substitutions for the second ink ranging from stronger to weaker. These are excellent starting points for your own creations. There's nothing wrong with tweaking the Duotone Curves to fine-tune your results, but you'll want to print some tests first to make sure you're not adding too much ink.

Testing duotones is tough because you *can't* proof them unless you've made a duotone out of process colors (which really makes it a quadtone). If you select a preset with inks not available on your printer, you won't get an accurate proof. The best you can do is contact your printing company and see if they'll print you a test on the paper they'll use when they print the final image. If you don't need the proof right away, they may be able to hold onto it and slide it in with another job that uses a similar ink and paper combo.

Figure 16-18:
Top: Once you pick a Preset, peek at the curves for each new ink; Notice that the curve for the black ink is reduced to make room for the other inks, which have straight, full-ink curves.

Bottom: If you choose Quadtone from the Type menu and "CMYK wm" from the Preset menu (the wm stands for warm), you can add a nice warm tone to your image (see page 317). If you're working with a CMYK image, this is a fine choice; however, if you're working with a grayscale document and you don't want to add many different inks, go for one of the Duotone options, which will add one ink instead of three.

6. **Save your document as an EPS or PDF.**

Here's yet another opportunity to chat with your printing company! Give 'em a ring and ask if they prefer EPS or PDF format for duotones or multi-tones. If they say EPS, ask them which settings they prefer, choose File → Save As, and then pick Photoshop EPS from the Format pop-up menu.

In the EPS Options dialog box (Figure 16-19, bottom), choose an 8-bit option from the Preview pop-up menu and pick Binary from the Encoding pop-up menu. Unless your printing company tells you otherwise, leave the rest of the options turned off and click OK. To save your duotone as a PDF file instead, you can use the same settings you used to save a spot color image in the previous section.

Figure 16-19:
As you can see, the difference between a grayscale image (top) and a quadtone (bottom) can be impressive.

Proofing Your Image Onscreen

When it comes to sending images out for print, it'd be nice to peek into the future and *see* what they'll look like first. Happily, Photoshop can create an onscreen proof simulation known as a *soft-proof,* a straightforward process using the same color profiles you've learned about in the previous sections. Here's how to do it:

1. **Calibrate your monitor using the tools described earlier in this chapter on page 618.**

   If you haven't calibrated your monitor, soft-proofing is a galactic waste of time.

2. **Open an RGB image you intend to print.**

   You can soft-proof either RGB or CMYK images, but it's especially cool to proof an RGB image and see what it will print like in CMYK without having to color convert it first!

3. **Choose Window → Arrange → New Window to create a second window showing a copy of your image.**

   Position the windows so they're side-by-side by choosing the 2-Up display from the Application bar's Arrange Documents menu (new in CS4).

4. **Click within the right window to activate it and then choose View → Proof Setup → Custom.**

5. **In the resulting dialog box, turn on the Preview checkbox (shown in Figure 16-20, top).**

6. **From the "Device to Simulate" menu, choose the profile for your final printer.**

   If your image is headed to a printing press, pick your old profile friend, "U.S. Sheetfed v2".

7. **Choose Perceptual from the Rendering Intent menu and turn on Black Point Compensation.**

   This setting makes sure that Photoshop maps your black values and converts them to blacks in your final print, which helps preserve the contrast of your original.

8. **In the "Display Options (On-Screen)" area, turn on the Simulate Paper Color option.**

   Watch your onscreen proof change as you turn this option on and off.

9. **Sit back and examine the differences between your left and right windows.**

   You can apply soft-proofing to other printers like your inkjet printer or a digital press (see page 654). All you need is a calibrated monitor and an accurate printer, along with a paper-specific profile to achieve good results. That said, soft-proofing isn't 100 percent accurate, but it's better than nothing and you'll almost always find it useful. It's also a good tool to help control your client's expectations, especially when the client is printing on low-quality (cheap) paper.

Figure 16-20:
Top: Turning on Preview lets you see the results of your proof settings without clicking the OK button.

Bottom: Notice that the image on the right is slightly more desaturated and has lower overall contrast than the original image on the left (which looks kind of flat). You can also select other profiles and see how they affect the soft-proofing results.

Printing Color Separations

To keep from encountering unexpected printing costs, it's a good idea to print your separations (also called *seps* around the water cooler) to make sure another color hasn't sneaked its way into your document—especially if you've toyed with some spot colors that you're not going to use. Honestly, though, you probably won't use Photoshop to print separations at all—in most cases, you'll place an RGB or CMYK image in a page-layout program (like InDesign), along with text and other images, and let *it* print the separations. The page-layout program does the final printing using *its* print dialog box. However, just in case you ever *do* need to print separations from Photoshop, here's how to do it:

1. **Open a CMYK image and choose File → Print.**

2. **Choose your printer model from the Printer menu.**

   Your "printer" can be anything from a printing press to a PDF file.

3. **Click Page Setup and choose your paper size and orientation.**

   If you pick 8.5×11 and then click the "Print Paper in Landscape Mode" button, the image prints horizontally instead of vertically so you can get more on the page.

4. **Choose Output from pop-up menu at the top right of the Print dialog box (see Figure 16-21).**

Figure 16-21:
Most likely, you'll never need to print separations from within Photoshop, but if you do need to, these settings will make it happen.

5. **Turn on the printer marks you want to include in your print.**

   Turn on Corner Crop Marks so you can see where your document will be trimmed when it's printed. Turn on Include Vector Data if you want any vector info in your image to print as hard-edged PostScript vectors. Many high-end commercial printing presses are PostScript, so this option is usually available. Whether you print your vector info as vectors or as rasterized pixels really depends on what you want (if you want the artwork to be super crisp, print them as vectors). Peek at the image preview on the left side of the Print dialog box to see if your image looks the way you want it to.

6. From the pop-up menu at the upper right, choose Color Management and turn on the Document option (Figure 16-21, bottom).

To choose separations in the next step, you have to choose Document rather than Proof.

7. Choose Separations from the Color Handling pop-up menu.

8. Click Print to send your separations directly to your printer.

If you picked PDF as your printer, the PDF Options dialog box opens.

Printing Proofs

If you're working in a prepress environment—and especially if you're not printing to a digital press (covered in the next section)—you're often proofing on a different printer than the one that will print your document. For example, you might print a proof using an inkjet, but your final image will print on a commercial offset printing press. In that situation, your proof printer can print a *simulation* of what will happen on the printing press. Simulating an image involves reining in the much larger color gamut of the proof printer to include only the colors reproducible on the printing press. You can prepare a simulation in Photoshop using profiles, along with the proofing function you learned about in the previous section. Here's how to do it:

1. Pop open an image and choose File → Print.

2. Pick your proofing printer from the Printer pop-up menu.

For this example, choose Epson Stylus Photo R2400.

3. Click the Page Setup button and enter your paper dimensions.

Click OK to return to the Print dialog box.

4. Choose Color Management from the pop-up menu at the top right of the Print dialog box and turn on the Proof option.

The Proof option lets Photoshop know you intend to print a proof on *one* printer (your inkjet printer) and simulate it on *another printer*, which you can choose from the Profile pop-up menu shown in Figure 16-22 (left).

5. From the Color Handling menu, choose Photoshop Manages Color.

If you choose Printer Manages Color, which you might do if your color-conversion tool is a special RIP set up for proofing (see the box on page 654 for more on RIPs), Photoshop has zero effect on your color and all the color conversion occurs at the RIP. You can't soft-proof your image using the Print dialog box, but you can still do it using the Proofing tools in the View menu (see the previous section on soft-proofing).

Figure 16-22:

Left: Choose Proof in the Color Management section to tell Photoshop that you want to print on one printer as it if were another.

Right: Turn on the Gamut Warning checkbox beneath the preview to see colors that may not print on press (they appear in gray).

6. From the Printer Profile menu, choose the printer/paper/quality profile for the printer you'll use to print the proof.

   For this example, choose "SPR2400 on Premium Luster Paper" using the Best Printer setting.

7. From the Proof Setup menu, pick either **Working CMYK** or **Current Custom Setup** as the proof profile for the print simulation.

   Pick the Current Custom Setup (in this case, the "Coated GRACoL 2006" profile mentioned earlier on page 635) to use the Custom soft-proofing profile you set up in the previous section.

8. **Turn on Simulate Paper Color for the best simulation.**

9. On the left side of the Print dialog box, turn on all three options: Match Print Colors, Gamut Warning, and Show Paper White.

   These options let you see an onscreen view of your image and indicate which, if any, colors might not print on the simulated printer because they're out-of-gamut on your GRACoL press (Figure 16-22, right). For the fun of it, test the Gamut Warning results using both coated and uncoated paper stock to see how the paper affects the printed image.

10. Click Print to summon your printer's Print dialog box.

    Adjust the settings if you need to, but be sure to deactivate the printer's color management. In the Print dialog box, turn Color Settings off to keep the printer driver from interfering with the color management voodoo you've got going on in Photoshop. If you pick Printer Manages Color from the Color Handling menu in the Print dialog box, you can manage the color through your printer driver or RIP (see the box on page 654).

11. **Click Print and wait eagerly to see what your proof looks like.**

Isn't it amazing what you can do with color profiles? Quick, go tell everyone you know how cool this stuff is and watch their eyes glaze over.

Printing on a Digital Press

In the past, when you prepared a document for a commercial printer, you would—and in many case still do—convert your images to the CMYK color mode (see the previous section on commercial offset printing) *before* you inserted them in a page-layout document and certainly before you fired them off to the printing company. However, that process is changing because an increasing number of printers also use *digital presses.*

Digital presses work just like laser printers or copiers; they use electrostatic charges to transfer images from cylinders to the print surface. Like commercial offset presses, digital presses are primarily CMYK printers though they use *toners* instead of inks (which is why they can't print spot color inks). Some digital presses like the Kodak Nexpress offer additional toner spot-color printing, but they're limited to very specific colors like red, green, or blue. Rather than being used for special objects like logos, these additional spot colors typically expand the gamut of the CMYK toners, much like light cyan and light magenta in inkjet printers.

Printing RGB Images on a Digital Press

A digital press uses toner instead of ink, and it handles images much like expanded gamut inkjet printers (see page 625). Because the RGB to CMYK-Plus conversion occurs at the *printing press's* processing RIP (see the box below) using a built-in profile specific to that press and the paper you're using, you'll be dealing with RGB images the whole time instead of converting them to CMYK. That's great news because, as you learned at the beginning of this (exhausting!) chapter, the RGB mode provides you with the widest range of printable colors.

FREQUENTLY ASKED QUESTION

Meet the RIP

I thought RIP meant "rest in peace." What the heck does that have to do with printing?

Quite a lot actually, and it has nothing to do with a funeral blessing.

The acronym RIP refers to a device known as a Raster Image Processor. It's a term you'll often hear tossed around at commercial printing services (also called *service bureaus*). RIPs are processors that convert your image

and document info into print-ready formats that specific printers and other output devices understand. You can think of them as sophisticated and powerful printer drivers (the little programs that power your home printer). Some RIPs can convert RGB color-mode files to CMYK, but others prefer to receive CMYK images. Ask your printing company which color mode it prefers before you send your file.

Printing CMYK Images on a Digital Press

If your images are already in CMYK mode, it's okay to leave them that way. Most digital presses recognize CMYK values and print them well enough. That said, you may want to confirm with your printing company that the press will use *your* current CMYK values rather than converting your image to another color mode and then back to CMYK on the press. This type of color shuffling can lead to unpredictable, and usually terrible, results. Keep in mind that your CMYK images will be darker and more saturated if they're printed on a digital press than they will if they're printed on a conventional ink-based printing press.

Printing Spot Colors on a Digital Press

Since digital presses don't print conventional spot color inks, any spot colors you've assigned in Photoshop or a page-layout program get converted into CMYK or CMYK-Plus colors, depending on the toners used on the press. This conversion happens automatically using a built-in spot-to-process color look-up table. Basically, you've got two choices for handing spot colors on a digital press:

- Leave the spot color in Photoshop and let the RIP automatically convert it to process color.

- Convert the spot color to process color yourself.

Because RIP uses expanded gamut color look-up tables customized for that printer, letting it convert the spot color typically yields better results, especially if the digital press is using one of its additional digital spot color toners to simulate the original spot color ink (talk about a tongue-twister).

If you plan on leaving the spot color in your image, be sure you use the name provided by Photoshop when you created the color. For example, Pantone 810C is a proper color name whereas "Logo spot color" isn't. Since the digital press can't print standard spot colors, it converts them to CMYK or CMYK-Plus process colors. For the RIP on the digital press to identify the spot color properly and produce the best simulation of that color, your spot color needs a standard color name that the RIP can use to find that color in its little black conversion book (or rather, color look-up table).

Since these toner-based digital presses are becoming more common in commercial printing companies, it's important to know which kind of press your image or document will end up on. If it's destined for one that uses gamut-expanding digital spot toners, leave your images in RGB mode to take full advantage of the expanded color gamut of the press itself.

Printing Several Images on a Page

Sometimes, of course, you'll want or need to print multiple images on a single page, especially if you want to review them and proof the content or if you're printing family reunion photos, and so on. Photoshop used to have—note the verb tense—three very handy tools to help you quickly and easily organize, format, and print multiple images on a single page. Those tools *used* to include PDF Presentation, Picture Package, and Contact Sheet. They were wildly useful, and nary a one of 'em made it into Photoshop CS4 though a crippled version of Contact Sheet is available in Bridge (see Appendix C).

The good news is that you can at least download and use CS3 versions of Picture Package and Contact Sheet. For PDF files, you can use the new "Output to PDF" option in Bridge (see page 101 in Chapter 3).

Using Picture Package and Contact Sheet

You can fetch the Picture Package and Contact Sheet plug-ins from Adobe's Web site (*www.adobe.com*) or copy one or both from a version of Photoshop CS3 (if it's still hanging around on your hard drive). If you go the CS3 route, you have to grab a couple of files to make the plug-ins work. Here's what you need to do:

1. Locate the Contact Sheet plug-in in the Photoshop CS3 → Plug-Ins → Automate folder and copy it into the same folder in Photoshop CS4, as shown in Figure 16-23.

2. Copy the entire Layouts folder from Adobe Photoshop CS3 → Presets into the same folder in Photoshop CS4.

   Photoshop stores the template presets for both Contact Sheet and Picture Package in the Layout folder.

3. Restart Photoshop CS4 and choose File → Automate → Contact Sheet II or Picture Package.

4. In the resulting dialog box, configure either Contact Sheet II or Picture Package to your heart's desire.

5. Preview your handiwork and click Print.

Who knows, maybe Adobe will buckle under the public outcry and include these two popular tools in some future version!

Recap: Stress-Free Printing Tips

Congratulations! You've just waded through a ton of dense information. Some of it you'll remember and some of it you won't, but, no matter what, it's here whenever you need to refer to it. As a recap, here's a quick list of some of the most important tips:

- **Calibrate your monitor with an external calibration tool.** These tools are the only way you can accurately view and proof your images onscreen.

- **Resize your images to the print dimensions** *before* **you print.** Resizing before you print lets you make sure your image prints at the size you expect. Besides, a smaller image prints faster.

Figure 16-23:
Top: Because neither Picture Package nor Contact Sheet was updated and included in CS4, you may encounter unexpected weirdness if you use them. Try downloading new versions from Adobe's Web site if your own CS3 versions of the Contact Sheet plug-in and Layout folder cause problems.

Bottom: Once you've copied the files and restarted Photoshop, both plug-ins should appear in the File → Automate menu as shown here.

- **Make sure you have enough resolution.** After you resize your image, make sure you have between 200 and 300 ppi to produce a high-quality print. Resolution is discussed in Chapter 6 on page 221.

- **Sharpen your image if you've made it substantially smaller.** Any time you change the number of pixels in your image it'll soften (blur) just a bit. A final round of sharpening can help you get some focus back.

- **Simplify your images before printing.** Though it's not essential, flattening layers and removing alpha channels makes your document less complex, making the file size smaller so it prints faster and more reliably.

- **Proof, convert, and print with printer- and paper-specific profiles.** Now that you've seen how powerful profiles can be, take the time to download and use them (or make your own). Using proper profiles lets you proof, change color modes, and print your images with the most reliable, most predictable, and highest-quality results.

- **Know your target color mode.** Be sure to choose the correct color mode for your image, whether it's RGB for expanded gamut printers like inkjets and digital presses or CMYK for commercial printing presses. And remember to use RGB mode images when you're printing to expanded gamut inkjets and digital presses.

- **Choose a high-quality print file format.** Use compression-free, print-compatible file formats like TIFF, PDF, and EPS for saving, sending, and printing your images.

- **Save editable PSD files.** Saving your Photoshop document in its native format lets you go back and edit your layers, alpha channels, and so on whenever you want. When you're creating a version to print, duplicate the file or use File → Save As to make a copy so you don't overwrite the original.

- **Use real names for spot colors.** When you're printing spot colors, use the name built into Photoshop instead of your own custom name to increase the chance it'll be recognized by other applications like InDesign or by RIPs that may have to convert it to process colors during the printing.

- **Use duotone or multi-tone presets.** When you're creating duotones or multitonal images, be sure to use the presets rather than adding additional colors yourself (at least, as a starting point). The presets make sure your original black ink and any additional inks are properly controlled by Duotone Curves that reduce the total ink used during printing, which keeps you from losing details and contrast because your image is dripping with ink.

- **Communicate with your printing company.** Find out at the beginning of your project which file formats and settings your printing company needs. Knowing ahead of time exactly what the company expects from you can help keep your client's project from going past its deadline and over its budget.

Photoshop and the Web

Preparing graphics for a Web site is a journey into the unknown. You've got no idea what kind of monitor folks will use to view your graphic, how fast (or slow) their Internet connection is, or what kind of Web browser they've got. It's a proposition riddled with variables that you have no control over; all you can do is prepare your graphic well and hope for the best.

Your challenge as a designer boils down to finding a balance between image quality and file size. Premium-quality, minimally compressed JPEGs look stunning under almost any conditions. But if your site visitor has a pokey dial-up connection, she might decide to click elsewhere rather than waiting for the darn thing to download. On the other hand, if you try to satisfy the slowest common denominator by making ultra-lightweight images, you'll deprive those with a broadband (high-speed) Internet connections from seeing impressive detail you've lovingly created.

Luckily, there are several tricks for keeping file sizes down *and* retaining quality. That's what this chapter is all about. You'll learn which size and file format to use when creating images destined for the Web. You'll also discover how to make animations; craft *favicons* (those tiny, graphics you see in Web browsers' address bars); mock up Web pages; and publish professional-looking online photo galleries.

Creating Web- and Email-Friendly Images

Whether you're designing an image destined for life on the Web or creating an email-friendly version of your latest digital photo, you need to follow three very specific steps to create a high-quality image that will also download quickly:

1. **Adjust the dimensions of your image.**

   The first thing you need to do is decide how big your image should be. In some cases, someone else may give you the size (like when you're instructed to make a Web banner or ad). At other times, you choose the size (like when you email a digital photo, send a sample design to a client, or post an image in an online discussion forum). And if you're designing graphics for smart phones and other mobile devices, you have some very specific sizes (and even file formats) to consider. All of these situations are discussed in this section.

2. **Decide which file format you want to use.**

   The two most common choices are JPEG and GIF. A relative newcomer, PNG, has a lot to offer, but it isn't compatible with all browsers. See page 663 for the pros and cons of each Web-friendly format.

   NOTE   As you learned in Chapter 2, you should always save your master file as a PSD file (Photoshop document) so you can open, edit, and resave it as often as you want without losing quality (each time you save a JPEG, your computer recompresses the graphic, degrading the image's quality). The PSD format also lets you retain any layers you created during the editing process.

3. **Save and compress the file.**

   When you're finally ready to create the version of your image that's going to live online, you can squeeze it down to the smallest size possible using the "Save for Web & Devices" dialog box. You'll learn all about using this massive dialog box, beginning on page 665.

If you follow each of these steps, you'll end up with images that match the dimensions you want, look great, and download quickly. The following pages will show you how to do all of those things.

Resizing Your Image

As you learned in Chapter 6, resolution matters when you print—it doesn't mean a hill of beans when you're preparing images for the Web or an email. In the online realm, it's the *pixel dimensions* that matter most. If you reduce your image's pixel dimensions first, you won't force unsuspecting folks to download an image that's so large it takes over their whole screen, and you'll end up with a smaller file size, which means it'll download faster.

NOTE   If you're emailing an image to someone who *does* need to print it, send him a full-size version in one of the print-friendly formats discussed on page 619. Be sure to compress the file into a .zip or .sit file before you send it so it transfers as fast as possible (see the Note on page 620).

If you're a graphic designer, someone may tell you the pixel dimensions for your project. If that's the case, you can create a new document at that size (page 37) to start with. If you're emailing a digital photo or sample design or posting an image to an online forum, you can choose the size. If the size is up to you, here are a few all-purpose pixel dimensions you can use as guidelines:

- **800 (width) × 600 (height) or 600 × 800.** Use this size if you're sending a design or photo sample to a client and your recipient doesn't need to print the image. The image is almost big enough to fill a Web browser window (unless your viewer has a 30-inch screen, that is), so she won't have to scroll very much (if any) to see the whole thing.

- **640 × 480 (or 480 × 600).** Use these dimensions if you're emailing a photo or posting an image to an online forum. These dimensions produce an image big enough to see well and a file size of less than 1 megabyte (so it transfers nice and fast).

- **320 × 240 (or 240 × 320).** These dimensions work well if you're emailing multiple photos or posting to an online forum that contains a lot of images. If your recipient has a slow Internet connection, she'll appreciate the smaller file size. And if you crop it wisely—see page 202—these dimensions will produce a photo that's big enough for your subject to be identifiable.

- **100 × 133 (or 133 × 100).** If you're creating headshots for the company staff Web page—a great way to humanize your firm, especially if it offers a service—100 × 133 makes a nice, small portrait. If you're building a catalog page with a ton of product thumbnails (small preview pictures), this size won't bog down the whole page. Linking the thumbnail to a full-sized version lets visitors view an enlargement if they want to.

Once you pick a size, flip back to Chapter 6 for step-by-step instructions on how to resize your images without losing quality.

Resizing Web images visually

Sometimes, it's easier just to choose the size you want for your resized image by looking at it. You can use the Zoom tool to decrease the size of your image until it looks right on your screen and then enter that zoom percentage in the Image Size dialog box. Here's how it works:

1. **Open the image you want to resize and zoom in or out until it looks like it's the right size on your screen.**

   Grab the Zoom tool in the Application bar at the top of your screen and click within your image to zoom in or Option-click (Alt-click on a PC) to zoom out. If you want to use a keyboard shortcut instead, press ⌘ and the + or – key (Ctrl and the + or – key on a PC) to zoom in or out (respectively).

2. **Make a note of the zoom percentage shown in the document tab, title bar, or status bar.**

   You can find the zoom percentage in several places: in your document's tab at the top of your screen, in its title bar if you're using floating windows (page 63), and in the status bar at the bottom left of your document window (page 57). The last two are circled in Figure 17-1.

Figure 17-1:
Top: After you use the Zoom tool to visually resize your image onscreen, make a note of the zoom percentage shown in the title bar or status bar (both are circled).

Bottom: Pop open the Image Size dialog box and enter the percentage in the Document Size section (circled here).

3. **Open the Image Size dialog box by choosing Image → Image Size.**

   At the bottom of the resulting dialog box, make sure the Resample Image checkbox is turned on. You can also open this dialog box by pressing ⌘-Option-I (Ctrl+Alt+I on a PC).

4. **Change the Width and Height pop-up menus to "percent".**

If the Constrain Proportions checkbox at the bottom of the dialog box is turned on, the second menu will change automatically when you change the first one.

5. **Type the zoom percentage into the Width or Height field.**

Again, if the Constrain Proportions checkbox is turned on, you have to enter the percentage only in one field or the other.

6. **Choose Bicubic Sharpener from the Method pop-up menu at the bottom of the dialog box.**

When you make an image smaller, you lose some details, but with this particular method you won't lose quite so many (see page 220 for more info on these methods).

7. **Click OK when you're finished to close the Image Size dialog box.**

Now you can upload your image to the Web (or fire it off in an email) knowing you did your part to be a respectful Web citizen. Your mom would be proud.

TIP   To make up for the bit of quality you lose when you make your image smaller, you can give it another round of Unsharp Mask (see page 428).

Choosing the Best File Format

Once you've resized your image, you need to save it in a format that's not only compatible with both the Web and email but also reduces the image to the smallest possible file size. As you learned back in Chapter 2 (page 46), those formats include JPEG, PNG, GIF, and WBMP (see Figure 17-2). The one you pick depends on how many colors are in your image and whether it has any transparent areas.

TIP   No matter which file format you choose, be sure to crop the image as close to the artwork edges as you can before you save it. That way, you shave off extra pixels you don't need. The Image → Trim command can come in especially handy for that particular job (see page 215).

Use the following list to determine which format to use:

- **Use JPEG for photos.** This format supports millions of colors though as you learned back on page 627, it's a "lossy" format, meaning it throws away pixels to compress your image into a smaller file size. However, you can choose the level of compression in the "Save for Web & Devices" dialog box, discussed later in this chapter. You can set the amount of compression with a number scale 0–100 (0 is the most compression and lowest quality; 100 is the least compression and highest quality) or by using the Quality pop-up menu, discussed later in this chapter.

- **Use GIF for images with solid blocks of color.** If you're dealing with line art (black and white with no shades of gray) or an image made from areas of solid

Figure 17-2:
Once you learn each format's strengths and weaknesses, it's easy to decide which one to use when. Here's a prime example for two of the three formats: Use JPEG for photos (top left) and use GIF for solid blocks of colors (bottom left) or line art (right).

color (logos, comic strip art, and so on), GIF is the way to go (see Figure 17-2). It supports fewer colors, so it doesn't work very well on photos. GIFs can be lossy or not; it's up to you. If you want to make 'em lossy, use a 0–100 scale (it works just the opposite of JPEGs: 0 is lossless and 100 is full-on lossy). To make the file sizes smaller without resorting to lossy compression, you can limit the number of colors you include in your image to anywhere between 2 and 256 (fewer colors equal a smaller file size).

• **Use GIF or PNG for images with a transparent background.** Use this format when you want a graphic (a logo, say) to blend seamlessly into the background of a Web page. If you've painstakingly deleted the background in your image, JPEG won't work since Photoshop automatically sticks a solid background behind any empty spaces in a JPEG. Only GIF or PNG lets you use transparent regions instead.

The newer PNG-8 is a lossless format (meaning it doesn't throw away any pixels) that can create a higher-quality file at smaller file sizes than a GIF. The PNG-24 format supports 256 levels of transparency so it produces the highest-quality transparent image of all though the file size is substantially larger than a PNG-8 or GIF. The drawback to PNGs is that some older Web browsers— Internet Explorer 6 in particular—don't display transparent PNGs properly and stick a white background behind them. PNG is still a relatively new kid on the file format block, so hopefully this problem won't be around forever. If you know your Web audiences will view your site on outdated browsers, stick with GIF. If you think they'll have the latest and greatest browsers, go with PNG.

- **Use PNG for super high-quality files.** If quality is more important than download speed, save your image as a PNG-24. For example, if you're a photographer trying to sell your images, use PNG-24 for the enlarged versions in your portfolio so your potential clients can see every last detail in your images.

- **Use GIF for animations.** If you want to combine several images into an automatic slide show, you need to save it as an animated GIF. These animations are handy when you have too much ad copy to fit in a small space on a Web site; an animated GIF lets you cycle through the ad content automatically. You'll learn how to create an animated GIF from start to finish, beginning on page 671.

- **Use WBMP (Wireless Bitmap) for black-and-white images headed for mobile devices.** If you're designing black-and-white images for handheld devices (cellphones, smart phones, and so on), choose WBMP. It supports only black and white pixels (you can't use it for color), and it gives you crispy text and logos that remain readable on those itty-bitty screens.

FREQUENTLY ASKED QUESTION

A Farewell to Web-Safe Colors

Dude, do I still have to use Web-safe colors in my graphics? It feels so 1990.

Negative, good buddy. Computer monitors have come a long way over the years, and they can now display a much wider range of colors than they used to. Heck, today's iPods and cellphones display more colors than the monitors of the early '90s! For that reason, there's no need to stick with the boring, 256-color Web-safe palette.

However, if you're convinced that the majority of your audience is afflicted with prehistoric monitors—the ones that can display only 256 colors—you can find the Web-safe palette in the Color Picker by turning on the Only Web Colors checkbox at the bottom left of the dialog box (page 457).

You can also convert other colors to their Web-safe equivalents by using the Color Table section in the "Save for Web & Devices" dialog box (see page 659).

These days, it's more important to make sure you have decent contrast in your images. Sure, you can upload them and see how they look on as many monitors or devices as you can get your hands on, but you can't possibly see how your images look on *every monitor* (though the "Save for Web & Devices" dialog box [page 665] and Adobe Device Central [page 671] can help with that problem, as discussed later in this chapter).

The cold, hard fact is that your images will look darker on some monitors and lighter on others—that's just the way it is. But as long as you have a decent amount of contrast between those colors, your images will still look good.

Save and Compress Your File

The "Save for Web & Devices" dialog box can save your image *and* compress the heck out of it at the same time. It also gives you four big preview windows—one for your original image and three others—so you can monitor your image's quality while you're trying to squeeze it into a smaller file size (see Figure 17-3).

Connection speed
menu

Tools   Preview tabs   Format   Options menu

Figure 17-3:
In this Texas-sized dialog box, you can see up to four preview windows of your image in various file formats at different levels of compression. Below each preview you see the file format, the file size, and an estimate of how long the image takes to download at a given connection speed. You can use the tiny pop-up menu to the right of the time estimate (it looks like a down-arrow with four tiny lines) to choose a speed for the estimate.

Set browser preview   Color values

You saw this dialog box in action when you resized a JPEG back in Chapter 6 (page 231). To explore even *more* of its settings, follow these steps:

1. **With your image open, choose File → "Save for Web & Devices" and, in the resulting dialog box, click the 4-Up tab.**

   At the top of the dialog box, you'll notice four tabs that let you see your original image alongside three previews that show what the image looks like if you change it in particular ways. The most useful are the 2-Up and 4-Up options. Use 2-Up if you already know the format you want to use and 4-Up if you want to make some more comparisons. (Optimize gives you no comparison at all and shows only the new image.)

2. **Click the preview window to the right of the original and, at the top right of the dialog box, choose a file format from the Preset pop-up menu.**

   The Preset menu contains a list of frequently used file format/compression level combinations for the formats previously mentioned. Photoshop changes the various quality and color settings on the right side of the dialog box for you and displays the file size and estimated download time below the preview. (You can change the connection speed Photoshop uses to calculate the download time by clicking the tiny icon to the right of the listed speed as shown in Figure 17-3.) If you don't want to go the preset route, you can also pick the format from the pop-up menu *underneath* the Preset menu and then adjust the quality/color settings manually, as discussed in the next step.

TIP   You can make Photoshop automatically fill in the remaining two preview windows by choosing Repopulate Views from the "Save for Web & Devices" dialog box's option menu (see Figure 17-3). Photoshop looks at the file format of the currently selected preview window and then loads up the other windows with previews of the same format at lower compression or color settings.

3. **Adjust the quality and color settings for the format you picked.**

Each item in this menu has its own entourage of settings related to quality and color. Here's the lowdown on what they all mean:

- **JPEG.** This format is the one you'll probably use most often. You can set the compression level using the Quality pop-up menu, which includes five settings from low (highest compression, smallest file size) to maximum (least compression, largest file size). You can fine-tune the quality by using the numeric quality field to its right (0 is the highest compression, smallest file size and 100 is the least compression, largest file size).

- **Optimized.** Normally an image has to download completely before it appears in a Web browser, but if you turn on the Progressive checkbox, your image loads a little bit at a time (row by row), sort of like a waterfall effect. Turning on this checkbox creates a slightly smaller, though somewhat less compatible file. Leave it off if your audience is likely to be using older Web browsers.

- **Embed Color Profile.** If you want the image's color profile (page 617) to tag along with the file, turn this checkbox on. On the off chance that the viewer's monitor can actually *read* the profile correctly (some of them can't), the colors will appear more accurate. If the monitor can't read the profile, you've added a little file size for nothing (which is why you should probably leave it off).

- **Blur.** Use the Blur field to run a slight Gaussian Blur on the image (page 591) to reduce its file size a little more. For a decent-quality image, you can get away with a setting of 0.1–0.5 pixels, but anything higher looks terrible.

- **Matte.** The Matte color swatch lets you pick a color to use in place of any transparent (or partially transparent) pixels in your image. Since JPEG doesn't support transparency, those pixels will become white. You can use the swatch to pick another color instead. Transparency options are discussed later on page 668.

- **GIF and PNG.** You get similar options for both these formats. Near the top right is the most crucial setting, the Color pop-up menu, which controls the number of colors you use to create your image (shown in the Color Table a little lower in the dialog box). If you reduce the number of colors in the image, you can greatly reduce its file size (though Photoshop will substitute the closest match for the missing colors, which can produce some weird-looking images). Both GIF and PNG-8 let you choose anywhere between 2 and 256 colors. PNG-24, on the other hand, gives you 16.8 million colors…period.

- **Color reduction method.** This pop-up menu lives below the Format menu. If you've reduced the number of colors as described earlier, this menu lets you pick the method Photoshop uses when it tosses them out. From the factory, it's set to Selective, which makes Photoshop keep colors that your eyes can see though it favors colors in broad areas (like a sky) and those that are safe for the Web. Perceptual favors only those colors that your eyes can see, and Adaptive creates a palette from the most dominant colors in the image (like greens and blues for landscape images and peachy colors for portraits). Restrictive uses only the Web-safe palette (see the box on page 665), and Custom lets you modify the color palette yourself (eek!) using the Color Table section of the dialog box. Choose Black and White, Grayscale, Mac OS, and Windows to use those respective color palettes. The Selective method usually produces the most visually pleasing color palette, so feel free to leave this menu alone.

- **Dither method and amount.** If your image contains colors that the viewer's monitor can't display, you can fake 'em with a process called *dithering*. Use the pop-up menu on the left to set the dither method (or to turn dithering on or off) and the numeric field to its right to set the amount. A high dither amount (percentage) produces more accurate color; the tradeoff is larger file size (try an amount between 80 percent and 90 percent). If you're desperate to make the file smaller, lower the dither amount. As far as how it does what it does, Diffusion simulates missing colors with a random pattern that's not too noticeable, so it's usually the best choice. Pattern simulates missing colors with a square pattern (which can sometimes create a weird color seam), and Noise uses a random pattern that doesn't spread across the whole image (so you won't get a weird seam). If you choose No Dither, Photoshop won't fake any colors. Since you never know how many colors folks' monitors are set to display (256 vs. thousands or millions), it's a good idea to leave the dither method and amount set to Diffusion; however, if file size is more important than quality, choose No Dither.

- **Transparency and Matte.** If you've deleted the background in your image, turn on the Transparency checkbox. If you want to change partially transparent pixels (those around the edges; see Figure 17-4) to a certain color, click the Matte swatch and pick a color from the resulting Color Picker. You can also choose a matte color from within your image by choosing Eyedropper from the Matte pop-up menu. Grab the Eyedropper tool at the far left of the dialog box—not the one in the Tools panel—and then click a color in the image (the color you clicked shows up in the square color swatch beneath the Eyedropper tool). Use the pop-up menu below the Transparency option to turn dithering on or off for the matte color, and use the numeric field to its right to set the dither amount. You'll typically leave transparency dithering off.

Figure 17-4:
As you can see here, the edges of a transparent image with a drop shadow looks much better as a PNG-24 (bottom left) than a GIF (top right) because the PNG-24 can display so many more colors. But, as the file sizes beneath each preview show, the PNG-24 is also much larger, so it takes longer to download.

If file size is more important than download speed, you can use the Matte menu to change the partially transparent pixels of the shadow to the color of your destination background (bottom right). This trick makes the shadow look nice and soft again because Photoshop mixes the matte color with the shadow. It also keeps you from seeing edge halos—leftover pixels from the image's original background.

- **Interlaced, Web Snap, Lossy.** Turn on the Interlaced checkbox to make the image appear a little at a time in your visitor's Web browser. If you want to convert your colors to the Web-safe color palette (see the box on page 665), use the Web Snap slider (the higher the number, the more Web-safe colors you get). Use the Lossy slider to lower the quality of your GIF which makes the file size smaller. (Lossy isn't available for the PNG-8 or PNG-24 formats.) You'll typically leave these settings turned off or set to 0, but feel free to experiment with them if you're feeling frisky.

- **WBMP.** If you've made a black-and-white image that's destined for a cell-phone or other hand-held device with an itsy-bitsy screen, choose this format. Since you're dealing only with black and white pixels, you just need to decide whether to turn on dithering (page 668) and, if you turn it on, to set the amount. Out of the box, it's set to Diffusion at 88 percent.

TIP If you're saving a graphic that has to weigh in at a certain size (like a Web banner ad), you can choose "Optimize to File Size" from the "Save for Web & Devices" dialog box's options menu. In the resulting dialog box, enter the target size and select a Start With option. Choose Current Settings to make Photoshop use the settings in the "Save for Web & Devices" dialog box. If you want Photoshop to pick a format, choose Auto Select GIF/JPEG. If you're dealing with an image that contains slices, you can choose to optimize the current slice, each slice, or all of 'em. Click OK to make Photoshop try to get your image as close to the target size as possible. You may still have some tweaking to do afterward, but Photoshop will do most of the work for you.

4. **Make sure the "Convert to sRGB" checkbox is turned on.**

   If you leave this option turned on, Photoshop converts your image to sRGB, a color space designed to mimic the characteristics of a Windows monitor. Since the majority of monitors *are* attached to Windows computers, leave it on.

5. **Use the Preview pop-up menu to see what your image looks like on a Mac or Windows computer with no color management or with the document's current color profile (page 617). This setting doesn't change your image; it just lets you see it through the eyes of someone with a different monitor.**

6. **Set the Metadata pop-up menu to None.**

   This pop-up menu lets you include the information Photoshop captured from your camera (metadata) or the copyright and contact info you stored using the File Info dialog box discussed later in this chapter (page 686). As you might suspect, including data with your document increases its file size. If you're trying to make your image's file size as small as possible, set it to None.

7. **Use the Color Table to edit the colors in your image.**

   This chart of color swatches lets you change or delete colors in your image. If your viewers are certain to have super old monitors, you can use the tiny Color Table panel menu to shift the colors in a GIF or PNG-8 image to Web-safe colors. If you need to make your file size even smaller, you can delete colors by clicking the swatch of the color you want to zap and then clicking the little trash can icon at the bottom right of the Color Table (shown in Figure 17-3). If you want certain colors to be transparent, you can select the swatch and click the transparency button below the table (it looks like a white-and-gray checkerboard). And finally, if the look of the Color Table scares you, don't panic; you'll probably never use it.

8. **When you're finished, click Save.**

   Photoshop opens the Save dialog box letting you pick a storage space and enter a name for your new file.

   TIP If you decide you've got some image editing left to do, but you want Photoshop to remember your current settings, click Done instead.

On the left side of the dialog box, you'll see a row of tools including:

- **Hand.** This tool lets you move the image around within the preview windows just like the regular Hand tool. You can also press the space bar (or H) to activate it and then move your mouse to see another part of the image.

- **Slice Select.** If you've mocked up a Web page and sliced it accordingly (see page 678), you can use this tool to select those slices for saving in specific formats. Its keyboard shortcut is C.

- **Zoom.** You can use this one to zoom in and out of your image just like the Zoom tool in your Tools panel, though it's faster to press ⌘-+ or – (Ctrl-+ or – on a PC). Alternatively, in the field at the bottom left of the dialog box, you can enter a zoom percentage or you can choose a preset from the pop-up menu. You can also Ctrl-click (right-click on a PC) within the preview window and choose a zoom percentage from the shortcut menu. Keyboard shortcut: Z.

- **Eyedropper.** Use this tool to snatch colors from the image in your preview window. It's helpful when you're creating a matte color for a transparent background as discussed previously on page 668. Keyboard shortcut: I.

- **Eyedropper Color.** This color swatch shows the current color of the Eyedropper.

- **Toggle Slices Visibility.** If you want to see the slices in your image, click this button. Slicing is discussed later in this chapter on page 678. Keyboard shortcut: Q.

The buttons at the bottom of the dialog box include:

- **Device Central.** If you're designing for a cellphone or other mobile device, this button launches a program that lets you preview the image on several devices. On the left side of the resulting window, choose your device and click the Emulator tab in the middle to see what your image looks like on that device (see Figure 17-5).

- **Preview.** To see what your image looks like in a Web Browser, click this button (it uses the main browser on your computer). To choose a specific Web browser installed on your computer, use the pop-up menu to the Preview menu's right and navigate to that browser.

- **Save, Cancel, Done.** Once you have all the settings just right, click the Save button to save your image and then, in the Save dialog box, give it a name. If you want to bail and do nothing, click the Cancel button. Clicking Done makes Photoshop remember the current settings and close the dialog box. Holding Option (Alt on a PC) changes the last two buttons to Reset and Remember.

Animating a GIF

You may think that creating an animation is a complicated process, but it's really not. In Photoshop, all it means is that you're creating a slideshow that plays automatically. You can control which images the program uses, the amount of time it

Figure 17-5:
Adobe Device Central has a ton of device-specific preview frames that you can use to see what your graphic looks like. You can use the panel on the left side of the window to load more devices from the Online Library. Use the options on the right to set the brightness of the display screen, and so on.

displays each one, whether it *loops* the slideshow (automatically starts over), and so on. This kind of control is really handy when you're making Web site ads. For example, if you're designing a 140-pixel × 140-pixel ad for your costume shop, you need to include a logo, a few costume samples, and a 10%-off coupon. Since you'll never fit all that into a tiny space, you can make an animated GIF that cycles through several images automatically.

The first step is to create the images you want to string together. (Each image needs its own layer.) Once you're ready to go, follow these steps:

1. **Open the Animation panel by choosing Window → Animation.**

   At the bottom of the Application Frame (page 11) or toward the bottom of your document if you've got the Application Frame turned off, find the long horizontal panel called "Animation (Frames)". Each frame serves as a placeholder for the image you want to show onscreen. As soon as you open the Animation panel, you see one frame representing what's currently visible in your Layers panel.

   NOTE   In Photoshop CS4 Extended (page 1), you can make animations using frames, as discussed here, or by using a more complicated timeline. Adobe's online help system (page 729) has more about that feature.

123456 (6-digit #)
Red gr Blu

POWER USERS' CLINIC

Matching and Snatching Colors on the Web

If you're designing an image destined for an existing Web page, you may find yourself in a color-matching conundrum. If you need to match the color scheme (page 452) or the colors in a company logo, you can do it by finding out the *hexadecimal* values of the colors involved.

The hex number, as it's affectionately called, is a six-digit, alphanumeric programming code for color values. The first two digits represent red, the next two represent green, and the last two represent blue (since your image appears only onscreen, RGB values are the only ones that matter). You can find a color's hex number in several different ways:

- Choose Window → Info and, from the panel menu, choose Panel Options. From the Mode menu, choose Web Color and then click OK. When you mouse over to the color, its hex number appears in the Info panel.

- Using the Eyedropper tool (page 459), Ctrl-click (right-click on a PC) any color in an open Photoshop document. From the resulting shortcut menu, choose Copy Color As HTML and paste the hex number into your HTML editor by choosing Edit → Paste.

- Using the Eyedropper tool, click a color in an open Photoshop document to load it as your foreground color chip. When you click the foreground chip to open the Color Picker, the color's hex number appears at the bottom of the dialog box in the field labeled # (see page 457 for more on the Color Picker).

- You can snatch color from anywhere on your screen, whether it's on your desktop or in a Web browser. Just click your foreground color chip to open the Color Picker, mouse over to your Photoshop document, and then click somewhere within the document itself. *Outside* Photoshop, hold the mouse button as you hover over the color you want to snatch, and then release your mouse button. As long as you click *within* your document first, your cursor remains an eyedropper no matter where you drag it.

At the bottom of the Color Picker dialog box (page 457), you can enter the hex number in the field marked # or use it in your favorite HTML editor when you're building the Web page.

---

2. **Add another frame.**

   At the bottom of the Animation panel, click the "Duplicate selected frames" icon (it looks like a piece of paper with a folded corner) as shown in Figure 17-6 (where it's labeled New Frame) to create a new placeholder for the next image in your animation. Initially, it contains the same image as the starter frame (don't worry; you'll fix that in the next step).

3. **In the Layers panel, use the visibility eyes to show only the layer containing the next image in your animation.**

   When you turn off the visibility of every layer *except* the one you want to show next, Photoshop displays the visible layer in the new frame you just created in step 2. That's all there is to it! There's no dragging or dropping, just showing and hiding using the layers' visibility eyes.

Selected frame

Panel menu

Set loop

Start

Back

Forward

End

Tween

New frame

Delete

Frame delay

Figure 17-6:
Top: Use the playback buttons at the bottom of the Animation panel to move through your animation frame by frame. Photoshop highlights the selected frame as shown here. You can also click a frame to select it.

Bottom: Open the Set Loop Count dialog box by clicking the Set Loop Count triangle (labeled, top) and choosing Other. The dialog box lets you determine how many times your animation plays. If you want it to keep playing without stopping, click the triangle and select Forever.

4. **Repeat steps 2 and 3 until you've made all the frames of your animation.**

5. **Press the Play button to see the slideshow.**

   Photoshop displays your slideshow in the main document window. The images flash by quickly, but don't worry—you'll learn how to make 'em stick around longer in the next section.

You did it! You created your first animated GIF. There's still some work to do, but you're more than halfway there.

Editing Your Animation

Once you've made all the frames in your animation, you can edit your masterpiece using the following controls:

- **Frame delay.** To control the length of time each image is visible, use the pop-up menus at the bottom of each individual frame (shown in Figure 17-6). To open one of the menus, click the down arrow near the bottom of a frame. Photoshop gives you a list of options ranging from No Delay to "10 seconds". If you want to enter a duration that's not listed, choose Other and type a number in the Set Frame Delay dialog box. You can set a duration for each frame or change several at once by Shift- or ⌘-clicking (Ctrl-clicking on a PC) to select multiple frames and then changing the duration of one of the selected frames.

- **Set Loop Count.** If you want the animation to play over and over, you can set it to loop a certain number of times. Click the down-pointing triangle at the bottom left of the Animation panel and choose Once, "3 Times", Forever, or Other from the pop-up menu. If you choose Other, Photoshop opens the dialog box shown in Figure 17-6, bottom, where you can enter any number you want.

- **Rearrange frames.** To change the frames' order, simply drag them into place.

- **Delete frames.** Just like almost every panel in Photoshop, this one has its own little trash can icon. If you want to zap a frame, select it and then click the trash can or drag it onto the trash can. If you want to delete more than one frame, select them first by Shift- or ⌘-clicking (Ctrl-clicking on a PC) and then click the trash can. In the resulting "Are you sure?" dialog box, click Yes.

- **Tween frames.** Right from the get-go, you don't have any kind of transition between your frames; the animation works just like a regular slideshow, in which one frame abruptly gives way to the next. If you want to make the frames fade in and out, you can add *tweening* (short for "in-betweening"). Just tell Photoshop *which* frames you want to tween and how many frames of fading you want to add to make Photoshop add the new frames for you automatically. When you play the animation, the frames seem to blend softly into one another. Figure 17-7 has the details.

Figure 17-7:
Top: If you want to fade the first frame shown in Figure 17-6 into the second, select the first frame and then click the Tween button (circled, bottom) and choose Next Frame from the Tween With pop-up menu. Enter 5 in the "Frames to Add" box and then click OK.

Bottom: Here, Photoshop has added five additional frames (numbered 2–6) that gradually change opacity. When you play the animation, it'll look like the text and dog images fade together. For a more gradual fade between frames, enter 10 in the "Frames to Add" box.

NOTE   Once you start adding tweened frames, you should speed up the whole animation's frame duration so it doesn't take forever to play.

You can create all kinds of special effects using tweening though you'll need to experiment and play around with it to learn what you can do. It's all about setting up a layer for each frame, creating the frames, and then adjusting what you want to happen *between* each frame. For example, if you move the contents of a layer in one frame, you can use tweening to make it look like the object is moving. You can also turn layer styles (page 119) on or off, add solid-color frames to make the animation look like it fades to that color, and so on. The creative possibilities are endless!

Saving Your Animation

When you've got the animation just right, you need to do just a couple of things before you post it on the Web. Of course, you need to save it as a Photoshop (PSD) document so you can go back and edit it later. You also need to:

- **Optimize it.** If you choose Optimize Animation from the Animation panel menu, you end up with a slightly smaller file size, which makes the animation download faster and run more smoothly. The resulting Optimize Animation dialog box contains two settings:

  — **Bounding Box** crops each changed frame to the part that's different from the previous frame. It's like running the Trim command (page 215) on each frame, so that each frame is cropped closely to the content.

  — **Redundant Pixel Removal** makes unchanged pixels transparent in subsequent frames, which makes the file size a little smaller.

  Both settings are turned on from the factory, but Photoshop doesn't apply them until you choose Optimize and then click OK.

- **Save it as an animated GIF.** Last but not least, choose File → "Save for Web & Devices" and, in the upper right of the dialog box that appears, choose GIF from the unlabeled format pop-up menu (it's right below the Preset menu). When you choose GIF, Photoshop activates the Animation section at the bottom right of the dialog box, giving you one last chance to change the Looping Options and preview your handiwork. When you've finished, click Save and say out loud, "I'm an animator."

Designing a Web Site Favicon

You know those tiny little icons on the left edge of your Web browser's address bar (see Figure 17-8)? They're called *favicons* (short for "favorites icons"), and they're great for adding a bit o' branding to your Web pages. They not only show up in your Web browser, they also appear in news feeds (clickable headlines from your favorite Web sites that you can access through special newsreader software or your favorite Web browser). Creating them in Photoshop is a snap, and you'll be designing them like a pro after you read this section.

First, spend some quality time looking at other favicons. Your goal is to brand your Web site with a graphic that's exactly 16 pixels×16 pixels—no more, no less. It's tough to design anything recognizable that small, but it can be done. For example, you might use a portion of your logo rather than the whole thing or your company's initials rather than the whole name. To get an idea of what works and what doesn't, spend some time Web surfing to see what other folks are using.

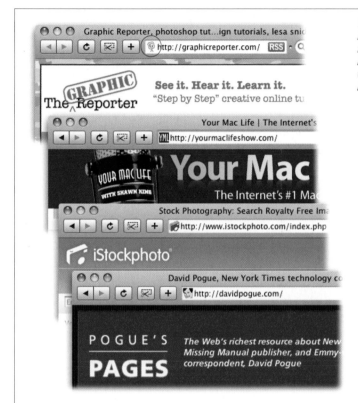

Figure 17-8:
Here's an example of four different favicons for various Web sites (the top one is circled). Designing favicons is a good way to test your design skills since you're limited to 16 pixels square!

Next, you need to download a plug-in that lets Photoshop save the file in the Windows Icon (ICO) file format. You can download a free plug-in called ICO Format from *www.telegraphics.com.au/sw/*. Just quit Photoshop and follow the instructions on page 711 to install it. When you relaunch Photoshop, you should see ICO appear in the Format pop-up menu of the Save As dialog box.

Now you're ready to create your tiny work of art:

1. **Create a new document that's 64 × 64 pixels.**

   Choose File → New or press ⌘-N (Ctrl+N on a PC) to make a new document. While your favicon will ultimately be 16 pixels × 16 pixels, that's too small a size to work with initially. To save yourself some eyestrain, start out with a larger, 64 pixel × 64 pixel canvas; you'll reduce its size later.

2. **Create or place your artwork in the new document.**

   If you designed a logo using Adobe Illustrator, choose File → Place to open it as a Smart Object (page 115). If you're creating art in Photoshop, be sure to turn off anti-aliasing so the edges are nice and crisp (especially important on text as discussed on page 555).

3. **If you need to, resize the artwork to fit the canvas.**

   To resize your artwork, press ⌘-T (Ctrl+T on a PC) to summon Free Transform and then drag one of the corner handles (see page 245 for more on using Free Transform). When you're happy with the size, press Return (Enter) to let Photoshop know you've finished.

4. **Resize the document.**

   When your design is done, choose Image → Image Size. Make sure the Constrain Proportions checkbox at the bottom of the dialog box is turned on and set the Width or Height field to *16 pixels* (Photoshop automatically changes the other field to 16), and then click OK.

5. **Sharpen your image if you need to.**

   If your design looks a bit blurry, run the Unsharp Mask filter (see page 428).

6. **Save your file in the ICO format and name it "favicon".**

   Choose File → Save As and pick Windows Icon (ICO) from the Format pop-up menu at the bottom of the dialog box and then click Save.

That's it! You've created your very first favicon. If a client asked you to create a favicon and send it to her, email the *favicon.ico* file and let her add it to her Web site. If you created it for your own site, you're ready to upload the file to the root level of your Web site where your index (home) page lives. (If you have no idea what that last sentence means, check out *Creating a Web Site: The Missing Manual, Second Edition.*)

Be aware that not all Web browsers support favicons, and some even want you to bury a link to the favicon in the code of each Web page. If you want to take that extra step, you can insert the following code somewhere within the <head> section of your Web pages:

```
<link rel="SHORTCUT ICON" href="/favicon.ico">
```

If you've got a big Web site, adding that line of code can be time consuming, so you may want to use the "Find and Replace" command found in most HTML editors so you can search for a piece of code that appears in every page like the closing </title> tag. For example, you could search for *</title>* and Replace it with *</title><link rel="SHORTCUT ICON" href="/favicon.ico">*.

Creating Web Page Mockups and Image Maps

As you've learned throughout this book, Photoshop is an amazingly powerful image editor, which means it's great for designing Web pages. In fact, Photoshop has a tool that'll let you slice your design into Web-friendly pieces that, when clicked, lead to whatever Web address you want to link them to. Photoshop even churns out the proper code that you can paste into your own Web page using your favorite HTML editor.

But does all that mean you should use Photoshop to build a Web site? Heck, no. Remember back in Chapter 14 when you learned that even though Photoshop has a powerful text tool, you shouldn't use it to create a book? The same principle applies here. While you *could* use the program to build real Web pages, you shouldn't; you're much better off using a program that's made for the job (Dreamweaver, for example). That said, the Slice tool comes in really handy in a few situations:

- **Building a Web site prototype.** If you've designed a Web site for a client in Photoshop and want to give him an idea of how the site will look and behave, you can use the Slice tool to get it done fast. If you slice up your design and assign different hyperlinks to navigation bars, you can give your client a good idea of how the navigation in the final Web site will feel.

- **Making an image map.** If you want to add hyperlinks to certain portions of a single image, you can do it with the Slice tool.

- **Making an image-heavy page load a little bit faster.** Chopping images into pieces makes them load a little at a time instead of in one big piece. (This problem will be less of an issue as more people get fast Internet connections.)

Slicing an Existing Image

Once you've created an image that you want to slice, you can use the Slice tool (shown in Figure 17-9) to draw the regions by hand or you can make Photoshop create slices from individual layers by choosing Layer → New Layer Based Slices. You can also make Photoshop slice your images according to the guides you've drawn (discussed later in this section).

Figure 17-9:
The Slice and Slice Select tools in the Crop toolset look like little X-Acto knives.

Here's how to slice and dice a Web page mockup:

1. **Turn on Photoshop's Rulers and draw individual guides around the areas you want to slice.**

   Instead of drawing each slice yourself, make Photoshop do the hard work by dragging a few well-placed guides around each slice you want to make. Turn on your Rulers by pressing ⌘-R (Ctrl+R on a PC) and then click within the horizontal ruler and drag downward to drop a horizontal guide. Do the same thing to create vertical guides until you've placed a guide around every slice you want to make as shown in Figure 17-10.

2. **Press C to grab the Slice tool.**

   The Slice tool, which looks like a tiny X-Acto knife, hides in the Crop toolset.

Figure 17-10:
As you can see here, Photoshop created individual slices from the guides. A bounding box and a tiny number appear at the top left corner of each slice; Photoshop numbers each one, beginning at the top left to bottom right of your document. If you draw the slices yourself, the number appears in a blue box. If you make Photoshop draw the slices for you, the number appears in a gray box.

3. **Trot up to the Options bar and click the Slices From Guides button.**

   In less than a second, Photoshop draws slices around your images, following the guides you placed in the first step. If you opted out of drawing guides first, you can slice areas yourself by clicking where you want the slice to begin and then dragging diagonally to the right. When you let go of your mouse button, Photoshop puts a blue bounding box around the slice. This kind of slice is called a *user-slice*. To account for the rest of your image (the areas you haven't yet sliced), Photoshop draws other slices (called *auto-slices*) automatically and marks them with a gray bounding box. These are Auto-slices are discussed in the next section.

   TIP If you've drawn a slice that's perfectly suited for another graphic, you can duplicate it by Option-dragging (Alt-dragging on a PC) the slice onto another image. If you want to draw a perfectly square slice, hold Shift as you drag.

Modifying Slices

Once you've created a slice, you may need to move it or change it in some way. If so, you have to select it using the Slice Select tool. Press Shift-C to activate the tool or, if the Slice tool is active, you can grab the Slice Select tool temporarily by pressing ⌘ (Ctrl on a PC). When you let go of the modifier key, Photoshop switches back to the regular Slice tool.

To select a slice, just click it. Its bounding box turns brown and little dots appear in the center of each line as shown in Figure 17-11.

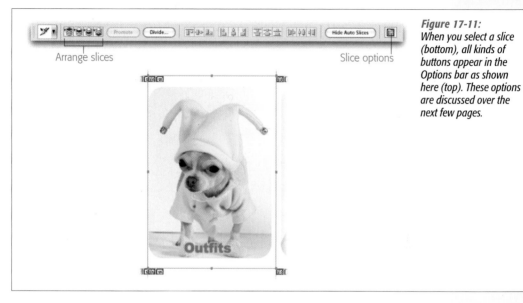

Arrange slices

Slice options

Now you're ready to:

- **Resize the slice.** Once you select a slice, you can drag any corner or center handle (they look like tiny solid circles) to make it bigger or smaller.

- **Move the slice.** Click within the slice and then drag it to another location. To restrict your drag horizontally or vertically, hold the Shift key as you drag.

   TIP   If you want your slices to snap to guides, other slices, or objects, choose View → Snap To. (Unless you've previously turned it off, this option is already turned on.)

- **Promote slices.** You can change a layer- or auto-based slice to a user-slice by clicking the Promote button in the Options bar. Auto-slices can't be edited because they were made by Photoshop, For example, if you place guides and let Photoshop make the slices for you as described in the previous section, you can't move or resize any of those slices until you promote them to user-slices (as shown in Figure 17-12). Similarly, layer-based slices are tied to the pixel content of that layer. To change the slice itself or the layer contents, you have to promote the slice to a user-slice first.

- **Arrange slices.** Because the Slice tool draws only rectangles, you have to overlap slices to make other shapes. In that case, you may need to fiddle with their stacking order by first selecting the slice with the Slice Select tool and then clicking the Bring Forward or Send Backward buttons (and so on) shown in Figure 17-11 (top).

- **Align slices.** You can align slices just like you can align layers (page 71). Using the Slice Select tool, just Shift-click to select more than one slice and then click the appropriate alignment button in your Options bar.

- **Divide slices.** If you need to slice a slice (oy!), select it with the Slice Select tool and click the Divide button in the Options bar. In the Divide Slice dialog box, turn on the Divide Horizontally Into or Divide Vertically Into checkbox, enter the number of slices you want to create, and then click OK.

- **Combine slices.** Select two or more slices by Shift-clicking with the Slice Select tool. Next, Ctrl-click (right-click on a PC) and choose Combine Slices from the resulting shortcut menu. Combining slices is helpful when Photoshop has created a few too many auto-slices and you want to combine them so they'll load as one image.

- **Copy and paste slices.** You can copy and paste a slice by selecting it and then pressing ⌘-C (Ctrl+C). Next, open the target document and press ⌘-V (Ctrl+V). The slice and graphics from the associated layers appear in your new document, but they're all on one layer (which means you can't edit them individually—you have to go back to your original document to do that).

- **Give it a URL.** If you want to transport visitors to a particular Web address when they click a slice, select the slice and click the Slice Options button shown in Figure 17-11 or just double-click the slice itself. In the resulting Slice Options dialog box, enter the full Web address into the URL field (for example, enter *http://www.petstumes.com*). The next section also discusses Slice Options.

- **Delete it.** To delete a slice, select it with the Slice Select tool and press Delete (Backspace on a PC).

- **Hide.** If you find a document riddled with slice borders and numbers distracting, you can hide them temporarily by pressing ⌘-H (Ctrl+H on a PC).

- **Lock.** To lock your slices so they can't be changed, choose View → Lock Slices.

- **Clear.** To zap all your slices, choose View → Clear Slices.

Slice Options

Once you've drawn your slices and put them in the right spot, you can start controlling how they behave in your Web browser by setting Slice Options (see Figure 17-13).

Figure 17-13:
If you click the Slice Options button at the top right of the Options bar (shown in Figure 17-11), you open a dialog box that lets you give each slice a custom name and a URL. You can also open this box by double-clicking the slice with the Slice Select tool.

> **TIP** To change the color of the slices lines, choose Photoshop → Preferences → "Guides, Grids, & Slices" (Edit → Preferences → "Guides, Grids, & Slices" on a PC). In the Slices section at the bottom of the dialog box, use the pop-up menu to change the line color. You can turn off the Show Slice Numbers checkbox here, too.

The Slice Options dialog box lets you control the following:

- **Slice Type.** Most of your slices consist of an image, though they can also be solid blocks of color or plain text. If you want to create an empty space that you can fill with HTML color or HTML text later, choose No Image from this pop-up menu. A "Text Displayed in Cell" field appears that lets you enter text that will be (bet you can't guess) displayed in that cell.

• **Name.** Straight from the factory, your slices get generic names that include the document name and a number. If you want to use a name that's more descriptive (and useful), enter it here.

• **URL.** One of the big benefits of slicing images is that it lets you make part of the image act as a hyperlink that takes visitors to another Web page. Enter the full URL here to make that happen. Photoshop doesn't actually embed this info into your image; instead, it stores the info in a separate HTML file that you can use to copy and paste into your own Web page.

> **NOTE** Assigning a hyperlink to part of your image is also called creating an *image map*. If you hear image maps mentioned at the water cooler, you'll be in the know!

• **Target.** This field determines where the hyperlink opens. For example, to make the hyperlink open the URL in another browser window, enter *_blank* into this field (complete with underscore). If you want the page to load within the same window, leave this field blank.

• **Message Text.** Almost every Web browser has a status bar at the bottom of the window to let folks know what's going on in the background. For example, when you type a URL into your browser's address bar and press Return (Enter on a PC), you'll see some kind of "loading" message. If you enter text in this field, you can send messages in the status bar (like a love note to your visitors: "Dude! Thanks for clicking!"). But since few folks ever look down that far, your efforts may be in vain.

• **Alt Tag.** Because some folks surf the Web with their graphics turned off, you can use this field to give your image an alternate text description. Visually impaired people using Web readers—special software that speaks the contents of Web pages—hear this text read to them. The text also pops up as a balloon or tooltip when visitors hover over it with their mouse.

• **Dimensions.** This info lets you know the width and height of your slice, along with its X and Y coordinates.

• **Slice Background Type.** If you've chosen "No Image for Slice Type", you can use this pop-up menu to give the selected cell a color. If your slice has any transparent pixels, this color will show through the transparent areas. Your choices include None, Matte (page 668), White, Black, and Other (which summons the almighty Color Picker).

Saving Slices

Once you've set all the options for your slices, it's time to save them to use on the Web (finally!). Use the File → "Save for Web & Devices" dialog box to set all those glorious file type, compression, and other options discussed earlier in this chapter. (If you use File → Save As, all your slice options will fly right out the window.)

On the left side of the "Save for Web & Devices" dialog box, click the Slice Select tool to grab each slice so you can apply different format and compression settings to each one (though if you're building a Web site prototype, choosing one file format for the whole thing probably works just fine). When you've finished, click OK and tell Photoshop where you want to save the files. If you've assigned URLs to the slices, be sure to choose "HTML and Images" from the Format pop-up menu at the bottom of the Save Optimized As dialog box as shown in Figure 17-14. (Be sure to change the Format menu back to Images the next time you use the Save As dialog box.)

Figure 17-14:
Left: If you've chosen to save both HTML and Images, it's a good idea to make a folder first—that way all your files are saved together in one place.

Right: Once the slices have been saved, you can open the folder and see your images, along with the HTML document containing code you can use in your very own Web page.

TIP An alternative to slicing and dicing the images yourself is to buy a plug-in called Site-Grinder, which will build your entire, fully functional Web site from your layered Photoshop document. See page 726 for details.

Protecting Your Images Online

Being able to share your images with the world via the Web is a glorious thing, but, in doing so, you risk having your images stolen (gasp!). It's frighteningly easy for thieves to snatch photos from your Web site to sell or use as their own, so it's important to take a few extra steps to protect them. You can deter these evil-doers in several different ways, including posting smaller versions of your image (page 231), embedding copyright info, adding watermarks, or using Zoomify (see the box on page 690). Read on for the scoop on each option.

Embedding Copyright Info

One of the simplest ways to protect your work is to embed your copyright and contact information into your image file by choosing File → Info. Sadly, it won't keep folks from stealing your image (heck, they won't even see it unless they choose File → Info themselves), but it *might* make them think twice about taking it if they do find a name attached to it. Alternatively, you can declare that the image is in the public domain, granting anyone and everyone a license to use it. See Figure 17-15 for more info.

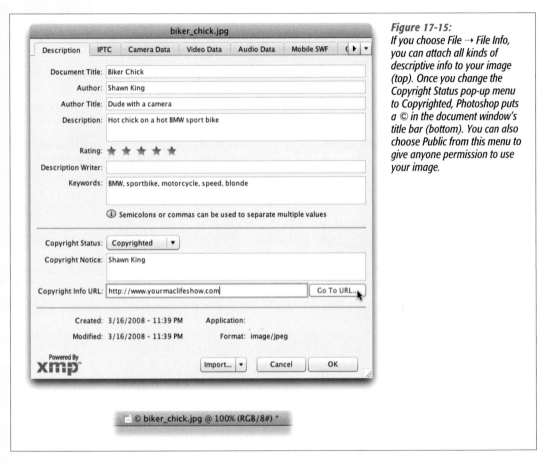

Figure 17-15:
If you choose File → File Info, you can attach all kinds of descriptive info to your image (top). Once you change the Copyright Status pop-up menu to Copyrighted, Photoshop puts a © in the document window's title bar (bottom). You can also choose Public from this menu to give anyone permission to use your image.

Watermarking Your Images

One of the best ways to protect your images online is to add a *watermark*—a recognizable image or pattern that you either place atop your image (as shown in Figure 17-16, bottom) or embed into it invisibly. A watermark is a great deterrent because would-be thieves will have one *heck* of a time trying to erase the watermark. You can add a watermark in Photoshop in a couple of ways:

- **Use custom shapes to add an opaque copyright symbol or logo.** The simplest way to watermark an image is to stick a big ol' copyright symbol (or your logo) on top of the image (this process is called *visual watermarking*). If you make the logo partially see-through, folks can still see the image but won't, presumably, steal it because of the huge graphic stamped on top of it.

- **Use the Digimarc filter.** This paid service creates a nearly invisible watermark by adding noise to your image (this process is called *digital watermarking*). It's not cheap, but you also get other features like image linking and tracking, online backups, and visual watermarking. Pricing depends on the number of images you use it on: $80 per year for 1,000; $200 for 3,000; and $500 for 5,000. You can learn all about it by visiting *www.digimarc.com/mypicturemarc*.

Since you've already plunked down good money on both Photoshop and this book, here's how to watermark your images *free* using the Custom Shape tool:

1. **Open the soon-to-be-watermarked image and grab the Custom Shape tool.**

   You can find the tool in the Shape toolset, or you can grab it by pressing Shift-U repeatedly (it looks like a rounded star).

2. **Set your foreground color chip to light gray.**

   If you set the foreground color now, you won't need to change the watermark's color later on. At the bottom of the Tools panel, click the foreground color chip, pick a light gray from the resulting Color Picker, and then click OK.

3. **Open the Custom Shape menu and choose the copyright symbol.**

   Up in the Options bar, click the down-pointing arrow to the right of the word Shape to open the menu of presets (see Figure 17-16, top). Scroll down until you see the copyright symbol (©), and then click once to select it.

4. **Draw the shape onto your image.**

   Mouse over to your image, click once where you want the shape to begin, and then Shift-drag diagonally to draw the shape. Holding Shift keeps the symbol perfectly square, instead of squished. When you let go of the mouse, Photoshop adds a Shape layer to the document. If you want to resize the shape, summon Free Transform by pressing ⌘-T (Ctrl+T on a PC).

5. **Add a "Bevel and Emboss" Layer style.**

   To give your watermark a little depth, you can tack on a Layer style. Click the tiny *fx* at the bottom of your Layers panel and choose "Bevel and Emboss" from the pop-up menu. If you want to fiddle with the settings, feel free (though they're probably fine the way they are). Click OK to close the Layers Styles dialog box.

   TIP   The shape's gray outline can make it darn difficult to see a preview of the Layer style you're about to apply. Luckily, you can hide the outline by pressing ⌘-H (Ctrl+H on a PC).

Figure 17-16:
*Top: The Custom
Shape tool makes
creating your own
watermark a snap.*

*Bottom: If you change
the blend mode to
Hard Light and lower
the opacity to about
50 percent, you can
create a nice,
professional-looking
watermark.*

6. **Grab the Type tool and type your name below the copyright symbol.**

Press T to fetch the Type tool, mouse over to your image, and then click where you want the text to start (Photoshop adds a Type layer to your document). You can type whatever you want though it's a good idea to include "Copyright" followed by the current year and your name or studio name. To change the font and type size, double-click the Type layer in the Layers panel and tweak the Options bar's settings (Arial Black is usually a good choice). Flip back to Chapter 14 for more on formatting text.

7. **Copy the Shape layer's style to the Type layer to make the text look similar to the copyright symbol.**

   You can copy a Layer style from one layer to another by Option-dragging (Alt-dragging on a PC) the style layer to the new layer (your cursor turns into a double-headed arrow when you drag). In this example, Option (Alt) click the layer named "Bevel and Emboss" and then drag it to the new layer and release your mouse button. If you don't press Option (Alt) *before* you start to drag, you'll *move* the Layer style instead (if that happens, just press ⌘-Z or Ctrl+Z to undo and then try it again).

8. **Change the Shape and Type layers' blend modes to Hard Light.**

   If you change the Shape and Type layers' blend modes, you can make your watermark see-through. Over in the Layers panel, select the Shape layer and change its blend mode to Hard Light using the pop-up menu at the top of the Layers panel (see page 267 for more on blend modes). Then select the Type layer and do the same thing. Unfortunately you can't select both layers and change their blend modes at the same time, so you have to change each one separately.

9. **Lower the Shape and Type layers' opacity to 50 percent.**

   To keep your watermark from overpowering the image, you can lower its opacity to 50 percent using the slider at the top of the Layers panel. You can't adjust the opacity of two layers at a time; once again you have to adjust each one separately.

   TIP You can save a step by merging the Shape and Type layers *before* you change their blend modes and opacity. Just Shift-click to select both layers and then press ⌘-E (Ctrl+E on a PC). The only downside is that you can't edit your text once the layers are merged.

10. **Save the file and upload it to the Web.**

    Enjoy peace of mind knowing that it'd take someone *weeks* to clone away your watermark.

Protecting your images takes a bit of effort, but it's well worth it. In fact, watermarking is exactly the type of thing you should record as an action. Just follow the instructions in Chapter 18 for creating a new action (page 699) and then repeat the steps in this list. You can even include the bit about embedding copyright info in your file (page 686). Once you've created the action, you can run it on a whole folder of files and save yourself tons of time!

Building Online Photo Galleries

Once you've massaged and tweaked your images to perfection, why not have Photoshop prepare a ready-for-the-Web photo gallery, complete with thumbnails and enlargements, like the one shown in Figure 17-17? (Actually, *Bridge* has done all the work using the new Adobe Output Module, but that doesn't make it any less cool.)

Zoomify Your Enlargements

It can be dangerous to post a full-sized image on the Web—you're practically giving thieves permission to steal it. But if you're a photographer and you want folks to see all the intricate details of your work, you can protect your images by using a Photoshop feature called Zoomify.

Instead of posting your image as one high-quality piece, Zoomify chops it into pieces and displays it in a Flash-based window with controls that visitors can use to zoom in on and move around within your image. (People who view your image need to have Flash installed on their computers, but if they don't, their browser should prompt them to get it.) Instead of seeing the whole thing at the enlarged size, they see only one piece at a time, so they can't grab it by taking a screen shot or downloading the whole image.

To use Zoomify, follow these steps:

1. Adjust the image's size using the techniques discussed in Chapter 6. This step is optional; if you want to upload a full-size image from your camera, feel free (though it won't work on files in Raw format).

2. Choose File → Export → Zoomify.

3. In the Zoomify Export dialog box, use the Output Location section to choose where you want to save the file and give it a name.

4. In the Image Tile Options section, choose an image quality. Use the Quality text box, pop-up menu, or slider to set the quality of your image's individual pieces. In the background, Zoomify chops up your image into a bunch of pieces that it reassembles when your visitor chooses to look at that area. Leave the Optimize Tables checkbox turned on so Photoshop optimizes the compression tables for each tile.

5. Enter a width and height (in pixels) for the Zoomify window to determine how large it is in your visitor's Web browser window.

6. Click OK when you've finished; Zoomify creates a block of code that you can paste into your Web page. If you leave the "Open In Web Browser" checkbox turned on, Photoshop opens your Web browser to show you what your Zoomify window will look like.

Now, just open the HTML document that Zoomify made, copy and paste the code into your Web page, and then upload the page and image pieces that Zoomify created to your server. After that, folks who look at your image online can see all its exquisite details but can't swipe it and claim it as their own.

NOTE In previous versions of Photoshop, you could create a gallery by choosing File → Automate → Web Gallery, but in CS4 that feature has been moved to the new Adobe Output Module in Bridge (and you get a lot more options than before). But if you're nostalgic and you like the old Web Gallery better, you can download it from *www.adobe.com* or grab it from Photoshop CS3 if you've got that version. On your hard drive, go to the Adobe Photoshop CS3 folder and open Plug-Ins → Automate and find the *WebContactSheetII.plugin* file. Then drag the file into the same folder in the Photoshop CS4 application folder. You have to restart Photoshop, but the Web Gallery should work…as terribly as it used to!

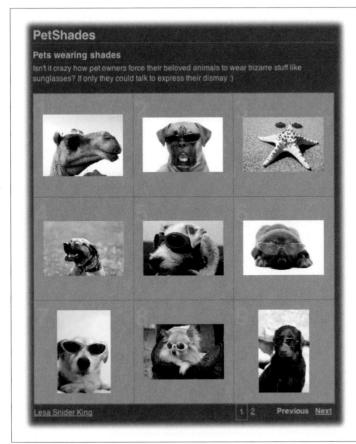

Figure 17-17:
Bridge offers a handful of beautiful photo gallery templates built like the one shown here. These templates let you plug in your own photos and, in return, you get ready-to-use HTML pages that you can upload to your own Web site.

Here's how to create a Web gallery using Bridge's new Adobe Output Module:

1. **Place the images in a single folder.**

   It's a lot easier to grab all the images you want to post online if you stick them in a folder first.

2. **Fire up Adobe Bridge.**

   You'll learn tons about Bridge in Appendix C. For now, launch it by pressing the Bridge icon in the Application bar at the top left of the Photoshop window (it's a red square with "Br" in the center).

3. **On the left side of the Bridge window, use the Folders panel to navigate to your images.**

   Your images appear at the bottom of the Bridge window in the Content panel.

4. **In the Content panel, arrange your images in the order you want them to appear in the gallery.**

   A vertical blue line appears as you drag an image around. When you get it in the right place, just let go of your mouse button.

5. **Select the images for your gallery.**

   If you've changed your mind about including only one or two images, here's your chance to select the photos you want to place in the gallery. You can ⌘-click (Ctrl-click on a PC) to select just a few or press ⌘-A (Ctr+A) to select them all.

6. **At the top of the Bridge window, click the Output button (which looks like a piece of paper with a folded corner) and choose "Output to Web or PDF" as shown in Figure 17-18, top.**

   On the right side of the Bridge window, Bridge opens the Output panel. You can also open this panel by clicking the word Output at the top of the Bridge window (which switches you to the Output workspace).

7. **Click the Web Gallery button at the top of the Output panel.**

   Bridge displays all kinds of settings that let you customize how your Web gallery looks.

8. **In the Options panel, choose HTML Gallery from the Template pop-up menu.**

   There aren't very many templates to choose from, but for a basic photo gallery, this one is tough to beat (as shown in Figure 17-17).

9. **In the Site Info section, add a title, caption, and description.**

   You can add all sorts of information in the Output panel, including a title, caption, and description of your gallery, as well as your name, email address, and copyright info. These extra tidbits appear at the top and bottom of your Web page (respectively), as shown in Figure 17-17.

10. **Scroll down to the Options panel's Color Palette section and edit the background, text, and link colors.**

    To change your gallery's colors, just click the little color swatch and choose something else from the Color Picker.

11. **In the Appearance section, set the number of columns and rows, and pick a preview size.**

    Unless you change these settings, your gallery has three rows and columns, and the previews are medium sized. If it needs to, Bridge builds more pages to accommodate your images.

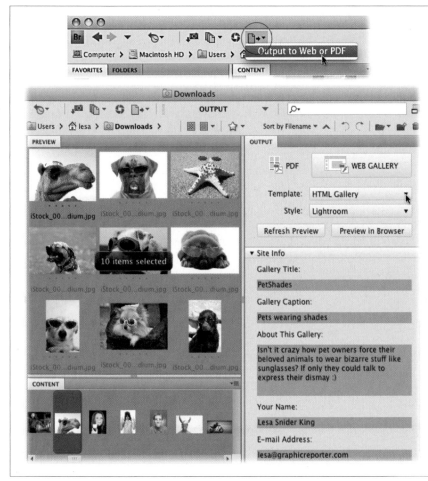

Figure 17-18:
Top: Bridge CS4 (which comes with Photoshop) has a new Output menu (circled) that lets you create a Web gallery or PDF page.

Bottom: When you choose Web Gallery, Bridge adds all kinds of options to the Output panel that you can use to customize the look of your gallery. Unfortunately, there's no way to save these changes so you can use them again later (bummer!). Thankfully, Bridge remembers the last Web Gallery settings you used.

12. Back near the top of the Output panel, click the Refresh Preview button and then, in the middle of the Bridge window, click the Content Preview tab to see a preview of your Web Gallery within Bridge.

If you'd rather see your Web Gallery in a real Web browser, click the "Preview in Browser" button instead. Bridge works away and eventually displays your gallery in your Web browser. Depending on the number of images in your gallery, this process may take a while.

13. If everything looks good, head back to Bridge (if necessary) and scroll down to the Create Gallery section of the Output panel to tell Bridge whether to save the gallery to your hard drive or upload it to the Web. (If you want to make changes in Bridge, scroll to the appropriate Output panel section and tweak the settings.)

At the bottom of the Output panel, you can give your gallery a name and save it to your hard drive or upload it to your Web server. If you choose to upload it, you need to enter your Web site's FTP (file transfer protocol) settings, along with your login and password.

14. Click Save if the gallery is headed for your hard drive or Upload if it's bound for the Web.

The only downside to using Bridge to make photo galleries is that you have to keep clicking the Refresh Preview to update the Content Preview panel within Bridge, and if you decide to preview the gallery in a real Web browser, Bridge takes awhile to make it happen. Also, you can't save changes to your templates (though Bridge does remember the last settings you used) or add your own. Hopefully, Adobe will improve all those features in the next version of Bridge.

Working Smarter with Actions

It's fun to spend hours playing and working in Photoshop, but once you've used the program for a while, you'll start to notice that you repeat the same steps over and over on most of your images. At first, the repetition probably won't bother you—it's actually good while you're learning—but when a deadline approaches and the boss is eyeing you impatiently, you need a way to speed things up.

Luckily, Photoshop includes all manner of automated helpers (some of which you've already learned about), including:

- The Image Processor script, which resizes images and changes their formats (page 238).

- The "Layer Comps to Files" script, which exports images you can turn into a PDF file (page 101).

- Automated photo stitching with Photomerge (page 286).

- Automated aligning and blending of layers with the Auto-Align and Auto-Blend Layers commands (Chapter 7, beginning on page 283).

- The new Adobe Output Module, which can build Web galleries (page 689), rename numerous files at once, and build Picture Packages and Contact Sheets (both discussed in Appendix C).

One of the best timesavers of all, however, is *actions*—an all-purpose, amazingly customizable system for automating mundane tasks like adding or duplicating layers, running filters with specific settings, and so on. You can use actions to record nearly every keystroke and menu choice you make and then play them back on another image or a whole *folder* of images. Because Photoshop doesn't make you waste time pressing keys or clicking a mouse when you're running actions, it can blast through them at warp speed. Just imagine how much time you'll save!

This chapter shows you how to use the actions that come with Photoshop and how to create, edit, and save your own. You'll also learn how to create drag-and-drop actions called *droplets*—icons you can drop other files on to trigger an action—as well as where to find and how to install actions made by other folks. By the time you're finished reading, you'll be working ten times smarter (and faster) instead of harder.

The Actions Panel

Actions let you record, play, and edit your keystrokes using the Actions panel (Figure 18-1). You can open it by clicking its icon in the panel dock on the right side of your screen (it looks like the triangular play button on a DVD player) or by choosing Window → Actions.

TIP   You can also open the Actions panel by pressing Option-F9 (Alt+F9 on a PC).

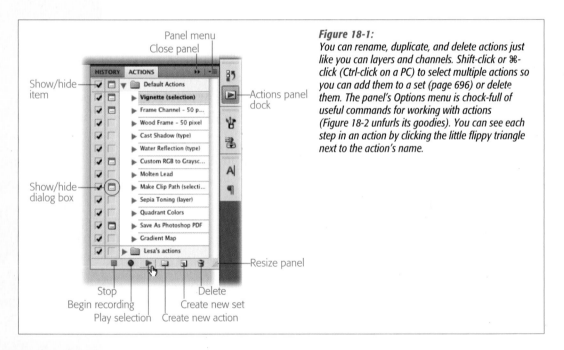

Figure 18-1:
You can rename, duplicate, and delete actions just like you can layers and channels. Shift-click or ⌘-click (Ctrl-click on a PC) to select multiple actions so you can add them to a set (page 696) or delete them. The panel's Options menu is chock-full of useful commands for working with actions (Figure 18-2 unfurls its goodies). You can see each step in an action by clicking the little flippy triangle next to the action's name.

TIP   Photoshop includes a special workspace (page 15) designed for creating and using actions. To switch to that workspace, choose Window → Workspace → Automation.

The controls in the Actions panel are pretty straightforward. The Stop, Record, and Play buttons do what you'd expect: They stop, record, and play actions. The "Create new set" button at the bottom of the panel (it looks like a folder) lets you store actions in a set just like you can store layers in a group (page 98). You can create a brand-new action by clicking the "Create new action" button and duplicate an action by dragging it atop that same button or by Option-dragging (Alt-dragging on a PC) it up or down in the panel. Duplicating an action comes in handy when you want to run the same filter more than once within an action or when you want to edit a copy of an action to make it do something slightly different (which is faster than rerecording the action from scratch).

The Actions panel has three unlabeled columns that let you:

- **Turn steps on or off.** The first column lets you turn individual steps in an action on or off via a checkbox next to each step. This option is useful if you've made a fairly complex action and only want to run, say, half of it. For example, if you created an action that stamps all visible layers (page 95), sharpens your image (Chapter 11), and then saves it as a TIFF file (page 46), you can turn off the "save" step and stop at sharpening instead. To turn off a step, click the checkmark to the left of its name. To turn off *all* the steps in an action or all the actions in a set, click the checkmark to the left of the action's or set's name. To turn off all steps *except* the one you've selected, Option-click (Alt-click on a PC) its checkmark.

  TIP In the Actions panel, a *black* checkmark next to an action's name means Photoshop will run all the steps in that action. A *red* checkmark means the action will stop at some point and wait for you perform another task like painting or drawing on an image or entering a value like the Radius for a feather effect.

- **Turn dialog boxes on or off.** The next column is for turning dialog boxes associated with the action's steps on or off. When you're creating an action, you can design it so that, at a certain point, it stops and opens a dialog box that prompts you to enter settings like feather amount, filter values, and so on. If the action needs your input, you see a little square with three dots in this column next to the action's name (it's supposed to look like a tiny dialog box); if the action doesn't need your input, the column is empty. If you'd rather not be bothered by dialog boxes, you can turn them off by clicking the square with the dots in it to make Photoshop use the settings you entered when you originally recorded the action. Turning dialog boxes on and off is handy when you're using Photoshop's built-in actions because entering different values changes the action's effect on your image. For example, you can change the feather setting in the Vignette action to create a softer edge.

  TIP A tiny *black* dialog box icon to the left of the action's name means that *all* the steps in that action need your input. A tiny *red* dialog box icon means that some do actions and some don't.

• **Expand or collapse an action.** The third column in the Actions panel lists each action's name and keyboard shortcut (if you've assigned one). If you want to see the individual steps within an action, you can expand the action by clicking the little flippy triangle to the left of its name—handy when you want to turn off individual steps as explained earlier or explore the inner workings of a built-in action.

TIP To expand or collapse all the actions in a set or all the steps in an action, Option-click (Alt-click on a PC) the action or step's flippy triangle.

Straight from the factory, Photoshop displays your actions as a list (see Figure 18-1) though you can make it display them as clickable buttons instead (see Figure 18-2). Just open the Actions panel menu and choose Button Mode. Now, instead of running an action and then pressing the play button, you can trigger the action by clicking its button. Unless you're creating or editing actions, this is the way to roll.

Figure 18-2:
One drawback to using Button mode is that it doesn't let you edit actions or create new ones. You also can't turn individual steps in an action on or off. Bummer!

Using Actions

Photoshop comes loaded with dozens of built-in actions, though only a smidgeon of them appear in the main part of Actions panel. Seven more sets of built-in actions are tucked away in the panel's menu (shown in Figure 18-2): Commands, Frames, Image Effects, Production, Text Effects, Textures, and Video Actions.

(To load one of these additional sets, simply select it from the menu to make Photoshop add it to the panel's main list.) Each set includes several actions that you can use as is or edit if you want to.

For example, if you think the Spatter Frame action (part of the Frames set) is boring with its 15-pixel spray radius, you can bump it up to 25 pixels instead. (Editing actions is discussed later in this chapter.) You can also duplicate that particular step to make the Spatter filter run twice.

> **TIP** An easy way to duplicate an action you want to edit is to Option-drag (Alt-drag on a PC) it to a different set.

To use one of the program's built-in actions, follow these steps:

1. **Open an image.**

   With most actions you simply need to open the image and you're ready to invoke the action magic. (You don't even have to unlock the Background layer.)

2. **If necessary, select the part of your image you want to work with.**

   Occasionally, you have to make a selection before you use some of the built-in actions (for instance, the ones with "selection" in parentheses after their names like "Vignette (selection)" [see Figure 18-3]).

3. **Select an action.**

   Over in your Actions panel, click an action to select it.

   > **NOTE** If you're in Button mode (page 698), simply clicking an action's name triggers that action, so you can skip this step.

4. **Click the Play button.**

   Click the little play button at the bottom of the Actions panel to run the action. Before you can blink, Photoshop is finished and dusting off its hands. If Photoshop displays a dialog box that it requires your input, the action pauses while you enter settings; once you click OK, it continues on its merry way.

   > **TIP** To play just one step of an action—without playing any of the steps that follow—simply double-click that step in the Actions panel. (You have to click the flippy triangle next to the action's name to see its steps.) You can also select the step in the Actions panel and then ⌘-click (Ctrl-click on a PC) the play button.

Creating Actions

When you're trying to decide which kind of action to record, start by thinking of any repetitive tasks you often perform. For example, back in Chapter 4 you learned that a simple one-pixel black border adds a classy touch to an image headed for a Web site, newspaper, or newsletter (page 168). If you add those borders regularly, that task is a great candidate for an action.

Figure 18-3:
Top: Photoshop's built-in actions include "Vignette (selection)". To use it, you first have to create a selection.

Bottom: Another useful built-in action adds a sepia tone to your image, as shown here. In both cases, the action created all the layers shown here except for the original Background layer (which shows you what the original images looked like).

> **TIP** Before you record your first action, it's a good idea to create a new *set* (group) for it to live in (you can also drag new actions into an existing set). There's no limit to how many sets you can make or how many actions you can add to each one. If you forget to make a set before you record an action, you can drag and drop the action into a set later. You can also move actions between sets, but they can only live in one set at a time.

Here's how to create an action that places a black border around your image:

1. **Open an image.**

   To record the steps, you have to perform them, so you need to open an image to play with.

2. **Open your Actions panel and create a new set.**

   Open the Actions panel using one of the methods described on page 696 and then click the folder icon at the bottom of the panel. In the resulting dialog box, enter a name for your set (see Figure 18-4) and then click OK.

   > **TIP** For reasons known only to Adobe, you can't assign F1 as a shortcut key on a PC.

WORKAROUND WORKSHOP

Different Files, Different Results

When you're recording actions, it's important to realize that not only is Photoshop recording every step *exactly* as you perform it, it's also memorizing info about your document. It remembers stuff like file size, color mode, layer names, and foreground color chip.

For that reason, if you try to run an action on a file that's in a different color mode (page 40) or a different size than the original, you may encounter unexpected results. For example, if you create an action that applies a 20-pixel feather to a selection in a 320 × 240 pixel image and then run it on a 3,888 × 2,492 pixel image, you won't get the same results. (In fact, you'll barely see the feather, if at all.) Since the document dimensions of those two images differ so much, you have to create two separate actions: One for the smaller file and one with a higher feather amount for the bigger file.

When you use certain tools while you're creating actions, Photoshop also records the tool's position within the image by snagging coordinates from your vertical and horizontal rulers (page 64). Among these tools are Marquee, Slice, Gradient, Magic Wand, Lasso, Shape, Path, Eyedropper, and Notes. If you run an action involving these tools on files of varying size, you'll run into problems. For example, if you record an action that includes drawing an Elliptical Marquee in the center of a document and then run that action on a different-sized file, the document's center won't be in the same place. The fix is to change the unit of measurement for your rulers to *percentages* (page 33) before you record the action. That way, Photoshop records your cursor's location as a *relative* position instead of an absolute one.

Figure 18-4:
Top: Keep your Actions panel organized by storing your actions in sets. This also lets you keep the actions you've made (or downloaded; see page 709) separate from Photoshop's built-in actions.

Bottom: In the New Action dialog box, give your action a name and assign it a keyboard shortcut for easy access. The shortcut can be a function key (the F-keys at the top of your keyboard) and, if you want, a modifier key (Shift or ⌘ [Ctrl or Alt on a PC]) to give you even more options. By combining F-keys and modifiers, you can create as many as 60 custom shortcuts for your actions (depending on the size of your keyboard).

3. Click the "Create new action" button.

The new action button looks like a piece of paper with a folded corner (just like the "Create new layer" and "Create new channel" buttons). In the resulting dialog box, give your action a short but meaningful name, like *Black border*. You can also assign it a function-key shortcut and a color (you can see these colors only when you're in Button mode [page 698], but they're super handy). When everything looks good, click Record to close the dialog box and start recording your action.

NOTE   You can edit these settings after you've recorded the action by selecting the action and then choosing Action Options from the Actions panel menu or by double-clicking the action set or action name.

4. **Perform the steps you want to record.**

Once you click Record, the circle button at the bottom of the Actions panel turns red to let you know Photoshop is recording nearly every keystroke and mouse click you make (it doesn't record some things like brushstrokes). To record the border action, consider whether you'll always start out with a locked Background layer. If so, start by double-clicking the Background to make it editable. If not, click the square Stop button at the bottom of the Actions panel, double-click the Background layer to unlock it *before* you start recording your action, and then click the Record button again.

Next, press ⌘-A (Ctrl+A on a PC) to select your whole image and then head up to the Edit menu and choose Stroke. Be sure to enter a pixel value even if the correct pixel value is already there—you never know what you might change in the Stroke dialog box between now and when you run the action. (Since Photoshop's settings are sticky [page 14] you need to make sure your action includes resetting anything that may have changed in any dialog boxes you open.) Click the Inside radio button for Location (even if it's already set to Inside) and then choose Black from the Use pop-up menu (even if it's already selected).

TIP   If you record a File → Save As command, don't enter a name for the document. If you do, Photoshop will use that exact file name every time you run the action, no matter what your original document was named. Instead, use the Save As dialog box to navigate to another folder on your hard drive and let Photoshop save the edited document *there*, with its original filename. That step tells Photoshop to save the edited version of your image in the folder you selected without renaming the file.

5. **Click Stop.**

Once you've finished recording, click the Stop button at the bottom of the Actions panel (it turns black) or press the Escape key.

6. **Choose File → Revert and test your action on the open image.**

To make sure your action works, return your image to its original state, select the new action, and then click the play button. (Might as well give her a spin while she's fresh!) If you run into problems, you can delete the action by dragging it to the trash can icon at the bottom of the panel and have another go at it or edit the action using the techniques discussed later in this chapter.

Give yourself a big pat on the back for successfully recording your first action.

TIP   If you make a mistake while you're recording an action, just click the Stop button. Delete the bad steps by dragging them to the trash can icon and then choose Edit → Step Backward until you get back to the last good step. Then, click the Record button and continue.

Action Errors

Recording actions is usually a trial-and-error operation—it can be a bit challenging to get them just right. If Photoshop encounters *any* condition that varies from what you recorded, it displays an error dialog box.

One of the most common errors is Layer Unavailable because most folks don't realize that Photoshop captures *layer names* when you record an action. For instance, if you start an action by double-clicking the Background layer to make it editable, Photoshop searches for a layer named Background when you run that action. If it doesn't find it, you'll be greeted with an error dialog box that says the object "layer Background" is unavailable. At that point

you can either continue running the action (click Continue) or stop right there (click Stop). If you've chosen to proceed and Photoshop *can* finish out the steps, it will. If it can't, you get (surprise!) another error dialog box expressing Photoshop's regret.

Admittedly, having to click Continue once in awhile is no biggie, but it brings your action to a screeching halt. To cut down on this type of error, use keyboard shortcuts to select layers. That way Photoshop records the *shortcuts* instead of specific layer names. See the box on page 77 for a huge list of shortcuts for selecting and moving layers.

Running Actions on a Folder

To really make actions work for you, you can run them on more than one file (this technique is called *batch processing* or *batching*). It takes an extra step or two, but it's worth it. For example, remember the black-border action you created in the previous section? You can run it on all your open files or on a folder of files instead of opening each one individually. Just imagine how much time you could save!

Here's how to run an action on more than one file:

1. **Open the files or place them in a folder.**

   Photoshop's Batch command works on all open files or a whole folder (unless you're using Bridge, as noted in step 3 below), so depending on how many files you want to work on, you'll probably want to stick 'em in a folder first.

2. **Choose File → Automate → Batch.**

   In the resulting dialog box (Figure 18-5), choose the action you want to run from the Action menu.

   TIP   You can also record actions that trigger other actions, which is *extremely* helpful when you're batch processing. Instead of running the actions on the files one after another, you can simply run the action that triggers the rest. This process is serious action voodoo and not recommended for beginners.

3. **Select source files or folders to process.**

   Use the Source pop-up menu to tell Photoshop whether to run the action on all open files or on a folder. If you pick Folder, click the Choose button and navigate to the folder with your images. You can also choose Import to snatch files

Figure 18-5:
To reap the full reward of using actions, use this dialog box to run them on multiple files (batches). You can choose to process files in folders within a master folder (turn on "Include All Subfolders"), which is especially handy if you use nested folders to organize your images.

parked in your scanner or in an attached digital camera. If you've selected a few files in Adobe Bridge (see Appendix C), you can run the action on those files by selecting Bridge.

4. **Adjust other settings if needed.**

Turn on the "Override Action 'Open' Commands" checkbox if you have a step in your action that opens a file. That way, Photoshop opens the files you've selected in the Source menu instead of hunting for the filename recorded in the action. Leave this checkbox off if you recorded the action to open a *specific* file that's necessary for the action to work properly like when you're using Match Color to snatch the color from one image and apply it to others (see page 326).

If you've chosen Folder as a source and the folder you want to work with contains *other* folders of images that you want Photoshop to process, turn on Include All Subfolders.

If you want to bypass any options associated with the Open dialog box, turn on the Suppress File Open Options Dialogs checkbox. This hides the options in Photoshop's Open dialog box so you can open a group of images without seeing the Open dialog box for each one (handy if you batch process Camera Raw images from your digital camera).

Finally, turn on the Suppress Color Profile Warnings checkbox if you want Photoshop to always use its own color profile (page 617) instead of asking you if it's okay.

5. **Tell Photoshop where you want to save the processed files.**

From the Destination pop-up menu, you can choose None to have Photoshop leave your files open *without* saving them (not a good idea if you're running the action on hundreds of files). Choose "Save and Close" to overwrite the originals and close the file.

If you want to preserve your originals, choose Folder and then click the Choose button to tell Photoshop where it should save the new files.

If you've got any "Save As" steps in your action, turn on the "Override Action 'Save As' Commands" checkbox and Photoshop uses the settings you've specified in this dialog box. If you don't turn on this checkbox, Photoshop saves your images twice: once where you specified in your original action and a second time in the location you set when you began batch processing.

6. **If you want to rename the resulting files, enter a naming scheme in the File Naming section.**

You can name the new files anything you want. Choose "DocumentName" from the first pop-up menu to have Photoshop keep the original filename, or enter something else in the field. You can also rename files with the current date (in several formats), using an alphabetical code or numeric serial number, and so on. Keep the second field in the same row set to "extension" so you don't encounter any problems with incompatible file formats down the road.

7. **Turn on the appropriate Compatibility checkbox(es) based on where the files are headed.**

If you know your images will be opened or stored on a computer that runs a different operating system, be sure to turn on the checkboxes for each system your file is likely to end up on. For example, if you're using a Mac and your images are destined for a Unix-based Web server or a Windows-based file server, check Mac and Unix or Windows. It's OK to check all three compatibility formats.

8. **Choose an error-handling method from the Error pop-up menu.**

Last but not least, tell Photoshop what to do if it encounters an error while it's running the action. Your options are Stop For Errors and "Log Errors to File". If you choose the latter, Photoshop writes down all the errors in a text file and continues to process your images; click the Save As button below this pop-up menu to tell the program where you want it to save that text file.

9. **Click OK to run the action.**

Sit back in your chair and smile smugly as Photoshop does all the work for you (and cross your fingers that you don't get any errors!).

Managing Actions

If you don't get your action quite right the first time (which is perfectly normal when you're first starting out), you can go back and edit it though, honestly, it's usually easier to start over from scratch. That said, a few commands in the Actions panel menu can help you get misbehaving actions working:

- **Record Again.** When you choose this option, Photoshop runs through all the steps in the action and opens all the dialog boxes associated with it so you can adjust their settings.

- **Insert Menu Item.** For some unknown reason, you can't record any items in the View and Window menus when you're creating an action, but you can insert them—or any other menu item—using this command, either while you record the action or after. Simply select the step directly above where you want the menu item to go, or, if you want to insert the menu item at the end of the action, select the action's name. Then choose Insert Menu Item from the Actions panel menu and, when the Insert Menu Item dialog box appears, select the item and then click OK. If the menu item pops open a dialog box, Photoshop won't record any settings, so you'll have to enter them when you run the action.

  There's no way that you or anyone else running an action can turn off a dialog box that you've added using the Insert Menu Item command (though you can turn off *other* action dialog boxes—see page 696), so it's a good way to *force* whoever is running the action to enter a particular menu's settings. You can use this command to insert any menu item you want, even ones like a feather radius that you can record in an action.

- **Insert Stop.** Use this command to pause the action so you can do something that you can't record, like paint with the Brush tool, draw with the Pen tool, and so on. (You can even include a dialog box that says what to do next, like "Use the Brush tool to paint a happy face now". After you've done what you need to do, click the Play button in the Actions panel to run the rest of the action's steps.) To add a stop after a particular step, select the step in the Actions panel and then choose Insert Stop (see Figure 18-6).

- **Insert Path.** Photoshop can't record the act of drawing a path, but you can use this command to insert a path you've already drawn. Just open the Paths panel (page 506), select the one you want, and then choose this command.

- **Action Options.** This command opens the Action Options dialog box so you can edit the action's name, keyboard shortcut, and color (this works on custom actions as well as built-in ones). You can also open this dialog box by Option-double-clicking (Alt+double-clicking on a PC) the action or rename an action by double-clicking its name in the Actions panel.

- **Playback Options.** If you can't figure out where an action has gone wrong, you can make Photoshop play the action more slowly by selecting this command. In the resulting dialog box, you can choose Accelerated (normal speed), Step By

Figure 18-6:
Top: When you insert a stop into an action, you can include instructions for the person who's running the action. The message appears when that person triggers the stop point in the action (you can enter any message you want). If you want to let folks continue with the action after they've preformed the step described by the message, turn on the Allow Continue checkbox.

Bottom: Here's what you see when you run the action and hit the stop point. Since a continue button wasn't allowed, your only choice is to click Stop. After you've performed the part that couldn't be recorded, click the Play button in the Actions panel to finish the action.

Step (Photoshop completes each step and refreshes the screen before going to the next step), or "Pause For _ _ Seconds" (Photoshop pauses between each step for the number of seconds you specify).

Editing Actions

If you want to rearrange the actions in your Actions panel, just drag an action to a lower or higher position in the panel. When you see a highlighted line where you want it to go, release your mouse button. Rearranging actions is helpful when you want to keep certain actions together so they're easier to spot (handy when you're in Button mode). You can also drag and drop steps *within* an action to rearrange them. To change an action's settings (such as the feather amount), just double-click the relevant step while an image is open, enter a new amount in the resulting dialog box, and then click OK.

> **NOTE**   Clicking OK actually runs the command associated with the dialog box (Feather, for example), but you can always undo it by pressing ⌘-Z (Ctrl+Z on a PC). Photoshop still remembers the new settings you entered.

You can also add steps to an action—just select the step that comes *before* the one you want to add and click the record button. Perform the new steps you want to add, and then click the Stop button. Photoshop adds the new steps below the one you first selected.

If you want to get rid of a step, action, or set of actions, just select what you want to delete and drag it onto the trash can icon at the bottom of the Actions panel. You can also select items and then Option-click (Alt-click on a PC) the Delete button (this method bypasses the "Are you sure?" dialog box). To do a *thorough* spring cleaning of your Actions panel, choose Clear All Actions from the Actions panel menu and, when Photoshop asks if you *really* want to delete everything (including Photoshop's Default Actions set), click OK.

TIP If you want to get Photoshop's Default Actions set back after you use the Clear All Actions option, just choose Reset Actions from the Actions panel menu.

Creating Droplets

Droplets are actions that you trigger by dragging and dropping files onto a special icon. As self-contained mini-applications, they can live outside Photoshop on your desktop, in your Dock (or taskbar on a PC), or on someone else's computer.

It's easy to create a droplet from an action. Just follow these steps:

1. **Over in the Actions panel, select an action.**

   You can't put the cart before the horse! To make a droplet, you've got to record the action first.

2. **Choose File → Automate → Create Droplet.**

   The resulting dialog box looks like the Batch dialog box shown in Figure 18-5. Click the Choose button at the top to tell Photoshop where to save your droplet and then set the other options according to the advice on page 709.

3. **Click OK when you're finished.**

   Your droplet (which looks like the one shown in Figure 18-7, top) appears wherever you specified.

Figure 18-7:
Top: Your droplet looks like a big, fat blue arrow.

Bottom: To use a droplet, drag and drop a file or folder on top of its icon. If Photoshop isn't currently running, it launches automatically.

Sharing Actions

When it comes to actions, lots of folks don't mind sharing—there are tons of actions floating around on the Web. Most are free, but some require you to register with a particular Web site, and some folks make you pay for the more useful and creative ones. Sharing actions is pretty easy; the only requirement is that you save your actions as a set (page 696) and then upload them to a Web site. That's what this section is all about.

Sharing Droplets

I want to send my extra special Mac droplet to a Windows computer. Is that legal?

Sure! It's within your Photoshop User Bill of Rights to share droplets between computers with different operating systems; however, the droplet won't work unless you know these secrets:

- Save the droplet with a *.exe* extension, which tells a Windows computer that it's an executable file—in other words, a program you can run (this extension isn't necessary on a Mac).

- If you created the droplet on a Windows computer and want to move it to a Mac, drag it onto the Photoshop CS4 icon to make Photoshop update it so it works on the Mac.

- File name references aren't supported between operating systems, so if your action includes an Open or Save As step that references a specific file, the action pauses and demands the filename from the poor soul who's using the droplet. If that happens to you, find and select the file Photoshop is asking for so the droplet can work just like it did on the computer it came from.

Installing Actions

One of the best action resources is the Adobe Studio Exchange Web site (*www.adobe.com/exchange*). Others include *www.atncentral.com*, *www.panosfx.com*, and *www.actionfx.com*. (These sites are also great resources for brushes, textures, and so on.) Most of these sites arrange their goodies by program, so you'll have to choose Photoshop and then Actions. Downloading and analyzing actions made by other folks can help you learn what's possible. That said, actions that are short and sweet—expand canvas, add new layer and fill it with white, and so on—can be even more useful than particularly complex ones because you'll use them more often.

Here's how to install somebody else's action:

1. **Download the action or set to your computer.**

   What you're actually downloading is an ATN file. Save it somewhere that you'll remember (like on your desktop).

2. **Drag and drop the action into the Photoshop program window as shown in Figure 18-8.**

   You can also load a new action by choosing Load Action from the Actions panel menu. Either way, it appears in your Actions panel.

3. **Select the action and give it a spin.**

   Test drive your new action by opening an image, selecting the action, and then pressing the Play button. That's the only way to find out whether it's lame-o.

Saving Your Actions

Photoshop temporarily stores the actions you create in a special spot on your hard drive. If you reinstall or upgrade the program, there's a darn good chance your

Figure 18-8:
You can quickly install an action by dragging and dropping the ATN file into the Photoshop window. You won't see anything happen, but it shows up in your Actions panel instantly.

actions will get zapped in the process. If you've grown fond of them, you need to save them so you can back them up *outside* the Photoshop application folder. That way you can reload them if they accidentally get deleted. As a bonus, once you save your actions you can share them with others by uploading them to sites like Adobe Studio Exchange, discussed in the previous section.

Here's what you need to do:

1. **In the Actions panel, select an action set.**

   You can save only actions that are part of a set—you can't save individual actions.

2. **Choose Save Actions from the Actions panel options menu.**

   In the resulting dialog box, Photoshop prompts you to save the file in the Presets folder though you can put it anywhere you want. To guard against losing your actions when you reinstall or upgrade Photoshop, save them somewhere else. No matter where you save them, if you add or edit the set later, be sure to pick the same spot or you'll end up with multiple versions of the action set.

3. **Click Save.**

   Photoshop creates an ATN file that you can move between computers, back up to an external hard drive, or share with the world via the Web.

   TIP   On the Mac, Photoshop saves your actions in *Home/Library/Application Support/Adobe/ Adobe Photoshop CS4/Presets/Actions*. On a Windows computer, it saves them in *C:\Documents and Settings\[your user name]\Application Data\Adobe\Adobe Photoshop CS4 Settings\Presets\ Actions.* (You can also use the Windows "Save in" pop-up menu in the Save dialog box to see where Photoshop hides your actions.)

Beyond Photoshop: Plug-Ins

With enough patience, practice, and keyboard shortcuts burned into your brain, you can get smokin' fast in Photoshop. But you'll never be as fast as a computer. As you've learned, some things—like creating complex selections, correcting colors, extensive skin retouching, and so on—are darned difficult, so they're going to take you a long time no matter how fast you get.

That's where plug-ins come in handy. Think of them as helper programs that run inside Photoshop (though a few run outside Photoshop, too) and let you do the hard stuff faster. You can get plug-ins from all kinds of Web sites, and they range from free to pricey. The really good ones give you amazing results in seconds, rather than the hours it would take to do the same thing yourself (if you can do it at all). Plus, the newer ones do their thing on a separate layer and can run as Smart Filters (page 588), so you don't even have to duplicate your original layer first. Nice.

In this chapter, you'll learn how to add and remove these little jewels, as well as how to store them somewhere other than your Photoshop CS4 folder (it's safer that way). You'll also be introduced to some of the most amazing plug-ins on the market today that will run on your Mac or PC.

Adding and Removing Plug-Ins

To install a plug-in on a Mac, download it or copy it from the installer disc it shipped with and then drag it from wherever it's saved on your computer into the Plug-ins folder (see Figure 19-1, top) in *Applications/Adobe Photoshop CS4/Presets/ Plug-ins*. (You can also store plug-ins elsewhere as discussed on page 713.) On a PC, download the plug-in or copy it from the installer disc. It should be an .exe file (executable), so you can run it to install a program. Simply find the file on your computer and double-click it.

NOTE If you have trouble installing a plug-in, contact the person or company who created it for help.

If Photoshop is running, quit the program (File → Quit [File → Exit on a PC]) and then relaunch it. When Photoshop reopens, you should see the plug-in listed at the bottom of the Filter menu. Some plug-ins come with an installer (like the one in Figure 19-1, bottom), which may also include an uninstaller (handy if you want to get rid of the plug-in later).

Figure 19-1:
On a Mac, you can install a plug-in manually by dragging it into Photoshop's Plug-ins folder (top) or by using the installer provided by the folks who created the plug-in (bottom). On a PC, simply run the plug-in's .exe file.

NOTE If a plug-in deals with *batch processing* (modifying multiple files at once), you may find it in the File → Automate menu instead of the Filter menu. If it deals with selections or masking (page 105), you may find it in the Select menu.

To remove a plug-in, open your Plug-Ins folder and drag it to the Trash. (On a PC running Windows Vista, go to Start → Control Panel → Classic View → "Programs and Features" → "Uninstall a program"; in Windows XP, go to Start → Settings → Control Panel → "Add or Remove Programs". Then select the plug-in from the list of programs and click Uninstall [in Vista] or Change/Remove [in XP].) The next time you launch Photoshop, you'll see neither hide nor hair of the banished plug-in.

Managing Plug-Ins

Photoshop expects you to store plug-ins in its Plug-ins folder, so that's where it looks each time you launch the program. That's all well and good, but there's an awfully good chance your plug-ins will get zapped if you upgrade to a new version of Photoshop or reinstall the current one. The same is true of actions (Chapter 18), brushes (page 476), and so on. (See page 733 in Appendix B for more on backing up those extra goodies.)

To protect your precious plug-ins, it's wise to store them somewhere else, but you have to tell Photoshop where you put them by choosing Photoshop → Preferences → Plug-Ins (Edit → Preferences → Plug-Ins on a PC). Turn on the Additional Plug-Ins Folder checkbox and then click Choose to navigate to the folder where you've decided to store your plug-ins. Click OK when you're finished, drag the plug-ins you want to move from Photoshop's Plug-ins folder to the location you just picked, and then relaunch Photoshop to make your changes take effect. Photoshop won't stop peeking inside the original plug-ins folder; it just takes a gander inside the *new* folder, too. If you want to move a plug-in to the new folder, just drag it from the original folder (shown in Figure 19-1) to the new one.

> **TIP**   If Photoshop starts acting weird after you install a plug-in, you may want to temporarily disable the plug-in to see if it's the culprit by finding it on your hard drive and adding a tilde (~) to the beginning of its file name. Some manufacturers install their plug-ins in a new folder; for example, you'll find a folder called Mask Pro inside your plug-in folder. In that case, you can put the tilde at the beginning of the folder's name to disable everything inside. Either way, adding the tilde means the plug-in won't load the next time you launch Photoshop. When you want the plug-in to load again, just delete the tilde and relaunch Photoshop.

In the following pages, you'll find brief descriptions of some of the most amazing plug-ins on the market. Each one performs its own special brand of magic like noise removal, color enhancement, or special effects—one even turns your Photoshop document into a fully functional Web page!

These plug-ins range in price from $70 to $500, but don't let that scare you; you can find tons of cheaper (and even free) offerings on the Web (though you may very well get what you pay for). Don't be alarmed if you don't see what you want in this list of plug-ins—it's simply impossible to list them all here.

Dude, Where's My Plug-In?

Help! I don't see my plug-in in the Filter menu. Did it load or what?

Peace, dear grasshopper. You can find out whether your plug-in loaded in a couple of ways.

When Photoshop encounters a plug-in that won't load, it presents you with a dialog box that says, "One or more plug-ins are currently not available on your system. For details, see Help → System Info."

If you don't see that dialog box and your plug-in is still missing, take a look at the list of loaded plug-ins (and there's a slew of 'em!) by choosing Photoshop → About Plug-In (Help → About Plug-In on a PC). Because so many Photoshop features are actually plug-ins (most filters, import and export commands, and so on), the list is a mile long, so you may need to scroll to see if Photoshop loaded the one in question.

If your plug-in is on the list but isn't loading, about the only thing you can do is install a fresh copy or, better yet, see if a newer version is available from the developer's Web site. Keep in mind that some plug-ins continue to work with newer versions of Photoshop, but some don't.

> **TIP** For a comprehensive list of Photoshop plug-ins, visit *www.adobe.com/products/plugins/ photoshop*. And why are some of them called "third-party" plug-ins? Because they're made by someone other than Adobe.

Noise Reducers

If you've taken a photo in low light (in a dark restaurant, say), or if you set your camera to a high ISO (a setting that increases your camera's sensitivity to light), chances are you've got a ton of *noise*—grainy-looking speckles—in your image. While you'll find a couple of noise-reducing tricks in Chapter 11, if the image is *really* important, you should spring for a noise-reducing plug-in instead.

Noiseware

This plug-in is relatively new, but it has quickly become the noise reducer of choice for professional photographers. Instead of blurring the whole image to make the noise less visible, Noiseware analyzes the image and reduces noise only in the parts of the image that really need it. You also get a handy before-and-after view so you can see what it did. It's available from *www.imagenomic.com* and costs around $50.

> **TIP** You can often get plug-ins much cheaper if you buy them bundled together. Be sure to look for special deals on the developer's Web site.

Dfine

This plug-in also reduces the noise in your image in a very simple and nondestructive way. When you launch it and click its Measure button, Dfine scours your image for noise in areas without much detail (where noise is easiest to see). Start by trying the factory setting and then increase or decrease the noise-reduction level using the sliders (see Figure 19-2). When you find a setting you like, click OK to make Dfine copy the currently selected layer and apply the noise reduction to the duplicate instead of the original.

Thanks to Nik Software's spiffy *control points* technology, Dfine lets you reduce noise in certain areas of your image without making a mask. It also figures out which kind of camera you used to take the photo and then applies the right amount of noise reduction for your particular model (which makes sense because the camera introduces noise in the first place). You can buy Dfine for $100, but it's cheaper if you buy it along with other Nik Software products, like Sharpener Pro, Color Efex Pro, Viveza, and more (*www.niksoftware.com*).

Figure 19-2:
Dfine's handy split-screen view lets you see how much noise the plug-in removes from your image before you commit to the change. Here you see the original image on the left side of the red vertical line and the result on the right.

TIP One nice thing about Nik Software's plug-ins is that they all use the same window layout—once you learn how to use one, you can easily use them all.

Noise Ninja

Long considered the gold standard of noise-reduction software (though the newer Noiseware may have changed that), photographers and newspapers have used this plug-in for years. It helps reduce noise (speckled imperfections) and grain (textured imperfections) while it preserves details. It can tackle 16-bit images (see the box on page 43), do batch processing, and work as a Smart Filter (page 588). It'll set you back about $80 (*www.picturecode.com*).

Making Selections and Masking

As you've learned in previous chapters, selecting stuff like hair and fur is really hard. Sure, you can learn some tricks, but a plug-in specifically designed for that task can make your life a heck of a lot easier and save you tons of time. That said, you'll need a bit of patience when you start working with masking plug-ins because they're not for the faint of heart. With practice, though, you can use them to create selections you just can't make any other way.

Fluid Mask

Fluid Mask is a powerful plug-in helps that makes easy work of masking around complex areas like hair or fur. As soon as you open Fluid Mask, it analyzes your image and marks what it thinks are edges with blue lines (see Figure 19-3) so you can mark which edges you want to keep and which ones you want to zap and then create a cutout of your image to send back to Photoshop to use as a mask. You can also save your project and return to it later—a nice touch. Fluid Mask costs about $240 (*www.vertustech.com*).

Figure 19-3:
These blue lines mark the edges that Fluid Mask found in the image. If you use a combination of the plug-in's tools (on the left), you can mark areas you want to keep and ones you want to throw away.

Mask Pro

Mask Pro helps you pick the precise colors you want to keep or remove as you build image masks. It gives you two eyedroppers to work with: Use one to select colors you want to keep and the other to select colors you want to throw away (see Figure 19-4). Then, you can use its Magic Brush to paint away the background while the program helps you along by referring to the Keep and Drop color palettes you made.

Mask Pro can also extract partial color from a pixel, leaving you with a partially transparent pixel—important when you're selecting hair or fur (the edges are so soft that they have to be partially see-through to blend in with a new background). You can also view the image in mask mode, which helps you see what the selection looks like because it's displayed in shades of gray (just like a layer or channel mask). Mask Pro can work with 16-bit images and works as a Smart Filter though you have to turn the layer into a Smart Object first (see page 115); otherwise, the plug-in deletes the selected pixels as soon as you apply it. It costs around $160 (*www.ononesoftware.com*).

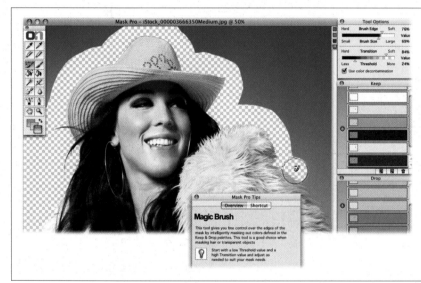

Figure 19-4:
Because masking plug-ins are inherently complex, the folks who created Mask Pro help you get up to speed by including "Show Me How" videos and tips (shown here).

NOTE   When you install an onOne Software plug-in like Mask Pro, it shows up in the Filter menu and in a brand-*new* menu between Window and Help called "onOne".

Color Correction and Enhancement

The plug-ins in this category can spruce up or adjust the color in your images and produce a startling array of special effects while they're at it. Read on for the scoop.

Viveza

As you've learned in previous chapters, before you adjust the color of a specific part of your image, you need to select it. Not so with Viveza. Since this plug-in made its debut in early 2008, it has revolutionized selective color and light adjustments. If you mark the areas you want to change with *control points* (the small gray circles shown in Figure 19-5), you can adjust the saturation, brightness, and contrast of individual areas at warp speed. Viveza performs all its magic on its own duplicate layer, so you don't have to worry about it destroying your original image. It's available from *www.niksoftware.com* and costs around $250.

Figure 19-5:
By dropping lots of control points on your image (the little gray dots), you can adjust each area's saturation, brightness, and contrast individually. Notice that the contrast and saturation of the woman's jeans and the grass have been increased while the man's red shirt has been desaturated and the sky remains untouched.

Color Efex Pro

If you could buy just one plug-in, Color Efex Pro would be a darn good choice. Using the same control points as other Nik Software plug-ins, this one lets you selectively apply 52 enhancement filters and over 250 effects to your images—all nondestructively. You can use them to enhance images in creative ways, as well as to fix color casts, smooth skin, and so on (see Figure 19-6). Drop as many control points as you want and use them to set the effect's opacity in certain areas of your image or click the Brush button to paint the effect where you want it. The price ranges from $100 for 15 filters to $300 for all 52, and it's available from *www.niksoftware.com*.

PhotoTune

This plug-in lets you correct color and skin tones easily. It's actually made up of two separate programs: ColorTune and SkinTune. The ColorTune part works like an eye exam, asking you which of two images you like better (see Figure 19-7). Through a series of six steps based on the choice you make, ColorTune resets your black and white points (page 370), applies curves for brightness and contrast (page 379), and so on. Since it's incredibly simple, it's great for newbies or those who (rightly!) fear the

Figure 19-6:
Top: This split-screen preview shows you before and after versions of an image. This particular filter, called Bleach Bypass, creates a high-contrast grunge look. (If this look interests you, head over to page 721 and read about LucisArt Pro.)

Bottom: The Glamour Glow filter gives the original image (left) a seriously dreamy look (right). But because Color Efex Pro applies the effect on another layer, you can always lower its opacity to blend it with the original.

Curves dialog box. If you're more advanced (or brave), you can skip to the fine-tune panel and adjust the settings manually. You can also take a snapshot of your image and compare it with other versions that use different settings.

SkinTune, the other half of PhotoTune, is designed to produce accurate skin color based on the subject's ethnicity. Just click a patch of skin and then select the person's ethnicity from a pop-up menu (shown in Figure 19-8). SkinTune presents you with a row of color swatches similar to that particular skin tone (click the one that looks best to you). It also zaps any color cast from the skin and removes the same cast from the rest of the photo. You can take a snapshot of your image and compare it with other versions produced with different settings, as well as save your settings and apply them to similar images later. Both ColorTune and SkinTune work as Smart Filters, but you have to convert your image layer to a Smart Object first. PhotoTune costs $160, and it's available from *www.ononesoftware.com*.

Figure 19-7:
ColorTune asks you to pick the better of two images in a series of six steps. It's by far the easiest way to color correct your images.

Figure 19-8:
After you choose your subject's ethnicity, you can pick from a row of color swatches developed by the folks at onOne Software. They took countless photos of people and assembled their skin tones into a massive database of over 400,000 different skin types. That's a lot of skin!

PhotoTools

This plug-in includes more than 150 photographic effects developed by the onOne team, as well as 100 extra effects from Photoshop guru Jack Davis and wedding photographer Kevin Kubota. PhotoTools helps you create beautiful portraits and vignettes, combine multiple effects into a layer mask, and more. You can export several versions of your image with different color profiles (page 617), which is handy if the result is headed to a printer or the Web. You can also apply a *watermark* (a partially transparent graphic) to your files that helps protect them from copyright violators when you post them on the Web. This plug-in does its thing on its own brand-new layer so it's nondestructive, and it can also batch process images. The pro edition costs $260 and the standard edition, without the effects from Jack Davis and Kevin Kubota, costs $160 (*www.ononesoftware.com*).

Miscellaneous Plug-ins

Most of the plug-ins covered in this section relate to specific tasks like enhancing detail, making enlargements, building Web sites, and so on, but some also alter color.

LucisArt

This plug-in has been around for several years and, while it's popular in scientific and medical circles, it's only recently begun to make a splash in the creative realm. Using a process originally developed to enhance details in images captured with electron microscopes, it lifts more detail from your image than you knew was there. Using only the luminance (lightness) info from your image, it extracts details without destroying highlights or shadows or shifting color (though you can control the color with a slider because you may *want* to shift the color a little).

You can vary your image in thousands of ways by tweaking just a couple of sliders, and though you could possibly reproduce some of these effects with Photoshop, you'd never know these possibilities exist if you didn't use this software first. You can use this plug-in to tweak individual channels or work on the composite channel (page 174), and you can also blend the original back into the processed image using a slider. Figure 19-9 gives you a taste of what you can do with LucisArt. The pro version will set you back $595, but if you make your living working with images, it's money well spent; a light version that offers fewer settings and gives you limited control over mid-range contrast patterns and reducing scan lines is available for $340 (*www.lucisart.com*).

Silver Efex Pro

This plug-in isn't a black-and-white converter; it's a virtual black-and-white *darkroom*. It helps you create stunning black-and-white images (see Figure 19-10) from your color images (though you can also use it to improve images that are already black and white). It has more than 20 black-and-white presets and also lets you create your own. You can make global adjustments using the sliders or drop control points to tweak the brightness, contrast, and structure (level of detail) in specific areas without affecting the whole image. The control points let you quickly sharpen certain parts of your image, like eyes, the pattern on clothing, and so on. You can also add a color filter just as if you'd put a filter on your camera lens. Silver Efex Pro lets you choose from 18 different film types to simulate the look

Figure 19-9:
Top: You can use LucisArt to smooth the details of your image to create a beautiful watercolor effect.

Bottom: If you enhance the details in your image and then smooth the overall picture slightly, you can get a high-contrast grunge effect (right) similar to the effect used in the movie 300.

and grain of real film, add tints, or burn the edges of your image. It works as a Smart Filter and costs about $200 (*www.niksoftware.com*).

Genuine Fractals

If you need to enlarge an image, this plug-in will save your bacon. It lets you create printable versions of even low-resolution images (like those made for the Web or captured with a low-quality setting on your digital camera). It can blow images up

Figure 19-10:
Silver Efex Pro, currently the most powerful black-and-white plug-in, helps you create the look of black-and-white images captured on real film. If you want to add a little grain to your image, you can pick from several different options that look like real film grain.

to over 1,000 percent to make honkin' big panoramas, enlarge still frames from old videos to create higher-quality versions, and so on. It can scale any Photoshop document—even if it's brimming with Smart Object layers (page 115), paths (page 497), or Type layers (page 537)—without losing resolution or harming the image's quality. Just pick the pixels dimensions (if you know them), enter a percentage for the enlargement, or enter the print size and resolution you want (page 221). If your image's proportions don't match those of the paper size you pick, Genuine Fractals offers you a cropping grid. It also batch processes images. The pro version costs $300 and the standard version, without CMYK image support, runs $160 (*www.ononesoftware.com*).

PhotoFrame

This plug-in can help you get super creative with your images by adding frames and textures. PhotoFrame includes approximately 1,000 frames, including film edges, backgrounds, ornamental overlays, and tape (see Figure 19-11). You can change the color and blend mode (page 267) of each element, as well as resize them (either individually or together). The plug-in places each added element on its own layer—in a layer group—so it doesn't change your original image. If you had the forethought to add a layer mask to the image before you framed it, the frame gets applied to the mask; otherwise, it gets put on its own brand-new layer. If you have something selected before you launch the plug-in, you can frame just that part of your image. The pro version runs $260 and the standard version, with fewer frames and no Aperture or Lightroom support, is $160 (*www.ononesoftware.com*).

Figure 19-11:
Top: PhotoFrame has a library of over 1,000 frames, overlays, backgrounds, and so on. You can rate your favorite frames using stars.

Bottom: In addition to frames, you can add all kinds of other embellishments like cursive text and ornamental objects. The tabbed palette on the right lets you customize each element's color, blend mode, opacity, and so on.

FocalPoint

Like popular tilt lenses (page 592), this plug-in lets you create interestingly blurred backgrounds and shallow depth-of-field effects by controlling exactly which part of your image is in focus. Since it mimics a real tilt lens, you don't have to worry about swapping lenses while you're out shooting. You use a "focus bug" to control which part of your image is in focus (Figure 19-12): Use its "legs" to rotate the aperture shape and size, and its "antennae" to control the amount of blur, as well as the transition between the blurry and unblurry bits (otherwise known as the blur's feather amount). You can also add a vignette to darken or lighten the edges of your image and save your settings as a preset to use again later. You can also use it for batch processing images. It costs $160, and you can get it from *www.ononesoftware.com*.

Sharpener Pro

As you learned in Chapter 11, sharpening is a bit of an art. It's hard to judge the amount of sharpening you need for a print based on what you seen onscreen. With this plug-in, you choose the type of printer and paper you're going to use and

Figure 19-12:
*The FocalPoint plug-in's
"focus bug" actually
looks like a bug, as
shown here. Use it to
control the size and
angle of the blur.*

Sharpener Pro applies the appropriate amount of sharpening. You can use the Structure slider to control the amount of details in the edges and the Focus slider to apply more sharpening to areas that are slightly out of focus. Drop as many control points as you want to apply more or less sharpening to specific areas (like eyes). You don't even have to worry about duplicating or stamping (Chapter 3) your layers before you use this plug-in—it does all that for you. It costs $200, and it's available from *www.niksoftware.com*.

Eye Candy

This ever-popular set of special effects plug-ins comes in three flavors. The Impact set includes over 200 presets for metal, glass, gel, and so on. The Nature set includes more than 500 presets for natural phenomenon like fire, ice, and smoke. The Textures set includes over 200 presets for your reskinning pleasure like lizard, fur, and stone. The Eye Candy plug-ins run about $100 each and are available from *www.alienskin.com*.

Xenofex

This plug-in helps you create realistic lightning and clouds, as well as distortions like Flag, TV, and Rip Open. You can also use it to turn your photos into jigsaw puzzles, constellations, and really cool mosaics. You can buy it from *www. alienskin.com* for $130.

SiteGrinder

If you've designed a Web site in Photoshop and shudder at the thought of slicing it up and turning it into actual code, this plug-in will do it for you in just two steps (see Figure 19-13). SiteGrinder builds a Web page based on *CSS* (Cascading Style Sheets) straight from Photoshop so you never have to *see* (much less tweak) any code. You can also make photo galleries, Flash slideshows, CSS-based menus and other amazing stuff without losing the design you've painstakingly crafted in Photoshop. The magic lies in naming your layers and layer groups things like "button," "rollover," "pop-up," and so on, so the plug-in can figure out how each part of your Web page should work. The pro version is $350 and the basic (which doesn't include several features like QuickTime, Flash, image gallery, and form support) is $130 (*www.medialab.com*).

Figure 19-13:
If you've mocked-up a Web page in Photoshop using layers (shown in the background), SiteGrinder can turn it into an HTML reality in minutes. In the foreground you can see the SiteGrinder dialog box alerting you that it's examined your document.

YouSendIt

If you need to transfer a large file to a client and don't want to fool with *FTP* (file transfer protocol) software, you can use this free plug-in to send it via an email link instead. To use it, choose File → Export. After you pick which kind of file you want to send (a JPEG at full size or 50 percent, a PSD file, and so on), YouSendIt pops open a form where you can enter an email address and a personal message (see Figure 19-14). You have to register with their Web site to use YouSendIt, and the free account has some size limitations. If you want more options, you can get them for a nominal fee. It's available from *www.yousendit.com*.

Figure 19-14:
As soon as you click the Send It button (bottom), YouSendIt uploads the file to its servers and emails a link to your recipient, who simply clicks the link to download your file.

Troubleshooting and Getting Help

Nobody's perfect, and that includes Photoshop *and* the folks who created it. Programmers can't anticipate how every single person who uses a program will push, prod, and poke it—and on what kinds of computers and under what circumstances. So don't be alarmed if at some point Photoshop acts strangely or just can't figure out how to make something work. If that happens, there are resources aplenty, both inside Photoshop and elsewhere that can help solve your dilemma.

The Online Help Desk

Nestled snuggly within Photoshop's Help menu is the program's own Help system, which gives you access to answers to common questions and links to tons of tutorials. You can take it for a test drive by choosing Help → Photoshop Help. When you do, Photoshop launches your Web browser and takes you to the page shown in Figure B-1. At the top of the page is a handy search field that can help you hunt down the info you seek, and on the left side of the page is a list of help topics. You can enter a choice word or two into the search field (the fewer the words, the better) or scan through the topics. Since this help page pulls its answers from Adobe's online database, you need an active Internet connection to use it.

> **TIP** Adobe's online help is great when you're somewhere with Internet access, but not so great when you're on a plane, on location for a photo shoot, or have an unreliable Internet connection. If you know of features you want to bone-up on when you're offline, you can download PDF versions of help topics. Just find the topic you want and then click the PDF icon in the upper-right corner of the page to download it. Sweet!

Figure B-1:
Adobe has hundreds of
pages of online
information and tips.
Since it's all Web-based,
Adobe can keep it
updated, and users can
add their comments.

When Good Tools Go Bad

Sometimes tools have minds of their own and insist on misbehaving no matter how firmly you press the keys or how loudly you curse. Before you announce your copy of Photoshop possessed by the Dark Lord of Mordor, make sure you:

• **Check the Options bar's settings.** If a brush isn't working, you may have changed its opacity or blend mode and forgotten to change it back. Remember, settings in the Options bar and some panels (like the Character and Paragraph panels) are *sticky*, meaning they don't change unless you change them. (See page 13 for more on the Options bar.)

• **Make sure you're on the right layer.** If you're not, nothing will work like you expect. Your tools won't seem to have any effect because the changes are happening on a different layer than you expect, most likely on a layer you can't see. Take a look at the Layers panel and, if the right layer isn't selected, click to select the layer you want to affect and have another go at it. (Chapter 3 teaches you all about layers.)

• **Check for stray selections.** If you've got marching ants somewhere on your image, it can make all kinds of tools act up. For example, a tiny selection can cause your Crop tool to make a microscopic box, make filters to run in just one area, keep you from activating the Type tool, and so on. Even if you can't *see* a selection, try pressing ⌘-D (Ctrl+D on a PC) or choosing Select → Deselect just for good measure. Then have another go with the tool and see what happens. (See Chapter 4 for more on selections.)

Believe it or not, these three tips will probably fix the majority of your problems. If the trouble persists, see if you can find the solution listed in the next several pages.

Mysterious Resizing when Dragging Layers

When you drag layers between documents (page 90), you might think that items have changed size along the way. They didn't, though—it only *looks* like they changed size because the document you dragged the layer into is set to a different zoom level, or the documents' resolution doesn't match. Remember from Chapter 6 that resolution controls the size of your pixels, so if you drag a layer from a 72-ppi document into a 300-ppi one, your pixels go from really big to really small. The fix is to *downsample* (see the Note on page 226) the higher-resolution document. (See Chapter 6 for more on resizing.)

Can't Save in Certain Formats

Here's an oldie but goodie: Let's say you're poised and ready to save your image but the Save As dialog box (page 46) doesn't list the file format you want. If that happens, there's a good chance your image is in a funky color mode (page 40). For example, Indexed color mode (which is used for GIFs) doesn't let you save in as many file formats as RGB color mode (see Figure B-2). To fix this problem, take a trip up to Image → Mode and try switching your document to RGB mode instead, and *then* saving it.

Disabled Filters

Have you ever opened the Filter menu only to find that the name of the filter you want to run is grayed out and unavailable? If so, you can bet the farm your image is in CMYK mode or 16-bit RGB. Several filters won't run on anything other than 8-bit RGB images, including whole filter categories like Artistic, Brush Strokes, Sketch, Texture, and Video. To use the unavailable filters, choose Image → Mode → 8 Bits/Channel. Then head back up to the Filter menu and run your filter.

> **TIP**   If your image is in 8-bit RGB mode but you still can't use some of the filters, check to see if you're editing a Smart Object (page 115). As you learned on page 588, not all filters run as Smart Filters.

Uneditable Images

As you know, you can't use all of Photoshop's editing features in every color mode. If you're suddenly locked out of using *any* of the buttons or menus in the Layers panel (like masks, Adjustment layers, opacity—the whole nine yards), your image is probably in Indexed mode (see Figure B-3). Choose Image → Mode → RGB Color and you'll be able to use all the Layers panel's controls.

Resetting Tools

If a tool is behaving erratically, you can give it an attitude adjustment by resetting it to its factory-fresh settings. Grab the problem tool and then Ctrl-click (right-click on a PC) the tool's preset menu at the far left of the Options bar. Choose Reset Tool from the shortcut menu that appears and see if that helps. If you want to reset *all* your tools, choose Reset All Tools from the shortcut menu instead.

Figure B-2:
When you go to save a file, Photoshop lists only formats that are compatible with your document's color mode (top). For example, an image in Indexed mode (bottom left) supports far fewer formats than an image in RGB mode (bottom right).

Figure B-3:
Indexed mode is great for limiting the number of colors in an image you want to post on the Web, but it also limits other stuff like your ability to edit the darn thing using layers. If the Layers panel includes a locked layer named Index (as shown here), you've found the culprit. Switch to RGB mode to regain control.

Trashing Photoshop's Preferences

If Photoshop won't launch, crashes a lot, or is acting funky, you can try zapping its preferences (Chapter 1 covers preferences). Damaged preference files can cause all those problems and more, and in many cases starting fresh fixes the problem. Follow these steps to delete Photoshop's preferences:

1. **Quit Photoshop if it's running.**

   Choose Photoshop → Quit Photoshop (File → Exit on a PC) or press ⌘-Q (Ctrl+Q).

2. **Relaunch Photoshop while pressing ⌘-Opt-Shift (on a PC, press Ctrl+Alt+Shift while choosing Photoshop from the Start menu).**

   Press and hold this three-key combo while you launch the program. Don't release the keys until you see the dialog box described in the next step!

3. **In the resulting dialog box (Figure B-4), click Yes.**

   Photoshop asks whether you want to delete your settings file, which is where the program stores your preferences. (If you somehow happened upon this dialog box by mistake or just change your mind, click No to continue launching the program without deleting your preferences.)

Figure B-4:
You don't have to go hunting for Photoshop's preferences files to delete them; the program takes care of the dirty work for you—if you know the secret keyboard shortcut!

The only problem with this fix is that you'll have to reapply any custom settings you had, like extra scratch disk settings (see Appendix A, online at *www. missingmanuals.com*), guide colors (page 63), and so on. But hey, at least Photoshop is running again!

Backing Up Presets, Plug-ins, and Actions

Sometimes all the tricks listed above just don't work, and you have to resort to drastic measures: Uninstalling and reinstalling Photoshop. Huge bummer! In that case, be sure to back up any custom presets you've made like actions, brushes, swatches, and so on, and make copies of any third-party plug-ins you've installed (unless you have the installers or the DVD for your add-ons lying around).

All of your custom goodies are stashed in the *Users/[your home directory]/Library/ Application Support/Adobe/Adobe Photoshop CS4/Presets* folder. On a PC running Windows Vista, they live in *C:\Users\[your name]\AppData\Roaming\Adobe\Adobe Photoshop CS4\Presets;* in Windows XP they live in *C:\Program Files\Adobe\Adobe Photoshop CS4\Presets.* Copy the Presets folder to someplace safe, like an external FireWire or USB hard drive. Any plug-ins you added are in the Plug-ins folder, which is inside the Adobe Photoshop CS4 program folder, so copy those, too.

Once your files are copied safely to somewhere other than the Adobe Photoshop CS4 folder, head over to Appendix A—online at *www.missingmanuals.com*—for the scoop on uninstalling the program.

Beyond This Book

Thanks to a vast number of gifted trainers, great magazines, and helpful Web sites devoted to the program, Photoshop users will never be left out in the cold. It is, after all, the most popular piece of software to date. Adobe's Web site is a great place to start rooting around for additional info. You'll find a design center with written and video tutorials (*www.adobe.com/designcenter*), along with some of the most active forums you'll ever run across. Folks post and reply to questions so often it'll leave you wondering whether they've got real jobs!

But some of the best content isn't available from Adobe—it's posted online by a wide variety of sources. Aside from the author of this book's own Web site (which appears first in the list below), there are a bazillion other sites bursting with useful, well-written tutorials, shortcuts, and downloads. All the resources listed below are free unless otherwise noted, so visit them all and bookmark the ones you like best. Also included are some of the most amazing Photoshop instructors and authors out there. If you ever get a chance to take one of their classes, you'll be glad you did!

- **The Graphic Reporter.** Your author is on a mission to teach the world to create better graphics. To that end, she created this free tutorial site. You'll find a new tutorial posted weekly, along with all kinds of other madness and mayhem (*www.graphicreporter.com*).

- **Kelby Training.** Your author teamed up with Kelby Training to produce several online training courses about both Photoshop and Photoshop Elements. You'll also find other courses by some of the best instructors and photographers in the country (*www.kelbytraining.com/instructors/lesa-snider-king.html*).

- **The National Association of Photoshop Professionals** (NAPP) is the world's largest professional Photoshop organization. Its Web site is loaded with articles, tutorials, and tips, plus it's the organization that publishes *Photoshop User* magazine. A $99 yearly membership fee gets you the magazine, access to a 24-hour help desk, discounts for PhotoshopWorld.com conferences, and a slew of other benefits (*www.photoshopuser.com*).

- **Planet Photoshop** is a news and tutorial hub for the Photoshop community. It's managed by Kelby Training (*www.planetphotoshop.com*).

- **Scott Kelby** is the man behind NAPP, PhotoshopTV (*www.photoshopusertv.com*), Kelby Training, *Photoshop User* magazine, *Layers* magazine, and an amazingly long list of books. He knows a thing or two about Photoshop and digital photography and has plenty to say about them (*www.scottkelby.com/blog*).

- **Dave Cross** is a Photoshop trainer, speaker, author, and another one of the guys behind PhotoshopTV (*http://davecross.blogspot.com*).

- **Ben Willmore** is an author and professional photographer who travels the world teaching folks how to use Photoshop (*www.digitalmastery.com*).

- **Jack Davis** is a talented photographer, Photoshop trainer, and author of the popular Photoshop WOW books (*www.adventuresinphotoshop.com*).

- **Taz Tally** is a professional photographer, author, trainer, and an expert on all things prepress (*www.tazseminars.com*).

- **Richard Harrington** is the author of *Photoshop for Video, Third Edition* (Focal Press, 2007). He travels the world teaching folks about motion graphics (*www.photoshopforvideo.com*).

- **Deke McClelland** is an author, trainer, and podcaster extraordinaire (*www.deke.com*).

- **Terry White** is Adobe's Director of North American Creative Pro Technical Sales, and writes for *Layers* magazine. He's also the author of *Secrets of Adobe Bridge* (Adobe Press, 2005) and co-author with Scott Kelby of *InDesign CS/CS2 Killer Tips* (New Riders Press, 2005). He discusses tech topics and Photoshop on his blog *www.terrywhite.com/techblog*.

- **CreativePro.com** is packed with useful information for Photoshop fans, graphic designers, and creative professionals. It covers industry news and offers tips and tricks for all the Adobe Creative Suite programs (*www.creativepro.com*).

- **Design Tools Monthly** collects all the news that's important to folks in the graphic design world—including digital photographers—and serves it up every month in easy-to-digest bits along with tips, fonts, and software updates (*www.designtoolsmonthly.com*).

Using Adobe Bridge

As digital images start to pile up on your hard drive, the ability to sift through them quickly and efficiently becomes more and more important. Enter Adobe Bridge CS4, an image-browsing and organizing program that's been shipping with Photoshop for several years. Browsing through your images in previous versions of Bridge was a painfully slow process, and the program's workspace wasn't very intuitive. But in CS4, Bridge got a speed boost, a flattering makeover, and a new Review mode (page 740) that'll make photographers squeal with joy.

In the following pages, you'll learn the basics of browsing, importing, and rating your images in Bridge. By the end of this appendix, you'll be able to find your favorite photos and plop them into a super-slick slideshow in no time.

Browsing Your Photos

If you're working in Photoshop, you can open Bridge by clicking the Launch Bridge button in the Application bar (page 12)—it looks like a square with the letters *Br* inside it. If Photoshop *isn't* running, you can double-click the Bridge icon in the Adobe Bridge application folder (on a PC, go to Start → Programs → Adobe Bridge CS4). Either way, you see the window shown in Figure C-1.

The Bridge window shows you a variety of info about your images in collapsible panels. You can use the Folders panel on the left to navigate to a specific spot on your hard drive to view the images stored there. When you click a folder in this panel, Bridge displays its contents as thumbnails in the Content panel (use the slider at the bottom of the Bridge window to control how big those thumbnails are). Click an image in the Content panel to see a larger version of it in the Preview panel on the right.

Figure C-1:
You can use Bridge to browse all the images on your hard drive, not just the ones you've imported using Bridge. The various panels shown here harbor different kinds of info, and they're all resizable and movable. To move a panel, drag its tab; to resize a panel, drag the bar that divides it from other panels; and to combine panels, drag one panel's tab into another panel.

TIP For quick access to certain folders, add them to Bridge's Favorites panel. Select the folder in the Folders or Contents panel and then choose File → Add to Favorites. From now on, you'll have one-click access to that folder in the Favorites panel.

At the top of the Bridge window are controls that help you find the files you want (shown in Figure C-1):

- **Forward and back arrows.** Click these buttons to move through the folders you've recently viewed. For example, if you went to your Racing Photos folder and then opened the Winners Circle folder inside it, click the back arrow to return to the Racing Photos folder. (These buttons don't select files, just folders.)

- **Go to parent or Favorites.** Like the back arrow, this menu lets you move up a folder level. For example, if you're perusing the Midnight Madness folder that lives inside your Photoshop World folder, you can use this menu to quickly pop into the Photoshop World folder (which is called the *parent* folder because it's one level above the Midnight Madness folder in your computer's file-organization family tree). You can also use this menu to access folders that you've added to the Favorites panel.

- **Go to recent files/folders.** This menu lists all the files and folders you've recently viewed, and it includes a list of files and folders categorized by the program that made them. When you choose a file or folder from this menu, Bridge displays a preview of the item along with its location on your hard drive.

- **Path bar.** This outrageously useful bar is a clickable, virtual trail of breadcrumbs that helps you keep track of where you are. It shows you which folder you're in; if you want to jump to a different spot in the trail, simply click the name of another folder in this bar. Since the Path bar shows you how you arrived at the folder you're in, you always know exactly where you are (and the clickable links offer you a fast track backwards). If you don't see this bar, choose Window → Path Bar.

- **Search bar.** If you know the name of the file you're looking for but don't remember where it lives, type its name (or the first few letters of it) into this field and then press Return (Enter on a PC). Bridge scours your hard drive and shows you a list of the files that best match what you were searching for.

TIP   If you don't have a big monitor but want to keep Bridge open—so you can drag and drop images from it into Photoshop, say—click the "Switch to Compact Mode" button in Bridge's upper-right corner and the Bridge window shrinks down to a more manageable size. Click this button again to expand the window back to normal size.

Importing and Managing Photos

Bridge makes importing images a snap, and you can make it perform all kinds of wonderful housekeeping chores for you. For example, it can automatically rename your photos and add keywords, descriptions, and copyright info to each file. You can also have it back up your files as part of the import process (though you need to have an external drive plugged in). If you've got a DVD drive, it can burn copies of your images to a DVD, which is a good way to make backups you can store somewhere else.

To import images, make sure your card reader is attached (see the box on page 742) and then choose File → "Get Photos from Camera" or click the tiny camera icon at the top of the Bridge window. The first dialog box you see isn't very impressive; its most redeeming feature is the Advanced Dialog button at the bottom left. Click it to summon the Adobe Bridge CS4 Photo Downloader (Figure C-2). At the top of the dialog box you can tell Bridge where to save your precious images by clicking the Choose button. The dialog box also lets you pick which images you want to import (turn on the appropriate checkboxes like the one circled in Figure C-2), give your images meaningful names, and tell Bridge to back up your images by turning on the Save Copies To checkbox. Once you've got the options just right, click Get Photos and then sit back and relax.

Customizing the Bridge Window

You can customize your Bridge workspace just like you can in Photoshop, or use one of its built-in layouts. Near the middle of the Bridge window is a list of workspaces that arrange the panels in a variety of ways—see Figure C-1. (These workspaces aren't new—they've been in Bridge since the first version, but until now they were stuffed at the bottom-right corner of the window and cryptically labeled 1, 2, 3.) Here's what each one does:

- **Essentials.** This is the workspace arrangement you see when you first open Bridge: The Folders panel is on the left, the Content panel is in the middle, and the Preview panel is on the right. It's a handy workspace for sifting through the files on your hard drive.

- **Filmstrip.** This workspace is great for looking at photos you've imported. The Folders panel is still on the left, but the Content panel is down at the bottom of the window as a wide, thin strip, and the Preview panel takes center stage. Photographers like this workspace because it gives them a nice big preview.

- **Metadata.** This workspace shows you all kinds of info about your images. There's no big Preview panel

in this workspace; the Content panel takes center stage and shows you a list that includes the date each file was created, its size, type, and so on. The Folders panel appears on the left along with the Metadata panel, which shows you statistics about the file like its dimensions, resolution, and so on.

- **Output.** This workspace sticks the Folders panel on the left, Content panel in the middle, and the new Output panel on the right. The Output panel lets you create PDFs and Web galleries, as explained later in this chapter.

If these workspaces don't float your boat, you can make your own. Once you've moved and resized the panels just the way you like, click the tiny down-pointing triangle to the right of the Output button and choose New Workspace. Give it a meaningful name and then click Save. Your new workspace appears as a button at the top of the Bridge window. If you want to get rid of it, click the triangle again, choose Delete Workspace, select the offending workspace in the resulting dialog box, and then click Delete. (You can only delete custom workspaces, not the built-in ones.)

TIP The first time you choose File → "Get Photos from Camera", Bridge asks if you want it to automatically launch each time you attach a card reader (or plug in your camera's USB cable). If you want to use Bridge to import all your photos, click Yes. This will save you a couple of clicks each time you import images because Bridge will automatically launch and open the Photo Downloader dialog box.

Using Review Mode

After you import images, you can use Bridge CS4's new Review mode to see them in a giant, floating carousel (see Figure C-3). It's a quick and easy way to view your images full-screen, mark the ones you don't like, and apply star ratings to the ones you do.

NOTE You can also mark images as rejected in the main Bridge window. Simply select the image's thumbnail and then press Option-Delete (Alt+Backspace on a PC).

Figure C-2:
*Importing your images
with Bridge is a huge
timesaver. If you've got
an external hard drive
plugged in, you can turn
on the "Save Copies To"
checkbox and sleep
better knowing you have
extra copies of your
photos.*

To use Review mode, select a folder in the Folders panel or choose multiple images
in the Content panel by ⌘ (Ctrl on a PC) or Shift-clicking them. (If the images are
next to each other, click the first image and then Shift-click the last one. If they're
not, click the first image and then ⌘-click [Ctrl-click] the others.) Then press ⌘-B
(Ctrl+B on a PC) or click the Refine button at the top of the Bridge window (it
looks like a stack of paper) and choose Review Mode. Either way, Bridge takes over
your screen and displays all your images on a gray background. By using the left
and right arrow buttons at the bottom-left corner of your screen, you can flip
through your images quickly. To exit Review mode and return to the Bridge window, click the X in the bottom-right corner of your screen or press Esc.

> **TIP**   To rotate your images in Review mode, select an image, press and hold ⌘ (Ctrl on a PC)
> and then press the left or right bracket key. Pressing ⌘-] rotates your image clockwise, and press-
> ing ⌘-[rotates it counterclockwise.

Sorting and Filtering Images

Bridge gives you a lot of flexibility when it comes to viewing your image collection. For example, you can use the Sort menu at the top of the Bridge window (see
Figure C-4 to arrange your images by name, date modified, size, and so on. You
can also choose to sort them manually, which lets you use the Content panel to
drag them into any order you want. Sorting is also a quick way to toss the images
you've rejected (page 740). To do that, choose Show Rejected Items Only from the
Sort Menu, and then choose File → Move To Trash.

Tips for Importing Photos

Here are a few pointers for importing photos from your digital camera quickly and safely that will also help you find the little buggers on your hard drive later on:

- **Always use a card reader to import photos.** The slowest way to import photos is by using the USB cable that came with your camera. (It's sweet that the camera manufacturer included it, but those cables are super cheap and you don't have to use them.) The USB cable's low quality makes using it dangerous—the cheaper the cable, the greater the chance that something will go wrong. Fortunately, you can avoid this risk by getting a *card reader*, which imports photos much faster and more reliably. You simply take the memory card out of your camera, stick it in the card reader, and connect the reader to your computer. Card readers are inexpensive (you can get a SanDisk ImageMate 12-in-1 for under $15) and most models can read several different kinds of memory cards (that's what the 12-in-1 stands for), which is a nice bonus if you have more than one brand of camera.

- **Erase memory cards only in your camera.** Most photo importing/organizing software offers to erase photos from your memory card after it imports them onto your computer. Resist the urge to say yes, and instead stick the memory card back into your camera, then use the *camera's* menus to reformat the card to erase your images. This protects

you from losing files if there's some kind of crash or stall while they're importing, which can corrupt your photos (and if the software has already erased them from the memory card, you can't re-import them). And many folks believe that reformatting memory cards rather than erasing them helps reduce the risk of cards getting corrupted and losing your photos. To learn how to reformat your memory card, dig out the manual that came with your camera.

- **Give photos meaningful names.** Instead of sticking with the completely useless names your camera assigns to each photo, give them meaningful names when you import them. Programs like Bridge can automatically number the files for you and tack on a name like *Photoshop World*. You've got to admit that the name *Photoshop World 08_1.jpg* is a lot more descriptive than *DCS_00102.jpg*.

- **Use several small memory cards instead of one big one.** No matter how well you care for them, memory cards—like any storage device—can fail and lose all the precious images that were stored on 'em. For that reason, consider carrying four 2 GB cards instead of a single 8 GB card; that way, you'll lose fewer photos if one of your memory cards goes south.

TIP To see a quick preview of an image, just select the file you want to view and then tap the space bar, and Bridge shows you a full-screen preview of your image. This very welcome feature is new in Bridge CS4. Press the space bar again to go back to the Bridge window.

The Filter panel lets you weed out images by displaying only those that match certain criteria, like a specific star rating (see Figure C-4). (If you don't see the Filter panel, choose Window → Filter Panel.) If you didn't use Review mode to rate your images when you imported them (page 739), you might want to rate them now so you can quickly view your best images. Rating and sorting is handy if you're a stock photographer: You can give future submissions a 5-star rating and then find them quickly using the 5-star filter.

Renaming Multiple Files

If you forgot to rename your photos when you imported them or if you'd like to rename other files on your hard drive, you don't have change their names one at a time—that'd take days. Instead, you can have Bridge rename entire folders of images for you using a simple process called *batch renaming.*

From the Refine menu at the top of the Bridge window (it looks like a stack of paper), choose Batch Rename or just press Shift-⌘-R (Shift+Ctrl+R on a PC). The Destination Folder section of the resulting dialog box lets you choose to rename your images without moving them, or move or copy them to a different folder. The New Filenames section includes several options for customizing your file names. Click one of the fields on the left side of this section to see the following options in a drop-down menu:

- **Text.** Choose this option to add your own text to the beginning of the file names. For example, if you shot a series of photos at Photoshop World, you could add "PhotoshopWorld" to the beginning of to your images' names.

- **New Extension** adds whatever you enter in this field to the end of your image name, replacing the original extension. Beware, though: Changing or adding a new extension to your file name doesn't change the file format, so your computer may not know what kind of file you really have if, for example, you add a .TIF extension to the end of a .JPG file.

- **Current Filename** leaves the file name that's already assigned to each image in place and adds your other custom name changes to it.

- **Preserved Filename** tells Bridge to keep the original metadata file name—the one assigned by your camera—as part of the new file name.

- **Sequence Number** adds a unique number to each image. You pick the starting number and Bridge counts up by one for each file it renames.

- **Sequence Letter** works just like Sequence Number, but it adds a unique *letter* to each file name instead.

- **Date Time** adds a date and time stamp to each file's name.

- **Metadata** lets you include metadata (page 53) in each file name. You can choose from several pieces of info that your camera embedded in your image files.

- **Folder Name** includes the name of the folder your images are in as part of the new file name.

You can add and remove items from the New Filenames section by clicking the + or – button to the right of each option. Be sure to remove items you don't plan on using so Bridge doesn't include info you don't want. (At the bottom of the Batch Rename dialog box, Bridge shows you a preview of your new file naming scheme.)

In the Options section, turn on the "Preserve current file-name in XMP Metadata" checkbox to leave the original file name that's stored in the file's metadata alone. If there's a chance your renamed images will end up on different computer platforms, be sure to turn the Compatibility checkboxes for the appropriate operating systems. For example, if you use a Mac but your client uses PCs and Unix computers, turn on the Windows and Unix checkboxes.

When you're satisfied with your brilliant file renaming scheme, click Rename and Bridge renames your files.

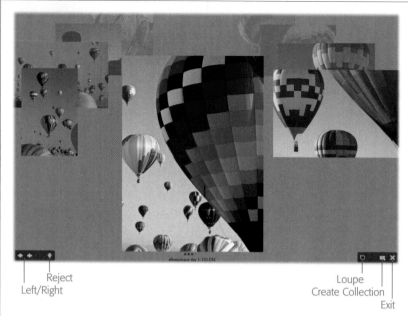

Figure C-3:
In Review mode, press ⌘-1, 2, 3, 4, 5 (Ctrl+1, 2, 3, 4, 5 on a PC) to give an image a rating of 1 to 5 stars, or press the down arrow button in the lower-left part of the window to reject an image (mark it as one you don't like). Once you've rejected images, you can filter them out and delete them in one fell swoop, as the next section explains. If you want to take a closer look at part of your image, click the Loupe button in the window's bottom-right corner or just click the image.

Reject
Left/Right

Loupe
Create Collection

Exit

TIP   If you've filtered your images but now want to see them all, press Opt-⌘-A (Alt+Ctrl+A on a PC) to remove the filter.

If you applied keywords when you imported your files, you can use those keywords to filter your images. Just open the Filter panel and you'll see a list of keywords applied to the files in the folder you're viewing. Click a keyword (it'll turn bold) and the Content panel displays only images with that particular keyword.

Grouping Images into Collections

Another way to organize your images is to put them into folders called *collections*. Bridge lets you create two types of collections:

- **User-defined collections** are ones you make by dragging and dropping images into a special folder. To create this kind of collection, click the Collections panel at the bottom-left part of the Bridge window or choose Window → Collection. Then click the New Collection button (shown in Figure C-5, top), give your collection a name, and press Return (Enter on a PC). Next, use the Folders or Favorites panel to find the images you want to include and then drag them into the red folder Bridge created.

TIP   You can create a user-defined collection while you're in Review mode by clicking the Create Collection button shown in Figure C-3.

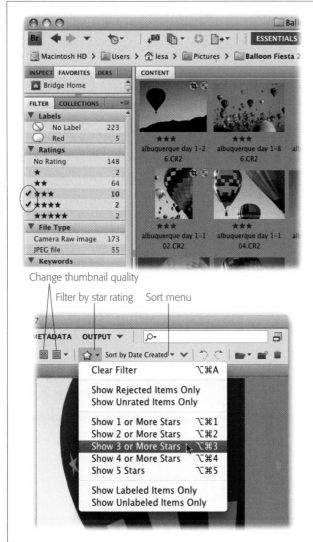

Figure C-4:

Top: The Filter panel (Window → Filter Panel) can help you limit the images Bridge displays. For example, if you've rated your images, you can filter your image collection by clicking the panel's stars (circled). In this example, Bridge is displaying just the 2- and 3-star images. To filter your images using other criteria like the date they were created or their orientation, Ctrl-click (right-click on a PC) the Filter panel and then choose an item from the resulting menu.

Bottom: You can also use the star menu at the top of the Bridge window to filter your images. The Sort menu to its right lets you control the order in which Bridge displays the thumbnails. If Bridge is taking a long time to display images as you scroll or after you filter them or perform a search, you can use the icons shown here to lower the thumbnails' quality, which makes Bridge draw them a little faster.

- Bridge creates **Smart Collections** according to criteria you set in the dialog box shown in Figure C-5 (bottom). Just click the New Smart Collection button at the bottom of the Collections panel and enter your criteria in the resulting dialog box. Click save when you're finished and Bridge finds the images that match your requirements. If you've told Bridge to look through your whole hard drive, this might take a while!

Figure C-5:
Top: Once you've created a user-defined collection, you can drag several photos into it at once, as shown here. You can tell this is a user-defined collection because its folder is red.

Bottom: With a Smart Collection, you use the Smart Collection dialog box (left) to tell Bridge which photos to fetch. Use the "Look in" pop-up menu to tell Bridge where to look for the images and then set criteria using the pop-up menus below it. To add more criteria, click the + button. Once you've made the Smart Collection, you can go back and tweak your criteria by clicking the Edit Smart Collection button (right). Smart Collections have blue folders, as shown here.

Opening Images in Camera Raw

One of the many benefits of organizing and browsing your images in Bridge is that it works with the Camera Raw plug-in (page 53). Bridge gives you lots of ways to open your images in Camera Raw:

• Double-click a Raw file and Camera Raw pops right open.

• Select an image in the Content panel and then press ⌘-R (Ctrl+R on a PC). This method lets you open Raw files, JPEGs, and TIFFs in Camera Raw.

• Select an image and then choose File → "Open in Camera Raw".

• Ctrl-click (right-click) the image and choose "Open in Camera Raw" from the shortcut menu that appears.

• Select an image and then click the shutter icon at the top of the window.

Once you've edited an image in Camera Raw, a couple of microscopic icons will appear next to the image's preview in Bridge's Content panel (see Figure C-6). If you've got several images that need the same edits, you can copy the changes from one image and apply them to others right here in Bridge. All you do is Ctrl-click (right-click on a PC) the image in the Content panel and then choose Develop Settings → Copy Settings from the resulting shortcut menu. Then select the images you want to apply the edits to, Ctrl-click (right-click) them, choose Develop Settings → Paste Settings, and Bridge applies those same edits to those images. Now that's working smarter instead of harder!

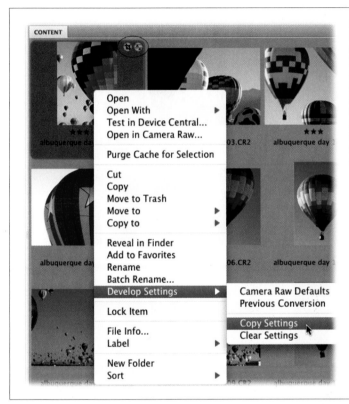

Figure C-6:
When you edit an image in Camera Raw and then click Done in the Camera Raw window, tiny icons representing the kinds of edits you made appear next to the image in Bridge. The icons circled here indicate that the image was cropped and its exposure was changed. Ctrl-clicking (right-clicking) an image in Bridge's Content panel brings up this shortcut menu, which includes all kinds of timesavers.

Showing Off Your Work

Bridge gives you several ways to display your work, including a nifty slideshow generator and the new Adobe Output Module that lets you create PDFs and Web galleries.

Making a Slideshow

If you need to show your work to a client or family member, you can quickly filter your top-rated images (see the figure on page 744) and have Bridge play them as a full-screen slideshow. Here's how:

- **To start an instant slideshow,** select a folder or several images by Shift- or ⌘-clicking (Ctrl-clicking on a PC) them, and then choose View → Slideshow. That's it! Your photos immediately appear onscreen, one after the other (each one stays onscreen for five seconds). To exit the slideshow, press Esc. You can also start a slideshow by pressing ⌘-L (Ctrl+L on a PC).

- **To customize the slideshow settings first,** choose View → Slideshow Options or press Shift-⌘-L (Shift+Ctrl+L). In the resulting dialog box you can make your slideshow repeat, control how many seconds each image stays onscreen, resize the slideshow window to fit your monitor, and add transitions between slides (see Figure C-7). The only thing you *can't* do is add music (though you can always open iTunes and play music in the background).

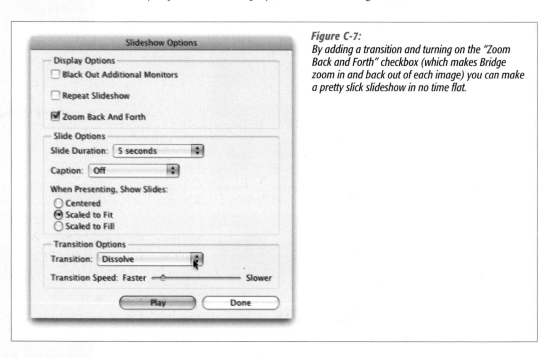

Figure C-7:
By adding a transition and turning on the "Zoom Back and Forth" checkbox (which makes Bridge zoom in and back out of each image) you can make a pretty slick slideshow in no time flat.

TIP   To create a slideshow you can export, use the PDF option explained in the next section.

Exporting Images as PDFs

PDFs are really handy because you can open them on any kind of computer without having to buy any software. Bridge has a couple of templates you can use to create PDFs, and a slew of settings you can use to customize exactly how your

PDFs look. Just select the image(s) you want to export and click the word Output at the top of the Bridge window to switch to the Output workspace (see the box on page 740), which displays the Output panel shown in Figure C-8 on the right side of the Bridge window (you'll need to use the scroll bar on the panel's right side to see all the settings).

At the top of the Output panel, make sure the PDF button is selected, and then choose a template from the Template pop-up menu. To see a preview of the template you picked, click the Preview tab in the center of the Bridge window (circled in Figure C-8). You don't have very many templates to choose from, but you can customize them using the Output panel's various settings. If you want your PDF to run as a slideshow, be sure the Playback options are turned on (they're about halfway down the panel). When everything looks good, click the Save button at the bottom of the Output panel and Bridge exports your file as a PDF.

Figure C-8:
The Template menu doesn't give you many options and, unfortunately, you can't add your own. But for those mourning the loss of Contact Sheets in Photoshop CS4, you can tweak the various settings to create a contact sheet here (you can't save your settings as a preset for future use, though). As you make changes in the Output panel, you have to click the Refresh Preview button (circled) to make Bridge update what's shown in the Output Preview tab.

NOTE Page 101 covers exporting layer comp files as PDFs.

The galactic bummer is that, once you get your PDF looking good, you can't *save* any of the settings you've painstakingly entered in the Output panel—though thankfully Bridge remembers the last settings you used. Perhaps future versions of the program will let you save template settings and create custom templates.

Creating a Picture Package

Sadly, your days of using Photoshop to print multiple photos at popular sizes all on one sheet of paper are over—unless you download and install the *older* version of the plug-in. Head to page 656 to learn how.

Making a Web Gallery

You can also use Bridge to make a quick online gallery of your images. Heck, it'll even upload the images for you! Flip back to page 689 for the scoop.

Index

Colophon

Sarah Schneider and Adam Witwer provided quality control for *Photoshop CS4: The Missing Manual*. Lucie Haskins wrote the index.

The cover of this book is based on a series design originally created by David Freedman and modified by Mike Kohnke, Karen Montgomery, and Fitch (*www.fitch.com*). Back cover deisgn, dog illustration, and color selection by Fitch.

David Futato designed the interior layout, based on a series design by Phil Simpson. This book was converted by Abby Fox to FrameMaker 5.5.6. The text font is Adobe Minion; the heading font is Adobe Formata Condensed; and the code font is LucasFont's TheSansMonoCondensed. The illustrations that appear in the book were produced by Robert Romano and Jessamyn Read using Macromedia FreeHand MX and Adobe Photoshop CS3.